£37·20

NOT TO BE
REMOVED
FROM THE
LIBRARY.

D1423365

WITHDRAWN

SYMPOSIA OF THE
SOCIETY FOR EXPERIMENTAL BIOLOGY

NUMBER XXXIX

POLYTECHNIC LIBRARY
WOLVERHAMPTON

ACC No. 586655   CLASS

CONTROL

591.77
PHY

D22

DATE -7 NOV. 1986   SITE RS

PROCEEDINGS OF A MEETING
HELD IN ST. ANDREWS, SCOTLAND
SEPTEMBER 1984

SYMPOSIA OF THE
SOCIETY FOR EXPERIMENTAL BIOLOGY

SYMPOSIA OF THE
SOCIETY FOR EXPERIMENTAL BIOLOGY

NUMBER XXXIX

PHYSIOLOGICAL ADAPTATIONS OF MARINE ANIMALS

EDITED BY

M. S. LAVERACK

Published for the Society for Experimental Biology
by The Company of Biologists Limited, Department of Zoology,
University of Cambridge, Downing Street, Cambridge CB2 3EJ

© The Society for Experimental Biology 1985

*Typeset and Printed by the Pindar Group of Companies, Scarborough,
North Yorkshire*

Published by The Company of Biologists Limited,
Department of Zoology, University of Cambridge,
Downing Street, Cambridge CB2 3EJ

© Society for Experimental Biology 1985

*Typeset and Printed by the Pindar Group of Companies,
Scarborough, North Yorkshire*

ISBN 0 948601 00 0

CONTENTS

Printed in Great Britain © Society for Experimental Biology 1985

INTRODUCTION

This volume stems from the meeting held at the University of St. Andrews from 11 to 13 September 1984. It was intended to assist in commemorating the centenary of the beginning of the St. Andrews Fisheries Laboratory (later to become the Gatty Marine Laboratory). During the course of the ensuing 100 years various types of work have been carried out in St. Andrews, from the taxonomy of polychaetes, to the rearing of the early stages of food fish; from natural history to physiology, from endocrinology of elasmobranchs to the nervous systems of marine invertebrates.

The general background of the Society for Experimental Biology covers all aspects of form and function and the design of the symposium was to reflect a wide spectrum of activities of the membership interested in marine organisms. Thus papers were delivered that ranged from the metabolic rates and biochemical actions of intertidal animals, through problems of osmoregulation and its control, to behaviour and to sensory and motor aspects of locomotion. The result is a set of chapters that indicate the breadth of investigations on marine animals carried out under the term 'Physiological Adaptations of Marine Animals', or under the preliminary title given to the meeting 'Experimental Marine Biology'.

The organizer records his special thanks to the Society for Experimental Biology for its assistance in all phases of the planning and execution of the symposium, to the Royal Society, the Royal Society of Edinburgh, the Company of Biologists and the University of St. Andrews for their financial help. The participation of Dr. D. C. Weeks (Plant Biology, University of St. Andrews) as local secretary, and of Christina Lamb and Florence McAndie in a variety of ways is gratefully acknowledged.

M. S. Laverack

February 1985.

Printed in Great Britain © Society for Experimental Biology 1985

ENVIRONMENTAL PHYSIOLOGY

F. JOHN VERNBERG

Director, Belle W. Baruch Institute for Marine Biology and Coastal Research, University of South Carolina, Columbia, SC 29208, U.S.A.

Introduction

The sea is not only an important component of the biosphere in terms of the amount of the earth's surface it covers (approximately 71 %), but it also is a highly complex environment in which a rich diversity of habitats is found. These habitats vary in structure from soft benthic oozes to rocky intertidal shores to various pelagic zones. The combinations and inter-relationships of the numerous abiotic and biotic factors in the sea also vary from habitat to habitat. Marine organisms, occupying various habitats in this ecologically diverse environment, have evolved to exhibit functional adaptations to the unique environmental complex in which they live. It is small wonder that biologists were delightfully challenged to answer the question of how marine organisms functionally respond to their environment, a discipline known as physiological ecology to some scientists and environmental physiology to others. Since this discipline, whatever you may call it, blends field and laboratory approaches, it forms the backbone of the theme of this symposium – Physiological Adaptations of Marine Animals.

Marine studies have progressed through various phases ranging from descriptive studies of the geological, physical, chemical, and biological attributes of the sea to varying levels of sophisticated experimental inves-tigation both in the field and in the laboratory. During the 100-year period since the founding of the St. Andrews Fisheries Laboratory, much progress in oceanography has occurred and scientists associated with this laboratory have contributed to these advances. The organizers of this symposium and the Society for Experimental Biology are to be commen-ded for combining the centenary of marine science in St. Andrews and a re-examination of the past, present, and future of experimental marine biology.

This opening paper has been assigned the challenging, but unattain-able, task to review the background of physiological marine biology and to present a general introduction of the major environmental factors which organisms encounter and the general types of organismic responses

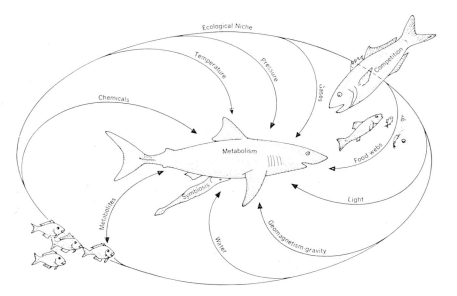

Fig. 1. Interactions of an organism and its environment.

to these factors. Later, other papers will analyse in depth (no pun intended) our current knowledge of how biological entities functionally cope with specific abiotic and biotic factors, such as osmotic pressure, light, chemicals, and food.

The organismic–environmental complex

A dynamic interaction exists between the internal environment of an organism and its external milieu (Fig. 1). Changes in the ambient environment influence the organism and, in turn, it may have homeostatic mechanisms which enable the internal milieu to be regulated and maintained in a relatively unchanged state; if it lacks the physiological machinery to regulate, the internal environment may change to resemble the state of the new external environment. Gradations between regulation and conformity occur and an organism may be able to regulate the response to one environmental factor while exhibiting the response of a conformer to a second factor. Further, this great variability in response between a regulator and a conformer may change during the organism's ontogeny or state of acclimation. Rather than allowing this great variation in response patterns to depress investigators, variability should stimulate our inquiry into the nature of adaptive phenomena.

For purposes of study, the external environmental complex in which an organism lives can be divided into abiotic and biotic factors. The principal abiotic factors are chemical (major and minor elements, organic and inorganic compounds, pH, and dissolved gases), physical (temperature, hydrostatic pressure, tidal phenomena, currents, osmotic pressure, light, geophysical forces, sound, and density), and geological (sedimentation, substratum, and earthquakes). Biotic factors include competition (intraspecific and interspecific), predator–prey interaction, symbiosis, and population and community dynamics. Of special significance to the experimental marine biologists is that many of these factors may vary independently of each other and different biotic and abiotic factors may act in concert. For example, predation by adults may increase with elevated temperatures and low light intensity but not be influenced by salinity, whereas predation by larvae may be markedly inhibited by low salinity and high temperature and stimulated only by high light intensity.

Although there is a tendency for marine biologists to study the influence of only a single factor on an organism at a time, data from these studies may have limited applicability to understanding how organisms function in a complex environment which consists of many (often independently varying) factors. The need to maintain a holocoenotic view of the environment is vital to insure that the results of our studies have ecological significance. On the other hand, 'single-factor' studies do provide valuable insight into how specific physiological processes respond to an environmental change. For a number of reasons, including an increased awareness of the importance of multiple factor interaction, better instrumentation for simulating complex environments, and the awesome advances in statistical and computer technologies, an ever-increasing number of multiple-factor studies are appearing (Vernberg, 1978).

When an organism is exposed to a gradient of factor expression under experimental conditions, typically there is a low and high level beyond which an organism is unable to survive; the points at the lower and upper portions of the environmental gradient are commonly known as the lower and upper lethal level (Fig. 2). In the middle portion of the gradient, the organism survives and each physiological function exhibits a variable response depending on whether the organism is a regulator or a conformer. This broad middle region of the gradient which supports life is commonly referred to as the zone of compatibility (biokinetic zone, tolerance zone), whereas the region outside this zone is known as the zone of lethality (zone of resistance). In general the dividing line between the point of death and survival is that point at which 50 % of a population sample indefinitely survives a given exposure. This point is not easy to determine in all cases and it could vary with such factors as acclimation,

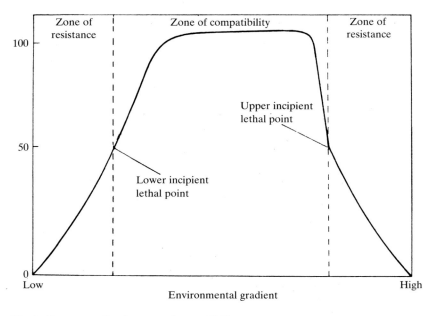

Fig. 2. The zones of resistance and compatibility.

sex, size, stage of life cycle, or starvation. Although this 50 % number has value for comparative purposes, it may not be ecologically significant because how much of a population has to be killed before a species disappears – 50, 80, 95, or 100 %?

Historical perspective

Although most of the marine biologists working before the 1880's were concerned with describing which plants and animals were found where, Semper (1881) reviewed the literature and emphasized the experimental approach in his book 'Animal Life as Affected by the Natural Conditions of Existence'. Discussions of such topics as respiratory gases, water currents, drought, and the effects of pressure of ocean depths were included. Of note, he also emphasized the importance of biotic factors including symbiotic interactions. Another important contribution to experimental biology was the two volume series of Davenport (1897, 1899) entitled 'Experimental Morphology'. These volumes contained an excellent early history of experimental work as it related to physiology and ecology. In these volumes, Davenport raised a number of questions. For example, he was very concerned about the effects of high temperature on organisms and how animals respond. He asked the question, What are the mechanisms behind the acclimatization of organisms to new thermal regimes? Although it is tempting to think that our current generation of scientists are attacking new problems, there is evidence that many problems are persistent and have been known for a long time but are now being addressed with newer sophisticated techniques. During the early part of the 20th century, there was a marked increased interest in analysing the physiological response of animals in respect to their ecology. This trend was beautifully exemplified by the work of V. E. Shelford. In particular, in his 1915 paper, he stated 'ecology is that branch of general physiology which deals with the organisms as a whole, with its general life processes as distinguished from the more special physiology of organs'. In this paper he stressed the importance of what he termed physiological life histories. Under this term he considered such things as metabolic rate, functional and activity rhythms, latency of eggs, time and condition of reproduction, and behaviour in relation to environmental conditions. Shelford stressed the need to study all stages in the life history of an organism and emphasized the relationship between laboratory results and determination of physiological life history parameters in nature.

An early and often cited paper, in which the differential effect of temperature on the rate of pulsation in a jellyfish from one population in Nova Scotia and a second at the southern tip of Florida was reported, is that of Mayer (1914). He noted that the northern population reached the same maximum rate of pulsation at lower temperatures than did the southern group. Although there was a region of the thermal gradient in which an overlap in response occurred, the northern population beat over a much lower temperature range, about 0 to 20 °C, than the species from Florida whose thermal range was 12 to 36 °C. In 1916, Krogh suggested that the respiratory rate of cold-blooded animals from warm and cold waters would show differences which could be correlated with their respective habitats. He suggested that there was some form of metabolic adaptation so that the species from the cold waters would have a metabolic rate at their habitat temperature which would be somewhat similar to that of a tropical species, determined at its higher environmental habitat temperature. Although it is beyond the scope of this paper to give a comprehensive history of environmental physiology of marine organisms, several papers will be cited.

In 1936, three papers were published which represented important contributions to the problem of how animals from different latitudes respond to environmental factors. Thorson (1936) compared the larval development, growth, and metabolism of lamellibranchs from cold Arctic waters and animals from warmer oceans. In general, he found that species with a northerly distribution have a higher metabolic rate than southerly distributed species of the same genus at the same temperature. At any one latitude there are interspecific differences which need to be taken into account. For example, epifaunal forms or species have a higher rate of oxygen consumption than do burrowing species. Thus, the rate of oxygen consumption can be correlated with the mode of life of the individual species as well as with geographical differences. Sparck (1936) reported similar results in studying molluscan species from the marine waters of Denmark and the Mediterranean Sea. He suggested that if northern species moved to warm waters the increased metabolic rate would cause the animal to starve to death, thus limiting its southern distribution. On the other hand the northern distribution of southern forms would be limited by the thermal influence on larval development and reproduction. Fox (1936, 1939) and Fox & Wingfield (1937) published papers of crustaceans and polychaete worms from such diverse thermal regimes as Sweden, England, and Greenland. They found marked differences in various physiological measurement such as beating of the scaphognathite, cellular respiration, heart rate, respiratory movements, and the influence of body size.

In general, the data from these three principal investigators demonstrated that northern species will function at a faster rate than closely related southern species when compared at similar temperatures. The Second World War interrupted studies on the experimental biology of marine organisms, but after the war Scholander and co-workers began studies on the environmental physiology of marine organisms. In 1953, they published an extensive paper comparing the metabolic – temperature responses of many species from the Arctic and tropical regions. Their work was extremely stimulatory to the development of experimental biology of marine organisms. The excellent review papers of Bullock (1955) and Prosser (1955) focused attention on the vital interdependence of an organism's environment and its internal physiological machinery. Following this period of time, many papers, books, new journals, and symposia proceedings appeared dealing with various aspects of experimental marine biology. The following papers in this volume will refer in more detail to advances in specific research areas.

Environmental components of the sea

As general background to the other papers in this volume which present detailed analyses of the functional response of marine organisms to a restricted number of environmental factors, a review of the environmental components of the sea and a few examples of how one organism responds to them is presented. As indicated earlier, the sea will be considered to consist of two major types of environmental factors: abiotic and biotic.

Abiotic Factors

Chemical

The sea represents a giant water-filled pitcher in which is found a complex array of chemical entities including 'natural' and 'man-introduced' substances. A number of reference books contain lists of compounds found in the sea and discuss their chemical dynamics.

In general, chemicals in seawater are divided into two major groups: major and minor elements. All elements present in concentrations less than one part per million by weight are classified as a minor element. The major constituents are few in number, but contribute significantly to determining the salinity level. The most significant major constituents in terms of abundance are chloride, sodium, sulphate, magnesium, calcium, potassium, bicarbonate, bromide, strontium, boron, and fluoride. In general, the concentration of major elements is relatively constant in the sea, but in regions of reduced salinity as in estuaries and coastal waters the concentration is reduced but the ratio of each element to another is fairly constant. However, the concentration of minor elements may vary with water masses or with depth. Although the concentrations of major and minor elements are markedly different, elements of both groups have pronounced physiological effects on organisms. One of the major environmental barriers that open ocean organisms face when attempting to invade estuaries is the decreased salinity and decreased osmotic concentration of the water. Organisms have used various functional responses to adapt to changing salinity. If the chemical composition of an organism's body fluids changes in response to ambient changes, the organism is referred to as a conformer; if the chemical composition is unchanged, it is a regulator. When referring to external osmoconcentration, the terms osmoregulator or osmoconformer are used; in reference to specific ions, the terms ionic regulator or ionic conformers are applied. Four generalized types of osmoregulatory responses have been observed 1) osmoregulation, 2) osmoconformer, 3) hyperosmoregulation in dilute media, and 4) hyper- and hypo-osmoregulation (Fig. 3). Although an organism may be placed in one of these groups, marked gradations between groups occur, in that species differ in their intensity of response.

For example, within the group 3 category some organisms may regulate better than others. Within a species, the type of response may vary due to external and intra-organismic factors. A few examples illustrate this point. Adult mud crabs (*Sesarma reticulatum*) are able to hyperregulate in dilute seawater, but the larval stages are osmoconformers (Foskett, 1977). Body size has been shown to affect osmoregulatory ability; small-sized flounder are more sensitive to fluctuation in ambient osmocon-centration than a large-sized animal (Hickman, 1959). After acclimation to concentrated seawater (175 % seawater) for 65–75 days the crab *Hemigrapsus oregonensis* showed significant hypoosmotic regulation, whereas little regulation was observed after 3 days (Gross, 1963). Earlier Lockwood (1962) proposed five principal types of osmoregulatory

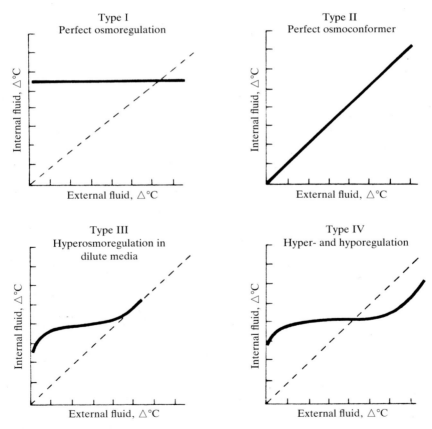

Fig. 3. Generalized patterns of osmoregulatory responses. The dotted line is the line of osmoticity.

mechanisms which are utilized by marine animals in meeting the stress of osmotic fluctuations: 1) reduced permeability of body surface, 2) active uptake or extrusion of ions, 3) regulation of body water volume, 4) conservation of salts or water by the excretory organs, and 5) regulation of cellular osmotic concentrations. Detailed discussions of osmoregulatory mechanisms are presented in a paper by Davenport (this volume).

In addition to playing a significant role in adapting to salinity changes, ionic regulation is important in organisms maintaining buoyancy (see review of Gordon & Belman, 1981).

Minor elements vary in their functional significance to marine organisms. Some minor elements serve as a means of communication both on an intra- and an interspecific basis; some trace metals are important in metabolic processes; some substances serve as food; and some man-introduced substances are harmful. Because of the development of extremely sensitive microchemical techniques, major research efforts on chemical–biological interactions are underway on the qualitative and quantitative composition of sea water, the distribution in time and space of chemical elements and their end products, and the functional significance of these minor elements and their end products to marine organisms. Some questions about the importance of minor elements are

1) the role of dissolved organic matter, amino acids and other elements in the nutrition of marine organisms (see review of Jorgensen, 1976);

2) the role of minor elements in communication between marine organisms and how are they detected (see review of Laverack, 1968; also Atema, this volume);

3) the effects of man-introduced compounds on the physiology of marine organisms.

Another important group of substances dissolved in seawater which profoundly influence marine organisms is dissolved gases. In the open sea oxygen concentrations generally are not functionally limiting, although concentrations may vary with depth in the water column and differ seasonally or climatically. In most oceans, a water layer of reduced oxygen concentration is found at intermediate depths. This region, called the oxygen minimum layer, may have concentrations of oxygen less than $0.5 \, \text{ml} \cdot \text{litre}^{-1}$, whereas water above and below this layer may have concentrations in excess of $6 \, \text{ml} \cdot \text{litre}^{-1}$. In one species found in this layer, *Gnathophausia ingens* (a mysid crustacean), some data are available on how it has become functionally adapted to inhabit this habitat. Childress (1968) showed that this species lives largely aerobically at oxygen concentrations as low as $0.2 \, \text{ml} \cdot \text{litre}^{-1}$, with a relatively constant rate of oxygen consumption of $0.8 \, \text{ml} \, O_2 \cdot \text{kg}^{-1} \cdot \text{ml}^{-1}$ at $5 \, °\text{C}$. The ability of this species to maintain aerobic metabolism appears to result from a combination of several physiological and morphological factors. These include 1) large gill surface areas (between 5 and $15\,cm^3 \cdot g^{-1}$); 2) low diffusion distances across the gills ($1 \cdot 5$–$2 \cdot 5\,\mu m$); 3) high ventilation volumes (up to 8 body volumes $\cdot$ min^{-1}); 4) high utilization of the available oxygen in the respiratory streams (50–80%); 5) rapid blood flows through the gills (turnover time, 2–3 min); and 6) relatively low routine metabolic rates (Childress, 1968, 1971; Belman & Childress, 1976).

In estuaries, low concentrations of oxygen and high levels of hydrogen sulphate occur in a number of habitats. Vernberg (1972, 1983) reviewed the literature on how marine organisms cope with hypoxic and anoxic conditions. Typically animals from oxygen-poor waters have the following characteristics: 1) the critical level of oxygen tension below which the organism becomes an oxyconformer is lower than that of organisms from well-aerated waters; 2) they possess long-lasting internal oxygen reservoirs (gas bubble pools of respiratory pigments with high oxygen affinity); 3) the oxygen consumption rate is reduced; and 4) if large oxygen reservoirs do not exist, the organisms rely on anaerobic metabolic pathways. Gnaiger (1983) surveyed the literature on calorimetry and thermodynamics of anoxibiosis and suggested the following: during hypoxia grossly inefficient pathways sustain high metabolic rates for a short time. In contrast, when subjected to long-term environmental anoxia, low steady-state heat dissipation is associated with the more efficient succinate, propionate, and acetate pathways. Theede, Ponat, Hiroki & Schlieper (1969) and Theede (1973) have discussed the effects of H_2 on bottom-dwelling organisms. A more detailed discussion of current research trends in respiration is presented by Taylor (this volume).

Hydrostatic pressure

With every 10 metre decrease in water depth, the hydrostatic pressure exerted on aquatic species increases by 1 atm. Macdonald (1975) and George (1981) have excellent reviews on the diverse effects of hydrostatic pressure on molecular, biochemical, bioenergetic, and behavioural responses of marine organisms.

Temperature

The open ocean and coastal environments exhibit a wide range of different thermal conditions. The temperature of ocean water may vary from $-2°$ to $+30°C$. In the tropics the annual fluctuation is less than

2 °C and about 4 °C in polar waters, and in the region of middle latitudes the range may be about 8 °C. Vertical stratification may be observed from a surface temperature of 30 °C to a bottom temperature of about 0 °C. Hence pelagic species may occur either over wide temperature ranges both geographically (populations) and daily (individuals), or may live in what are often completely thermally stable environments. In the intertidal zone and estuaries, thermal regimes may exhibit a much wider range of temperatures. The winter air temperatures could be very low depending on the latitude, while the summer air temperature could be in excess of 40 °C. Not only may there be extreme seasonal changes in thermal regimes but wide daily fluctuations may occur.

Temperature is a pervasive environmental factor and influences many physiological and behavioural processes. Hence, over the years, patterns of physiological responses to temperature and to temperature changes have been the subject of considerable interest and have been extensively studied. The effects of temperature on metabolism and activity in invertebrates are reviewed in detail by Kinne (1964), Vernberg & Vernberg (1972), Hochachka & Somero (1973), Wieser (1973), and Hoar (1975).

One example of thermal effects on oceanic animals is presented. Off the east coast of the United States, the waters near Cape Hatteras represent a zone of marked thermal discontinuity: north of the Cape the Virginian current brings cold waters to the south, while to the south the Gulf Stream brings warm water to the north. Where the two currents meet off Cape Hatteras a dynamic thermal zone is created. Cerame-Vivas & Gray (1966) described discrete faunal assemblages north of the Cape, in the inshore water south of the Cape and in the Gulf Stream. The offshore fauna south of the Cape (both the inshore and the Gulf Stream assemblages) survived high temperatures better than the cold-water fauna found north of the Cape. In addition, these warm-water species did not survive either the low winter temperature of 4 °C, which is characteristic of the waters north of the Cape, or the low winter temperature of 10 °C of the waters between the Gulf Stream and the shore south of the Cape. The few species which have wide geographical limits were able to shift their lethal limits by seasonal acclimation phenomena. Similar general trends were exhibited by larval Crustacea from this area of the sea: zoeae of warm-adapted species were less resistant to both low temperature and low salinity than cold-adapted species (Vernberg & Vernberg, 1970). The metabolic–temperature (M–T) response of animals from these distinctly different regions reflected similar trends: the cold-water species had M–T curves shifted to the left of those from the Gulf Stream organisms (Vernberg & Vernberg, 1970).

Tidal phenomena and periodicity

The rise and fall of the tides has created a distinctive habitat, the intertidal zone. This rhythmic ebbing and flowing of seawater is an environmental factor to which intertidal organisms must cope. In many regions of the world published tide tables exist which not only list the time of high and low tide, but indicate the extent of tidal excursion. The magnitude of tidal change varies geographically from a few inches to more than 40 feet in the Bay of Fundy. At any one site, the tidal amplitude varies depending on the phase of the moon: spring tides, which is the time of maximum tidal change, occur during new and full moon, while during neap tides the least change in tidal elevation takes place. The type of tide is different in various geographical regions: typically the tide changes twice a day (a semidiurnal tide) with the time between succeeding high tides being 12·4 hours, but some regions have only one high tide per day (averaging 24·8 hours) which is known as a diurnal tide. Macmillan (1966) and recent physical oceanography texts have excellent discussions of the complexity of tidal phenomena.

Organisms have been influenced by tidal changes as observed in various physiological and behavioural responses; including locomotion, respiration, reproduction, osmoregulation, and feeding (see symposium proceedings by DeCoursey, 1976; Naylor & Hartnoll, 1979).

In addition to tidal rhythmicity, other cyclic phenomena occur in the sea which significantly influence marine organisms. Symposia proceedings edited by DeCoursey (1976) and Naylor & Hartnoll (1979) deal with the response of organisms to many types of periodicities, including diurnal, semilunar, seasonal and annual cycles. Naylor (this volume) deals with this topic in great depth.

Light

One abiotic factor which is very variable is light. It varies in quality and intensity both on a rhythmic (*i.e.* daily and seasonal) and an arhythmic (*i.e.* changes in cloud cover) basis. The amount of solar radiation penetrating the sea depends, in part, on two factors: 1) the amount of radiation immediately above the sea, which is largely determined by the angle of incidence of radiation; and 2) the surface reflectivity. When penetrating seawater, the beam of light is both scattered and absorbed, so that radiation decreases with depth. The percentage of light penetrating various depths is not the same in different bodies of water. The spectral distribution of light also changes with depth and the degree of change differs in various water columns. The angular distribution of light in the sea may be important as a cue in orientation. Also the polarization pattern of light in the sea, which changes with the sun's position, may aid in animal orientation.

Light is of great biological significance, although it should be pointed out that 90 % of the sea bottom is without light. Herring (this volume) and Lythgoe (this volume) discuss light and its influence on marine animals.

Currents

The movement of oceanic waters influences the distribution of many organisms. They respond to these currents by passively moving with the water mass, actively swimming into the currents, or some combination of these two responses. Different types of oceanic currents have been described: tidal, surface, deep, subsurface, rip, longsore, and offshore to mention a few. To the physiological ecologist, it is important to understand the functional mechanisms which enable organisms to detect currents and to respond. Other contributors to this volume will address some aspects of this problem, especially Wardle and Strickler.

Buoyancy

There are marked density gradients in the sea and these differences help determine currents and water movements. Related to the general problem of an organisms maintaining a position in the ocean, as it must do in response to currents, is how is it able to inhabit different depths. If the density of an organism varies significantly from that of seawater, the organism would be expected to either rise or sink until it reaches a depth where the two densities are equal unless energy is expended by active movements.

Density

Density increases with depth, but the increase is not necessarily uniform. The heaviest or densest waters are found at the ocean bottom. The lightest or least dense waters are found at sea level. In some regions of the deep sea, the density is constant for some depth. But in other areas, called pycnoclines, density increases rapidly with a small change in depth. Such regions are quite stable. A water column is stable (has little tendency to mix vertically) if less dense water is above heavier water and if there is a sharp gradation in density. In some cases, less-dense water may lie below heavy water, which makes the water column unstable. When density is the same over a wide region, the region has neutral stability. Two water masses with the same density may have different temperatures and salinities; it is not too unusual to find warm waters below cold waters or less-saline waters below more-saline waters. Yet the water structure will still be stable. Structural and physiological mechanisms have been described which enable organisms to regulate buoyancy so that they can conserve energy and passively occupy different depths.

Sound

In recent years there has been much research on sound in the sea, especially the non-biotic characteristics as applied to military interests. However, the importance of understanding the significance of how organisms detect and respond to sound has not been neglected (Diemer et al., 1980).

Sound in seawater has certain physical properties which makes it an excellent media for animal communication. Sound travels faster through water than through air. The velocity of sound in seawater depends on salinity, temperature, and pressure. For water with a salinity of 34·85‰ and a temperature of 0 °C, the velocity would be 1445 m · sec^{-1}. Increasing the salinity by 1 percent increases the velocity by 1·5 m · sec^{-1}. Raising the temperature 1 °C will increase it by 4 m/sec; and a 1000 m increase in depth will increase it by about 19 m · sec^{-1}. Knowledge of all three of these factors is necessary in order to specify the velocity of sound at a particular depth. Of course, both salinity and temperature are affected by seasonal changes and they vary with latitude; velocity will vary accordingly.

Other abiotic factors

Many other abiotic factors have been demonstrated to influence the distribution and survival of aquatic organisms. They are listed without benefit of much discussion, not because of a diminished importance to plants and animals, but because of space limitations in this volume and also because less is known of the physiological mechanisms used to cope with these factors. The geomagnetic field of the earth is not constant and varies geographically. Earlier Brown (1962) reported that marine organisms can detect and are physiologically responsive to these differences. The type of substratum profoundly influences the distribution of organisms. This is well demonstrated in that the free-swimming larval stage of many benthic species are physiologically attracted to a specific substratum at the time of settling (Crisp, 1974).

The type and amount of sediment affects both pelagic and benthic organisms. In the case of filter-feeding crustaceans, increased sediment load can inhibit feeding while other crustaceans can detect and ingest certain sediments as a potential food source (Grahame, 1983). Although the hydrogen ion concentration of seawater is relatively constant (pH about 8), microhabitats of higher or lower pH values occur and result in altering the physiology and behaviour of organisms (Vernberg & Vernberg, 1972).

Biotic factors

The interaction between organisms can influence their functional stability and behaviour. Hence it is not surprising that physiological processes have evolved which are adaptive to environmental biotic stresses. The functional capability of organisms to respond to both physical and biotic factors plays a significant role in determining success in intra-and interspecific competition. Earlier Croghan (1961) suggested that as organisms invaded brackish and estuarine waters, mechanisms of osmoregulation came into being. An organism in a dilute medium uses a considerable amount of energy for osmotic regulation, but if these organisms can increase the efficiency of osmoregulation, they require less energy. If less energy were required for osmoregulation, less food would be needed by the organism for this function so that more energy would be available for other phases of the life processes and, ultimately, the species could gain a competitive advantage. Croghan concluded that the major adaptations to a dilute medium all reduce the amount of energy required to maintain a steady state.

Symbiotic relationships between organisms represent varying degrees of functional interdependence between the host and symbiont. For example in some mutualistic associations the two species do not associate continuously and their dependency may be very limited. For example, the cleaner shrimp removes ectoparasites from fish on an irregular basis, however, in other relationships the metabolism of both partners is supplemented such as observed in some gut microflora and animals. In commensalism and parasitism, a greater degree of physiological interdependence is observed. In extreme cases of parasitism, certain life history stages of a parasite are metabolically dependent on the host and in many cases the parasite is dependent on one species. Not only is the physiological adaptation of host and symbiont an intriguing research field (Vernberg, 1974) but results of these studies have pinpointed the need for physiologists investigating a specific function, such as osmoregulation, in one species to be aware that the response of a parasitized animal may be markedly different from that of a non-parasitized individual.

Population studies

At another level of biological organization, the physiological response to environmental stress of populations of a species has been studied. Although this symposium is devoted more to the environmental physiology of organisms, knowledge of population responses is related to and is dependent on organismic studies. Examples of two types of study are presented: 1) population bioenergetics and 2) modelling of population physiology.

Population energetics

The need for energy by a biotic system to survive, whether it be a cell, an organism, or a population of organisms, is well documented. Obtaining energy and its utilization by a living system is influenced by environmental factors. This method of accounting for energy input and energy usage is referred to as developing an energy budget. The commonly accepted equation for estimating the energy budget is as follows:

$$C = P + R + F + U,$$

$$\text{where } P = P_r + P_g \text{ and } P_g = B + E.$$

Each component may be measured in kilocalories per unit time (1 KCal = 4·184 KJ). C is the energy content of the food consumed by the population; P, the total energy produced as flesh or gametes; P_g, the energy content of the tissue due to growth and recruitment; B, the net increase in energy content of standing stock; E, elimination, or energy content lost to the population through mortality; P_r, the energy content of the gametes liberated during spawning; R, the energy lost due to metabolism (respiration); F, the energy lost as faeces; and U, the energy lost as urine or other exudates.

Obviously, the development of an energy budget is a complex process involving determination of various functional processes. Although it is beyond the scope of the present paper to present a detailed review of bioenergetics, some examples of recent studies will indicate current problems.

Because energy intake is basic to organismic survival, it is not unexpected that various mechanisms have evolved in marine organisms. Dissolved organic substances may be removed by organisms from the surrounding seawater (see review, Jorgensen, 1976) and or by ingesting larger particles (see review, Pandian, 1975). One of the basic problems in developing an energy budget is to determine energy input to an organism. Under laboratory conditions input has been estimated for a number of species, but the question can be raised – Is this what the organism eats in the field? In many cases the natural diet of marine animals is unknown let alone data on quantitative aspects of ingestion.

Another important component of bioenergetics is respiration. Numerous variables have been shown to influence oxygen uptake (Vernberg & Vernberg, 1972). Wu & Levings (1978) also determined the rate of respiration and its contribution to the annual energy budget for barnacles (*Balanus glandula*) during their first year after settlement. Approximately 67 % of the energy was lost in respiration with egg production being the second major component at 12·3 %.

The energy balance of a species may be different depending on where it lives. For example, Griffiths (1981) reported that the energy budget of a mussel population (*Choromytilus meridionalis*) living intertidally was distinct from that of a subtidal population (Fig. 4). Upper-shore mussels had a reduced growth rate and reduced metabolism during aerial exposure computed for the first years of growth when compared with subtidal forms. Although she calculated that the energy requirements of the intertidal population was half that of totally submerged animals, the

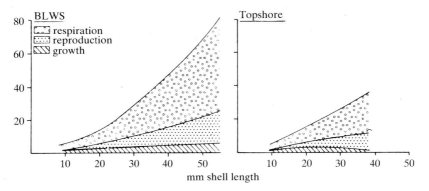

Fig. 4. Calculated energy requirements for growth, reproduction, and respiration in sublittoral and topshore mussels during the first five years of growth (Griffiths, 1981).

amount of energy allotted to reproduction in both populations was not markedly different.

Modelling

One approach to integrating various physiological responses of organisms to improve understanding of the population in a complex ecological setting is modelling. One example of utilizing field and laboratory data to develop a conceptual model of major energy flows through a population of *Uca pugilator* as affected by mercury is represented (Vernberg, McKellar & Vernberg, 1978). The conceptual model (Fig. 5) involves a knowledge of population structure, energy input, respiration, egestion, mortality, temperature, salinity and various mercury concentrations, reproduction, development, and abiotic factors. Based on available data, transfer coefficients between various components of the model were calculated and used to simulate population changes over a 4-year span (Fig. 6). Using this model, it is predicted that even low levels of mercury will dramatically reduce populations of *Uca* in an estuary. This modelling approach can be used to gain insight into which physiological functions are most sensitive to environmental change at different stages in the life history of an organism. One of the important objectives of physiological ecologists is to understand how organisms respond to their environment.

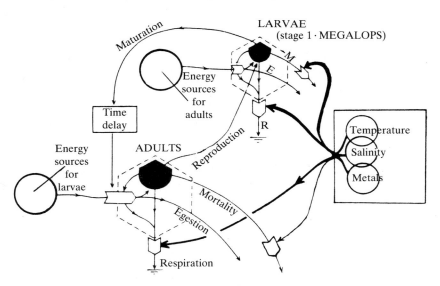

Fig. 5. Conceptual model of major energy flows in marine invertebrates Vernberg *et al.*, 1978).

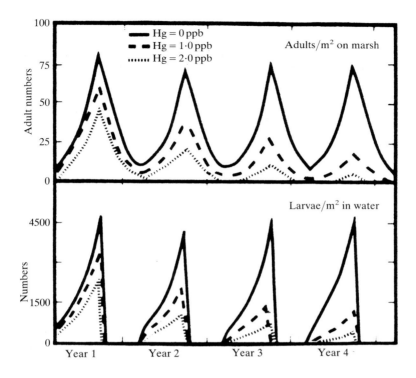

Fig. 6. Simulated annual fluctuations of adult and larval numbers of fiddler crabs under control conditions and when exposed to low levels of mercury (Vernberg *et al.*, 1978).

We are beginning to understand how separate physiological systems function, but we need to know how the responses of the various systems are integrated so that there is continuity of biotic systems through time.

Multiple factor interaction

Since Alderdice (1972), Salisbury (1975), Vernberg (1975), and Vernberg (1978) have reviewed and discussed many papers dealing with this topic, a comprehensive review is not attempted; rather, it will emphasize some distinct research areas. In some cases, two or more factors may interact to produce a synergistic response, which is defined as the cooperative action of discrete agencies, such that the total effect is greater than the sum of the two effects taken independently. A multiple factor effect is simply the expression of the influence of two or more factors on some response of an organism. The data from this type of study can be

statistically analysed to determine the nature and significance of interactions (see review of Alderdice, 1972).

Lethal limits

One of the classic papers demonstrating the effects of three factors
(salinity, temperature, and dissolved oxygen concentration) on the survival of an adult aquatic animal, the American lobster, is that of McLeese
(1956). A sublethal but stressful exposure to one factor may become
lethal when an animal is exposed concurrently to a second sublethal but
stressful factor. The net result is a reduction in the size of the zone of
compatibility. For example, when salinity is optimal, the lobster can
survive at a higher temperature than it can when exposed to low salinity
and elevated temperature. Larval states are also sensitive to multiple
factor exposure, as seen in the work of Vernberg, DeCoursey & O'Hara
(1974). In this case the multiple effects of temperature, salinity, and
cadmium also reduced the size of the compatibility zone for larval fiddler
crabs.

Laboratory determination of the response to temperature and salinity
does not always correlate with the occurrence of that species in the field.
For example, Bradley (1975) reported that the thermal tolerance of the
copepod *Eurytemora affinis* determined at various salinities, with or
without acclimation, varied with season. He also reported that the
tolerance level and differences between populations greatly increased
with salinity. The seasonal distribution of this copepod, however, is contrary to what would be predicted on the basis of his data. Bradley suggested that other copepod species have a competitive advantage during the
summer and fall and thereby restrict populations of *E. affinis*. In contrast,
after determining the salinity and temperature tolerances and the salinity
preferences of the meiofaunal species *Derocheilocaris typica*, Kraus &
Found (1975) found that this species was distributed in nature by active
selection of tolerable and avoidance of intolerable salinity – temperature
regimes. Distribution patterns were in general agreement with laboratory
findings, unlike the work of Bradley (1975).

The role of other environmental factors also has been studied. Roland
& Ring (1977) reported on the interrelations of cold, freezing, and
desiccation tolerances of the limpet *Acmaea digitalis*. The freezing
tolerance of the intertidal mollusc *Modiolus demissus* increased after
acclimation to either low temperature or high salinity (Murphy & Pierce,
1975). It was proposed that low-temperature acclimation does not act to
increase freezing tolerance by reducing the amount of tissue water frozen,

but rather it increases cellular tolerance to greater levels of dehydration by an unspecified mechanism.

Vargo & Sastry (1977) analysed the combined effects of two other environmental factors, dissolved oxygen and temperature, on the tolerance limits of five zoeal stages and megalops of the crab *Cancer irroratus*. In general, these larval states appear to have the capacity to tolerate a wider range of temperature and oxygen conditions than they encounter in the natural environment.

The interaction of abiotic and biotic factors can influence measures of tolerance. For example, Rippingale & Hodgkin (1977) reported that the brackish-water copepod *Sulcanus conflictus* is rarely found in salinities above 25‰. Yet in laboratory studies this species will thrive in high salinities if excess food is available. It is suggested that the high energy demands for osmoregulation are not met in natural field conditions.

Wallis (1976) has published a simple multifactorial model using response-surface analysis for studies relating to power-station cooling systems. He incorporated salinity, temperature, temperature shock, exposure time, and mortality responses as well as some sublethal effects.

Larval development and growth

Various papers have dealt with the effects of environmental factors on the development of embryos and larvae (see review of Sastry, 1983). Earlier Alderdice & Forrester (1968) demonstrated that developmental abnormalities occurred in *Parophrys vetulus* eggs when exposed to certain temperature–salinity combinations. The effects of cadmium and salinity on the larval development of two estuarine crabs, *Rhithropanopeus harrisii* and *Callinectes sapidus*, subjected to either constant or cycling temperature were reported by Rosenberg & Costlow (1976). Cycling temperature appeared to lengthen survival times. The megalops were more tolerant of cadmium than were the zoeal stages. Christiansen & Costlow (1975) reported on the effects of salinity and cyclic temperature on *R. harrisii*. Christiansen, Costlow & Monroe (1977), recently studied the effects of the juvenile hormone mimic ZR–515 (Altosid), salinity, and cyclic temperatures on this same species. No significant synergism between Altosid, salinity, and temperature was reported. The amphipod *Corophium triaenonyx* inhabits parchment tubes in fouling communities on wood and concrete jetties. The eggs are more sensitive to salinity than are adults. The optimum range for development is between 27·5 and 30‰ and a constant temperature of 28 °C (Shyamasundari, 1976).

In 1975, Lough reevaluated the literature on the combined effects of temperature and salinity on survival and growth of bivalve larvae using response-surface techniques. Generally, tolerance to both temperature and salinity were greater in the late veliger larvae than in the developing embryos. Each species had its own specific characteristic response pattern, which changed as the larvae approached the adult condition. In all species there was a significant temperature–salinity interaction in relation to growth. Cain (1975) subjected larvae of the bivalve *Rangia cuneata* to combinations of temperature and salinity. Embryos were relatively insensitive to thermal shock. In addition, growth was reduced in lower salinities. The combined effects of temperature and salinity resulted in a higher level of mortality than the sum of the mortalities for either of the two factors alone.

Fish development is also influenced by environmental factors. Hamor & Garside (1976) subjected embryos of the Atlantic salmon, *Salmo salar*, to various combinations of temperature, dissolved oxygen, and water exchange. Survival during embryogenesis and during the hatching period was limited primarily by oxygen supply. Water exchange and temperature were next in importance, but all three were statistically significant in affecting development.

Reproduction

Asexual reproduction in an intertidal zone sea anemone, *Haliplanella luciae*, was influenced by exposure to both fluctuating temperature and immersion (Johnson & Shick, 1977). Significantly different numbers of fissions were observed under these various test conditions.

Other reproductive phenomena can be influenced by environmental factor interactions. De Vlaming (1975) reported that at any time during the year a long-photoperiod warm-temperature regime stimulated gonadal development to the prespawning condition or induced spawning in the cyprinid fish *Notemigonus crysoleucas*. Neither photoperiod nor temperature acting alone would stimulate final gonadal maturation. Although spermatocyte formation, proliferation, and the early stages of vitellogenesis occurred independently with respect to imposed conditions, final gonadal maturation and the rate of gametogenesis depend on specific environmental conditions. Rouquette (1976) reported that temperature and light influenced ovary development, formation of periodic sexual characteristics, and egg laying of the crab *Pachygrapsus marmoratus*. Recently Sastry (1983) reviewed the influence of environmental factors on reproduction of crustaceans.

Behaviour

Environmental factor interactions also influence the behaviour of many species of organisms. Both the hard-shell clam *Mercenaria mercenaria* and the Atlantic surf clam *Spisula solidissima* experience extremes of temperature and dissolved oxygen during their burrowing activity. For each species a thermal zone of optimum activity was determined; above and below this zone burrowing declined with changing temperature. Exposing *Mercenaria* to low oxygen conditions $(1 \, \text{mg} \cdot \text{litre}^{-1})$ for 3 weeks did not severely impair burrowing (Savage, 1976).

Another behavioural response, thermal preference, has been studied in relation to thermal acclimation and salinity in the fishes *Fundulus heteroclitus* and *F. diaphanus* (Garside & Morrison, 1977) and *Gasterosteus aculeatus* (Garside, Heinze & Barbour 1977). Both species of *Fudulus* preferred higher temperatures in a salinity approximating that of the typical habitat. In *Gasterosteus* the preferred temperatures increased through thermal acclimation, ranging from 5 to 25 °C. However, values for the freshwater tests were about 2 °C lower at each acclimation point than those for sea water tests. Differences might be due to differentials in metabolic loading brought on by osmoregulative stresses.

Acute changes in temperature and salinity affect pulsation rates in the ephyrae of the jellyfish *Aurelia aurita* (Dillon, 1977). The rate increases with temperature, although a Q_{10} of 0·97 was found between 20 and 25 °C. When salinity is reduced acutely, the pulsation rate is increased for about a 2-day period.

Physiological responses

Numerous physiological processes are influenced by interaction of multiple environmental factors (Kinne, 1963, 1964; Vernberg & Vernberg, 1970, 1972; Alderdice, 1976; Vernberg, 1978). Only a few will be cited here.

Water loss

Humidity affects the rate of water loss in the shore crab *Carcinus maenas* and the subtidal crab *Portunus marmoreus* (Ahsanullah & Newell, 1977). *Portunus* loses water more readily than *Carcinus*, probably because of differences in relative gill areas.

Metabolic rate

The results of numerous investigations of the effects of temperature, salinity, and other factors on the metabolic rates of aquatic organisms have been published. The metabolic rate of the goby *Gillichthys mirabilis* increased with increasing temperature, decreased with decreasing ambient oxygen, but remained constant over a wide range of salinities (Courtois, 1976). Nelson, Armstrong, Knight & Li (1977) found that the distribution and migration of juvenile *Macrobrachium rosenbergii* in natural habitats was correlated with their metabolic responses to temperature and salinity. Working with the mysid *Neomysis intermedia*, Simmons & Knight (1975) measured respiration at different combinations of temperature and salinity at three seasons of the year. This species is found in freshwater and in salinities up to 18‰. Unlike the goby, their metabolic rate decreases as salinity is increased. As temperature increases, metabolic rate increases. These workers found seasonal changes that may be related to reproduction and to the type of food available. The metabolic rate of the isopod *Idotea chelipes* from Lake Veere, The Netherlands, is influenced by temperature and salinity in such a manner as to suggest the need for energy for osmoregulatory activities (Vlasblom, Graafsmar & Verhoeven 1977). Dimock & Groves (1976), working with thermal–salinity effects on the respiration rate of the estuarine crab *Panopeus herbstii* concluded that these two factors showed significant interaction. The amphipod *Gammarus fossarum* showed partial metabolic regulation in waters of decreasing oxygen content. In the microhabitat of this species, slowly running water is preferred, with a maximal temperature of 22 °C (Franke, 1977).

A unique environment in the ocean is the oxygen minimum layer, which may have oxygen levels less than $0.5 \, \text{ml} \cdot \text{litre}^{-1}$. The copepod *Gaussia princeps* exhibits a diurnal vertical migration, but may spend days below a depth of 400 m in the oxygen minimum layer. Extending some of his earlier work on *G. princeps*, Childress (1977) observed the effects of pressure, temperature, and oxygen consumption of this midwater species. At all temperature–pressure combinations, *G. princeps* displays a very low metabolic rate compared to shallow-living copepods. A higher rate of oxygen consumption was exhibited at the shallower night-time depths and a much lower rate (partially anaerobic) at deeper daytime depths. Hydrostatic pressure significantly affected oxygen consumption at pressures as low as 28 atm. These responses can be correlated with the ecology of this species. Bivalve molluscs may also be exposed to periods of anoxia. Bayne & Livingstone (1977) reported that *Mytilus edulis* acclimated with respect to rates of oxygen consumption after being maintained at reduced oxygen tensions for more than 5 days. Temperatures of 10 to 22 °C did not influence the capacity to acclimate.

Metabolic responses of excised gills of the crab *Hemigrapsus nudus* to temperature and salinity adaptation were reported by Hulbert, Schneider & Mood (1976a). These workers also investigated the effects of temperature and salinity on the intermediary metabolism of excised gill homogenates of this species (Hulbert *et al.*, 1976b). At the subcellular level Thomson, Sargent & Owen (1977) reported the influence of acclimatization temperature and salinity on Na^+,K^+-dependent adenosine triphosphate and fatty acid composition in the gills of the eel *Anguilla anguilla*. They concluded that temperature and not salinity determines the degree of unsaturation of gill lipids. The Arrhenius plot showed a different discontinuity for microsomal Na^+,K^+-ATPase from gills of freshwater eels than that for preparations from gills of seawater eels. In another study, temperature and thermal acclimation influenced the osmotic properties and the non-electrolyte permeability of liver and gill mitochondria from the rainbow trout, *Salmo gairdneri* (Hazel & Schuster, 1976).

Osmoregulation

In 1979, Vernberg & Silverthorn, Bouquegneau & Gilles, and Gilles & Jeuniaux reviewed the literature on the interaction between osmoregulation and environmental factors. As is to be expected, environmental factors differ in their ability to influence the osmoregulating ability of marine organisms. For example, when temperature falls some species cannot osmoregulate, while, in contrast, other species are not influenced. Frequently those animals which cannot osmoregulate at lower temperatures migrate to higher salinity waters. Larvae and adults may show different responses to salinity and temperature. Species also show marked differences in their ability to osmoregulate in a media of fluctuating salinity. Pollutants affect the osmoregulating of some species but not always in a predictable manner.

Other physiological processes

Other physiological processes also have been studied when the organism is subjected to multiple environmental factors. Duman & DeVries (1974) found that temperature and photoperiod influenced the production of a macromolecular substance that functions as an antifreeze in the blood serum of a fish. From a biogeographic point of view, it was interesting to note that apparent genetic differences exist between Alaska and California populations of *Anoplarchus purpurescens* in that the

California fishes were unable to produce antifreeze when acclimated to cold temperatures.

Endocrine changes can result when levels of environmental factors are changed. For example, McKeown & Peter (1976) found that photoperiod and temperature influenced the release of prolactin from the pituitary gland of the goldfish, *Carassius auratus*. In fiddler crabs, Silverthorn (1975) reported that temperature and thermal acclimation affected the production of a 'hormone-like' factor, which influenced oxygen consumption. Regeneration and moulting of fiddler crabs are influenced by light, temperature, and salinity (Weis, 1976).

In summary, studies of multiple environmental factors and their interactions have involved many diverse organisms inhabiting aquatic systems. These studies have included numerous abiotic factors, both natural and man-induced, and biotic factors. An organism is faced with a complex environment, and it is a natural evolution in our scientific thinking to investigate multiple factor effects and interactions in terms of organismic responses. We need more coordinated field and laboratory studies to answer environmentally oriented questions. A better definition of the characteristics of the microenvironment in which a species lives is required to design laboratory studies that simulate the environment. Experiments need to be designed to help explain and describe the functional mechanisms involved in an organism's responses to multiple factors. As we begin to understand one level of complexity, we encounter an entirely different and higher level of complexity. It is the excitement of trying to understand the next higher level of complexity that compels us to continue research.

Contribution No. 569 of the Belle W. Baruch Institute for Marine Biology and Coastal Research.

References

AHSANULLAH, M. & NEWELL, R. C. (1977). The effects of humidity and temperature on water loss in *Carcinus maenas* (L) and *Portunus marmoreus* (Leach), *Comp. Biochem. Physiol.* **56A**, 593–601.

ALDERDICE, D. F. (1972). Chapter 12 Factor combination. In *Marine Ecology*, Vol. 1, Part 3 (ed. O. Kinne), pp. 1659–1722. New York: Wiley-Interscience, Inc.

ALDERDICE, D. F. (1976). Some concepts and descriptions of physiological tolerance: rate-temperature curves of poikilotherms as transects of response surfaces. *J. Fish. Res. Board Can.* **33**, 299–307.

ALDERDICE, D. F. & FORRESTER, C. R. (1968). Some effects of salinity and temperature on early development and survival of the English sole *(Parophrys vetulus)*. *J. Fish. Res. Board Can.* **25**, 495–521.

BAYNE, B. L. & LIVINGSTONE, D. R. (1977). Responses of *Mytilus edulis* L. to low oxygen tension: acclimation of the rate of oxygen consumption. *J. comp. Physiol.* **114**, 129–142.

BELMAN, B. W. & CHILDRESS, J. J. (1976). Circulatory adaptations to the oxygen minimum layer in the bathypelagic mysid *Gnathophausia ingens*. *Biol. Bull. Mar. biol. Lab., Woods Hole* **150**, 15–37.

BOUQUEGNEAU J. M. & GILLES R. (1979). Osmoregulation and pollution of the aquatic medium. In *Mechanisms of Osmoregulation in Animals*, (ed. R. Gilles), pp. 563–580. New York: Wiley Interscience.

BRADLEY, B. P. (1975). The anomalous influence of salinity on temperature tolerances of summer and winter populations of the copepod *Eurytemora affinis*. *Biol. Bull. Mar. biol. Lab., Woods Hole* **148**, 26–34.

BROWN, F. A., JR. (1962). Response of the planarian *Dugesia* and the protozoan *Paramecium* to very weak horizontal magnetic fields. *Biol. Bull. Mar. biol. Lab., Woods Hole* **123**, 264–281.

BULLOCK, T. H. (1955). Compensation for temperature in the metabolism and activity of poikilotherms. *Biol. Rev. Cambridge Philos. Soc.* **30**, 311–342.

CAIN, T. D. (1975). Combined effects of changes in temperature and salinity on early stages of *Rangia cuneata*. *Va. J. Sci.* **25**, 30–31.

CERAME-VIVAS, M. J. & GRAY, I. E. (1966). The distributional pattern of benthic invertebrates of the continental shelf off North Carolina. *Ecology* **47**, 260–270.

CHILDRESS, J. J. (1968). Oxygen minimum layer, vertical distribution and respiration of the mysid *Gnathophausia ingens*. *Science* **160**, 1242–1243.

CHILDRESS, J. J. (1971). Respiratory adaptations to the oxygen minimum layer in the bathypelagic mysid *Gnathophausia ingens*. *Biol. Bull. Mar. biol. Lab., Woods Hole* **141**, 109–121.

CHILDRESS, J. J. (1977). Effects of pressure, temperature and oxygen on the oxygen-consumption rate of the midwater copepod *Gaussia princeps*. *Mar. Biol.* **39**, 19–24.

CHRISTIANSEN, M. E. & COSTLOW, J. D., JR. (1975). The effect of salinity and cyclic temperature on larval development of the mud-crab *Rhithropanopeus harrisii* (Brachyura: Xanthidae) reared in the laboratory. *Mar. Biol.* **32**, 215–221.

CHRISTIANSEN, M. E, COSTLOW, J. D., JR. & MONROE, R. J. (1977). Effects of the juvenile hormone mimic ZR-515 (Altosid) on larval development of the mud-crab *Rhithropanopeus harrisii* in various salinities and cyclic temperatures. *Mar. Biol.* **39**, 269–279.

COURTOIS, L. A. (1976). Respiratory responses of *Gillichthys maribilis* to changes in temperature, dissolved oxygen and salinity. *Comp. Biochem. Physiol.* **53A**, 7–10.

CRISP, D. J. (1974). Factors influencing the settlement of marine invertebrate larvae. In *Chemoreception in Marine Organisms*, (eds P. T. Grand and A. M. Mackie), pp. 177–265. New York: Academic Press.

CROGHAN, P. C. (1961). Competition and mechanisms of osmotic adaptation. In *Mechanisms in Biological Competition*, pp. 156–167. *Soc. exp. Biol.* Symposium No. **15**.

DAVENPORT, C. B. (1897–1899). *Experimental Morphology*. Vols I and II. London and New York: Macmillan Publishing Co.

DECOURSEY, P. J. (1976). *Biological Rhythms in the Marine Environment*. No. 4, 283 pp. Columbia, SC: University of South Carolina Press.

DE VLAMING, V. L. (1975). Effects of photoperiod and temperature on gonadal activity in the cyprinid teleost, *Notemigonous crysoleucas*. *Biol. Bull. Mar. biol. Lab., Woods Hole* **148**, 402–415.

DIEMER, F. P., VERNBERG, F. J. & MIRKES, D. Z. (1980). *Advanced Concepts in Ocean Measurements for Marine Biology*. No. 10, 572 pp. Columbia, SC: University of South Carolina Press.

DILLON, T. M. (1977). Effects of acute changes in temperature and salinity on pulsation rates in ephyrae of the scyphozoan *Aurelia aurita*. *Mar. Biol.* **42**, 31–35.

DIMOCK, R. V., JR. & GROVES, K. H. (1976). Interaction of temperature and salinity on oxygen consumption of the estuarine crab *Panopeus herbstii*. *Mar. Biol.* **33**, 301–308.

DUMAN, J. G. & DEVRIES, A. L. (1974). The effects of temperature and photoperiod on antifreeze production on cold water fishes. *J. exp. Zool.*. **190**, 89–98.

FOSKETT, J. K. (1977). Osmoregulation in the larvae and adults of the grapsid crab *Sesarma reticulatum* Say. *Biol. Bull. Mar. biol. Lab., Woods Hole* **153**, 505–526.

FOX, H. M. (1936). The activity and metabolism of poikilothermal animals in different latitudes. I. *Proc. Zool. Soc. London.* 1936, 945–955.

FOX, H. M. (1939). The activity and metabolism of poikilothermal animals in different latitudes. V. *Proc. Zool. Soc. Lond. A.* **109**, 141–156.

FOX, H. M. & WINGFIELD, C. A. (1937). The activity and metabolism of poikilothermal animals in different latitudes. II. *Proc. Zool. Soc. London, Ser. A.* **107**, 275–282.

FRANKE, U. (1977). Experimental investigations of the respiration of *Gammarus fossarum* Koch 1835 (Crustacea-Amphipoda) in relation to temperature, oxygen concentration and water movement, *Arch. Hydrobiol. Supplement B.* **48**, 369–411.

GARSIDE, E. T. HEINZE, D. G. & BARBOUR, S. E. (1977). Thermal preference in relation to salinity in the threespine stickleback, *Gasterosteus aculeatus* L., with an interpretation of its significance. *Can. J. Zool.* **55**, 590–594.

GARSIDE, E. T. & MORRISON, G. C. (1977). Thermal preferences of mummichog, *Fundulus heteroclitus* L., and banded killifish, *F. diaphanus* (LeSueus), (Cyprinodontidae) In relation to thermal acclimation and salinity. *Can. J. Zool.* **55**, 1190–1194.

GEORGE, R. Y. (1981). Functional adaptations of deep-sea organisms. In *Functional Adaptations of Marine Organisms*, (eds. F. J. Vernberg & W. B. Vernberg), pp. 229–332, New York: Academic Press.

GILLES, R. & JEUNIAUX, CH. (1979). Osmoregulation and ecology in media of fluctuating salinity. In *Methanisms of Osmoregulation in Animals*, (ed. R. Gilles), 581–610. New York: Wiley Interscience.

GNAIGER, E. (1983). Heat dissipation and energetic efficiency in animal anoxibiosis: Economy Contra Power. *J. exp. Zool.* **228**, 471–490.

GORDON, M. S. & BELMAN, B. W. (1981). Pelagic Macrofauna. In *Functional Adaptations of Marine Organisms*, (ed. F. J. Vernberg & W. B. Vernberg), pp. 231–277. New York: Academic Press.

GRAHAME, J. (1983). Adaptive aspects of feeding mechanisms. In *Environmental Adaptations*, Vol. 8 of Biology of Crustacea Series, (eds. F. J. Vernberg & W. B. Vernberg), pp. 65–107. New York: Academic Press.

GRIFFITHS, R. J. (1981). Aerial exposure and energy balance in littoral and sublittoral *Choromytilus meridionalis* (Kr.) (Bivalvia). *J. exp. Mar. Biol. Ecol.* **52**, 231–241.

GROSS, W. J. (1963). Acclimation to hypersaline water in a crab. *Comp. Biochem. Physiol.* **9**, 181–188.

HAMOR, T. & GARSIDE, E. T. (1976). Development rates of embryos of Atlantic salmon, *Salmo salar* L., in response to various levels of temperature, dissolved oxygen, and water exchange. *Can. J. Zool.* **54**, 1912–1917.

HAZEL, J. R. & SCHUSTER, V. L. (1976). The effects of temperature and thermal acclimation upon the osmotic properties and nonelectrolyte permeability of liver and gill mitochondria from rainbow trout *(Salmo gairdneri)*. *J. exp. Zool.* **195**, 425–438.

HICKMAN, C. P. (1959). The osmoregulatory role of the thyroid gland in the starry flounder, *Platichthys stellatus*. *Can. J. Zool.* **37**, 997–1060.

HOAR, W. S. (1975). *General and Comparative Physiology*. 848 pp. Englewood Cliffs, New Jersey: Prentice-Hall, Inc.

HOCHACHKA, P. W. & SOMERO, G. N. (1973). *Strategies of Biochemical Adaptation*. 358 pp. Philadelphia: Saunders.

HULBERT, W. C., SCHNEIDER, D. E. & MOON, T. W. (1976a). Temperature and salinity adaptation in the purple shore crab *Hemigrapsus nudus*: An *in vitro* physiological study with excised gills. *Mar. Biol.* **36**, 217–222.

HULBERT, W. C. SCHNEIDER, D. E. & MOON, T. W. (1976b). Temperature and salinity adaptation in the purple shore crab *Hemigrapsus nudus*: An *in vitro* metabolic flux study with excised gills. *Mar. Biol.* **36**, 223–231.

JOHNSON, L. L. & SHICK, J. M. (1977). Effects of fluctuating temperature and immersion on asexual reproduction in the intertidal sea anemone *Haliplanella luciae* (Verrill) in laboratory culture. *J. exp. Mar. Biol. Ecol.* **28**, 141–149.

JORGENSEN, C. B. (1976). August Putter, August Krogh, and modern ideas on the use of dissolved organic matter in aquatic environments. *Biol. Rev. Cambridge Philos. Soc.* **51**, 292–328.

KINNE, O. (1963). The effects of temperature and salinity on marine and brackish water animals. I. Temperature. *Oceanogr. Mar. Biol. A. Rev.* **1**, 301–340.

KINNE, O. (1964). The effects of temperature and salinity on marine and brackish water animals. II. Salinity and temperature salinity combinations. *Oceanogr. Mar. Biol. A. Rev.* **2**, 281–339.

KRAUS, M. G. & FOUND, B. W. (1975). Preliminary observations on salinity and temperature tolerances and salinity preferences of *Derocheilocaris typica*. *Cah. Biol. mar.* **16**, 751–762.

KROGH, A. (1916). *Respiratory Exchange of Animals and Man*. London: Green.

LAVERACK, M. S. (1968). On the receptors of marine invertebrates. *Oceanogr. Mar. Biol. Ann. Rev.* **6**, 249–234.

LOCKWOOD, A. P. M. (1962). The osmoregulation of Crustacea. *Biol. Rev.* **37**, 257–305.

LOUGH, R. C. (1975). A reevaluation of the combined effects of temperature and salinity on survival and growth of bivalve larvae using response surface techniques. *Fish. Bull.* **73**, 86–94.

MACDONALD, A. G. (1975). *Physiological Aspects of Deep Sea Biology*. London and New York: Cambridge Univ. Press.

MACMILLAN, D. H. (1966). *Tides*. New York: American Elsevier Publishing Co., Inc.

MAYER, A. G. (1914). The effects of temperature upon tropical animals. *Pap. Tortugas Lab.* **6**, 3–24. Carnegie Institute, Washington, DC.

MCKEOWN, B. A. & PETER, R. E. (1976). The effects of photoperiod and temperature on the release of prolactin from the pituitary gland of the goldfish, *Carassius auratus* L. *Can. J. Zool.* **54**, 1960–1968.

MCLEESE, D. W. (1956). Effects of temperature, salinity and oxygen on the survival of the American lobster. *J. Fish. Res. Board. Can.* **13**, 247–272.

MURPHY, D. J. & PIERCE, S. K. JR. (1975). The physiological basis for changes in the freezing tolerance of intertidal molluscs. *J. exp. Zool.* **193**, 313–322.

NAYLOR, E. & HARTNOLL, R. G. (1979). Cyclic phenomena in marine plants and animals. In *Proceedings of the 13th European Marine Biology Symposium Isle of Man, 27 September – 4 October 1978*. Oxford: Pergamon Press.

NELSON, S. G., ARMSTRONG, D. A., KNIGHT, A. W. & LI, H. W. (1977). The effects of temperature and salinity on the metabolic rate of juvenile *Macrobrachium rosenbergii* (Crustacea: Palaemonidae), *Comp. Biochem. Physiol.* **56A**, 533–537.

PANDIAN, T. J. (1975). Mechanisms of heterotrophy. In *Marine Ecology*, vol. 2 (ed. O. Kinne), pp. 61–249. New York: Wiley.

PROSSER, C. L. (1955). Physiological variation in animals. *Biol. Rev.* **30**, 229–262.

RIPPINGALE, R. J. & HODGKIN, E. P. (1977). Food availability and salinity tolerance in a brackish water copepod. *Aust. J. Mar. Freshwater Res.* **28**, 1–8.

ROLAND, W. & RING, R. A. (1977). Cold, freezing and desiccation tolerance of the limpet *Acmaea digitalis* (Eschscholtz). *Cryobiology.* **14**, 228–235.

ROSENBERG, R. & COSTLOW, J. D. JR. (1976). Synergistic effects of cadmium and salinity combined with constant and cycling temperatures on the larval development of two estuarine crab species. *Mar. Biol.* **38**, 291–303.

ROUQUETTE, M. P. (1976). Etude de la fonction de reproduction chez les femelles du crabe *Pachygrapsus marmarotus* (F.), et de differents facterus qui liu sont lies (I). *Cah. Biol. Mar.* **17**, 387–403.

SALISBURY, F. B. (1975). Multiple factor effects on plants. In *Physiological Adaptation to the Environment*. (ed. F. J. Vernberg). New York: Thomas Y. Crowell Co.

SASTRY, A. N. (1983). Ecological aspects of reproduction. In *Environmental Adaptations*, Vol. 8 of The Biology of Crustacea Series. (eds. F. J. Vernberg and W. B. Vernberg), pp. 179–270. New York: Academic Press.

SAVAGE, N. B. (1976). Burrowing activity in *Mercenaria mercenaria* (L.) and *Spisula solidissima* (Dillwyn) as a function of temperature and dissolved oxygen. *Mar. Behav. Physiol.* **3**, 221–234.

SCHOLANDER, P. F., FLAGG, W., WALTERS, V. & IRVING, L. (1953). Climatic adaptation in arctic and tropical poikilotherms. *Physiol. Zool.* **26**, 67–92.

SEMPER, K. G. (1881). *Animal Life as Affected by the Natural Conditions of Existence*. New York: Appleton.

SHELFORD, V. E. (1915). Principles and problems of ecology as illustrated by animals. *Journal of Ecology*. **3**, 1–23.

SHYAMASUNDARI, K. (1976). Effects of salinity and temperature on the development of eggs in the tube building amphipod *Corophium triaenonyx* Stebbing. *Biol. Bull. Mar. biol. Lab., Woods Hole* **150**, 286–293.

SILVERTHORN, S. (1975). Hormonal involvement in thermal acclimation in the fiddler crab *Uca pugilator* (Bosc). I. Effect of eyestalk extracts on whole animal respiration. *Comp. Biochem. Physiol.* **50A**, 281–283.

SIMMONS, M. A. & KNIGHT, A. W. (1975). Respiratory response of *Neomysis intermedia* (Crustacea: Mysidacea) to changes in salinity, temperature and season. *Comp. Biochem. Physiol.* **50A**, 181–193.

SPARCK, R. (1936). On the relation between metabolism and temperature in some marine lamellibranchs, and its zoogeographical significance. *Biol. Medd.* (5) 13.

THEEDE, H. (1973). Comparative studies on the influence of oxygen deficiency and hydrogen sulphide on marine bottom invertebrates. *Neth. J. Sea Res.* **7**, 244–252.

THEEDE, H., PONAT, A., HIROKI, K. & SCHLIEPEN, C. (1969). Studies on the resistance of marine bottom invertebrates to oxygen-deficiency and hydrogen sulphide. *Mar. Biol.* **2**, 325–337.

THOMSON, A. J., SARGENT, J. R. & OWEN, J. M. (1977). Influence of acclimitization temperature and salinity on $(Na^+ + K^+)$-dependent adenosine triphosphatase and fatty acid composition in the gills of the eel, *(Anguilla anguilla)*. *Comp. Biochem. Physiol.* **56B**, 223–228.

THORSON, G. (1936). The larval development, growth, and metabolism of arctic marine bottom invertebrates compared with those of other seas. *Medd. Gronland.* (6) 100.

VARGO, S. L. & SASTRY, A. N. (1977). Acute temperature and low dissolved oxygen tolerances of brachyuran crab *(Cancer irroratus)* larvae, *Mar. Biol.* **40**, 165–171.

VERNBERG, F. J. (1972). Dissolved gases-animals. In *Marine Ecology*. Vol. 1 (ed. O. Kinne), pp. 1491–1526. New York: Wiley (Interscience).

VERNBERG, F. J. (1978). Multiple factor and synergetics stresses in aquatic systems. In *Energy and Environmental Stress in Aquatic Systems*. (eds. H. Thorp & J. Gibbons). Washington, DC. Technical Information Center, US Dept. Energy.

VERNBERG, F. J. (1983). Respiratory adaptations. In *Environmental Adaptations* Vol. 8 *The Biology of Crustacea Series*. (eds. F. J. Vernberg & W. B. Vernberg), pp. 1–42. New York: Academic Press.

VERNBERG, F. J. & SILVERTHORN, S. Y. (1979). Temperature and osmoregulation in aquatic species. In *Mechanisms of Osmoregulation in Animals*. (ed. R. Gilles), pp. 537–562. New York: Wiley Interscience.

VERNBERG, W. B. (1974). *Symbiosis in the Sea*. 276 pp. Columbia, SC: University of South Carolina Press.

VERNBERG, W. B. (1975). Multiple factor effects on animals. In *Physiological Adaptation to the Environment*. (ed. F. J. Vernberg), pp. 521–538. New York: Croswell-Collier.

VERNBERG, W. B. & VERNBERG, F. J. (1970). Metabolic diversity in oceanic animals. *Mar. Biol.* **6**, 33–42

VERNBERG, W. B. & VERNBERG, F. J. (1972). *Environmental Physiology of Marine Animals.* Berlin and New York: Springer-Verlag.

VERNBERG, W. B., DeCOURSEY, P. J. & O'HARA, J. (1974). Multiple factor effects on physiology and behaviour of the fiddler crab, *Uca pugilator.* In *Pollution and Physiology of Marine Organisms.* (ed. F. J. Vernberg & W. B. Vernberg), pp. 381–426. New York: Academic Press.

VERNBERG, W. B., McKELLAR, H., JR. & VERNBERG, F. J., (1978). Toxicity studies and environmental impact assessment.*Environmental Management* **2**(3), 239–243.

VLASBLOM, A. G., GRAAFSMA, S. J. & VERHOEVEN, J. T. A. (1977). Survival, osmoregulatory ability, and respiration of *Idotea chelipes* (Crustacea, Isopoda) from Lake Veere in different salinities and temperatures. *Hydrobiologia* **52**, 33–38.

WALLIS, R. L. (1976). Some uses of multifactorial response surface analysis in temperature tolerance studies. *Aust. J. Mar. Freshwater Res.* **27**, 487–498.

WEIS, J. S. (1976). Effects of environmental factors on regeneration and molting in fiddler crabs. *Biol. Bull. Mar. biol. Lab., Woods Hole* **150**, 152–162.

WIESER, W. (1973). *Effects of Temperature on Ectothermic Organisms.* 298 pp. New York, Heidelberg, Berlin: Springer-Verlag.

WU, R. S. S. & LEVINGS, C. D. (1978). An energy budget for individual barnacles *(Balanus glandula). Mar. Biol.* **45**, 225–235.

Printed in Great Britain © *Society for Experimental Biology 1985*

METABOLIC ADAPTATIONS OF INTERTIDAL INVERTEBRATES TO ENVIRONMENTAL HYPOXIA (A COMPARISON OF ENVIRONMENTAL ANOXIA TO EXERCISE ANOXIA)

A. DE ZWAAN

Laboratory of Chemical Animal Physiology, State University of Utrecht, Padualaan 8, NL-3508 TB Utrecht, The Netherlands

and V. PUTZER

Institut für Zoologie, Universität Innsbruck, Peter-Mayr Str. la, A-6020 Innsbruck, Austria

Summary

By comparing environmental anaerobiosis with exercise anaerobiosis it appears that animals with high anoxia tolerance use (partly) different types of metabolic reactions to sustain energy metabolism, whereas low tolerance animals (Arthropoda, Echinodermata, Vertebrata) use the same pathway under both conditions. During exercise anaerobiosis the classical glycolysis (lactate pathway) is a main pathway among all multicellular organisms, although in marine invertebrates – except the Arthropoda and Echinodermata – it mostly does not terminate in lactate. During environmental anaerobiosis Cnidaria, Mollusca, Annelida and Sipunculida first couple additional pathways for energy extraction to the glycolytic pathway (the aspartate – succinate pathway) and later deviate the main carbon flow of glycogen at the level of phosphoenolpyruvate towards succinate, propionate and acetate production. Metabolic adaptations to anoxic cellular conditions in these groups are high fuel stores, increased ATP yield by anaerobic sources, formation of easily excretable (volatile) end products, an aspartate-dependent system for transport of hydrogen through the inner membrane of the mitochrondrion and a rapid recovery from anaerobic metabolism.

During anaerobic conditions three sources can contribute to the anaerobic power output, endogenous stores of both ATP and phosphagen and catabolism. Anaerobic power output rates have been calculated for a number of Mollusca, Annelida and Crustacea. Extreme anoxia resistance is coupled to a strongly reduced metabolic rate. In animals with high aspartate stores, the aspartate – succinate pathway and phosphagen hydrolysis can provide sufficient ATP during environmental anaerobiosis; however, with exercise anaerobiosis when ATP turnover rates may be increased by a factor of 20, pyruvate derivatives simultaneously accumulate in high amounts relative to succinate.

Introduction

Organisms living in the intertidal zone experience aquatic and aerial conditions. A number of them have an inadequate oxygen supply at a cellular level when they are faced with a lack of aerated sea water at low tide. They have generally developed impressive anaerobic capacities. Representatives of most of the invertebrate phyla have been subjects of studies of metabolic responses on imposed anaerobic conditions. Some species have been studied in greater detail and appeared to be good models for the phyla to which they belong. Examples are the sea mussel *Mytilus edulis*, the annelid *Arenicola marina* and the intertidal 'worm' *Sipunculus nudus*. From these comparative studies a number of general characteristics of anaerobic metabolism have been recognized which facilitate living in a habitat with large oxygen fluctuations. A number of these characteristics will be discussed in this paper.

In order to explain which specific metabolic adaptations may occur to environmental hypoxia we have compared the sources and pathways for ATP supply when environmental change blocks or reduces oxygen supply (environmental anaerobiosis) with the condition that due to locomotory activity the energy demand exceeds the capacity of the aerobic energy production (exercise anaerobiosis).

High fuel stores for anaerobic metabolic ATP formation

Glycogen is an important source of energy during anaerobiosis. During long-term anaerobiosis it gradually becomes the sole catabolic fuel after an initial stage in which simultaneously stored aspartate or malate can be utilized. Glycogen is therefore found in reasonable to high amounts in muscle and other tissues of invertebrates which show high anoxia tolerance (Table 1). In bivalves and gastropods values normally exceed 1 % of the wet weight (this equals 10 mg or about 60 μmoles glycosyl units), but is somewhat lower in cephalopods (Gäde & Zebe, 1973; De Zwaan & Wijsman, 1976; Livingstone, 1982; Livingstone & De Zwaan,

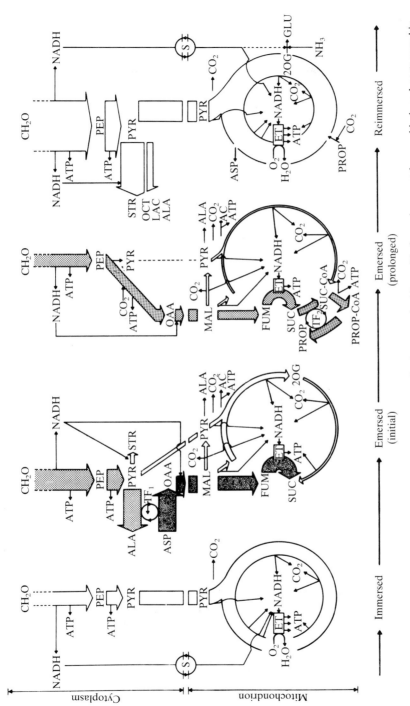

Fig. 1. A metabolic map to account for the degradation of glycogen (and aspartate) with aerobiosis, environmental anaerobiosis and postanaerobic recovery. From the left to the right, the pathways represent gradual transitions in the carbon flow, which occur in the course of long-term anaerobiosis. The width of the bars is an indication of the relative carbon flux through the given part of the pathway. (Redrawn after De Zwaan, 1983).
Abbreviations: CH_2O, glycogen; ET, electron-transfer-chain; OCT, octopine; PROP, propionate; AC, acetate; STR, strombine; S, malate-aspartate shuttle; TF_1, transfer of amino group from aspartate to alanine by amino-transferase reactions; TF_2, transfer of CoA by acyl-CoA transferase.

Table 1. Levels ($\mu moles \cdot g^{-1}$ wet weight) of glycogen (glycosyl units), aspartate and phosphagen in different invertebrates

Organism	Tissue	Glycogen	Aspartate[1]	Phosphagen	Reference
A Mollusca					
Mytilus edulis	AM	86·3–234†[1]	4–14†[1]	2–85†[2]	[1]Zurburg et al. 1979; [2]Zurburg & Ebberink, 1981
Crassostrea virginica	AM	61·7–493†	6·7	n.d.	Galtsoff, 1964; Eberlee et al. 1983
Cardium edule	AM[1]F[2]	101[1]	4·5[2]	6·5[2]	[1]Gäde & Zebe, 1973; [2]Gäde & Meinardus, 1981
Cardium tuberculatum	F[1]TA[2]	n.d.	5·8[2]	24·0[1]	Meinardus & Gäde, unpublished
Placopecten magellanicus	AM[c]/AM[p]	25/62	1·5/0·5	5·1/22·3	De Zwaan et al. 1980
Lima hians	AM	n.d.	2·7	21·9	Gäde, 1983b
Anodonta cygnea††	AM	148	0·07	n.d.	Gäde & Zebe, 1973; De Zwaan et al. 1984
Nassa mutabilis	F	n.d.	5·7	9·3	Gäde et al. 1984
Buccinum undatum	F[1]TA[2]	97[2]	7·3[2]	8·5[1]	Koormann & Grieshaber, 1980; Kluytmans & Zandee, 1983
Littorina littorea	TA	42	5·1	n.d.	Kluytmans & Zandee, 1983
Lymnea stagnalis††	TA,F[2]	96[1]	0·13[2]	n.d.	[1]Kluytmans & Zandee, 1983; [2]De Zwaan et al. 1976
Cepaea nemoralis†††	TA	80	0·96	n.d.	Kluytmans & Zandee, 1983
Helix pomatia†††	TA	58	0·98	n.d.	Kluytmans & Zandee, 1983
B Sipunculida					
Sipunculus nudus	BWM	n.d.	1·5	34	Pörtner et al. 1984

Table 1. *cont.*

Organism	Tissue	Glycogen	Aspartate[1]	Phosphagen	Reference
C Annelida					
Arenicola marina	BWM	62†	8·8†	7·4–14·4†	Schöttler et al. 1983; Siegmund & Grieshaber, 1984
Nephtys hombergii	TA	n.d.	5·6†	n.d.	Schöttler, 1982
Nereis diversicolor	TA	94†	3·8†	n.d.	Schöttler, 1978
Nereis pelagica	TA	n.d.	1·5†	n.d.	Schöttler, 1979
Nereis virens	TA	n.d.	3·4†	n.d.	Schöttler, 1979
Tubifex sp.††	TA	56–222†	0·6†	1·74†	Seuss et al. 1982; Hoffmann, 1981
Lumbriculus variegatus††	TA	136	1·3(9)	2·03	Putzer, 1984
Hirudo medicinalis††	TA	40	0·3(7)	n.d.	Zebe et al. 1981
D Crustacea					
Cirolana borealis††	TA	66†	1·1†	n.d.	De Zwaan & Skjoldal, 1979
Artemia salina	TA	60	0·8	n.d.	Bernaerts, 1982
Cherax destructor	TM	37	n.d.	25	England & Baldwin, 1983
Crangon crangon	TM	25†	0·9†	21†	Onnen & Zebe, 1983
Upogebia pugettensis	TA	44	0·5	n.d.	Zebe, 1982
Callianassa californiensis	TA	24	0·9	n.d.	Zebe, 1982
Orconectes limosus	TM	77	n.d.	21	Gäde et al. 1984

† calculated from dry weight, using a water content of 80%; †† fresh water invertebrates; TA, total animal; TM, tail muscle; BWM, body wall musculature; AM, adductor muscle; AM_c, adductor muscle catch part; AM_p, adductor phasic part; F, foot; n.d., not determined; [1] Values in brackets give levels of malate.

1983). In the annelids *Nereis diversicolor, Arenicola marina, Tubifex sp.* and *Lumbriculus variegatus* values are above 1·5 % (Schöttler, 1978; Zebe, Salge Wieman & Wilps 1981; Seuss, Hipp & Hoffmann 1983; Putzer, 1984), whereas for the leech *Hirudo medicinalis* a value of 0·6 % was found (Zebe *et al.*, 1981). Values of crustacean species which can survive experimental anoxia for one to two days range between 0·3 and about 1·25 % (Gäde, 1983a).

Aspartate is another important substrate of anaerobic metabolism in marine annelids and molluscs (Table 1). Concentrations vary in a range from 1·5 to 15 μmoles per gram wet weight (or 0·02–0·2 %). In marine crustaceans values are usually below 1 μmole and aspartate is here not of quantitative importance as energy substrate during anaerobiosis.

Aspartate is utilized at the onset of anaerobiosis, but due to its low concentration relative to glycogen its role is usually limited to the first 5 to 10 h (Collicutt & Hochachka, 1977; Schöttler, 1980; Gäde, 1983a). In fresh water invertebrates high steady state levels of malate instead of aspartate may be present. In larvae of the midge *Chaoborus crystallinus* levels of 15·6 μmole were found (Englisch, Opalka & Zebe, 1982), in *Hirudo medicinalis* 7 μmoles (Zebe *et al.*, 1981) and 9 μmoles in *Lumbriculus variegatus* (Putzer, 1984). During environmental anaerobiosis both aspartate and malate are utilized and converted into succinate.

Anaerobic ATP generating pathways

In the presence of an adequate supply of oxygen the malate aspartate shuttle can compete better for cytosolic NADH than pyruvate oxidoreductases (see Fig. 1, immersed). When during low tide oxygen availability becomes limited, gradually more and more NADH will be reoxidized in the cytosol by lactate dehydrogenase. The so-called classical glycolysis has two sites at which ATP is generated at substrate level. Vertebrates, Echinoderms and Arthropods rely mainly on the classical glycolysis for anaerobic energy production, both with exercise and environmental anoxia. Lactate is the prime end product formed from pyruvate, sometimes accompanied by accumulation of small amounts of alanine (Zebe 1982; England & Baldwin, 1983; Onnen & Zebe, 1983; Gäde, 1984). The same can be stated for other invertebrates with exercise anaerobiosis. In many marine invertebrates, however, the classical glycolysis does not terminate in lactate accumulation. Except for the Arthropoda and Echinodermata, lactate dehydrogenase is usually replaced by enzymes which catalyse the reductive imination of an amino acid and pyruvate. The iminocarboxylic acid products thus formed are collectively called opines. To date three opines have been identified in marine invertebrates: octopine, strombine and alanopine. The amino acid co-substrates of pyruvate are arginine, glycine and alanine, respectively. Octopine was first isolated from the muscle of *Octopus octopoda* by Morizowa (1927), strombine in the tissue of the gastropod *Strombus gigas* (Sangster, Thomas & Tingling, 1975) and alanopine from the muscle of the squid *Todarodes pacificus* (Sato, Sato & Tsuchiya 1977). Van Thoai & Robin (1959) demonstrated the synthesis of octopine from arginine and pyruvate, in the presence of NADH, by octopine dehydrogenase. A dehydrogenase which synthesized D-strombine from glycine and pyruvate in the presence of NADH was first isolated from the adductor muscle of the oyster *Crassostrea gigas* (Fields, 1976; Fields *et al.*, 1980). This enzyme was called 'alanopine dehydrogenase' because it also catalysed formation of alanopine from alanine and pyruvate in the presence of NADH. With the discovery of the opine dehydrogenases it became apparent that marine invertebrates may have up to four pyruvate oxidoreductases in their muscular tissues which together represent a considerable potential for the reduction of pyruvate. The identification and distribution of opine dehydrogenases in metazoa have recently been discussed (Livingstone, De Zwaan, Leopold & Marteïjn, 1983; De Zwaan & Dando, 1984).

Due to a lack of routine methods for opine determination in crude tissue extracts it took until 1981 for the unequivocal *in vivo* formation of strombine and alanopine in relation to anaerobiosis to be demonstrated. Meanwhile four methods for analyses of opines have been published (see Fiore, Nicchitta & Ellington, 1984) and over the last three years a respectable number of papers reporting *in vivo* production of opines have appeared. We have summarized those studies in which at least the formation of one opine was reported (see Table 2).

Preference for octopine formation appears to be related to high resting steady state values of phosphoarginine, which in swimming bivalves and cephalopods range between 20 and 30 μmoles per gram wet weight (Table 1). *Cardium tuberculatum*, which can display strenuous escape movements with its foot, has a comparable high resting value (Table 1). As is clear from Table 2, octopine is the preferred pyruvate derivative in these mobile molluscs, formed during exercise and postexercise recovery. Whelks (*Buccinum undatum, Nassa mutabilis, Nassarius coronatus, Busycon contrarium*) and other gastropods which exhibit vigorous escape activities have steady state levels of phosphoarginine which are lower (around 10 μmoles) and in these animals not all pyruvate may be used for octopine formation. In the gastropod *Strombus luhuanus*, for example, both octopine and strombine are formed at about equal amounts during

Table 2. *Accumulation of various pyruvate derivatives and activities of pyruvate oxidoreductases ($\mu moles \cdot min^{-1} \cdot g^{-1}$ wet weight) in several marine invertebrates*

Species	Tissue	Pyruvate derivative					Condition	Reference
		A	A/S	S	O	L		
A Nemertina								
Cerebratulus lacteus	TA	n.d. / 3		n.d.	+ / 50	− / 0·5	exercise	Gäde, 1983c
B Mollusca								
Littorina littorea	F	+ / 13†		3	− / −	+ / 7	anoxia	Storey et al. 1982; Kluytmans & Zandee, 1983
Strombus luhanus	F	230	+ / +++		+ / − / 585	− / 5	exercise / recovery	Baldwin & England, 1982a,b
Buccinum undatum	F	n.d. / 9†		n.d.	+++ / 87	− / 3	exercise	Koormann & Grieshaber, 1980
Nassarius coronatus	F	n.d. / n.d. / n.d.		n.d. / n.d. / n.d.	+++ / − / 159	− / +++/+ / 40	exercise / recovery/anoxia	Baldwin et al. 1981
Nassa mutabilis	F	n.d. / n.d. / 1		n.d. / n.d. / 13	+++ / − / 139	+ / ++ / 6	exercise / recovery	Gäde et al. 1984
Busycon contrarium	V	+ / 97			++ / 283	28	anoxia	Fiore et al. 1984; Gäde & Ellington, 1983; Ellington, 1981b
Lima hians	AM	n.d. / n.d. / 5		n.d. / n.d. / 4	++++ / − / 60	− / − / <0·1	exercise / anoxia/recovery	Gäde, 1981; Gäde, 1983

Table 2. *cont.*

Species	Tissue	Pyruvate derivative					Condition	Reference
		A	A/S	S	O	L		
Limaria fragilis	AM	3	+	37	− / <0·2	− / <0·2	exercise	Baldwin & Morris, 1983
Cardium tuberculatum	F	−		−	++	−	exercise	Gäde, 1980; Meinardus & Gäde, 1984
		+ / 21		18	117	++ / 4	anoxia	
Busycon contrarium	RM	163	+	150	507	30	anoxia	Ellington, 1982*b*
			++		−	+	recovery	
Pecten alba	AM	n.d.		n.d.	++++ / 58	<0·1	exercise	Baldwin & Opie, 1978
Pecten jacobaeus	AM	n.d.		n.d.	++++	−	exercise	Grieshaber & Gäde, 1977
Pecten maximus	AM	n.d.		n.d.	++	−	exercise	Gäde *et al.* 1978
		1†		1	+++ / 22	<0·1	recovery	
Chlamys opercularis	AM	n.d.		n.d.	−	−	exercise	Grieshaber, 1978
		0·8†		0·5†	++/+++ / 27	3	recovery: water/air	
Placopecten magellanicus	AM	n.d.		n.d.	++	−	exercise	De Zwaan *et al.* 1980; Livingstone *et al.* 1981
		n.d.		n.d.	+++ / 30	<0·2	recovery	
Argopecten irr. concentr.	AM	−		+	++++	−	exercise	Fiore *et al.* 1984; Chih & Ellington, 1983
		7		+	98	−	anoxia	

Table 2. *cont.*

Species	Tissue	A	A/S	S	O	L	Condition	Reference
Mytilus edulis	AM	–		++	–	–	anoxia	De Zwaan & Zurburg, 1981;
				+++	++	+	forced valve closure	Siegmund & Grieshaber, 1983;
				++++	+++	+	aminooxyacetate	De Zwaan et al. 1983b
				+++	+	++	recovery	
		3†		5	18	13		
Crassostrea angulata	AM	+		+			anoxia	Siegmund & Grieshaber, 1983
		36†		37				
Crassostrea virginica	V		+				anoxia	Foreman & Ellington, 1983
			++				aminooxyacetate	
Crassostrea virginica	AM	+		+			anoxia	Eberlee et al. 1983
		++		++				
		20		19		0.3	recovery	
Geukensia demissa	AM		+			–	anoxia	Nicchitta & Ellington, 1983
			++			–	recovery	
		1			5	3		
Modiolus squamosus	AM		++			+++	anoxia	Nicchitta & Ellington, 1983
			++			–	recovery	
		13				1–2		
Nucula nitida	TA	+		++			anoxia	Siegmund & Grieshaber, 1983

Table 2. *cont.*

Species	Tissue	Pyruvate derivative					Condition	Reference
		A	A/S	S	O	L		
C Annelida								
Arenicola marina	BWM	+++		+++		−	digging	Siegmund & Grieshaber, 1983;
		n.d.		n.d.		++	anoxia	Siegmund & Grieshaber, 1984;
		47†		6	−	1	mercaptopicolinate	Schöttler & Wienhausen, 1981
D Sipunculida								
Sipunculus nudus	BWM	−		++	+++	−	digging	Pörtner *et al.* 1984
	IRM			++	+	−	digging	
	IRM			+	++	−	electrical	
	BWM	49		9	445	<0·05	anoxia	
	IRM	30		13	228	<0·05	anoxia	
	BWM			+++			recovery	Vögeler *et al.* 1984

Production of pyruvate derivatives (µmoles · g⁻¹ · wet weight) is presented by a range within the absolute change in concentration falls. Ranges are as follows: +, 0–1 µmoles; ++, 1–4 µmoles; +++, 4–8 µmoles and ++++, more than 8 µmoles.

† After Livingstone *et al.* 1983; −, not detectable; n.d., not determined; V, ventricle; RM, radula retractor muscle; IRM, introvert retractor muscle; other tissue abbreviations as for Table 1; A, alanopine; A/S, alanopine and/or strombine; S, strombine; O, octopine; L, lactate, the numbers give the corresponding oxidoreductase activity.

exercise (Baldwin & England, 1982a,b). In *Sipunculus nudus* octopine formation appears also to depend on the levels of phosphoarginine. The body wall muscle contains 30 μmoles phosphoarginine and the introvert retractor muscle 12 μmoles: during digging exercise the former muscle accumulates mainly octopine, and the latter strombine. Detailed studies have revealed that there is usually little integration between phosphoarginine breakdown and octopine formation (Livingstone De Zwaan & Thompson, 1981; Gäde, Carlsson & Melnaraus, 1984). At the onset of muscular activity ATP supply is almost completely at the expense of hydrolysis of phosphagen which leads to a rapid and large rise in arginine concentration when high amounts of arginine phosphate are available. This in turn activates octopine dehydrogenase which subsequently leads to octopine formation. In *Arenicola marina* alanopine is formed during digging activity (Siegmund & Grieshaber, 1984). In this animal the lack of octopine formation is due to the absence of octopine dehydrogenase which is a common feature of annelids (Livingstone *et al.*, 1983).

Alanopine and strombine appear to be primarily formed with environmental anaerobiosis and postanaerobic recovery (Table 2). Only in those animals with octopine dehydrogenase as the sole pyruvate oxidoreductase, may octopine be formed during environmental hypoxia (De Zwaan Thompson & Livingstone, 1980). A first indication that opine formation might occur during environmental anaerobiosis came from studies by Collicutt & Hochachka (1977). They postulated that alanopine was probably the unidentified metabolite formed in anoxic oyster heart. The accumulation of opines during environmental anaerobiosis appears to be more pronounced during the first hours (De Zwaan & Zurburg, 1981; Pörtner *et al.*, 1984).

Since the opine dehydrogenases are functionally analogous to lactate dehydrogenase, replacement of lactate by opine formation does not result in a higher ATP output per glycosyl unit. Therefore there has been much speculation about other possible functional reasons for opine formation. Suggested advantages above lactate formation have been summarized and discussed by Fields (1983).

In the Annelida, the Mollusca and 'lower Invertebrata phyla' there is a large metabolic diversity in anaerobic energy supply during environmental anaerobiosis. The accumulation pattern of end products varies from species to species, from tissue to tissue within the species and with the season. Nevertheless certain basic patterns can be recognized in the metabolic events occurring during long-term anaerobiosis. It has been established in the time course of anaerobiosis that gradual transitions occur in the carbon flow. This is illustrated in Fig. 1. There is a transition stage lasting up to 10 h or even longer (Fig. 1 emersed, initial) followed by a stage in which an anaerobic steady state is reached (Fig. 1, emersed, prolonged). In the transition stage an opine is formed as well as succinate (De Zwaan & Zurburg, 1981; Pörtner *et al.*, 1984; Siegmund & Greishaber, 1984). Succinate is derived from aspartate (Table 3,I,0–4h). Its formation is coupled with alanine formation from glycogen. The carbohydrate – alanine and the aspartate – succinate route are coupled by a set of transaminase reactions (Felbeck, 1980; De Zwaan, De Bont & Verhoeven, 1982). When aspartate pools are depleted glycogen can be converted into succinate (Fig. 1, emersed, prolonged). This is initiated by the formation of oxaloacetate from phosphoenolpyruvate by PEP-carboxykinase (Schöttler & Wienhausen, 1980), an enzyme generally found in invertebrates muscle as opposed to vertebrates. From the mainstream of carbon towards succinate there is a deviation of a small part of malate which is used in routes containing oxidative steps in order to generate NADH for the fumarate reduction into succinate (Schöttler, 1977; De Zwaan & Zurburg, 1981). This mostly leads to acetate accumulation in addition to succinate and propionate. In this phase succinate is no longer an end product but a mainstream product. In four reaction steps succinate is converted into propionate with the release of an equimolar amount of CO_2 (Schroff & Zebe, 1980; Schulz & Kluytmans, 1983). In the route malate–propionate there are two sites of ATP formation, one is coupled to the reduction of fumarate (Schöttler, 1977, Holwerda & De Zwaan, 1979) and the other to the decarboxylation of D-methylmalonyl-CoA (Schroff & Zebe, 1980; Schulz & Kluytmans, 1983; see also Fig. 1, emersed, prolonged). The route glycogen – malate already has two sites of ATP formation; this means that there is an increase by a factor of 2 compared to the classical glycolysis. Formation of propionate (and CO_2), succinate and acetate therefore considerably increases the yield of ATP per glycosyl unit when compared to lactate production (see for stoichiometric equations and ATP yield of glycogen fermentations, De Zwaan, 1983). Moreover, these products are highly soluble and can be easily released by diffusion into the surrounding water. This is a good strategy against metabolic acidosis. In crustaceans the succinate-propionate pathway has been established, but its role is less important than in molluscs and annelids (see Table 3, III).

Postanaerobic recovery

Intertidal species which have to sustain regularly low oxygen partial pressures need a quick reestablishment of normoxic cellular conditions.

This subject has been recently reviewed by Ellington (1983).

ATP and phosphagen levels are recharged very rapidly during recovery. This recharging, as well as the resynthesis of aspartate and glycogen, the clearance of acidic end products and the resumption of normal activities such as feeding increase the energy demand. This high energy demand is met by elevated oxygen consumption rates and in addition mostly an anaerobic component (see Fig. 1, reimmersed) within the first 4 h of recovery. Various pyruvate derivatives may accumulate (see Table 2). Strombine formation could be established in the posterior adductor muscle of the bivalves *Mytilus edulis* (De Zwaan *et al.*, 1983b) *Geukensia dimissa* and *Modiolus squamosis* (Nicchitta & Ellington, 1983), the body wall musculature of *Sipunculus nudus* (Vogeler, Pörtner & Grieshaber 1984) and the pedal retractor muscle of Strombidae (Baldwin & England, 1982). Octopine is accumulated in the adductor muscle of the scallops *Pecten maximum* (Gäde, Weeda & Gabbott, 1978), *Chlamys opercularis* (Grieshaber, 1978) and *Placopecten magellanicus* (Livingstone *et al.*, 1981). Lactate accumulated after establishing normoxic conditions in various crustaceans (*Crangon crangon*, Onnen & Zebe, 1983; *Orconectes limosus*, Gäde, 1984; *Nassarius coronatus*, Baldwin Lee & England, 1981) and acetate in some annelids (*Arenicola marina*, Schöttler, Fahrenholz & Weinhausen, 1981; *Lumbriculus variegatus*, Putzer unpublished). It could be argued that especially muscle tissue would basically function in an anaerobic manner even when oxygen is available. However, clearance of succinate is usually within one hour indicating that succinate oxidase will be operative at the expense of oxygen. It is therefore more likely that the energy demand temporarily exceeds the maximum capacity of aerobic ATP yielding processes.

Reoxidation of cytosolic NADH

With a tight coupling of the glycogen–alanine and the aspartate– succinate pathway in the transition stage (Fig. 1, emersed, initial), absolute changes in the concentration of succinate, alanine and aspartate should be equal. For foot (Meinardus & Gäde, 1981), adductor muscle (Gäde, 1983b, De Zwaan *et al.*, 1982, 1983), ventricle (Ellington, 1981a,b, Gäde & Ellington, 1983) of molluscs and body wall muscle of annelids (Schöttler, 1980) there appears to be indeed a one-to-one stoichiometry between aspartate utilization and L-alanine accumulation (in *Arenicola marina* there is also an equimolar accumulation of D-alanine). However, the ratio of succinate accumulation and aspartate utlilization is about 0·5. In the presence of the aminotransferase inhibitor aminooxyacetate

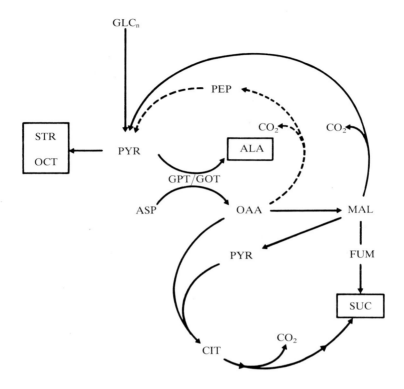

Fig. 2. A metabolic map showing routes for the simultaneous utilization of glycogen (GLC$_n$) and aspartate (ASP) and for the conversion of aspartate into alanine (ALA) via oxaloacetate (OAA), malate (MAL) and pyruvate (PYR) with an equimolar release of CO_2. The decarboxylation reaction is assumed to be catalysed by malic enzyme. Theoretically the route could be also via oxaloacetate and phosphoenolpyruvate (PEP) (dashed line). The enzyme involved, PEP-carboxykinase, is inhibited by 3-mercaptopicolinate, but it was found that this inhibitor displayed no effect on the conversion of aspartate into alanine. *Abbreviations:* GLC$_n$, glycogen; STR, strombine; OCT, octopine; GPT, glutamate-pyruvate-transaminase; GOT, glutamate-oxaloacetate-transaminase.

changes in concentration of aspartate, alanine and succinate are almost absent (De Zwaan *et al.*, 1982, De Zwaan, De Bont & Hemelraad 1983a, Foreman & Ellington, 1983). It is clear that the formation of succinate is at the expense of twice the amount of aspartate. We assume that succinate is not only coupled to aspartate utilization in a direct manner, but also indirectly, by converting aspartate into alanine. In the latter a key step is the decarboxylation of malate by malic enzyme. Both routes of aspartate utilization are depicted in Fig. 2. Evidence cannot only be derived from the observed discrepancy between formed succinate and utilized aspartate, but also from radiolabel studies. In isolated ventricles of oyster incubated for 3h with U-[^{14}C]aspartate, 43·4 % of the label appeared in end products derived from pyruvate and 41 % in succinate (Collicutt & Hochachka, 1977). Experiments in which U-[^{14}C]aspartate was anaerobically metabolized by *Arenicola marina* revealed that incorporation of radiolabel into succinate and alanine was almost equal (Zebe, 1975). In another experiment with labelled aspartate, after 120 min anaerobic incubation, 20 % of the radioactivity metabolized was accounted for by CO_2. The decarboxylation step in the aspartate – alanine conversion is probably not catalysed by PEP-carboxykinase (indicated in Fig. 2 by a dashed line), because in that case 3-mercaptopicolinate would have displayed an inhibitory effect on this conversion (De Zwaan *et al.*, 1983a).

It has been argued by one of us (see De Zwaan *et al.*, 1983a) that the aspartate – alanine conversion is a consequence of a reorganization of the malate – aspartate shuttle. When tissues become anoxic mitochondrial malate dehydrogenase will no longer catalyse the oxidation of malate into oxaloacetate, but instead catalyse the reverse reaction due to a retarded withdrawing of oxaloacetate. Malic enzyme can now take over the role which malate dehydrogenase previously played in the malate – aspartate shuttle. Since pyruvate is now formed instead of oxaloacetate, glutamate oxaloacetate transaminase will be replaced by glutamate pyruvate transaminase. Functionally the aspartate – alanine conversion (Fig. 2) replaces in this manner the malate – aspartate shuttle in transferring cytoplasmic hydrogen from the cytosol through the inner mitochondrial membrane. When both routes of aspartate utilization are coupled then the mitochondrial aspartate conversion into malate (and finally into succinate and/or propionate) will reoxidize an equimolar amount of cytosolic NADH and thus repays for an equimolar amount of glycolytically formed pyruvate. The coupling of the cytosolic GAPDH reaction and the mitochondrial malate dehydrogenase reaction for maintaining redox balance occurs indirectly via the decarboxylation of aspartate into alanine. The coupling of the aspartate – succinate pathway with the glycogen – alanine pathway on one hand and its connection with the 'aspartate-coupled hydrogen transfer system' on the other hand is schematically depicted in Fig. 3 (light dotted bars). This concept explains the observed discrepancy between aspartate utilization and succinate formation. The overall reaction is namely: pyruvate + 2 aspartate → 2 alanine + CO_2 + malate. A topographic separation is obtained between the sites of operation of opine dehydrogenases (cytosol) and pyruvate glutamate transferase (mitochondrion), so preventing them competing for pyruvate within the same cell compartment.

In resting vertebrate muscle lactate accumulation does not occur, because of a higher affinity of the malate – aspartate shuttle for cytoplas-

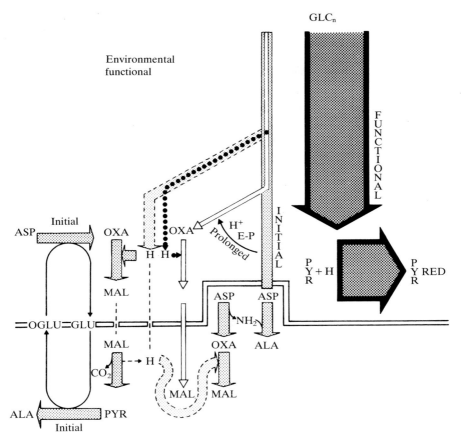

Fig. 3. Three possible pathways for anaerobic ATP supply: The aspartate–(malate) succinate pathway (light dotted), the glycogen–(malate) succinate pathway (open) and the classical glycolytic pathway (heavy dotted). PYR RED can either be lactate or an opine. The width of the bars is an indication of the relative flux capacity or scope for anaerobic power out put. It is shown that the aspartate–succinate pathway is coupled with the glycogen–alanine pathway for nitrogen transfer and to the aspartate–alanine conversion for hydrogen transfer through the inner mitochondrial membrane. A gradual switch from the aspartate–succinate route (INITIAL) to the glycogen–succinate route (PROLONGED) is indicated. This switch is initiated by the carboxylation of phosphoenolpyruvate (PEP) into oxaloacetate (OXA). The PEP-branchpoint is indicated with the regulatory signals that are thought to be important in the transition of the carbon flow: acidification (H^+) and covalent phosphorylation of pyruvate-kinase (E-P).
Abbreviations: OGLU, 2-oxo glutarate; GLCn, glycogen; ASP, aspartate; MAL, malate; PYR, pyruvate; ALA, alanine; GLU, glutamate.

mic NADH than for lactate dehydrogenase. A comparable situation occurs in anaerobic marine invertebrate muscle with high aspartate reserves. As long as the energy demand is not too high, so that more NADH is generated in the glycolytic pathway than can be transferred by the 'aspartate-coupled hydrogen transport system', then pyruvate oxidoreductases will be depleted of reduced co-enzyme. Evidence for a higher affinity for cytosolic NADH by the 'aspartate-coupled hydrogen transfer system' could be derived from *in vitro* and *in vivo* studies in which fluxes through pathways were manipulated with inhibitors. Instead of discussing separate experiments we have summarized the results obtained with oyster ventricle (Foreman & Ellington, 1983) and adductor muscle of the sea mussel (De Zwaan *et al.*, 1983a,b) in the form of a scheme (Fig. 4). In the middle panel of Fig. 4 we see how the transaminase inhibitor aminooxyacetate blocks both aspartate conversion into alanine and into succinate. Therefore ATP output linked to the aspartate – succinate conversion is lost. However, the aspartate – alanine conversion also does not occur and can therefore not compete with the pyruvate oxidoreductases for NADH. This results in extra opine formation which compensates for the lost of ATP. When, however, the glycolytic flux is reduced with iodoacetate (right panel of Fig. 4), no opine formation is observed, whereas accumulation of succinate decreased. A reduced glycolytic flux means also a reduced NADH production rate; consequently the capacity of the aspartate – alanine conversion is sufficient to deal with all generated NADH. As additional evidence it was observed that the ratio of changes in the levels of alanine, aspartate and succinate was maintained at 1:1:0·5. This fixed ratio of accumulation can be used to determine the moment of succinate production from glycogen. This point is indicated when the ratio of changes in succinate and aspartate begins to exceed a value of 0·5. In *Mytilus edulis* (De Zwaan *et al.*, 1983a) and *Arenicola marina* (Schötter, 1980) and probably generally in intertidal invertebrates with a high aspartate pool this transition will not fall within the time period of anaerobiosis normally occurring in the intertidal habitat. The switch in carbon source for succinate formation from aspartate to carbohydrate needs namely several regulatory adjustments at the level of the conversion of phosphoenolpyruvate and is a gradual process taking place over hours (De Zwaan & Dando, 1984). Coupling aspartate utilization to both energy production and NADH reoxidation is an important adaptation, because it leads to a more economic use of glycogen than the classical glycolysis.

Marine crustaceans at the onset of the transition from aerobic to anaerobic metabolism obligatorily switch to the lactate pathway, because of their lack of high aspartate stores (Table 1). *Nereis pelagica* and *Placopecten magellanicus* also have very low aspartate pools relative to other representatives of their taxonomic group (Table 1). They also mainly use the classical glycolysis during natural anaerobiosis. These two

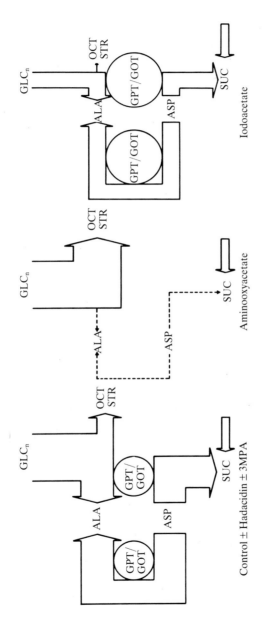

Fig. 4. The effect of metabolic inhibitors on the carbon flow (the width of the bars is an indication of the relative carbonflux) of the glycolytic pathway (terminating in alanine or opines), the aspartate–succinate pathway and the aspartate–alanine conversion (in detail depicted in Fig. 3). Hadacidin, 3-mercaptopicolinate (3-MPA), aminooxyacetate and iodoacetate are inhibitors of purine nucleotide cycle, PEP-carboxykinase, transaminases and glycolysis, respectively.
Abbreviations: As for Fig. 2 and Fig. 4.

Table 3. ATP turnover rate ($\dot{M}$ ATP: μmoles ATP · g^{-1} wet weight · min); comparison of ATP equivalents derived from ATP, phosphagen and anaerobic catabolism (given as percentage of total ATP turnover rate) and the flow (μmoles metabolite · g^{-1} wet weight · min) of glycosyl units ($\dot{M}$ C_6) and oxaloacetate ($\dot{M}$ C_4) through the glycolytic and succinate pathway respectively, during environmental hypoxia or anoxia (A) and muscular exercise (B) in different tissues of several invertebrate species

Species	Tissue	$\dot{M}$ ATP	%			$\dot{M}$		Reference
			ATP	GP	CAT	C_6	C_4	
I MOLLUSCA and Bunodosoma c. (CNIDARIA)								
A Environmental								
0–4 h								
Nassa mutabilis	F	0.036	0	48	52	0.004	0.004 A	Gäde et al. 1984
Cardium tuberculatum	F	0.030	0	67	23	0.003	0.001 A	Gäde, 1980
Cardium edule	F	0.035	0	46	54	0.006	0.002 A	Meinardus & Gäde, 1981
Mytilus edulis	AM	0.032	9	60	31	0.003	0.002 A	Ebberink et al. 1981
Modiolus squamosus	AM$_p$	0.049	2	3	95	0.024	0.011 A	Nicchitta & Ellington, 1983
	AM$_t$	0.020	7	42	51	0.0004	0.009 A	Nicchitta & Ellington, 1983
Geukensia dem. gran.	TA	0.021	0	20	80	0.003	0.005	Nicchitta & Ellington, 1983
Lima hians	AM	0.121	4	65	31	0.007	0.008 A	Gäde, 1983b
>10 h								
Cardium edule	F	0.005	n.d.	6	≤94	0.001	0.001 G	Meinardus & Gäde, 1981
Mytilus edulis	AM	0.008	0	0	100	0.002	0.003 G	Ebberink et al. 1981
Geukensia dem. gran.	TA	0.008	0	0	100	0.001	0.002 G	Ho & Zubkoff, 1982
Lima hians	AM	0.021	14	24	52	0.003	0.004	Gäde, 1983b
Bunodosoma cavernata	TA	0.003	1.8	n.d.	98.2	0.0006	0.0005 G	Ellington, 1981a; Ellington, 1982a

Table 3. *cont.*

Species	Tissue	$\dot{M}$ ATP	%			$\dot{M}$		Reference
			ATP	GP	CAT	C_6	C_4	
B Exercise								
Buccinum undatum	F	0·800	4	32	64	0·160	n.d.	Koormann & Grieshaber, 1980
Nassarius coronatus	F	1·400	n.d.	36	≤64	0·290	n.d.	Baldwin et al. 1981
Strombus luhanus	F	2·900	n.d.	41	≤59	0·590	n.d.	Baldwin & England, 1982a
Nassa mutabilis	F	10·600	2	51	47	1·750	n.d.	Gäde et al. 1984
Limaria fragilis (+O_2)	AM	3·9(10·5)	11	83	6	0·09(0·26)	n.d.	Baldwin & Lee, 1979; Baldwin & Morris, 1983
Argopecten irradians	AM	9·700	7	50	43	1·350	0·090	Chih & Ellington, 1983
Lima hians	AM	11·600	2	59	39	0·150	n.d.	Gäde, 1981
Cardium tuberculatum	F	11·080	1	88	11	0·450	0·001	Gäde, 1980
Placopecten magellanicus	AM	12·600	13	69	18	0·780	0·080	De Zwaan et al. 1980
Chlamys opercularis	AM	15·400	22	78	0	0·000	n.d.	Grieshaber, 1978
Hapalochlaena maculosa	M	16·000	9	44	47	2·500	n.d.	Baldwin & England, 1980

Table 3. *cont.*

| Species | Tissue | Ṁ ATP | % | | | Ṁ | | Reference |
			ATP	GP	CAT	C_6	C_4	
II ANNELIDA and Sipunculus n. (SIPUNCULIDA)								
A Environmental anoxia: 0–24 h; 12–48 h‡								
Sipunculus nudus	BWM	0·028	0	32	68	0·005	0·004 G	Pörtner *et al.* 1984
Arenicola marina	BWM	0·040	1	12	87	0·006	0·008 G 0·001 A	Schöttler *et al.* 1983; Surholt, 1977
Nephtys hombergii	TA	0·032	n.d.	n.d.	≤100	0·005	0·010 G 0·001 A	Schöttler, 1982
Nereis diversicolor	TA	0·042	1	n.d.	≤99	0·009	0·009 G 0·001 A	Schöttler, 1979
Nereis pelagica	TA	0·020	3	n.d.	≤97	0·006	0·003 G 0·0004 A	Schöttler, 1979
Nereis virens	TA	0·028	1	n.d.	≤99	0·007	0·004 G 0·001 A	Schöttler, 1979
Tubifex sp.‡	TA	0·039	0	0	100	0·006	0·013 G	Seuss *et al.* 1983
Lumbriculus variegatus‡	TA	0·058	0	0	100	0·009	0·017 G	Putzer, 1984
Hirudo medicinalis	BWM	0·045	0	n.d.	≤100	0·006	0·011 G 0·004 M	Zebe *et al.* 1981

Table 3. *cont.*

Species	Tissue	$\dot{M}$ ATP	%			$\dot{M}$		Reference
			ATP	GP	CAT	C_6	C_4	
B Exercise								
Sipunculus nudus	BWM	0·680	0	43	57	0·129	0·003 A	Pörtner *et al.* 1984
Nereis virens	TA	0·428	n.d.	n.d.	≤100	0·143	n.d.	Schöttler, 1979
Nereis pelagica	TA	0·615	n.d.	n.d.	≤100	0·205	n.d.	Schöttler, 1979
Nereis diversicolor	TA	0·626	n.d.	n.d.	≤100	0·209	n.d.	Schöttler, 1979
Hirudo medicinalis	BWM	0·307	3	n.d.	≤97	0·099	0·000	Zebe *et al.* 1981
Arenicola marina	BWM	2·934	5	20	75	0·648	0·255 A	Siegmund & Grieshaber, 1984
Lumbriculus var. (+O$_2$)	TA	2·5(3·3)	4	20	76	0·650(0·09)	0·000	Putzer, 1984; Kaufmann, 1984
III CRUSTACEA								
A Environmental								
<16 h								
Callianassa californiensis	TA	0·020	n.d.	n.d.	≤100	0·007	0·0004 A	Zebe, 1982
Upogebia pugettensis	TA	0·040	n.d.	n.d.	≤100	0·013	0·0003 A	Zebe, 1982
Orconectes limosus	TM	0·036	0	27	73	0·008	0·0020 G	Gäde, 1984
Cirolana borealis	TA	0·054	n.d.	n.d.	≤100	0·017	0·0014 G	De Zwaan & Skjoldal, 1979
B Exercise								
ca. 60″								
Cherax destructor	TM	32·700	9	72	19	2·000	n.d.	England & Baldwin, 1983
Crangon crangon	TM	24·310	7	88	5	0·370	n.d.	Onnen & Zebe, 1983
Orconectes limosus	TM	16·900	0·5	90	0·5	0·500	n.d.	Gäde, 1984

Tissue abbreviations: M, mantle; AM, adductor muscle; other tissue abbreviations as for Table 1.
Abbreviations in the C_4 column: A, aspartate; G, glycogen; M, malate.
GP, guanidino phosphate; CAT, catabolism.

species (Schöttler, 1979; De Zwaan et al., 1980) and crustaceans in general (Hammen, 1976) appear to have a low anoxic resistance. In some fresh water species high malate stores may be an adaptation to a sudden transition to anoxic conditions (see Table 1). Other fresh water animals seem to switch to lactate production (for example gastropods). Tubifex has neither high aspartate nor malate pools, but is known to withstand complete anoxia for over 4 months. It has been argued that Tubifex is adapted to a life under permanent anoxic conditions (Famme & Knudsen, 1984) and therefore may be able to switch immediately to the glycogen – succinate pathway when faced with a sudden large decrease in oxygen partial pressure.

Metabolic rate

We have calculated the anaerobic power output (or ATP turnover rate) for a number of invertebrates in connection with environmental and exercise anaerobiosis. This is obtained by summation of the rate of utilization of ATP, the rate of utilization of phosphagen and the rate of end product formation (multiplied by an ATP equivalent factor). The results are presented in Table 3. For the Mollusca the average value for the first 4 h of anoxia, as well as for 'long-term anoxia' (> 10 h) was calculated. These two periods correspond to the transition stage and the anaerobic steady state stage, respectively. As is clear from Table 3 (part I), the ATP turnover rate is a factor three to six lower in the steady state stage. This is due to the fact that phosphoarginine pools are depleted (see low percentage contribution of phosphagen in Table 3I, > 10 h) and to a lowered glycolytic flux. The latter is caused by the cessation of opine formation and the switch in the glycogen conversion from alanine towards succinate formation (see Ṁ C6 and Ṁ C4 values in Table 3). The lower the metabolic rate, the longer the animal will survive imposed anaerobic conditions. The ATP turnover rates for long-term environmental anaerobiosis vary within the examined molluscs in the range $0\cdot005-0\cdot021$ (μmoles g^{-1} wet weight. min), in the annelids in the range $0\cdot020-0\cdot058$ and in the crustaceans in the range $0\cdot020-0\cdot054$. When we compare these rates with the corresponding aerobic resting rates (derived from oxygen consumption rates of quiescent, well-adapted animals) it appears that molluscs can on average reduce their metabolic rate about 75 times, and both the annelids and crustaceans about 10 times (De Zwaan & Van den Thillart 1985); however, the crustaceans can only use the lactate pathway, whereas anaerobic metabolism of annelids and molluscs is well adapted to anaerobic survival.

The ATP turnover rate during exercise is at least two orders of magnitude higher than during environmental anaerobiosis. Swimming bivalves (Table 3I, exercise) and especially crustaceans (Table 3III, exercise) show high metabolic rates, which correspond to a high steady state level of phosphoarginine in the resting animal (Table 1) and a high utilization rate of this compound during exercise. However, the increase of the ATP turnover rate is in part also due to a large increase in the glycolytic flux (see $\dot{M}$ C_6 values in Table 3). The fraction of glycogen that is converted into succinate under these conditions (see $\dot{M}$ C_4 in Table 3) is marginal in comparison to environmental anaerobiosis and most of it is now converted into a pyruvate derivative.

Relationship between metabolic rate and anaerobic pathway: summary

We have described three main anaerobic pathways. They are shown in Fig. 3: 1. the classical glycolytic pathway, 2. the aspartate – succinate pathway and 3. the glycogen – succinate pathway. The aspartate – succinate pathway is coupled to the glycogen – alanine pathway and to the aspartate – alanine conversion for H-transport through the inner mitochondrial membrane. In marine invertebrates (except for arthropods and probably echinoderms) the type of anaerobic pathway depends on the ATP power output. Each pathway has its intrinsic scope for ATP power output. The glycogen – succinate pathway has the lowest scope, followed by the aspartate – succinate pathway, whereas the classical glycolytic pathway has by far the highest ATP-yielding capacity. However, the affinity for NADH of the aspartate – succinate pathway is higher than that of the terminal dehydrogenase of the glycolytic pathway. The aspartate – succinate pathway will therefore always be in operation, both with environmental and exercise anaerobiosis. We have seen that the ATP turnover rate is strongly reduced with environmental anaerobiosis and the energy supply can therefore largely be covered by the aspartate – succinate pathway. During exercise anaerobiosis the ATP turnover rate is relatively very high. The aspartate – succinate pathway will operate at its maximum rate, but due to its low capacity and the short duration of burst activities, it hardly leads to the accumulation of detectable amounts of succinate. Therefore during exercise anaerobiosis, the energy needs will largely be paid by the classical glycolytic pathway.

References

BALDWIN, J. & ENGLAND, W. R. (1980) A comparison of anaerobic energy metabolism in mantle and tentacle muscles of the blue ringed octopus *Hapalochlaena maculosa* during swimming. *Aust. J. Zool* **28**, 407–412.

BALDWIN, J. & ENGLAND, W. R. (1982a) Multiple forms of octopine dehydrogenase in *Strombus luhuanus* (Mollusca, Gastropoda, Strombidae): Genetic basis of polymorphism, properties of the enzymes, and relationship between the octopine dehydrogenase phenotype and the accumulation of anaerobic end products during exercise. *Biochem. Genetics* **20**, 1015–1025.

BALDWIN, J. & ENGLAND, W. R. (1982b) The properties and functions of alanopine dehydrogenase and octopine dehydrogenase from the pedal retractor muscle of Strombidae (Class Gastropoda). *Pacific Science* **36**, 381–364.

BALDWIN, J. & LEE, A. K. (1979) Contributions of aerobic and anaerobic energy production during swimming in the bivalve mollusc *Limaria fragilis* (family Limidae). *J. comp. Physiol.* **129**, 361–364.

BALDWIN, J., LEE, A. K. & ENGLAND, W. R. (1981) The functions of octopine dehydrogenase and D-lactate dehydrogenase in the pedal retractor muscle of the dog whelk *Nassarius coronatus* (Gastropoda: Nassariidae). *Marine Biology* **62**, 235–238.

BALDWIN, J. & MORRIS, G.M. (1983) Re-examination of the contributions of aerobic and anaerobic energy production during swimming in the bivalve mollusc *Limaria fragilis* (family Limidae). *Aust. J. Mar. Freshw. Res.* **34**, 909–914.

BALDWIN, J. & OPIE, A. M. (1978) On the role of octopine dehydrogenase in the adductor muscles of bivalve molluscs. *Comp. Biochem. Physiol.* **61B**, 85–92.

BERNAERTS, F. (1982) Het aerobe en anaerobe metabolisme van *Artemia*. Thesis, University Antwerpen, Belgium.

CHIH, C. P. & ELLINGTON, W. R. (1983) Energy metabolism during contractile activity and environmental hypoxia in the phasic adductor muscle of the bay scallop *Argopecten irradians concentricus*. *Physiol. Zool.* **56**, 623–631.

COLLICUTT, J. M. & HOCHACHKA, P. W. (1977) The anaerobic oyster heart: Coupling of glucose and aspartate fermentation. *J. comp. Physiol.* **115**, 147–157.

DE ZWAAN A. (1983) Carbohydrate Catabolism in Bivalves. In *The Mollusca* Vol. 1, (ed. P. V. Hochachka) p 137–175. New York: Academic Press.

DE ZWAAN, A. & DANDO, P. R. (1984) Phosphoenolpyruvate-pyruvate metabolism in bivalve molluscs. *Molec. Physiol.* **5**, 285–310.

DE ZWAAN, A., DE BONT, A. M. T. & HEMELRAAD, J. (1983a) The role of phospheoenolpyruvate carboxykinase in the anaerobic metabolism of the sea mussel *Mytilus edulis* L. *J. comp. Physiol.* **153**, 267–274.

DE ZWAAN, A., DE BONT, A. M. T. & NILSSON, P. (1984) Anaerobic energy metabolism in two organs of the fresh water mussel *Anodonta cygnea* L. *Abstract in the First Int. Congress C.P.B. Liege Belgique.*

DE ZWAAN, A., DE BONT, A. M. T. & VERHOEVEN, A. (1982) Anaerobic energy metabolism in isolated adductor muscle of the sea mussel *Mytilus edulis* L. *J. comp. Physiol.* **149**, 137–143.

DE ZWAAN, A., DE BONT, A. M. T., ZURBURG, W., BAYNE, B. L. & LIVINGSTONE, D. R. (1983b) On the role of strombine formation in the energy metabolism of adductor muscle of a sessile bivalve. *J. comp. Physiol.* **149**, 557–563.

DE ZWAAN, A., MOHAMED, A. M. & GERAERTS, W. P. M. (1976) Glycogen degradation and the accumulation of compounds during anaerobiosis in the fresh water snail *Lymnaea stagnalis*. *Neth. J. Zool.* **26**, 549–557.

DE ZWAAN, A. & ZURBURG, W. (1981) The formation of strombine in the adductor muscle of the sea mussel *Mytilus edulis*. *Mar. Biol. Lett.* **2**: 179–192.

De Zwaan, A. & Skjoldal, H. R. (1979) Anaerobic energy metabolism of the scavenging isopod *Circolana borealis* (Lilljeborg). *J. comp. Physiol.* **129**, 327–331.

De Zwaan, A., Thompson, R. J. & Livingstone, D. R. (1980) Physiological and biochemical aspects of the valve snap and valve closure response in the giant scallop *Placopecten magellanicus. J. comp. Physiol.* **137**, 105–114.

De Zwaan, A. & Van den Thillart, G. (1985) Low and high power output modes of anaerobic metabolism: Invertebrate and lower vertebrate strategies. (In press).

De Zwaan, A. & Wijsman, T. C. M. (1976) Anaerobic metabolism in bivalva (Mollusca). Characteristics of anaerobic metabolism. *Comp. Biochem. Physiol.* **54B**, 313–324.

Ebberink, R. H. M., Zurburg, W. & Zandee, D. I. (1979) The energy demand of the posterior adductor muscle of *Mytilus edulis* in catch during exposure to air. *Mar. Biol. Lett.* **1**, 23–31.

Eberlee, J. C., Storey, J. M. & Storey, K. B. (1983) Anaerobiosis, recovery from anoxia, and the role of strombine and alanopine in the oyster *Crassostrea virginica. Can. J. Zool.* **61**, 2682–2687.

Ellington, W. R. (1981a) Effect of anoxia on the adenylates and the energy charge in the sea anemone *Bunodosoma cavernata* (Bosc). *Physiol. Zool.* **54**, 415–422.

Ellington, W. R. (1981b) Energy metabolism during hypoxia in the isolated, perfused ventricle of the whelk, *Busycon contrarium* Conrad. *J. comp. Physiol.* **142**, 457–464.

Ellington, W. R. (1982a) Metabolic responses of the sea anemone *Bunodosoma cavernata* (Bosc) to declining oxygen tensions and anoxia. *Physiol. Zool.* **55**, 240–249.

Ellington, W. R. (1982b) Metabolism at the pyruvate branch point in the radula retractor muscle of the whelk *Busycon contrarium. Can. J. Zool.* **60**, 2973–2977.

Ellington, W. R. (1983) The recovery from anaerobic metabolism in invertebrates. *J. exp. Zool.* **228**, 431–444.

England, W. R. & Baldwin, J. (1983) Anaerobic energy metabolism in the tail musculature of the australian yabby *Cherax destructor* (Crustacea, Decapoda, Parastacidae): Role of phosphagens and anaerobic glycolysis during escape behavior. *Physiol. Zool.* **56**, 614–622.

Englisch, H., Opalka, B. & Zebe, E. (1982) The anaerobic metabolism of the larvae of the midge *Chaoborus crystallinus. Insect Biochem* **12**, 149–155.

Famme, P. & Knudson, J. (1984) Metazoan life under permanent anoxic conditions? *Abstract in the First Int. Congress C.P.B. Liege Belgique.*

Felbeck, H. (1980) Investigations in the role of the amino acids in anaerobic metabolism of the lugworm *Arenicola marina* L. *J. comp. Physiol.* **137**, 183–192.

Fields, J. H. A. (1976) A dehydrogenase requiring alanine and pyruvate as substrates from oyster adductor muscle. *Fed. Proc.* **37**, 1687.

Fields, J. H. A. (1983) Alternatives to lactic acid: Possible advantages. *J. exp. Zool.* **228**, 445–457.

Fields, J. H. A., Eng, A. K., Ramsden, W. D., Hochachka, P. W. & Weinstein, B. (1980) Alanopine and strombine are novel imino acids produced by a dehydrogenase found in the adductor muscle of the oyster *Crassostrea gigas. Archs Biochem. Biophys.* **201**, 110–114.

Fiore, G. B., Nicchitta, C. V. & Ellington, W. R. (1984) High-performance liquid chromatographic separation and quantification of alanopine and strombine in crude tissue extracts. *Anal. Biochem.* **139**, 413–417.

Foreman, R. A. & Ellington, W. R. (1983) Effects of inhibitors and substrate supplementation on anaerobic energy metabolism in the ventricle of the oyster *Crassostrea virginica. Comp. biochem. Physiol.* **74B**, 543–547.

Gäde, G. (1980) The energy metabolism of the foot muscle of the jumping cockle, *Cardium tuberculatum*: Sustained anoxia versus muscular activity. *J. comp. Physiol.* **137**, 177–182.

GÄDE, G. (1981) Energy production during swimming in the adductor muscle of the bivalve *Lima hians*: Comparison with the data from other bivalve molluscs. *Physiol. Zool.* **54**, 400–406.

GÄDE, G. (1983a) Energy metabolism of arthropods and molluscs during environmental and functional anaerobiosis. *J. exp. Zool.* **228**, 415–429.

GÄDE, G. (1983b) Energy production during anoxia and recovery in the adductor muscle of the file shell, *Lima hians*. *Comp. Biochem. Physiol.* **76B**, 73–78.

GÄDE, G. (1983c) How does the nemertean *Cerebratulus lacteus* meet the energy demand during environmental and functional anaerobiosis? *Proc. ESCBP, Taormina*, pp 179–180.

GÄDE, G. (1984) Effects of oxygen deprivation during anoxia and muscular work on the energy metabolism of the crayfish *Orconectes limosus*. *Comp. Biochem. Physiol.* (In press).

GÄDE, G., CARLSSON, K. H. & MEINARDUS, G. (1984) Energy metabolism in the foot of the marine gastropod *Nassa mutabilis* during environmental and functional anaerobiosis. *Marine Biology* **80**, 49–56.

GÄDE, G. & ELLINGTON, W. R. (1983) The anaerobic molluscan heart adaptation to environmental anoxia. Comparison with energy metabolism in vertebrate hearts. *Comp. Biochem. Physiol.* **76A**, 615–620.

GÄDE, G. & MEINARDUS, G. (1981) Anaerobic metabolism of the common cockle *Cardium edule*. V. Changes in the level of metabolites in the foot during aerobic recovery after anoxia. *Marine Biology* **65**, 113–116.

GÄDE, G., WEEDA, E. & GABBOTT, P. A. (1978) Changes in the level of octopine during the escape responses of the scallop, *Pecten maximum* L. *J. comp. Physiol.* **124**, 121–127.

GÄDE, G. & ZEBE, E. (1973) The anaerobic pathway in molluscan muscles. *J. comp. Physiol.* **85**, 291–301.

GALTSOFF, P. S. (1964) The american oyster, *Crassostrea virginica*. *Fish Bull 64* Washington, D.C: U.S. Govt. Printing Office.

GRIESHABER, M. (1978) Breakdown and formation of high-energy phosphates and octopine in the adductor muscle of the scallop, *Chlamys opercularis* (L.), during swimming and recovery. *J. comp. Physiol.* **126**, 269–276.

GRIESHABER, M. & GÄDE, G. (1977) Energy supply and the formation of octopine in the adductor muscle of the scallop, *Pecten jacobaeus* (Lamarck). *Comp. Biochem. Physiol.* **58B**, 249–252.

HAMMEN, C. S. (1976) Respiratory adaptations: Invertebrates. In *Estuarine Processes* Vol. **1**, (ed. Wiley M.) pp 347–355.

HO, M. S. & ZUBKOFF, P. L. (1982) Anaerobic metabolism of the ribbed mussel *Geukensia demissa*. *Comp. Biochem. Physiol.* **73B**, 931–936.

HOFFMANN, K. H. (1981) Phosphagens and phosphokinases in *Tubifex sp. J. comp. Physiol.* **143**, 237–243.

HOLWERDA, D. A. & DE ZWAAN, A. (1979) Fumarate reductase of *Mytilus edulis* L. *Mar. Biol. Lett.* **1**, 33–40.

KAUFMANN, R. (1984) Relationship of activity and respiration of *Lumbriculus variegatus* (Oligochaeta) at various temperatures and under declinig oxygen conditions. *Abstract in the First Int. Congress C.P.B. Liege Belgique.*

KLUYTMANS, J. H. & ZANDEE, D. I. (1983) Comparative study of the formation and excretion of anaerobic fermentation products in bivalves and gastropods. *Comp. Biochem. Physiol.* **75B**, 729–732.

KOORMANN, R. & GRIESHABER, M. (1980) Investigations on the energy metabolism and on octopine formation of the common whelk, *Buccinum undatum* L. during escape and recovery. *Comp. Biochem. Physiol.* **65B**, 543–547.

LIVINGSTONE D. R. (1982) Energy production in the muscle tissue of different kinds of molluscs. In *Exogenous and Endogenous Influences on Metabolic and Neural Control*, (ed. A. D. F. Addink & N. Spronk pp 257–274.

LIVINGSTONE, D. R. & DE ZWAAN, A. (1983) Carbohydrate metabolism of gastropods. In *The Mollusca* Vol. 1, (ed. P. W. Hochachka) pp 177–242 New York: Academic Press.

LIVINGSTONE, D. R., DE ZWAAN, A., LEOPOLD, M. & MARTEIJN, E. (1983) Studies on the phylogenetic distribution of pyruvate oxidoreductases. *Biochem. Syst. Ecol.* 11, 415–425.

LIVINGSTONE, D. R., DE ZWAAN, A. & THOMPSON, R. J. (1981) Aerobic metabolism, octopine production and phosphoarginine as sources of energy in the phasic and catch adductor muscles of the giant scallop *Placopecten magellanicus* during swimming and the subsequent recovery period. *Comp. Biochem. Physiol.* 70B, 35–44.

MEINARDUS, G. & GÄDE, G. (1981) Anaerobic metabolism of the common cockle, *Cardium edule* – IV. Time dependent changes of metabolites in the foot and gill tissue induced by anoxia and electrical stimulation. *Comp. Biochem. Physiol.* 70B, 271–277.

MEINARDUS, G. & GÄDE, G. (1984) Why does the cockle *Cardium tuberculatum* possess three different enzymes with the same function in anaerobic metabolism? *Abstract in the First Int. Congress C.P.B. Liege Belgique.*

MORIZAWA, K. (1927) The extractive substances in *Octopus octopodia. Acta Sch. Med. Univ. Imp. Kioto.* 9, 285–298.

NICCHITTA, C. V. & ELLINGTON, W. R. (1983) Energy metabolism during air exposure and recovery in the high intertidal bivalve mollusc *Geukensia demissa granosissima* and the subtidal bivalve mollusc *Modiolus squamosus. Biol. Bull* 165, 708–722.

ONNEN, T. & ZEBE, E. (1983) Energy metabolism in the tail muscles of the shrimp *Crangon crangon* during work and subsequent recovery. *Comp. Biochem. Physiol.* 74A, 833–838.

PÖRTNER, H. O., KREUTZER, U., SIEGMUND, B., HEISLER, N. & GRIESHABER, M. K. (1984) Metabolic adaptation of the intertidal worm *Sipunculus nudus* to functional and environmental hypoxia. *Marine Biology* 79, 237–247.

PUTZER, V. (1984) Energy production and glycolytic flux during functional and environmental anoxia in *Lumbriculus variegatus. Abstract in the First Int. Congress C.P.B. Liege Belgique.*

SANGSTER, A. W., THOMAS, S. E. & TINGLING, N. L. (1975) Fish attractants from marine invertebrates: Arcamine from *Arca zebra* and strombine from *Strombus gigas. Tetrahedron* 31, 1135–1137.

SATO, M., SATO, Y. & TSUCHIYA, Y. (1977) Studies on the extractives of molluscs. I. α-Iminodipropionic acid isolated from the squid muscle extracts. *Nippon Suisan Gakkaishi* 43, 1077–1079.

SCHÖTTLER, U. (1977) The energy-yielding oxidation of NADH by fumarate in anaerobic mitochondria of *Tubifex sp. Comp. Biochem. Physiol.* 58B, 151–156.

SCHÖTTLER, U. (1978) Investigations of the anaerobic metabolism of the polychaete worm *Nereis diversicolor* M. *J. comp. Physiol.* 125, 185–189.

SCHÖTTLER, U. (1979) On the anaerobic metabolism of three species of *Nereis* (Annelida). *Mar. Ecol. Prog. Ser.* 1, 249–254.

SCHÖTTLER, U. (1980) The energy metabolism during facultative anaerobiosis: Investigations on annelids. *Verh. Dtsch. Zool. Ges* 1980, 228–240.

SCHÖTTLER, U. (1982) An investigation on the anaerobic metabolism of *Nephtys hombergii* (Annelida: Polychaeta). *Marine Biology* 71, 265–269.

SCHÖTTLER, U., FAHRENHOLZ, S. & WIENHAUSEN, G. (1981) Investigations on the recovery metabolism of *Arenicola marina* after anaerobiosis. *Verh. Dtsch. Zool. Ges.* 1981, 270.

SCHÖTTLER, U. & WIENHAUSEN, G. (1980) The importance of the phosphoenolpyruvate carboxykinase in the anaerobic metabolism of two marine polychaetes. *In vivo* investigations on *Nereis virens* and *Arenicola marina. Comp. Biochem. Physiol.* 68B, 41–48.

SCHÖTTLER, U., WIENHAUSEN, G. & ZEBE, E. (1983) The mode of energy production in the lugworm *Arenicola marina* at different oxygen concentrations. *J. comp. Physiol.* 149, 547–555.

SCHROFF, G. & ZEBE, E. (1980) The anaerobic formation of propionic acid in the mitochondria of the lugworm *Arenicola marina. J. comp. Physiol.* 138, 35–41.

SCHULZ, T. K. F. & KLUYTMANS, J. H. (1983) Pathway of propionate synthesis in the sea mussel *Mytilus edulis* L. *Comp. Biochem. Physiol.* **75B**, 365–372.

SEUSS, J., HIPP, E. & HOFFMANN, K. H. (1982) Oxygen consumption, glycogen content and the accumulation of metabolites in *Tubifex* during aerobic-anaerobic shift and under progressing anoxia. *Comp. Biochem. Physiol.* **75A**, 557–562.

SIEGMUND, B. & GRIESHABER, M. K. (1983) Determination of *meso*-alanopine and D-strombine by high pressure liquid chromatography in extracts from marine invertebrates. *Hoppe-Seyler's Z. Physiol. Chem.* **364**, 807–812.

SIEGMUND, B. & GRIESHABER, M. K. (1984) Opine metabolism of *Arenicola marina* L. *Abstract in the First Int. Congress C.P.B. Liege Belgique.*

STOREY, K. B., MILLER, D.C., PLAXTON, W. C. & STOREY, J. M. (1982) Gas-liquid chromatography and enzymatic determination of alanopine and strombine in tissues of marine invertebrates. *Anal. Biochem.* **125**, 50–58.

SURHOLT, B. (1977) Production of volatile fatty acids in the anaerobic carbohydrate catabolism of *Arenicola marina*. *Comp. Biochem. Physiol.* **58B**, 147–150.

VAN THOAI, N. & ROBIN, Y. (1959) Métabolisme des dérivés guanidylés. VIII Biosynthése de l'octopine et répartition de l'enzyme l'opérant chez les invertébrés. *Biochim. Biophys. Acta.* **35**, 446–453.

VOGELER, S., PÖRTNER, H. O. & GRIESHABER, M. K. (1984) Recovery from anaerobiosis of the intertidal worm *Sipunculus nudus* L.: Concentrations of anaerobic metabolites and events in the acid base status. *Abstract in the First Int. Congress C.P.B. Liege Belgique.*

ZEBE, E. (1975) *In vivo* Untersuchungen über den Glucose-Abbau bei *Arenicola marina* (Annelida, Polychaeta). *J. comp. Physiol.* **101**, 133–145.

ZEBE, E. (1982) Anaerobic metabolism in *Upogebia pugettensis* and *Callianassa californiensis* (Crustacea, Thalassinidea). *Comp. Biochem. Physiol.* **72B**, 613–617.

ZEBE, E., SALGE, U., WIEMAN, C. & WILPS, H. (1981) The energy metabolism of the leech *Hirudo medicinalis* in anoxia and muscular work. *J. exp. Zool.* **218**, 157–163.

ZURBURG, W. & EBBERINK, R. H. M. (1981) The anaerobic energy demand of *Mytilus edulis*. Organ specific differences in ATP-supplying processes and metabolic routes. *Mol. Physiol.* **1**, 153–164.

ZURBURG, W., KLUYTMANS, J. H., PIETERS, H. & ZANDEE, D. I. (1979) The influence of seasonal changes on energy metabolism in *Mytilus edulis* L. – II. Organ specificity. In *Cyclic Phenomena in Marine Plants and Animals*, (ed. E. Naylor & R. G. Hartnoll) pp 292–300.

Printed in Great Britain © *Society of Experimental Biology 1985*

TIDALLY RHYTHMIC BEHAVIOUR OF MARINE ANIMALS

E. NAYLOR

School of Animal Biology, University College of North Wales, Bangor,
Gwynedd LL57 2UW, U.K.

Summary

The best general hypothesis for the control of 'spontaneous' tidal and daily patterns of behaviour in coastal animals postulates an endogenous physiological pacemaker system which generates approximate periodicity, together with environmental adjustment of the clock(s) to local time. Free-running endogenous rhythms of circatidal, circadian, circasemilunar and circalunar periodicity have been demonstrated in a number of species in constant laboratory conditions, in some cases clarifying hitherto poorly understood aspects of the behavioural repertoire of animals in the sea.

Entrainment of circatidal rhythmicity has been demonstrated using cycles of simulated tidal variables such as temperature, hydrostatic pressure, salinity and wave action. The crab *Carcinus* shows increased locomotor activity after changes of salinity (halokinesis); responses to 34‰ salinity entrain the endogenous clock, but responses to salinities above or below 34‰ are purely exogenous and do not persist in constant conditions after entrainment. Phase responsiveness of circatidal rhythms to pulses of tidal variables has been demonstrated in several species; phase response curves show marked differences from those of circadian rhythms.

The endogenous basis of tidal and diel behaviour in marine molluscs and crustaceans involves matching spontaneous rhythms of neuroelectrical activity. Also, in decapod crustaceans a peptidic neurodepressing hormone (NDH) modulates neuroelectrical and behavioural rhythmicity. NDH is produced rhythmically in the eyestalk neurosecretory complex, perhaps partly under the control of other clock components elsewhere in the CNS.

The physiological basis of circasemilunar, lunar (and annual) rhythms of behaviour has not been studied, but studies of synchronization of these rhythms have been undertaken. In some localities it has been shown experimentally that light intensities equivalent to moonlight are sufficient to entrain such rhythms. In other localities where moonlight is a less reliable cue the *relative* timing of tidal and daily variables has been shown to be important. So far there is no evidence that synchronization is achieved by *absolute* differences between tidal variables at neap and spring tides.

Introduction

Early studies of tidally rhythmic behaviour of marine animals and its possible control by physiological 'clocks' were particularly influenced by claims which were often anecdotal rather than experimental. There was scepticism of 'la phenomene de l'anticipation reflexe' described by Bohn & Pieron (1906), a reluctance to accept the possibility of direct control of behaviour by moonlight (Korringa, 1957), and such overt criticism of the biological clock concept that Cole (1957) published a paper demonstrating biological clocks in the unicorn. Subsequent studies then often sought to determine whether the rhythms were *either* endogenous *or* exogenous (see Naylor, 1976). Since most investigators control only selected environmental variables, and since many studies have demonstrated so-called 'temperature-independence', Brown (1960, 1972) proposed that tidal and daily rhythmic behaviour was controlled exogenously by 'residual geophysical periodic variables'.

In the past 25–30 years extensive studies by a number of workers (see Enright, 1975; Naylor, 1976; DeCoursey, 1983) coupled with improved techniques of statistical analysis (Enright, 1965; Williams, J. A. & Naylor, 1978; Broom, 1979; Harris & Morgan, 1983) have demonstrated that the best general hypothesis for the control of 'spontaneous' behavioural rhythms postulates an endogenous physiological pacemaker system which generates the approximate basic periodicity, coupled to environmental cycles which exogenously adjust the internal clock to local time. Even now, however, the two parts of the general hypothesis tend to be studied separately. Moreover, relatively little attention has been paid by many workers to the adaptive aspects of behavioural rhythmicity (Naylor, 1976). It seems reasonable to assume that genetic fitness is enhanced by temporal patterning of behaviour but, as Enright (1970) and DeCoursey (1983) point out, most authors have merely ignored or speculated about fitness. The present review therefore presents arguments concerning the need for an integrated approach, alongside the reductionist approach, in experimental studies of the clock problem in marine animals. The rhythmic behaviour of coastal species in relation to tidal rise and fall will be shown to be of particular interest in comparison with those animals which show only circadian rhythms. Regional variations in tidal patterns present interesting contrasts with seasonal and latitudinal variation in photoperiod, making it of particular importance to relate laboratory studies to behaviour in the sea. In addition, it will be emphasized that there are contrasts with circadian rhythms concerning the multiplicity of environmental variables which entrain circatidal and related rhythms, and in the phase responsiveness of circatidal rhythms to such variables. Finally the question of the physiological basis of circatidal rhythmicity will be addressed.

Tidal patterns of behaviour

There is now good evidence that many coastal marine animals when kept in the laboratory away from the influence of tides, exhibit endogenously controlled rhythms of circatidal periodicity in their patterns of behaviour and physiology. Unequivocal evidence of persistent circatidal rhythms of locomotor activity was first obtained in the late 1950's for the crabs *Uca* (Bennett, Shriner & Brown, 1957) and *Carcinus* (Naylor, 1958). Since that time numerous other examples of endogenous circatidal rhythms of locomotion, respiration and colour change have been reported for many organisms from diatoms to invertebrates and fish (see Enright, 1975; Naylor, 1976; DeCoursey, 1983). Recently, too, Cronin & Forward (1979) and Forward & Cronin (1980) have demonstrated endogenous circatidal rhythms of vertical swimming, swimming speed and phototaxis in the zoea larvae of the estuarine crab *Rhithropanopeus harrisii*, and Forward (1980) has demonstrated circatidal rhythmic changes in the phototaxis responses of the beach amphipod *Synchelidium*.

Ecological significance

Some examples of rhythmic swimming or walking behaviour have been related to observations of the experimental animals in the field. The shore crab *Carcinus*, for example, is active at high tide on the shore and in the laboratory (Naylor, 1958). The endogenous component of rhythmicity controls a cessation of activity in anticipation of low tide, permitting the crabs to seek shelter from avian predators and from desiccation (Fig. 1A) (Naylor, 1976). Likewise the sand-beach isopod *Eurydice pulchra* avoids being carried away with the falling tide by ceasing to swim and by burrowing in the sand before the tide has fully ebbed (Fig. 1B), thus maintaining its normal pattern of zonation on the beach (Jones & Naylor, 1970; Alheit & Naylor, 1976). Similarly, spontaneous swimming on rising tides by crab

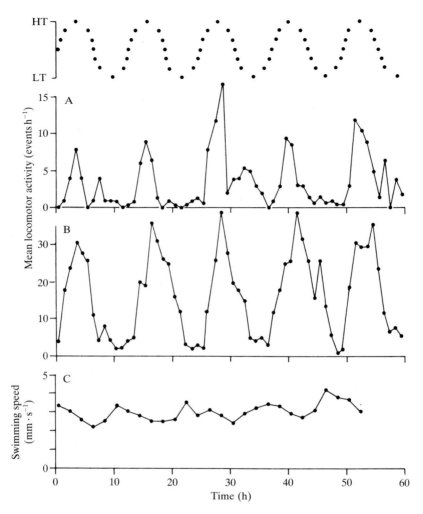

Fig. 1 Endogenous free-running circatidal rhythms of three marine crustaceans in constant conditions in the laboratory.
(A) *Carcinus maenas* walking rhythm of three crabs in tilting box actographs (After Naylor, 1963), (B) *Eurydice pulchra* swimming rhythm recorded as numbers (of five individuals) swimming past an infrared light source (After Jones & Naylor, 1970), and (C) *Rhithropanopeus harrisii* zoea rhythm of swimming speed, each point recorded as the mean of 45 observations (After Forward & Cronin, 1980). Top trace: schematic outline of 'expected' tidal regime; HT – high tide, LT – low tide.

larvae (Fig. 1C) (Forward & Cronin, 1980) is adaptive for retention in tideswept estuaries. In contrast, some shore organisms, such as sessile barnacles which are structurally well adapted to withstand desiccation and to resist predators at low tide show spontaneous shell opening and closing patterns which are stochastic (Sommer, 1972). These animals appear not to make use of endogenous timing to control their behaviour; they simply close their shell aperture as a direct response to the falling tide (Naylor, 1976). However, there are few studies involving concurrent field and laboratory experiments which permit better understanding of the adaptive aspects of tidal rhythmicity (see Palmer, 1974).

A problem which can arise in attempting to assess the adaptive significance of rhythmicity is illustrated by recent studies on a New Zealand mud crab *Helice crassa* (Williams, B. G., Naylor & Chatterton, 1985). Recordings of locomotor activity of *Helice* in constant conditions in the laboratory showed that it has an endogenous circatidal rhythm with peak activity at the times of high tide on the shores from which the animals were collected. The phasing of this circatidal rhythm was unexpected since the species can be seen on the surface of the mudflats at low tide, engaged in feeding on fine particulate matter and in the maintenance of their burrows. Similar field observations have been reported by Fielder & Jones (1978), and the general view in the literature is that these crabs are, on the shore, active at low tide. To study this apparent discrepancy, field experiments were carried out in which a grid of pitfall traps was set out on a sheltered beach where the crabs occurred abundantly (Williams, B. G. *et al.*, 1985). The traps were emptied at intervals over one or more complete tidal cycles, all the traps being accessible by wading at high tide. Fig. 2A, B illustrates that catches in the pitfall traps were clearly greatest at the times of high tide, contrary to the literature reports that *Helice* is low-tide active. The spontaneous circatidal locomotor activity rhythm of the crab (Fig. 2C) also shows peaks at expected times of high tide, coincident with the peaks of catch in the pitfall traps. Similar results were obtained for another crab *Macrophthalmus* which occurs lower down the shore in the same locality (Williams, B. G. *et al.*, 1985). In the light of these experiments it is interesting to note that though Beer (1959) and Fielder & Jones (1978) record that *H. crassa* is most active at low tide, the latter authors noted that the crabs seldom forage farther than 20 cm from the burrow when exposed to air. This presumably explains why although they are evident on the surface at low tide they are not abundantly caught in pitfall traps at that time.

Concurrent field and laboratory experiments clearly demonstrate a hitherto undetected aspect of the behavioural repertoire of *Helice* which appears to undertake extensive movements on the mud surface at high tides (Williams, B. G. *et al.*, 1985). In fact there are also differences in such behaviour dependent upon whether it is studied at spring tides or at neaps, as will be discussed below (pp. 79). Other marine species for

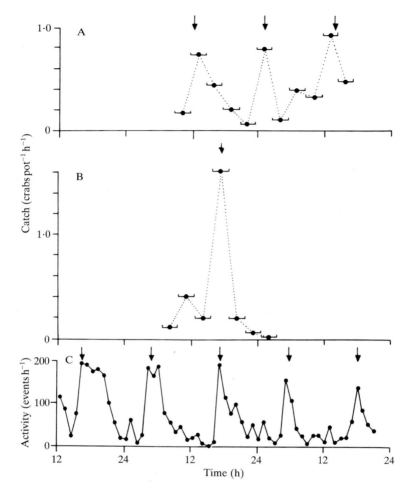

Fig. 2. Field catches and endogenous locomotor activity rhythm of the crab *Helice crassa* on a muddy shore in New Zealand.
(A) Number of crabs collected in a grid of 20 traps (crabs. $\text{trap}^{-1}.\text{h}^{-1}$) emptied at 3 h intervals (horizontal bars) over three consecutive tides, (B) similar catches of crabs carried out concurrently with (C) which records the total hourly walking activity of five crabs in infrared beam actographs over a period of five periods of expected high tide (arrows) in constant dim light and at constant 15 °C (After Williams, B. G., Naylor, E. & Chatterton, T. D., 1985).

which apparent discrepancies between field and laboratory rhythms have been reported include the commercially fished prawn *Nephrops norvegicus* which shows spontaneous nocturnal locomotor activity in the laboratory but which is caught in trawls mainly by day (Atkinson & Naylor, 1976; Hammond & Naylor, 1977; Moller & Naylor, 1980).

Entrainment by simulated tides

The generally accepted hypothesis for the control of tidal and daily rhythms of behaviour postulates that endogenously controlled inexact rhythms free-run in constant conditions. In nature the free-running rhythms are corrected by entraining exogenous factors in order that the naturally expressed behaviour is synchronized to the environmental regime. Such entraining factors determine the precise period and phase of the inexact endogenous process.

In field experiments using animals kept in perforated or closed containers tethered below or between tidemarks, or floating, the possible role of a number of tidal variables has been assessed. From such experiments it has been hypothesized that endogenous circatidal rhythmicity is at least partially entrained by wave action in the amphipod *Synchelidium* (Enright 1965), by hydrostatic pressure in the amphipod *Corophium* (Morgan 1965) and by hydrostatic pressure and temperature cycles in the crab *Carcinus* (Williams, B. G. & Naylor, 1969). Laboratory experiments confirming such hypotheses have been carried out for a number of coastal species. Entrainment to tidal cycles of simulated wave action has been demonstrated in the isopods *Excirolana* (Enright, 1965) and *Eurydice* (Jones & Naylor, 1970), and to simulated tidal changes of hydrostatic pressure in the isopod *Eurydice* (Jones & Naylor, 1970), the crab *Carcinus* (Naylor, Atkinson & Williams, B. G., 1971) and in the shore fish *Blennius pholis* (Gibson 1971). Similar entrainment to artificial tidal cycles of temperature has been demonstrated in *Carcinus* (Williams, B. G. & Naylor, 1969), *Bathyporeia* (Fincham, 1970) and *Corophium* (Holmström & Morgan, 1983b), and to immersion cycles in *Uca* (Lehmann, Neumann & Kaiser, 1974) and *Corophium* (Holmström & Morgan, 1983b). Square-wave and sinusoidal changes in the salinity over a tidal time base have also been shown to entrain persistent circatidal locomotor rhythmicity in *Carcinus* (Taylor & Naylor, 1977, Bolt & Naylor, 1984) (Figs 3, 4).

There have been relatively few studies of the limits of entrainment by cyclical variables (Naylor, 1982; DeCoursey, 1983; Naylor & Williams, B. G., 1984b) except for studies such as those reported for the entrainment of locomotor rhythms by cycles of hydrostatic pressure change in *Carcinus* (Naylor & Atkinson, 1972). In those experiments the crabs demonstrated clear-cut responses to environmentally realistic pressure cycles of tidal periodicity, with increased activity at periods of raised pressures of up to 0·6 atm above ambient atmospheric pressure. There was a threshold of response which is below 0·1 atm above ambient, with induced activity and subsequent endogenous activity more or less equal at 0·1, 0·2, 0·3 and 0·6 atm. There was, however, a linear relationship between the average amount of locomotor activity and the number of imposed tidal pressure cycles from 1 to 6. Also the crabs were most responsive to pressure entrainment in late summer and it has been suggested (Naylor & Atkinson, 1972) that there is seasonality in the extent to which different tidal variables are used as zeitgebers, with temperature most effective during the spring and early summer.

Interaction of exogenous and exogenous factors during entrainment

In many entrainment experiments using tidal simulations, periods of high activity induced at a particular phase of the imposed environmental variable are followed by high activity at 'expected' times of that phase of the variable in constant conditions after treatment. However, in experiments in which the shore crab *Carcinus maenas* was exposed to square-wave changes of salinity of tidal periodicity, Taylor & Naylor (1977) reported an additional and different kind of response. During treatment the crabs responded with increased locomotor activity after each change of salinity, but in constant salinity after treatment the crabs showed peak activity only at the times of expected full seawater (34‰ salinity) (Fig. 3). These responses occurred in crabs exposed for 42 h to alternating 6 h periods at 34 and 20‰ before being recorded at constant 34 or at 20‰ after treatment, and in others exposed to 6 h periods at 34 and 48‰ before recording at 34‰ or at 48‰ after treatments. From those experiments and from salinity choice chamber experiments by Thomas, Lasiak & Naylor (1981) a hypothesis was developed which relates the rhythmic behaviour of *Carcinus* to the crab's wider behavioural repertoire. The crab appears to be able to detect and avoid both hypersaline and hyposaline media and, when presented with a choice, appears to select salinities between 27–41‰. Avoidance of unfavourable salinities appears to be effected by a behavioural response to changed salinity which can be defined as halokinesis. This response is clearly exogenous; it does not persist at constant salinity after treatment. In contrast the repeated responses to exposure to ambient seawater, which are followed by peaks of activity at times of expected 34‰ after treatment, appear to be involved in the entrainment process of the endogenous clock. The proposed differences in the responses to alternate phases of square-wave salinity change are supported by the apparently longer latency times of responses to ambient salinity compared with responses to reduced salinity (Fig. 3).

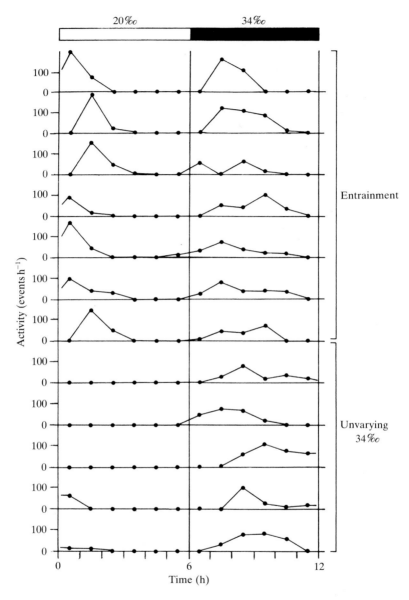

Fig. 3. Mean hourly locomotor activity records of five *Carcinus maenas* subjected to 42 h of 6 : 6 h cycles of 20‰ : 34‰ salinity, followed by 30 h at continous 34‰ (After Taylor & Naylor, 1977).

To test the hypothesis outlined above Bolt & Naylor (1985) have recently carried out experiments in which *Carcinus* were exposed to sinusoidal changes of salinity in phase and in antiphase with salinity changes such as would be experienced by crabs on an estuarine shore. Where the imposed salinity cycle was in antiphase with the 'expected' salinity cycle (Fig. 4B) the exogenous response to low salinity initially enhanced the endogenous component of circatidal rhythmicity giving pronounced 'tidal' peaks. However, later in the experiment, activity was also induced at the times of high salinity and these, but not the low salinity peaks, persisted after treatment. The distinction between an exogenous halokinesis response to low salinity, and endogenous reentrainment to high salinity seems clear. In Fig. 4A the imposed salinity cycle was in phase with the 'expected' pattern of tides. Here low salinity times of the imposed cycle initially induced high peaks of locomotor activity. Later, however, the high salinity events reinforced the endogenous component, which persisted in constant conditions after treatment. These experiments clearly indicate that it is important to distinguish between apparent entrainment of behaviour and true entrainment of underlying physiological oscillators.

It is also necessary to assess responses to cyclical environmental variables against the background of possible endogenous, phasic changes in responsiveness to such variables. Singarajah, Moyse & Knight-Jones (1967), for example, reported that the planktonic nauplius larvae of *Elminius modestus* and *Balanus balanoides* were photonegative at noon and photopositive in the afternoon, even in constant conditions. More recently, too, Forward (1980) has demonstrated that the sand-beach amphipod *Synchelidium* is more negatively phototaxic and less sensitive to light on rising tides than on falling tides. Such temporal patterns must clearly be taken into account when characterizing so-called 'typical' behavioural responses of animals (Naylor, 1982).

Finally, it is necessary to relate general behavioural responses to clock-controlled behaviour when assessing seasonal differences in the expression of locomotor activity rhythms, some of which are reported to be lost in winter. *Carcinus*, for example, does not express tidal rhythmicity in winter when locomotor activity is recorded in crabs kept in full seawater or in moist air. Yet Bolt & Naylor (1985) have recently shown that clear circatidal rhythmicity is expressed in winter-caught crabs recorded in low salinity. Evidently low temperatures in winter override but do not completely suppress the ability of the crabs to show endogenous circatidal rhythmicity. Similarly, the degree of expression of circatidal rhythmicity varies where local tides are markedly diurnal (Williams, B. G. *et al.*, 1985). Also there are often considerable variations in tidal behaviour at spring and neap tides, particularly in species living high on shores with extensive tides. Lack of reinforcement of endogenous

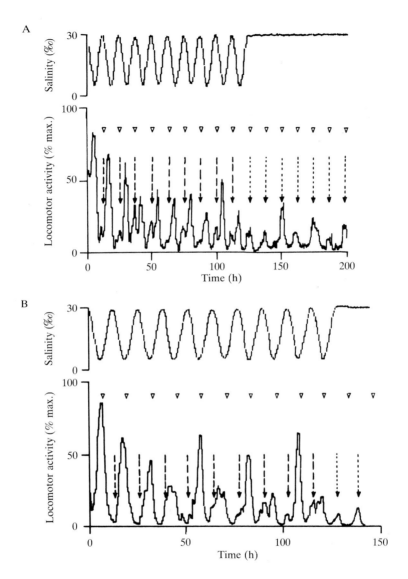

Fig. 4. Hourly activity values of eight freshly collected *Carcinus maenas* exposed to artificial tides of sinusoidal change of salinity, followed by a period at continuous high salinity.

(A) With imposed high salinity time at times of 'expected' high tide, (B) with imposed high salinity times at times of 'expected' low tide. (Triangles: expected high tide times; vertical arrows: times of high or expected high salinity. All records at constant 15 °C in continuous darkness (After Bolt & Naylor, 1985).

rhythmicity at neap tides is correlated with apparent loss or imprecise expression of tidal rhythms in the prawn *Palaemon elegans* (Rodriguez & Naylor, 1972) and in the mud crab *Helice crassa* (Williams, B. G. *et al.*, 1985). Springs/neaps variations in spontaneous locomotor behaviour have also been reported in a number of other organisms (see pp. 78).

Phase responsiveness to pulses of tidal variables

Since circatidal rhythms are entrained in nature by environmental cycles, the question arises as to whether particular phases of the environmental cycle are more critical for entrainment. Presumably in order to entrain to a particular environmental variable, an organism must exhibit a differential responsiveness to phase shifting by that stimulus. Many circadian rhythms, for example, which are typically entrained by light/dark transitions, show phase responsiveness to pulses of light of as little as 1 h duration or less (Pittendrigh, 1981; Daan, 1982; DeCoursey, 1983). Phase-response curves (PRC) can be plotted, indicating the extent of phase delays or advances which are induced by light pulses applied at various stages of a free-running rhythm of animals kept in continuous dim light in the laboratory. Among coastal animals, the circadian locomotor rhythm of the high shore amphipod *Talitrus saltator* has been shown to respond phasically to 2 h pulses of white light of 400 lux intensity at various times throughout the 24 h cycle (Williams, J. A., 1980). When *Talitrus* were kept in continuous dim light, pulses of white light applied from before dusk until around midnight induced delays of up to 4 h in the phase of the free-running rhythm. In contrast, 2 h pulses applied between midnight and dawn induced phase advances of up to 4 h. In *Talitrus*, which exhibits a free-running circadian rhythm of period slightly greater than 24 h, entrainment in nature can be envisaged as occurring by the generation of slight phase advances induced by the dawn light cue. The same process also presumably brings about seasonal adjustment of the predawn nocturnal peak of locomotor activity, the phase of which varies according to annual changes in photoperiod (Williams, J. A., 1980).

Despite the considerable amount of information available on phase responsiveness of circadian rhythms in protists to vertebrates, in response to pulses of light, temperature and chemical substances (DeCoursey, 1983), there is relatively little information available on phase responsiveness of circatidal rhythms. Such data are of interest not only concerning the problem of entrainment, but also in relation to the question as to whether circatidal rhythms are 'real' or whether they should be regarded as twin-peaked circadian oscillations. PRC's of a true circatidal rhythm would be expected to be unimodal over a tidal (12·4 h) time base, whereas a twin-peaked circadian rhythm might be expected to show a PRC which is unimodal over a diel (24 h) time base.

In an attempt to test this hypothesis Enright (1976a, b) subjected the intertidal isopod *Excirolana chiltoni* to 2 h pulses of water agitation simulating high tide at different times throughout the day. These experiments yielded a PRC which was symmetrically bimodal over a 24 h time base, which could be interpreted as supporting the idea of circatidal rather than circadian rhythmicity. Despite that possible explanation, Enright (1976a, b) concluded that the free-running rhythm of *Excirolana* was not truly circatidal but most probably a tidally synchronized circadian activity rhythm. There are, however, marked diurnal inequalities of tidal amplitude in the locality in S. California where the experiments were carried out (Barnwell, 1976; Klapow, 1976), which may limit the extent to which the interpretation of the *Excirolana* PRC can be generalized for tidal rhythms as a whole (Naylor, 1982; Naylor & Williams, B. G., 1984b).

Recently several authors have addressed this problem in experiments on animals from localities where tides show only small diurnal inequalities. Petpiroon & Morgan (1983) studied the responses of *Littorina nigrolineata* to short pulses of immersion, and Holmström & Morgan (1983a) and Harris & Morgan (1984) studied the responses of the swimming rhythm of *Corophium volutator* to pulses of sub-zero temperature and to high salinity (40‰), respectively. Also, Naylor & Williams, B. G. (1984a) subjected the crab *Hemigrapsus edwardsii* to 3 h artificial tidal pulses of immersion at low temperature (10 °C) (Fig. 5) and Reid (In litt.) subjected *Eurydice pulchra* to 2 h pulses of simulated tidal agitation. Each of these experiments (Fig. 6) demonstrated phase responsiveness to the pulses of artificial 'tides' illustrating the mechanism whereby circatidal endogenous rhythms are entrained in nature. The time base of the pattern of response in each case was tidal rather than diel (Fig. 6). Therefore all phase-response data, including those for *Excirolana*, derived so far for tidal rhythms, suggest that such rhythms are entrained by each tidal rise and fall. If that is so then tidal rhythms should be regarded as having an endogenous physiological basis which is truly circatidal rather than semicircadian (see also Neumann, 1981). However, further testing of that hypothesis is required, for example, by attempts to induce independent phase shifts in circatidal and circadian rhythms in animals which exhibit both kinds of rhythmicity.

A striking difference between PRC's for circadian and circatidal rhythms concerns the relatively small phase shifts induced in the latter

E. NAYLOR

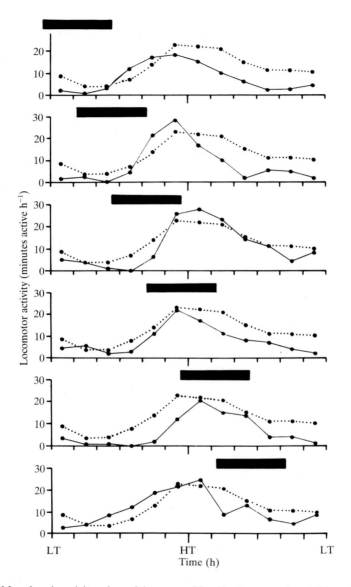

Fig. 5. Mean hourly activity values of six groups of five *Hemigrapsus edwardsii* (continuous lines) recorded over a period of 36–48 h after exposure to a 3 h period of simulated high tide (shaded bars) at various times throughout the expected tidal cycle, compared with untreated controls (dotted lines). All recordings carried out at 15 °C, in moist air and in continuous dim red illumination; and during the 3 h tidal pulses crabs were immersed in seawater at 10 °C. (HT expected high tide; LT 'expected' low tide.) (After Naylor & Williams B.G. 1984a).

compared with the former. This is only partially explained by the smaller period length of circatidal rhythms. More extensive phase shifts are often apparent in selected individually recorded animals (Enright, 1976a) but on a population basis it appears that the underlying oscillators controlling circatidal rhythms of coastal animals are relatively stable when compared with those controlling circadian rhythms. These differences may have adaptive value in that the phase of circadian rhythms, unlike circatidal rhythms, is often continuously adjusted in relation to seasonal changes in photoperiod (Naylor & Williams, B. G., 1984b). In addition, the multiplicity and seasonal variability of potential time cues in coastal environments suggest that extensive phase shifting by single pulses of

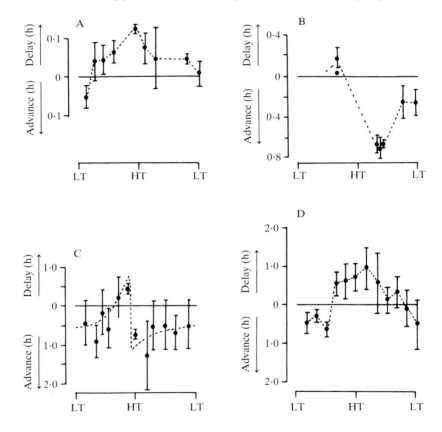

Fig. 6. Phase-response curves of the circatidal locomotor rhythms of four coastal species subjected to single tidal pulses at various times throughout the 'expected' tidal cycle.
(A) *Corophium volutator* subjected to 3 h pulses of high salinity ($40^0/_{00}$) (after Harris & Morgan, 1984a), (B) *Littorina nigrolineata* subjected to immersion in seawater after acclimation in moist air, (after Petpiroon & Morgan, 1983), (C) *Hemigrapsus edwardsii* subjected to 3 h pulses of immersion at 10 °C and recorded subsequently in moist air at 15 °C (after Naylor & Williams, 1984a), (D) *Eurydice pulchra* subjected to 2 h pulses of simulated tidal agitation (after Reid, In litt.). (HT: 'expected' high tide; LT: 'expected' low tide).

individual variables might in general be unlikely (Naylor 1982). Finally
in this context it is appropriate to emphasize that differential responses
of circatidal rhythms to changing temperature (Naylor, 1963; Williams &
Naylor, 1969; Holmström & Morgan, 1983a) confirm the need to question earlier generalizations in the literature (pp. 64) that endogenous
rhythms are strictly 'temperature-independent'.

Tidal effects on long-period rhythms

Many marine animals show not only short-period rhythms of tidal and
diel periodicity but also semilunar, lunar and annual rhythms of behaviour
and reproduction (Naylor, 1976, 1982; Olive & Garwood, 1983). Moreover it is becoming evident that some of the long-period rhythms are also
under the control of endogenous mechanisms which are phased by environmental variables. Responses to lunar illumination have been postulated on
a number of occasions as a controlling factor in long-term rhythms and understandable scepticism has been expressed concerning that view (Korringa, 1957; Caspers, 1984). However, the hypothesis has been confirmed experimentally in studies on the reproductive behaviour of the polychaete
Platynereis dumerilii (Hauenschild 1960) and the intertidal midge *Clunio
marinus* (Neumann, 1967, 1978). In *Clunio* the larvae and pupae are
restricted to the lowest levels of the intertidal zone and are exposed to air
only at low spring tides. Copulation between newly emerged winged males
and wingless females, and subsequent egg-laying, must take place in air.
Emergence of adult flies from the pupae therefore takes place only at low
spring tides, and hence at semilunar intervals. Cultures of the midge kept in
LD 12:12 exhibit only 24 h rhythmicity of emergence, but cultures exposed
to simulated moonlight (0·3 lux) during a sequence of four nights every
month, show a circasemilunar emergence rhythm. Even one such sequence
of three 'moonlight' nights is sufficient to re-establish the rhythm, thus suggesting that it is truly endogenous (Neumann, 1976, 1978).

Despite increasing evidence that moonlight may directly control some
aspects of long-term rhythmic behaviour (Naylor, 1976, 1982) it is also
important to consider the direct effects of tides upon such rhythms. Clearly in many parts of the world moonlight would be an unreliable zeitgeber
owing to the irregularities of cloud cover. Additional 'semilunar' cues
could derive from the springs/neaps pattern of tides, and 'lunar' cues
from inequalities between new and full moon spring tides.

Semilunar and lunar rhythms

Apart from the *Platynereis* and *Clunio* rhythms referred to above,
lunar or semilunar rhythms of locomotion or reproduction have been

widely reported in a number of invertebrates (Naylor, 1982; Olive & Garwood, 1983; DeCoursey, 1984). In fish, too, lunar cycles have been reported in otolith increments, behavioural thermoregulation, and the thyroxine surge of salmonids prior to migration (Gibson, 1978; Grau *et al.*, 1981; Kavaliers, 1982; Campena, 1984). Experimental demonstrations of such behaviour patterns have been reported, for example, in the swimming of high shore prawns (Rodriguez & Naylor, 1972) and isopods (Enright, 1972); Fish & Fish, 1972; Fincham, 1973; Kensley, 1974; Alheit & Naylor, 1976; Hastings & Naylor, 1980; Hastings, 1981a), and in the respiration rate of the isopod *Eurydice pulchra* (Hastings, 1981b). Similar rhythms of locomotion or reproduction have been shown in marine amphipods (Preece, 1971; Fincham, 1972; Fish, 1975; Benson & Lewis, 1976; Williams, J. A., 1979; Dieleman, 1979) and in a number of coastal species of crabs (De Vries, Epifanio & Dittel, 1984; DeCoursey, 1984; Williams, B. G. *et al.*, 1985).

The function of semilunar rhythms has been related to the maintenance of breeding synchrony (Neumann, 1976, 1978) and the synchronous release of larvae or young (Williams, J. A., 1979; DeCoursey, 1984). They may also contribute to position maintenance in strongly tidal coastal localities and estuaries. For example the sand beach isopod *Eurydice pulchra* exhibits spontaneous emergence from sand and enhanced tidal swimming rhythms after the times of maximum spring tides. This appears to provide a mechanism whereby the isopods avoid stranding in sand above high water mark at the times of neap high tides (Alheit & Naylor, 1976). Similarly, Dieleman (1979) has demonstrated peaks of spontaneous swimming at the time of spring tides in the estuarine amphipods *Gammarus zaddachi* and *G. chevreuxi*. Such temporal patterns of behaviour ensure that swimming is least likely at neap tides when downstream transport by river flow would be hazardous.

Many lunar (c. 30 day), as distinct from semilunar, rhythms of behaviour are also directly associated with the spring/neaps cycle. They occur in localities where at times there are considerable inequalities between those spring tides associated with the new moon and those with the full moon. In such circumstances lunar modulation of tidally rhythmic behaviour has been reported in the swimming rhythm of the isopod *Excirolana chiltoni* in S. California (Enright, 1972; Klapow, 1976) and in the walking rhythm of the New Zealand crab *Helice crassa* (Williams, B. G. *et al.*, 1985).

So far, few of these long-term rhythms have been shown to free run as circalunar or circasemilunar rhythms in constant conditions in the laboratory. Moreover little attempt has been made to ascertain whether such rhythms are generated by the beat effect of endogenous circatidal and circadian rhythms (Bunning & Müller, 1961; Barnwell, 1968) or whether they are controlled directly by endogenous oscillators of approximately 15 or 30 day periodicity. For the free-running circalunar rhythm of the isopod *Excirolana* Enright (1972) favoured the latter hypothesis. That conclusion is also supported by recent demonstrations of free-running circasemilunar locomotor rhythms in the amphipod *Talitrus* (Williams, J. A., 1979) and the isopod *Eurydice* (Reid & Naylor, 1985). Since *Talitrus* exhibits circadian but not circatidal rhythmicity (Bregazzi & Naylor, 1972; Williams, J. A., 1980), yet still exhibits circa-semilunar rhythmicity, it provides clear evidence against the 'beat' hypothesis. In *Eurydice*, which exhibits both circadian and circatidal rhythmicity the expression of these two rhythms showed great variability over 50–60 days in constant conditions in the laboratory, yet a clear circasemilunar pattern of total daily swimming activity was apparent (Fig. 7A). Here again, therefore, the 'beat' hypothesis seems an unlikely explanation for the control of the semilunar rhythm.

Experimental evidence of tidal synchronization of semilunar rhythms has built up in recent years. However, so far there appears to be no evidence that this is achieved by *absolute* differences between tidal variables at neaps and springs (Neumann, 1978; Hastings, 1981a). Hastings (1981a), for example, could detect no significant differences between the wave turbulence profiles at spring and neap tides on a beach where *Eurydice pulchra* is known to exhibit semilunar rhythmicity (Hastings & Naylor, 1980). A less economical, but so far more likely hypothesis, is that springs/neaps cues derive from the *relative* timing of tidal and daily environmental variables. Evidence for this is provided by laboratory experiments on *Clunio* (Neumann, 1978) and *Eurydice* (Hastings, 1981a; Reid & Naylor, 1985) in which circasemilunar rhythms were entrained using pulses of artificial wave turbulence applied at those times of day when high spring tides occur on the shores where the animals were collected (Fig. 7B).

The corollary of the hypothesis outlined above is that to permit synchrony of behaviour at a particular stage of the neaps/springs cycle then populations in different localities should exhibit differences in the phase relationships of the entrainment factors. For example, races of *Clunio* from Helgoland and Normandy both show maximum emergence during the low water of spring tides, but there is a 2 h difference in the timing of low tide between the two localities. When entrained in the laboratory to the same combination of light–dark cycle and wave simulation, the induced circasemilunar rhythms of the two races showed a phase difference

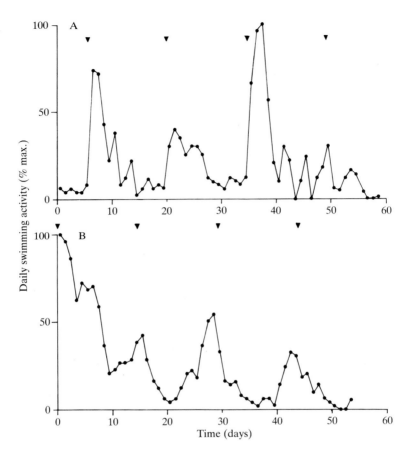

Fig. 7. Total daily swimming activity of 20 *Eurydice pulchra* recorded in constant conditions for 50–60 days in the laboratory.
(A) Freshly collected animals, (B) animals kept initially in the laboratory, then entrained with 2 h agitation every 12 h (around noon and midnight) for 4 days in LLDD. (Arrow heads are at expected maximum tides (A) and at 14–15 days intervals from end of entrainment (B)). (After Reid & Naylor, 1985.)

of 3 days. This difference corresponds well with the time difference between afternoon low spring tides in the two localities (Neumann 1978). Differences in the phase relationships of tidal turbulence and light–dark cycles as entraining cues for a circasemilunar rhythm also occur in different populations of the sand beach isopod *Eurydice*. Populations from the Isle of Man and from North Wales where high spring tides occur around 1200 and 2400 h entrain most successfully when artificial tides are induced around noon and midnight, and least successfully when artificial tides are applied around dawn and dusk (Hastings, 1981a; Reid & Naylor,

1985). In contrast, populations of *Eurydice* from the South Wales coast where high spring tides occur around dusk and dawn, the circasemilunar rhythm of emergence and swimming is least effectively cued by artificial tides induced at noon and midnight (Reid, In litt.). Those populations respond best to simulated tidal action at the times of dusk and dawn.

Apart from wave turbulence the only other tidal variable which has been investigated as a possible time cue for lunar and semilunar rhythms is that of temperature. The fortnightly interaction of the tidal cycle and daily solar cycle in summer induces a pattern of heating of beach sediments which is greater when a low tide occurs around noon. This has been shown to generate 14- to 15-day differences of up to 5 °C in beach sediment temperatures (de Wilde & Berghuis, 1979). Vugts & Zimmerman (1975) have suggested that interaction of the tidal cycle and daily cycle of solar radiation may phase control the semilunar rhythm of the amphipod *Talorchestia quoyana*. However, there is little experimental evidence in favour of this view and in any event there are likely to be considerable regional variations in the magnitude of the temperature cues generated by this phenomenon (Naylor, 1982). In contrast there is recent experimental evidence (Neumann & Heimbach, 1984) that *tidal* temperature cycles, like those of wave turbulence, when combined with the 24 h light /dark cycle, influence the semilunar rhythm of emergence of the intertidal midge *Clunio marinus*.

Annual rhythms

There are several examples in the literature of fairly precisely timed annual rhythms of behaviour in marine animals (Naylor, 1976, 1982). However, these accounts are largely observational with relatively little quantitative data available. Moreover, it has yet to be ascertained that such rhythms are circa-annual, in the sense that they free run in constant conditions. Also little experimental work has been done on the nature of their environmental cues.

A recent paper by Caspers (1984) collates the known spawning dates of the Pacific Palolo *Eunice viridis* on the Samoan Islands over a period from 1843–1982. Apart from one or two very sporadic spawnings at other times of the year, spawning in any one year occurs on up to 3 nights at the times of the third quarter of the moon in October or November. It may occur in each of those two months, dependent upon the precise solar/ lunar relationship which varies on the 19-year metonic cycle. A plot of the tabulated data of Caspers (1984) on a 19-year form estimate (Fig. 8) demonstrates that the first or only spawnings occur on an annual cycle of

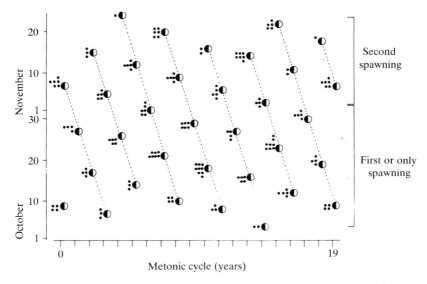

Fig. 8. Plots of the recorded spawning dates of the Pacific Palolo (*Eunice viridis*) on the Samoan Islands from a discontinuous series of observations from 1843–1982. All dates are plotted on the 19-year metonic cycle and the times of the third quarters of the moon are indicated; thus, for example, the points for years 0 and 19 are based on data for 1982, 1944, 1925 and 1868 (Data from Caspers, 1984).

356 ± 15 days. A second spawning may occur over a subsequent period of about 14 days dependent upon the timing of the initial spawning.

Most spawning takes place on the day of the third quarter of the moon and is therefore coincident with a period of neap tides. The adaptive significance of this pattern may be to produce larvae at times when tidal flushing is least likely to sweep them away from the parental reefs, as has been suggested for some corals (Kojis & Quinn, 1982; Hughes, 1983). A similar pattern is also exhibited by the Atlantic Palolo *Eunice fucata* around the Dry Tortugas Islands which spawns on either the third or the first lunar quarters dependent upon the relative timing of those events during the spawning month of July (Clark & Hess, 1940). Such a pattern is certainly consistent with a neaps-spawning hypothesis. However, it is difficult to envisage a mechanism whereby the low amplitude tides of neaps act to synchronize Palolo spawning, particularly in view of the lack of spawning by *E. viridis* on the neap tides of the first lunar quarter. This is so despite the fact that, whereas in some years the third lunar quarter neaps are smaller in amplitude than those of the first quarter, in other years the opposite is true.

So far then there is little evidence to indicate the lunar cues of the reproductive behaviour of the Pacific Palolo. Moreover, there has been a reluctance to accept the possibility of direct control by moonlight (Caspers, 1984), despite the fact that Clark & Hess (1940) postulated such a mechanism for the Atlantic Palolo, and despite experimental evidence in favour of moonlight synchronization of reproduction in the polychaete *Platynereis* (Hauenschild, 1960) and the midge *Clunio* (Neumann, 1978). In *E. fucata* Clark & Hess (1940) suggested that spawning is inhibited at full moon because the worms remain in their burrows and at new moon because the epitokal region is not attracted to the surface. At the lunar quarters the light intensity is below the threshold for photonegative behaviour by the anterior region of the worms yet high enough to induce upward swimming in the epitokes. Such an explanation, however, cannot readily be extended to *E. viridis* which appears never to spawn on the first lunar quarter (Fig. 8) . Further experimental study of these long-term rhythms is clearly required to ascertain the extent of their control by endogenous factors and their synchronization by primary or secondary lunar factors. However, it would not be surprising if endogenous rhythmicity were shown to be an important component of many annual reproductive rhythms of marine invertebrates (Naylor, 1976; Olive & Garwood, 1983).

Physiological basis of rhythmic behaviour in marine animals

The search for physiological components of clock control of rhythmic behaviour in marine animals has so far concentrated particularly upon circadian aspects of rhythmicity in molluscs, crustaceans and unicellular organisms such as *Gonyaulax* and *Euglena*. Among molluscs it has been shown that isolated portions of the parietovisceral ganglia and the optic cup of *Aplysia* are capable of exhibiting circadian oscillations in neuroelectrical output (Strumwasser, 1971; Jacklett & Geronimo, 1971). Indeed the nervous system of molluscs as a whole is capable of generating a variety of patterned impulse activity, based on both endogenous mechanisms in single neurons or the properties of reticular systems (Dorsett, 1979). The fundamental period of these oscillators is often measured in seconds, but the output may be modulated by sensory or neuroendocrine influences to produce behavioural cycles of a much greater length (Dorsett, 1979).

In decapod crustaceans there is also good evidence of matching rhythms of behaviour and spontaneous neuroelectrical activity (Arechiga, Huberman & Naylor, 1974). Moreover there is considerable evidence in favour of an inhibitory hormonal clock component in the eyestalk which modulates locomotor and neural activity (Arechiga *et al.*,

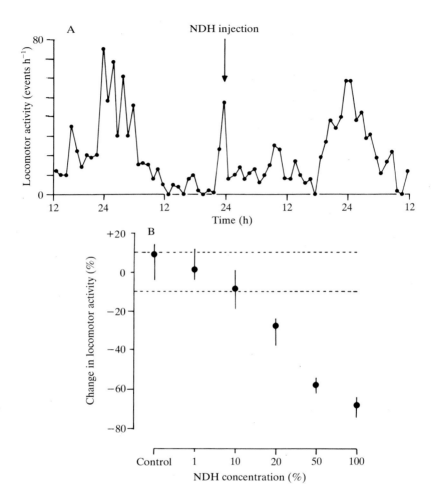

Fig. 9. Effects of injecting NDH-containing fractions of eyestalk extracts on the circadian locomotor rhythm of *Carcinus maenas*.

(A) Hourly activity of one crab over a period of 72 h injected with 0·25 ml of partially purified extract (concentration index 100) at the time of the arrow, (B) Mean percentage change of locomotor activity in the 12 h period following injection of various concentrations of partially purified extract. The change in activity is determined from a comparison between the 12 h period after injection and the equivalent period 24 h earlier. Concentration is given as a percentage of the total protein content of the fraction, with 100% = 1890 μg/ml. Circles and bars represent the mean and range of at least three replicates; the horizontal dashed lines are ±10% confidence limits of expected daily variation in activity. (After Arechiga *et al.*, 1979).

1974; Arechiga & Naylor, 1976; Keller, 1983). Occasional hypoactivity induced by eyestalk ablation and hyperactivity induced by injected crude eyestalk extract (Cooke & Sullivan, 1982) has been explained as a postoperative shock response to eyestalk ablation (Naylor & Williams, B. G., 1968) or a response to exaggerated potassium levels in injected un-purified eyestalk extract (Williams, J. A. *et al.*, 1979a). The eyestalk hormonal factor which inhibits neural activity, neurodepressing hormone (NDH), appears to be a small peptide (Arechiga *et al.*, 1974), which in Sephadex columns co-elutes with markers between $1-1\cdot3 \times 10^3$ relative molecular mass (M_r) (Huberman *et al.*, 1979). NDH also appears to act as an inhibitor of locomotor activity (Fig. 9) and is cross reactive between different species of decapod crustaceans (Arechiga, Williams, Pullin & Naylor, 1979).

The question as to how NDH can be distinguished from other peptidic eyestalk hormones (Cooke & Sullivan, 1982) has been addressed by Arechiga, Garcia & Rodriguez-Sosa (1984). Of the hormones postulated so far, erythrophore concentrating hormone (ECH) and distal retinal pigment hormone (DRPH) have been fully characterized in terms of amino acid composition, and crustacean hyperglycaemic hormone (CHH) has been partially characterized (Cooke & Sullivan, 1982; Keller, 1983; Arechiga *et al.*, 1984). Among these CHH, unlike NDH, does not dialyse and is species specific, whilst DRPH has a different elution time from NDH in Sephadex columns and it does not inhibit neuronal activity. ECH has a relative molecular mass of 1000, which is close to that of NDH, but the two elute with different retention times in high-pressure liquid chromatography. Moreover, ECH does not affect the discharge of neurons known to be inhibited by NDH, and NDH has no effect on tegumentary chromatophores (Arechiga *et al.*, 1984). Recent studies by Webster (1985) demonstrate that moult inhibiting hormone (MIH) is of larger M_r ($6-14 \times 10^3$) than NDH.

NDH therefore appears to be quite distinct from other peptidic hor-mones postulated so far in the decapod crustacean eyestalk. Moreover there is sufficient evidence (Arechiga *et al.*, 1979; Arechiga & Huberman, 1980; Arechiga *et al.*, 1984) to postulate that blood-borne NDH is secreted rhythmically and that it interacts with synaptic mediators to adjust circadian neuronal activity and locomotor rhythmicity (Fig. 9). Such a role for NDH may also be valid in the control of tidal rhythmicity. Experiments by Naylor, Smith & Williams (1973) and Williams *et al.* (1979a) showed inhibition of tidal rhythmicity by an eyestalk factor and different potency of inhibition of locomotion by eyestalk extracts, depending upon the phase of the tidal cycle at which the samples were taken. In addition, based upon evidence of temporal cytological changes in neurosecretory cells of isolated eyestalks, Williams, J. A. *et al.*, (1979b) advanced a tentative hypothesis that NDH is synthesized and released rhythmically by cells of type 5 in Hanstrom's organ of the *Carcinus* medulla terminalis.

A picture is emerging, therefore, of rhythmic neuroendocrine modulation as a clock component in the physiological control of neural and locomotor rhythms in decapod crustaceans. However, it has yet to be ascertained whether rhythmicity is an inherent property of the neuroendocrine cells or whether they are under the influence of other 'clocks' located elsewhere. In addition the interrelationships of circadian and circatidal rhythmicity require further study at this level of organization.

At the cellular level a number of models have been proposed for the action of circadian and circatidal oscillators. These include the membrane hypothesis (Njus, Sulzman & Hastings, 1974), the protein synthesis or 'chronon' hypothesis (Ehret & Trucco, 1967) and a combination of these two in the coupled translation–membrane model of Schweiger & Schweiger (1977). Tests of the first hypothesis have been carried out using applications of ethanol and various membrane active drugs such as valinomycin, all of which have been shown to affect the phase or period of free-running circatidal rhythms, for example in the marine isopod *Excirolana* (Enright, 1971) and the amphipod *Corophium* (Harris & Morgan, 1984b), and the circadian rhythms of the dinoflagellate *Gonyaulax* (Sweeney, 1976, Dunlop, Taylor & Hastings, 1980) and the optic nerve of *Aplysia* (Jacklett, 1980, 1982). Similarly, tests of the 'chronon' hypothesis have been carried out using drugs to inhibit the translation of DNA to protein. One such drug, cycloheximide, had little efect when added to seawater in which free-running circatidal rhythms were being recorded for *Excirolana chiltoni* (Enright, 1971) and *Corophium volutator* (Harris & Morgan, 1984b). However, whereas Enright (1971) concluded that cycloheximide may not have penetrated the tissues of *Excirolana*, Harris & Morgan (1984b) argued that it had done so in *Corophium*. The latter authors concluded that cycloheximide had little effect on the phase and period of the *Corophium* rhythm, thus favouring the membrane hypothesis rather than the 'chronon' hypothesis from their experiments. In contrast, however, NDH as a possible clock component of the *Carcinus* rhythm clearly appears to be dependent upon a ribosomal protein synthesis mechanism (Gainer, Loh & Neale, 1982). Moreover, NDH synthesis is inhibited by cycloheximide, puromicine and emetine (Arechiga *et al.*, 1984).

In conclusion it is too early to determine whether clock function at the cellular level is more likely to be dependent upon the protein synthesis model, the chronon model or a combination of both. Further work is required on chemical perturbations of physiological components of rhythmic processes, and possible phase-response curves derived therefrom. It is also necessary to establish whether the 'responses observed are effects upon basic clock components or on some aspect of the coupling mechanisms between separate components of the physiological clock mechanism. Finally, it is required to demonstrate whether clocks at the cellular level are circadian, semicircadian or truly 'tidal'.

References

ALHEIT, J. & NAYLOR, E. (1976). Behavioural basis of intertidal zonation in *Eurydice pulchra* Leach. *J. exp. Mar. Biol. Ecol.* **23**, 135–144.

ARECHIGA, H., HUBERMAN, A. & NAYLOR, E. (1974). Hormonal modulation of circadian neural activity in *Carcinus maenas* (L.). *Proceedings of the Royal Society of London, B* **187**, 299–313.

ARECHIGA, H., GARCIA, U. & RODRIGUEZ-SOSA, L. (1984). Neurosecretory role of the crustacean eyestalk in the control of neuronal activity. In *Model Neural Networks and Behaviour.* (ed. A. I. Selverston) New York: Plenum Press.

ARECHIGA, H. & HUBERMAN, A. (1980). Peptide modulation of neuronal function in crustaceans. In *The Role of Peptides in Neuronal Function*, pp. 317–349. Place: Marcel Deklu, Inc.

ARECHIGA, H. & NAYLOR, E. (1976). Endogenous factors in the control of rhythmicity in decapod crustaceans. In *Biological Rhythms in the Marine Environment.* (ed. P. J. DeCoursey) pp. 1–16, University of South Carolina Press.

ARECHIGA, H., WILLIAMS, J. A., PULLIN, R. S. V. & NAYLOR, E. (1979). Cross-sensitivity to neurodepressing hormone and its effect on locomotor rhythmicity in two different groups of crustaceans. *Gen. comp. Endocr.* **37**, 350–357.

ATKINSON, R. J. & NAYLOR, E. (1976). An endogenous activity rhythm and the rhythmicity of catches of *Nephrops norvegicus* (L.). *J. exp. Mar. Biol. Ecol.* **25**, 95–108.

BARNWELL, F. H. (1968). The role of rhythmic systems in the adaptation of fiddler crabs to the intertidal zone. *Am. Zool.* **8**, 569–583.

BARNWELL, F. H. (1976). Variation in the form of the tide and some problems it poses for biological timing systems. In *Biological Rhythms in the Marine Environment.* (ed. P. J. DeCoursey) pp. 161–187, University of South Carolina Press.

BEER, C. G. (1959). Notes on the behaviour of two estuarine crab species. *Trans. R. Soc. N.Z.* **86**, 197–203.

BENNETT, M. F., SHRINER, J. & BROWN, F. A. (1957). Persistent tidal cycles of spontaneous motor activity in the fiddler crab *Uca pugnax*. *Biol. mar. biol. Lab., Woods Hole* **112**, 267–275.

BENSON, J. A. & LEWIS, R. D. (1976). An analysis of the activity rhythm of the sand beach amphipod *Talorchestia quoyana*. *J. comp. Physiol.* **105**, 339–352.

BOHN, G. & PIERON, H. (1906). Le rhythme des marees et la phenomene de l'anticipation reflexe. *C. r. Séanc. Soc. Biol., Paris* **61**, 660–661.

BOLT, S. R. L. & NAYLOR, E. (1985). Interaction of endogenous and exogenous factors controlling locomotor activity rhythms in *Carcinus* exposed to tidal salinity cycles. *J. exp. mar. Biol. Ecol.* (in press).

BREGAZZI, P. E. & NAYLOR, E. (1972). The locomotor activity rhythm of *Talitrus saltator* (Montagu) (Crustacea, Amphipoda). *J. exp. Biol.* **57**, 375–391.

BROOM, D. M. (1979). Methods of detecting and analysing activity rhythms. *Biology of Behaviour* **4**, 3–18.

BROWN, F. A. (1960). Response to pervasive geophysical factors and the biological clock problem. *Cold Spring Harb. Symp. quant. Biol.* **25**, 57–71.

BROWN, F. A. (1972). The 'clocks' timing biological rhythms. *Am. Scient.* **60**, 756–766.

BUNNING, E. & MÜLLER, D. (1961). Wie messen Organismen lunare Zyklen? *Z. Naturf.* **166**, 391–395.

CAMPENA, S. E. (1984). Lunar cycles of otolith growth in the juvenile starry flounder *Platichthus stellatus*. *Marine Biology* **80**, 239–246.

CASPERS, H. (1984). Spawning periodicity and habitat of the palolo worm *Eunice viridis* (Polychaeta, Eunicidae) in the Samoan Islands. *Marine Biology* **79**, 229–236.

CLARK, L. B. & HESS, H. W. (1940). Swarming of the Atlantic Palolo worm, *Leodice fucata*. *Carnegie Publications* **524**, 21–27.

COLE, L. C. (1957). Biological clocks in the unicorn. *Science* **125**, 874.

COOKE, I. M. & SULLIVAN, R. E. (1982). Hormones and secretion. In *The Biology of Crustacea*. (ed. D. E. Bliss), vol. **3**, 205–290. New York: Academic Press.

CRONIN, T. W. & FORWARD, R. B. (1979). Tidal vertical migration: an endogenous rhythm in estuarine crab larvae. *Science* **205**, 1020–1022.

DAAN, S. (1982). Circadian rhythms in plants and animals. In *Biological Timekeeping* (ed. J. Brady), pp. 11–32 Cambridge C.U.P.

DeCOURSEY, P. J. (1983). Biological Timing. In *The Biology of Crustacea* (ed. D. E. Bliss), vol. **7**, 107–162. New York: Academic Press.

DE VRIES, M. C., EPIFANIO, C. E. & DITTEL, A. I. (1984). Lunar rhythms in the egg hatching of the subtidal crustacean *Callinectes arcuatus* Ordway (Decapoda: Brachyura). *Estuarine Coastal and Shelf Science* **18**.

DE WILDE, P. A. W. & BERGHUIS, E. M. (1979). Cyclic temperature fluctuations in a tidal mud-flat. In *Cyclic Phenomena in Marine Plants and Animals*. (ed. E. Naylor & R. G. Hartnoll) pp. 435–441, Oxford: Pergamon Press.

DIELEMAN, J. (1979). Swimming rhythms, migration and breeding cycles in the estuarine amphipods *Gammarus chevreuxi* and *Gammarus zaddachi*. In *Cyclic Phenomena in Marine Plants and Animals*. (ed. E. Naylor & R. G. Hartnoll), pp. 415–422. Oxford: Pergamon Press.

DORSETT, D. A. (1979). Physiological control of short-term cyclic activities in opisthobranch molluscs. In *Cyclic Phenomena in Marine Plants and Animals*. (ed. E. Naylor & R. G. Hartnoll), pp. 443–450. Oxford: Pergamon Press.

DUNLAP, J., TAYLOR, W. & HASTINGS, J. W. (1980). The effects of protein synthesis inhibitors on the *Gonyaulax* clock. I. Phase-shifting effects of cycloheximide. *J. comp. Physiol* **138**, 1–8.

EHRET, C. F. & TRUCCO, E. (1967). Molecular models of the circadian clock. I. The chronon concept. *J. theor. Biol.* **15**, 240–262.

ENRIGHT, J. T. (1965). Entrainment of a tidal rhythm. *Science* **147**, 864–867.

ENRIGHT, J. T. (1970). Ecological aspects of endogenous rhythmicity. *Am. Rev. Ecol. Syst.* **1**, 221–238.

ENRIGHT, J. T. (1971). The internal clock of drunken isopods. *Z. vergl. Physiol.* **75**, 332–346.

ENRIGHT, J. T. (1972). A virtuoso isopod: circa-lunar rhythms and their tidal fine structure *J. comp. Physiol.* **77**, 141–162.

ENRIGHT, J. T. (1975). Orientation in time: endogenous clocks. *Marine Ecology* **2**, 917–944.

ENRIGHT, J. T. (1976a). Resetting a tidal clock: a phase response curve for *Excirolana*. In *Biological Rhythms in the Marine Environment*. (ed. P. J. DeCoursey). pp. 103–114, University of South Carolina Press.

ENRIGHT, J. T. (1976b). Plasticity in an isopod's clockworks: shaking shapes form and affects phase and frequency. *J. comp. Physiol.* **107**, 13–37.

FIELDER, D. R. & JONES, M. B. (1978). Observations of feeding behaviour in two New Zealand mud crabs (*Helice crassa* and *Macrophthalmus hirtipes*). *Mauri Ora* **6**, 41–46.

FINCHAM, A. A. (1970). Rhythmic behaviour of the intertidal amphipod *Bathyporeia pelagica*. *J. mar. biol. Ass. U.K.* **50**, 1057–1068.

FINCHAM, A. A. (1972). Rhythmic swimming and rheotropism in the amphipod *Marinogammarus marinus* (Leach). *J. exp. mar. Biol. Ecol.* **8**, 19–26.

FINCHAM, A. A. (1973). Rhythmic swimming behaviour of the New Zealand sand beach isopod *Pseudaega punctata* (Thomson). *J. exp. mar. Biol. Ecol.* **11**, 229–237.

FISH, J. D. (1975). Development, hatching and brood size in *Bathyporeia pilosa*. *J. mar. biol. Ass. U.K.* **55**, 357–368.

FISH, J. D. & FISH, E. (1972). The swimming rhythm of *Eurydice pulchra* Leach and a possible explanation of intertidal migration. *J. exp. mar. Biol. Ecol.* **8**, 195–200.

FORWARD, R. B. (1980). Phototaxis of a sand-beach amphipod: physiology and tidal rhythms. *J. comp. Physiol.* **135**, 243–250.

FORWARD, R. B. & CRONIN, T. W. (1980). Tidal rhythms of activity and phototaxis of an estuarine crab larva. *Biol. Bull. mar. biol. Lab., Woods Hole*, **158**, 295–303.

GAINER, H., LOH, Y. P. & NEALE, E. A. (1982). The organization of post-translational precursor processing in peptidergic neurosecretory cells. In *Proteins of Nervous Systems: Structure and Function.* (eds: B. Haber, J. R. Perez-Polo & J. D. Coulter), pp. 131–145, New York: Alan Liss Inc.

GIBSON, R. N. (1971). Factors affecting the rhythmic activity of *Blennius pholis* (Teleostei). *Animal Behaviour* **19**, 336–343.

GIBSON, R. N. (1978). Tidal and lunar rhythms in fish. In *Rhythmic Activity of Fishes* (ed. J. E. Thorpe), pp. 201–213, New York: Academic Press.

GRAU, E. G. W. W., DICKHOF, R. S., BERN, H. A. & FOLMAR, L. C. (1981). Lunar phasing of the thyroxine surge preparatory to seaward migration of salmonid fish. *Science*, **211**, 607–609.

HAMMOND, R. D. & NAYLOR, E. (1977). Effects of dusk and dawn on locomotor activity rhythms in the Norway lobster *Nephrops norvegicus*. *Marine Biology* **39**, 253–260.

HARRIS, G. J. & MORGAN, E. (1983). Estimates of significance in periodogram analysis of damped oscillations in a biological time series. *Behav. Anal. Let.* **3**, 221–230.

HARRIS, G. J. & MORGAN, E. (1984a). The effects of salinity changes on endogenous circa tidal rhythm of the amphipod *Corophium volutator* (Pallas). *Mar. behav. Physiol.* **10**, 199–217.

HARRIS, G. J. & MORGAN, E. (1984b). The effects of ethanol, valinomycin and cycloheximide on the endogenous circatidal rhythm of the estuarine amphipod *Corophium volutator* (Pallas). *Marine Behaviour and Physiology* **10**, 219–233.

HASTINGS, M. H. (1981a). The entraining effect of turbulence on the circatidal activity rhythm and its semilunar modulation in *Eurydice pulchra*. *J. mar. Biol. Assoc. U.K.* **61**, 151–160.

HASTINGS, M. H. (1981b). Semilunar variations of endogenous circatidal rhythms of activity and respiration in the isopod *Eurydice pulchra*. *Marine Ecology, Progress Series* **4**, 85–90.

HASTING, M. H. & NAYLOR, E. (1980). Ontogeny of an endogenous rhythm in *Eurydice pulchra*. *J. exp. mar. Biol. Ecol.* **46**, 137–145.

HAUENSCHILD, C. (1960). Lunar periodicity. In *Biological Clocks. Cold Spring Harbor Symposia in Quantitative Biology* **25**, 491–497.

HOLMSTRÖM, W. F. & MORGAN, E. (1983a). The effects of low temperature pulses on rephasing the endogenous activity rhythm of *Corophium volutator* (Pallas). *J. mar. biol. Assoc. U.K.* **63**, 851–860.

HOLMSTRÖM, W. F. & MORGAN, E. (1983b). Laboratory entrainment of the rhythmic swimming activity of *Corophium volutator* (Pallas) to cycles of temperature and periodic inundation. *J. mar. biol. Assoc. U.K.* **63**, 861–887.

HUBERMAN, A., ARECHIGA, H., CIMET, A., DE LA ROSA, J. & ARAMBURO, C. (1979). Isolation and purification of a neuro-depressing hormone from the eyestalk of *Procambarus bouvieri* (Ortmann). *Eur. J. Biochem.* **99**, 203–208.

HUGHES, R. N. (1983). Evolutionary ecology of colonial reef-organisms, with particular reference to corals. *Biol. J. Linn. Soc.* **20**, 39–58.

JACKLETT, J. N. (1980). Protein synthesis requirement of the *Aplysia* circadian clock, tested by active and inactive derivatives of the inhibitor anisomycin. *J. exp. Biol.* **85**, 33–42.

JACKLETT, J. W. (1982). Circadian clock mechanisms. In *Biological Timekeeping* (ed. J. Brady), pp. 173–188, C.U.P.

JACKLETT, J. W. & GERONIMO, J. (1971). Circadian rhythm: population of interacting neurons. *Science* **174**, 299–302.

JONES, D. A. & NAYLOR, E. (1970). The swimming rhythm of the sand beach isopod *Eurydice pulchra*. *J. exp. Mar. Biol. Ecol.* **4**, 188–199.

KAVALIERS, M. (1982). Endogenous lunar rhythm in the behavioural thermoregulation of a teleost fish, the white sucker, *Catastomus commersoni*. *Journal of Interdisciplinary Cycle Research* **13**, 23–27.

KELLER, R. (1983). Biochemistry and specificity of the neurohaemal hormones in Crustacea. In *Neurohaemal Organs of Arthropods: their Development, Evolution, Structures and Functions* (ed. A. P. Gupta) pp. 118–148. Springfield, Illinois: C. C. Thomas.

KENSLEY, B. (1974). Aspects of the biology and ecology of the genus *Tylos* Latreille. *Ann. S. Afr. Mus.* **65**, 401–471.

KLAPOW, L. A. (1976). Lunar and tidal rhythms of an intertidal crustacean. In *Biological Rhythms in the Marine Environment* (ed. P. J. DeCoursey), pp. 215–224, University of South Carolina.

KOJIS, B. L. & QUINN, N. J. (1982). Reproductive ecology of two faviid corals (Coelenterata: Scleratinia). *Marine Ecology Progress Series* **8**, 251–255.

KORRINGA, P. (1957). Lunar periodicity. *Mem. Geol. Soc. Amer.* **67**, 917–934.

LEHMANN, U., NEUMANN, D.& KAISER, H. (1974). Gezeitenrhthmische und spontane Aktivitatsmuster von Winkerkrabben. I. Ein neuer Ansatz zur quantitaven Analyse von Lokomotionrhythmen. *J. comp. Physiol.* **91**, 187–221.

MOLLER, T. H. & NAYLOR, E. (1980). Environmental influence on locomotor activity in *Nephrops norvegicus* (Crustacea: Decapoda). *J. mar. biol. Assoc. U.K.* **60**, 103–113.

MORGAN, E. (1965). The activity rhythm of the amphipod *Corophium volutator* (Pallas) and its possible relationship to changes in hydrostatic pressure associated with tides. *J. Anim. Ecol.* **34**, 731–746.

NAYLOR, E. (1958). Tidal and diurnal rhythms of locomotory activity in *Carcinus maenas* (L.). *J. exp. Biol.* **35**, 602–610.

NAYLOR, E. (1963). Temperature relationships of the locomotor rhythm of *Carcinus*. *J. exp. Biol.* **40**, 669–679.

NAYLOR, E. (1976). Rhythmic behaviour and reproduction in marine animals. In *Adaptation to Environment: Essays on the Physiology of Marine Animals* (ed. R. C. Newell), pp. 393–429, London: Butterworths.

NAYLOR, E. (1982). Tidal and lunar rhythms in animals and plants. In *Biological Timekeeping* (ed. J. Brady), pp. 33–48, Cambridge: C.U.P.

NAYLOR, E. & ATKINSON, R. J. A. (1972). Pressure and the rhythmic behaviour of inshore animals. *Symp. Soc. exp. Biol.* **26**, 345–415.

NAYLOR, E., ATKINSON, R. J. A. & WILLIAMS, B. G. (1971). External factors influencing the tidal rhythm of shore crabs. *J. Interdisciplinary Cycle Research* **2**, 173–180.

NAYLOR, E., SMITH, G. & WILLIAMS, B. G. (1973). Role of the eyestalk in the tidal activity rhythm of the shore crab *Carcinus maenas* (L.). In *Neurobiology of Invertebrates* (ed. J. Salanki), pp. 423–429, Budapest: Hungarian Academy of Sciences.

NAYLOR, E. & WILLIAMS, B. G. (1968). Effects of eyestalk removal on rhythmic locomotor activity in *Carcinus*. *J. exp. Biol.* **49**, 107–116.

NAYLOR, E. & WILLIAMS, B. G. (1984a). Phase-responsiveness of the circatidal locomotor activity rhythm of *Hemigrapsus edwardsii* (Hilgendorf) to simulated high tide. *J. mar. Biol. Assoc. U.K.* **64**, 81–90.

NAYLOR, E. & WILLIAMS, B. G. (1984b). Environmental entrainment of tidally rhythmic behaviour in marine animals. *Zool. J. Linn. Soc.* **80**, 201–208.

NEUMANN, D. (1967). Genetic adaptation in emergence time of *Clunio* populations to different tidal conditions. *Helgolander wiss meeresunters* **15**, 163–171.

NEUMANN, D. (1976). Entrainment of a semilunar rhythm. In *Biological Rhythms in the Marine Environment* (ed. P. J. DeCoursey), pp. 115–127, University of South Carolina Press.

NEUMANN, D. (1978). Entrainment of a semilunar rhythm by simulated tidal cycles of mechanical disturbance. *J. exp. mar. Biol. Ecol.* **35**, 73–85.

NEUMANN, D. (1981). Tidal and lunar rhythms. In *Handbook of Behavioural Neurobiology. IV. Biological Rhythms* (ed. J. Aschoff), pp. 351–380, New York: Plenum Press.

NEUMANN, D. & HEIMBACH, F. (1984). Time cues for semilunar reproduction rhythms in European populations of *Clunio marinus*. II. The influence of tidal temperature cycles. *Biol. Bull. mar. biol. Lab., Woods Hole* **166**, 509–524.

NJUS, D., SULZMAN, F. & HASTINGS, J. W. (1974). Membrane model for the circadian clock. *Nature* **248**, 116–120.

OLIVE, P. J. W. & GARWOOD, P. R. (1983). The importance of long term endogenous rhythms in the maintenance of reproductive cycles of marine invertebrates: a re-appraisal. *Int. J. Invert. Reproduction* **8**, 339–347.

PALMER, J. D. (1974). *Biological Clocks in Marine Organisms*. 173pp. New York: John Wiley & Sons.

PETPIROON, S. & MORGAN, E. (1983). Observations on the tidal activity rhythm of the periwinkle *Littorina nigrolineata* (Gray). *Marine Behaviour and Physiology* **9**, 171–192.

PITTENDRIGH, C. S. (1981). Circadian systems: Entrainment. In *Handbook of Behavioural Neurobiology, Vol. 4. Biological Rhythms*, pp. 95–124, New York and London: Plenum Press.

PREECE, G. S. (1971). The swimming rhythms of *Bathyporeia pilosa* (Crustacea: Amphipoda). *J. mar. biol. Assoc. U.K.* **51**, 777–791.

REID, D. G. & NAYLOR, E. (1985). Free-running, endogenous semi lunar rhythmicity in a marine isopod crustacean. *J. mar. biol. Assoc. U.K.* (in press).

RODRIGUEZ, G. & NAYLOR, E. (1972). Behavioural rhythms in littoral prawns. *J. mar. biol. Assoc. U.K.* **52**, 81–95.

SCHWEIGER, H. G. & SCHWEIGER, M. (1977). Circadian rhythms in unicellular organisms: an endeavour to explain the molecular mechanism. *Int. Rev. Cytol.* **51**, 315–342.

SINGARAJAH, K. V., MOYSE, J. & KNIGHT-JONES, E. W. (1967). The effects of feeding upon the phototactic behaviour of cirripede nauplii. *J. exp. mar. Biol. Ecol.* **1**, 144–153.

SOMMER, H. H. (1972). Endogene und exogene Periodike in der Aktivität eines mederen Krebses (*Balanus balanus* L.). *Z. vergl. Physiol.* **76**, 177–192.

STRUMWASSER, F. (1971). The cellular basis of behaviour in *Aplysia*. *Psychiatric Research* **8**, 237–257.

SWEENEY, B. M. (1976). Pros and cons of the membrane model for circadian rhythms in the marine algae *Gonyaulax* and *Acetabularia*. In *Biological Rhythms in the Marine Environment* (ed. P. J. DeCoursey), pp. 63–76, University of South Carolina Press.

TAYLOR, A. C. & NAYLOR, E. (1977). Entrainment of the locomotor rhythm of *Carcinus* by cycles of salinity change. *J. mar. biol. Assoc. U.K.* **57**, 273–277.

THOMAS, N. J., LASIAK, T. A. & NAYLOR, E. (1981). Salinity preference behaviour in *Carcinus*. *Marine Behaviour and Physiology* **7**, 277–283.

VUGTS, H. F. & ZIMMERMANN, J. T. F. (1975). Interaction between the daily heat balance and the tidal cycle. *Nature* **255**, 113–117.

WEBSTER, S. G. (1985). Neurohormonal control of ecdysteroid biosynthetics by *Carcinus maenas* Y organs, and preliminary characterisation of the putative moult-inhibiting hormone (MIH). *Gen. comp. Endocrinol.* (in press).

WILLIAMS, B. G. & NAYLOR, E. (1969). Synchronization of the locomotor tidal rhythm of *Carcinus*. *J. exp. Biol.* **51**, 715–725.

WILLIAMS, B. G., NAYLOR, E. & CHATTERTON, T. D. (1985). The activity patterns of New Zealand mud crabs under field and laboratory conditions. *J. exp. mar. biol. Ecol.* **89**, 269–282.

WILLIAMS, J. A. (1979). A semi-lunar rhythm of locomotor activity and moult synchrony in the sand-beach amphipod *Talitrus saltator*. In *Cyclic Phenomena in Marine Plants and Animals* (ed. E. Naylor and R. G. Hartnoll), pp. 407–414, Oxford: Pergamon Press.

WILLIAMS, J. A. (1980). The light-response rhythm and seasonal entrainment of the endogenous circadian locomotor rhythm of *Talitrus saltator* (Crustacea: Amphipoda). *J. mar. biol. Assoc. U.K.* **60**, 773–785.

WILLIAMS, J. A. & NAYLOR, E. (1978). A procedure for the assessment of significance of rhythmicity in time-series data. *Journal of Chronobiology* **5**, 435–444.

WILLIAMS, J. A., PULLIN, R. S. V., WILLIAMS, B. G., ARECHIGA, H. & NAYLOR, E. (1979a). Evaluation of the effects of injected eyestalk extract on rhythmic locomotor activity in *Carcinus*. *Comp. Biochem. Physiol.* **62A**, 903–907.

WILLIAMS, J. A., PULLIN, R. S. V., NAYLOR, E., SMITH, G. & WILLIAMS, B. G. (1979b). The role of Hanstrom's organ in clock control in *Carcinus maenas*. In *Cyclic Phenomena in Marine Plants and Animals* (ed. E. Naylor and R. G. Hartnoll), pp. 459–466, Oxford: Pergamon Press.

Printed in Great Britain © *Society for Experimental Biology 1985*

TEMPERATURE ADAPTATION OF ENZYME FUNCTION IN FISH MUSCLE

IAN A. JOHNSTON

Department of Physiology and Pharmacology, University of St. Andrews, St. Andrews, Fife KY16 9TS, Scotland, U.K.

Summary

Temperature directly affects the performance of fish muscle through a variety of extrinsic and intrinsic mechanisms. A common observation is that (a) species adapted to different temperatures over evolutionary time scales, or (b) individuals exposed to temperature change from periods ranging from minutes to months are able to adjust muscle performance so as to partially offset the effects of temperature change. The underlying mechanisms are complex, involve a variety of levels of organization (behavioural, organismic, tissue and molecular) and probably vary with the time scale of adaptation to temperature. The present essay considers the extent to which interspecific differences in the structural and functional characteristics of muscle enzymes contribute to adjustments in contractile performance at different body temperatures.

Introduction

Different fish species inhabit water ranging in temperature from $-2\,°C$ in Antarctica to $+40\,°C$ in thermal hot springs. The daily and/or seasonal temperature variation experienced by a particular species can range from a fraction of a degree Centigrade to more than $25\,°C$ (see Sverdrup, Johnson & Fleming, 1942 for a description of temperature variation in the oceans).

Although an acute reduction in body temperature will result in a decrease in muscle performance, a degree of temperature compensation of activity patterns is often observed between species adapted to different thermal environments or for individuals following a period of acclimation to low temperature (Hazel & Prosser, 1974). A large number of extrinsic and intrinsic factors determine muscle performance. The former include the arrangement of muscle fibres, tendons and ligaments, fibre recruitment patterns, hormone titres, and the supply of nutrients and oxygen by the blood stream. Intrinsic factors include the amounts, properties and spatial relationships of contractile proteins, internal and external membranes, and metabolic enzymes. Clearly, the mechanisms underlying thermal compensation of locomotory performance in ectotherms are complex and may involve a large number, but not necessarily all of these factors.

The present essay considers the effects of temperature on muscle enzymes and the extent to which their structural and kinetic properties reflect the characteristic thermal environments of different species. The catalytic potential and regulatory properties of enzymes *in vivo* are dependent on ionic strength, pH, the concentrations of substrates, cofactors and modulators (inhibitors/activators), and in some cases the presence of low relative molecular mass solutes, and/or the binding of the enzyme to membrane phospholipids or other proteins (see Somero, 1983). In many cases there is uncertainty about how these factors vary with temperature *in vivo*. Thus, although modern chromatographic techniques make it relatively easy to purify a large number of enzymes to homogenity, it is difficult to design *in vitro* experiments which enable the regulatory and catalytic capacities of most metabolic enzymes to be assessed under conditions that approximate to those found *in vivo*. For example, the temperature dependence of enzyme–ligand binding properties of M_4-lactate dehydrogenase varies according to whether assays are carried out at constant or variable pH (Wilson, 1977; Yancey & Somero, 1978). Since the pH of body fluids and tissues increases as water temperature falls (Reeves, 1977), the latter conditions are likely to be of more physiological significance. However, patterns of acid–base regulation are complex and appear to vary with time, body compartment, and between species (Heisler, 1980; Walsh & Moon, 1982). In addition, substrate turnover by a particular enzyme *in vivo* is dependent on the activities, concentrations and degree of activation of other enzymes in the same metabolic pathway. It is often difficult, therefore, to assess the contribution of particular kinetic and structural traits of single enzymes to muscle function as a whole. Since locomotory performance and survival are functions of the whole organism, many characteristics at lower levels of organization are likely to be neutrally selective.

Enzymes of energy metabolism

Allelic variants

Many enzyme loci are polymorphic. There is electrophoretic evidence for directional changes in the frequency of particular allozymes within a species, which are correlated with changes in latitude and hence mean environmental temperature. For example, Johnson (1977) observed changes in LDH allelic frequency for the crested blenney *(Anoplarchus purpurescens)* along the Puget Sound, U.S.A. and Merritt (1972) found a latitudinal cline for LDH polymorphism in the fathead minnow *(Pimephales promelas)*. The extent to which this genetic variability might be considered 'adaptive' for function at particular environmental temperature ranges remains controversial. In order to determine the possible adaptive nature of these polymorphisms, one approach is to establish both the structural and functional properties of a large number of enzyme loci in relation to *in situ* temperate regime. Powers and co-workers have carried out one of the best and most comprehensive studies of this kind for fish, using the common killifish *(Fundulus heteroclitus)* the range of which extends from Port au Port Bay, Newfoundland to Mantanzas River, Florida. Powers & Place (1978) sampled liver, eye and white muscle tissue at 22 localities over a 4-year period and studied spatial variation in allelic frequencies for four unlinked genetic loci, Ldh-B, Mdh-A, Gpi-B and Pgm-B. Stable clinal variations in gene frequencies were found for Ldh-B, Mdh-A and Gpi-B loci, together with relatively small changes in PgM-A for its three alleles (see Fig. 1). One of the problems with the correlative approach is the possibility of migration, linkage and hybridization of populations which have diverged genetically

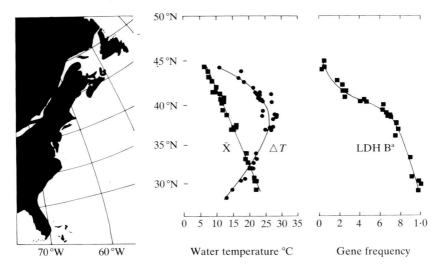

Fig. 1. Adapted from Powers & Place (1978). Mean ($\bar{X}$) and range (ΔT) of temperature along the eastern seaboard of the U.S.A. correlated with the frequency of the LDH B^a gene from tissues of the common killifish *(Fundulus heteroclitus)*.

either through selection or random fixation of selectively neutral alleles. For example, geographical patterns of allelic variation could arise simply because of migration and gene flow between genetically dissimilar populations. Alternatively, if such clines are maintained by selective pressures imposed by a steep thermal gradient then some adaptive differences in the kinetic properties of particular allelic variants would be predicted. Place & Powers (1979) investigated the temperature and pH dependence of K_{cat} and K_m for the LDH-B^aB^a, LDHB$^aB^b$ and LDH B^bB^b allozymes of *Fundulus* in the direction of pyruvate reduction. At low temperatures (10 °C) and pH (6·5) the 2nd-order rate constant K_{cat}/K_m for LDH-B^bB^b the allozyme common to Northern latitudes was more than twice that for LDH-B^aB^a the allozyme common to Southern waters (see Fig. 2). The reaction rate for the heterozygous phenotype under these conditions did not represent a simple average of the two homozygous allozymes. Similar results for the temperature dependence of K_{cat}/K_m at subsaturating pyruvate concentrations were obtained at both constant pH and constant relative alkalinity [constant $[OH^+]/[H^+]$]. However, at saturating pyruvate concentrations the kinetic properties of the various allozymes were indistinguishable. Since *in vivo* LDH is thought to operate at pyruvate concentrations at or below the K_m, Place & Powers (1979) considered that these results were consistent with the allozyme characteristic of Northern latitudes, being a 'better' catalyst at low temperatures. However, many more such clines at different enzyme loci need to be investigated to establish the extent to which enzyme polymorphisms are important in temperature compensation of metabolism.

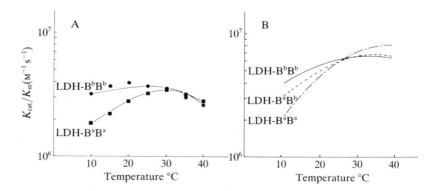

Fig. 2. Adapted from Place & Powers (1979). K_{cat}/K_m for lactate dehydrogenase allozymes from tissues of the common killifish (*Fundulus heteroclitus*) measured at (A) constant pH (7·5) and (B) at a constant ratio $[OH^-]/[H^+] = 1$.

Interspecific variation

In relaxed muscle, intracellular substrate concentrations are main-tained at or below the K_m values for most enzymes (Fersht, 1977). This has several important consequences: (1) in the case of allosteric enzymes, only small changes in K_m resulting from modulator binding can result in relatively large changes in reaction velocity and (2) it provides a substan-tial reserve capacity for increasing reaction rate during exercise. Somero and coworkers have carried out some elegant kinetic studies on M_4 lactate dehydrogenase and pyruvate kinase from the white muscle of a wide range of species with different body temperatures (Low, Bada & Somero, 1973; Somero, 1975; Low & Somero, 1976; Yancey & Somero, 1978; Somero, 1978; Graves & Somero, 1982; Hochachka & Somero, 1973). Their basic findings are as follows:–

1. Although K_m increases with increasing temperature providing pH is allowed to vary with temperature using an imidazole buffer system ($\triangle pH/\triangle T = -0.018u/°C$) then K_m values are highly conserved be-tween species.

2. K_{cat} values are higher for homologous enzymes from cold- than warm-adapted species (Fig. 3A).

3. The free energy of activation ($\triangle G^{\ddagger}$) for some enzymes is slightly lower in cold- than warm-adapted animals. As body temperature increases there are larger changes in the relative contributions of the enthalpy ($\triangle H^{\ddagger}$) and entropy ($\triangle S^{\ddagger}$) components to the free energy of activation ($\triangle G^{\ddagger}$). Both $\triangle H^{\ddagger}$ and $\triangle S^{\ddagger}$ are found to increase markedly with rising body temperature such that increases in $\triangle H^{\ddagger}$ largely compensate for increases in $\triangle S^{\ddagger}$ (Fig. 3B) (N.B. The overall free energy change is negative due to the increased entropy of the system (enzyme, ligands, cell water) following catalyses.

4. Enzymes isolated from animals with low body temperatures are more susceptible to thermal denaturation at high temperatures than those from warm-bodied species suggesting a less-rigid tertiary and/or quaternary structure.

Somero has suggested a compromise between structural and functional traits in enzyme evolution which links the requirement to conserve enzyme–ligand binding properties within an appropriate range with adjustments in substrate turnover number. According to this hypothesis, animals operating at low temperatures (low kinetic energy in the cell) would require relatively few weak bonds to stabilize the enzyme–substrate–cofactor complex during the formation of the active state. Since relatively few weak bonds need to be disrupted to form the reaction

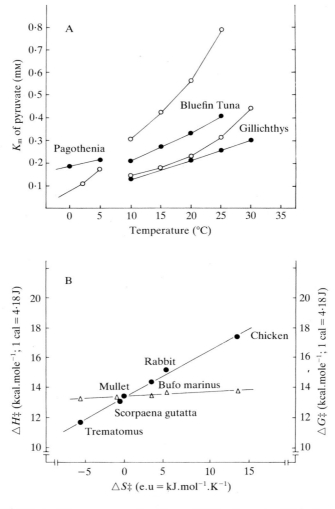

Fig. 3. (A) Effects of temperature on the apparent Michaelis constant (K_m) of pyruvate for M_4-lactate dehydrogenase purified from fish white muscles. Open symbols were determined at constant pH of 7·4 at all temperatures whereas closed symbols represent data obtained using imidazole buffer set to pH 7·2 at 20 °C and allowed to vary freely with temperature. (Adapted from Yancey & Somero, 1978). (B) Relative contribution of enthalpy and entropy of activation to the free energy of activation for pyruvate kinases from fish white muscles assayed in direction of pyruvate reduction. (Data from Low & Somero, 1976)

products, this would keep the free energy of the reaction ($\triangle G^{\ddagger}$) relatively low and the reaction rate relatively high, thus providing an important mechanism for temperature compensation of metabolic rate at low temperatures. Conversely, since weak bonds formed during the conformational events accompanying catalyses are relatively easily disrupted by small inputs of thermal energy, relatively more would be required to maintain tertiary and quaternary structure in the case of enzymes operating at high body temperatures (high kinetic energy in the cell). Since more weak bonds may be required to maintain K_m at or below substrate or cofactor concentrations, more bonds need to be disrupted to form the reaction products resulting in a relatively higher ($\triangle G^{\ddagger}$) and reduction in K_{cat}. The total entropy change for a warm-adapted enzyme would therefore be relatively high, resulting in an increased enthalpy contribution to $\triangle H^{\ddagger}$ relative to a homologous enzyme from a cold-adapted animal. Although this hypothesis is appealing and consistent with the conservation of K_m and K_{cat} and adjustments of steady state thermodynamic activation parameters observed between species (see also Borgman & Moon, (1975)), it is unfortunately difficult to test experimentally.

Whatever the mechanistic interpretation of the above results, it is significant that differences in kinetic properties are noted for species for which there is only a 5–8 °C difference in mean water temperature. Graves & Somero (1982) investigated enzyme polymorphism in more than 22 enzyme loci and determined the kinetic properties of white muscle M_4 LDH for four cogeneric species of eastern Pacific Barracudas (genus *Sphyraena*). The ranges of the four species (*S. argentea, S. lucasana, S. ensis, S. idiastes*) which have similar morphology and ecologies, overlap only slightly, midrange water temperatures varying from 18 °C for *S. argentea* to 26 °C for the tropically distributed *S. ensis* (Fig. 4). Graves & Somero (1982) found electrophoretic evidence that the most closely related species (*S. lucasana* and *S. idiastes*) had been separated for at least 3–4 million years. Three electrophoretically distinct M_4 LDH's were found with each species monomorphic for its particularly allele. Interestingly the two temperate Barracudas shared an allele of slow anodal mobility with identical kinetic properties although they were separated by 7000 km of ocean across the tropics and at least 5 million years of evolutionary history. The turnover numbers (K_{cat}) of LDH's at 25 °C were inversely related to average habitat temperature (T_m), which would tend to offset temperature effects on metabolic rate such that at T_m K_{cat} values are similar (Fig. 4). Although K_m was temperature dependent, when pH was allowed to vary with temperature using imidazole buffer ($\triangle pH/\triangle T = 0.018$ u/ °C), values were found to be highly conserved (Fig. 4) falling within the range reported for other species (0.15–0.30 mM pyruvate). The active site of LDH contains a histidine at residue 195 which needs to be protonated in order to bind pyruvate.

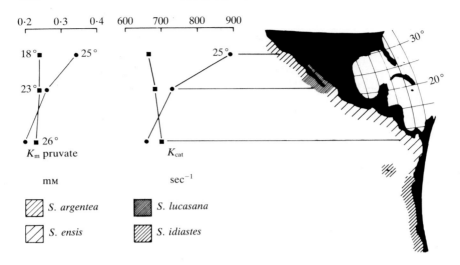

Fig. 4. (Data from Graves & Somero (1982)). Distribution of eastern Pacific barracudas (genus *Sphyraena*) together with the kinetic properties of white muscle M_4-lactate dehydrogenases from *S. argentea*, *S. lucasana* and *S. ensis*. Values of K_{cat} and K_m in the direction of pyruvate reduction were determined from Arrhenius plots and K_m-*versus*-temperature plots respectively. Measurements were made at 25 °C (squares) and at the approximate midrange temperatures (cT_M) of each species (circles).

Somero has suggested that conservation of the fractional dissociation state of this imidazole group with temperature will tend to stabilize K_m values.

Seasonal acclimation

Mechanisms for increasing metabolic flux following acclimation to low temperature include (1) changes in metabolite concentrations (Walsh & Somero, 1982), (2) increases in enzyme concentration (Sidell, 1983) (Fig. 5) (3) post-transitional modifications of proteins — often reversible phosphorylation reactions, and (4) changes in the expression of different isozymes. There is relatively little evidence for the last two mechanisms having a major role in seasonal adjustments in metabolic rate (see Johnston, 1983).

Most studies on seasonal acclimation in fish have dealt with freshwater species which often experience much larger variations in water temperatures between summer and winter than marine species. However, the effects of several months' acclimation to either 5 or 25 °C on energy metabolism of muscle from striped bass (*Morone saxatilis*) has been shown to be broadly similar to that described for freshwater species (Jones & Sidell, 1982).

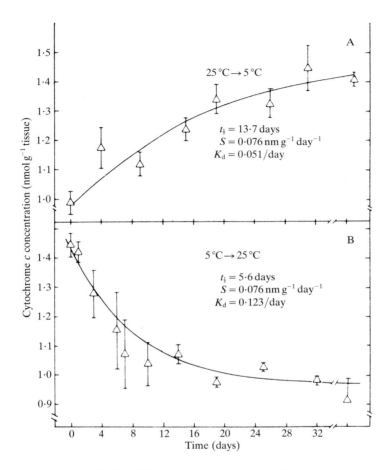

Fig. 5. Adapted from Sidell, (1977). Changes in green sunfish (*Lepomis cyanellus*) muscle cytochrome c concentrations during acclimation between 5 and 25 °C. S, zero-order rate constant for synthesis; K_d, first order rate constant for degradation; $t_{\frac{1}{2}}$, time taken for 50% change in concentration.

Cold acclimation in striped bass is associated with a 75 % increase in oxygen consumption of muscle homogenates and corresponding increases in the activity of tricarboxylic acid cycle and electron transport chain enzymes (Fig. 6) (Jones & Sidell, 1982). Increases in aerobic capacity with cold acclimation are particularly marked for red muscles and are associated with increases in the surface ($Sv_{(mt,f)}$) and volume densities ($Vv_{(mt,f)}$) of mitochondria. For example, $Vv_{(mt,f)}$ for red myotomal muscle fibres of Crucian carp are 28 % for 5 °C and 14 % for 25 °C-acclimated individuals (Johnston, 1982a). Increases in mitochondrial volume and surface density would have the effect of enhancing the rate of ATP provision at low temperatures in the muscles of cold-acclimated fish and may also serve to offset the effects of temperature on the rate of diffusion of metabolites between the mitochondrial compartment and cytoplasm (Johnston & Maitland, 1980; Sidell, 1983). Sidell (1977) investigated the turnover of cytochrome C in tissues of the green sunfish (*Lepomis*

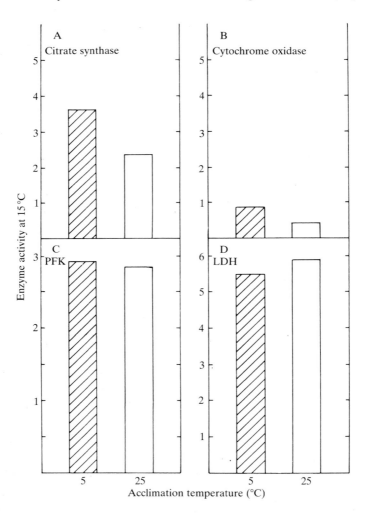

Fig. 6. Adapted from Jones & Sidell (1982). Effects of acclimation to either 5 or 25 °C on enzyme activities in homogenates prepared from the red muscle of the striped bass (*Morone saxatilis*). Assays were carried out at 15 °C, and expressed as units · mg^{-1} protein for phosphofructokinase (PFK) and lactate dehydrogenase and as units · mg x10^{-1} protein for citrate synthase and cytochrome oxidase.

cyanellus) acclimated to either 5 °C or 25 °C using [δ^{14}C] amino laevulinic acid a non-reutilizable precursor of haem. He found that temperature decreased the rate of synthesis of cytochrome C to a lesser extent than that of degradation resulting in a net increase in concentration for a minimum energetic demand for protein synthesis (Fig. 5).

There is a variety of evidence for changes in the relative importance of different substrates following acclimation to different body temperatures (Hazel & Prosser, 1974). For example, in striped bass oxidation of ^{14}C-1-palmitate by red muscle was two times higher in fish acclimated to 5 °C compared to 25 °C. In contrast, ^{14}C-U-glucose was oxidized at a higher rate by the red muscle of warm-acclimated bass (Jones & Sidell, 1982). A general finding with studies of goldfish, green sunfish and striped bass is either no change, or slight decreases in the maximal activities of glycolytic enzymes following cold acclimation (Shacklee *et al*, 1977; Sidell, 1980) (Fig. 6). Preferred fuels may vary according to changes in food availability as well as changes in temperature with different seasons. Stone & Sidell (1981) found that the increase in capacity for fatty acid composition by mitochondria from cold-acclimated striped bass was correlated with an increase in hepatic lipid stores. Thus, as food availability declines during the autumn and winter, dietary lipid insufficiencies may be offset by mobilization of triglyceride stores in liver and mesenteric fat depots (Jones & Sidell, 1982).

Contractile proteins

Contractile proteins provide a particularly favourable model for studies of temperature adaptation of enzyme function since at least some of the experimental problems outlined above for metabolic enzymes are overcome. The catalytic (myosin ATPase), structural (myosin, actin, M-protein, α-actin) and regulatory (tropomyosin-troponins) proteins are organized into myofibrils so that their relative concentrations and geometrical relationships are defined by the myofilament lattice. Skeletal muscle is thought to operate at saturating concentrations of MgATP^{-2} (the substrate for myosin ATPase) and Ca^{2+}, which activate contraction by binding to sites on the regulatory subunit troponin C. Skinned fibre preparations in which the external membrane is removed, either by dissection or detergent treatment, allow the ionic composition of the solution bathing the myofilaments to be manipulated and both enzyme activity and mechanical work to be measured simultaneously (see Fig. 7).

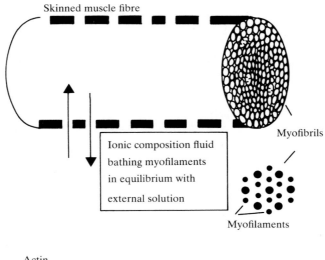

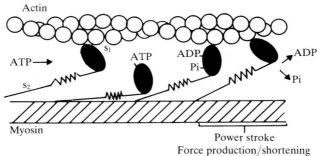

Fig. 7. Diagrammatic representation of (A) skinned fibre model for studying muscle contractile and biochemical properties and (B) a model for the crossbridge cycle. Adapted from Shriver (1984). Linking ATP hydrolysis to force production. The force generating step of the cycle is depicted as a rotation of the crossbridge head (SI) from 90° to 45° with concomitant stretching of the S-2 elastic element and release of ADP + P_i.

Interspecific variation

Myosins from North Sea fish readily undergo a side-by-side aggregation reaction on isolation resulting in the loss of ATPase activity (Connell, 1961). A variety of methods have been developed to purify these 'unstable' types of myosin (Mackie & Connell, 1964; Focant & Huriaux, 1976). However, even the best methods yield preparations low in enzymic activity. Myosins isolated from the white muscle of warm-water fish, e.g. tuna, (Richards, Chung, Menzel & Olcott, 1967) are less susceptible to aggregation and yield preparations of comparable ATPase activity to those obtained for mammals and birds. Myofibril and actomyosins from

cold-water fish have high ATPase activities and are stable on storage at
0 °C for several days (Johnston & Walesby, 1977; Johnston, 1982b).

Johnston & Walesby (1977) demonstrated a positive correlation be-
tween the half life of denaturation ($t_{\frac{1}{2}}$d) of myofibrillar ATPase activity at
high temperature (37 °C) and the average water temperature at which different fish species were adapted (Fig. 8). At low protein concentrations
and ionic strength (see Johnston & Walesby, 1977 for details) $t_{\frac{1}{2}}$d varied
from around 1·5 minute for Antarctic fish to over 500 mins in *Oreochromis*
a tilapia species adapted to temperatures of 35–42 °C in a thermal hot
spring. Experiments of this kind suggest large differences in the tertiary
and quaternary structures of different myosins according to adaptation
temperature but do not provide any information on the thermal stabilities
of the proteins at the much lower temperatures found *in vivo*.

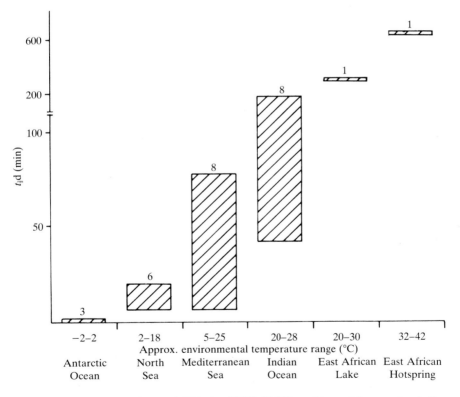

Fig. 8. Adapted from Johnston & Walesby, (1977). Half-line of thermal denaturation ($t_{\frac{1}{2}}$d)
of fish myofibrillar ATPase activity at 37 °C. Values were determined from first-order rate
constants of denaturation under identical conditions (50 mM-KC1, 40 mM-Tris-HC1
0·05 mg.ml⁻¹ myofibrils pH 7·5). The number of species studied from each environmental
temperature range is shown, see original publication for further details.

Mg^{2+}-activated actomyosin ATPase activities are 10–30 times higher at 0 °C for polar than tropical fish species (Johnston, Walesby, Davison & Goldspink, 1977) (Fig. 9A). These results suggest that crossbridge cycle times and shortening speeds should show substantial cold compensation. However, recent studies utilizing skinned fibre preparations have shown that unloaded contraction speeds at 0 °C are in the range of

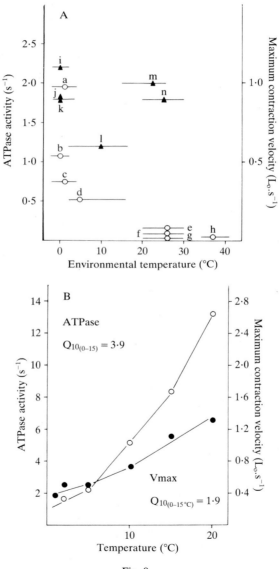

Fig. 9

0·5–1·5 muscle lengths. s^{-1} ($L_0.s^{-1}$) regardless of the adaptation temperature of the fish (Fig. 9A). Skinned fibres differ from isolated myofibril suspension in that the lattice structure of the contractile proteins is preserved and subject to the stresses associated with force generation. There is a variety of evidence to suggest that both the rate of ATP hydrolysis by myosin and its coupling to the power stroke of the crossbridge cycle are critically dependent on mechanical stresses imposed on the active site (see Tregear & Marston, 1979; Shriver, 1984). Johnston & Sidell (1984) in a study of *Myoxocephalus scorpius* muscle have shown that the Mg^{2+}-activated ATPase of isolated myofibrils has a different temperature dependence to that of unloaded contraction velocity (V_{max}) of skinned fibres measured under similar ionic conditions. For example, between 0 and 15 °C V_{max} for muscle shortening increased 1·5 times compared with 8 times for Mg^{2+}-ATPase activity (Fig. 9B). This suggests that either the rate constants for ATP splitting are very different in the two preparations and/or that the coupling of ATPase and mechanical cycles of crossbridges varies with temperature. Maximum contraction velocities for fully activated white myotomal muscle fibres have been determined at different temperatures of a variety of relatively stenothermal fishes (Fig. 10). Any compensatory increases in V_{max} at low temperatures in cold-adapted species (if they occur at all) would appear to be within the variation expected for animals with different body shapes and swimming behaviours.

Q_{10} values for both red and white muscle fibres from relatively stenothermal species are around 2·0 regardless of adaptation temperature (Fig. 10A) (Johnston & Brill, 1984). Again this contrasts with results for

---

Fig. 9. (A) Myofibrillar ATPase activity (open symbols) and maximum contraction velocity of skinned fibres from white muscle (closed symbols) determined at 0 °C. (a) *Champsocephalus gunnari*; (b) *Notothenia neglecta*, (Johnston & Walesby, 1977); (c) *Notothenia rossii* (Johnston *et al*, 1977); (d) *Myoxocephalus scorpius*, (Johnston & Walesby, 1977) (North Sea); (e) *Abudefduf oxydon* (Johnston *et al*, 1977) (Indian Ocean); (f) *Pomatocentrus uniocellatus* (Johnston *et al*, 1977); (g) *Dascyllus carneus* (Johnston & Walesby, 1977) (Indo-Pacific); (h) *Tilapia grahami* (Hot-springs equatorial soda-lake) (Johnston *et al*, 1977); (i) Icefish *Chaenocephalus aceratus*; (j) *Notothenia rossii*; (k) *Trematomus hansoni* (Johnston & Harrison, 1984) (Antarctic species); (l) Bullrout *Myoxocephalus scorpius* (North Sea) unpublished results; (m) Pacific Blue Marlin (*Maikaira nigricans*) Johnston, unpublished results; (n) Blue Crevally *Carangus melampygus* (Johnston & Brill, 1984). V_{max} was determined at 5 °C and the 0 °C value extrapolated from the Q_{10} relationship. See original publications for experimental details. (B) Effects of temperature on ATPase activity (s^{-1}) (open circles) of isolated myofibrils and maximum contraction velocity (solid symbols) of skinned fibres (muscle lengths.s^{-1}) isolated from the white muscle of the bullrout *Myoxocephalus scorpius*. Measurements were carried out under similar ionic conditions, see Johnston & Sidell, (1984), for details.

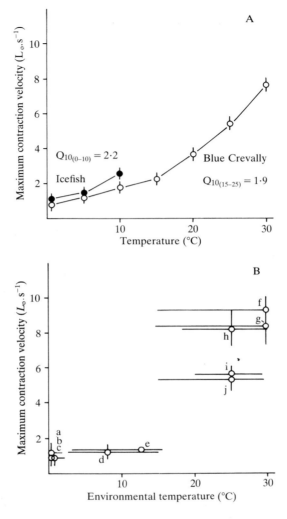

Fig. 10. (A) Effects of temperature on maximum unloaded contraction velocity (V_{max}) (muscle lengths, $L_o.s^{-1}$) for skinned fibres isolated from the white muscle of Icefish (*Chaenocephalus aceratus*) (Antarctica -2 to $+2$ °C) (Johnston, 1985) and Blue Crevally (*Carangus melampygus*) (surface waters, Pacific Ocean 22–28 °C) (data from Johnston & Brill, 1984). The 0 °C value of V_{max} for Blue Crevally was extrapolated from measurements at 5 °C using the experimentally determined Q_{10} relationship. (B) V_{max} ($L_o.s^{-1}$) for skinned fibres isolated from the white muscle of (a) Icefish *Chaenocephalus aceratus*); (b) *Notothenia rossii*; (c) *Trematomus hansoni* (Johnston & Harrison, 1985); (d) cod (*Gadus morhua*) (Altringham & Johnston, 1982); (e) *Myoxocephalus scorpius* (Johnston & Sidell, 1984); (f) Pacific Blue Marlin (*Maikaira nigricans*); (g) Blue Crevally (*Carangus melampygus*); (h) Dolphin fish (*Coryphaena hippurus*); (i) Skipjack tuna (*Katsuwonus pelamis*); (j) Kawakawa (*Euthynuus affinis*) (Pacific Ocean). The approximate environmental temperature range of each species is indicated by a horizontal line.

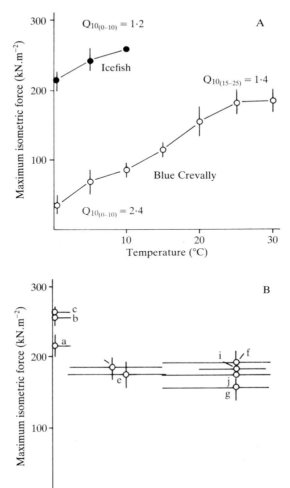

Fig. 11. (A) Effects of temperature on maximum isometric force production (P_o) (kN.m^{-2}) for skinned fibres isolated from the white muscle of the Icefish (*Chaenocephalus aceratus*) (Antarctica $-2\,°C$ to $+2\,°C$) (Johnston, 1985) and Blue Crevally (*Carangus melampygus*) (surface waters, Pacific Ocean 22–28 °C) (data from Johnston & Brill, 1984). The 0 °C value for Blue Crevally was extrapolated from a P_o determination at 5 °C using a Q_{10} value of 2·4. (B) Maximum isometric force (kN.m^{-2}) at 0 °C for skinned fibres isolated from the white muscles of (a) Icefish (*Chaenocephalus aceratus*); (b) *Notothenia rossii*; (c) *Trematomus hansoni* (Johnston & Harrison, 1985); (d) cod (*Gadus morhua*) (Altringham & Johnston, 1982); (e) *Myoxocephalus scorpius* (Johnston & Sidell, 1984): (f) Pacific Blue Marlin (*Maikaira nigricans*); (g) Blue Crevally (*Carangus melampygus*); (h) Dolphin fish (*Corypheana hippurus*); (i) Skipjack tuna (*Katsuwonus pelamis*); (j) Kawakawa (*Euthynuus pelamis*) (Pacific Ocean) (Johnston & Brill, 1984). The approximate environmental temperature range of each species is indicated by a horizontal line.

myofibril suspensions in which the activation enthalpy ($\triangle H^{\ddagger}$) for the Mg-ATPase of 17 species was found to be positively correlated with adaptation temperature (Johnston & Walesby, 1977; Johnston *et al*, 1977).

In contrast, maximum Ca^{2+}-activated force production (P_o) would appear to show a high degree of interspecific temperature compensation (Fig. 11). At $0\,°C$ P_o for the white muscles of Antarctic species are toward the upper range reported for teleosts ($230–270\ kN.m^{-2}$) and around 5–12 times higher than for various tropical fish at this temperature (Johnston & Brill, 1984; Johnston & Salamonski, 1984; Johnston & Harrison, 1985). P_o values for white myotomal muscles of various species measured at their normal body temperatures are similar (Fig. 11).

The maximum power output of a muscle fibre is dependent on the degree of curvature of the force–velocity relationship. A variety of empirical equations (hyperbolic–linear, exponential–linear) have been used to describe the P–V curve. Hill's (1938) equation for muscle shortening provides a good fit for data at loads below $0·7–0·8\ P_o$ for most muscles and is probably the most widely used:–

$$V\ (P + a) = b\ (P_o - P)$$

where P = load, P_o = maximum isometric force, v = contraction speed and a and b are constants. Maximum power output is produced at loads corresponding to $(a^2 + a)^{\frac{1}{2}} - a/P_o$ which corresponds to around $0·25–0·35$ P_o for most fish muscles. Hill's constant a/P_o provides an estimate of the degree of curvature of the force–velocity relationship. For muscles with equivalent values of V_{max} and P_o a decrease in curvature (higher (a/P_o)) would result in an increase in maximum power output. The thermodynamic significance of different shaped a/P_o values in unclear. Woledge (1968) investigated the thermal and mechanical properties of tortoise rectus femoris muscle and compared his results with Hill's data on frog sartorius muscle. He found that the lower a/P_o values obtained for the slow contracting tortoise muscle at $0\,°C$ was associated with an increased ratio of work to heat and work relative to the frog muscle (i.e. an increased amount of isotonic work per mole of ATP).

The degree of curvature of the P–V relation for white fibres was found to be independent of temperature over the range $0–15\,°C$ for *Myoxocephalus scorpius* (Johnston & Sidell, 1984) and $15–25\,°C$ for *Maikaira nigricans* (Johnston & Salamonski, 1984) (Fig. 12). These temperatures are within the normal range for these species. In contrast, for *Chaenocephalus aceratus* which lives at a near constant $-1\,°C$ a/P_o decreased from $0·27$ at $-1\,°C$ to $0·14$ at $+10\,°C$ (Johnston, 1985). It is not known whether there are systematic differences in the shape of the P–V

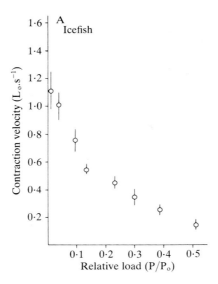

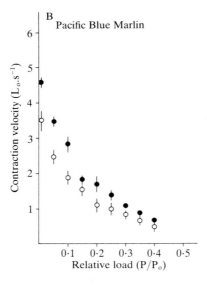

Fig. 12. Force–velocity relationships for maximally activated skinned fibres isolated from the white muscle of (A) Icefish (*Chaenocephalus aceratus*) (Antarctica −2 to +2 °C) at 0 °C (Johnston & Harrison, 1985) and (B) Pacific Blue Marlin (*Maikaira migricans*) (Pacific Ocean, 15 to 28 °C) (Johnston & Salamonski, 1984). Experiments at 15 °C (open symbols), and at 25 °C (closed symbols).

I. A. JOHNSTON

Table 1. *Summary of force–velocity characteristics of skinned fibres isolated from the white myotomal of teleosts with different characteristic body temperatures*

Parameter/Units	Species/(temperature)			
	Icefish*	Pacific Blue Marlin†	Common Carp‡	
			7 °C-acclimated	23 °C-acclimated
	(0 °C)	(25 °C)	(7 °C)	
Maximum isometric force (P_o) kN.m^{-2}	214 ± 14	176 ± 15	178 ± 15	76 ± 10
Unloaded contraction velocity (V_{max}) $L_o.s^{-1}$)	$1 \cdot 1 \pm 0 \cdot 1$	$5 \cdot 3$	$1 \cdot 2 \pm 0 \cdot 02$	$0 \cdot 6 \pm 0 \cdot 04$
a/P_o	$0 \cdot 24$	$0 \cdot 12$	$0 \cdot 30$	$0 \cdot 33$
b	$0 \cdot 26$	$0 \cdot 64$	$0 \cdot 35$	$0 \cdot 19$
Maximum power output (W.Kg^{-1})	23	57	19	7

* Icefish (*Chaenocephalus aceratus*) data from Johnston & Harrison (1985).

† Pacific Blue Marlin (*Maikaira nigricans*) data from Johnston & Salamonski (1984).

‡ Common carp (*Cyprinus carpio* L.) were acclimated to either 7 °C or 23 °C for 1–2 months. Data from Johnston, Sidell & Driedzic, (1985).

curve in muscles from fish with different body temperatures. Nevertheless the available evidence suggests a substantial degree of temperature compensation between species with respect to power output at optimal load. For example, maximum power outputs for skinned fibres from white muscle are 27 W.Kg^{-1} for the haemoglobin-less Antarctic fish (*Chaenocephalus aceratus*) at 0 °C, 24 W.Kg^{-1} for cod (*Gadus morhua*) at 5 °C and 37 and 55 W.Kg^{-1} for Pacific Blue Marlin (*Maikaira nigricans*) determined at 15 and 25 °C, respectively. (See Table 1).

The relatively low temperature dependence of V_{max} and power output for Pacific Blue Marlin ($Q_{(10(15-25 °C)} = 1 \cdot 3$) is of interest. In common with many large pelagic fishes, Blue Marlin undertake vertical migrations between warm surface ($+ 28 °C$) and cooler deeper waters (15 °C at 100 m). During these migrations, individuals may experience changes in water temperature of up to 19 °C in under 2h (Carey & Robison, 1981). Istiophorids have a specialized heat-producing tissue, rich in mitochondria, associated with certain extrinsic eye muscles and brain, warming these tissues at up to 10–14 °C above ambient (Carey, 1982). This, in association with rete mirabile which conserve the heat produced, is thought to maintain brain temperatures during vertical migrations stabilizing the various sensory and integrative functions and learned behaviour associated with prey capture. Unlike tuna which possess similar brain and eye heat exchangers, Marlin muscle temperatures are close to ambient water temperatures. Natural selection in this species appears to have favoured contractile proteins which function relatively independently of temperature over the range 15–25 °C.

Some tuna and lamanid sharks have internalized red muscle which, during high-speed cruising, is maintained at 8–10 °C above ambient water temperatures by counter-current vascular heat exchangers (Stevens & Neil, 1978). A number of advantages for maintaining 'warm red muscles' have been proposed including an increased myoglobin-mediated O_2 flux, and enhanced rates of lactate catabolism (Stevens & Carey, 1981). V_{max} and P_o for maximally activated muscle fibres from Skipjack tuna and Kawakawa are similar to those of other tropical fish at the same temperature (Johnston & Brill, 1984). Interestingly, however, Q_{10} (15–25 °C) for V_{max} for red (3·1) and to a lesser extent white (2·5) fibres are significantly greater than for homologous fibres in fish that do not maintain elevated muscle temperatures. At constant temperature, for a given load, white fibres contract at 2·5 times the speed of red fibres (Fig. 13). In a 1 Kg Skipjack tuna, around 28 % of the muscle bulk is composed of the internalized red muscle. During swimming at high speed, a large proportion of white muscle motor units are recruited and at constant temperature the slower contracting red fibres will presumably contribute little to the total power output. However, one possibility is that the establishment of a temperature gradient between red and white muscles and the relatively high Q_{10} of red fibres would allow both fibre types to contribute to power production at the higher range of swimming speeds. This might be advantageous for a fish that has a high proportion of red muscle and is specialized for high speed swimming. Measurements of the temperature gradient through the body, and muscle recruitment patterns, in free swimming fish would be needed to test this idea.

A commonly observed phenomenon with skinned fibre preparation is the failure to relax completely following activation resulting in postcontraction or 'residual' tension. Residual tension appears to vary with the length and degree of activation with muscle fibre type and with temperature. It is rarely observed for relatively short activations (<3 min) at temperatures within the normal range experienced by a particular species. For example, residual tension increases progressively from zero at 10 °C to 75% P_o at 20 °C for white muscle fibres from the Antarctic species *Chaenocephalus aceratus*. At temperatures above 22 °C fibres contract spontaneously in relaxing solution (10^{-9}M [Ca^{2+}]) following skinning (unpublished results). In contrast, muscle fibres from Skipjack

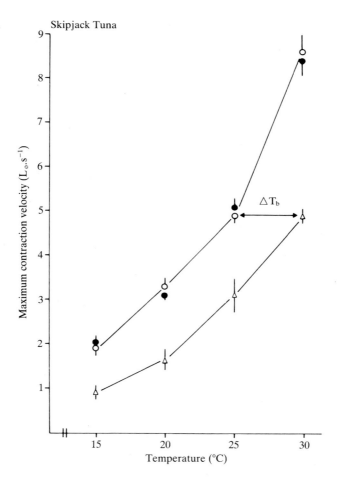

Fig. 13. Effect of temperature on unloaded contraction velocity of skinned fibres isolated from the superficial red (closed circles), deep internalized red (open triangles) and white muscle (open circles) from Skipjack tuna (*Katsuwonus pelamis*). T_b shows the maximum temperature gradient between internal red and white muscle reported by Stevens & Neill (1978). Note the similar contraction speeds for red and white muscle fibres for an 8–12 °C temperature difference. (from Johnston & Brill, 1984).

tuna show no residual tension up to 30 °C (Johnston & Brill, 1984) and fibres from the iliofibularis muscle of the desert iguana *Dipsosaurus dorsalis* relax completely up to 45 °C (Johnston & Gleeson, 1984). While the origin of postcontraction tension is unclear, it appears to involve the formation of abnormal crossbridge linkages since contraction velocity is markedly reduced. Although of little direct significance for muscle function *in vivo*, inter-specific variations in the development of residual tension clearly reflect differences in the structures of myosins which are related in some way to their function at different body temperatures.

Acclimation

Natural selection over evolutionary time periods has resulted in muscle fibres which have broadly similar mechanical power outputs in spite of differences in body temperature of 20 °C or more. However, for most species, V_{max} has a Q_{10} of around 2·0 and consequently muscle performance will fall sharply in response to an acute drop in body temperature. Many species are adapted to environments (e.g. tide pools, salt marshes) with highly variable temperatures. For example, *Fundulus heteroclitus*, which inhabit tidal creeks along the Northeastern seaboard of the U.S.A. may experience temperatures of 30 °C during low tide on hot summer days falling to 12 °C at high tide. Sidell, Johnston, Moerland & Goldspink, (1983) found that the $pCa^{2+} - Mg^{2+} - $ ATPase relationship and specific activity of white muscle myofibrils was relatively insensitive to temperature over the range 10–30 °C. However, no differences in the properties of the ATPase were found in populations of fish maintained at water temperatures of 5, 15 and 25 °C for several months (Sidell *et al*, 1983). Instead, there is evidence that *Fundulus* become inactive at winter temperatures (<5 °C) and hibernate in the mud. However, there are many fish, particularly in fresh water and shallow seas (e.g. Adriatic) that experience large, seasonal variations in body temperature and yet remain active and feed throughout the coldest part of the year.

Johnston, Davison & Goldspink (1975) showed that the properties of Mg^{2+} ATPase of myofibrils from goldfish (*Carassius auratus*) white muscle are modified by several months acclimation to temperatures of either 1 °C or 26 °C. At 0 °C, ATPase activity was four times higher for myofibrils from cold- than warm-acclimated populations. Penney & Goldspink (1981) acclimated goldfish to a range of temperatures and found that myofibrillar ATPase activity did not vary continuously with acclimation temperatures but attained steady states at upper and lower compensation limits of 26 °C and 10 °C, respectively. Johnston, Sidell & Driedzic (1985) acclimated another cyprinid fish *Cyprinus carpio* L. to either 8 °C or 23 °C for 1–2 months and investigated the force–velocity relationship of red and white muscle fibres. For warm-acclimated fish, the Q_{10} for maximum power output for red and white fibres was around 2·0. The acute effects of low temperature on muscle performance were found to be largely offset by a period of acclimation to low temperature. Maximum isometric force (P_o) was around 70% higher and V_{max} 100%

higher at 7 °C in muscles from cold-acclimated individuals (Fig. 14). There were also qualitative differences in the properties of skinned fibres at high temperatures between cold- and warm-acclimated fish. Fibres isolated from cold-acclimated carp showed up to 75% residual tension following 2-minute activations at 23 °C (Johnston, Sidell & Driedzic, 1985) reflecting structural differences in the myofibrillar proteins. Altringham & Johnston (1985) determined the ATPase activity of skinned fibres during maximal isometric concentrations by inhibiting endogenous

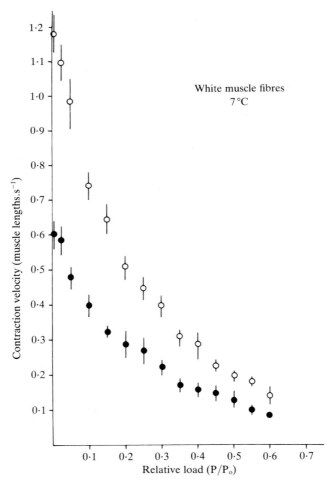

Fig. 14. Force–velocity curves for skinned fibres isolated from white myotomal muscle of common carp (*Cyprinus carpio* L) acclimated for 1–2 months to either 7 °C (open circles) or 23 °C (closed circles). Experiments were carried out at 7 °C at maximal Ca^{2+}-concentrations. (adapted from Johnston, Sidell & Driedzic, 1985).

creatine phosphokinase and measuring ADP production using High Performance Liquid Chromatography. At 7 °C, ATP turnover per myosin head was 50% lower (1·85 and 2·84 $ATPS_1^{-1}s^{-1}$) and 'work' (force time integral) obtained for each ATP hydrolysed was 50% higher in fibres from cold- than warm-acclimated fish.

It is not known whether temperature compensation of the contractile properties of fish muscle involve changes in gene expression or post-translational modifications of particular proteins. It is of interest that changes in ATPase activity with temperature acclimation are only evident for natural actomyosin and not for preparations from which the Ca^{2+}-regulatory proteins have been removed, suggesting the cooperative involvement of several myofibrillar proteins (Johnston, 1979).

To date, the kind of acclimatory changes in contractile properties reported for carp and goldfish have not been observed for any marine fish. Moerland & Sidell (unpublished results, 1984) found no differences in the properties of myofibrillar ATPase of muscle from striped bass (*Morone saxatilis*) acclimated for several months to either 5 or 25 °C. However, a number of other acclimatory mechanisms have been observed including changes in the proportion of different fibre types (goldfish, Johnston & Lucking, 1978; striped bass, Jones & Sidell, 1982 and changes in the threshold swimming speed for recruitment of white muscle fibres (Rome, Loughna & Goldspink, 1984) which may allow the maintenance of locomotory activity at low temperatures without the necessity for modifications in the P–V relation of muscle fibres.

The author's work is supported by grants from the Natural Environment Research Council.

References

ALTRINGHAM, J. D. & JOHNSTON, I. A. (1982). The pCa-tension and force-velocity characteristics of skinned fibres isolated from fish fast and slow muscles. *J. Physiol.* **333**, 421–449.

ALTRINGHAM, J. D. & JOHNSTON, I. A. (1985). Simultaneous measurement of force production and ATPase activity in skinned muscle fibres isolated from carp, acclimated to different environmental temperatures. *Pflügers Archs* (in press).

BORGMAN, U. & MOON, T. W. (1975). A comparison of lactate dehydrogenases from an ectothermic and an endothermic animal. *Can. J. Biochem.* **53**, 998–1004.

CAREY, F. G. (1982). A brain heater in swordfish. *Science, N.Y.* **216**, 1327–1329.

CAREY, F. G. & ROBISON, B. H. (1981). Daily patterns of swordfish observed by acoustic telemetry. *Fishery Bull. Fish. Wildl. Serv. U.S.* **79**, 277–292.

CONNELL, J. J. (1961). The relative stabilities of the skeletal muscle myosins of some animals. *Biochem. J.* **80**, 503–509.

FERSHT, A. (1977). *Enzyme Structure and Mechanism* pp. 246. San Francisco: Freeman.

FOCANT, B. & HURIAUX, F. (1976). Light chains of carp and pike skeletal muscle myosins. Isolation and characterisation of the most anodic light chain on alkaline pH electrophoresis. *FEBS Letters* **65**, 16–19.

GRAVES, J. E. & SOMERO, G. N. (1982). Electrophoretic and functional enzymic evolution in four species of Eastern Pacific barracudas from different thermal environments. *Evolution* **36**, 97–106.

HAZEL, J. R. & PROSSER, C. L. (1974). Molecular mechanisms of temperature compensation in poikilotherms. *Physiological Reviews* **54**, 620–677.

HEISLER, N. (1980). Regulation of acid-base status in fishes. In *Environmental Physiology of Fishes*. NATO Advanced Study Institute Series A: Life Sciences (Ed. M. A. Ali) pp. 123–162. New York and London: Plenum Press.

HILL, A. V. (1938). The heat of shortening and the dynamic constants of muscle. *Proc. R. Soc.* B, **126**, 136–195.

HOCHACHKA, P. W. & SOMERO, G. N. (1973). *Strategies of Biochemical Adaptation* 358pp. Philadelphia: W. B. Saunders.

JOHNSON, M. S. (1977). Association of allozymes and temperature in the crested blenny *Anoplarchus purpurescens*. *Mar. Biol.* **41**, 147–153.

JOHNSTON, I. A. (1979). Calcium regulatory proteins and temperature acclimation of actomyosin from a eurythermal teleost (*Carassius auratus* L.). *J. comp. Physiol.* **129**, 163–167.

JOHNSTON, I. A. (1982a). Capillarisation, oxygen diffusion distances and mitochondrial content of carp muscles following acclimation to summer and winter temperatures. *Cell Tissue Res.* **222**, 325–337.

JOHNSTON, I. A. (1982b). Biochemistry of myosins and contractile properties of fish skeletal muscle. *Molecular Physiology* **2**, 15–29.

JOHNSTON, I. A. (1983). Cellular response to an altered body temperature: the role of alterations in the expression of protein isoforms. *Soc. Exp. Biol. Seminar Series* (ed. A. Cossins & P. Sheterline). **17**, 121–143.

JOHNSTON, I. A. (1985). Effects of temperature on force-velocity relationship of skinned fibres isolated from Icefish (*Chaenocephalus aceratus*) skeletal muscle. *J. Physiol.* R. (in press).

JOHNSTON, I. A. & WALESBY, N. J. (1977). Molecular mechanisms of temperature adaptation in fish myofibrillar adenosine triphosphates. *J. comp. Physiol.* **119**, 195–206.

JOHNSTON, I. A. & LUCKING, M. (1978). Temperature induced variation in the distribution of different types of muscle fibre in the goldfish (*Carassius auratus*). *J. comp. Physiol.* **124**, 111–116.

JOHNSTON, I. A. & MAITLAND, B. (1980). Temperature acclimation in crucian carp (*Carassius carassius* L morphometric analyses of muscle fibre ultrastructure. *J. Fish. Biol.* **17**, 113–125.

JOHNSTON, I. A. & GLEESON, T. T. (1984). Thermal dependence of contractile properties of red and white fibres isolated from the iliofibularis muscle of the desert iguana (*Dipsosaurus dorsalis*). *J. exp. Biol* **111**, (in press).

JOHNSTON, I. A. & BRILL, R. (1984). Thermal dependence of contractile properties of single skinned muscle fibres isolated from Antarctic and various warm water marine fishes including Skipjack tuna (*Katsuwonu pelamis*) and Kawakawa (*Euthynuus affinis*). *J. comp. Physiol.*, **155**, 63–70.

JOHNSTON, I. A. & HARRISON, P. (1985). Contractile and metabolic characteristics of muscle fibres from Antarctic fish. *J. exp. Biol.* (in press).

JOHNSTON, I. A. & SALAMONSKI, J. (1984). Power output and force-velocity relationship of red and white muscle fibres from the Pacific Blue Marlin (*Maikaira nigricans*). *J. exp. Biol.* **111**, 171–177.

JOHNSTON, I. A. & SIDELL, B. D. (1984). Differences in the temperature dependence of muscle contraction velocity and myofibrillar ATPase activity in a cold-temperature teleost. *J. exp. Biol.* **111**, 179–189.

JOHNSTON, I. A., DAVISON, W. & GOLDSPINK, G. (1975). Adaptations in Mg^{2+}-activated myofibrillar ATPase activity induced by temperature acclimation. *FEBS Lett* **50**, 293–295.

JOHNSTON, I. A., WALESBY, N. J., DAVISON, W. & GOLDSPINK, G. (1977). Further studies on the adaptation of fish myofibrillar ATPases to different cell temperatures. *Pflügers Archs*, **371**, 257–262.

JOHNSTON, I. A., SIDELL, B. D. & DRIEDZIC, W. R. (1985). Force-velocity characteristics and metabolism of carp muscle fibres following temperature acclimation. *J. exp. Biol.* (in press).

JONES, P. L. & SIDELL, B. D. (1982). Metabolic responses of striped bass (*Morone saxatilis*) to temperature acclimation. II. Alterations in metabolic carbon sources and distributions of fibre types in locomotory muscle. *J. exp. Zool.*, **219**, 163–171.

LOW, P. S., BADA, J. L. & SOMERO, G. N. (1973). Temperature adaptation of enzymes: roles of the free energy, the enthalpy and the entropy of activation. *Proc. natn. Acad. Sci. U.S.A.*, **70**, 430–432.

LOW, P. S. & SOMERO, G. N. (1976). Adaptation of muscle pyruvate kinases to environmental temperatures and pressures. *J. exp. Zool.*, **198**, 1–11.

MACKIE, I. M. & CONNELL, J. J. (1964). Preparation and properties of purified cod myosin. *Biochim. Biophys. Acta*, **93**, 544–552.

MERRITT, R. B. (1972). Geographical distribution and enzymatic properties of lactate dehydrogenase allozymes in the fathead minnow, *Pimphales promelas*. *Am. Nat.*, **106**, 173–184.

PENNEY, R. F. & GOLDSPINK, G. (1981). Compensation limits of fish muscle myofibrillar ATPase enzyme to environmental temperature. *J. therm. Biol.*, **4**, 269–272.

PLACE, A. R. & POWERS, D. A. (1979). Genetic variation and relative catalytic efficiencies: Lactate dehydrogenase B allozymes of *Fundulus heteroclitus*. *Proc. natn. Acad. Sci., U.S.A.* **76**, 2354–2358.

POWERS, D. A. & PLACE, A. R. (1978). Biochemical genetics of *Fundulus heteroclitus* (L.) 1. Temporal and spatial variation in gene frequencies of Ldh-B, Mdh-A, Gpi-B and Pgm-A. *Biochemical Genetics*, **16**, 593–607.

REEVES, R. (1977). The interaction of body temperature and acid-base balance in ectotherms. *Ann. Rev. Physiol.* **39**, 559–586.

RICHARDS, E. G., CHUNG, C.-S., MENZEL, D. B. & OLCOTT, H. S. (1967). Chromatography of myosin on diethylaminoethyl-Sephadex A-50. *Biochemistry*, **6**, 528–540.

ROME, L.C., LOUGHNA, P. T. & GOLDSPINK, G. (1984). Muscle fibre activity in carp as a function of swim speed and muscle temperature. *Am J. Physiol.* (In press).

SHAKLEE, J. B., CHRISTIANSEN, J. A., SIDELL, B. P., PROSSER, C. L. & WHITT, G. S. (1977). Molecular aspects of temperature acclimation in fish: contributions of changes in enzymic activities and isoenzyme patterns to metabolic reorganisation in the green sunfish. *J. exp. Zool.* **201**, 1–20.

SHRIVER, J. W. (1984). Energy transduction in myosin. *TIBS July*, pp. 322–328.

SIDELL, B. (1977). Turnover of cytochrome c in skeletal muscle of green sunfish (*Lepomis cyanellus* R.) during thermal acclimation. *J. exp. Zool.* **199**, 233–250.

SIDELL, B. D. (1980). Responses of goldfish (*Carassius auratus* L.) muscle to acclimation temperature: alterations in biochemistry and proportions of different fibre types. *Physiol. Zool.* **53**, 98–107.

SIDELL, B. D. (1983). Cellular acclimatisation to environmental change by quantitative alterations in enzymes and organelles pp. 103–120. In *Cellular Acclimatisation to Environmental change* (eds A. Cossins & P. Shertertine) *Soc. exp. Biol. Seminar Series Symposia* Cambridge: Cambridge University Press.

SIDELL, B. D., JOHNSTON, I. A., MOERLAND, T. S. & GOLDSPINK, G. (1983). The eurythermal myofibrillar protein complex of the mummichog (*Fundulus heteroclitus*): adaptation to a fluctuating thermal environment. *J. comp. Physiol. B*. **153**, 167–173.

SOMERO, G. N. (1975). The role of isozymes in adaptation to varying temperatures pp. 221–234. In *Isozymes II. Physiological Function* (ed. C. L. Markert pp. 890. New York: Academic Press.

SOMERO, G. N. (1978). Temperature adaptation of enzymes: Biological optimisation through structure-function compromises. *Am. Rev. Ecol. Syst.* **9**, 1–29.

SOMERO, G. N. (1983). Environmental adaptation of proteins: strategies for the conservation of critical functional and structural traits. *Comp. Biochem.* **76A**, 621–633.

STEVENS, E. D. & NEILL, W. H. (1978). Body temperature relations of tunas, especially skipjack. In *Fish Physiology*, Vol. 7 (eds W. S. Hoar & D. J. Randall) pp. 316–356. New York: Academic Press.

STEVENS, E. D. & CAREY, F. G. (1981). One "why" of the warmth of warm-bodied fish. *Am. J. Physiol.* **240**, R151–155.

STONE, B. B. & SIDELL, B. D. (1981). Metabolic response of striped bass (*Morone saxatilis*) to temperature acclimation I. Alterations in carbon sources for hepatic energy metabolism. *J. exp. Zool.* **218**, 371–379.

SVERDRUP, H. U. M., JOHNSON, M. W. & FLEMING, R. H. (1942). *The Oceans* pp. 1087. New York: Prentice-Hall.

TREGEAR, R. T. & MARSTON, S. B. (1979). The crossbridge theory. *Ann. Rev. Physiol.* **41**, 723–736.

WALSH, P. J. & MOON, Y. W. (1982). The influence of temperature on extracellular and intracellular pH in the American eel, *Anguilla rostrata* (Le Sueur). *Respir. Physiol.* **50**, 129–140.

WALSH, P. J. & SOMERO, G. N. (1982). Interactions among pyruvate concentration pH, and Km on pyruvate in determining *in vivo* Q_{10} values of the lactate dehydrogenase reaction. *Can. J. Zool.* **60**, 1293–1299.

WILSON, T. L. (1977). Interrelations between pH and temperature for the catalytic rate of the M_4 isozyme of lactate dehydrogenase (EC 1.1.1.27) from goldfish (*Carassius auratus* L.). *Arch. Biochem. Biophys.* **179**, 378–390.

WOLEDGE, R. C. (1968): The energetics of tortoise muscle. *J. Physiol.* **197**, 685–707.

YANCEY, P. H. & SOMERO, G. N. (1978). Temperature dependence of intracellular pH: its role in the conservation of pyruvate apparent Km values of vertebrate lactate dehydrogenases. *J. comp. Physiol.* **125**, 129–134.

Printed in Great Britain © *Society of Experimental Biology 1985*

CONTROL AND CO-ORDINATION OF GILL VENTILATION AND PERFUSION

E. W. TAYLOR

Department of Zoology & Comparative Physiology, University of
Birmingham, Birmingham B15 2TT

Introduction

When Professor Laverack invited me to contribute to this centenary symposium on the biology of marine animals I was reminded of my good fortune in being a member of the audience at a previous symposium of the Society for Experimental Biology in St. Andrews in 1965. The topic for that meeting was Nervous and Hormonal Mechanisms of Integration and partially in recognition of the influence it had on the development of some of my research interests I have chosen that general theme, as it applies to control of gill function. This account is restricted to a consideration of external respiration (i.e. between the animal and seawater), and more particularly the uptake of oxygen, in some fish (particularly the dogfish *Scyliorhinus canicula*) and decapodan crustaceans. The elimination of carbon dioxide over gills has not been considered as this is in relative terms not a problem for water breathers because of its very high solubility in water and is complicated by its association with acid–base balance and ionoregulation (Randall, 1982). The emphasis throughout is on the control of rates of oxygen uptake resulting from alterations in the patterns of gill ventilation and perfusion, which ultimately, together with their detailed morphology, determine the relative effectiveness of the respiratory gas-exchange surfaces. A brief description of the functional morphology of gills and their ventilation and perfusion leads to a consideration of receptors monitoring gill function then to the control of respiratory and cardiac rhythms and their temporal relationships. There have been a number of useful reviews of respiratory gas exchange in water breathers which represent a suitable background to this account; notably those by Hughes & Shelton (1962); Shelton (1970); Johansen (1971) and Randall (1970; 1982) on fish and Taylor (1982); Wilkens (1981) and McMahon & Wilkens (1983) on crustaceans. Dejours (1975) reviewed the principles of comparative respiratory physiology, and the symbols used to represent respiratory variables are largely taken from his account.

Oxygen uptake from seawater is by physical diffusion, a process obeying Fick's Law which states that the quantity of oxygen passing over an exchange surface ($\dot{M}_{O_2}$ in moles O_2 min^{-1}kg^{-1} tissue) is governed by Krogh's diffusion constant (K), which is a measure of relative O_2 conductance of the exchange surface, its surface area (A), thickness (x) and the gradient for diffusion expressed as partial pressure ΔP_{O_2}. This may be expressed as a simple equation:

$$M_{O_2} = K.A.\frac{\Delta P_{O_2}}{x}$$

Both A and x describe the morphology of the exchange surfaces or gills which in order to maximize their effectiveness are characterized by a large surface area (A) and a relatively thin epithelial layer separating seawater from blood (x). Of equal importance in determining $\dot{M}_{O_2}$ is ΔP_{O_2} and this can be controlled by alterations in the relative rates of ventilation of the gills with water and perfusion with blood. Indeed the detailed pattern of ventilation and perfusion of the gills can change their effective diffusive conductance as well as altering ΔP_{O_2}.

Seawater is a difficult medium from which to extract oxygen. Oxygen supply is limited by partial pressure and solubility coefficient and this latter physical constant is reduced by an increase in temperature and salinity. Warm, salty water has a relatively low oxygen content and large volumes must be presented to the exchange surfaces of active animals in order that sufficient oxygen may be extracted to fuel aerobic metabolism. This presents an additional problem as water is a relatively dense and viscous medium. The momentum of the ventilatory stream is sustained by unidirectional ventilation. Nevertheless, the high work rates demanded from respiratory muscles during periods of reduced O_2 supply (hypoxia) or increased demand (exercise) may significantly increase total oxygen demand (Jones, 1971). These problems have of course been successfully overcome both by extant species and their early ancestors and some ways in which optimal rates of oxygen uptake are attained with the minimum of energy expenditure are described in this review.

The functional anatomy of gills

The gills of fishes are borne on pharyngeal arches supported by bone or cartilage as double rows of horizontally stacked filaments, separate in teleosts but attached to a central interbranchial septum in elasmobranchs (Fig. 1). Each filament bears rows of vertically stacked lamellae (sometimes termed secondary lamellae) on its dorsal and ventral

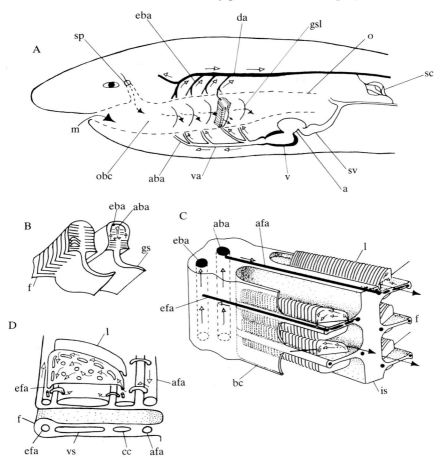

Fig. 1. Schematic diagrams of the gills and their blood supply in the dogfish *Scyliorhinus canicula* L. (A) Side view of anterior half of animal to show general plan of gill ventilation and perfusion. The fourth gill arch has been drawn as if exposed; (B) dorsolateral view of 2 gill arches to show the gill septa, stacked filaments and lamellae; (C) laterodorsal view of portion of single gill arch to show details of filaments with canopy and lamellae and their blood supply; (D) dorsolateral view of two filaments to show details of their blood supply, which is described in the text. a, atrium; aba, afferent branchial artery; afa, afferent filament artery; bc, branchial canopy; cc, corpora cavernosa; da, dorsal aorta; eba, efferent branchial artery; efa, efferent filament artery; f, filament; gs, gill septum; g sl, gill slit; is, interbranchial septum; l, lamella; m, mouth; o, oesophagus; obc, oro-branchial cavity; s, spiracle; sc, systemic circulation; sv, sinus venosus; v, ventricle; va, ventral aorta; vs, venous sinus. Diagram (C) is modified from Cooke, 1980. Water flow —▶ ; blood flow —▷

surfaces. These are flattened structures, presenting a large surface area to the surrounding seawater. The total area of the secondary lamellae and the thickness of their epithelial surfaces varies between species according to their relative requirements for oxygen transfer, with fast-swimming species such as the tuna having a large gill area combined with a short diffusion distance (Hughes & Morgan, 1973). Each lamella is perfused with a sheet of blood running between pillar cells which hold the upper and lower epithelial layers together (Randall, 1982) and cover approximately 10 % of the surface of the lamella rendering it not available for gas exchange (Farrell, Sobin, Randall & Crosby, 1980). Gill structure is essentially similar in decapodan crustaceans (Fig. 2), though their exchange surfaces are structurally homologous to the filaments of fish gills (i.e. they lack secondary lamellae). The epithelial layers on the lamellae of crab gills are separated by a haemocoelic space traversed by pillar cells and are covered by a layer of chitin (Figs 3 & 4). Chitin is relatively impermeable to oxygen which may account for the relatively large gill areas and high rates of ventilation observed in many active crustaceans (Taylor, 1982).

Fish ventilate their gills unidirectionally by means of a double-action pump. Hughes & Shelton (1958) divided ventilation in the trout into four phases with the opercular suction pump (phase 1) and buccal pressure pump (phase 3) separated by periods of transition when differential pressure across the resistance offered by the gill lamellae was much reduced or in some species briefly reversed. A similar dual pump was described by Hughes (1960) in elasmobranch fish which lack an operculum but generate suction in the parabranchial cavities enclosed by the gill septa over each gill slit (Fig. 1). Ventilation in crustaceans is achieved by the rapid oscillations of a pair of specialized appendages, the scaphognathites which draw water into the branchial chambers, acting as force-suction pumps (Taylor, 1982).

Perfusion of the gill lamellae in fish is direct from the heart, which pumps deoxygenated blood, via the ventral aorta and afferent branchial arteries to the afferent filament arteries. Blood flow then separates into a respiratory route which runs via the lamellae where it is oxygenated,

---

Fig. 2. Schematic diagram of a transverse section through a large, posterior gill from *Carcinus maenas*, to show the morphology of a single lamella on one side of the gill shaft. *Carcinus* has phyllobranchiate gills with stacks of flat lamellae inserted into a central shaft which extends between the main afferent vessel (aff) on the outer (epibranchial) surface of the gill and the efferent vessel (eff) which runs along the inner (hypobranchial) surface. Haemolymph flows up the afferent vessel and through rows of open apertures into the haemocoel of each lamella between radiating lines of pillar cells (pc). Towards the efferent vessel the pillar cells fuse into complete partitions forming efferent channels (ec) which may collect haemolymph from discrete areas of the lamella. The openings from these channels into the efferent vessels are restricted by groups of cells which may act as valves (v). Other labels: art, lamellar artery; ip, intralamellar partition; mc, marginal canal; mg, mucus gland; nep, nephrocytes; ner, nerve. (From Taylor & Taylor, 1985).

then enters the efferent filament arteries which lead to the systemic circulation. Before entering the lamellae the afferent filament arteries of elasmobranchs drain into a corpora cavernosa, which may act as a hydraulic skeleton supporting the filaments or as a pulse-smoothing

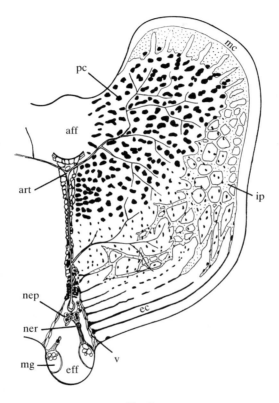

Fig. 2

capacitance vessel proximal to the exchange surfaces (Wright, 1973; Cooke, 1980). This respiratory route interconnects with a non-respiratory blood pathway at various points. Some blood leaves the respiratory, arterio-arterial route to enter a large central canal or venous sinus in the filament which is in turn connected to large sinuses in the interbranchial septum and gill arch. This blood then drains back to the heart along an arterio-venous, non-respiratory route. The complexity of gill perfusion is indicated on Fig. 1 and has been described in detail for teleosts (Laurent & Dunel, 1980; Dunel & Laurent, 1980) and elasmobranchs (Cooke, 1980; de Vries & de Jager, 1984; Metcalfe & Butler, 1985). The venous

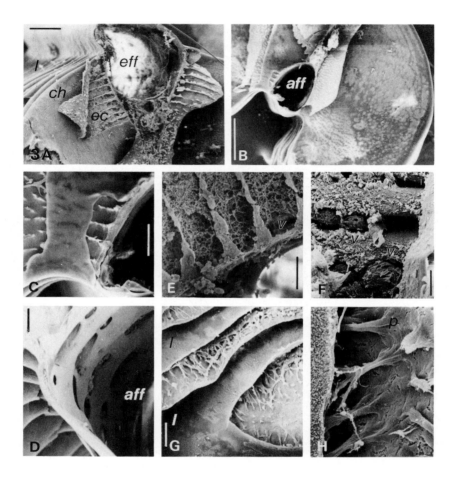

Fig. 3 for legend see p.130

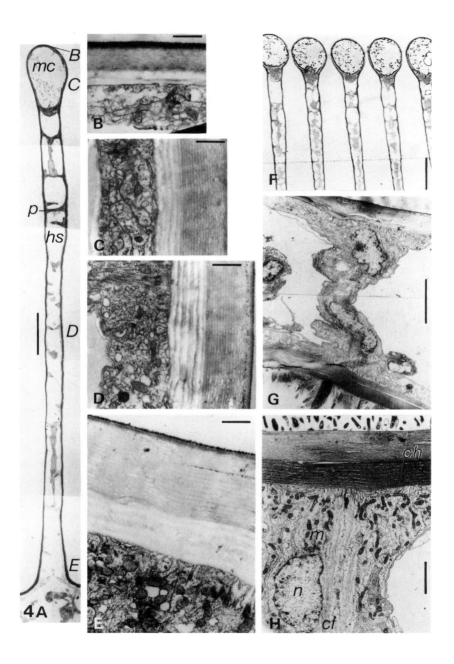

Fig. 4 for legend see p.130

drainage from the gill filaments is thought to arise primarily or solely from the efferent side of the arterio-arterial route with the respiratory and non-respiratory routes supplied in series, while the non-respiratory route and the systemic circulation are perfused in parallel (Metcalfe & Butler, 1985). It seems possible that the venous sinuses subserve a nutritional role rather than representing a variable blood shunt which bye-passes the respiratory exchange surfaces as suggested by Steen & Kruysse (1964). Potential shunts do, however, exist on fish gills. Cooke (1980) pointed out that the basal one-fifth of the filaments on dogfish gills lie in a ventilatory dead space, where water flow is excluded by the branchial canopy (Fig. 1). Also, the basal channels in each gill lamella are buried beneath the gill filament epithelium. Blood passing through either of these routes cannot participate in gas exchange and if this is a variable proportion of total flow then it constitutes a potential mechanism for control of the effectiveness of oxygen uptake into the systemic circulation.

In crustaceans the heart pumps oxygenated blood returning from the gills which receive deoxygenated blood from large venous sinuses (Taylor, 1982). Several arteries leave the heart in decapodan crustaceans to supply organs anteriorly, posteriorly and ventrally. These bear cardio-arterial valves at their exits from the heart which are controlled by neurohormones released from the ligament nerve terminals close to the heart. Octopamine closes the posterior valve and relaxes the anterior valves indicating that the peripheral distribution of haemolymph may be controlled, possibly to favour perfusion of the anterior CNS (Kuramoto & Ebara, 1984). The gills (Fig. 2) possess valves on the entrances to the

---

Fig. 3. Scanning electron micrographs of gill lamellae from *Carcinus maenas*: (A) ventral surface of gill to show efferent vessel (*eff*) with efferent channels (*ec*) leading into it from a gill lamella (l) revealed by fracturing of the chitin (*ch*) and epithelial cells; (B) view of afferent vessel (*aff*) showing openings into gill lamellae and outlines of pillar cells visible through the chitin; (C) close-up of openings from afferent vessel into gill lamella; (D) view down afferent vessel to show regular array of unimpeded openings into lamellae, (E) close-up of openings from lamella into efferent vessel, which are apparently impeded by a layer of cells (*v*); (F) end-view of efferent openings, showing valve-like structures (*v*); (G) broken edges of lamellae (*l*) showing pillar cells; (H) close up of pillar cells (*p*) including stumps of broken pillars. Scale bars: A, 200 μm; B, 400 μm; C, D & G, 50 μm; E & F, 25 μm.

Fig. 4. Transmission electron and light micrographs of gill lamellae from *Carcinus maenas*; (A) T.S. of whole gill lamella near efferent vessel to show marginal canal (*mc*); pillar cells (*p*); haemocoelic spaces (*hs*); (B-E) sections through gill lamellae taken from the positions indicated on (A); (F) T.S. of tips of five lamellae to indicate their spacing and rigidity, confered by the covering of chitin; (G) T.S. gill lamella through pillar cells which are modified epithelial cells, fused in the central line; (H) T.S. pillar cell and chitin showing nucleus (*n*); mitochondria, (*m*); collagen-like fibres, (*cf*). Scale bars: A, 150 μm; B–E, 1 μm; F, 100 μm; G, 10 μm; H, 2 μm.

efferent (hypobranchial) vessels which rectify flow through the lamellae (Taylor & Taylor, 1985) and they receive a direct supply of arterial blood from the heart which may have a nutritive function (Taylor & Greenaway, 1979). Very high rates of ventilation in disturbed crabs may indicate large ventilation dead space in the branchial chambers (Johansen, Lenfant & Mecklenberg, 1970).

There is abundant evidence for the existence of counter-current exchange of oxygen between water and blood over the gill lamellae of fish (Hughes & Shelton, 1962). Experimentally this has been demonstrated by examples of measured oxygen tension in arterialized blood (Pa, O_2) exceeding that in mixed expired water (P_{E,O_2}) in both teleosts (e.g. Steen & Kruysse, 1964) and elasmobranchs (Grigg, 1970a). Similar evidence is lacking in crustaceans, though Hughes, Knights & Scammell (1969) described a possible counter current over the gills of *Carcinus maenas* and the physiological evidence ($P_{a,O_2} > P_{E,O_2}$) may be masked by a large ventilation dead space or water shunts in fish (Short, Taylor & Butler, 1979) and crustaceans (Johansen *et al.* 1970).

The rates of water ($\dot{V}_w$) and blood ($\dot{V}_b$) flow over the counter-current exchanger at the gills are matched according to their relative capacities to carry oxygen (Hughes & Shelton, 1962). Typically in fish the $\dot{V}_w/\dot{V}_b$ ratio is 10–20 (e.g. Piiper & Schumann, 1967) or higher, reflecting the enhanced O_2 capacity of the blood conferred by haemoglobin in the red blood cells (Randall, 1970). In the haemoglobinless ice fish cardiac output ($\dot{V}_b$) is relatively high and $\dot{V}_w/\dot{V}_b$ is less than 3 (Holeton, 1970) and experimentally induced anaemia reduces the ratio in trout due to a large increase in $\dot{V}_b$ (Cameron & Davis, 1970). Crustaceans with their limited O_2 capacity in the haemolymph similarly have relatively high $\dot{V}_b$ when active and low ventilation/perfusion ratios (Taylor & Wheatly, 1980; Taylor, 1982). The diffusive conductance of the exchange surface on the gills is a measure of their functional area (A), thickness (x) and value for Krogh's constant (K) but may be assessed as rate of oxygen uptake $\dot{M}_{O_2}$ related to mean oxygen gradient over the gills using equations proposed by Hughes & Shelton (1962) modified by Scheid & Piiper (1976) and applied to the dogfish by Short *et al.* (1979). Recently, Metcalfe (1983) demonstrated that diffusive conductance could be reliably assessed in the dogfish from measurements of $\dot{M}_{O_2}, P_{a,O_2}$ and P_{I,O_2}. The effectiveness of gas exchange (E) which is the ratio between actual and maximum possible gas transfer in a counter-current exchange system represents another index of the functional performance of gills suggested by Hughes & Shelton (1962). These means of assessment of gill performance are based on the 'Fick principle' which assumes that oxygen uptake is limited to the gills and is reflected in the O_2 partial pressures measured in blood and water afferent and efferent to the exchange surfaces. Complications are introduced by the arterio-venous blood drainage from the gills which does not enter the systemic circulation and by the existence of a small but variable degree of O_2 exchange over the skin of fish (Nonnotte & Kirsch, 1978). The latter component, which may become significant during hypoxia in the dogfish (Metcalfe & Butler, 1982) is precluded in crustaceans by their calcified exoskeleton which effectively prevents O_2 uptake over the general body surface, though the ventral abdomen is available for limited exchange in macrurans such as the lobster (Thomas, 1954). Application of the Fick equation is complicated in crustacean studies by the lack of a sampling site for mixed venous haemolymph (Taylor, 1982; Taylor & Greenway, 1984).

Changes in oxygen availability

The ability of marine animals to control the relative diffusive conductance and effectiveness of oxygen transfer over their gills has been assessed by exposing them to hypoxic water. The pattern of responses observed varies between species and between individuals, with temperature and with levels and rates of exposure to hypoxia (Shelton, 1970; Butler & Taylor, 1971, 1975). The 'typical' hypoxic response in a water-breathing fish or crustacean is an increase in ventilation rate, $\dot{V}_w$ and a reflex bradycardia, which may result in a reduction in cardiac output $\dot{V}_b$. Consequently, the $\dot{V}_w/\dot{V}_b$ ratio is further increased to compensate for the lower O_2 capacity of the water and the diffusion time for blood to equilibrate and potentially saturate with oxygen in the gill lamellae is increased. This interpretation of the response often proves oversimplistic.

The increase in ventilation has been described in a number of teleost species (e.g. Randall & Shelton, 1963; Saunders & Sutterlin, 1971) though it has only recently been detected in unrestrained dogfish which show a 50 % increase in ventilatory frequency during hypoxic exposure (Metcalfe & Butler, 1984a). Ultimately the efficacy of increasing V_w may be limited by the high respiratory cost of ventilation and by the decrease in effectiveness at high rates of $\dot{V}_w$ (Hughes, 1964; Jones, 1971). As well as increasing the rate of delivery of oxygen, increased $\dot{V}_w$ may cause turbulent water flow at the exchange surfaces, breaking up stationary water layers close to the lamellae which may present a major obstacle to gas exchange (Piiper & Scheid, 1975). Hyperventilation may serve to blow off CO_2, causing a respiratory alkalosis with a subsequent Bohr shift on the respiratory blood pigment, increasing its affinity for oxygen and thus facilitating oxygen transfer to the blood. This latter mechanism has been substantiated for the crayfish during hypoxia (Wheatly & Taylor, 1981) but in the trout (Holeton & Randall, 1967) tench (Eddy, 1974) and dogfish (Butler & Taylor, 1975) the respiratory alkalosis is countered by a metabolic acidosis during hypoxia.

A reflex hypoxic bradycardia is a well-established response to hypoxia in both fish (e.g. Randall & Shelton, 1963; Butler & Taylor, 1971) and crustaceans (Taylor, 1982); though when given time to 'settle' both dog-

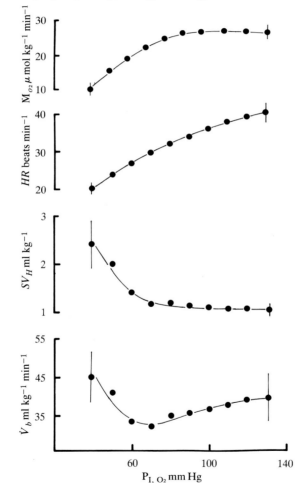

Fig. 5. *Scyliorhinus canicula*. The effects of progressive hypoxia at 17 °C on rate of oxygen consumption ($\dot{M}_{O_2}$); heart rate (*HR*); cardiac stroke volume (SV_H); and cardiac output, ($\dot{V}_b$). The hypoxic bradycardia was compensated by an increase in SV_H resulting in maintenance of $\dot{V}_b$ at the normoxic level. $\dot{M}_{O_2}$ fell due to reduced saturation of the blood with oxygen at ambient P_{O_2} levels below 70 mmHg. (Adapted from Butler & Taylor, 1975).

fish (Butler, Taylor & Davison, 1979) and lobsters (Butler, Taylor &
McMahon, 1978) showed no cardiac response to moderate hypoxia. The
hypoxic bradycardia does not necessarily imply a reduction in blood flow.
In dogfish the bradycardia which developed during progressive hypoxia
was compensated by a proportional increase in cardiac stroke volume
(Figs. 5 & 6A) and an identical response was described for the trout by
Holeton & Randall (1967). It was only during exposure to extreme
hypoxia that the reduction in heart rate was sufficient to reduce cardiac
output (Fig. 6B).

The absence of a reduction in $\dot{V}_b$ calls into question the functional
significance of the hypoxic bradycardia. Taylor, Short & Butler (1977)

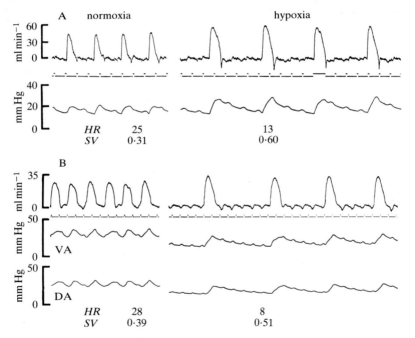

Fig. 6A. Blood flow (ml min^{-1}) and pressure (mm Hg) recorded from the ventral aorta of a
dogfish (female 0·85 kg) at 12 °C during normoxia (P_{I,O_2} 140 mmHg) and moderate hypoxia
(P_{I,O_2} 36 mm Hg). Values of heart rate (HR) and stroke volume (SV) are given below the
traces. The hypoxic bradycardia was accompanied by an increase in pulse pressure and cardiac
stroke volume, with no change in cardiac output. (Adapted from Butler & Taylor, 1975).

Fig. 6B. Blood flow (ml min^{-1}) and pressure (mm Hg) in the ventral aorta (VA) and dorsal
aortic blood pressure (DA) recorded from a dogfish (female 1.05 kg) at 15 °C during normoxia (P_{I,O_2} 130 mmHg) and hypoxia (P_{I,O_2} 29 mmHg). Values for heart rate, stroke volume
and cardiac output are given below the traces. The increase in stroke volume was insufficient
to compensate for the bradycardia and cardiac output fell. Blood pressure in both aortae
is markedly pulsatile and the traces include pressure and flow pulses generated by ventilatory movements. (Adapted from Taylor et al., 1977).

calculated a reduction in apparent power output of the dogfish heart during hypoxia which may reduce overall oxygen demand. More recently, however, Taylor & Barrett (1985a) were able to demonstrate a reduction in diffusive capacity and effectiveness of O_2 transfer into the blood of hypoxic dogfish when the bradycardia was prevented by injection of atropine. Apparently the bradycardia subserved a respiratory role which did not involve a reduction in cardiac output.

A possible mechanism whereby oxygen uptake may be enhanced by a bradycardia in the absence of a change in cardiac output was described by Randall (1982). Farrell *et al.* (1980) described changes in perfusion of gill lamellae as transmural hydrostatic pressure varied. At pressures below 30 cm H_2O some vascular spaces and whole lamellae remained closed. During a hypoxic bradycardia the pulse pressure developed in the branchial circulation may increase (Fig. 6) and this could serve to open previously poorly perfused vascular spaces in the gill lamellae increasing the effective surface area for gas exchange (A). Farrell *et al.* (1980) suggested that the pillar cells will not stretch, so that distension of the blood spaces must occur around these cells with a resultant decrease in diffusion distance (x). As these changes will occur most readily in the marginal and central regions of the lamellae then blood may be shunted preferentially away from the basal regions which do not take part in respiratory gas exchange. These changes are summarized diagrammatically in Fig. 7. Farrell, Daxboeck & Randall (1979) also suggested that pulsatile blood flow may enhance oxygen transfer over the gill lamellae as reported for mammalian lungs and Randall (1982) stated that the gill lamellae of eels had been observed to flutter in the ventilatory stream and to stiffen as each pulse of blood entered the vascular spaces, which may enhance oxygen transfer (Fig. 7). Increased cardiac output may also result in recruitment of additional, previously unperfused lamellae. Some filaments have all lamellae perfused whereas others have none (Booth, 1979; Farrell *et al.* 1979) and most frequently the proximal lamellae are perfused whilst the more distal are not. In dogfish the proximal lamellae are covered by the canopy and if the increased pulse pressure, resulting from hypoxic bradycardia, caused the perfusion of more distal lamellae this would increase the effective area available for respiratory gas exchange. The mechanisms described by Farrell and his coworkers were present in isolated perfused gills and resulted from physical changes in the compliance of the branchial vasculature, in the absence of neuronal or hormonal influences. The blood vessels in intact teleosts have neurally and hormonally regulated smooth muscle with a maintained tone (Wood, 1974) and the differential perfusion of gill lamella reported from intact

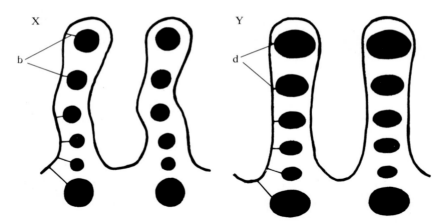

Fig. 7. Schematic diagram of blood spaces between pillar cells in a cross section of fish gill lamellae. X, represents a period when blood pressure and flow are near the minimum attained during each cardiac cycle in the resting fish. Y, illustrates probable changes in vascular dimensions and the rigidity of the lamellae with blood pressure and flow at a maximum following ventricular systole, when cardiac stroke volume is elevated during hypoxia or exercise. In Y diffusion distances (d) are reduced and a greater proportion of the total, increased blood volume is passing through the lamellar subregions with the shorter diffusion distances. These changes could result in an increase in diffusive conductance. (Adapted from Farrell *et al.* 1980).

trout (Booth, 1979) may be actively regulated. In normoxic trout 60 % of lamellae were perfused and during hypoxia or following injection of adrenaline this proportion was reduced in the first gill arch but markedly increased in the last gill arch, with an overall increase in lamellar perfusion approaching 30 %. Similar changes in gill perfusion could result in the increases in diffusive conductance during hypoxia reported for fish (Randall, 1970) and crustaceans (e.g. Wheatly & Taylor, 1981).

Receptors in the respiratory and cardiovascular systems

The aquatic environment often varies markedly in oxygen content and this is reflected immediately as an internal change, across the counter current on the gills. Some fish and crustaceans show behavioural avoidance reactions to hypoxia (e.g. Jones, 1952; Taylor & Wheatly, 1980), whereas in the dogfish prolonged hypoxia may suppress activity (Metcalfe & Butler, 1984a). The physiological responses typically include an increase in ventilation rate and reduction in heart rate as described above. Studies of these hypoxic responses have given indirect evidence for the existence of oxygen receptors at various sites in the ventilatory stream or blood system but as yet no definitive study of an oxygen receptor has been reported. Many studies support the existence of O_2 receptors on or near the gills which monitor environmental P_{O_2} (see Shelton, 1970; Johansen, 1971; Taylor, 1982). The gill arches in fishes are innervated by cranial nerves IX and X and it is these nerves which innervate the carotid and aortic bodies of mammals. Bilateral section of IX and X abolished the hypoxic bradycardia in the trout (Smith & Jones, 1978) but in elasmobranchs did not affect the hypoxic response (Satchell, 1959) and Butler, Taylor & Short (1977) found it necessary to bilaterally section cranial nerves V, VII, IX and X to abolish the hypoxic bradycardia in the dogfish. Their conclusion was that O_2 receptors are distributed diffusely in the orobranchial and parabranchial cavities which agreed with the diffuse distribution of putative receptors in the pharynx of trout and salmon (de Kock, 1963). Saunders & Sutterlin (1971) were unable to record any change in the level of afferent nervous activity from branchial branches of the vagus nerve during hypoxic exposure of the sea raven, *Hemitripterus americanus*. In contrast Laurent (1967) recorded oxygen chemoreceptor activity from branches of cranial nerve IX innervating the pseudobranch in the tench. This organ is derived from the spiracle which is open in elasmobranchs and as it receives arterialized blood flowing from the gills it is ideally sited to monitor P_{a,O_2} levels. Smith & Davie (1984) concluded that O_2 receptors were innervated by IX in the salmon but bilateral denervation of the pseudobranch in the trout had no effect on the changes in ventilation volume following exposure to hypoxia and hyperoxia (Randall & Jones, 1973). Daxboeck & Holeton (1978) found that irrigation of the anterior region of the respiratory tract of the trout with hypoxic water caused a reflex bradycardia but no change in ventilation, implying that different receptors are involved in the induction of the two overt responses to hypoxic exposure. Saunders & Sutterlin (1971) observed an increase in 'breathing amplitude' in the sea raven when the dorsal aorta was perfused with hyperoxic blood, and also when perfusing the dorsal aorta with normoxic blood during ambient hypoxia, which they regarded as evidence for both central and peripheral sites of oxygen receptor activity. Eclancher & Dejours (1975) observed a ventilatory and cardiac response to an intravascular injection of cyanide but no response to cyanide in the ventilatory water stream of teleosts, which indicates that the P_{O_2} receptors are located internally. Randall (1982) reviewed evidence for the oxygen receptors being sensitive to arterial blood oxygen content or rate of delivery of oxygen to the receptor which would be singularly appropriate as oxygen supply is thought to be limited by rate of perfusive conductance ($\dot{V}_b.C_{a,O_2} - C_{v,O_2}$) in fish and Bamford (1974) concluded that the most important site of oxygen detection in the trout is the brain. This is in contrast to crustaceans in which the chitin covering the gills may cause the rate of oxygen supply to the tissues to be dependent on diffusive conductance at the gills and there is abundant circumstantial evidence for the existence of externally placed P_{O_2} receptors in the branchial chambers of crustaceans (Taylor, 1982). Recently evidence has accumulated for the existence of venous P_{v,O_2} receptors in fish, first postulated by Taylor, Houston & Horgan (1968). Exposure of the dogfish to progressive hyperoxia caused an initial tachycardia, towards the atropinized heart rate, indicating a reduction in vagal tone, followed by a secondary reflex bradycardia at high $P_{,O_2}$ levels which corresponded with an increase in P_{v,O_2} (Fig. 8). This response was mimicked by injection of hyperoxaemic blood into the venous system (Barrett & Taylor, 1984a). This evidence suggests that fish may possess receptors monitoring, P_{O_2} levels on both the afferent and efferent sides of the countercurrent exchanger, potentially enabling them to match the relative flow rates of water and blood over the gill lamellae in order to optimize respiratory gas exchange, saturating the blood with oxygen whilst minimizing the energy cost of ventilation and perfusion.

The respiratory muscles in fish contain length and tension receptors, in common with other vertebrate muscles, and the gill arches bear a number of mechanoreceptors with various functional characteristics. Satchell & Way (1962) characterized mechanoreceptors on the branchial processes of the dogfish and Sutterlin & Saunders (1969) described receptors on the gill filaments and gill rakers of the sea raven. Current unpublished work by P.J.F. de Graaf (1985) described slowly adapting position receptors on the gill arches and phasic receptors on the gill filaments and rakers of the trout. He interpreted their function as maintenance of the gill sieve and detection of and protection from clogging or damaging material. Mechanical stimulation of the gill arches is known to elicit the 'cough' reflex in fish (e.g. Satchell, 1959).

These mechanoreceptors will be stimulated by the ventilatory movements of the gill arches and filaments and afferent information reaching the brain in the IXth and Xth cranial nerves is known to influence the respiratory rhythm with breathing rate slowing in teleosts and increasing in elasmobranchs following transection of the branchial nerves or paralysis of the ventilatory muscles (Johansen, 1971; Barrett & Taylor, 1985a; Ballintijn, 1985). Stimulation of branchial mechanoreceptors by increasing rates of water flow may be the trigger for the cessation of active ventilatory movements during ram ventilation in fish (Johansen, 1971; Randall, 1982). Although there are mechanoreceptors distributed profusely around the inhalent apertures and general surface of the bran-

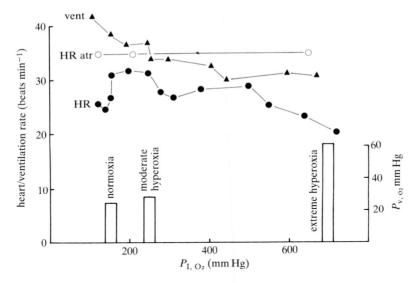

Fig. 8. Effect of exposure of the dogfish to progressive hyperoxia at 15 °C on venous oxygen tension (P_{v,O_2}) ventilation rate (vent, ▲) and heart rate in both normal (H.R., ●) and atropinised (H.R.atr, ○) fish. An initial tachycardia, towards the atropinised rate, in moderate hyperoxia was followed by a bradycardia in extreme hyperoxia which accompanied an increase in P_{v,O_2}. Ventilation rate decreased towards heart rate in moderate hyperoxia.

chial chambers in crustaceans a leading role in the control of ventilation is played by the oval organ located on the scaphognathite. Imposed movement of the scaphognathite can entrain the central respiratory pacemaker neurones (Young & Coyer, 1979).

Historical evidence for the existence of baroreceptor type responses in elasmobranchs, responsible for regulating blood pressure by reflex alteration of heart rate and peripheral vascular resistance were reviewed by Johansen (1971). Recent studies on the dogfish, which involved repeated sampling and reinjection of blood, revealed that the resultant changes in blood pressure were largely uncompensated and that the reflex bradycardia induced by injecting 5–10 ml of hyperoxaemic blood did not compensate for the associated increase in blood pressure (Barrett & Taylor, 1984a). In contrast, Wood & Shelton (1980) interpreted increases in heart rate from reduced hypoxic rates in the trout, which paralleled reductions in arterial blood pressure induced by haemorrhage, as interaction between baroreceptor and chemoreceptor drive. Haemorrhage reduced blood pressure but did not result in a compensatory change in cardiac frequency in normoxic trout.

Control of ventilation

The respiratory muscles in fish operate around the jaws and gill arches and are innervated by cranial nerves with their motoneurones in the brainstem. This complicates the differentiation between neurones generating the respiratory rhythm and the motoneurones they drive, which supply the respiratory muscles. Neurones which fire rhythmically in phase with ventilation have been located throughout the medulla oblongata of fish (Ballintijn, 1981). They comprise the motor nuclei of the Vth (trigeminal), VIIth (facial), IXth (glossopharyngeal) and Xth (vagus) cranial nerves together with the descending trigeminal nucleus and the reticular formation alongside the motonuclei. Recent ablation experiments and recordings of central activity suggest that the respiratory rhythm generator (RRG) neurones are located in the reticular formation which has efferent and afferent connections with all the motonuclei (Ballintijn, 1985). Electrical stimulation of respiratory muscles altered the firing pattern of respiratory motoneurones in the carp with some reacting as part of a peripheral proprioceptive control loop whilst others integrated proprioceptive information from several muscles (Ballintijn & Bamford, 1975). Stimulation of sensory fibres leaving branchial vagal ganglia altered the duration of the ventilatory cycle and could produce movements similar to a cough; whilst continual stimulation had a synchronizing effect on the ventilatory rhythm (Ballintijn, Roberts & Luiten, 1983). There are also projections to the RRG and respiratory motoneurones from mesencephalic neurones, stimulation of which may cause phase switching or entrainment and may end ventilatory pauses (Ballintijn, 1985). The neurones in the different motonuclei innervate muscles which generate the complex series of movements involved in ventilation. They all burst rhythmically, with phase relationships dependent upon the muscles they innervate. The neurones are not clustered according to the phase relation between their activity and ventilation. Adjacent neurones may have different firing patterns and their functional role has been assessed by simultaneous recordings of e.m.g.'s from the respiratory muscles (e.g. Ballintijn & Alink, 1977). A typical recording is shown in Fig. 9. Another way of studying the phase relationships of activity in the respiratory motoneurones is to monitor the efferent activity in the nerves supplying the ventilatory muscles. In the dogfish the onset of bursts of activity in the mandibular branch of the Vth cranial nerve, supplying muscles in the jaw, preceded activity in the glossopharyngeal IXth which innervates the 1st gill arch by a mean of 152 m.s. (Fig. 10). This in turn preceded activity in the four branchial branches of the Xth

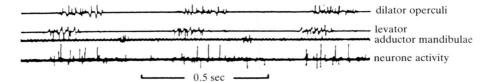

Fig. 9. Simultaneous recordings of e.m.g. from different respiratory muscles (top three traces) and a respiratory motoneurone located in the hindbrain of the carp which fired in phase with activity recorded from the dilator operculi. (Adapted from Ballintijn & Alink, 1977).

vagus nerve, which fired simultaneously, by about 30 m.s. (Barrett & Taylor, 1985a). This independent innervation of the first gill arch may have a functional significance as Grigg (1970b) found that during experimentally induced hypoxia the Port Jackson shark (*Heterodontus portusjacksoni*) relaxed the septum over the first gill slit causing it to flare open and admit inhalent water which reappeared from the other gill slits. This ability may enable the fish to continue gill ventilation whilst its mouth is obstructed during feeding.

The control of ventilation in decapodan crustaceans was reviewed by Taylor (1982) and most recently by Bush, Simmers & Pasztor (1985). The scaphognathites are driven by antagonistic sets of levator and depressor muscles, each supplied with motoneurones from the CNS. These motoneurones show periodic oscillations in membrane potential with waves of depolarization and superimposed spikes in phase with activity in synergistic motor nerves and in antiphase with antagonistic motor bursts. These oscillators depend upon periodic inhibition, interrupting tonic excitation, mediated by a small group of non-spiking interneurones

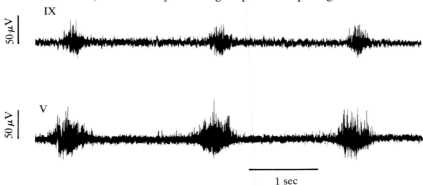

Fig. 10. Efferent activity recorded simultaneously from the glossopharyngeal (IX) and the mandibular (V) cranial nerves of a dogfish, innervating respiratory muscles in the gill arches and jaw. The onset of bursts of activity in V preceded the bursts in IX by 150 m.s. (Adapted from Barrett & Taylor, 1985,a).

which show cyclical, probably endogenous, oscillations in membrane potential and are in turn influenced by 'higher order' non-spiking 'integrating' neurones. Synaptic interaction between motoneurones, feedback onto premotor neurones and stimulation of mechanoreceptors, including the oval organ, can all influence the ventilatory motor rhythm.

Control of the heart and branchial circulation

The fish heart is composed of typical vertebrate cardiac muscle fibres with contraction initiated by a propagated muscle action potential from a myogenic pacemaker and generating a characteristic e.c.g. waveform (Randall, 1968; Satchell, 1971). The isolated heart continues to beat and to respond to perfusion with appropriate putative transmitters (Capra & Satchell, 1977a). Heart beat is influenced by intrinsic mechanisms such as the relationship between the force of contraction and stretch applied to the muscle fibre known as the Frank–Starling relationship. The increase in diastolic filling time, which accompanies cardiac slowing, can, therefore, result in an increase in cardiac stroke volume. Short, Butler & Taylor, (1977) concluded that the compensatory increases in cardiac stroke volume which maintained cardiac output during induced cardiac slowing in the dogfish were wholly attributable to the Frank–Starling relationship, and this represents a self-regulating feature of cardiac function.

The heart is supplied with inhibitory parasympathetic innervation via the vagus nerve, which terminates on the heart as a plexus of fibres limited to the sinus venosus in elasmobranchs (Young, 1933) but spreading over the atrium in teleosts (Young, 1936). The inhibitory effect is mediated via muscarinic cholinoreceptors associated with the pacemaker and myocardium (Holmgren, 1977). Recently inhibitory purinoceptors have been detected in the dogfish atrium (Meghji & Burnstock, 1984). The heart typically operates under a degree of inhibitory vagal tone which varies with physiological state and environmental conditions. In the dogfish cholinergic vagal tone, assessed as the proportional change in heart rate following atropinization, increased with an increasing temperature of acclimation (Taylor et al. 1977). In the trout vagal tone on the heart, although higher than in the dogfish at all temperatures, decreased at higher temperatures (Fig. 11), but the cardioacceleration induced by adrenaline injection into atropinized fish increased with temperature (Wood, Pieprzak & Trott, 1979). Heart rate in dogfish restrained in a standard set of experimental conditions at 15°–17°C varied directly with P_{O_2}, so that hypoxia induced a reflex bradycardia and a normoxic vagal

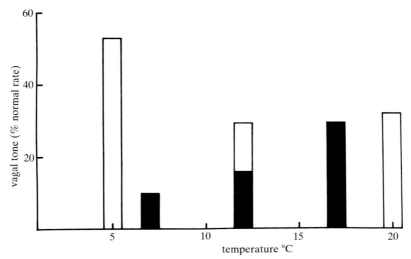

Fig. 11. The effect of release of normoxic vagal tone, by injection of atropine, on heart rate in the trout (□) and dogfish (■), at a range of acclimation temperatures. The increase in heart rate following atropinization is plotted as a percentage of the normal rate. Vagal tone increased with temperature in restrained dogfish, whilst vagal tone was highest at low temperatures in the trout. (data on dogfish from Taylor *et al.*, 1977; on trout from Wood *et al.*, 1979).

tone was released by exposure to moderate hyperoxia (Taylor *et al.* 1977; Barrett & Taylor, 1984a). These data imply that the level of vagal tone on the heart in dogfish is determined peripherally by graded stimulation of P_{O_2} receptors and variations in this inhibitory tone may result in a reflex bradycardia or tachycardia. There is little morphological or physiological evidence for sympathetic innervation of the elasmobranch heart (Young, 1933; Short *et al.*, 1977). The reported effects of adrenaline and noradrenaline on the elasmobranch heart are variable (Nilsson, 1983) but a positive chronotropic and large inotropic effect, mediated by a β-adrenoreceptor mechanism, has been described for the isolated heart (e.g. Capra & Satchell, 1977a) and it remains possible that some degree of cardioregulation may be exercised by catecholamines, released by activity in sympathetic preganglionic fibres from the chromaffin tissue located in the posterior cardinal sinus, and released directly into the venous drainage to the heart (Johansen, 1971). The levels of circulating catecholamines are extremely high in the dogfish, possibly in some way compensating for the lack of sympathetic innervation of the heart and gills, and the levels increase during hypoxia (Butler, Taylor, Davison & Capra, 1978). Their major effect on oxygen uptake may be vasodilatation of the branchial vasculature (Capra & Satchell, 1977b). There is no evidence for vasomotor innervation of elasmobranch gills (Nilsson, 1983;

Metcalfe & Butler, 1984b) but an intrinsic vasoconstriction during deep hypoxia (Satchell, 1962) may be released by a rise in circulating catecholamines (Butler *et al.* 1978) and it remains possible that these vasomotor effects on the branchial vasculature involve variations in the relative proportion of total blood flow directed through the parallel arterio-arterial and arterio-venous routes, or changes in the patterns of perfusion of the gill lamellae, described above.

In teleosts the heart receives both a cholinergic vagal supply and an adrenergic sympathetic supply. Goldfish at 25 °C had a calculated parasympathetic tone (released by atropine) of 66 % of intrinsic heart rate whilst sympathetic tone was 22 % and a rapid cardioacceleration induced by enforced swimming was abolished by the sympathetic β antagonist propranalol (Cameron, 1979). A normoxic vagal tone was absent in trout stressed by experimental conditions (Wood & Shelton, 1980). There are sympathetic ganglia associated with cranial nerves IX and X in teleosts and the branchial nerves are mixed vago/glossopharyngeo-sympathetic trunks (Nilsson, 1983). Stimulation of these nerves may produce a cholinergically mediated constriction of the arterio-arterial pathway whereas stimulation of the adrenergic fibres favours blood flow through this respiratory route rather than the arterio-venous route. Despite the clear demonstration of mixed autonomic innervation of the heart and branchial vasculature in teleosts it remains probable that much of the functional control of gill perfusion is exercised via circulating catecholamines (Nilsson, 1983).

The crustaceans heart is single chambered and beats at systole against the elasticity of suspensory ligaments. It responds to stretch by an increase in the force and rate of contraction. Crustacean muscle fibres do not conduct action potentials, consequently the heart possesses a neurogenic pacemaker in the form of a cardiac ganglion. This can function independently of the CNS producing rhythmical discharges which cause the heart to contract. Heart rate is governed by inhibitory and excitatory inputs from the CNS as well as by circulating hormones released from the pericardial glands situated close to the heart. The circulatory system is an open haemocoel, continuous with the interstitial fluid space in the tissues, although recent evidence suggests that there may be a circulatory and a non-circulatory component of this space (Taylor, Tyler-Jones & Wheatly, 1985). Until recently there was no evidence for control of the peripheral circulation but Taylor & Greenaway (1984), using injected microspheres, have shown that haemolymph may be shunted from the gills to air-breathing structures during aerial exposure of the land crab *Holthuisana transversa*.

Vagal innervation of the heart in the dogfish

The existence of a varying level of inhibitory vagal tone on the heart of the experimentally restrained dogfish prompted an investigation of vagal output to the heart. The heart in the dogfish is supplied with two pairs of cardiac vagi, a branchial cardiac branch leaves the fourth branchial nerve and a visceral cardiac branch is supplied from the visceral branch of the vagus, on either side of the animal (Taylor *et al.*, 1977). Experiments involving transection and electrical stimulation of these nerves revealed that the branchial cardiac branches are more effective in cardioinhibition than the visceral cardiac branches (Short *et al.*, 1977), accounting for the majority of normoxic vagal tone and the reflex bradycardia during

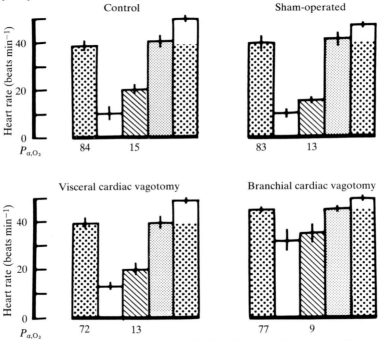

Fig. 12. Mean values (± S.E.) of heart rate before, during and on recovery from rapid hypoxia and following atropinization in control and selectivity vagotomized fish. The columns are respectively: ▦, initial (normoxic) heart rate; □, the transient, intense bradycardia immediately following rapid exposure to hypoxia; ▨, the stable, hypoxic heart rate after approximately 1 min exposure to hypoxia; ▨, the heart rate on recovery from hypoxia. The final column indicates mean normoxic heart rate following atropinization, the spotted portion of this column indicates the initial normoxic heart rate and the clear portion of this column is an indication of the degree of vagal tone exerted by the portion of the vagus which was intact prior to atropinization. The initial normoxic and stable hypoxic P_{a,O_2} values are given below the relevant columns for each category of animal. (From Taylor *et al.*, 1977).

hypoxia (Fig. 12). Recordings from a branchial cardiac branch contained high levels of spontaneous efferent activity, separable into two types of unit. Some, typically smaller, units fired sporadically and increased their firing rate during hypoxia (Fig. 13A). These non-bursting units seem to play the major role in initiating the reflex hypoxic bradycardia and may also determine the overall level of vagal tone on the heart. Other, larger units fired in rhythmical bursts which were synchronous with ventilatory movements (Taylor & Butler, 1982). Recordings from the less-effective visceral cardiac branches consisted of bursting units alone and their motor function is as yet unclear (Barrett & Taylor, 1985a). Their primary function may be sensory (Short *et al.* 1977). The bursts recorded from branchial cardiac branches continue in decerebrate, paralysed dogfish, and are synchronous with efferent activity in branchial branches of the vagus which innervate respiratory muscles (Fig. 13B). This evidence alone suggests that the bursting activity originates in the CNS through some interaction, either direct or indirect, with the RRG. Retrograde intraxonal transport has been used to locate vagal preganglionic motoneurones (VM) in the hindbrain of the dogfish (Barrett, Roberts & Taylor, 1984; 1985a). The vagal motor column extends over about 5 mm in the medulla both rostral and caudal of obex with the motoneurones supplying axons to various organs located sequentially (i.e. branchial branches from the rostral end and visceral branches from the caudal end of the motor column). The majority of VM are located medially, close to the wall of the fourth ventricle, but the branchial cardiac branch is unique in having some of its cardiac vagal motoneurones (CVM) located as a ventrolateral group of neurones which supply axons solely to this branch of the vagus (Barrett & Taylor, 1985b). Extracellular recordings from CVM identified in the hindbrain of decerebrate, paralysed dogfish by antidromic stimulation of a branchial cardiac branch revealed that neurones located in the medial division were spontaneously active, firing in rhythmical bursts which contributed to the bursts recorded from the intact nerve (Fig. 14A). Neurones located in the ventrolateral division were either spontaneously active, firing regularly or sporadically but never rhythmically, or were silent (Barrett & Taylor, 1984b; 1985c). It seems that the two types of efferent activity described in the branchial cardiac branches of the vagus have separate origins in the CNS which may indicate a separation of function. All of the spontaneously active CVM from both divisions and some of the silent CVM fired in response to mechanical stimulation of a gill arch (Fig. 14) which infers that they could be entrained to ventilatory movements in the spontaneously breathing fish and that both may be responsible for the reflex bradycardia recorded

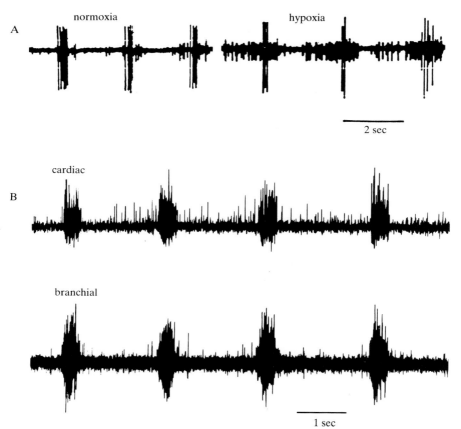

Fig. 13A. Efferent activity recorded from the left branchial cardiac branch of the vagus of a decerebrate dogfish in normoxia (P_{I,O_2} 150 mmHg) and hypoxia (P_{I,O_2} 45 mmHg). The smaller, sporadically active units markedly increased firing rate during hypoxia, whilst the larger, rhythmically bursting units were less active. (From Taylor & Butler, 1982).

Fig. 13B. Simultaneous recordings of efferent activity in the 3rd branchial branch (branchial) and the branchial cardiac branch (cardiac) of the left vagus from a decerebrate, paralysed dogfish. The persistence of rhythmic bursting activity in both nerves indicates that it is generated in the CNS and not by stimulation of mechanoreceptors on the gill arches. The sporadically active units which are present in recordings from the cardiac nerve are absent from the branchial nerve. (From Barrett & Taylor, 1985, a).

in response to mechanical stimulation (Taylor & Butler, 1982). Randall (1966) recorded bursting activity from the cardiac vagus of the tench which he concluded could either originate peripherally from stimulation of receptors on the gills or blood stream dorsal to the gills (i.e. efferent vessels) or may result from connection between the vagal and respiratory centres in the medulla.

The origin of the respiration-related bursting activity in the medial

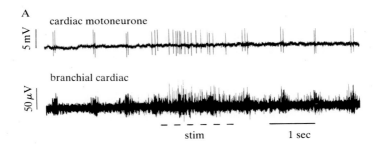

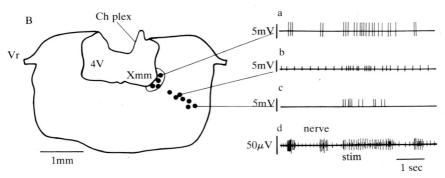

Fig. 14A. Activity recorded extracellularly from a cardiac vagal motoneurone (cardiac motoneurone) located medially in the hindbrain of the dogfish, just rostral to obex, which supplied its axon to the branchial cardiac branch of the vagus. The neurone was spontaneously active, firing rhythmically and contributing to the bursts of activity recorded from the whole nerve (branchial cardiac). Mechanical stimulation of the gill septa (stim) induced a marked increase in activity both in the motoneurone and in the cardiac nerve. (Adapted from Barrett & Taylor, 1985,c).

Fig. 14B. Schematic diagram of the location and properties of cardiac vagal motoneurones (●) in the hindbrain of the dogfish. The representative section of the medulla is taken just rostral to obex. All CVM in a medial location (a) were spontaneously active, firing rhythmically and contributing to the bursting activity recorded from the whole nerve (d). The CVM in the ventrolateral group were divisible into spontaneously active units which fired regularly or sporadically (b) but did not burst, or normally silent units (c) which fired in response to mechanical stimulation of the gill septa (Stim.), as did all the spontaneously active units. Other silent ventrolateral CVM did not fire during mechanical stimulation and these do not appear on the diagram. Ch plex, choroid plexus; Vr, vagal rootlet; Xmm, medial motonucleus of X; 4V, 4th ventricle.

group of CVM is of particular interest because respiratory modulation of CVM has been observed in mammals. The sensitivity of mammalian CVM to inputs from arterial baroreceptors and chemoreceptors is reduced during inspiration and when their excitability is raised experimentally they fire in the postinspiratory and expiratory phases of ventilation and are silent during inspiration, when the phrenic nerve is firing (Spyer, 1982). This modulation, which is the central origin of sinus arrhythmia in the mammal, is thought to arise from direct, inhibitory synaptic contact between collaterals from respiratory vagal motoneurones (RVM) and CVM. Direct connections between bursting CVM and RVM are possible in the dogfish hindbrain as both are located in the medial division of the vagal motor column with an overlapping rostrocaudal distribution (Barrett *et al.* 1985a). As the bursts are synchronous (Fig. 13B) the innervation of CVM is likely to be excitatory rather than inhibitory and it is equally possible that a direct drive from the RRG operates on the RVM and the CVM. Activity in both the CVM and RVM may be modulated by afferent input from gill mechanoreceptors stimulated by ventilatory movements and by chemoreceptors in various locations. The possible connections to and from the RRG, RVM and CVM are summarized diagrammatically in Fig. 15.

There is a possible parallel between the distribution of CVM in the dogfish and that established in mammals, with the medial group of CVM the equivalent of the mammalian dorsal vagal motor nucleus (DVN) and the ventrolateral group being the possible evolutionary antecedent of the mammalian nucleus ambiguus (NA) as postulated by Barrett *et al.* (1984). The ventrolateral group of neurones are all CVM and constitute 8 % of the total VM in the dogfish. In teleosts the ventrolateral group constitute 11 % of VM and some contribute axons to branchial branches of the vagus which may have a vasomotor function, absent in elasmobranchs. In the amphibian *Xenopus laevis* the ventrolateral group rises to 32 % of identified VM, possibly in association with the development of air-breathing structures, which are innervated from the NA in mammals (Barrett, Taylor & Metcalfe, 1985b). A clear evolutionary line in the progressive ventrolateral migration of VM may be established between elasmobranch fish and mammals.

If this topographical distribution proves to be truly homologous then it may reflect functional divisions between the medial and ventrolateral CVM. In mammals CVM in the NA give rise to myelinated axons which may exert the major chronotropic influence over the heart whereas CVM in the DVN give rise to unmyelinated fibres which exert a negative inotropic effect on the heart (Spyer, 1982). The non-bursting units recorded from the branchial cardiac vagi of the dogfish arise from the ventrolateral group of VM (i.e. the equivalent of the NA) and appear to exert the major chronotropic effect on the heart. The bursting units arise from the DVN but their fibres are myelinated and there is no evidence for nervous control of cardiac stroke volume in the dogfish (Short *et al.* 1977). The functional role of the bursting CVM is not clear though it seems probable that they serve to relate heart beat to ventilation, which reopens

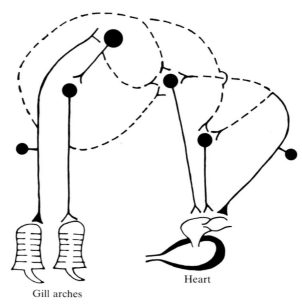

Fig. 15. Diagram of the possible connections between vagal motoneurones in the hindbrain of the dogfish which control and coordinate gill ventilation and heart rate. There are several established connections: 1) the respiratory rhythm generator neurones (RRG) show endogenous bursting activity which drives respiratory motoneurones (RVM); 2) the RVM innervate the intrinsic muscles in the gill arches; 3) the activity of the RRG is modulated by feedback from mechanoreceptors and possibly chemoreceptors located on or near the gills and innervated by vagal sensory neurones (RVS). Heart rate is controlled by inhibitory input from the vagus nerve which receives axons from cardiac vagal motoneurones (CVM) which are topographically and functionally separable into: 4) a ventrolateral group, some of which fire continuously and may be responsible for reflex changes in heart rate (e.g. hypoxic bradycardia) and for the varying level of vagal tone on the heart, and 5) a medial group, which burst rhythmically and may cause the heart to beat in phase with ventilation. Other more speculative connections may determine the activity in the CVM; 6) collaterals from neighbouring RVM may have an excitatory effect on bursting medial CVM (or release a tonic inhibition); 7) the RRG may connect directly to medial CVM; 8) stimulation of receptors on the gill arches may directly modify activity in medial and some ventrolateral CVM; 9) stimulation of receptors in the cardiovascular system close to the heart innervated by vagal sensory neurones (CVS) may affect vagal outflow to the heart. This diagram is highly schematic and ignores the existence and possible roles of interneurones and inputs from and to higher centres in the CNS. Efferent termination, λ; afferent termination, $\blacktriangle$.

an historical debate over the possible existence and functional significance of cardiorespiratory synchrony in fish.

Cardiorespiratory synchrony revisited

A link between heart beat and ventilation in fish was first noted by Schoenlein (1895) who described 1:1 synchrony in *Torpedo marmorata*.

This observation has recently been repeated (Fig. 16). Lutz (1930) demonstrated that the cardiac vagus was involved in the maintenance of this link, and a full account of the reflex coordination of heart beat with ventilation in the dogfish was published by Satchell (1960). He found that the heart contracted at intervals which approximated to a simple multiple (1–4) of the duration of the ventilatory cycle, with each beat tending to be initiated at the mouth-opening phase. He concluded that coordination was reflexly controlled with mechanoreceptors on the ventilatory apparatus constituting the afferent limb and the cardiac vagus the efferent limb of a reflex arc. Just as sinus arrhythmia in mammals was previously attributed to stimulation of lung receptors and baroreceptors and is now known to be at least partially centrally generated; cardiorespiratory synchrony in the dogfish could originate centrally with the respiration-related bursting units causing the heart to beat in a particular phase of the ventilatory cycle.

The supposed functional significance of cardiorespiratory synchrony relates to the importance of matching relative flow rates of water and blood over the counter current at the gill lamellae. Although virtually continuous both water and blood flow over the lamellae are markedly pulsatile. Recordings of differential blood pressure and gill opacity in the dogfish revealed a brief period of rapid blood flow through the lamellae early in each cardiac cycle (Satchell, 1960) and as the e.c.g. tended to occur at or near the mouth-opening phase of the ventilatory cycle this could result in coincidence of the periods of maximum flow rate of blood and water during each cardiac cycle (Shelton, 1970). The improvement in gill perfusion and consequent oxygen transfer resulting from changes in transmural pressure and intralamellar blood flow, described by Farrell *et al.* (1980) may be further improved by synchronization of the pressure pulses associated with ventilation and perfusion. Cardiorespiratory synchrony may, by a combination of these effects, increase the relative

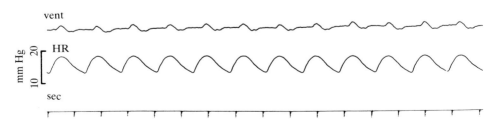

Fig. 16. Ventilation rate (vent), measured as orobranchial water pressure, and heart rate (HR), measured as ventral aortic blood pressure, in an unrestrained electric ray, *Torpedo marmorata* stationary on the bottom of a large tank of aerated seawater at 23 °C. There is 1:1 synchrony between heart beat and ventilation. (Taylor & Barrett – unpublished).

efficiency of respiratory gas exchange (i.e. maximum exchange for minimum work).

One problem with this proposal is that ventilation rate is usually faster than heart rate in experimental dogfish so that if one ventilatory cycle coincides appropriately with heart beat then the second or third in a sequence will occur in a wholly inappropriate phase of the cardiac cycle (Shelton, 1970). Data from other investigations also question the proposal. Teleosts do not show such clear coordination, there is merely a statistical probability that the heart will beat more often in a particular phase of ventilation (i.e. loose phase coupling) though synchrony developed in the trout during progressive hypoxia (Shelton, 1970). In the restrained dogfish ventilation rate was approximately twice heart rate and they showed a drifting relationship (Taylor & Butler, 1971). A typical recording is shown in Fig. 17. Hughes (1972) explored evidence for phase coupling between ventilation and heart beat in dogfish released into a fish box which included a movement restrictor. Very sophisticated analysis of a lot of data using event correlograms revealed that in some cases the heart tended to beat in a particular phase of the ventilatory cycle, for short periods. Analysis using polar coordinates revealed some significant coupling at varied phase angles between the two rhythms with individual fish varying in both the degree of coupling and the phase angle, during a period of observation.

The absence of synchrony, or even consistent close coupling, as opposed to a drifting phase relationship, was most often attributable to changes in heart rate (Fig. 17) which was more variable than ventilation rate (Taylor & Butler, 1971; Hughes, 1972). This may be reliably interpreted in the dogfish as variations in cardiac vagal tone, possibly exerted by changes in the rate of firing of the non-bursting units recorded from the branchial cardiac nerves. Activity in these units is high in the restrained dogfish when cardiorespiratory synchrony is absent (Taylor & Butler, 1971; 1982). A decrease in vagal tone on the heart, such as that recorded during exposure to moderately hyperoxic water (Fig. 8), causes heart rate to rise towards ventilation rate suggesting that in the undisturbed fish a 1:1 synchrony may occur. This proves to be the case. When dogfish were allowed to settle in large tanks of running, aerated seawater at 23 °C they showed 1:1 synchrony between heart beat and ventilation for long periods (Taylor & Barrett, 1985b). This relationship was abolished by atropine (Fig. 18A) confirming the role of the vagus in the maintenance of synchrony and providing a hypothetical role for the bursting units recorded from the cardiac vagi. Whenever the fish was spontaneously active or disturbed the relationship broke down due to a reflex bradycardia and

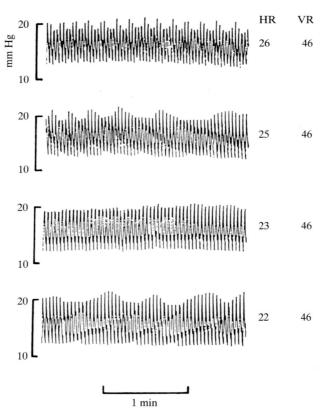

Fig. 17. Ventral aortic blood pressures recorded from a restrained dogfish in normoxic water at 12 °C. Each pressure trace includes two small pressure pulses arising from ventilatory movements and the position of these pulses can be used to judge the temporal relationships between the two rhythms. Heart rate (HR) and ventilation rate (VR) in beats min^{-1} are listed at the side of the traces. Over the 40 min period covered by these traces heart rate slowed progressively from slightly more to slightly less than half ventilation rate, passing through a period when the two rhythms had a 2:1 ratio. Normally they showed a drifting relationship. (From Taylor & Butler, 1971).

acceleration of ventilation (Fig. 18B). In disturbed fish the 2:1 relationship between ventilation and heart rate characteristic of the experimentally restrained animal was re-established (Fig. 19) and it is possible that the elusiveness of data supporting the proposed existence of cardiorespiratory synchrony is due to experimental procedures which increase vagal tone on the heart exerted by the non-bursting units, and mask the more subtle control exerted by the bursting units recorded from the cardiac vagi. Short periods of 1:1 synchrony were observed in unrestrained cod (Jones, Langille, Randall & Shelton, 1974). If this hypothesis can be validated then synchrony may serve to maximize the

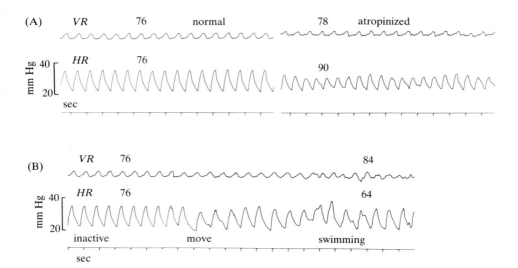

Fig. 18A. Ventilation rate (VR), measured as orobranchial water pressure, and heart rate (HR) measured as ventral aortic blood pressure (beats min^{-1}) recorded from an unrestrained dogfish enclosed in a large tank of running seawater at 23 °C. When the animal was stationary, resting on the bottom of the tank (normal), the two rates were identical and there were clear signs of maintained synchrony. Atropinisation (atropinised) caused an increase in heart rate and loss of synchrony.

Fig. 18B. When the normal, inactive animal moved (move) and then spontaneously commenced swimming it showed a bradycardia and then an increase in ventilation rate so that ventilation became considerably faster than heart beat, a condition previously observed in disturbed or restrained animals. (From Taylor & Barrett, 1985 b).

efficiency of respiratory gas exchange in the 'resting' animal. In the dogfish at least this probably represents a large proportion of their life span because they are observably rather inactive animals, spending a lot of time resting on the substratum, both in aquaria and on the sea bed. Synchrony may yet be observed in cruising fish as gentle swimming movements, due to contraction of lateral bands of aerobic red muscle, may often entrain to the ventilatory rhythm (Satchell, 1968) but the relationship breaks down in 'disturbed' animals when 'efficiency' makes way for emergency and they rely on the large blocks of anaerobic white muscle for sprint swimming. This whole discussion is of course hypothetical because we need to know much more in detail about the beat by beat control of ventilation and blood flow over the surfaces of the gill lamellae and the resultant instantaneous effects on respiratory gas exchange before this relationship can be properly understood. What emerges from current work is that a potent mechanism for the generation of cardiorespiratory synchrony may exist in the dogfish in the form of the bursting

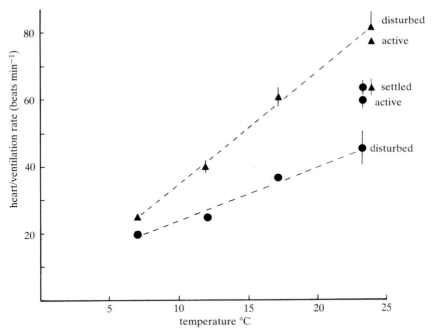

Fig. 19. Heart rate (●) and ventilation rate (▲) at a range of acclimation temperatures in the dogfish. At 7 °C, 12 °C and 17 °C ventilation rate was higher than heart rate in restrained animals. At 23 °C unrestrained animals allowed to settle in a large tank of running seawater (settled) had identical rates of ventilation and heart beat (64 ± 2 beats min^{-1}). Spontaneous bouts of slow swimming (active) were accompanied by a marked increase in ventilation and a slight bradycardia. Fish which were disturbed and swimming vigorously showed a further small increase in ventilation rate and a pronounced bradycardia (disturbed). In disturbed fish ventilation rate was approximately twice heart rate as reported in restrained fish. The divided lines extrapolate the values from restrained fish to disturbed fish. In settled fish when inhibitory vagal tone on the heart was low there was clear evidence of cardiorespiratory synchrony. (Data at 7°, 12° and 17 °C from Taylor *et al.* 1977; at 23 °C from Taylor & Barrett, 1985 b).

units present in recordings of efferent activity in the cardiac vagi. When the vagus nerves of the dog were stimulated once each cardiac cycle the degree of cardioinhibition (lengthening of the cardiac cycle) observed was critically dependent upon the timing of the stimulus, relative to the phase of the cardiac cycle (Levy, Martin, Iano & Zieske, 1969). Such repetitive stimuli tended to entrain the S-A nodal pacemaker cells and when brief bursts of stimulation were delivered the tendency for heart beat to synchronize with the stimulus was considerable (Levy, Iano & Zieske, 1972). Such entrainment could explain the 1:1 synchrony observed in 'settled' dogfish and the apparent loose coupling observed in 'disturbed' animals may arise from interactions between the effects of the bursting and non-bursting units when vagal tone is relatively high. These relationships are currently being investigated in the hope that we can successfully extrapolate from dogs to dogfish and perhaps eventually back again because it is always possible that comparative physiologists can uncover mechanisms which ultimately are of interest to mammalian and, therefore, medical research.

Most of my work was performed in Birmingham and I am indebted to Professor O. E. Lowenstein both for my presence here and the continuing stimulation I derive from having witnessed his dedication to research. The work has also required several trips to marine biological stations or departments between 1970 and 1984 including the M.B.A. Plymouth, the Gatty Laboratory, St. Andrews, the Zoology Department, University of Swansea and the Laboratoire de Neurobiologie Comparee at Arcachon. The author wishes to acknowledge the hospitality and help given by the respective directors and their staff in these establishments, particularly Professor Eric Denton, Professor Mike Laverack, Professor E. W. Knight-Jones and Professor Maurice Moulins. The trip to Arcachon in 1984 was funded from the European Science Exchange Programme, administered by the Royal Society to whom I am most grateful for their support. Parts of our research have been funded by the Science and Engineering Research Council with grants to the author and to postgraduate students. The names of my coworkers appear in the references to our work, they are in no way implicated in this particular interpretation of our joint efforts. The manuscript was processed by Mrs. Jean Hill and the illustrations photographed by Ms. Debbie Palmer. The S.E.M. pictures were taken with help from Mrs. Sue Dipple, Centre for Materials Science, University of Birmingham.

References

BALLINTIJN, C. M. (1981). Neural control of respiration in fish and mammals In *Exogenous and Endogenous Influences on Metabolic and Neural Control.* (ed. A. D. F. Addink & N. Spronk) Oxford: Pergamon Press.

BALLINTIJN, C. M. (1985). Evolution of central nervous control of respiration in vertebrates. In *Neurobiology of the Cardiorespiratory System* (ed. E.W. Taylor) Manchester University Press.

BALLINTIJN, C. M. & ALINK, G. M. (1977). Identification of respiratory motoneurones in the carp and determination of their firing characteristics and interconnections. *Brain Res.* **136**, 261–276.

BALLINTIJN, C. M. & BAMFORD, O. S. (1975). Proprioceptive motor control in fish respiration. *J. exp. Biol.* **62**, 99–114.

BALLINTIJN, C. M., ROBERTS, B. L. & LUITEN, P. G. M. (1983). Respiratory responses to stimulation of branchial vagus nerve ganglia of a teleost fish. *Respir. Physiol.* **51**, 241–257.

BAMFORD, O. S. (1974). Oxygen reception in the rainbow trout *Salmo gairdneri. Comp. Biochem. Physiol.* **48A**, 69–76.

BARRETT, D. J., ROBERTS, B. L. & TAYLOR, E. W. (1984). The topographical organisation of vagal motoneurones in the dogfish *Scyliorhinus canicula* L. *J. Physiol. Lond.* **350**, 32P.

BARRETT, D. J., ROBERTS, B. L. & TAYLOR, E. W. (1985a). The location and distribution of vagal preganglionic motoneurones in the brainstem of the dogfish *Scyliorhinus canicula* L. *J. comp. Neurol.* (submitted).

BARRETT, D. J. & TAYLOR, E. W. (1984a). Changes in heart rate during progressive hyperoxia in the dogfish *Scyliorhinus canicula* L.: evidence for a venous oxygen receptor. *Comp Biochem. Physiol.* **78A**, 697–703.

BARRETT, D. J. & TAYLOR, E. W. (1984b). Characteristics of cardiac vagal motoneurones in the dogfish, *Scyliorhinus canicula* (L.) *J. Physiol. Lond.* **354**, 59P.

BARRETT, D. J. & TAYLOR, E. W. (1985a). Spontaneous efferent activity in branches of the vagus nerve controlling heart rate and ventilation in the dogfish. *J. exp. Biol.* (in press).

BARRETT, D. J. & TAYLOR, E. W. (1985b). The location of cardiac vagal preganglionic neurones in the brainstem of the dogfish. *J. exp. Biol.* (in press).

BARRETT, D. J. & TAYLOR, E. W. (1985c). The characteristics of cardiac vagal preganglionic motoneurones in the dogfish. *J. exp. Biol.* (in press).

BARRETT, D. J., TAYLOR, E. W. & METCALFE, J. D. (1985b). The location and distribution of vagal preganglionic motoneurones in the hindbrain of lower vertebrates. In *Neurobiology of the Cardiorespiratory System* (ed. E.W. Taylor) Manchester University Press.

BOOTH, J. H. (1979). The effects of oxygen supply, epinephrine and acetylcholine on the distribution of blood flow in trout gills. *J. exp. Biol.* **83**, 31–39.

BUSH, B. M. H., SIMMERS, A. J. & PASZTOR, V. M. (1985). Neural control and modulation of gill ventilation in crabs and lobsters. In *Neurobiology of the Cardiorespiratory System* (ed. E.W. Taylor) Manchester University Press.

BUTLER, P. J. & TAYLOR, E. W. (1971). Response of the dogfish (*Scyliorhinus canicula* L.) to slowly induced and rapidly induced hypoxia. *Comp. Biochem. Physiol.* **39A**, 307–323.

BUTLER, P. J. & TAYLOR, E. W. (1975). The effect of progressive hypoxia on respiration in the dogfish (*Scyliorhinus canicula*) at different seasonal temperatures. *J. exp. Biol.* **63**, 117–130.

BUTLER, P. J., TAYLOR, E. W., CAPRA, M. F. & DAVISON, W. (1978). The effect of hypoxia on the levels of circulating catecholamines in the dogfish, *Scyliorhinus canicula. J. comp. Physiol.* B, **127**, 325–330.

BUTLER, P. J., TAYLOR, E. W. & DAVISON, W. (1979). The effect of long term moderate hypoxia on acid-base balance, plasma catecholamines and possible anaerobic end products in the unrestrained dogfish, *Scyliorhinus canicula. J. comp. Physiol.* B, **132**, 297–303.

BUTLER, P. J., TAYLOR, E. W. & McMAHON, B. R. (1978). Respiratory and circulatory changes in the lobster (*Homarus vulgaris*) during long-term exposure to moderate hypoxia. *J. exp. Biol.* **73**, 131–146.

BUTLER, P. J., TAYLOR, E. W. & SHORT, S. (1977). The effect of sectioning cranial nerves V, VII, IX and X on the cardiac response of the dogfish *Scyliorhinus canicula* to environmental hypoxia. *J. exp. Biol.* **69**, 233–245.

CAMERON, J. S. (1979). Autonomic nervous tone and regulation of heart rate in the goldfish, *Carassius auratus. Comp. Biochem. Physiol.* **63C**, 341–349.

CAMERON, J. N. & DAVIS, J. C. (1970). Gas exchange in rainbow trout with varying blood oxygen capacity. *J. Fish. Res. Bd. Canada.* **27**, 1069–1085.

CAPRA, M. F. & SATCHELL, G. H. (1977a). Adrenergic and cholinergic responses of the isolated saline-perfused heart of the elasmobranch fish, *Squalus acanthias. Gen. Pharmac.* **8**, 56–65.

CAPRA, M. F. & SATCHELL, G. H. (1977b). The adrenergic responses of isolated saline-perfused prebranchial arteries and gills of the elasmobranch *Squalus acanthias. Gen. Pharmac.* **8**, 67–71.

COOKE, I. C. R. (1980). Functional aspects of the morphology and vascular anatomy of the gills of the Endeavour dogfish *Centrophorus scalpratus* (McCulloch) (Elasmobranchii: Squalidae). *Zoomorphologie* **94**, 167–183.

DAXBOECK, C. & HOLETON, G. F. (1978). Oxygen receptors in the rainbow trout, *Salmo gairdneri. Can. J. Zool.* **56**, 1254–1259.

DEJOURS, P. (1975). *Principles of Comparative Respiratory Physiology*. New York: American Elsevier Publishing Co.

DE GRAAF, P. (1985). Mechanoreceptor activity in the gills of the carp. *Soc. exp. Biol. Leeds meeting* (poster).

DE KOCK, L. L. (1963). A histological study of the head region of two salmonids with special reference to pressor and chemoreceptors. *Acta anat.* **55**, 39–50.

DE VRIES, R. & DE JAGER, S. (1984). The gill in the spiny dogfish *Squalus acanthias*: respiratory and nonrespiratory function. *Am. J. Anat.* **169**, 1–29.

DUNEL, S. & LAURENT, P. (1980). Functional organisation of the gill vasculature in different classes of fish. In *Epithelial transport in the Lower Vertebrates*. (ed. B. Lahlou). Cambridge University Press.

ECLANCHER, B. & DEJOURS, P. (1975). Control de la respiration chez les Poissons teleosteens: existence de chemorecepteurs physiologiquement analogues aux chemorecepteurs des Vertebres superieurs. *C.r. Lebd. Séanc. Acad. Sci. Paris, Ser.* D. **280**, 451–453.

EDDY, F. B. (1974). Blood gases of the tench (*Tinca tinca*) in well-aerated and oxygen-deficient waters. *J. exp. Biol.* **60**, 71–83.

FARRELL, A. P., DAXBOECK, C. & RANDALL, D. J. (1979). The effect of input pressure and flow on the pattern and resistance to flow in the isolated perfused gill of a teleost fish. *J. comp. Physiol.* **133**, 233–240.

FARRELL, A. P., SOBIN, S. S., RANDALL, D. J. & CROSBY, S. (1980). Intralamellar blood flow patterns in fish gills. *Am. J. Physiol.* **239**, R428–436.

GRIGG, G. C. (1970a). Water flow through the gills of Port Jackson sharks. *J. exp. Biol.* **52**, 565–568.

GRIGG, G. C. (1970b). Use of the first gill slits for water intake in a shark. *J. exp. Biol.* **52**, 569–574.

HOLETON, G. F. (1970). Oxygen uptake and circulation by a haemoglobinless antarctic fish (*Chaenocephalus aceratus* Lomberg) compared with three red-blooded antarctic fish. *Comp. Biochem. Physiol.* **34**, 457–471.

HOLETON, G. F. & RANDALL, D. J. (1967). The effect of hypoxia upon the partial pressure of gases in the blood and water afferent and efferent to the gills of rainbow trout. *J. exp. Biol.* **46**, 317–327.

HOLMGREN, S. (1977). Regulation of the heart of a teleost, *Gadus morhua*, by autonomic nerves and circulating catecholamines. *Acta Physiol. Scand.* **99**, 62–74.

HUGHES, G. M. (1960). The mechanism of gill ventilation in the dogfish and skate. *J. exp. Biol.* **37**, 11–27.

HUGHES, G. M. (1964). Fish respiratory homeostasis. *Symp. Soc. exp. Biol.* **18**, 81–107.

HUGHES, G. M. (1972). The relationship between cardiac and respiratory rhythms in the dogfish, *Scyliorhinus canicula*. *J. exp. Biol.* **57**, 415–434.

HUGHES, G. M., KNIGHTS, B. & SCAMMELL, C. A. (1979). The distribution of P_{O_2} and hydrostatic pressure changes within the branchial chambers in relation to gill ventilation of the shore crab *Carcinus maenus* L. *J. exp. Biol.* **51**, 203–220.

HUGHES, G. M. & MORGAN, M. (1973). The structure of fish gills in relation to their respiratory function. *Biol. Rev.* **48**, 419–475.

HUGHES, G. M. & SHELTON, G. (1958). The mechanism of gill ventilation in three freshwater teleosts. *J. Exp. Biol.* **35**, 807–823.

HUGHES, G. M. & SHELTON, G. (1962). Respiratory mechanisms and their nervous control in fish. *Adv. comp. Physiol. Biochem.* **1**, 275–364.

JOHANSEN, K. (1971). Comparative physiology: gas exchange and circulation in fishes. *Ann. Rev. Physiol.* **33**, 569–612.

JOHANSEN, K., LENFANT, C. & MECKLENBERG, T. A. (1970). Respiration in the crab *Cancer magister*. *Z. vergl. Physiol.* **70**, 1–19.

JONES, D. R. (1971). Theoretical analysis of factors which may limit the maximum oxygen uptake of fish: the oxygen cost of the cardiac and branchial pumps. *J. theor. Biol.* **32**, 341–349.

JONES, D. R., LANGILLE, B. L., RANDALL, D. J. & SHELTON, G. (1974). Blood flow in dorsal and ventral aortas of the cod, *Gadus morhua*. *Am. J. Physiol.* **226**, 90–95.

Jones, J. R. E. (1952). The reactions of fish to water of low oxygen concentration. *J. exp. Biol.* **29**, 403–415.

Kuramoto, T. & Ebara, A. (1984). Neurohormonal modulation of the cardiac outflow through the cardioarterial valve in the lobster. *J. exp. Biol.* **111**, 123–130.

Laurent, P. (1967). La pseudobranchie des teleosteens: preuves electrophysiologique de ses fonctions chemoreceptrice et baroreceptrice. *C.r. Lebd. Séanc Acad. Sci., Paris, Ser D*, **264**, 1879–1882.

Laurent, P. & Dunel, S. (1980). Morphology of gill epithelia in fish. *Am. J. Physiol.* **238**, R147–159.

Levy, N. N., Iano, T. & Zieske, H. (1972). Effects of repetative bursts of vagal activity on heart rate. *Circ. Res.* **30**, 286–295.

Levy, N. N., Martin, P. J., Iano, T. & Zieske, H. (1969). Paradoxical effect of vagus nerve stimulation on heart rate in dogs. *Circ. Res.* **25**, 303–314.

Lutz, B. R. (1930). Reflex cardiac and respiratory inhibition in the elasmobranch *Scyllium canicula. Biol. Bull. mar. Lab., Woods Hole*, **59**, 170–178.

McMahon, B. R. & Wilkens, J. L. (1983). Ventilation, perfusion and oxygen uptake. In *Biology of Crustacea* Vol. 5. (ed. L. H. Mantel & D. E. Bliss), New York: Academic Press.

Meghji, P. & Burnstock, G. (1984). The effect of adenyl compounds on the heart of the dogfish, *Scyliorhinus canicula. Comp. Biochem. Physiol.* **77C**, 295–300.

Metcalfe, J. D. (1983). A reappraisal of the estimation of the oxygen partial pressure difference between blood and water across the gills of the dogfish (*Scyliorhinus canicula*). *J. Physiol. Lond.* **338**, 54P.

Metcalfe, J. D. & Butler, P. J. (1982). Differences between directly measured and calculated values for cardiac output in the dogfish: a criticism of the Fick method. *J. exp. Biol.* **99**, 255–268.

Metcalfe, J. D. & Butler, P. J. (1984a). Changes in activity and ventilation in response to hypoxia in unrestrained, unoperated dogfish (*Scyliorhinus canicula*). *J. exp. Biol.* **108**, 411–418.

Metcalfe, J. D. & Butler, P. J. (1984b). On the nervous regulation of gill blood flow in the dogfish (*Scyliorhinus canicula*). *J. exp. Biol.* **113**, 253–267.

Metcalfe, J. D. & Butler, P. J. (1985). The functional anatomy of the gills of the dogfish (*Scyliorhinus canicula*). *J. Zool. Lond.* (in press).

Nilsson, S. (1983). *Autonomic Nerve Function in the Vertebrates*. Berlin: Springer-Verlag.

Nonnotte, G. & Kirsch, R. (1978). La respiration cutanee chez un Selacien (*Scyliorhinus caniculus* L.). *C.r. Lebd. Séanc. Acad. Sci., Paris*. Ser.D. **286**, 1597–1599.

Piiper, J. & Scheid, P. (1975). Gas transport efficacy of gills, lungs and skin: theory and experimental data. *Respir. Physiol.* **23**, 209–221.

Piiper, J. & Schumann, D. (1967). Efficiency of O_2 exchange in the gills of the dogfish, *Scyliorhinus stellaris. Respir. Physiol.* **2**, 135–148.

Randall, D. J. (1966). The nervous control of cardiac activity in the tench (*Tinca tinca*) and the goldfish (*Carassius auratus*). *Physiol. Zool.* **39**, 185–192.

Randall, D. J. (1968). Functional morphology of the heart in fishes. *Am. Zool.* **8**, 179–189.

Randall, D. J. (1970). Gas exchange in fish. In *Fish Physiology* (ed. W. S. Hoar & D. J. Randall). New York: Academic Press.

Randall, D. J. (1982). The control of respiration and circulation in fish during exercise and hypoxia. *J. exp. Biol.* **100**, 275–288.

Randall, D. J. & Jones, D. R. (1973). The effect of deafferentation of the pseudobranch on the respiratory response to hypoxia of the trout (*Salmo gairdneri*). *Respir. Physiol.* **17**, 291–301.

Randall, D. J. & Shelton, G. (1963). The effects of changes in environmental gas concentrations on the breathing and heart rate of a teleost fish. *Comp. Biochem. Physiol.* **9**, 229–239.

SATCHELL, G. H. (1959). Respiratory reflexes in the dogfish. *J. exp. Biol.* **36**, 62–71.

SATCHELL, G. H. (1960). The reflex co-ordination of the heart beat with respiration in the dogfish. *J. exp. Biol.* **37**, 719–731.

SATCHELL, G. H. (1962). Intrinsic vasomotion in the dogfish gill. *J. exp. Biol.* **39**, 503–512.

SATCHELL, G. H. (1968). A neurological basis for the co-ordination of swimming with respiration in fish. *Comp. Biochem. Physiol.* **27**, 835–841.

SATCHELL, G. H. (1971). *Circulation in Fishes* Cambridge University Press.

SATCHELL, G. H. & WAY, H. K. (1962). Pharyngeal proprioceptors in the dogfish *Squalus acanthias* L. *J. exp. Biol.* **39**, 243–250.

SAUNDERS, S. R. L. & SUTTERLIN, A. M. (1971). Cardiac and respiratory responses to hypoxia in the sea raven, *Hemitripterus americanus*, and an investigation of possible control mechanisms. *J. Fish. Res. Bd. Canada.* **28**, 491–503.

SCHEID, P. & PIIPER, J. (1976). Quantitative functional analysis of branchial gas transfer: theory and application to *Scyliorhinus stellaris* (Elasmobranchii). In *Respiration of Amphibious Vertebrates* (ed. G. M. Hughes). New York: Academic Press.

SCHOENLEIN, K. (1895). Beobachtungen uber Blutkreislauf und Respiration bei einigen Fischen. *Z. Biol.* **32**, 511–547.

SHELTON, G. (1970). The regulation of breathing. In *Fish Physiology* Vol IV (ed. W. S. Hoar & D. J. Randall). New York. Academic Press.

SHORT, S., BUTLER, P. J. & TAYLOR, E. W. (1977). The relative importance of nervous, humoral and intrinsic mechanisms in the regulation of heart rate and stroke volume in the dogfish *Scyliorhinus canicula*. *J. exp. Biol.* **70**, 77–92.

SHORT, S., TAYLOR, E. W. & BUTLER, P. J. (1979). The effectiveness of oxygen transfer during normoxia and hypoxia in the dogfish (*Scyliorhinus canicula* L.) before and after cardiac vagotomy. *J. comp. Physiol.* **132**, 289–295.

SMITH, F. M. & DAVIE, P. S. (1984). Effects of sectioning cranial nerves IX and X on the cardiac response to hypoxia in the coho salmon, *Oncorhynchus kisutch. Can. J. Zool.* **62**, 766–768.

SMITH, F. M. & JONES, D. R. (1978). Localisation of receptors causing hypoxic bradycardia in trout (*Salmo gairdneri*) *Can. J. Zool.* **56**, 1260–1265.

SPYER, K. M. (1982). Central nervous integration of cardiovascular control. *J. exp. Biol.* **100**, 109–128.

STEEN, J. B. & KRUYSSE, A. (1964). The respiratory function of teleostean gills. *Comp. Biochem. Physiol.* **12**, 127–142.

SUTTERLIN, A. M. & SAUNDERS, R. L. (1969). Proprioceptors in the gills of teleosts. *Can. J. Zool.* **47**, 1209–1212.

TAYLOR, E. W. (1982). Control and co-ordination of ventilation and circulation in crustaceans: responses to hypoxia and exercise. *J. exp. Biol.* **100**, 289–319.

TAYLOR, E. W. & BARRETT, D. J. (1985a). Evidence of a respiratory role for the hypoxic bradycardia in the dogfish *Scyliorhinus canicula* L. *Comp. Biochem. Physiol.* **80A**, 99–102.

TAYLOR, E. W. & BARRETT, D. J. (1985b). Cardiorespiratory synchrony in unrestrained dogfish. (in preparation).

TAYLOR, E. W. & BUTLER, P. J. (1971). Some observations on the relationship between heart beat and respiratory movements in the dogfish *Scyliorhinus canicula* L. *Comp. Biochem. Physiol.* **39A**, 297–305.

TAYLOR, E. W. & BUTLER, P. J. (1982). Nervous control of heart rate: activity in the cardiac vagus of the dogfish. *J. Appl. Physiol.* **53**, 1330–1335.

TAYLOR, E. W., SHORT, S. & BUTLER, P. J. (1977). The role of the cardiac vagus in the response of the dogfish *Scyliorhinus canicula* to hypoxia. *J. exp. Biol.* **70**, 57–75.

TAYLOR, E. W., TYLER-JONES, R. & WHEATLY, M. G. (1985). The effects of aerial exposure on water balance and the distribution of body water in the freshwater crayfish *Austropotamobius pallipes* (Lereboullet). *J. comp. Physiol.* (submitted).

TAYLOR, E. W. & WHEATLY, M. G. (1980). Ventilation, heart rate and respiratory gas exchange in the crayfish *Austropotamobius pallipes* (Lereboullet) submerged in normoxic water and following 3 h exposure in air at 15 °C. *J. comp. Physiol.* **138**, 67–78.

TAYLOR, H. H. & GREENAWAY, P. (1979). The structure of the gills and lungs of the arid-zone crab, *Holthuisana* (*Austrothelphusa*) *transversa* (Brachyura-Sundathelphusidae) including observations on arterial vessels within the gills. *J. Zool. Lond.* **189**, 359–384.

TAYLOR, H. H. & GREENAWAY, P. (1984). The role of the gills and branchiostegites in gas exchange in a bimodally breathing crab, *Holthuisana transversa*: Evidence for a facultative change in the distribution of the respiratory circulation. *J. exp. Biol.* **111**, 103–121.

TAYLOR, H. H. & TAYLOR, E. W. (1985). Observations of valve-like structures and evidence for rectification of flow within the gill lamellae of the crab *Carcinus maenas* (L.). *Zoomorphology* (submitted).

TAYLOR, W., HOUSTON, A. H. & HORGAN, J. D. (1968). Development of a computer model simulating some aspects of cardiovascular-respiratory dynamics of salmonid fish. *J. exp. Biol.* **49**, 477–493.

THOMAS, H. J. (1954). The oxygen uptake of the lobster (*Homarus vulgaris* Edw.) *J. exp. Biol.* **31**, 228–251.

WHEATLY, M. G. & TAYLOR, E. W. (1981). The effect of progressive hypoxia on heart rate, ventilation, respiratory gas exchange and acid-base status in the crayfish *Austropotamobius pallipes*. *J. exp. Biol.* **92**, 125–141.

WILKENS, J. L. (1981). Respiratory and circulatory coordination in decapod crustaceans. In *Locomotion and Energetics in Arthropods* (ed. C. F. Herreid & C. R. Fourtner). New York: Plenum Press.

WOOD, C. M. (1974). A critical examination of the physical and adrenergic factors affecting blood flow through the gills of the rainbow trout. *J. exp. Biol.* **60**, 241–265.

WOOD, C. M., PIEPRZAK, P. & TROTT, J. N. (1979). The influence of temperature and anaemia on the adrenergic and cholinergic mechanisms controlling heart rate in the rainbow trout. *Can. J. Zool.* **57**, 2440–2447.

WOOD, C. M. & SHELTON, G. (1980). The reflex control of heart rate and cardiac output in the rainbow trout: interactive influences of hypoxia, haemorrhage, and systemic vasomotor tone. *J. exp. Biol.* **87**, 271–284.

WRIGHT, D. E. (1973). The structure of the gills of the elasmobranch *Scyliorhinus canicula Z. Zellforsch. mikrosk. Anat.* **144**, 489–509.

YOUNG, R. E. & COYER, P. E. (1979). Phase co-ordination in the cardiac and ventilatory rhythms of the lobster *Homarus americanus*. *J. exp. Biol.* **82**, 53–74.

YOUNG, J. Z. (1933). The autonomic nervous system of selachians. *Q.J. microsc. Sci.* **75**, 571–624.

YOUNG, J. Z. (1936). The innervation and reactions to drugs of the viscera of teleostean fish. *Proc. R. Soc. Lond. Ser.* B. **120**, 303–318.

Printed in Great Britain © Society for Experimental Biology 1985

CIRCULATING RESPIRATORY PIGMENTS IN MARINE ANIMALS

ANDRE TOULMOND *

Université Pierre-et-Marie-Curie, Paris and Station Biologique, Roscoff, France

Summary of Contents

* *Reprint request*: Laboratoire de Biologie et Physiologie marines, Université Paris VI, Bâtiment A, 4 place Jussieu, F–75230 Paris Cedex 05, France.

I. Introduction

Most animals depend on aerobic metabolism for their energy supplies and the maintenance of this process involves the constant flow of oxygen from its source in the external medium to the sites of utilization in the mitochondria. The evolution from a unicellular ancestor of large, active, multicellular animals composed of complex and fragile organs, and with a high and regulated body temperature, was possible only in so far as the problem of continuous transport of increasingly large quantities of oxygen was resolved (see Dejours, 1981).

Three solutions to this problem coexist among modern animal species, probably corresponding to three successive stages in the evolution of transport mechanisms. In the very small organisms, the mitochondria are separated from the external medium by such a short distance that passive diffusion alone satisfies the metabolic oxygen requirements. Certain recent hypotheses suggest that this process may have operated in the large organisms with a characteristic leaf-like structure that once constituted the Ediacarian fauna (see Cloud & Glaessner, 1982; Seilacher, *in* Lewin, 1984). The evolutionary failure of these aquatic Metazoa, which seem to have disappeared leaving no descendants, is perhaps related to the fact that strictly diffusive oxygen transfer is only really efficient in an air environment. It is utilized successfully by the arthropods whose tracheal system reduces the distance separating the external medium and the deepest mitochondria to less than one micrometer. The fact that the largest arachnids and insects are relatively small clearly indicates that even under these conditions, simple diffusion soon reaches the limits of its possibilities.

In most phyla, diffusion is therefore complemented by a convective transport of oxygen. Once the gas has crossed the more or less complex and specialized exchange surface (epidermis, lining of digestive cavity, gills, lungs), it dissolves in a physiological fluid set in motion by a variety of anatomical structures ensuring oxygen distribution to the organs. Provided that the metabolic activity is not too great, this type of system may be sufficiently effective to cover the requirements of large and quite complex organisms such as certain fish.

This efficacy is limited, however, by the very low solubility of oxygen in physiological fluids. The surface area of the exchange surfaces, the volume of the carrier fluid, the size and power of the pumps ensuring its displacement, cannot increase indefinitely. The appearance in this fluid of metalloproteins, usually coloured and capable of reversibly binding molecular oxygen, constitutes evolution's final response to the problem of cellular oxygen supply. These 'respiratory pigments' are said to be 'circulating' because they are found in one or several of the organism's extracellular fluid compartments. They may be contrasted with the non-circulating respiratory pigments, only briefly mentioned here, which are localized in the cells of various fixed organs: muscles (myoglobins, myohaemerythrins), nervous system, ovaries, eggs (see Schindelmeiser, Kuhlmann & Nolte, 1979; Ochs, Ochs & Burton, 1980; Ruppert & Travis, 1983; Durliat, 1984; Schreiber & Parkhurst, 1984).

The marine fauna are much more varied than the terrestrial since, unlike the latter, they include representatives of all the known phyla (see Sverdrup, Johnson & Fleming, 1942). Amongst these phyla there is such a diversity of circulating respiratory pigments that to discuss them involves reviewing practically the whole category of these proteins. As in addition the study of respiratory pigments has considerably intensified over the last twenty years, an exhaustive bibliographic analysis like those of Manwell (1960*a*) and Prosser (1973) is impossible within the limits of this essay. This synopsis will therefore be restricted to the most recent findings concerning the structures, properties and adaptations of the circulating respiratory pigments, with special attention to those of marine animals. More details will be found in the text references; the numerous recent partial reviews by Klotz, Klippenstein & Hendrickson (1976), Wells & Dales (1976), Antonini & Chiancone (1977), Weber (1978), Chung & Ellerton (1979), Lontie & Gielens (1979), Vinogradov, Shlom, Kapp & Frossard (1980), Vinogradov, Kapp & Ohtsuki (1982), Van Holde & Miller (1982), Toulmond & Truchot (1982), Ellerton, Ellerton & Robinson (1983), Perutz (1983), Klotz & Kurtz (1984) and Ghidalia (1984); the monographs of Fermi & Perutz (1981), Imai (1982) and Dickerson & Geis (1983); and several 'Symposium Volumes': Bannister (1977), Wood (1980), Lamy & Lamy (1981), Bonaventura, Bonaventura & Tesh (1982) and Wood (1983). The rarer reviews concerning the more strictly physiological aspects of the problem include Johansen & Weber (1976), Mangum (1976 *a,b,* 1980, 1982, 1983*a*), Weber (1978, 1980, 1982) and Bonaventura & Bonaventura (1980).

II. Localization and distribution

The anatomical localization of circulating respiratory pigments is extremely variable. The pigments are found in the blood of a closed circulatory system (nemerteans, annelids, phoronids, cephalopods and vertebrates) or in the haemolymph of an open circulatory system (arthropods and most molluscs). In these organisms, pulsatile organs located along the course of the vessels ensure that the blood or haemolymph circulates in a more or less perfectly one-way manner. Circulating respiratory pigments may also be found in the coelomic fluid (in certain annelids, sipunculids, echiuroids and priapulids); here, there is a mixing, not a true circulation. The peristaltic contractions of the body wall ensure the renewal of the oxygen-carrying fluid at the exchange organ and at the utilizing organ. Usually, mixing is improved by the activity of cilia covering the coelomic cavity walls. In certain echinoderms, a respiratory pigment circulates in the water-vascular and haemal systems derived from the coelomic compartment. In some nematodes, a pigment may be found in the perivisceral cavity directly derived from the embryonic blastocoele.

Apart from this diversity in the nature and embryonic origin of the fluid compartment, the pigment may also be localized in two ways in the compartment. Intracellular pigment is contained in cells suspended in the fluid (blood corpuscles, erythrocytes, coelomocytes); extracellular pigment is dissolved in the fluid (see Table 1 and 2).

In a given animal two different pigments may be found in two anatomically distinct compartments. This frequently occurs in the sipunculids

Table 1. *Distribution of circulating respiratory pigments in marine animals*

1) Haem pigments	
Haemoglobins	Nemertines, polychaete annelids, echiuroids, phoronids, bivalves, ophiuroids, holothuroids, vertebrates.
Erythrocruorins	Annelids, pogonophorans, entomostracan crustaceans, bivalves.
Chlorocruorins	4 polychaete annelid families (sabellids, serpulids, flabelligerids, ampharetids).
2) Haemocyanins	Molluscs (amphineurans, gastropods, cephalopods), arthropods (*Sacculina*, malacostracan crustaceans, xiphosurans).
3) Haemerythrins	Polychaete annelids of the genus *Magelona*, sipunculids, priapulids, brachiopods).

Table 2. *Main characteristics of the three classes of circulating respiratory pigments*

Class	Haem pigments	Haemocyanins	Haemerythrins
Colour* deoxy	purple red	colourless	colourless
oxy	bright red	blue	violet-pink
Metal	Fe	Cu	Fe
Metal:O_2	Fe:O_2	2Cu:O_2	2Fe:O_2
Pigment deoxy-	Fe^{2+}	Cu^+	Fe^{2+}
oxy-	Fe^{2+}	Cu^{2+}	Fe^{3+}
Localization†	IC or EC	EC	IC
Frequency‡	33%	9%	4%

* in concentrated solutions
† IC: intracellular; EC: extracellular
‡ % of total number of living animal classes (see Mayr, Linsley & Usinger, 1953)

and in the polychaete annelids. An extreme example is provided by the polychaete *Serpula vermicularis*, whose blood contains two different extracellular pigments (see Terwilliger, 1978).

The distribution of circulating respiratory pigments in the different groups of marine animals does not seem to follow any logical rule. All the representatives of many groups, including some of the most important, lack pigments altogether, for instance all marine protozoans, all poriferans, cnidarians, ctenophorans, bryozoans, chaetognaths, hemichordates, tunicates (haemovanadin does not exist, see Macara, McLeod & Kustin, 1979; Balwin, McCabe & Thomas, 1984) and cephalochordates. It is also the case for most bivalves. In the echinoderms, a pigment has been found only in a few holothurians and ophiurans. In the annelids and crustaceans, the distribution of a pigment within the different orders, families or even genera, often seems apparently to be completely random. Also, several different circulating respiratory pigments may coexist within a given group (the annelids for example, Table 1). The phylum *Vertebrata* is doubly exceptional: all its members, save a few very rare exceptions, possess i) a circulating respiratory pigment ii) of one same class and structural type.

III. Classification

Circulating (and non-circulating) respiratory pigments may be divided into three classes corresponding each to a different structure of the site reversibly combining with the oxygen molecule (Table 2).

A) *Haem pigments*

The active site consists of a single iron atom in the ferrous state (Fe^{2+}), whether the pigment is oxygenated or not. The iron atom is coordinated with the four nitrogen atoms of a tetrapyrrole ring (the iron porphyrin nucleus) and a histidine residue of the globin polypeptide chain. Haem pigments are always dichroic: concentrated solutions are red and dilute solutions are yellow, except for the chlorocruorins, so named by Lankester (1868) because of their green colour, which is related to the replacement of one of the two vinyl residues ($CH = CH$) of the haem by a formyl residue (CHO) (Fischer & Von Seemann, 1936). Although haem pigments vary widely in molecular structure, they have similar spectrophotometric properties, as the absorption bands in the visible part of the spectrum are related to the presence of the haem group (see Prosser, 1973). Haem pigments are able to fix small molecules other than oxygen (see Dickerson & Geis, 1983), for instance carbon monoxide for which they have an extraordinarily high affinity. Haem pigments are by far the most widely distributed pigments in the living world in general and among marine animals in particular (Table 1 and 2). Two subclasses of this heterogeneous group may be provisionally identified: i) the haemoglobins, always localized in circulating cells, and which should be distinguished from myoglobins and other non-circulating intracellular haem pigments; ii) the erythrocruorins and chlorocruorins, a very heterogeneous subclass including all the extracellular circulating haem pigments.

B) *Haemocyanins*

The active site consists of two copper atoms in the cuprous state (Cu^+) in the deoxygenated molecule. Recent findings suggest that the two copper atoms are in the cupric state (Cu^{2+}) in the oxygenated molecule (see Wilson *et al.*, 1981). The two copper atoms are coordinated with six amino acids of the polypeptide chain carrying the active site and, in the spiny lobster, these are thought to be six histidine residues (Gaykema *et al.*, 1984). Haemocyanin solutions are deep blue when the pigment is oxygenated and colourless when it is reduced. They can bind with carbon monoxide, although their affinity for this gas is much less than that of the haem pigments, and the nature of the CO-binding mechanism is still uncertain (Van Holde & Miller, 1982; Ellerton *et al.*, 1983). The haemocyanins are much less widely distributed than the haem pigments (Table 1 and 2).

C) *Haemerythrins*

The active site consists of two iron atoms in the ferrous state (Fe^{2+}) in the deoxygenated pigment, and in the ferric state (Fe^{3+}) when the pigment is combined with oxygen. These two iron atoms are coordinated with at least five histidines, a glutamate and an aspartate of the polypeptide chain (Klotz & Kurtz, 1984). Haemerythrin solutions are coloured violet–pink when the pigment is oxygenated and colourless when it is deoxygenated. Heamerythrins do not combine with carbon monoxide. These rare pigments are found only in marine animals, in zoological groups of minor importance (Table 1 and 2).

IV. Molecular structure

The molecular structure of each of the three classes of circulating respiratory pigments is far from homogeneous. The intracellular, low relative molecular mass pigments are conventionally contrasted with the extracellular, high relative molecular mass pigments (Table 3). The quaternary structure of the respiratory pigments is now well-enough known to permit another grouping and to demonstrate, on the one hand, the structural heterogeneity of classes with the same active site and, on the other, the presence of structural features shared by molecules of different classes. I propose to classify provisionally the circulating respiratory pigments into three structural types, irrespective of the constitution of the active site: i) *protomeric pigments* in which the native molecule is composed of protomers; ii) *heteromeric pigments* in which the native molecule is composed of protomers *and* polypeptide chains not carrying an active site; iii) *multidomain pigments* in which the native molecule is composed of multidomain polypeptide chains, each with several active sites (Table 3).

A) *Protomeric pigments*

The native molecule is composed of protomers, each protomer being operationally defined as a single polypeptide chain carrying a single active site. The protomers are in most cases assembled non-covalently and weakly linked by salt bridges, Van der Waals forces or hydrogen bonds. They may therefore be separated with a detergent (such as sodium dodecyl sulphate, SDS), urea, highly concentrated salt solutions, a chelating agent such as EDTA, or alkaline solutions. The circulating intracellular pigments haemoglobin and haemerythrin and the arthropod haemocyanins belong to this first type.

Table 3. *Molecular structure of circulating respiratory pigments*

Item	Relative molecular mass $\times 10^{-3}$	Mean protein weight *per* O_2-binding site $\times 10^{-3}$	Type	Number of protomers*	Number of polypeptides without O_2-binding site	Number of multidomain polypeptides†	Number of domains *per* polypeptide
A) INTRACELLULAR PIGMENTS							
Haemoglobins	14–130	14–17	Protomeric	1-2-4-8-(n)	0	0	0
Haemerythrins	40–110	12–15	Protomeric	2-3-4-8	0	0	0
B) EXTRACELLULAR PIGMENTS							
Haemocyanins (arthropods)	400–3,000	75	Protomeric	6-12-24-48	0	0	0
Erythro- + Chlorocruorins (annelids, pogonophorans)	3,000–4,000	21–30	Heteromeric	12×12?	12×6?	0	0
Haemocyanins (molluscs)	3,500–9,000	50	Multidomain	0	0	10–20	8
Erythrocruorins (molluscs)	1,700–12,000	15–20	Multidomain	0	0	10–40	10–20
Erythrocruorins (crustaceans)	250	17	Multidomain	0	0	2	7–8

* one protomer=one polypeptide bearing one O_2-binding site
† one multidomain polypeptide=one polypeptide bearing more than one O_2-binding site

(1) *Haemoglobins* are small intracellular molecules existing as monomers, dimers, tetramers, octomers and, in some cases, n-mers of a protomer of relative molecular mass (M_r) 14 to 17×10^3. The tetrameric haemoglobin of mammals, a typical example, is composed of two α and two β protomers. Haemoglobins are found in the blood of certain nemerteans (see Poluhowich, 1970) and phoronids (Garlick, Williams & Riggs, 1979), in the haemolymph of certain bivalves (see Furuta & Kajita, 1983; Terwilliger, Terwilliger & Arp, 1983) and in the water-vascular system of numerous holothurians and two ophiurans (see Foettinger, 1880; Hajduk & Cosgrove, 1975; Terwilliger, 1980). They are present in the coelomocytes in representatives of five families of polychate annelids (*Glyceridae, Terebellidae, Ophelidae, Capitellidae,* and *Cirratulidae*) and in the echiuroids (see Weber, 1978). Erythrocytes or blood corpuscles of all adult vertebrates contain haemoglobin, with the notable exception of several species of ice-fishes (family *Chaenichthyidae*) which lack a blood respiratory pigment (Ruud, 1954; Johnston *et al.*, 1983).

Although vertebrate haemoglobin nearly always has a tetrameric structure, invertebrate haemoglobin may assume a wide variety of aggregation states. In the annelid genus *Glycera*, for example, mono-, di-, tetra-, octa-, and n-meric haemoglobin is found in different species. The structure of a protomer, however, is very similar to that of vertebrate haemoglobins. The tertiary structure of the monomeric haemoglobin of *G. dibranchiata*, for example, is very close to that of mammalian myoglobin and haemoglobin protomers. There is a 45 % sequence homology between its amino acid sequence and that of the haemoglobin of the cyclostome, *Petromyzon*, sperm-whale myoglobin, and the α and β chains of human haemoglobin. Such homology is not, however, the general rule. For example, the amino acid sequence of the haemoglobin of the terebellid *Enoplobranchus* is quite different not only from that of the lamprey and mammalian haemoglobins, but also from that of *G. dibranchiata* and two other terebellids, *Pista pacifica* and *Thelepus crispus*, suggesting that polychaete annelid haemoglobins may have multiple origins. Thus considerable caution is required if haemoglobin sequence homologies are used to determine possible phylogenetic relations within or between zoological groups (see Weber, 1978).

(2) *Haemerythrins* are small, intracellular molecules, existing as dimers, trimers, tetramers and above all octomers of a protomer with a M_r of between 12 and 15×10^3 (Ward, Hendrickson & Klippenstein, 1975; Klotz *et al.*, 1976; Klippenstein, 1980; Sieker *et al.*, 1981; Smith, Hendrickson & Addison, 1983). Haemerythrins are found in nucleated or non-nucleated cells which are suspended in the blood and/or coelomic

fluid of the sipunculids, in the coelomic fluid of the few priapulids that have been examined and of the brachiopods *Lingula* and *Glottidia* (Weber & Fänge, 1980) and in the blood of the polychaete annelids of the genus *Magelona* (see Wells & Dales, 1974; Weber, 1978). The tertiary and quaternary structure and the amino acid sequence of several haemerythrins are now known in detail (Klippenstein, 1980).

(3) *Arthropod haemocyanins*, always extracellular, have been demonstrated in the haemolymph of numerous arachnids (spiders, scorpions, *Uropygi, Amblypygi*), the limulids and a myriapod. Haemocyanins in crustaceans have been identified in the decapods, stomatopods, numerous isopods, a few amphipods, in the *Mysidacea* (see Ellerton *et al.*, 1983; Ghidalia, 1984) and, recently, in the cirriped parasite *Sacculina carcini* (Herberts & de Frescheville, 1981). Native arthropod haemocyanin molecules, of moderate to giant size, comprise an assembly of 6, 12, 24 or 48 protomers with an average relative molecular mass of approximately 75×10^3. The kidney-shaped protomer may be obtained by alkaline dissociation in the presence of EDTA of the basic unit common to all the arthropods, a hexamer formed by two layers of three protomers arranged in two alternate triangles (see Ellerton & Ellerton, 1982). This hexamer constitutes the native molecule of the haemocyanin of the spiny lobster, the isopod *Bathynomus giganteus*, and the shrimp *Penaeus setiferus*. Dodecamers (12-mers) composed of two hexamers in a staggered parallel arrangement are the native molecule in the haemolymph of the stomatopods, the isopod *Ligia exotica* and most of the decapod crustaceans. Thalassinid crustaceans and arachnids have 24-mers formed of two 12-mers in an antiparallel arrangement. The most highly aggregated molecule, found in the horseshoe crabs (*Xiphosura*), is a 48-mers structure with a M_r of approximately 3000×10^3. In a given species, there are generally several different polypeptide chains, each corresponding to a different protomer. The greater the degree of aggregation of the native molecule, the larger the number of different types of protomers. For example, six different protomers are found in the spiny lobster and 18 in the horseshoe crab. *In vitro* reassociation experiments show that the exact proportions of the different protomers must be respected to obtain the reassembly of molecules (see Bonaventura & Bonaventura, 1980; Van Holde & Miller, 1982; Ellerton *et al.*, 1983; Lamy *et al.*, 1983; Ghidalia, 1984). In some haemocyanins, a dimer composed of two disulphide-linked protomers has been isolated. Among the protomeric pigments, this dimer represents the sole known example of a covalent association between two protomers, which can therefore be separated only by the action of a reducing agent such as mercaptoethanol.

In a very few cases, it has been shown that such a dimer was necessary to obtain, *in vitro*, the reassociation of protomers into 12- or 24-mers (see Murray & Jeffrey, 1974; Jeffrey, Shaw & Treacy, 1978; Ellerton *et al.*, 1983; Pilz *et al.*, 1980; Rochu & Fine, 1984).

B) *Heteromeric pigments*

Erythrocruorins of the *Annelida* (*Polychaeta, Oligochaeta* and *Achaeta*) and probably the *Pogonophora* on the one hand, and the chlorocruorins on the other, constitute the heteromeric haem pigments which are always extracellular and are dissolved in the blood and/or the coelomic fluid. The M_r of the native molecule ranges from 3000 to 4000×10^3, corresponding to a sedimentation coefficient of approximately 60 S. Electron micrographs show each molecule as having a hexagonal structure of two superimposed rings, each formed of six polyhedric subunits with a M_r of approximately 300×10^3. In at least two polychaete annelid genera, *Nephthys* and *Oenone*, an additional subunit seems to fill the apparently empty space which is normally found in the centre of the hexagonal double ring. All the subunits seem to be the same, as dissociation at alkaline pH yields particles with a sedimentation coefficient of about 10 S, corresponding to one-twelfth of the native molecule (see Terwilliger, Terwilliger & Schabtach, 1976; Wells & Dales, 1976; Antonini & Chiancone, 1977; Weber, 1978; Chung & Ellerton, 1979; Garlik, 1980; Terwilliger, 1980; Terwilliger, Terwilliger & Schabtach, 1980; Vinogradov *et al.*, 1980; Vinogradov *et al.*, 1982).

Another common feature of heteromeric pigments is that to each haem there corresponds a protein weight between 21 and 30×10^3, much greater than the typical 14 to 17×10^3 of haemoglobin protomers. The dissociation of the subunits by SDS gives several types of polypeptide chains, some of which seem not to carry an active site. Finally, subunit dissociation by SDS in the presence of a reducing agent such as mercapto-ethanol shows that each is composed of i) non-covalently linked protomers, of M_r between 14 and 16×10^3, similar to that of haemoglobin protomers; ii) polypeptide chains without an active site, of M_r between 16 and 31×10^3, covalently linked together or with certain protomers by disulphide bridges. These chains, whose existence has been questioned (Garlik, 1980) may give cohesion to the subunit, although they perhaps have other functions as well. It seems, for instance, that the native molecule is assembled via these polypeptides. It is also possible that they play a role similar to that of the enzymatic systems in the vertebrate red blood cells which prevent the irreversible oxidation of the iron atom at the active site of the haemoglobin. Numerous but perhaps premature models have been proposed to describe the structure of the native molecule of heteromeric pigments (see Waxman, 1975; Chung & Ellerton, 1979; Pionetti & Pouyet, 1980; Frossard, 1982; Hendrickson, 1983).

C) *Multidomain pigments*

This class groups together the molluscan haemocyanins and the erythro-cruorins of the molluscs (gastropods and bivalves) and branchiopod crustaceans. They are all extracellular, in solution in the haemolymph. Their M_r varies enormously, between 220 and $12\,000 \times 10^3$, although under the electron microscope the native pigment molecule always has the shape of a disc or cylinder. The dissociation of the native molecule in alkali or SDS always gives polypeptide chains which carry from two to 20 active sites, corresponding to the same number of polypeptide 'domains' linked together, end to end, by covalent peptide bonds. The different domains may therefore only be separated by gentle proteolysis (see Lontie & Gielens, 1979; Bonaventura & Bonaventura, 1980; Van Bruggen, 1980; Van Holde & Miller, 1982; Ellerton *et al.*, 1983; Terwilliger & Terwilliger, 1983).

(1) *Molluscan haemocyanin* structure has been mostly studied in the gastropods. The main features of the description below probably also apply to the cephalopod haemocyanins which have not been so thoroughly investigated. In the gastropods (for example, *Helix*), the native molecule has a M_r of 9000×10^3, corresponding to a sedimentation coefficient of 100 S. It is a hollow cylinder which is partially closed at both ends by a 'collar'. In an alkaline medium and in the absence of Ca^{2+} and Mg^{2+}, the molecule may be cleaved into two halves, then into tenths and finally into twentieths which, under the electron microscope, look like strings of beads. The tenths correspond to two polypeptide chains which are linked by non-covalent bonds near their C-terminal ends. Each twentieth corresponds to a single polypeptide chain with a M_r of approximately 450×10^3, carrying eight active sites distributed in as many unequal, dissimilar domains, each representing 50×10^3 of protein. These domains cannot be further separated from each others without specific proteolytic treatments. Two of the eight domains are part of the collar and the six others part of the wall of the cylinder comprising the half-molecule. The collar domains are indispensable for the formation of the complete molecule and if they are removed by gentle trypsinolysis, the cylinders associate *in vitro* into long tubular polymers (see Lontie & Gielens, 1979).

In the cephalopods, the native molecule is smaller. Its M_r, between

3500 and 3750 × 10^3, is much less than that of the gastropod haemocyanin half-molecule (4350 × 10^3). At alkaline pH and in the absence of divalent cations, it too dissociates into 'multi-domain' polypeptide chains (see Bonaventura, Bonaventura, Miller & Van Holde, 1981).

(2) *Molluscan erythrocruorins* are found in the haemolymph of some of the freshwater pulmonate gastropods of the genera *Planorbis* and *Helisoma* and the bivalves of the families *Astartidae* and *Carditidae*. They have a M_r of between 1700 and 2000 × 10^3 (gastropods) or between 8000 and 12 000 × 10^3 (bivalves). The native molecules may be dissociated into giant polypeptide chains of M_r between 175 and 320 × 10^3 carrying 10 to 20 active sites (haems) corresponding to as many domains, each representing 15 to 17 × 10^3 protein. As in molluscan haemocyanins, these domains are linked together by covalent peptide linkages which seem to be heterogeneous, with very different susceptibilities to proteolysis (see Terwilliger & Terwilliger, 1978; Terwilliger, Terwilliger & Schabtach, 1978; Yager *et al.*, 1982; Terwilliger & Terwilliger, 1983).

(3) *Crustacean erythrocruorins* are found in the haemolymph of numerous species and, in particular, in freshwater and brackish-water branchiopods. The quaternary structure of these molecules is now becoming understood (Moens & Kondo, 1978; Van den Branden, D'Hondt, Moens & Decleir, 1978; Dangott & Terwilliger, 1980; Geelen *et al.*, 1982; Wolf, Van Pachtenbeke, Moens & Van Hauwaert, 1983; Daniel, 1983). The native molecule has a M_r of between 230 and 800 × 10^3 depending on the genus examined. It may be dissociated into two to 24 polypeptide chains each carrying two (*Lepidurus*) to eight (*Artemia*) active sites which correspond, here too, to as many domains separable only by proteolysis. Each domain represents from 14 to 23 × ^{3} protein, so that in certain cases the quantity of protein associated with the haem may be greater than for other haem pigments described above. Some of the values found, however, may be erroneous, as proteolysis yielded fragments which may not have corresponded to a whole number of domains (see Terwilliger & Terwilliger, 1983; Ghidalia, 1984).

D) *Comments*

A certain number of circulating respiratory pigments have been described that do not fit any of the three structural types discussed above: i) in the native erythrocruorin molecule dissolved in the perivisceral cavity fluid of the nematode parasite *Ascaris lumbricoides,* the subunit has a M_r of approximately 40 × 10^3 (see Terwilliger, 1980). If each subunit is a protomer, this pigment belongs to the first type, although it differs from all the other haem pigments in that the amount of protein associated with each haem group is more than twice the general average. So far, there is no evidence that this pigment is heteromeric or multidomain in type; ii) the erythrocytes of the bivalve *Barbatia reeveana* contain, apart from a normal tetrameric haemoglobin, a haem pigment with a M_r of approximately 430×10^3, made up of subunits with a M_r of approximately 34×10^3. Each subunit is composed of a polypeptide chain carrying two haems. This is the only known intracellular multidomain pigment (see Grinich & Terwilliger, 1980; Terwilliger & Terwilliger, 1983); iii) the native erythrocruorin molecule dissolved in the haemolymph of the larva of the dipteran *Chironomus* is composed of monomers or dimers of a protomer whose M_r is 14 to 17×10^3. The tertiary structure of this protomer and 20 % of its amino acid sequence are identical to those of sperm-whale myoglobin (see Terwilliger, 1980; Goodman, Braunitzer, Kleinschmidt & Aschauer, 1983). This is the only known extracellular haem pigment with the protomeric molecular structure of a haemoglobin (intracellular in our definition).

V. Multiple and polymorphic circulating pigments

The class and structural type of the circulating respiratory pigment are identical in all individuals of the same species. In many cases, however, the pigment is not homogeneous, and is present in several different molecular forms in the same individual (multiple pigments or isopigments), as may be demonstrated by simple electrophoretic techniques. Very often these multiple pigment systems are polymorphic, and the distribution of isopigments may differ from one individual to another. These isopigments generally have complementary functional properties, and it is generally accepted that the existence of a multiple, and in some cases polymorphic, pigment system represents an adaptive response enabling an efficient oxygen transport in an internal and/or external environment whose physicochemical characteristics vary (see Powers, 1980).

A) *Intracellular pigments*

Multiple haemoglobin systems are found in the erythrocytes of nearly all vertebrates. In the homeotherms, mammals and birds, there are few isohaemoglobins and a single component predominates. The number of components is larger in the reptiles and amphibians. It is maximum in the fishes where up to 25 different haemoglobins may be found in a single species (see Riggs, 1970; Powers, 1974, 1980; Bonaventura, Bonaventura & Sullivan, 1975; Perez & Maclean, 1976). Among seawater fishes, the toadfish *Opsanus tau* provides an excellent example. In the populations studied, 16 isohaemoglobins were identified, and six principal phenotypes none of which had a frequency greater than 0·27 (Fyhn & Sullivan, 1974). Bivalves (see Read, 1965; Djangmah, Gabbott & Wood, 1978; Como & Thompson, 1980) and annelids also have multiple haemoglobin systems. The haemoglobins of *Glycera dibranchiata* and *Glycera gigantea*, for example, are very heterogeneous, include five and six main components, respectively, and are probably polymorphic (see Weber, 1978).

Numerous multiple haemerythrin systems are also known. The trimeric coelomic haemerythrin of the sipunculid *Phascolosoma agassizii* is a mixture of 10 different molecular species, assembled from three different protomers. In *Phascolosoma lurco*, 20 different trimers may be separated, indicating that there are at least four types of protomer (see Klippenstein, 1980).

B) *Extracellular pigments*

Intact extracellular pigment molecules are probably at least as heterogeneous as the haemoglobins and haemerythrins. The higher the M_r of the pigment, however, the harder it is to demonstrate heterogeneity. Among the erythrocruorins, it is known that in the dipteran *Chironomus thummi thummi*, the hemolymph of the larva contains 12 different components: five are monomers, six are homodimers and the 12th is either a monomer or a homodimer (see Goodman *et al.*, 1983). The haemolymph of the branchiopod *Artemia salina* contains three different erythrocruorins, in proportions which vary with the age and sex of the individual examined (see Heip, Moens, Joniau & Kondo, 1978). Evidence for heterogeneity of annelid and molluscan erythrocruorins is practically non-existent.

As for the haemocyanins, it has long been known that snails' haemolymph contains several different molecular species. In *Helix pomatia* for example, haemocyanins α_1, α_2, β_s and β_c have been isolated (see Van Holde & Miller, 1982). Arthropod multiple haemocyanin systems may exist, as in strongly suggested by the demonstration of considerably heterogeneous protomers making up the native pigment molecules. For instance, each of the six protomers of the hexameric haemocyanin molecule in the spiny lobster has a different structure. In the horseshoe crab, the 48-meric pigment molecule is composed of at least 18 different protomers. Studies of decapod crustaceans suggest that these multiple subunit systems are also polymorphic (see Bonaventura *et al.*, 1975; Lamy *et al.*, 1981; Van Holde & Miller, 1982).

V. Origins of circulating respiratory pigments

The question of the origin and evolution of the circulating respiratory pigments is an extremely speculative one, to which exceedingly tentative answers may be given, until more is known about the primary and tertiary structures of these proteins, in particular the erythrocruorins and haemocyanins.

Since the structure of the active sites of the haem pigments, the haemocyanins and the haemerythrins is completely different, it seems probable that they do not have the same biochemical origin, and that they have appeared separately and evolved independently at the same time as the animal kingdom. It is generally believed that the circulating polymeric haem pigments, which are the most widespread, have as their common ancestor a monomeric intracellular myoglobin-like respiratory pigment derived, like cytochromes, cytochrome oxidases, catalases and peroxidases, from a more ancient haem protein (Wald & Allen, 1957). Considering intracellular localization of haemoglobin is the primitive state, certain authors believe that the erythrocruorins and chlorocruorins evolved secondarily, and that their particularly complex quaternary structure was selected for as an adaptation to the more severe constraints of the extracellular medium (Lehmann & Huntsman, 1961). Such constraints might also be responsible for the structure of the always extracellular haemocyanins which are supposed to derive, like tyrosinases, from a tyrosinase-like common ancestor protein (see Van Holde & Miller, 1982). According to these authors, the divergence between the protomeric haemocyanins of the arthropods and the multidomain haemocyanins of the molluscs would have occurred very early on, with the latter pigments the result of a preliminary massive gene multiplication which enabled the synthesis of giant multidomain polypeptides. Multidomain erythrocruorins in the molluscs and crustaceans may also have appeared by a similar mechanism.

The origins of the haemerythrins are even more obscure. Recent analysis of the protomers' structure suggest that they may be more closely related to the haemoglobins than has been thought (Sippl, 1983). The rarity of this type of pigment, its apparently residual distribution in a few primitive zoological groups with only a small number of species, suggest that it was a very early molecular configuration that did not have the evolutionary success of the other classes of respiratory pigments. The reason for its relative failure can perhaps be found in some intrinsic lack of plasticity of the molecule. The haemerythrins, unlike the haem pigments and haemocyanins, do not seem to be true allosteric molecules: the homotropic interactions are usually slight or null, and there is never any Bohr effect or Haldane effect (see below, section VII). On the other hand, the effects of temperature on the oxygen affinity are so considerable that the haemerythrin in animals living in temperate regions has been suggested to play a role in oxygen transport during only part of the year (Mangum, 1976*a*).

VII. Oxygen-binding properties

The characteristics of the reversible binding of a circulating respiratory pigment with oxygen should be such that the pigment may transport a sufficient quantity of this gas from the external medium to the tissues. The efficiency of this transfer, the flow economy of the carrier fluid, is related first to the potential quantity of combined oxygen in the circulating fluid, O_2-binding capacity or $C_{xO_2}^{max}$, which ultimately depends on the fluid's concentration of active sites. It is also related to the effective capacity for loading these sites in the gas-exchange organs and unloading them in the organs consuming oxygen. This double capacity is revealed by the pigment's oxygen saturation curve shape and its position in relation to various Po_2 values.

The shape of the curve is determined either by the absence (hyperbolic curve) or presence (sigmoid curve) of steric 'homotropic' interactions of facilitation occurring between the different active sites of the molecule, empirically quantified by the value of Hill's coefficient *n*, equal to one in the case of no interactions, and greater than one when there is interactions.

The curve's position depends on the O_2 affinity of the pigment, commonly quantified by the value of P_{50}, the partial pressure of oxygen at which 50 % of the active sites combine with one oxygen molecule. The O_2-affinity is a function of: i) the intrinsic structure of the pigment molecule (intrinsic affinity); ii) eventual steric 'heterotropic' interactions between the O_2-binding sites and various other molecular sites which may combine with 'allosteric effectors', mineral or organic ions or molecules; iii) the temperature.

Whatever the pigment in question, all the interactions within its molecule are usually analysed and interpreted in the framework of Wyman's theory of linked functions (1964) and the allosteric model proposed by Monod, Wyman & Changeux (1965). This model postulates that the pigment molecule may exist in two extreme steric states: i) a T ('Tense') state corresponding to the deoxygenated molecule (O_2-affinity constant K_T); ii) an R ('Relaxed') state, corresponding to the molecule almost completely saturated in oxygen (O_2-affinity constant K_R).

In this chapter, we will review in turn each of the factors that may affect the properties of a circulating respiratory pigment considered to be an oxygen transporter. Mammalian haemoglobin will frequently be used as a point of comparison as its molecular structure and properties are the best understood and explained. Note, however, that this pigment is only one particular case among many others.

A) *Oxygen-binding capacity of body fluids*

$C_{xO_2}^{max}$ varies enormously (see Prosser, 1973; Weber, 1978), from a value close to zero (gastropod opisthobranchs, see Ghiretti-Magaldi, Salvato, Tallandini & Beltramini, 1979) to 10 to 14 mmol $O_2.L^{-1}$. As a general rule, $C_{HcyO_2}^{max}$ is rather low in haemocyanin-containing haemolymphs. Values range between almost 0 and 2 mmol $O_2.L^{-1}$, the highest being observed in the cephalopods. $C_{HrO_2}^{max}$ is lower in coelomic fluids containing haemerythrin, 1 to 1·6 mmol $O_2.L^{-1}$, than in bloods carrying the same pigment ($C_{HrO_2}^{max} = 2·8$ mmol $O_2.L^{-1}$ in *Magelona*, Wells & Dales, 1974). Erythro- and ·chlorocruorin containing bloods may have very high $C_{ErO_2}^{max}$, particularly in the annelids, where values are similar and sometimes higher than those measured in lower vertebrates (5–6 mmol $O_2.L^{-1}$ in *Arenicola*). Finally, in fluids carrying haemoglobin, the values of $C_{HbO_2}^{max}$ are always moderately high to high, varying from 1·8 mmol $O_2.L^{-1}$ in the coelomic fluid of *Glycera* to 10 to 14 mmol $O_2.L^{-1}$ in the blood of marine diving birds and mammals.

$C_{xO_2}^{max}$ depends on the weight concentration of the pigment in the circulating fluid and on the mean protein mass associated with each active site (see Table 3). The protein mass per active site of intracellular pigments is relatively low and constant, 12·5 to 18×10^3. High $C_{HbO_2}^{max}$ values result from the sometimes enormous intracellular pigment concentrations (haemoglobin may account for up to 35 % of the fresh weight and 95 % of the dry weight of the mammalian red blood cell) and/or the high haematocrit values. In the case of extracellular pigments, the mean mass of protein per active site is usually higher. For haemocyanins, this can be 50 to 75×10^3, which may explain the low $C_{HcyO_2}^{max}$ values of bloods containing this pigment, in spite of the sometimes high pigment weight concentrations.

$C_{xO_2}^{max}$ values seem to be a compromise between the necessity of a sufficient oxygen transport, and a viscosity and colloid osmotic pressure that not only do not jeopardize the organism's water balance, but are compatible with the performances of the circulatory system. The polymerization of the functional units into giant molecules seems to be the solution which satisfies these three requirements (Lehmann & Huntsman, 1961; Mangum & Johansen, 1975; Snyder, 1978; Snyder & Mangum, 1982). Some authors have suggested that the large extracellular pigments ensure that they remain inside a given compartment. By contrast, Wells & Dales (1976) have shown that, in *Arenicola*, carbonic anhydrase, $M_r = 29 \times 10^3$, is present in the blood (which also contains an erythrocruorin of M_r approximately 3600×10^3) but not in the coelomic fluid: the vascular walls are apparently perfectly capable of retaining a molecule with a mass 100 times less than that of the respiratory pigment molecule.

B) *Homotropic interactions*

The oxygen equilibrium curve of a circulating respiratory pigment, the (number of oxygenated active sites/total number of active sites) as a function of Po_2, is generally sigmoid, showing that O_2-binding by the pigment molecule is a cooperative phenomenon, the saturation of one site increasing the oxygen affinity of the other sites. Hill's coefficient n is the slope of the equilibrium curve transformed in a Hill plot, log (number of oxygenated active sites/number of deoxygenated active sites) as a function of log Po_2. Hill's n gives an indication of the minimum number of active sites involved in the cooperation process. It has a maximum (n_{max}) but at both very low and very high saturation percentages, *i.e.* when all the pigment molecules are near either the deoxygenated T-state or the oxygenated R-state, it tends asymptotically to 1 (zero cooperativity, no interaction between the different active sites). The intersections of the two asymptotical straight lines with the x-axis give the values (in $Torr^{-1}$) of K_T and K_R, the O_2-affinity constants of the pigment molecule in the T- and R-states respectively. Physiologically, cooperativity allows for Po_2 values corresponding to n_{max}, a maximal O_2-loading or -unloading of the molecule for a corresponding minimal change of Po_2 in the carrier fluid, a property thought to be important for a respiratory pigment since it keeps the O_2-diffusion gradients at their maximal values at both ends of the O_2-transport system. This gives a maximal O_2 net flux for a minimal turnover of the circulating fluid.

The value of the coefficient n_{max}, which varies between 1 and 9, is to a certain degree independant of the number of active sites present in the native molecule. By definition, there is no cooperativity in a monomeric native molecule of circulating respiratory pigment. It is null or low, n_{max} 1 to 1·8 (Weber, 1978), in the native haemerythrin molecule whether this is trimeric or octameric. In contrast, n_{max} is high, 2·5 to 3, in the tetrameric haemoglobin molecule of mammals. The cooperativity of the haemocyanins is extraordinarily variable, n_{max} 1 to 9·3, and is very often null in multidomain haemocyanins (Van Holde & Miller, 1982; Mangum, 1982). That of annelid erythro- and chlorocruorins (12×12 active sites per native molecule) is high or very high: n_{max} may be greater than 6. Conversely, there is no cooperativity in the multidomain erythrocruorin of the bivalve *Cardita borealis*. Even though each of the 35 to 40 chains of the native molecule has 20 active sites, the pigment behaves like a monomeric one (Terwilliger & Terwilliger, 1978). Does it actually transport oxygen, or does it, like myoglobin, act as an oxygen store?

Generally speaking, the cooperativity of giant extracellular pigment molecules is more complex than that of the oligomeric intracellular pigment molecules. In the native molecule of annelid erythrocruorin, it seems to be confined to the interior of each of the 12 subunits (Weber, 1970). On the contrary, cooperativity of the haemocyanin molecule of *Octopus* seems to start in one subunit and then spread to two or three adjacent subunits, resulting in a particularly atypical oxygen equilibrium curve (Tallandini & Salvato, 1981).

C) *Heterotropic interactions*

For reasons that are not yet really understood, the intrinsic O_2-affinity of a given pigment depends on its particular molecular structure and varies considerably from one pigment to another. The data grouped by Weber (1980) show, for example, that the P_{50} of haem pigments is between 0·002 and 200 Torr, an extremely wide and significant range of values even if the fact that they were not always obtained under the same conditions is taken into account. The intrinsic O_2-affinity of a given pigment may be modulated within limits by various ions and molecules which are present in the physicochemical environment and which can bind to the pigment molecule at specific sites distinct from the O_2-binding sites. These substances are called allosteric effectors, because they modify the tertiary and quaternary structure of the molecule and increase or reduce the O_2-affinity by favouring the transition to the oxygenated R-state or the deoxygenated T-state. Hydrogen ions, molecular CO_2, inorganic salts and organic phosphates, whose effects on the affinity of vertebrate haemoglobins has been studied in great detail, all reduce the O_2-affinity of these pigments. Identical studies carried out on invertebrate pigments have shown that i) other substances may act as allosteric effectors; ii) the action of the whole of the allosteric effectors can be extraordinarily varied.

(1) *Hydrogen ions.* The O_2-affinity of a circulating respiratory pigment may depend on the hydrogen ion concentration, and therefore on the pH, of the carrier fluid. This 'Bohr effect' is conventionally quantified by the Bohr coefficient, $\emptyset = \Delta\log P_{50}/\Delta pH$; a molecular explanation of the Bohr effect has been given by Perutz and his group (see Kilmartin, 1972, 1976; Fermi & Perutz, 1981; Dickerson & Geis, 1983). In most cases, the affinity of the pigment decreases as pH decreases. This corresponds to the 'normal' or 'alkaline' Bohr effect, considered to be physiologically advantageous as it aids the unloading of oxygen in the tissues and the re-oxygenation of the pigment in the external exchange organs (see Bartels, 1972). The Bohr effect is not universal, pH has no effect on the O_2-affinity of haemerythrins (except that of *Lingula*, Manwell, 1960*b*). For haem pigments, the Bohr effect does not always exist but it can be very strong: the values of $\emptyset$ are between zero and $-1\cdot7$, the chlorocruorins having the maximum Bohr effect (see for example Weber, 1978). The normal Bohr effect is rarely zero and often large in haemocyanins, and $\emptyset$ is often less than -1 (Brix, Lykkeboe & Johansen, 1981; Mangum, 1983*a*). The Bohr effect is related to the percentage saturation of the pigment. For mammalian haemoglobins, the higher the percentage saturation, the less the Bohr effect measured by the ratio $\emptyset = \Delta\log P_{O_2}/\Delta pH$ (see, for example, Imai & Yonetani, 1975). On the contrary, for tuna haemoglobin (Ikeda-Saito, Yonetani & Gibson, 1983) or for *Arenicola* erythrocruorin (Weber, 1981), $\emptyset$ increases with the O_2-saturation of the pigment. In the first case, the O_2-unloading in the tissues is optimized, whereas in the second, it is the O_2-loading in the gills that is enhanced. These differing molecular adaptations may be related to the medium breathed: air in the mammals and water in the tuna and *Arenicola*.

In certain cases, lowering the pH causes not only a lesser affinity but also an apparent decrease of the active sites concentration in the carrying fluid. This strengthened Bohr effect constitutes the 'normal' Root effect, a property which plays a part in the fact that fish with gas bladders are able to secrete gaseous oxygen into the bladder at hydrostatic pressures of several tens of atmospheres (Root, 1931; Scholander & Van Dam, 1954; Blaxter & Tytler, 1978). The molecular explanation of the Root effect has been given (see Perutz & Brunori, 1982; Perutz, 1983). In carp haemoglobin, the substitution of two amino acids in a key position increases the stability of the T conformation of the molecule to such an extent that oxygen can no longer combine with the pigment, even at partial pressures of several tens of atmospheres.

The haemocyanins of numerous species of gastropod molluscs and that of *Limulus* all show, at physiological pH values, a 'reverse' or 'acidic' Bohr effect characterized by an increased affinity with decreased pH (see references in Ellerton *et al.*, 1983). In *Buccinum*, a 'reverse' Root effect is superimposed on the reverse Bohr effect: a fall in pH causes an apparent increase of the concentration of active sites in the haemocyanin solution (Brix, Lykkeboe & Johansen, 1979). The physiological significance of the reverse Bohr and Root effects is unclear.

(2) *Carbon dioxide.* Carbon dioxide binds reversibly to mammalian haemoglobin by reacting with each of the 4 α-NH_2 groups at the amino-terminal ends of the four protein chains to form carbamino compounds (α-$NHCOO^-$) which establish salt bridges with the other residues of the polypeptide chain, stabilizing the deoxy-T conformation of the molecule at the expense of the oxy-R conformation. This reduces the O_2-affinity of the pigment whereas, reciprocally, O_2-binding reduces the affinity of the pigment for CO_2. The formation of carbamino compounds was demonstrated in 1934 by Ferguson & Roughton who showed that at identical pH and P_{CO_2}, an oxyhaemoglobin solution contained less CO_2 than the same deoxygenated solution (see Roughton, 1970; Perrella, Rossi-Bernardi & Roughton, 1972).

The negative specific effect of CO_2 on the O_2-affinity of a pigment, due to an inhibitory heterotropic interaction between the O_2-binding sites and the CO_2-binding sites, has only been demonstrated and thoroughly understood in the case of mammalian haemoglobin (see Kilmartin, 1976). For other pigments, a very few but notable studies report the existence of a *reverse, positive* effect of CO_2 on O_2-affinity. Truchot (1973*a*) clearly showed that, at constant pH, the O_2-affinity of the haemocyanin of *Carcinus maenas* was increased by CO_2 which must therefore preferentially combine with the oxy-R form of the pigment. The same specific positive effect seems also to exist for the haemocyanins of *Busycon* (Mangum & Lykkeboe, 1979), *Sepia* (Lykkeboe, Brix & Johansen, 1980) and *Palaemon adsperus* (Weber & Hagerman, 1981), and for the erythrocruorin of *Arenicola marina* (Krogh-Rasmussen & Weber, 1979), but in these examples direct binding of CO_2 has never been demonstrated. Note that the whole of these animals are water breathers.

The physiological significance of the phenomenon is not clear. The formation of carbamino compounds by mammalian haemoglobin is generally supposed to favour the quick release of CO_2 in the lungs as the pigment combines with oxygen. In actual fact, according to Dill, Edwards

& Consolazio (1937), 30 % of the CO_2 contained in the expired air comes from the carbamino compounds, which represents only 5 % of the total CO_2 in the venous blood. However for Kilmartin (1976), the physiological role of the carbamino compounds, in mammals, is to reduce the O_2-affinity of the pigment, and variations in the concentration of CO_2, like those of DPG, would allow for an adaptive modulation of this affinity. In the invertebrates' pigments for which a positive specific effect of CO_2 has been described, the formation of carbamino compounds would correspond to the same, but inverse, function, that of an increase of the pigments' affinity.

(3) *Inorganic salts. In vitro*, an increased concentration of neural salts in the respiratory pigment solution causes a reduction in the O_2-affinity of vertebrate haemoglobins and *Limulus* haemocyanin, has no effect on the affinity of the erythrocruorins of *Artemia* and increases that of other erythrocruorins and haemocyanins. The increased ionic strength of the solution is not the cause, the effect is due to the specific action of the anions or cations (see Antonini, Amiconi & Brunori, 1972; Weber, 1980; Imai, 1982; Ellerton *et al.*, 1983).

The anions bind preferentially to and stabilize the deoxygenated, low O_2-affinity T forms of the haemoglobins. Chloride has a strong effect *in vivo*, except in the *Crocodilia*, whose haemoglobin is above all sensitive to bicarbonate ions (Bauer *et al.*, 1981; Perutz *et al.*, 1981). Chloride also specifically reduces the affinity of the haemocyanins of the horseshoe crab (Brouwer, Bonaventura & Bonaventura, 1977) and the snail, but it increases that of the decapod crustaceans (see Ellerton *et al.*, 1983).

Cations, especially the divalent cations such as Ca^{2+} and Mg^{2+}, preferentially bind to the oxygenated, high-O_2-affinity R forms of the decapod crustacean haemocyanins (Truchot, 1975; Ellerton *et al.*, 1983) and to the extracellular haem pigments of annelids and crustaceans (see Weber, 1980, 1981). These cations may also have a very pronounced effect on cooperativity.

(4) *Organic molecules*. Three categories of organic molecules, organic phosphates, lactates and urea, may combine with certain respiratory pigments and modify their O_2-affinity.

The O_2-affinity of vertebrate haemoglobins decreases with the increase of the intraerythrocytic concentration of various organic phosphates: 2,3–DPG, GTP, UTP, IDP, IPP, IHP, depending on the vertebrate group (see Bartlett, 1980). The molecular mechanism of these organic phosphate reactions is now well understood (see Benesch & Benesch, 1974; Kilmartin, 1976; Weber, 1982; Perutz, 1983). The effects of organic phosphates on invertebrate haemoglobins or haemerythrins are poorly known, apparently they also have a depressive action on the pigment O_2-affinity (see Weber, 1978, 1980).

Organic phosphates do not seem to affect the extracellular pigments. By contrast, at constant pH, lactates increase the affinity of several crustacean haemocyanins (Truchot, 1980), but decrease that of human haemoglobin (Guesnon, Poyart, Bursaux & Bohn, 1979) (see section VIII, B).

Urea increases the affinity of certain vertebrate haemoglobins, an effect seemingly due in part to a direct combination with the pigment molecule (see section VIII, A).

(5) *Hydrogen sulphide*. The toxic effects on most living organisms of hydrogen sulphide and its compounds are due to their capacity for inhibiting many enzyme systems, in particular the cytochromes of the respiratory chain (Evans, 1967). They bind irreversibly to human haemoglobin which is transformed into a sulphhaemoglobin whose O_2-affinity is more than two orders of magnitude lower than that of the native pigment (Carrico, Blumberg & Peisach, 1978). Numerous marine organisms, however, live in environments whose sulphide are 2 to 300 times the normally lethal concentrations. This is the case for part of the meiofauna (Fenchel & Riedl, 1970) and many mud- and sand-dwelling species.

Many studies of the mechanisms that enable these organisms to resist the toxic effects of sulphides have been made (see Theede, Ponat, Hiroki & Schlieper, 1969; Powell, Crenshaw & Rieger, 1979; Groenendaal, 1981). The erythrocruorins of *Arenicola marina* (Patel & Spencer, 1963a,b) and *Abarenicola marina* (Wells & Pankhurst, 1980), two burrowing annelids, do not form sulpherythrocruorins *in vitro*, and their affinity for oxygen is not affected by the presence of sulphides, whereas under the same conditions human haemoglobin is transformed, at least in part, into sulphhaemoglobin whose affinity for oxygen is multiplied by six (Wells & Pankhurst, 1980).

Recently, some remarkable biocoenoses have been discovered in association with the submarine thermal springs of the Galapagos Rift (Corliss *et al.*, 1979). One of the most spectacular constituent species is the vestimentiferan pogonophoran *Riftia pachyptila*, (Jones, 1980), whose blood contains an erythrocruorin with structural features and properties very similar to those of annelids (Terwilliger, Terwilliger & Schabtach, 1980). Like the other members of the biocoenose, *Riftia* lives in an environment rich in sulphide compounds brought up by the hot springs, but its blood contains a factor which prevents these substances from inhibiting cytochrome c oxidase (Powell & Somero, 1983). Arp & Childress (1983) have shown that *Riftia* blood contains, *in vivo*, up to $1 \cdot 1 \, \text{mmol.l}^{-1}$ of sulphides, and that it can accumulate more than $3 \, \text{mmol.l}^{-1}$ when dialysed, *in vitro*, against a $0 \cdot 1 \, \text{mmolar}$ sulphide solution. They suggest that *Riftia* blood transports oxygen as well as the hydrogen sulphide that is essential for the metabolism of the chemo-autotrophic bacteria living in symbiosis in the animal trophosome. As dialysis does not affect the capacity for accumulating sulphide, as the most abundant blood protein is the respiratory pigment and as the pigment does not form sulpherythrocruroin in the presence of H_2S, Arp & Childress (1983) suggest that this erythrocruorin may be responsible for the reversible binding and the transport of both O_2 and H_2S. This rather revolutionary hypothesis requires experimental substantiation.

D) *Temperature effects*

As O_2-binding is an exothermic reaction, a pigment's O_2-affinity decreases when the temperature increases. The effect of this factor on the affinity may be quantified by the value of ΔH, the apparent heat of oxygenation, usually calculated by using Van't Hoff's equation in the form

$$\Delta H = 2 \cdot 303 \, R \cdot \Delta \log P_{50} / \Delta (T^{-1}),$$

where R is the universal gas constant and T the absolute temperature.

ΔH is the total change in enthalpy of the pigment–oxygen–solvent system and corresponds to the algebraic sum of several terms. These, apart from the intrinsic heat of oxygenation of the pigment, are the heat of solution of oxygen in water ($-3 \, \text{kcal} \cdot \text{mol}^{-1}$ at $25 \, °C$); the heats of ionization of all known and unknown groups involved in the heterotropic interactions with the O_2-binding sites and in particular the groups responsible for the Bohr effect; the heats of ionization of the protein surface groups that interact with the solvent; and the heats of ionization of the groups responsible for the buffer capacity of the solvent (see Rossi-Fanelli, Antonini & Caputo, 1964; Collet & O'Gower, 1972). ΔH therefore represents a complex quantity and physiological interpretation of its variations requires caution.

The ΔH values of the vertebrate, annelid and echiurian haemoglobins are usually between -10 and $-15 \, \text{kcal} \cdot \text{mol}^{-1}$. The range is wider, -5 to -16 $\text{kcal} \cdot \text{mol}^{-1}$, in the annelid erythrocruorins (see Weber, 1978). The range of ΔH is maximum for the haemocyanins, 0 to $-38 \, \text{kcal} \cdot \text{mol}^{-1}$ (see Mangum, 1980; Jokumsen, Wells, Ellerton & Weber, 1981; Jokumsen & Weber, 1982). The haemerythrins are characterized by uniformly high oxygenation heats: ΔH values vary from -10 to $-20 \, \text{kcal} \cdot \text{mol}^{-1}$ (see Mangum, 1976a; Weber, 1978; Weber & Fange, 1980).

Low values of ΔH are interpreted as a molecular adaptation minimizing the effect of the temperature factor on the pigment O_2-affinity. This adaptation, of unknown mechanism, is thought to enable animals subjected to a wide temperature range to maintain a constant rate of oxygen transport. Many examples seem in fact to show that the apparent heat of oxygenation of a pigment is the greater the more stenothermal the animal's environment; the highest value known, $\Delta H = -38\,\text{kcal·mol}^{-1}$, is that of the haemocyanin of the isopod *Glyptonotus antarcticus* which lives in water whose temperature varies between 0·05 and −1·80 °C (Jokumsen *et al.*, 1981). In contrast, the haemocyanin of the hermit crab *Pagurus bernhardus* has an apparent heat of oxygenation of zero ($\Delta H = 0$), possibly in relation with the eurythermal conditions of the intertidal zone inhabited by this crustacean (Jokumsen & Weber, 1982).

In fishes, the properties of the haemoglobins of the tuna group are also remarkable. The apparent heat of oxygenation is low, $\Delta H = -1·8\,\text{kcal·mol}^{-1}$ (Rossi-Fanelli & Antonini, 1960), or even positive, $\Delta H = +1·7\,\text{kcal·mol}^{-1}$ (Cech, Laurs & Graham, 1984), which would correspond to a possible endothermal binding of molecular oxygen. In fact, in *Thunnus thynnus*, the effect of temperature on the O_2-affinity is a function of the percentage saturation of the pigment: *in vitro*, on cooling from 20 to 10 °C, the affinity at low saturation increases, and that at high saturation decreases (Carey & Gibson, 1977). The temperature of the deep musculature and certain viscera of tunas may be more than 20 °C higher than that of the water passing over the gills (Carey, Kanwisher & Stevens, 1984; Stevens & MacLeese, 1984). Heat conservation is ensured by thermal exchanges between the venous blood and the postbranchial arterial blood in the countercurrent retia mirabilia arranged in series on the vessels entering and leaving the red muscles (see Carey *et al.*, 1971). The pigment is subjected to sudden changes in temperature which could have a dramatic effect on its O_2-affinity if the ΔH values were those normal for a vertebrate haemoglobin, −10 to −14 kcal·mol^{-1}.

The haemoglobin of the bivalve *Anadara granosa* is also unique (Collett & O'Gower, 1972). The apparent heat of oxygenation varies considerably with the temperature, $\Delta H = -8\,\text{kcal·mol}^{-1}$ between 10 and 20 °C and $\Delta H = +10\,\text{kcal·mol}^{-1}$ between 25 and 35 °C. This extreme case resembles nevertheless the finding that ΔH of the erythrocruorin of *Arenicola* varies with the temperature (Toulmond, 1978–79).

VIII. Circulating respiratory pigments at work: a few examples

A) *Urea tolerance of elasmobranch haemoglobins*

The high salt concentration in sea water poses problems for the water–mineral balance of marine vertebrates. Teleosteans for example, which are hypoosmotic, continually lose water through their body surface and gills, and they compensate by drinking sea water. The initial problem is therefore replaced by that of how to eliminate the excess salts ingested with the sea water. Elasmobranchs (sharks, rays), holocephalans, the coelacanth *Latimeria*, and the crab-eating frog *Rana cancrivora* conserve water by being hyperosmotic with respect to the sea water, a consequence of the active retention of by-products of nitrogen metabolism, urea and methylamines, mainly trimethylamine oxide (TMAO), but also betaine and sarcosine. These different substances account for approximately 50 % of the total osmolarity of the blood and muscles (Gordon, Schmidt-Nielsen & Kelly, 1961; Robertson, 1975; Yancey *et al.*, 1982; Schmidt-Nielsen, 1983).

Urea strongly denatures proteins, whose structures (α-helix, tertiary and quaternary) it destabilizes by breaking non-covalent bonds, thereby seriously disturbing protein functional properties (Tanford, 1970). Nevertheless, the presence of urea in elasmobranch tissues is indispensable. The isolated shark heart contracts for hours if it is perfused with physiological saline having a high concentration of urea, but it rapidly deteriorates and stops beating in the absence of urea (Schmidt-Nielsen, 1983). Other results show that elasmobranch lactate dehydrogenases *in vitro* only function if the medium contains $0\cdot4$ M-urea (Yancey & Somero, 1978).

In the presence of urea, certain properties of human haemoglobin are completely modified. The tetramers dissociate into dimers and the O_2-affinity of the pigment increases considerably. In 0 to 5 M-urea, ray haemoglobin remains tetrameric, its cooperativity remains unchanged and its O_2-affinity increases only very slightly (Bonaventura, Bonaventura & Sullivan, 1974; Mumm, Atha & Riggs, 1978). Shark haemoglobin reactions to urea are more variable. The haemoglobin of the smooth dogfish *Mustelus canis* reacts like that of the rays (Bonaventura *et al.*, 1974), whereas that of the spiny dogfish *Squalus acanthias* behaves more like human haemoglobin since in the presence of $0\cdot5$ or 1 M-urea, the cooperativity of the pigment decreases (Hill's coefficient approaches 1) and its O_2-affinity increases (Weber, Wells & Rossetti, 1983). Nevertheless, this effect of urea is partially offset *in vitro* by the action of organic phosphates (Weber *et al.*, 1983), present at similar concentrations in the erythrocytes of the ray and shark (Wells & Weber, 1983), but which do not affect the ray's pigment affinity (Mumm *et al.*, 1978).

The stability in the presence of urea of the haemoglobin tetramer of the rays and certain sharks is thought to be linked to the existence of re-inforced electrostatic interactions at the points of contact between the protomers, because some amino acids in the polypeptide chains differ from those found at the same key positions in human haemoglobin and, probably, in that of *Squalus acanthias* (Bonaventura *et al.*, 1974). The higher O_2-affinity of ray haemoglobin at high NaCl concentrations, the dimerization of human haemoglobin in urea solutions, the fact that *Squalus* oxyhaemoglobin is a dimer whereas deoxyhaemoglobin is a tetramer, all support this hypothesis.

The increase, in the presence of urea, of the O_2-affinity of human and *Squalus* haemoglobins may also be partially due to a direct action of urea combining with the free carboxyl radicals of the polypeptide chain (Weber *et al.*, 1983). Binding of this type would explain that urea concentrations have been found to be higher in red blood cells than in plasma (Browning, 1978). Terminal carboxyl radical of the $\beta2$-protomer of the human haemoglobin molecule is responsible for 40 % of the Bohr effect (see Kilmartin, 1976). By combining with this carboxyl terminal, urea would prevent the proton binding responsible for the Bohr effect, thereby increasing the O_2-affinity of the pigment (Weber *et al.*, 1983). Urea may also transform spontaneously into cyanate and then carbamylate free NH2-radicals (Tanford, 1968), in particular the terminal amino ends of the polypeptide chains. As the α-amino radicals are at least partly responsible for ATP-binding in the human haemoglobin, their carbamylation would reduce ATP-binding and thereby also cause higher O_2-affinity of the pigment (Weber *et al.*, 1983). These authors in fact found that urea caused a reduced ATP activity in the spiny dogfish but a mechanism of this sort poses a problem (Bonaventura *et al.*, 1974): as carbamylation of the free NH2 groups is irreversible, and as urea is omnipresent in the elasmobranchs, their proteins should be highly carbamylated, unless these animals have developed biochemical mechanisms for decarbamylation or for elimination of the cyanate formed.

It has been suggested that the simultaneous presence in elasmobranch blood and tissues of urea and methylamines at a constant concentration ratio of 2:1 is not fortuitous (Yancey & Somero, 1979, 1980). Methylamines neutralize *in vitro* the adverse effects of urea on the function of all enzymes tested, elasmobranch or mammalian, and this neutralization is at a maximum when the urea/methylamines ratio is approximately 2:1. It is concluded that elasmobranch enzymes are not specifically adapted to the presence of urea. What about elasmobranch haemoglobin? Weber (1983) showed that TMAO had no effect on the affinity of the haemoglobin of *Squalus acanthias* in the presence or absence of urea and/or ATP. It is the ATP that neutralizes the disturbing effects of urea on this particular haemoglobin.

B) *Regulation of haemocyanin oxygen affinity in euryhaline crabs*

Near the coast and especially in estuaries, the salinity of sea water, elsewhere remarkably constant, may vary considerably in time and space, as it can be diluted by inland fresh water, or concentrated by evaporation in lagoons periodically isolated from the sea. Most marine animals cannot tolerate this osmotically unstable environment, and the brackish-water fauna comprises relatively few euryhaline species, but usually in very dense populations.

In certain of these species, the osmoconformers, the body fluid osmolarity changes in parallel with the variations of the external salinity. In others, the osmoregulators, these environmental changes are offset by the active absorption or excretion of salt which enables these animals to maintain more or less the constancy of the animal medium. The green crab *Carcinus maenas* and the blue crab *Callinectes sapidus* are osmoregulators though, like all euryhaline invertebrates, they control only imperfectly the ionic concentrations of their haemolymph. If the external salinity decreases, the internal osmolarity, although maintained above that of the ambient osmolarity, decreases appreciably, in parallel with a fall in the haemolymph concentration of the various inorganic ions. But some of these ions considerably influence the O_2-affinity of the crabs' haemocyanins. At physiological concentrations, the affinity increases with the calcium and, to a lesser extent, with the magnesium concentration, so that *in vitro*, and all other conditions being the same, the O_2-affinity of the blood pigment appears to be lower in animals acclimated to low salinities. In *Carcinus maenas*, this reduction may be quantitatively accounted for by the reduction in Ca^{2+} and Mg^{2+} alone (Truchot, 1973b, 1975; Mason, Mangum & Godette, 1983). *In vivo*, however, an additional factor is involved: after a sufficiently long stay in dilute sea water, the animals blood pH rises, and this, because of a normal Bohr effect, brings the O_2-affinity back to a value close to that observed in normal sea water (Truchot, 1973b, 1975). *Callinectes sapidus* behaves the same way (Weiland & Mangum, 1975), except that in this species, whereas the effect of Ca^{2+} on the pigment affinity of the pigment *in vitro* is three times as great as in *Carcinus maenas, in vivo* the physiological changes of Ca^{2+} explain only a very small part of the variations in affinity that accompany acclimation to a new salinity. Another, non-dialysable, and so far unidentified factor is therefore, no doubt, the cause (Mason *et al.*, 1983).

The higher blood pH following the crabs' acclimation to dilute sea water is probably due to ammonia produced, during the intracellular osmotic reequilibration, by deamination of part of the amino acid pool responsible for maintaining cell osmolarity. In both *Carcinus maenas* and *Callinectes sapidus*, acclimation to dilute sea water is accompanied by a reduction in this amino acid pool and an increase in blood NH_3 concentration (Gerard & Gilles, 1972; Mangum *et al.*, 1976). Even if this is not the complete explanation, the observed increase in pH compensates for the decrease in Ca^{2+} and Mg^{2+} concentrations, the oxygen saturation of the arterial blood is maintained, and oxygen transport is assured under the best possible conditions, in just the situation where the quantity of oxygen available may become limited (Mangum, 1976*b*).

The blue crab, for example, can live in water with a salinity that may vary over the extremely wide range of 0 to 75 ‰ . During the reproductive period, the adults may migrate up to 300 km to ocean waters from which the offspring must return. Swimming speeds may then exceed $1\,m\cdot s^{-1}$ (see Lynch, Webb & Van Engel, 1973; Booth, McMahon & Pinder, 1982). The quantity of oxygen available on the migration route may be much lower than normal (Mangum, 1976*b*), yet the crab, experiencing considerable salinity and temperature variations, metabolically requires more oxygen because of the greater osmotic and mechanical work performed. The muscles may metabolize anaerobically part of the time, with the production, as in all decapods, of lactic acid which may reduce the blood pH. But (if this occurs) the increase in blood lactate levels would increase the pigment's O_2-affinity.

In *Carcinus maenas*, the lactate, the main by-product of anaerobic metabolism, increases the *in vitro* O_2-affinity of haemocyanin without modifying the Bohr effect (Truchot, 1980), and the lactate effect has been confirmed in *Callinectes sapidus*, some other decapod crustaceans and in a stomatopod (Johnson & Becker, 1981; Mangum, 1983*a*,*b*). Lactate sensitivity is not shared by all haemocyanins: there is none in the haemocyanins of the molluscs or the chelicerates studied by Mangum (1983*b*), and, in crustaceans, the response is variable and sometimes absent. The lactate effect, where it exists, cannot totally account for the change in affinity of dialysed haemocyanins. There must be another, as yet unidentified dialysable factor (Truchot, 1980; Graham, Mangum, Terwilliger & Terwilliger, 1983; Mangum, 1983*a*,*b*).

The action of lactates is specific, and distinct from that of protons and divalent cations. Among the structural analogues and the final products of anaerobic metabolism that have been tested, only D-lactate, glycolate, and 2-methyl-lactate are slightly active (Graham *et al.*, 1983). Although haemocyanin only incompletely differentiates the two optical isomers of lactic acid, there is believed to be a direct heterotropic interaction between L-lactate and the O_2-binding site. A model for this allosteric interaction has been proposed by Graham *et al.*, (1983) (see also Mangum, 1983*c*). Johnson, Bonaventura & Bonaventura (1984) have shown that there is less than one lactate-binding site per O_2-binding site.

In summary, for the euryhaline crabs, at least three factors, the variation in the concentration of divalent cations, the variations caused by changes in the ammonia concentration and the lactates, all contribute to the stability of a fourth factor, haemocyanin O_2-affinity. This stability is essential for one function, the transport of oxygen. Overall, this processes correspond to an 'enantiostatic' type of regulation as defined by Mangum & Towle (1977).

C) *Adaptations to an intertidal way of life: lugworm erythrocruorin*

Between land and sea, between aquatic and aerial environments, the intertidal zone is a biotope characterized by the extreme instability of its abiotic ecological factors. The periodic disappearance of the liquid element is the most visible and spectacular sign of instability, for it deprives at least part of the intertidal fauna of water, the respiratory medium with which it exchanges oxygen and carbon dioxide at high tide. Burrowing organisms are at a greater disadvantage, as they cannot extract from the atmosphere, as do certain epigeal species, the indispensable oxygen for aerobic metabolism. For sand- and mud-dwelling species, the tidal cycle may in fact be a truly anoxic (low tide)–normoxic (high tide) cycle. Under these conditions, respiratory functions are made possible only by a variety of specific adaptations, anatomical, ethological, physiological and biochemical, some of which have been demonstrated and analysed in considerable detail (see Newell, 1979). Among the burrowing polychaete annelids, the lugworm *Arenicola marina* is one of the species intensively studied over the last few years.

The lugworm burrows in the sand to form an L-shaped gallery in which during high tide it maintains a tail-to-head current of normoxic sea water produced by appropriate movements of the muscular body wall (see Krüger, 1964; Wells, 1966). At low tide, the lugworm remains confined, sometimes for two-thirds of the tidal cycle, in the very hypoxic water standing in the lower part of the burrow. Its respiratory exchanges take place mainly across the 13 pairs of gills regularly spaced along the anterior two-thirds of the body length. The gills are irrigated in parallel by the prebranchial blood coming from the ventral vessel, and bathe in turn in the flux of water ventilated by the animal, this water becoming progressively hypoxic and hypercapnic as it moves forward in the gallery (see Mangum, 1976*c*). The body wall, which probably also participates in the respiratory exchanges, contains two different myoglobins which have a very high O_2-affinity (Weber & Pauptit, 1972). The relative volume of the closed circulatory compartment is equal or greater than that of the most active aquatic organisms (cephalopods, fishes, mammals), and represents 3 to 8 % of the total body volume (Toulmond, 1971a).

The blood has an ionic composition very close to that of sea water, and contains two dissolved proteins: carbonic anhydrase at a concentration close to that of human blood (Wells, 1973), and a typical annelid erythro-cruorin whose concentration ranges from 107 to 144 g·l^{-1} (Toulmond, 1973). This erythrocruorin is characterized by a high O_2-affinity, P_{50} approximately 2–3 Torr in vivo at 15 °C, and the cooperativity and normal Bohr effect are both strong (Toulmond, 1970a, 1973; Weber, 1970, 1972, 1981). The cooperativity and Bohr effect are particular in that they are very dependent on the percentage saturation of the pigment in oxygen, S_{O_2}. The oxygen association constant of the pigment molecule in the R state (K_R) varies much more with pH than does the corresponding constant for the T state (K_T) (Weber, 1981). Consequently, the Bohr coefficient, $\Delta \log P_{O_2}/\Delta pH$, decreases regularly from –0·83 to –0·25 when S_{O_2} falls from 95 to 10 %.

Given these observations, what is the efficiency of the pigment as an oxygen carrier? The high affinity for oxygen, in conjunction with maximum cooperativity and strong Bohr effect at high values of S_{O_2}, facilitate O_2-loading of the pigment by maintaining a maximum O_2-diffusion gradient in an external O_2-exchanger which is of a crosscurrent type (see Dejours, 1981). But at low S_{O_2}, the reduced cooperativity and Bohr effect should hinder the O_2-unloading of the pigment in the tissues. Oxygen transport can then be optimal only if the percentage saturation of the pigment remains high after the blood has passed through the organs taking up O_2. This implies that the flow of oxygen through these organs should be much greater than the metabolic demand. These two conditions seem to be satisfied in the lugworm: the blood has such a high O_2-binding capacity, 5 to 6 mmol·l^{-1}, that in vivo, in normoxic water at 15 °C, prebranchial blood pigment remains 90 % saturated. Nevertheless, if the pigment in the postbranchial blood is taken as 100 % saturated, it can be calculated that the transport of oxygen in combined form covers 50 to 70 % of the total O_2-consumption of the animal at 15 °C (Toulmond, 1973, 1975).

An O_2-transport system of this sort has several advantages: i) oxygen extraction from the flux of ventilated water is optimal, and the ventilatory yield is maximal: in the normoxic lugworm, O_2-extraction coefficients are around 80 % (Toulmond & Tchernigovtzeff, 1984); ii) the diffusion gradient between the blood and the muscles' respiratory pigments is maximum; iii) a maximum amount of oxygen can be stored in the blood for use during the ventilatory pauses occurring in normoxia, a reserve which is rapidly used up as the tide starts to go out, and when the animal stops ventilating altogether.

Several arguments suggest that the pigment plays a role in oxygen transport only during the normoxic external conditions of high tide: i) experimentally, ventilation is reduced when P_{O_2} in the water is less than 80 Torr, and stops completely when $P_{O_2} = 20$ Torr (Toulmond & Tchernigovtzeff, 1984). Recent findings suggest that the lugworm can detect the fall of P_{O_2} via primary sensory cells situated in the caudal epidermis (Toulmond, Tchernigovtzeff, Greber & Jouin, 1984; Jouin, Tchernigovtzeff, Baucher & Toulmond, 1985); ii) under natural conditions on the beach, pigment oxygenation falls spectacularly from the first hour of low tide onwards, and the percentage saturation approaches zero (Toulmond, 1973); iii) under the same conditions, P_{CO_2} of the prebranchial blood increases, pH decreases, this respiratory and metabolic acidosis reflecting on the one hand the retention of CO_2 and therefore the total disorganization of gas exchanges, and, on the other hand the start up of anaerobic metabolism with the consequent accumulation of acetic, propionic and succinic acids (Pionetti & Toulmond, 1980; Schöttler, Wienhausen & Zebe, 1983).

The blood acidosis is, however, limited by a particular characteristic of the buffering power of the erythrocruorin. This may be demonstrated by titrating the blood with either CO_2 (Toulmond, 1970*b*), or with a fixed acid or base (Toulmond, 1971*b*, 1977). These titrations show that, for physiological pH values, the buffering capacity of the pigment is suddenly increased by a factor of two when the pigment is oxygenated, and by a factor of six when it is deoxygenated, that is, during low tide. The pH value for which there is a maximum variation in the buffer capacity showing the same temperature-dependence as the pK of imidazole groups, it is most likely, therefore, that the characteristic buffer capacity of the erythrocruorin is due to a pH-dependent unmasking of an imidazole group, and that this unmasking is more gradual when the molecule is in the R-state than in the T-state (Toulmond, 1977).

Lugworm erythrocruorin is perhaps just a special case. It is possible that adaptations of the same type exist in other burrowing intertidal polychaetes, but the lack of concrete data and the diversity of the life habits of members of this group prevent any generalization for the moment.

IX. Conclusions

This review has emphasized the tremendous structural and functional diversity of circulating respiratory pigments. The causes of this diversity are multiple and some are very ancient. The three classes of respiratory pigments, haem pigments, haemocyanins and haemerythrins, have been selected for and have evolved while the animal kingdom was diversifying. The occurrence in a given modern species of a respiratory pigment belonging to one of the three classes thus depends on the history and on the phylogenetical relationships of the species, but it seems evident that the functional properties of the pigment must have been selected for more or less recently, in response to a specific set of constraints.

These constraints derive from the intrinsic properties of the solvent fluid and especially from its qualitative and quantitative inorganic and organic composition. They also depend on the structure and characteristics of the body fluid compartment, and internal and external O_2- and CO_2-exchangers. But most importantly, constraints arise from the fact that the compartment containing the respiratory pigment constitutes an interface between the external medium and the cellular compartment, and their intrinsic characteristics must have considerably influenced pigment structure and function. The extracellular pigments, which lack the stable, conventional cellular microenvironment provided to the intracellular pigments, ought to, and effectively do, show the greatest diversity of structures and properties. In these conditions, a true understanding of the whole of the circulating respiratory pigments is not possible without an extensive knowledge of the particular animal's whole respiratory gas exchange system, and of the characteristics and properties of the respiratory medium. Behaviour must also be taken into account, since in several cases it has been shown that animals, and specially invertebrates, actively create a specific external microenvironment.

The diversity of the respiratory pigments in marine species correspond to a maximum phylogenetic and structural heterogeneity and to a maximum variety of external environments. However, adaptations particular to the pigments of marine animals are probably fairly rare. Most, apart from those related to a life in a medium of high and sometimes variable salinity, can be found in fresh-water animals. The important adaptive differences between functional properties of respiratory pigments may be found perhaps only when pigments of aerial and aquatic animals are compared.

The author wishes to thank Drs J. de Frescheville, P. Dejours, W. Ghidalia, J. Lamy and J. P. Truchot for valuable discussions and comments, Mrs S. Dejours for editing the English of this article and Mrs F. Kleinbauer for her help in the material preparation of the manuscript. This work was partly supported by the Centre National de la Recherche Scientifique, Paris, J. E. n⁰ 960050.

References

ANTONINI, E., AMICONI, G. & BRUNORI, M. (1972). The effect of anions and cations on the oxygen equilibrium of human hemoglobin. In *Oxygen Affinity of Haemoglobin and Red Cell Acid Base Status*, (ed. M. Rorth & P. Astrup), pp. 122–129. Copenhagen: Munksgaard.

ANTONINI, E. & CHIANCONE, E. (1977). Assembly of multisubunit respiratory proteins. *Ann. Rev. Bioph. Bioeng.* **6**, 239–271.

ARP, A. J. & CHILDRESS, J. J. (1983). Sulfide binding by the blood of the hydrothermal vent tube worm *Riftia pachyptila*. *Science* **219**, 295–297.

BALDWIN, D., McCABE, M. & THOMAS, F. (1984). The respiratory gas carrying capacity of ascidian blood. *Comp. Biochem. Physiol.* **79A**, 479–482.

BANNISTER, J. V. (ed.) (1977). *Structure and Function of Haemocyanin*. Berlin: Springer–Verlag.

BARTELS, H. (1972). The biological significance of the Bohr effect. In *Oxygen Affinity of Hemoglobin and Red Cell Acid Base Status*. (ed. M. Rorth & P. Astrup), pp. 717–735. Copenhagen: Munksgaard.

BARTLETT, G. R. (1980). Phosphate compounds in vertebrate red blood cells. *Am. Zool.* **20**, 108–114.

BAUER, C., FORSTER, M., GROS, G., MOSCA, A., PERRELLA, M., ROLLEMA, H. S. & VOGEL, D. (1981). Analysis of bicarbonate binding to crocodilian hemoglobin. *J. biol. Chem.* **256**, 8429–8435.

BENESCH, R. E. & BENESCH, R. (1974). The mechanism of interaction of red cell organic phosphates with hemoglobin. *Adv. Protein Chem.* **28**, 211–237.

BLAXTER, J. H. S. & TYTLER, P. (1978). Physiology and function of the swimbladder. *Adv. comp. physiol. Biochem.* **7**, 311–367.

BONAVENTURA, C., BONAVENTURA, J., MILLER, K. I. & VAN HOLDE, K. E. (1981). Hemocyanin of the chambered *Nautilus*: structure-function relationships. *Arch. Biochem. Biophys.* **211**, 589–621.

BONAVENTURA, J. & BONAVENTURA, C. (1980). Hemocyanins: relationships in their structure, function and assembly. *Am. Zool.* **20**, 7–17.

BONAVENTURA, J., BONAVENTURA, C. & SULLIVAN, B. (1974). Urea tolerance as a molecular adaptation of elasmobranch hemoglobins. *Science* **186**, 57–59.

BONAVENTURA, J., BONAVENTURA, C. & SULLIVAN, B. (1975). Hemoglobins and hemocyanins: comparative aspects of structure and function. *J. exp. Zool.* **194**, 155–174.

BONAVENTURA, J., BONAVENTURA, C. & TESH, S. (eds) (1982). *Physiology and Biology of Horseshoe Crabs*. Prog. Clin. Biol. Res. Vol. 81. New York: A. R. Liss.

BOOTH, C. E., McMAHON, B. R. & PINDER, A. W. (1982). Oxygen uptake and the potentiating effects of increased hemolymph lactate on oxygen transport during exercise in the blue crab, *Callinectes sapidus*. *J. comp. Physiol.* **148**, 111–121.

BRIX, O., LYKKEBOE, G. & JOHANSEN, K. (1979). Reversed Bohr and Root shifts in hemocyanin of the marine prosobranch, *Buccinum undatum*. Adaptations to a periodically hypoxic habitat. *J. comp. Physiol.* **129**, 97–104.

BRIX, O., LYKKEBOE, G. & JOHANSEN, K. (1981). The significance of the linkage between the Bohr and Haldane effects in cephalopod bloods. *Respir. Physiol.* **44**, 177–188.

BROUWER, M., BONAVENTURA, C. & BONAVENTURA, J. (1977). Oxygen binding by *Limulus polyphemus* hemocyanin: allosteric modulation by chloride ions. *Biochemistry* **16**, 3897–3902.

BROWNING, J. (1978). Urea levels in plasma and erythrocytes of the southern fiddler skate, *Trygonorhina fasciata guanerius*. *J. exp. Zool.* **203**, 325–330.

CAREY, F. G. & GIBSON, Q. H. (1977). Reverse temperature dependence of tuna hemoglobin oxygenation. *Biochem. Biophys. Res. Commun.* **78**, 1376–1382.

CAREY, F. G., KANWISHER, J. W. & STEVENS, E. D. (1984). Bluefin tuna warm their viscera during digestion. *J. exp. Biol.* **109**, 1–20.

CAREY, F. G., TEAL, J. M., KANWISHER, J. W., LAWSON, K. D. & BECKETT, K. S. (1971). Warm-bodied fish. *Am. Zool.* **11**, 137–145.

CARRICO, R. J., BLUMBERG, W. E. & PEISACH, J. (1978). The reversible binding of oxygen to sulfhemoglobin. *J. biol. Chem.* **253**, 7212–7215.

CECH, J. J., LAURS, R. M. & GRAHAM, J. B. (1984). Temperature-induced changes in blood gas equilibria in the albacore, *Thunnus alalunga*, a warm-bodied tuna. *J. exp. Biol.* **109**, 21–34.

CHUNG, M. C. M. & ELLERTON, H. D. (1979). The physico-chemical and functional properties of extracellular respiratory hemoglobins and chlorocruorins. *Prog. Biophys. mol. Biol.* **35**, 53–102.

CLOUD, P. & GLAESSNER, M. F. (1982). The Ediacarian period and system: Metazoa inherit the Earth. *Science* **217**, 783–792.

COLLETT, L. C. & O'GOWER, A. K. (1972). Molluscan hemoglobins with unusual temperature dependent characteristics. *Comp. Biochem. Physiol.* **41A**, 843–850.

COMO, P. F. & THOMPSON, O. P. (1980). Multiple hemoglobins of the bivalve mollusc, *Anadara trapezia*. *Aust. J. biol. Sci.* **33**, 643–652.

CORLISS, J. B., DYMOND, J., GORDON, L. I., EDMOND, J. M., VON HERZEN, R. P., BALLARD, R. D., GREEN, K., WILLIAMS, D., BAINBRIDGE, A., CRANE, K. & VAN ANDEL, T. H. (1979). Submarine thermal springs on the Galapagos rift. *Science* **203**, 1073–1083.

DANGOTT, L. J. & TERWILLIGER, R. C. (1980). The subunit structure of *Daphnia pulex* hemoglobin. *Comp. Biochem. Physiol.* **67B**, 301–306.

DANIEL, E. (1983). Subunit structure of arthropods erythrocruorins. In *Structure and Function of Invertebrate Respiratory Proteins*, (ed. E. J. Wood), *Life Chem. Repts*, Sup. 1, pp. 157–163. London: Harwood.

DEJOURS, P. (1981). *Principles of Comparative Respiratory Physiology*. 2nd Ed., Amsterdam: Elsevier-North Holland Biomedical Press.

DICKERSON, R. E. & GEIS, I. (1983). *Hemoglobin: Structure, Function, Evolution, and Pathology*. Menlo Park, California: Benjamin–Cummings.

DILL, D. B., EDWARDS, H. T. & CONSOLAZIO, W. V. (1937). Blood as a physico-chemical system. XI. Man at rest. *J. biol. Chem.* **118**, 635–648.

DJANGMAH, J. S., GABBOTT, P. A. & WOOD, E. J. (1978). Physico-chemical characteristics and oxygen-binding properties of the multiple hemoglobins of the west African blood clam, *Anadara senilis* (L.). *Comp. Biochem. Physiol.* **60B**, 245–250.

DURLIAT, M. (1984). Occurrence of plasma proteins in ovary and egg extracts from *Astacus leptodactylus*. *Comp. Biochem. Physiol.* **78B**, 745–753.

ELLERTON, N. F. & ELLERTON, H. D. (1982). Quaternary structure of arthropod hemocyanins. *Biochem. Biophys. Res. Comm.* **108**, 1383–1387.

ELLERTON, H. D., ELLERTON, N. F. & ROBINSON, H. A. (1983). Hemocyanin. A current perspective. *Prog. Biophys. molec. Biol.* **41**, 143–248.

EVANS, C. (1967). The toxicity of hydrogen sulfide and other sulphides. *Quart. J. exp. Physiol.* **52**, 231–248.

FENCHEL, T. M. & RIEDL, R. J. (1970). The sulfide system: a new biotic community underneath the oxidised layer of marine sand bottoms. *Mar. Biol.* **7**, 255–268.

FERGUSON, J. K. W. & ROUGHTON, F. J. W. (1934). The chemical relationship and physiological importance of carbamino compounds of CO_2 with hemoglobin. *J. Physiol., Lond.* **83**, 87–102.

FERMI, G. & PERUTZ, M. F. (1981). *Haemoglobin and Myoglobin. Atlas of Molecular Structures in Biology*, (ed. D. C. Phillips & F. M. Richards), Vol. 2. Oxford: Clarendon Press.

FISCHER, H. & VON SEEMANN, C. (1936). Die Konstitution des Spirographishamins. *Hoppe-Seyler's Z. physiol. Chem.* **242**, 133–157.

FOETTINGER, A. (1880). Sur l'existence de l'hémoglobine chez les Echinodermes. *Arch. Biol.* **1**, 405–415.

FROSSARD, P. (1982). The erythrocruorin of *Eisenia fetida*. I. Properties and subunit structure. *Biochem. biophys. Acta* **704**, 524–534.

FURUTA, H. & KAJITA, A. (1983). Dimeric hemoglobin of the bivalve mollusc, *Anadara broughtonii*: complete amino acid sequence of the globin chain. *Biochemistry* **22**, 917–922.

FYHN, U. E. H. & SULLIVAN, B. (1974). Hemoglobin polymorphism in fishes. I. Complex phenotypic patterns in the toad fish, *Opsanus tau*. *Biochem. Genetics* **11**, 373–385.

GARLICK, R. L. (1980). Structure of annelid high molecular weight hemoglobins (erythrocruorins). *Am. Zool.* **20**, 69–77.

GARLICK, R. L., WILLIAMS, B. J. & RIGGS, A. F. (1979). The hemoglobins of *Phoronopsis viridis*, of the primitive invertebrate phylum *Phoronida*. Characterization and subunit structure. *Arch. Biochem. Biophys.* **194**, 13–23.

GAYKEMA, W. P. J., HOL, W. G. J., VEREIJKEIN, J. M., SOETER, N. M., BAK, H. J. & BEINTEMA, J. J. (1984). 3·2 Å structure of the copper-containing, oxygen-carrying protein *Panulirus interruptus* hemocyanin. *Nature* **309**, 23–29.

GEELEN, D., MOENS, L., HEIP, J., HERTSENS, R., DONCEEL, K. & CLAUWAERT, J. (1982). The structure of *Artemia sp.* haemoglobins – I. Isolation and characterization of oxygen binding domains obtained by limited tryptic digestion. *Intern. J. Biochem.* **14**, 991–1001.

GERARD, J. F. & GILLES, R. (1972). The free amino-acid pool in *Callinectes sapidus* (Rathbun) tissues and its role in the osmotic intracellular regulation. *J. exp. mar. Biol. Ecol.* **10**, 125–136.

GHIDALIA, W. (1984). Structural and biological aspects of pigments. In *The Biology of Crustacea*, (ed. D. E. Bliss), Vol. **9**, pp. 301–394. Orlando, Florida: Academic Press.

GHIRETTI-MAGALDI, A., SALVATO, B., TALLANDINI, L. & BELTRAMINI, M. (1979). The hemocyanin of *Aplysia limacina*: chemical and functional characterization. *Comp. Biochem. Physiol.* **62A**, 579–584.

GOODMAN, M., BRAUNITZER, G., KLEINSCHMIDT, T. & ASCHAUER, H. (1983). The analysis of a protein-polymorphism. Evolution of monomeric and homodimeric hemoglobins (erythrocruorins) of *Chironomus thummi thummi* (Insecta, Diptera). *Hoppe-Seyler's Z. physiol. Chem.* **364**, 205–217.

GORDON, M. S., SCHMIDT-NIELSEN, K. & KELLY, H. M. (1961). Osmotic regulation in the crab eating frog, (*Rana cancrivora*). *J. exp. Biol.* **38**, 659–678.

GRAHAM, R. A., MANGUM, C. P., TERWILLIGER, R. C. & TERWILLIGER, N. B. (1983). The effect of organic acids on oxygen binding of hemocyanin from the crab *Cancer magister*. *Comp. Biochem. Physiol.* **74A**, 45–50.

GRINICH, N. P. & TERWILLIGER, R. C. (1980). The quaternary structure of an unusual high-molecular-weight intracellular hemoglobin from the bivalve mollusc *Barbatia reeveana*. *Biochem. J.* **189**, 1–8.

GROENENDAAL, M. (1981). The adaptation of *Arenicola marina* to sulphide solutions. *Neth. J. Sea Res.* **15**, 65–77.

GUESNON, P., POYART, C., BURSAUX, E. & BOHN, B. (1979). The binding of lactate and chloride ions to human adult hemoglobin. *Respir. Physiol.* **38**, 115–129.

HAJDUK, S. L. & COSGROVE, W. B. (1975). Hemoglobin in an ophiuroid, *Hemipholis elongata*. *Am. Zool.* **15**, 808.

HEIP, J., MOENS, L., JONIAU, M. & KONDO, M. (1978). Ontogenetical studies on extra-cellular hemoglobins of *Artemia salina*. *Devl. Biol.* **64**, 73–81.

HENDRICKSON, W. A. (1983). Hierarchal symmetry in annelid hemoglobins. In *Structure and Function of Invertebrate Respiratory Proteins*, (ed. E. J. Wood), *Life Chem. Repts*, Sup. **1**, pp. 167–185. London: Harwood.

HERBERTS, C. & DE FRESCHEVILLE, J. (1981). Occurrence of hemocyanin in the rhizocephalan crustacea, *Sacculina carcini* Thompson. *Comp. Biochem. Physiol.* **70B**, 657–659.

IKEDA-SAITO, M., YONETANI, T. & GIBSON, Q. H. (1983). Oxygen equilibrium studies on hemoglobin from the bluefin tuna (*Thunnus thynnus*). *J. mol. Biol.* **168**, 673–686.

IMAI, K. (1982). *Allosteric Effects in Hemoglobin*. Cambridge: Cambridge University Press.

IMAI, K. & YONETANI, T. (1975). pH dependence of Adair constants of human hemoglobin. Non uniform contribution of successive oxygen bindings to alkaline Bohr effect. *J. biol. Chem.* **250**, 2227–2231.

JEFFREY, P. D., SHAW, D. C. & TREACY, G. B. (1978). Hemocyanin from the Australian freshwater crayfish *Cherax destructor*. Characterization of a dimeric subunit and its in-volvement in the formation of the 25S component. *Biochemistry* **17**, 3078–3084.

JOHANSEN, K. & WEBER, R. E. (1976). On the adaptability of hemoglobin function to environmental conditions. In *Perspectives in Experimental Biology*, (ed. P. S. Davis), pp. 219–234. Oxford, New York: Pergamon Press.

JOHNSON, B. A. & BECKER, D. J. (1981). Lactic acid as an allosteric modifier of the oxygen affinity of blue crab hemocyanin. *Am. Zool.* **21**, 951.

JOHNSON, B. A., BONAVENTURA, C. & BONAVENTURA, J. (1984). Allosteric modulation of *Callinectes sapidus* hemocyanin by binding of L-lactate. *Biochemistry* **23**, 872–878.

JOHNSTON, I. A., FITCH, N., ZUMMO, G., WOOD, R. E., HARRISON, P. & TOTA, B. (1983). Mor-phometric and ultrastructural features of the ventricular myocardium of the hemo-globin-less icefish *Chaenocephalus aceratus*. *Comp. Biochem. Physiol.* **76A**, 475–480.

JOKUMSEN, A. & WEBER, R. E. (1982). Hemocyanin-oxygen affinity in hermit crab blood is temperature independent. *J. exp. Zool.* **221**, 389–394.

JOKUMSEN, A., WELLS, R. M. G., ELLERTON, H. D. & WEBER, R. E. (1981). Hemocyanin of the giant antarctic isopod, *Glyptonotus antarcticus*: structure and effects of tem-perature and pH on its oxygen affinity. *Comp. Biochem. Physiol.* **70A**, 91–95.

JONES, M. L. (1980). *Riftia pachyptila*, new genus, new species, the vestimentiferan worm from the Galapagos rift geothermal vents (*Pogonophora*). *Proc. Biol. Soc. Wash.* **93**, 1295–1313.

JOUIN, C., TCHERNIGOVTZEFF, C., BAUCHER, M. F. & TOULMOND, A. (1985). Fine structure of probable mechano- and chemoreceptors in the caudal epidermis of the lugworm *Arenicola marina* (Annelida, Polychaeta). *Zoomorphology* **105**, 76–82.

KILMARTIN, J. V. (1972). Molecular mechanism of the Bohr effect. In *Oxygen Affinity of Haemoglobin and Red Cell Acid Base Status*, (ed. M. Rorth & P. Astrup), pp. 93–100. Copenhagen: Munksgaard.

KILMARTIN, J. V. (1976). Interaction of hemoglobin with protons, CO_2 and 2,3–diphosphoglycerate. *Br. Med. Bull.* **32**, 209–212.

KLIPPENSTEIN, G. L. (1980). Structural aspects of hemerythrin and myohemerythrin. *Am. Zool.* **20**, 39–51.

KLOTZ, I. M., KLIPPENSTEIN, G. L. & HENDRICKSON, W. A. (1976). Hemerythrin: alter-native oxygen carrier. *Science* **192**, 335–344.

KLOTZ, I. M. & KURTZ, D. M. JR. (1984). Binuclear oxygen carriers: hemerythrin. *Accounts Chem. Res.* **17**, 16–22.

KROGH–RASMUSSEN, K. & WEBER, R. E. (1979). Respiratory properties of erythrocruorin (extracellular hemoglobin) in the blood of the annelid, *Arenicola marina* with special reference to the influences of salinity and temperature. *Ophelia* **18**, 151–170.

KRÜGER, F. (1964). Versuche uber die Abhangigkeit der Atmung von *Arenicola marina* (Annelides Polychaeta) von Grosse und Temperatur. *Helgol. Wiss. Meeresunters.* **10**, 38–63.

LAMY, J., BIJHOLT, M. M. C., SIZARET, P.-Y., LAMY, J. & VAN BRUGGEN, E. F. J. (1981). Quaternary structure of scorpion (*Androctonus australis*) hemocyanin, localization of subunits with immunological methods and electron microscopy. *Biochemistry* **20**, 1849–1856.

LAMY, J. & LAMY, J. (eds) (1981). *Invertebrate Oxygen-binding Proteins: Structure, Active Site and Function.* New York and Basel: Dekker.

LAMY, J., LAMY, J., SIZARET, P.-Y., BILLIALD, P., JOLLES, P., JOLLES, J., FELDMANN, J. & BONAVENTURA, J. (1983). Quaternary structure of *Limulus polyphemus* hemocyanin. *Biochemistry* **22**, 5573–5583.

LANKESTER, E. R. (1868). Preliminary notice of some observations with the spectroscope on animal substances. *J. Anat. Physiol. norm. pathol., Paris* **2**, 114–116.

LEHMANN, H. & HUNTSMAN, R. G. (1961). Why are red cells the shape they are? The evolution of the human red cell. In *Functions of the Blood*, (ed. R. G. MacFarlane & A. H. T. Robb-Smith), pp. 73–148. New York, London: Academic Press.

LEWIN, R. (1984). Alien beings here on earth. *Science* **223**, 39.

LONTIE, R. & GIELENS, C. (1979). Molluscan and arthropodan hemocyanins. In *Metalloproteins*, (ed. U. Weser), pp. 62–72. Stüttgart: Thieme.

LYKKEBOE, G., BRIX, O. & JOHANSEN, K. (1980). Oxygen-linked CO_2 binding independent of pH in cephalopod blood. *Nature* **287**, 330–331.

LYNCH, M. P., WEBB, K. L. & VAN ENGEL, W. A. (1973). Variations in serum constituents of the blue crab, *Callinectes sapidus*: chloride and osmotic concentration. *Comp. Biochem. Physiol.* **44A**, 719–734.

MACARA, I. G., MCLEOD, G. C. & KUSTIN K. (1979). Vanadium in tunicates: oxygen-binding studies. *Comp. Biochem. Physiol.* **62A**, 821–826.

MANGUM, C. P. (1976a). Primitive respiratory adaptations. In *Physiological Adaptations to the Marine Environment*, (ed. R. C. Newell), pp. 191–278. London: Butterworth.

MANGUM, C. P. (1976b). The function of respiratory pigments in estuarine animals. In *Estuarine Processes*, (ed. M. L. Wiley), Vol. 1, pp. 356–380. New York: Academic Press.

MANGUM, C. P. (1976c). The oxygenation of hemoglobin in lugworms. *Physiol. Zool.* **49**, 85–99.

MANGUM, C. P. (1980). Respiratory function of the hemocyanins. *Am. Zool.* **20**, 19–38.

MANGUM, C. P. (1982). The functions of gills in several groups of invertebrate animals. In *Gills*, (ed. D. F. Houlihan, J. C. Rankin, & T. J. Shuttleworth), *Soc. exp. Biol. Sem. Ser.* **16**, pp. 77–97. Cambridge: Cambridge University Press.

MANGUM, C. P. (1983a). Oxygen transport in the blood. In *Biology of the Crustacea*, (ed. L. H. Mantel), Vol. 5, pp. 373–429. New York: Academic Press.

MANGUM, C. P. (1983b). On the distribution of lactate sensitivity among the hemocyanins. *Mar. Biol. Letters* **4**, 139–149.

MANGUM, C. P. (1983c). Adaptability and inadaptability among HcO_2 transport systems: an apparent paradox. *Life Chem. Repts.* **4**, 335–352.

MANGUM, C. P. & JOHANSEN, K. (1975). The colloid osmotic pressures of invertebrate body fluids. *J. exp. Biol.* **63**, 661–671.

MANGUM, C. P. & LYKKEBOE, G. (1979). The influence of inorganic ions and pH on oxygenation properties of the blood in the gastropod mollusc *Busycon canaliculatum*. *J. exp. Zool.* **207**, 417–430.

MANGUM, C. P., SILVERTHORN, S. U., HARRIS, J. L., TOWLE, D. W. & KRALL, A. R. (1976). The relationship between pH, ammonia excretion and adaptation to low salinity in the blue crab *Callinectes sapidus*. *J. exp. Zool.* **195**, 129–136.

MANGUM, C. & TOWLE, D. (1977). Physiological adaptation to instable environments. *Am. Scientist* **65**, 67–75.

MANWELL, C. (1960a). Comparative physiology: blood pigments. *Ann. Rev. Physiol.* **22**, 191–244.

MANWELL, C. (1960b). Oxygen equilibrium of brachiopod *Lingula* hemerythrin. *Science* **132**, 550–551.

MASON, R. P., MANGUM, C. P. & GODETTE, G. (1983). The influence of inorganic ions and acclimation salinity on hemocyanin-oxygen binding in the blue crab *Callinectes sapidus*. *Biol. Bull. mar. biol. Lab., Woods Hole* **164**, 104–123.

MAYR, E., LINSLEY, E. G. & USINGER, R. L. (1953). *Methods and Principles of Systematic Zoology*. New York: McGraw–Hill.

MOENS, L. & KONDO, M. (1978). Evidence for a dimeric form of *Artemia salina* extracellular hemoglobins with high-molecular-weight subunits. *Eur. J. Biochem.* **82**, 65–72.

MONOD, J., WYMAN, J. & CHANGEUX, J. P. (1965). On the nature of allosteric transitions. A plausible model. *J. mol. Biol.* **12**, 88–118.

MUMM, D. P., ATHA, D. H. & RIGGS, A. (1978). The hemoglobin of the common sting-ray, *Dasyatis sabina*: structural and functional properties. *Comp. Biochem. Physiol.* **60B**, 189–193.

MURRAY, A. C. & JEFFREY, P. D. (1974). Hemocyanin from the australian freshwater crayfish *Cherax destructor*. Subunit heterogeneity. *Biochemistry* **13**, 3667–3671.

NEWELL, R. C. (1979). *Biology of Intertidal Animals*. 3rd Ed., Faversham, Kent: Marine Ecological Surveys Ltd.

OCHS, R. L., OCHS, D. C. & BURTON, P. R. (1980). Axons of crayfish nerve cord contain intracellular hemocyanin. *J. Cell Biol.* **87**, 73a.

PATEL, S. & SPENCER, C. P. (1963a). Studies on the haemoglobin of *Arenicola marina*. *Comp. Biochem. Physiol.* **8**, 65–82.

PATEL, S. & SPENCER, C. P. (1963b). The oxydation of sulphide by the haem compounds from the blood of *Arenicola marina*. *J. mar. biol. Ass. UK.* **43**, 167–175.

PEREZ, J. E. & MCLEAN, N. (1976). Multiple globins and haemoglobins in four species of grey mullet (Mugilidae, Teleosta). *Comp. Biochem. Physiol.* **53B**, 465–468.

PERRELLA, M., ROSSI-BERNARDI, L. & ROUGHTON, F. J. W. (1972). The carbamate equilibrium between CO_2 and bovine haemoglobin at 25 °C. In *Oxygen Affinity of Hemoglobin and Red Cell Acid Base Status*, (ed. M. Rorth & P. Astrup), pp. 177–204. Copenhagen: Munksgaard.

PERUTZ, M. F. (1983). Species adaptation in a protein molecule. *Mol. Biol. Evol.* **1**, 1–28.

PERUTZ, M. F., BAUER, C., GROS, G., LECLERCQ, F., VANDECASSERIE, C., SCHNEK, A. G., BRAUNITZER, G., FRIDAY, A. E. & JOYSEY, K. A. (1981). Allosteric regulation of crocodilian haemoglobin. *Nature* **291**, 682–684.

PERUTZ, M. F. & BRUNORI, M. (1982). Stereochemistry of cooperative effects in fish and amphibian haemoglobins. *Nature* **299**, 421–426.

PILZ, I., GORAL, K., HOYLAERTS, M., WITTERS, R. & LONTIE, R. (1980). Studies by small-angle X-ray scattering of the quaternary structure of the 24-S component of the haemocyanin of *Astacus leptodactylus* in solution. *Eur. J. Biochem.* **105**, 539–543.

PIONETTI, J. M. & POUYET, J. (1980). Molecular architecture of annelid erythrocruorins. Extracellular haemoglobin of *Arenicola marina* (*Polychaeta*). *Eur. J. Biochem.* **105**, 131–138.

PIONETTI, J. M. & TOULMOND, A. (1980). Tide-related changes of volatile fatty acids in the blood of the lugworm, *Arenicola marina* (L.). *Canad. J. Zool.* **58**, 1723–1727.

POLUHOWICH, J. J. (1970). Oxygen consumption and the respiratory pigment in the fresh-water nemertean *Prostoma rubrum*. *Comp. Biochem. Physiol.* **36**, 817–821.

POWELL, E. N., CRENSHAW, M. A. & RIEGER, R. M. (1979). Adaptations to sulfide in the meiofauna of the sulfide system. I. ^{35}S-sulfide accumulation and the presence of a sulfide detoxification system. *J. exp. mar. Biol. Ecol.* **37**, 57–76.

POWELL, M. A. & SOMERO, G. N. (1983). Blood components prevent sulfide poisoning of respiration of the hydrothermal vent tube worm *Riftia pachyptila*. *Science* **219**, 297–299.

POWERS, D. A. (1974). Structure, function, and molecular ecology of fish hemoglobins. *Ann. N.Y. Acad. Sc.* **241**, 472–490.

POWERS, D. A. (1980). Molecular ecology of teleost fish hemoglobins: strategies for adapting to changing environments. *Am. Zool.* **20**, 139–162.

PROSSER, C. L. (ed.) (1973). *Comparative Animal Physiology.* 3rd Ed., Philadelphia, London: Saunders.

READ, K. R. (1965). The characterization of the hemoglobins of the bivalve mollusc *Phacoides pectinatus* (Gmelin). *Comp. Biochem. Physiol.* **15**, 137–158.

RIGGS, A. (1970). Properties of fish hemoglobins. In *Fish Physiology*, (ed. W. S. Hoar & D. J. Randall), Vol. 4, pp. 209–252. New York: Academic Press.

ROBERTSON, J. D. (1975). Osmotic constituents of the blood plasma and parietal muscle of *Squalus acanthias* L. *Biol. Bull. mar. biol. Lab., Woods Hole* **148**, 303–319.

ROCHU, D. & FINE, J. M. (1984). *Cancer pagurus* hemocyanin: subunit arrangement and subunit evolution in functional polymeric forms. *Comp. Biochem. Physiol.* **78B**, 67–74.

ROOT, R. W. (1931). The respiratory function of the blood of marine fishes. *Biol. Bull. mar. biol. Lab., Woods Hole* **61**, 427–456.

ROSSI-FANELLI, A. & ANTONINI, E. (1960). Oxygen equilibrium of haemoglobin from *Thunnus thynnus. Nature* **186**, 895–896.

ROSSI-FANELLI, A., ANTONINI, E. & CAPUTO, A. (1964). Hemoglobin and myoglobin. *Adv. Protein Chem.* **19**, 73–222.

ROUGHTON, F. J. W. (1970). Some recent work on the interactions of oxygen, carbon dioxide and haemoglobin. The seventh Hopkins memorial lecture. *Biochem. J.* **117**, 801–812.

RUPPERT, E. E. & TRAVIS, P. B. (1983). Hemoglobin-containing cells of *Neodasys* (Gastrotricha, Chaetonotida). I. Morphology and ultrastructure. *J. Morph.* **175**, 57–64.

RUUD, J. T. (1954). Vertebrates without erythrocytes and blood pigment. *Nature* **173**, 848–850.

SCHINDELMEISER, I., KUHLMANN, D. & NOLTE, A. (1979). Localization and characterization of hemoproteins in the central nervous tissue of some gastropods. *Comp. Biochem. Physiol.* **64B**, 149–154.

SCHMIDT-NIELSEN, K. (1983). *Animal Physiology. Adaptation and Environment. 3rd Ed.,* Cambridge: Cambridge University Press.

SCHOLANDER, P. F. & VAN DAM, L. (1954). Secretion of gases against high pressures in the swimbladder of deep sea fishes. I. Oxygen dissociation in blood. *Biol. Bull. mar. biol. Lab., Woods Hole* **107**, 247–259.

SCHÖTTLER, U., WIENHAUSEN, G. & ZEBE, E. (1983). The mode of energy production in the lugworm *Arenicola marina* at different oxygen concentrations. *J. comp. Physiol.* **149**, 547–555.

SCHREIBER, J. K. & PARKHURST, L. J. (1984). Ligand binding equilibrium and kinetic measurements on the dimeric myoglobin of *Busycon canaliculatum* and the comparative ligand binding of diverse non-cooperative heme proteins. *Comp. Biochem. Physiol.* **78A**, 129–135.

SIEKER, L. C., BOLLES, L., STENKAMP, R. E., JENSEN, L. H. & APPLEBY, C. A. (1981). Preliminary X-ray study of a dimeric form of hemerythrin from *Phascolosoma arcuatum. J. molec. Biol.* **148**, 493–494.

SIPPL, M. J. (1983). On the origin of the globins: structural relations between the globin exon products. In *Structure and Function of Invertebrate Respiratory Proteins*, (ed. E. J. Wood), *Life Chem. Repts*, Sup. **1**, pp. 223–224. London: Harwood.

SMITH, J. L., HENDRICKSON, W. A. & ADDISON, A. W. (1983). Structure of trimeric haemerythrin. *Nature* **303**, 86–88.

SNYDER, G. K. (1978). Blood viscosity in annelids. *J. exp. Zool.* **206**, 271–302.

SNYDER, G. K. & MANGUM, C. P. (1982). The relationship between the capacity for oxygen transport, size, shape, and aggregation state of an extracellular oxygen carrier. In *Physiology and Biology of Horseshoe Crabs*, (ed. J. Bonaventura, C. Bonaventura and S. Tesh). *Prog. Clin. Biol. Res.*, Vol. **81**, pp. 173–188. New York: A. R. Liss.

STEVENS, E. D. & McLEESE, J. M. (1984). Why bluefin tuna have warm tummies: temperature effect on trypsin and chymotrypsin. *Am. J. Physiol.* **246**, R487–R494.

SVERDRUP, H. U., JOHNSON, M. W. & FLEMING, R. H. (1942). *The Oceans. Their Physics, Chemistry and Biology.* New York: Prentice–Hall.

TALLANDINI, L. & SALVATO, B. (1981). Allosteric modulations in the oxygen binding of *Octopus vulgaris* hemocyanin. In *Invertebrate Oxygen-binding Proteins: Structure, Active Site and Function*, (ed. J. Lamy & J. Lamy), pp. 727–738. New York and Basel: Dekker.

TANFORD, C. (1968). Protein denaturation. *Adv. Protein Chem.* **23**, 121–282.

TANFORD, C. (1970). Protein denaturation. Part C. Theoretical models for the mechanism of denaturation. *Adv. Protein Chem.* **24**, 1–95.

TERWILLIGER, N. B. & TERWILLIGER, R. C. (1978). Oxygen binding domains of a clam (*Cardita borealis*) extracellular haemoglobin. *Biochem. Biophys. Acta.* **537**, 77–85.

TERWILLIGER, R. C. (1978). The respiratory pigment of the serpulid polychaete, *Serpula vermicularis* L. Structure of its chlorocruorin and hemoglobin (erythrocruorin). *Comp. Biochem. Physiol.* **61B**, 463–469.

TERWILLIGER, R. C. (1980). Structures of invertebrate hemoglobins. *Am. Zool.* **20**, 53–67.

TERWILLIGER, R. C. & TERWILLIGER, N. B. (1983). Oxygen binding domains in invertebrate hemoglobins. In *Structure and Function of Invertebrate Respiratory Proteins*, (ed. E. J. Wood), *Life Chem. Repts*, Sup. **1**, pp. 227–238. London: Harwood.

TERWILLIGER, R. C., TERWILLIGER, N. B. & ARP, A. (1983). Thermal vent clam (*Calyptogena magnifica*) hemoglobin. *Science* **219**, 981–983.

TERWILLIGER, R. C., TERWILLIGER, N. B. & SCHABTACH, E. (1976). Comparison of chlorocruorin and annelid hemoglobin quaternary structures. *Comp. Biochem. Physiol.* **55A**, 51–55.

TERWILLIGER, R. C., TERWILLIGER, N. B. & SCHABTACH, E. (1978). Extracellular hemoglobin of the clam, *Cardita borealis* (Conrad): an unusual polymeric hemoglobin. *Comp. Biochem. Physiol.* **59B**, 9–14.

TERWILLIGER, R. C., TERWILLIGER, N. B. & SCHABTACH, E. (1980). The structure of hemoglobin from an unusual deep sea worm (Vestimentifera). *Comp. Biochem. Physiol.* **65B**, 531–535.

THEEDE, H., PONAT, A., HIROKI, K. & SCHLIEPER, C. (1969). Studies on the resistance of marine bottom invertebrates to oxygen-deficiency and hydrogen sulphide. *Mar. Biol.* **2**, 325–337.

TOULMOND, A. (1970a). La fixation de l'oxygène par le sang chez l'Arénicole (*Arenicola marina* (L.), Annélide Polychète). *C. r. hebd. Séanc. Acad. Sci., Paris* **270**, 1368–1371.

TOULMOND, A. (1970b). La fixation du dioxyde de carbone par le sang chez l'Arénicole (*Arenicola marina* (L.), Annélide Polychète). *C. r. hebd. Séanc. Acad. Sci., Paris* **270**, 1487–1490.

TOULMOND, A. (1971a). Détermination du volume des compartiments coelomique et circulatoire de l'Arénicole (*Arenicola marina* (L.), Annélide Polychète. *C. r. hebd. Séanc. Acad. Sci., Paris* **272**, 257–260.

TOULMOND, A. (1971b). Sur une particularité du pouvoir tampon de l'hémoglobine d'Arénicole (*Arenicola marina* (L.), Annélide Polychète). *C. r. hebd. Séanc. Acad. Sci., Paris* **272**, 3184–3187.

TOULMOND, A. (1973). Tide-related changes of blood respiratory variables in the lugworm *Arenicola marina* (L.). *Respir. Physiol.* **19**, 130–144.

TOULMOND, A. (1975). Blood oxygen transport and metabolism of the confined lugworm *Arenicola marina* (L.). *J. exp. Biol.* **63**, 647–660.

TOULMOND, A. (1977). Temperature-induced variations of blood acid-base status in the lugworm, *Arenicola marina* (L.): I. *In vitro* study. *Respir. Physiol.* **31**, 139–149.

TOULMOND, A. (1978–79). Action du pH et de la température sur l'affinité pour l'oxygène de l'hémoglobine d'*Arenicola marina* (L.), Annélide Polychète. *Vie Milieu* **28–29**, 443–459.

TOULMOND, A. & TCHERNIGOVTZEFF, C. (1984). Ventilation and respiratory gas exchanges of the lugworm *Arenicola marina* (L.) as functions of ambient P_{O_2}. (20–700 torr). *Respir. Physiol.* **57**, 349–363.

TOULMOND, A., TCHERNIGOVTZEFF, C., GREBER, P. & JOUIN, C. (1984). Epidermal sensitivity to hypoxia in the lugworm. *Experientia* **40**, 541–543.

TOULMOND, A. & TRUCHOT, J. P. (1982). Les pigments respiratoires des invertébrés. In *Centenaire de l'Ecole Normale Supérieure de Saint-Cloud. Actes du Colloque de Biologie (17–18 Nov. 1982)*, pp. 241–265. Saint-Cloud.

TRUCHOT, J. P. (1973a). Action spécifique du dioxyde de carbone sur l'affinité pour l'oxygène de l'hémocyanine de *Carcinus maenas* (L.) (Crustacé Décapode Brachyoure). *C. r. hebd. Séanc. Acad. Sci., Paris* **276**, 2965–2968.

TRUCHOT, J. P. (1973b). Fixation et transport de l'oxygène par le sang de *Carcinus maenas*: variations en rapport avec diverses conditions de température et de salinité. *Neth. J. Sea Res.* **7**, 482–495.

TRUCHOT, J. P. (1975). Factors controlling the *in vitro* and *in vivo* oxygen affinity of the haemocyanin in the crab *Carcinus maenas* (L.). *Respir. Physiol.* **24**, 173–189.

TRUCHOT, J. P. (1980). Lactate increases the oxygen affinity of crab hemocyanin. *J. exp. Zool.* **214**, 205–208.

VAN BRUGGEN, E. F. J. (1980). Hemocyanin: the mystery of blue blood. *Trends Biochem. Sci.* 185–188.

VAN DEN BRANDEN, C., D'HONDT, J., MOENS, L. & DECLEIR, W. (1978). Functional properties of the hemoglobins of *Artemia salina* (L.). *Comp. Biochem. Physiol.* **60A**, 185–187.

VAN HOLDE, K. E. & MILLER, K. I. (1982). Haemocyanins. *Quart. Rev. Biophys.* **15**, 1–129.

VINOGRADOV, S. N., KAPP, O. H. & OHTSUKI, M. (1982). The extracellular haemoglobins and chlorocruorins of Annelids. In *Electron Microscopy of Proteins*, (ed. J. Harris), Vol. 3, pp. 135–164. New York: Academic Press.

VINOGRADOV, S. N., SHLOM, J. M., KAPP, O. H. & FROSSARD, P. (1980). The dissociation of annelid extracellular hemoglobins and their quaternary structure. *Comp. Biochem. Physiol.* **67B**, 1–16.

WALD, G. & ALLEN, D. W. (1957). The equilibrium between cytochrome oxidase and carbon monoxide. *J. gen. Physiol.* **40**, 593–608.

WARD, K. B., HENDRICKSON, W. A. & KLIPPENSTEIN, G. L. (1975). Quaternary and tertiary structure of haemerythrin. *Nature* **257**, 818–821.

WAXMAN, L. (1975). The structure of annelid and mollusc hemoglobins. *J. biol. Chem.* **25**, 3790–3795.

WEBER, R. E. (1970). Relation between functional and molecular properties of annelid haemoglobins. Interaction between haems in the haemoglobin of *Arenicola marina* L. *Comp. Biochem. Physiol.* **35**, 179–189.

WEBER, R. E. (1972). On the variation in oxygen-binding properties in haemoglobins of lugworms (Arenicolidae, Polychaeta). *Fifth Eur. mar. Biol. Symp.*, pp. 231–243. Padova: Piccin.

WEBER, R. E. (1978). Respiratory pigments. In *Physiology of Annelids*, (ed. P. J. Mill), pp. 393–446. London: Academic Press.

WEBER, R. E. (1980). Functions of invertebrate hemoglobins with special reference to adaptations to environmental hypoxia. *Am. Zool.* **20**, 79–101.

WEBER, R. E. (1981). Cationic control of O_2 affinity in lugworm erythrocruorin. *Nature* **292**, 386–387.

WEBER, R. E. (1982). Intraspecific adaptation of hemoglobin function in fish to oxygen availability. In *Exogenous and Endogenous Influences on Metabolic and Neural Control*, (ed. A. D. F. Addink & N. Spronk), Vol. 1, pp. 87–102. Oxford: Pergamon Press.

WEBER, R. E. (1983). TMAO (trimethylamine oxide)-independence of oxygen affinity and its urea and ATP sensitivities in an elasmobranch hemoglobin. *J. exp. Zool.* **228**, 551–554.

WEBER, R. E. & FANGE, R. (1980). Oxygen equilibrium of *Priapulus* hemerythrin. *Experientia* **36**, 427–428.

WEBER, R. E. & HAGERMAN, L. (1981). Oxygen and carbon dioxide transporting qualities of hemocyanin in the hemolymph of a natant decapod *Palaemon adsperus*. *J. comp. Physiol.* **145**, 21–28.

WEBER, R. E. & PAUPTIT, E. (1972). Molecular and functional heterogeneity in myoglobin from the Polychaete *Arenicola marina* (L.). Arch. Biochem. Biophys. **148**, 322–324.

WEBER, R. E., WELLS, R. M. G. & ROSSETTI, J. E. (1983). Allosteric interactions governing oxygen equilibria in the haemoglobin system on the spiny dogfish, *Squalus acanthias*. *J. exp. Biol.* **103**, 109–120.

WEILAND, A. L. & MANGUM, C. P. (1975). The influence of environmental salinity on hemocyanin function in the blue crab, *Callinectes sapidus*. *J. exp. Zool.* **193**, 265–274.

WELLS, G. P. (1966). The lugworm (*Arenicola*). A study in adaptation. *Neth. J. Sea Res.* **3**, 294–313.

WELLS, R. M. G. (1973). Carbonic anhydrase activity in *Arenicola marina* (L.). *Comp. Biochem. Physiol.* **46A**, 325–331.

WELLS, R. M. G. & DALES, R. P. (1974). Oxygenational properties of haemerythrin in the blood of *Magelona papillicornis* Muller (Polychaeta: Magelonidae). *Comp. Biochem. Physiol.* **49A**, 57–64.

WELLS, R. M. G. & DALES, R. P. (1976). Subunit organization in the respiratory proteins of the polychaeta. *Comp. Biochem. Physiol.* **54A**, 387–394.

WELLS, R. M. G. & PANKHURST, N. W. (1980). An investigation into the formation of sulphide and oxidation compounds from the haemoglobin of the lugworm *Abarenicola affinis* (Ashworth). *Comp. Biochem. Physiol.* **66C**, 255–259.

WELLS, R. M. G. & WEBER, R. E. (1983). Oxygenational properties and phosphorylated metabolic intermediates in blood and erythrocytes of the dogfish, *Squalus acanthias*. *J. exp. Biol.* **103**, 95–108.

WILSON, L. J., MERRILL, C. L., SIMMONS, M. G., TRANTHAM, J. M., BOTTOMLEY, L. A. & KADISH, K. M. (1981). A synthetic copper(I) oxygen-carrier as a hemocyanin model compound. In *Invertebrate Oxygen-binding Proteins: Structure, Active Site and Function*, (ed. J. Lamy & J. Lamy), pp. 571–588. New York and Basel: Dekker.

WOLF, G., VAN PACHTENBEKE, M., MOENS, L. & VAN HAUWAERT, M. L. (1983). Oxygen binding characteristics of *Artemia* hemoglobin domains. *Comp. Biochem. Physiol.* **76B**, 731–736.

WOOD, S. C. (ed.) (1980). Symposium on *Respiratory Pigments*, Annual Meeting of the American Society of Zoologists (27–30 December 1978, Richmond, Virginia). *Am. Zool.* **20**, 1–211.

WOOD, E. J. (ed.) (1983). *Structure and function of invertebrate respiratory proteins*. In *Life Chem. Repts*, Sup. 1. London: Harwood.

WYMAN, J. (1964). Linked functions and reciprocal effects in hemoglobin: a second look. *Adv. Protein Chem.* **19**, 223–286.

YAGER, T. D., TERWILLIGER, N. B., TERWILLIGER, R. C., SCHABTACH, E. & VAN HOLDE, K. E. (1982). Organization and physical properties of the giant extracellular hemoglobin of the clam, *Astarte castanea*. Biochem. Biophys. Acta **709**, 194–203.

YANCEY, P. H., CLARK, M. E., HAND, S. C., BOWLUS, R. D. & SOMERO, G. N. (1982). Living with water stress: evolution of osmolyte systems. *Science* **217**, 1214–1222.

YANCEY, P. H. & SOMERO, G. N. (1978). Urea-requiring lactate dehydrogenases of marine elasmobranch fishes. *J. comp. Physiol.* **125**, 135–141.

YANCEY, P. H. & SOMERO, G. N. (1979). Counteraction of urea destabilization of protein structure by methylamine osmoregulatory compounds of elasmobranch fishes. *Biochem. J.* **183**, 317–323.

YANCEY, P. H. & SOMERO, G. N. (1980). Methylamine osmoregulatory solutes of elasmobranch fishes counteract urea inhibition of enzymes. *J. exp. Zool.* **212**, 205–213.

Printed in Great Britain © *Society of Experimental Biology 1985*

OSMOTIC CONTROL IN MARINE ANIMALS

JOHN DAVENPORT

Animal Biology Group, Marine Science Laboratories, Menai Bridge,
Gwynedd, North Wales, U.K.

Summary

The sea is the home of two types of animal; primary marine inhabitants of wholly marine ancestry (mainly invertebrates) and secondary marine inhabitants (mainly fish and higher vertebrates) which have had a fresh-water or terrestrial phase in their evolutionary history. The former have blood osmolarities close to that of seawater, and only encounter osmotic problems at the sea's margins (e.g. intertidal zones, lagoons, estuaries) where salinities are different from the open sea; the latter have low blood concentrations and potentially have problems of salt loading and water loss in seawater.

Most primary marine inhabitants are stenohaline, live in the open sea and encounter no osmotic stress, and can tolerate little change in external salinity. The bulk of their euryhaline relatives living in the more demanding environments of littoral zones and estuaries rely heavily upon behavioural osmotic control. Sessile animals employ isolation responses (burrowing, shell valve closure etc.) when external salinities are stressful; mobile species have been little studied, but some are known to avoid deleterious salinities or choose optimum concentrations. The existence of predictive and reactive categories of behavioural osmotic control in mobile animals is suggested.

Intracellular osmotic regulation by changes in the size of the pool of non-essential amino acids is the basis of much penetration of brackish/hypersaline water by primary marine inhabitants; however, it is doubtful whether changes in amino acid concentration are rapid enough to prevent cellular swelling/shrinkage in animals exposed to short-term salinity fluctuations (e.g. in estuaries, splash-zone pools).

Extracellular osmoregulation is characteristic of fish, many euryhaline crustacea and a few representatives of other groups. It depends primarily on salt pumps (located usually at gut and/or gill) but low integumentary permeabilities to salt and water are equally essential. The permeability of teleost eggs to salt and water is given special consideration because of

their hypo-osmotic state and apparent absence of osmoregulatory structures.

In elasmobranchs and coelocanths the problems of salt loading and
water loss have effectively been met by separate mechanisms. Osmotic
water loss is opposed by high blood concentrations of urea (maintained
by renal reabsorption and low branchial permeability) which result in a
total blood osmolarity rather higher than that of the external medium.
Control of blood salt level in this group is still not fully understood; the
secretion of rectal fluid is not essential for survival, and appears to function mainly to achieve the rapid excretion of salt loads incurred by meals
of salt-rich invertebrates.

Marine insects, reptiles and birds have relatively impermeable integuments and lose little urinary water. However, they pick up salt in their
diet and employ a variety of structures (Malpighian tubules, various salt
glands) to excrete salt rich fluids with a higher osmolarity than seawater.

Evolutionary trends, particularly in terms of the early development of
cell-wall ion pumps, and the evolution of behavioural osmotic control,
are discussed.

Introduction

In the latter part of the nineteenth century it was discovered that animal
body fluids resembled seawater in their ionic composition. Together with
the observation that all animal phyla may be found in seawater, yet
several are missing in whole or in part from freshwater or land (e.g.
echinoderms, pogonophora, cephalopods), this ionic data formed the
basis of the generally accepted hypotheses of Haldane (1954), Bernal
(1954) and Oparin (1957) that the origin and early evolution of all living
organisms took place in the open sea. Adaptive radiation subsequently
led to the colonization of other environments; shores and estuaries,
streams and lakes, bog, mountain and desert. The spur for this radiation
presumably lay in the prize of access to unexploited habitats and energy
sources, but in order to achieve survival in more extreme habitats there
was a general tendency for a reduction in the overall ionic strength of
body fluids.

More recently still, the sea has been re-entered by animals from these
harsher environments, so in consequence there are broadly speaking two
categories of animals living in the sea with opposing ionic and osmotic
problems; primary and secondary inhabitants.

This paper is concerned with the behavioural, structural and
physiological means by which both types of marine animal control the

osmolarity of their cells and body fluids. The wider area of animal osmotic control has attracted much study in the past 60 years and the literature has been reviewed regularly at various levels (e.g. Krogh, 1939; Lockwood, 1963; Potts & Parry, 1964; Bentley, 1971; Maloiy, 1979; Gilles, 1979; Rankin & Davenport, 1981). In a short review it is therefore inappropriate to attempt an exhaustive treatment, so a general outline is given, with additional detail in a few areas which have perhaps attracted less attention than others.

Problems

The overriding purpose of osmotic control is to avoid or minimize osmotic gradients between the cells of animals and their environment, whether this be the external medium (in the case of protozoans, sponges and coelenterates) or the extracellular fluid. For primary marine inhabitants living in the open sea there are few strictly osmotic problems because intracellular and extracellular body fluids are close to isosmocity (ignoring slight discrepancies caused by Gibbs–Donnan equilibria) with the external medium, having a concentration of *ca.* 1000 mOsmoles kg^{-1}. Such animals excrete some ions (especially SO_4^{2-}) and metabolites isosmotically, so suffer bulk fluid loss and consequently require volume regulatory mechanisms. They also need ion uptake and extrusion sites to maintain discrepancies between body fluid and seawater ionic concentrations (see Table 1). However, *sensu strictu* they do not need osmotic control mechanisms unless exposed to the more stressful conditions at the sea's margins – in estuaries, lagoons and between the tidemarks. In these more demanding areas they can be exposed to media more concentrated or more dilute than oceanic seawater; intertidally they also run the risk of desiccation. In dilute media they will tend to take up water from the environment by osmosis and lose salts by diffusion; the reverse situation occurs in lagoons or pools concentrated by sun- or wind-driven evaporation. Strictly speaking, desiccation does not cause osmotic problems since osmosis can only take place between two liquid media. However, exposure to air of reduced relative humidity (R.H.) is a potential cause of increase in body fluid osmolarity, and loss of water, which must be countered or minimized.

Historically, most study of osmotic control in primarily marine animals has been carried out in temperate areas where the most likely stressor is that of reduced salinity encountered in estuaries or intertidally because of rain and terrestrial run off. Such hypo-osmotic stress may take two forms, though there is probably a continuum between them. First, there

Table 1. *Extracellular fluid ionic concentrations in some marine invertebrates (from Robertson, 1957), and in* Myxine *(from Bellamy & Chester-Jones, 1961)*

Group	Concentration of ions as percentage of seawater ionic concentrations					
	Na$^+$	K$^+$	Ca^{2+}	Mg^{2+}	Cl$^-$	SO$_4^{2-}$
A. Coelenterates						
Aurelia aurita	99	106	96	97	104	47
B. Echinoderms						
Marthasterias glacialis	100	111	101	98	101	100
C. Tunicates						
Salpa maxima	100	113	96	95	102	65
D. Annelids						
Arenicola marina	100	104	100	100	100	92
E. Crustaceans						
Maia squinado	100	125	122	81	102	66
Carcinus maenas	110	118	108	34	104	61
Nephrops norvegicus	113	77	124	17	99	69
F. Molluscs						
Pecten maximus	100	130	103	97	100	97
Sepia officinalis	93	205	91	98	105	22
G. Agnathans						
Myxine glutinosa	117	91	61	38	102	–

may be short-term (usually tidal) changes in environmental salinity, typical of drowned river valley estuaries (see Fig. 1), which impose continually changing concentration differences between the internal and external milieux. Secondly, there can be stable environmental salinities below those of the open sea; these are found mainly in lagoons and brackish seas (*e.g.* Chesapeake Bay, Baltic Sea). Hyperosmotic stress, caused by heightened external salinity is often assumed to be a largely tropical and subtropical phenomenon (especially of shallow lagoons), but occurs in temperate salt marshes just as in mangrove swamps, and is also a feature of high latitude intertidal pools where surface ice formation causes underlying salinity levels to rise dramatically (Ganning, 1971; Davenport, 1979a).

Secondary marine inhabitants have rather different osmotic problems. Animals which have had a freshwater phase in their ancestry (mainly fish) have low body fluid ionic concentrations, roughly one third that of seawater. They therefore tend to lose water by osmosis and take up salts by diffusion when in seawater. Animals of terrestrial ancestry (insects,

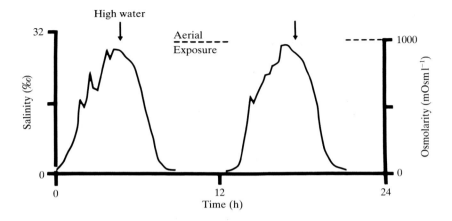

Fig. 1. Salinity changes during the tidal cycle at a point on the shore of the Conwy Estuary, North Wales (redrawn from Cawthorne, 1979).

reptiles, birds and mammals) have similar low blood ionic concentrations (having themselves had freshwater ancestry), but are generally adapted to conserve water, so are preadapted to some extent for life in the sea. However, they have problems in dealing with the salt loads associated with eating marine organisms and/or drinking high-salinity water. As with primary marine inhabitants, some species spend at least part of their life history feeding in, or moving through estuaries and the intertidal zone (e.g. migratory teleosts and elasmobranchs; some reptiles and birds) so may face alterations in the strength and direction of osmotic stress.

Solutions

It must first be emphasised that the majority of marine animals are stenohaline invertebrates which do not have the ability to control the osmotic pressure of their body fluids. If placed in diluted or concentrated seawater they soon die as their cells swell or shrink and intracellular ionic concentrations become inappropriate for enzyme function. The few remaining marine invertebrates are described as euryhaline since they may survive in media of a variety of osmolarities. However, most of them have no control over the osmolarity of their body fluids, which eventually become isosmotic with the external medium if that medium remains constant in osmolarity. Such animals are known as osmoconformers (see Fig. 2), and can only exert osmotic control by biochemical mechanisms at the cellular level, and, in some cases, by behavioural avoidance of

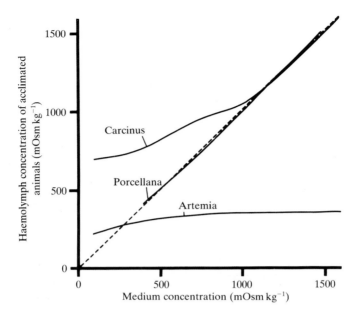

Fig. 2. A comparison of body fluid and ambient osmolarity for an osmoconformer (*Porcellana*), a hyperosmotic osmoregulator (*Carcinus*) and a hypo–hyperosmotic regulator (*Artemia*). The broken line represents isosmocity.

deleterious salinities. The bulk of intertidal, lagoon and estuarine invertebrate species fall into this category. Finally, there are a small number of species (mainly fish and crustaceans, but including a few annelids and gastropods) which are capable of maintaining differences between the osmolarity of their body fluids and the external medium by a variety of structural, physiological and biochemical means.

Behavioural osmotic control

Osmoconformers can only control the concentration of their body fluids by behavioural mechanisms, while osmoregulators often need to supplement their physiological or biochemical attributes by behavioural reactions when exposed to extreme salinities. There are several possible ways of subdividing behavioural responses to salinity, but it is probably easiest to consider sessile and mobile species separately:

1. Sessile species

Truly sessile animal species occurring in brackish water or hypersaline areas include barnacles, bivalve molluscs, bryozoa, tunicates and some annelids. Slow moving species with very limited ranges may also be considered here (e.g. limpets, chitons, lugworms). Basically, none of these animals can avoid changes in salinity by escape reactions (i.e. by physically moving from an unfavourable environment to a more attractive one). Most sessile species cannot tolerate prolonged tissue contact with low external salinities, and therefore deploy various behavioural mechanisms to minimize such contact.

First let us consider the hard-shelled epifaunal species (bivalves, barnacles, limpets and chitons). Milne (1940) was one of the first workers to note that estuarine bivalves closed their shell valves in response to freshwater influence when he studied mussels (*Mytilus edulis*) living in the Aberdeenshire River Dee. He found that mussels tightly adducted their shell valves as seawater concentrations fell, and therefore maintained high salinity levels within the mantle cavity. Accordingly, the mussels' tissues were exposed to a fraction of the external salinity range. This response has since been studied in greater detail (Davenport, 1979b; 1981). Mussels have peripheral salinity receptors on the tentacles of the inhalant siphon. These are sensitive to Na^+, Mg^{2+} and possibly to Cl^-, but not to other ions or the osmotic pressure of the external medium. The valve closure mechanism is a progressive three-part process. First, at an external salinity of *ca.* 26‰ the exhalant siphon of the mussel closes, and this action immediately stops effective mantle cavity irrigation (see Davenport, 1979c). Next the inhalant siphon is shut (at *ca.* 24‰) and finally the shell valves become tightly adducted at about 20‰. The net result of this behaviour is that the mantle cavity of *Mytilus* remains full of a fluid with a salinity of about 26‰ (often for many hours, even in freshwater) – only about 20% below that of full seawater (see Fig. 3). These values were derived in a simulated estuarine salinity regime in which salinities fluctuated between 34‰ and 0‰; in real estuaries, salinities may not rise as high on the flood tide, but the author has measured mantle fluid salinities of 25–28‰ in mussels bathed in near freshwater at low tide in the Conwy estuary. Obviously this type of isolation behaviour is extremely effective in reducing osmotic stress, but despite its efficiency there are some problems associated with the behaviour. First, if tissue isolation is to be effective, it is obvious that contact between the external medium and the mantle fluid has to be reduced to a minimum to prevent salt and water exchange. So how is a mussel to register that the conditions in the external environment have returned to favourable levels? Davenport (1981) showed that mussels did not periodically open their shell valves to test the external medium, but that diffusion of salts through the narrow gap between the shell valves to receptors on the

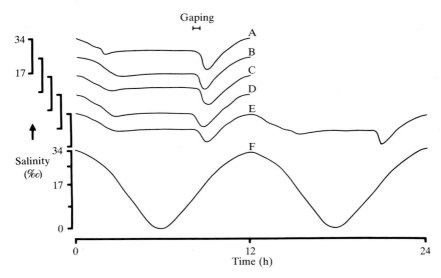

Fig. 3. Conductivity traces from the mantle fluid of five mussels (A–E) exposed to the sinusoidal salinity regime (F) shown below. Conductivity expressed as equivalent salinity; each trace is to the same vertical scale. From Davenport (1981).

tentaculate portion of the inhalant siphon (which also respond to falling salinities when the mussel is open and pumping) informs the mussel that it is safe to open again. Secondly, although isolation behaviour certainly protects mussels (or other sessile organisms behaving in similar fashion) against the adverse effects of low salinity, it also prevents animals from gaining food or oxygen from the environment during the period of isolation. This point is of ecological importance and discussed more fully elsewhere (Davenport, 1985).

Similar isolation mechanisms to that used by *Mytilus* have been demonstrated for a variety of other epifaunal invertebrates, including limpets, which can clamp themselves down onto rocky substrata and thereby trap high-salinity water around their tissues (e.g. *Acmaea limatula* – see Segal & Dehnel, 1962). In analogous fashion, a number of intertidal gastropods are capable of retreating into their shells and shutting out low-salinity water by closing the shell aperture with the operculum. However, gastropods can often be quite mobile forms, so will be discussed later in more detail.

The other group of hard-shelled epifauna which has attracted study consists of intertidal and estuarine barnacles. Like bivalves, these animals can isolate themselves from the environment; in their case by closing the opercular plates. In estuarine situations they can retain high-salinity water (>25‰) despite near freshwater external conditions (Cawthorne, 1979). Barnes & Barnes (1958) gave direct evidence for the existence of receptors (probably located on the soft lips of the opercular plates) which are sensitive to salinity and inorganic ions. If drops of water are placed on the closed opercular plates of *Balanus balanoides* the animals only open and protrude their cirri if the salinity is above *ca.* 17‰. Critical salinities causing cessation of activity and resumption of interaction with the external medium under simulated estuarine conditions were determined by Davenport (1976), and are shown in Table 2.

Soft-bodied sessile epifaunal animals (e.g. sponges, sea anemones, tunicates and bryozoa) are less common in estuaries than hard-shelled forms, and have also attracted little study in terms of their osmotic relations. All are believed to be osmoconformers and, if they have any responses at all, can only slow down osmotic equilibration with the external medium by behaviourally restricting the surface area of tissue exposed to the external medium, or by secreting mucus which effectively thickens the integument and consequently slows down water and ion movements. Thus, Shumway (1978) found that the sea anemone *Metridium senile* expelled water from the enteron, retracted its tentacles, and shrank as salinities fell, thereby reducing the effective surface area of the animal by several orders of magnitude; the author has also noted increased mucus production in this and other anemone species exposed to low salinities. More study of soft-bodied forms would be desirable; they would appear to be particularly suited to the study of the function of mucus.

Rocky substrata, on which epifaunal animals thrive, normally form relatively small portions of the areas of estuaries and other brackish water habitats. Gravel, sand and muddy substrata are far more extensive and support a rich fauna of sessile invertebrates. Kinne (1971) pointed out

Table 2. *Critical salinity levels for intertidal balanomorph barnacles exposed to a sinusoidal salinity regime of 12 h wavelength fluctuating between 33·3 and 6·7‰. (simplified from Davenport, 1976)*

Species	Mean salinities (‰)	
	a) Inducing activity cessation	b) Inducing activity onset
A. From Menai Strait		
Balanus crenatus	23·3	21·7
Balanus balanoides	23·6	23·3
Elminius modestus	22·0	19·5
B. From Conwy Estuary		
Balanus crenatus	19·1	19·4
Elminius modestus	20·4	24·4

that the interstitial salinity of estuarine substrata remains higher, and is far less variable than the salinity of the overlying water column, because of the denser nature of more saline water, combined with the slowness of diffusional processes between the water column and the interstices of the sediments. Animals living entirely within estuarine sediments (e.g. nematodes, protozoans) will therefore be exposed to relatively little osmotic stress by virtue of their infaunal habit. However, many members of the infauna, particularly larger forms, live in burrows within the substratum, but have to interact with the water column to gain food or an adequate supply of oxygen. Siphonate clams such as *Scrobicularia plana* and *Mya arenaria* are able to detect salinity changes in the water entering the inhalant siphon. *Mya arenaria* retracts its siphons and stops pumping when the salinity of the water column declines to about 10‰, while *Scrobicularia* simply becomes less active as the salinity falls (Bettison, 1982). Both responses are effective in dramatically slowing osmotic equilibration with the water column (Shumway, 1977). The means by which *Scrobicularia* detects salinity changes has been studied by Akberali & Davenport (1982), who found that changes in medium concentration were detected by the visceral ganglion which is situated at the base of the inhalant siphon (directly exposed to the inhalant stream) in this species. The ganglion proved to be sensitive to Ca^{2+}, Na^+ and Mg^{2+}, and thus differed somewhat from the detection mechanism of *Mytilus edulis*. Incidentally, it seems probable that a central rather than peripheral location for salinity reception is necessary in *Scrobicularia* because the long, extensible siphons of the species are regularly cropped by predators (particularly flatfish). The siphons regenerate readily, but if receptors were mounted upon them, cropping would cause temporary loss of salinity sensitivity.

The lugworm *Arenicola marina* (and related arenicolids) behaves in analogous fashion to these clams; when the water column salinity falls below about 20‰ the worms cease irrigating their burrows and retreat to the bottom of their mucus-lined tubes where the stable interstitial salinities allow them to survive despite their limited physiological euryhalinity and classic osmoconforming nature (Shumway & Davenport, 1977). Periodically the lugworms test the water column by briefly pumping water, but they quickly become inactive again if the salinity is still below 20‰. This sensitive behavioural mechanism allows the soft-bodied, highly permeable *Arenicola* to maintain its body fluid osmolarity within narrower limits than intertidal barnacles, and even matches the capability of osmoregulators such as the shore crab *Carcinus maenas* (Davenport, 1985).

A feature of all sessile animals which demonstrate effective behavioural osmotic control is that the response is remarkably symmetrical (Davenport, 1982); the salinity which triggers isolation from unfavourable salinities is close to that which stimulates a return to normal activity when salinities rise again. Poorly adapted animals (e.g. the offshore barnacle *Balanus hameri* and the hermit crab *Pagurus berhardus*) exhibit pronounced asymmetry (Davenport, 1976; Davenport, Busscchots & Cawthorne, 1980). They tend to isolate themselves at similar salinities to the better adapted forms (for most estuarine species about 20‰), but invariably fail to recover until exposed to high salinity for quite long periods. This suggests that, even though they reduce tissue contact with the medium to some extent, they are still affected osmotically and therefore need a period of time in concentrated media before resuming normal activity. There are obvious energetic advantages conferred by a symmetrical behaviour pattern; food and oxygen collection during any tidal cycle are maximized, as are scope for growth and scope for activity. This last point is worth considering a little further; the penetration of such sessile forms into estuaries is almost certainly not controlled by salinity directly (the animals can tolerate any external salinity between freshwater and full seawater for many hours in most cases), but by the balance between the energy gained during periods of exposure to high enough salinities to permit feeding or O_2 uptake, and the energy consumed during periods of isolation and anaerobiosis.

Before leaving the topic of sessile animals it has to be stressed that all of their behavioural responses are only of advantage in habitats featuring short-term fluctuations in environmental salinity; if they live in lagoons or brackish seas where salinities change over periods of weeks rather than hours, they cannot utilize isolation behaviour, but have to interact with their environment. Thus, *Mytilus* in the Baltic Sea live in salinities as low as 5–7‰, and are isosmotic with such media, while in drowned river valley habitats where environmental salinities may fall close to zero, their tissues rarely encounter salinities below 20–25‰ (Milne, 1940; pers. obs.).

2. *Mobile species*

The term 'mobile' covers a vast range of abilities, from that of an intertidal gastopod which may move no more than a few metres (and usually much less) during a tidal cycle, to powerful fish like salmon and trout which can traverse many kilometres of water in a day. Some fish are known to be capable of avoiding deleterious salinities, or selecting optimum ones (e.g. Bull, 1938), and it is most probable that migratory teleosts (e.g. eels and salmon) sense alterations in the salinity of their surroundings. However, most experimental studies have been carried out upon rather smaller and more convenient animals which do not travel so far.

Several intertidal and estuarine crustaceans, both nektonic and benthic, have evolved behavioural mechanisms which keep them away from water of unfavourable salinity (e.g. Barnes, 1939; Krijgsman & Krijgsman, 1954; Gross, 1957; Lagerspetz & Mattila, 1961; Jansson, 1962; McLusky, 1970; Davenport, 1972; Davenport & Wankowski, 1973; Bettison & Davenport, 1976). Most of these are osmoregulators like *Corophium volutator* which has a refined mechanism to discriminate finely between different seawater concentrations (it can detect differences of less than 2·5‰), and so keep it in preferred salinities between 10 and 30‰ (McLusky, 1970), or *Marinogammarus marinus* which has a cruder mechanism which simply keeps it away from very low salinities (Bettison & Davenport, 1976). However, some are osmoconformers, and one of these is the anomuran porcelain crab *Porcellana platycheles*, which lives intertidally in crevices and shallow pools (up to midtide level) and so is exposed to the influences of rain and runoff. The animal has three behavioural mechanisms which allow it to avoid (or extricate itself from) potentially damaging dilute media. First, when immersed, it can detect salinity gradients and move along them to areas of higher concentration. The receptors involved in this process appear to be located upon the antennules, since destruction of the latter inhibits salinity choice (Davenport, 1972). The receptors are sensitive to the osmotic pressure of the external medium rather than to any specific ion or group of ions. Secondly, the crabs can recognize a dangerous external salinity and climb upwards to get out of the water. Finally, they can use their second and third walking limbs to 'test' the salinity of pools before they immerse themselves (Davenport & Wankowski, 1973). This last attribute is shared by a number of tropical and subtropical land crabs, some of which are able to select pools appropriate to their state of hydration – they choose more dilute pools if their blood concentration is high (Gross, 1955).

A few mobile molluscs can also detect unfavourable salinity levels. Ganning (1971) and Davenport et al., (1980) showed that intertidal rock pools usually have stable bottom salinities close to ambient seawater levels. However, pools exposed to freshwater inflow may often have an almost fresh surface layer. For most of the pools' inhabitants the freshwater layer will have no impact upon their existence, but gastropods may climb the side walls of such pools and therefore encounter horizontal salinity interfaces. Recently the author (unpublished data) has found that the winkle *Littorina littorea* can detect such interfaces with its cephalic tentacles, and will not cross into the more dilute medium if the upper layer has a salinity below about 10‰.

Almost all study of behavioural responses to salinity has been directed at the problems of animals of marine ancestry encountering *reduced* salinities. However, animals of freshwater origin living at the landward end of estuaries potentially face the opposite problem; how to avoid being exposed to water of too *high* a salinity. This problem is no doubt exacerbated for smaller and weak swimming animals by the net current direction, which will almost always tend to take freshwater animals seawards. This would appear to be a fruitful area for study, but so far appear to have attracted little attention. An exception lies in some studies upon a small number of reptilian species, basically of freshwater ancestry and origin, which penetrate brackish, or even fully marine habitats to some extent (see Dunson 1984 for review). Truly marine reptiles (sea turtles and sea snakes) possess structural and physiological modifications which allow them to combat the salt loads imposed upon them. A few crocodilians and freshwater turtles are found in salt water in part of their range (this is far more common a situation than once realized) and survive mainly because of behavioural reactions, since their physiology is inadequate to cope with salt uptake and water loss. The diamondback terrapin (*Malacolemys centrata*) and the American crocodile (*Crocodilus acutus*) can withstand high salinities by choosing to drink fresh or brackish water when available; both species are heavily dependent upon rain, particularly when young and handicapped by unfavourable surface-area-to-volume ratios. In the tidal creeks of Virginia, snapping turtles (*Chelydra serpentina*) will catch and eat crabs when foraging in salt water, but retreat to the low salinity part of their habitat for most of their existence. Analogous behavioural response are exhibited by some saltmarsh insects. Insects are generally impermeable to salts and water, but their food (whether animal or plant) tends to contain large amounts of salts. To avoid salt loading problems some intertidal beetles forage mainly after rainstorms or select food of the lowest available salt content (Bro Larsen, 1952, 1953).

In the case of planktonic organisms of estuaries, it can be important to avoid both low and high salinities to maintain an estuarine position without being carried too far upstream or out to sea. Little direct evidence is available for holoplanktonic organisms, although Lance (1962) found that estuarine copepods (*Acartia spp.* and *Centropages spp.*) could not migrate readily through salinity discontinuities in the water column. However, the situation of meroplanktonic larvae of oysters and barnacles has attracted some attention.

There has long been controversy about the means by which oyster larvae maintain their upstream position in estuaries prior to settlement. It should be remembered that oyster larvae, like their parents, can close their (uncalcified) shell valves to exclude the external medium; when the valves close the propulsive velum has to be retracted so the larvae sink onto the substratum. Three stances, as yet unresolved, have been adopted by various researchers. Some believe that the larvae have no control over their destiny, and are simply moved around by water currents, presumably with some wastage of those larvae swept into inappropriate areas (Loosanoff, 1949; Korringa, 1952; Andrews, 1954). Secondly, Pritchard (1953) proposed that, in a two-layered estuarine situation (commonly found in poorly mixed estuaries where 'salt wedges' move landwards along the substratum on each flood tide), oyster larvae would only have to remain close to the seabed (perhaps because of phototrophic or geotrophic reactions), to stay in high-salinity water and move upstream. Finally, there are those workers who have suggested that the larvae do have direct reactions to salinity, becoming inactive at low salinity but starting to swim up off the bottom as salinity rises, thus being swept upstream on the flood tide (Nelson, 1912; Haskin, 1964; Wood & Hargis, 1971). Since the adult oysters have a well-developed closure reaction to lowered salinity (Bettison, 1982), the author is inclined to favour the third hypothesis. Salinity sensitivity has been demonstrated for the larvae of estuarine barnacles by Cawthorne & Davenport (1980). These larvae have rather more complicated problems because the release stage (nauplius) is an unprotected form which has no ability to isolate itself from the external medium; it needs to be carried seawards if it is to survive. This stage is at least given a good start because the eggs hatch to release nauplii into the mantle cavity of the adult barnacle; if the external salinity is below about 25‰, the adult remains tightly closed and does not release larvae until conditions are more favourable (this behaviour is almost certainly identical with the normal salinity reaction of the adult and should not be confused with parental care). The settlement stage (cyprid) can isolate itself (by closure of the carapace valves), is very dense, and needs to be carried upstream (though not too far) to exploit estuarine settlement sites. *A priori* it would appear that the nauplii ought to react to fluctuating salinities by ceasing to swim, whereupon they would sink into water of higher salinity where they could resume swimming and be carried seawards on the ebb. Cyprids ought also to respond to falling salinities by ceasing to swim, but in their case this would cause them to fall to the substratum, so that they would avoid being carried too

Table 3. *Salinities inducing cessation of swimming in barnacle larvae exposed to falling salinities (from Cawthorne & Davenport, 1980). Critical salinities are those which stop swimming in 50 % of larvae; they are shown with 95 % confidence intervals*

Species	Rate of fall in salinity ($\text{‰}h^{-1}$)	Critical salinities (‰)	
		A. Nauplius	B. Cyprid
Elminius modestus	16·75	8·8 ± 0·9	9·0 ± 1·3
	4·81	6·6 ± 0·3	8·3 ± 0·9
Balanus balanoides	16·75	12·3 ± 1·0	10·9 ± 1·0
	4·81	9·3 ± 1·0	9·1 ± 1·1

far upstream on the flood tide. Cawthorne & Davenport confirmed this hypothesis, and recorded the critical salinities which triggered cessation of swimming; these are shown in Table 3. These values are close to the lethal salinity limits for the larvae of the two species studied (*Balanus balanoides* and *Elminius modestus*), so the reactions will not only ensure proper placement within the estuary (at least in terms of salinity; suitable substrata are selected by other mechanisms), but will also promote survival.

3. *Future directions*

Information about behavioural osmoregulation is rather fragmentary; most information collected so far is concerned with sessile osmoconformers, and it would be desirable for osmoregulators and more mobile species to be investigated. Salinity reception has been studied to some extent, but in most cases the receptor sites have either not been identified, or only localized approximately by crude ablation studies. Unfortunately most of the species studied in greatest detail (bivalves and barnacles) are not easy for neurophysiologists to study because their protective shells inhibit invasive experiments.

The underlying basis of salinity reception is also interesting in that the few studies performed so far have revealed much variation between the sensing mechanisms of different intertidal and estuarine forms. *Porcellana* detects osmotic pressure differences; *Mytilus* relies upon the detection of Na^+, Mg^{2+} and Cl^-, while *Scrobicularia* responds to Ca^{2+} as well. Together with the variety of receptor sites, this variation suggests that the ability to cope behaviourally with salinity stress has evolved many times, and with much convergence. However, more study of closely related species might reveal trends which are at present obscure.

Particularly interesting is the role of salinity sensing in the behaviour of migratory animals that breed in or move through estuaries (e.g. migratory teleosts, *Eriocheir spp.*, penaeid prawns, *Macrobrachium spp.*). Do mitten crabs cease their seaward breeding migration when the external salinity reaches a given level? Do larval and juvenile penaeids move along salinity gradients to reach their estuarine nursery areas, or do they rely upon other cues?

In the field of behavioural thermoregulation in ectothermic aquatic animals (which have to swim or otherwise change their location to regulate their temperature) two categories have been recognized in the last few years; 'predictive thermoregulation' and 'reactive thermoregulation' (see Neil, 1979 for review). To achieve predictive thermoregulation a fish does not need to recognize and swim along thermal gradients; it simply has a) to recognize that its current thermal state is suboptimal, and b) to possess inherent reactions to this situation which transfer it to a more favourable thermal environment. For example; a rock-pool fish swimming at the surface of its pool on a hot day only has to react to high external temperature by swimming downwards to cooler water – the relation down = cold is predictable. In contrast, reactive thermoregulation involves the recognition of, and reaction to, temperature differences and gradients (i.e. 'decisions' are based upon recent experience). Reactive responses are regarded as more flexible than predictive reactions (the latter are vulnerable to any breakdown in the predicted relationship), but predictive responses are in most cases as effective, and often more rapid. The author feels that similar considerations may equally apply to behavioural osmotic control in mobile species. A crustacean moving along salinity gradients to escape from suboptimal salinities might be regarded as employing reactive behavioural osmotic control, while a bivalve larva swimming through a horizontal salinity interface and responding to a low external salinity by ceasing to swim (and therefore automatically sinking back into more saline water) might be described as employing predictive behavioural osmotic control. Generally speaking, the rather few reactions to salinity described so far either fall into the reactive category, or defy assignment because of the experimental/statistical design used. However, if more study of mobile species is carried out, then reliance upon predictable relationships (e.g. low salinity = up; high salinity = downstream) rather than salinity gradients ought to be considered.

Physiological and biochemical osmotic control

1. *Intracellular osmotic regulation*

It has been known for some 30 years that the fluid within animal cells is always isosmotic with, or very slightly hyperosmotic to the extracellular fluid (e.g. Conway & McCormack, 1953; Appelboom, Brodsky, Tutle & Diamond, 1958; Maffly & Leaf, 1959). No exceptions to this rule have yet been demonstrated. However, the osmotic effectors making up osmolarity inside and outside the cell are very different. Outside the cells of the majority of marine animals, virtually all osmolarity is due to inorganic ions (except in the case of elasmobranchs, coelocanths and a few other species which have substantial quantities of urea (and often trimethylamine oxide) in their blood). Intracellular osmotic pressure on the other hand is substantially created (<60–70 %) by the presence of organic molecules which are too large to pass through the cell membranes, but small enough to create an osmotic pressure (so-called 'colloid osmotic pressure'). Because of the resultant Gibbs-Donnan equilibrium, it would be expected that these organic molecules would create a higher osmotic pressure within the cell than outside, and that (since animal cell walls are elastic) there would be an inward isosmotic flow of water and ions (which can pass through the cell membrane) causing swelling and cell lysis. This does not happen because cells possess active volume regulatory processes based at least to some extent upon the active uptake of K^+ and the extrusion of Na^+ from the intracellular fluid ('$Na^+ - K^+$ exchange pump' – see Rorive & Gilles, 1979 for critique).

When a marine animal is transferred from seawater to a dilute medium the extracellular fluid becomes diluted; this reduction in concentration is necessarily more dramatic in osmoconformers than osmoregulators. There is therefore a tendency for the osmotic flow of water into the cells because of the intracellular colloid osmotic pressure. In plant cells the semirigid cellulose cell walls allow the build up of hydrostatic pressure to oppose this osmotic pressure, but in animal cells, swelling takes place. Obviously there is a corresponding tendency towards cell shrinkage if animals are transferred from water of low salinity to media of high osmolarity.

In some stenohaline invertebrates such disturbances in cell structure appear to be irreversible (save by returning the animal to its original medium) and are probably a major cause of death when these animals are exposed to salinity changes. However, euryhaline osmoconformers (invertebrates and hagfish) and osmoregulators all possess a mechanism to deal with the problem of cellular swelling/shrinkage. During the past 25 years, a large number of investigators, but notably the biochemists Florkin, Schoffeniels and Gilles, have found that cells from a great variety of organisms (including some bacteria and microalgae) can manipulate the intracellular colloid osmotic pressure by controlling the concentration of

Table 4. *Amino acid concentrations in the tissues of* Eriocheir sinensis.
Data from Bricteux-Gregoire et al., *(1962)*

Amino acid	Concentrations (μmol. 100 mg^{-1} wet wt)		Rise (%)
	in fresh water	in sea water	
Alanine	1·39	3·37	142·5
Arginine	2·99	4·13	107·5
Aspartic acid	0·29	0·86	196·6
Glutamic acid	0·84	2·11	151·2
Glycine	4·64	8·00	72·4
Isoleucine	0·08	0·24	200·0
Leucine	0·14	0·40	185·7
Lysine	1·16	1·38	18·9
Phenylalanine	0·00	trace	–
Proline	0·77	3·50	354·5
Serine	0·21	0·47	123·8
Taurine	1·67	2·06	23·3
Threonine	0·36	1·14	216·7
Tyrosine	0·00	trace	–
Valine	0·00	0·50	–
TOTAL	14·54	28·16	93·7
Blood osmolarity (mOsm kg^{-1})	550	1100	

free amino acids which make up a considerable proportion (usually
>60 %) of that colloid osmotic pressure. In animals exposed to low
salinities the size of the free amino acid pool decreases (thus reducing
total intracellular osmolarity), while if they are exposed to hyperosmotic
stress the amino acid concentration rises. Early in these studies it was
realized that not all intracellular amino acids were involved in this
mechanism; except for arginine, only the so-called 'non-essential' amino
acids were implicated. An example derived from the very euryhaline
Chinese mitten crab *Eriocheir sinensis* (Bricteux-Gregoire, Duchâteau-
Bosson, Jeuniaux & Florkin, 1962) is shown in Table 4. Amongst the non-
essential amino acids there is considerable interspecific variation in the
osmotic significance of the various amino acids, though proline, alanine
and glycine often dominate. In a few species, osmotic effectors other than
amino acids have been implicated; *Eriocheir* employs trimethlyamine
oxide to some extent. This area of research has been reviewed on several
occasions, and massively not too long ago by Gilles (1979). Present
biochemical research is concentrated upon the means by which the size
of the amino acid pool is manipulated. While there is considerable
controversy, and a complicated picture is emerging, it seems that control

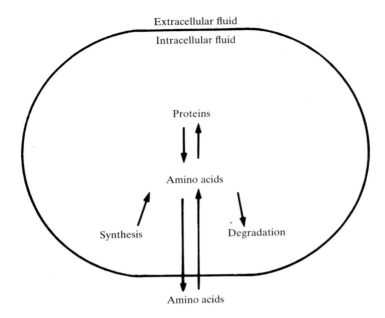

Fig. 4. Possible mechanisms of control of the intracellular amino acid pool (Gilles, 1979).

takes place at the cellular level by local feedback mechanisms, and that there is no evidence at present for direct nervous or hormonal control of intracellular colloid osmotic pressure. Possible mechanisms are indicated diagrammatically in Fig. 4. There is no particular reason to assume that a single mechanism is involved, indeed there is some evidence to suggest that alterations in the rate of amino acid efflux may explain much of the response to lowered salinity (see Gilles, 1979), while there is some support for the idea that raised amino acid levels in response to hyperosmotic stress are associated with increases in the concentration of protein-degrading enzymes (e.g. Moore, Koehn & Bayne, 1980). Schoffeniels & Gilles (1970) have also shown that the activities of some of the enzymes involved in amino acid synthesis and breakdown are profoundly altered by the salt content of their surroundings, which indicates another control route. However, in the case of at least some amino acids (proline, tyrosine, phenylalanine, leucine, isoleucine and valine), regulation appears to be primarily achieved by changes in permeability of the cell membranes. Thus, when an animal is transferred from seawater to a medium of lower salinity, there is an increased permeability of the cell walls (perhaps because of osmotic swelling?) to these amino acids, which diffuse into the blood along concentration gradients. In most cases the extruded amino acids are broken down elsewhere in the animal's body by oxidases, and the nitrogen excreted as NH_3. In *Eriocheir* it would appear that extruded proline is transported to the three posterior gill pairs of the crab, where it is degraded by proline oxidase, and the resultant NH_3 diffuses easily out into the surrounding medium.

There is no doubt that alterations in the size of the amino acid pool are effective in animals exposed to gradual changes in environmental salinity. Historically, it is probable that the penetration of brackish seas (e.g. the Baltic) by osmoconformers (e.g. *Mytilus, Asterias*) was only possible by a reduction in intracellular colloid osmotic pressure. However, some workers have implied that changes in free amino acid concentration are rapid enough to prevent cellular volume changes in animals exposed to short-term alterations in environmental salinity. For *Eriocheir* it appears (Gilles, 1979) that adjustments to a direct transfer from seawater to freshwater are accomplished in about 24 h, while compensation in the opposite direction takes much longer (>15 days); whatever the direction of transfer, some change in tissue hydration, and hence cell volume, does take place.

However, *Eriocheir* makes its breeding migrations between freshwater and seawater over long distances (often hundreds of kilometres) and so changes in environmental salinity are probably fairly slow. For animals exposed to regular tidal fluctuations in salinity (*ca.* 12·4 h wavelength) these responses would appear to be too slow to *prevent* cell volume changes. Shumway, Gabbott & Youngson (1977) investigated amino acid levels (measured as ninhydrin-positive substances, N.P.S.) in the adductor muscles of *Mytilus* acclimated to simulated tidal changes in salinity. They found that there was virtually no change in amino acid concentra-

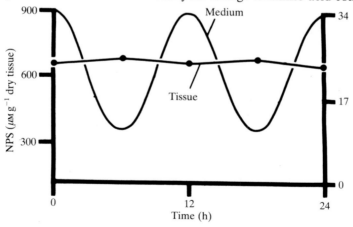

Fig. 5. Tissue amino acid concentrations (measured as ninhydrin-positive substances, NPS) in mussels, *Mytilus edulis*, exposed to fluctuating salinities (redrawn from Shumway *et al.*, 1977).

tion during the salinity fluctuations (see Fig. 5), although the tissue N.P.S. level was lower than in mussels taken from full seawater. This suggests that there is an overall reduction in the size of the amino acid pool of estuarine mussels to a level which minimizes the effects of alternating hypo- and hyperosmotic stress, but in the case of *Mytilus* there is the complicating factor of isolation behaviour in response to low salinity. More recently, Burton & Feldman (1982) have investigated free amino acid concentrations in the intertidal harpacticoid copepod *Tigriopus californicus*, which lives in splash-zone pools. These animals are extraordinarily euryhaline, being capable of withstanding abrupt salinity changes of considerable magnitude, and living indefinitely in media ranging from about 5–100‰. They are osmoregulators (McDonough & Stiffler, 1981), but still undergo great changes in haemolymph concentration when exposed to substantial alterations in environmental salinity. These features, coupled with their small size (which favours rapid ionic and osmotic equilibration) suggest that *Tigriopus* would be a most likely candidate for rapid intracellular osmotic adjustment. If acclimated to a variety of salinities for 10 days, *Tigriopus* shows the normal differences in amino acid levels, with proline being most important (see Fig. 6). However, responses to sudden osmotic stress are only a little quicker than in the far larger *Eriocheir*. Much adjustment to hypo-osmotic stress is accomplished in about 5 h (although complete equilibration takes at least 24 h) but, as with *Eriocheir*, adjustment to hyperosmotic stress takes several days. More tellingly, Burton & Feldman report that haemolymph concentration changes occur (accompanied by grossly obvious changes in animal volume) within about 20 min of the abrupt transfer between salinities, so this mismatch in timing suggests that cellular swelling and shrinkage is inevitable in animals exposed to short-term salinity fluctuations – which perhaps helps to explain the heavy reliance upon behavioural osmotic control in animals living in the intertidal zone and in the harsher estuarine environments, despite the fact that most of them are capable of regulating the size of their intracellular amino acid pools.

2. Salt pumps and permeability

Invertebrate osmoregulators and teleost fish are able to sustain osmolarity differences between their body fluids and the external medium. Most of the invertebrates are hyperosmotic regulators which are isosmotic with the medium at high salinities, but are hyperosmotic to dilute media. Marine teleosts are hypo-osmotic to the outside medium. To maintain these concentration differences, the animals require salts to be

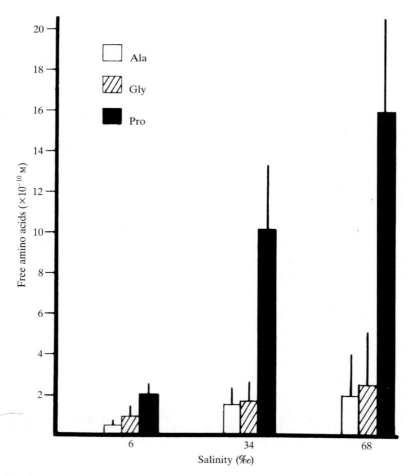

Fig. 6. Levels of free amino acids in copepods, *Tigriopus californicus*, acclimated to three different salinities. Symbols represent mean values ±s.D. (from Burton & Feldman, 1982).

actively pumped across the body wall (in this context the gut surface has to be considered part of the body wall) with concomitant osmotic water flow which has to be balanced by drinking or appropriate changes in urine production. Thus, an invertebrate maintaining a high blood concentration in a dilute medium tends to lose salts by diffusion and so has to pump salts inwards from the environment. This maintenance of a high blood osmolarity causes an osmotic inflow of water which has to be opposed by increased urine output. In most invertebrates the urine is isosmotic with the blood, so represents a route of salt loss, but a few euryhaline invertebrates (in which integumentary salt loss is fairly low) are capable of secreting a dilute (hypo-osmotic) urine which conserves body salt; this ability was first detected in the amphipod *Gammarus duebeni* (Lockwood, 1961).

In contrast, a marine teleost, with its low blood osmolarity, tends to gain salts by diffusion and lose water osmotically. To combat water loss the fish has to drink, but this causes salt uptake problems. Hirano & Mayer-Gostan (1976), working with seawater-adapted eels, found that the oesophagus is highly permeable to salts, but not to water, so salts diffuse from the gut fluid into the blood (thereby adding to the fish's salt-loading problem), effectively diluting the ingested seawater before it reaches the stomach. The eel stomach was found to be permeable to salts and water, so more salt diffuses into the blood, while water moves osmotically in the opposite direction to further dilute the gut fluid. By the time gut fluid enters the intestine it has half the osmolarity of seawater, but is still hyperosmotic to the blood. However, in the intestine there is an uptake of water, even though this is apparently against an osmotic gradient. This water uptake is known to require the active pumping of salts from gut fluid to blood (Skadhauge, 1974), so is known as 'solute-linked water flow', but how this is accomplished is still controversial. Local osmotic gradients, created in the intercellular spaces of the gut epithelium were invoked by Diamond & Bossert (1967) in their 'standing gradient hypothesis' (see Fig. 7) which has the attraction of not requiring water to move against osmotic gradients, but there are objections to facets of this hypothesis (see Kirschner, 1979; Rankin & Davenport, 1981 for discussion), and more work and finer techniques will be required for further progress. However, the net effect of drinking seawater is to help to solve the problem of osmotic water loss (also aided by minimal urine output), but to exacerbate the tendency to take up salts. Salt loading is opposed in marine teleosts by the active outward pumping of salts across the gills by the so-called 'chloride cells'.

Sites of active pumping of salts in primitive animals probably evolved originally as proton pumps required to control cell volume (Wilson & Maloney, 1976), which led in osmoregulating metazoans to pumps operating over wide areas of the body surface. More recently still, in evolutionary terms, there has been a tendency towards localization of the salt-pumping function to specialized areas of the integument – usually the gut and gills. Gill salt pumps have been extensively studied in crustaceans and fish, and it has become increasingly clear that the location on gills is highly appropriate because of the interlocking nature of ionic and respiratory exchange with acid–base balance and nitrogenous excretion (which largely occurs at the gills, in the form of NH_3, in aquatic animals).

Historically (mainly for technical and economic reasons – see Rankin & Davenport, 1981 for discussion), research concerned with salt pumps

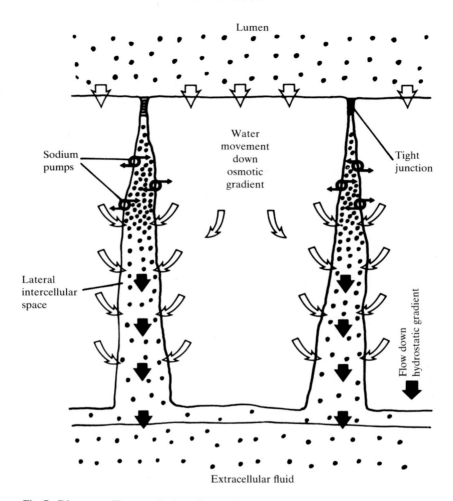

Fig. 7. Diagram to illustrate the 'standing gradient hypothesis' for solute-linked water flow across an epithelium. Density of dots is proportional to ion concentration. Open arrows represent water movement, solid arrows represent movement of solution. From Rankin & Davenport (1981), but based upon Diamond & Bossert (1967).

has been heavily concentrated upon the transport of Na^+, K^+ and Cl^+, although the ionic values presented in Table 1 indicate that a far wider range of pump mechanisms must exist. The literature devoted to active salt transport is extensive and cannot be handled in detail here. However, it should be pointed out that there are common histological and biochemical features of salt pumps which transcend phylogeny, even though their gross anatomical sites appear very different. The pumps require energy in the form of adenosine triphosphate (ATP) to drive them, and there are associated enzymes (Na^+, K^+-ATPase and Mg^{2+}-ATPase) which have been reported from a wide range of vertebrates and invertebrates. Typically there are correlations between the levels of these enzymes and the osmotic gradient between body fluids and the external medium; Jowett, Rhead & Bayne (1981), for example, found that enzyme activity in the gills of *Carcinus maenas* rose if the crab was transferred from seawater to more dilute media. Recently, several studies have also implicated the enzyme carbonic anhydrase in the osmoregulation process, particularly of crabs (e.g. Henry & Cameron, 1982) with falling salinities being accompanied by rising levels of the enzyme in the posterior two or three pairs of gills (where ATPases are also found *e.g.* Neufeld, Holliday & Pritchard, 1980). The function of this enzyme in salt pumping is not yet clear, although HCO_3^- is exchanged for Cl^- to remove CO_2 and take up Cl^- in freshwater animals, so a similar mechanism may operate in euryhaline crabs moving into brackish water.

The more euryhaline crustaceans and teleosts, particularly those capable of migrating between seawater and freshwater, are capable of pumping salts in either direction across the gills, so that they may extrude salts when external salinities are high, and absorb salts from dilute media. In teleosts it seems that the same cells are involved in both uptake and extrusion; the switch between the two functions may take days in migratory teleosts, although House (1963) demonstrated that the intertidal blenny, *Blennius pholis*, could switch in less than 5 min from pumping outwards in hyperosmotic media to pumping inwards in hypo-osmotic solutions ($<400\,$mOsmoles kg^{-1}). Davenport & Vahl (1979) found that the blenny maintained a near constant blood concentration when exposed to alternate 6 h periods in seawater and freshwater. In euryhaline crabs there is some confusion; some workers have implied that ion extrusion and uptake both take place across the posterior gills, but Watanabe & Yamada (1980) suggest that, in *Eriocheir japonicus* (a close relative of the Chinese mitten crab, with a similar lifestyle), there is a division of labour with the anterior gills being responsible for extrusion and the posterior gills dealing with uptake.

Salt pumps are essential if an aquatic animal is to be capable of osmoregulation, but just as crucial is the possession of a reduced permeability to water and salts to minimize the energy consumed in active processes which resist water and salt movements. As Kirschner (1979) points out, permeability measurements are difficult and our concepts of membrane and tissue permeability are rather primitive at present. However, it is well known that the integumentary permeability of osmoregulators is much lower than in related stenohaline marine osmoconformers. A moderately euryhaline crab such as *Carcinus maenas* shows half the water permeability of a marine form such as *Maja verrucosa*, while *Eriocheir sinensis* has a water permeability which is more than an order of magnitude less than that of *Carcinus* (see Kirschner, 1979 for review). Most fish, including rather surprisingly the osmoconforming hagfish (McFarland & Munz, 1965), have much lower permeabilities to salts and water than stenohaline invertebrates. Unfortunately (from an osmoregulation point of view!), a reduction in permeability cannot be carried too far because permeable structures (gills) are required for gaseous exchange. Only in the air-breathing marine reptiles, birds and mammals is there the possibility of extremely low integumentary permeabilities, and even amongst those animals the once-accepted idea of almost total impermeability is no longer viable for all species. Reptiles in particular have recently been shown to have more water-permeable skins than previously realized (Dunson, 1979; Minnich, 1979; Seymour, 1982; Lillywhite & Maderson, 1982), though Dunson & Stokes (1983) have recently revealed a fascinating adaptive feature of skin permeability in fully marine sea snakes. In these animals there is an asymmetry of permeability; water moves more readily inwards across the skin, while salts diffuse outwards more readily than inwards. This asymmetry is the opposite of that found in freshwater snakes.

The vitelline membrane of some marine teleost eggs has also been shown to have some interesting permeability characteristics. Both pelagic and demersal teleost eggs taken from the oviduct of the parent fish appear to be close to isosmocity with the maternal blood plasma (see Kjørsvik, Davenport & Lønning, 1984 for review) so the ovoplasm has an osmolarity of 300–400 mOsmoles kg^{-1}. When the eggs are laid they therefore encounter a substantially hyperosmotic external medium (*ca.* 1000 mOsmoles kg^{-1}), yet do not have the gut and gill salt pumps of their parents. The non-living chorion or eggshell is known to be freely permeable to salts and water in all species so far studied, and presents no barrier (e.g. Holliday, 1969; Potts & Eddy, 1973). However, many teleost eggs maintain near constant ovoplasm/yolk osmolarities from the time of spawning to hatching (e.g. Lønning & Davenport, 1980; Davenport, Lønning & Kjørsvik, 1981). Two explanations for this phenomenon are feasible; that eggs possess ion pumps which extrude salts from the ovoplasm, or that the vitelline membrane (which bounds the ovoplasm) itself must have a low permeability to salts and water. There is now strong evidence that permeability levels are low, especially in the more euryhaline species. Unfertilized cod, plaice and lumpsucker eggs all retain low osmolarities in full seawater for many hours despite their small size and high surface-area-to-volume ratios (Kjørsvik, unpublished data;

Holliday & Jones, 1967; Kjørsvik *et al.*, 1984), while fertilized lump sucker (*Cyclopterus lumpus*) eggs held in deionized distilled water showed only an 8% decline in ovoplasm concentration after 24 h (Kjørsvik *et al.*, 1984). More recently still (Davenport & Stene, in Press), the author has found that eggs of the capelin *Mallotus villosus* (a marine salmonoid teleost) can survive and develop for several weeks in deionized distilled water; this survival can only be attributed to a low-permeability vitelline membrane, since the capelin chorion is known to be extraordinarily permeable to water (Davenport & Vahl, 1984). The source of this low permeability in teleost eggs is not known, although the experiments of Potts & Eddy (1973) upon plaice (*Pleuronectes platessa*) eggs show that low permeability develops in the first few minutes after spawning, when a variety of histological changes are taking place during egg 'hardening'. Further structural and biochemical studies of the vitelline membrane should prove fruitful.

Before leaving the topic of permeability, mention should be made of the importance of mucus. This has already been touched upon in the consideration of behavioural osmotic control in soft-bodied epifaunal species, but mucus is also thought to be involved in the osmoregulation of teleost fish (see Solanki & Benjamin, 1982 for review). In this case mucus may not simply have a passive thickening function, but may also actively influence ion fluxes because glycoproteins secreted in mucus are polyanionic and therefore attract cations. However, in this context it is probable that mucus is more important to the ionic regulation of freshwater and migratory teleosts than to fully marine fish. Unfortunately, mucus probably has several functions (including lubrication and the exclusion of pathogens); also, in fish at least, mucus is often produced in abnormal quantities in crowded captive conditions, so study so far has been rather qualitative.

3. *Extracellular organic osmotic effectors*

In most marine animals the regulation of internal salt and water levels are closely related, but another adaptive approach has been adopted in some species which effectively separate their osmotic and ionic regulation to a large extent. This situation was first recognized in elasmobranch fish by Smith (1931, 1936), who found that much of the blood osmolarity of these animals was non-ionic and created by high blood urea ($CO(NH_2)_2$) levels. Subsequently it was found that some of the osmolarity was due to trimethylamine oxide (($CH_3)_3NO$, TMAO), and that the total osmolarity of the blood of sharks, skates and rays was slightly greater than the

J. Davenport

Table 5. *The composition of plasma and excretory fluids in* Squalus acanthias. *(simplified from Kirschner, 1979)*

Fluid	Concentrations (mmol l^{-1})							osmolarity (mOsm kg^{-1})
	Na	K	Cl	Mg	Ca	urea	TMAO	
Sea water	440	9	490	50	10	0	0	930
Plasma	250	4	240	1	3	350	70	1000
Urine	240	2	240	40	3	100	10	800
Rectal gland fluid	500	7	500	0	0	18	–	1000

osmoconcentration of seawater (see Table 5). Ionic levels in the blood of elasmobranchs are rather higher than in most teleosts, but still make up little more than half of the concentration present in seawater. The levels of blood urea in elasmobranchs are far above those which are toxic in other animals, and urea permeates the fishes' cells. However, the tissues of elasmobranchs are in fact dependent upon the presence of urea, to the extent that elasmobranch enzymes will not function *in vitro* in its absence. Because the total blood osmolarity is slightly above that of seawater, there is a tendency for osmotic uptake of water, and so the problem of water balance is effectively solved, since excess water is voided in the urine (which is appreciably more copious than in marine teleosts). Obviously there have to be mechanisms to maintain high blood urea levels; reabsorption in the kidney (Schmidt-Nielsen, 1972) and low gill permeability (Payan, Goldstein & Forster, 1973) are responsible. Urea is converted from NH_3 by the enzymes of the ornithine cycle, but trimethylamine oxide, which is also apparently conserved by low branchial and renal losses, appears to stem from dietary supply rather than metabolic processes. Few brackish water elasmobranchs are known, but those species which do move into salinities below those of the open sea simply reduce their blood urea levels as urine output rises to cope with increased osmotic inflow of water, and the resorption of urea becomes rather less effective (see Rankin & Davenport (1981) for discussion).

More obscure is the means by which elasmobranchs maintain their low internal ion concentrations. It seems likely (but not conclusively so) that elasmobranchs are not very permeable to salts (see Kirschner, 1979 for review), so uptake is probably much slower than in marine teleosts. In the early 1960's (e.g. Burger & Hess, 1960; Burger, 1962) it appeared that the secretion of a very salty fluid by the ATPase-rich rectal gland (a general feature of elasmobranchs) would completely explain the maintenance of salt balance. However, within a few years it was found that elasmobranchs not only survived removal of the rectal gland, but were able to maintain their low plasma ionic concentrations (Burger, 1965; Chan, Phillips & Chester-Jones, 1967). Removal of the gland did impair the ability to deal with a salt load (administered either as an injection of NaCl solution, or in the form of a large invertebrate meal), and it now appears that the main function of the gland is to deal with excess salt taken in at mealtimes. It has been found that fish without rectal glands exhibit an increased urine output, and since the urine is approximately isoionic with the blood, the kidneys must consequently be regarded as useful salt-loss routes. Finally, there is some evidence that salt may be excreted elsewhere in the body, perhaps at the gills (Maetz & Lahlou, 1966; Chan *et al.*, 1967), but again conclusive evidence is unavailable and the field of osmotic and ionic regulation is still remarkably open.

For some years the urea-based control of blood osmolarity was thought to be unique to elasmobranchs, but Pickford & Grant (1967) showed that the crossopterygian coelocanth *Latimeria chalumnae* showed similar blood Na^+ ($181 \, mmol \, l^{-1}$), Cl^- ($199 \, mmol \, l^{-1}$) and urea ($355 \, mmol \, l^{-1}$) levels to those of elasmobranchs. These workers were dealing with dead material and were not able to state with confidence whether coelocanth blood is hypo- or hyperosmotic to seawater; certainly it is very close to isosmocity, and will consequently cause little osmotic exchange of water with the external medium.

High blood urea levels have also been found in representatives of other vertebrate groups. The crab-eating frog, *Rana cancrivora*, which lives in mangrove swamps and tolerates salinities as high as about 28‰ has become well known since it was studied by Gordon, Schmidt-Nielsen & Kelly (1961). The frog has low blood urea levels when held in freshwater, but as the external salinity is increased the animal retains urea so that it remains hyperosmotic to the outside medium. Less-widely appreciated is the brackish water diamondback terrapin *Malaclemys centrata* which was extensively investigated by Gilles-Baillen (1970, 1973a, b) and shown to accumulate blood urea when external salinities are high (this chelonian can tolerate full seawater for months). Dunson (1979) suggests that the rise in blood urea of terrapins (which have extremely low skin per-meabilities to salt and water) exposed to seawater may simply reflect a strong antidiuresis, since there is a general rise in tissue NH_3, taurine and urea as well; he therefore believes that the high blood urea is probably not of great importance to the animal's water economy. This suggestion may conceivably indicate an evolutionary sequence for the more effective urea-based mechanisms in elasmobranchs and coelocanths as they moved (presumably intermittently at first) into the marine habitat from fresh or brackish water; an antidiuretic response in an animal with a fairly low permeability to salts, water and NH_3 would favour the retention of nitrogenous end products and a switch away from NH_3 towards the use of urea. Tissue dependence upon urea would follow, allowing a progressively greater plasma urea concentration to be attained.

Insects have high levels of organic compounds in their haemolymph (which is a nutrient rather than gas carrier because of the existence of tracheal respiration). No insect is known to live permanently submerged in full seawater, but a number live in close association with the sea, especially in saltmarsh habitats, and of course the sea skaters (e.g. *Halobates spp.*) live on the sea surface in mid ocean (see Cheng, 1976 for review). More than half of the blood osmolarity of insects may be made up of sugars and amino acids, but although salt regulation has been much studied in marine insects, rather less attention has been paid to the possibility that the size of the extracellular organic osmotic pool might be changed in response to external salinity levels. Partly this is probably because most insects have highly impermeable integuments and so tend not to suffer osmotic water loss in seawater. However, Sutcliffe (1961) did suggest that the saltmarsh trichopteran *Limnephilus affinis* (which *does* have a relatively water-permeable integument) raised haemolymph organic levels to maintain near isosmocity at high salinities. More recently, Edwards (1982) has found that larvae of the yellow-fever mosquito *Aedes aegyptii* accumulate free amino acids in the haemolymph to the extent that the blood is still hyperosmotic in water of about 10‰ (about the maximum tolerated by the larvae). This mechanism is obviously analogous in action to the urea-based mechanisms described above, but may also have affinities with the intracellular amino acid control described earlier. It would be interesting to know whether 'non-essential' amino acids predominate in this response too.

4. *Salt excretion in animals of terrestrial ancestry*

Reptiles, birds, mammals and insects are all air breathers with integuments which have low (in some cases near-zero) permeabilities to both water and salts. Marine representatives of these groups are therefore substantially preadapted for life in the sea. However, salt uptake in the diet (or by drinking if it occurs) causes salt-loading problems. This is obviated to some extent in fish-eating species (*e.g.* toothed whales, seals, sea otters, many birds) whose prey have low tissue ion levels, but is severe in herbivorous or invertebrate-eating species.

Marine mammals maintain blood concentrations slightly higher than do their terrestrial relatives; dolphin plasma is about 420 mOsmoles kg^{-1} compared with values of around 300 mOsmoles kg^{-1} for most terrestrial species. Because they breathe humid air and do not sweat, water loss in marine mammals is low and largely confined (<90 %) to urinary and faecal losses. Intake of Na$^+$ and Cl$^-$ in the diet is balanced by the secretion of concentrated urine. The water loss is balanced by free and metabolic water in the diet; no marine mammal is known to drink seawater (though it is difficult to see how krill-eating baleen whales can avoid taking in some seawater along with their food). The baleen whales (whose prey are invertebrates, isosmotic with seawater) were once thought to perhaps have problems in opposing chloride intake, but the available evidence suggests that they can produce urine concentrated enough to cope, even if they drink seawater (see Rankin & Davenport, 1981 for discussion). Presumably the hormonal control of water and salt balance (outside the scope of this review) is similar to that of terrestrial mammals.

Marine reptiles, birds and insects have rather different problems. All three groups possess urinary systems which are far more effective in restricting urinary water loss than the mammalian kidney, because they involve the excretion of colloidal urate salts rather than urea (which needs far more water to carry it). Also, in many species, the anatomical connection between urinary and gut systems allows the rectal reabsorption of urinary water so that mixed urine and faeces are semisolid (see Wall & Oschman, 1975 for a model of the function of insect rectal glands). Combined with dietary water, these mechanisms are effective in balancing the animals' water budgets, but leave a substantial salt-loading problem. This has been solved by the convergent evolution of extrarenal salt-secreting structures (analogous incidentally to elasmobranch rectal glands), which are capable of secreting very salt-rich fluids at fairly slow flow rates. In insects the Malpighian tubules, which empty into the gut at the junction between midgut and rectum, fulfil this function (see Maddrell, 1977 for discussion); in marine reptiles and birds there are a variety of salt glands situated in the head region which are capable of secreting almost pure NaCl solutions at concentrations up to more than twice that of seawater (see Peaker & Linsell, 1975; Peaker, 1979; Dunson, 1976; 1979 for review).

Evolutionary considerations

While it is generally agreed that life evolved originally in the sea, and there is a consensus about the broad evolutionary trends of ionic and

osmotic regulation in secondary marine inhabitants, there is some
controversy about the very early stages in the development of regulation
in primary marine inhabitants. Early recognition of the variability of body
fluid ionic concentrations in invertebrates (see Table 1) led to the
hypothesis that each species' internal ionic and osmotic condition reflected the composition of sea water at the time of the species' evolution (e.g.
McCallum, 1926), and that this composition was subsequently maintained by regulatory processes. Interpreted too narrowly, this hypothesis
becomes untenable because frequent changes in seawater ionic ratios and
overall concentration would be required, which current knowledge of
marine palaeochemistry (e.g. Holland, 1972) does not support. Potts and
Parry (1964) rejected the concept on the grounds that there was no good
reason to support the idea of internal ionic stability lasting for millions of
years, but the hypothesis has been revived more recently with some
success by Spaargaren (1978). Spaargaren argues that metabolic pathways *are* stable over long periods of geological time, that such pathways
are dependent upon particular ionic conditions, and that therefore the
conditions themselves ought to remain constant over long periods. He
also argues for the maintenance of particular internal osmolarities (the
sea has certainly changed in overall salt concentration in the past) rather
than for conservation of primitive ionic ratios, so avoids the objections
already mentioned to some extent.

The background to the early evolution of ion pumps is also obscure,
although it seems to be generally agreed that all current pumps developed
from the first active transport mechanisms which maintained cell volume
in primitive cells (Wilson & Maloney, 1976; see also Prusch, 1983 for
review). The origin of the earliest cell volume regulatory mechanisms,
presumably based upon $Na^+ - K^+$ exchange pumps (since high
intracellular K^+ levels appear to be universal) are, and will probably
remain obscure. A particular problem lies in the difficulty of imagining
how a primitive cell could exist *without* active mechanisms to oppose
osmotic water uptake caused by the presence within the cell of osmotically active molecules. Prusch (1983) states that ionic regulation and cell
volume control must have evolved at the same time, but this rather begs
the question; without a cell membrane enclosing non-permeating organic
molecules on one side there is no need for an ion pump; without an ion
pump any membrane will soon be disrupted by osmotic lysing. Perhaps
a partial escape from this dilemma lies in the apparent high level of
organic material in Precambrian seas (<30 % of total osmolarity; see
Spaargaren, 1978) which existed before microbiological activity removed
it (Bernal, 1954). If one assumes that equal concentrations of small,

osmotically active molecules were present on either side of the primitive cell membrane (unlike the present situation where external osmolarity is virtually all inorganic), then it is possible to envisage cell origin predating the necessity for ion pumps. Once ion pumps *were* developed, the foundation for the invasion of more demanding environments than the open sea were laid, but further progress required a) the ability to manipulate the size of the intracellular amino acid pool, and b) mechanisms for removing bulk fluid (i.e. as urine). These points have been dealt with extensively by other authors (see Prusch, 1983 for review), so will not be considered further here.

Earlier in this review it was stressed that the majority of intertidal and estuarine animals relied upon behavioural osmotic control rather than physiological/biochemical mechanisms. No attempt to explain the evolutionary basis of such behaviour appears to have been made. In a broader context Davenport (1985) has noted that behavioural homeostatic responses by animals seem to have been largely derived from responses which aid in the avoidance of predation. Most euryhaline osmoconformers showing behavioural reactions to salinity are filter feeders, sediment sorters or browsers (mainly annelids and molluscs), while most predators in osmotically demanding environments are effective physiological osmoregulators (fish, crustacea). The commonest behavioural responses to low salinity (across a broad spectrum of species) involve burrowing, closing shell valves/opercular plates, retracting siphons etc. All of these behaviour patterns are also seen in stenohaline, offshore relatives of the animals concerned when they are threatened by predators. Mechanisms for the avoidance of predators must obviously have arisen very early in evolution, and this process presumably favoured the development of anatomical specializations and peripheral chemoreceptor sites which make ideal preadaptations for the avoidance of deleterious salinities.

References

AKBERALI, H. B. & DAVENPORT, J. (1982). The detection of salinity changes by the marine bivalves *Scrobicularia plana* (daCosta) and *Mytilus edulis* L. *J. exp. mar. biol. Ecol.* **58**, 59–71.

ANDREWS, J. D. (1954). Setting of oysters in Virginia. *Natn. Shellfish Assoc. Proc.* **45**, 38–45.

APPELBOOM, J. W. T., BRODSKY, W. A., TUTLE, W. S. & DIAMOND, I. (1958). The freezing point depression of mammalian tissues after sudden heating in boiling distilled water. *J. gen. Physiol.* **41**, 1153–1169.

BARNES, H. & BARNES, M. (1958). Note on the opening responses of *Balanus balanoides* (L.) in relation to salinity and certain inorganic ions. *Veröff. Inst. Meeresforsch. Bremerh.* **5**, 160–164.

BARNES, T. C. (1939). Experiments on *Ligia* in Bermuda. VI. Reactions to common cations. *Biol. Bull. mar. biol. Lab., Woods Hole* **76**, 121–126.

BELLAMY, D. & CHESTER-JONES, I. (1961). Studies on *Myxine glutinosa* – 1. The chemical composition of the tissues. *Comp. Biochem. Physiol.* **3**, 175–183.

BENTLEY, P. J. (1971). *Endocrines and Osmoregulation*. New York: Springer-Verlag.

BERNAL, J. D. (1954). *The Origin of Life. New Biology*, **16**. London: Penguin Books.

BETTISON, J. C. (1982). A comparative study of the behaviour of bivalve molluscs in simulated estuarine conditions. PhD Thesis: University of Wales.

BETTISON, J. C. & DAVENPORT, J. (1976). Salinity preference in gammarid amphipods with special preference to *Marinogammarus marinus* (Leach). *J. mar. biol. Assoc. U.K.* **56**, 135–142.

BRICTEUX-GREGOIRE, S., DUCHÂTEAU-BOSSON, G. L., JEUNIAUX, C. L. & FLORKIN, M. (1962). Constituents osmotiquements actifs des muscles du crab chinois *Eriocheir sinensis* adapté a l'eau douce ou a l'eau de mer. *Arch. int. Physiol. Biochim.* **70**, 273–286.

BRO LARSEN, E. (1952). On subsocial beetles from the salt marsh, their care of progeny and adaptation to salt and tide. *Proc. 9th Int. Congr. Entomol. Amsterdam.* **I**, 502–506.

BRO LARSEN, E. (1953). Successionsstudier i et havendigsomrade, Skomargierstelten, Skallinen. *Georgr. Tiddsk.* **52**, 182–200.

BULL, H. O. (1938). Studies on conditional responses in fishes. Part VIII. Discrimination of salinity changes by marine teleosts. *Rep. Dove Mar. Lab.* **5**, 1–19.

BURGER, J. W. (1962). Further studies on the function of the rectal gland in the spiny dogfish. *Physiol. Zool.* **35**, 205–217.

BURGER, J. W. (1965). Roles of the rectal glands and the kidneys in salt and water excretion in the spiny dogfish. *Physiol. Zool.* **38**, 191–196.

BURGER, J. W. & HESS, W. N. (1960). Function of the rectal gland in the spiny dogfish. *Science* **131**, 670–671.

BURTON, R. S. & FELDMAN, M. W. (1982). Changes in free amino acid concentrations during osmotic response in the intertidal copepod *Tigriopus californicus*. *Comp. Biochem. Physiol.* **73A**, 441–445.

CAWTHORNE, D. F. (1979). Some effects of fluctuating temperature and salinity upon cirripedes. PhD Thesis: University of Wales.

CAWTHORNE, D. F. & DAVENPORT, J. (1980). The effects of fluctuating temperature salinity and aerial exposure upon larval release in *Balanus balanoides* and *Elminius modestus*. *J. mar. biol. Assoc. U.K.* **60**, 367–377.

CHAN, D. K. O., PHILLIPS, J. G. & CHESTER-JONES, I. (1967). Studies on electrolyte changes in the lip-shark *Hemiscyllium plagiosum* (Bennett), with special reference to hormonal influence on the rectal gland. *Comp. Biochem. Physiol.* **23**, 185–198.

CHENG, L. (ed)(1976). *Marine Insects*. Amsterdam: North Holland.

CONWAY, E. J. & MCCORMACK (1953). The total intracellular concentration of mammalian tissues compared with that of the extracellular fluid. *J. Physiol.* **120**, 1–4.

DAVENPORT, J. (1972). Salinity tolerance and preference in the porcelain crabs, *Porcellana platycheles* and *Porcellana longicornis*. *Mar. Behav. Physiol.* **1**, 123–138.

DAVENPORT, J. (1976). A comparative study of the behaviour of some balanomorph barnacles exposed to fluctuating seawater concentrations. *J. mar. biol. Assoc. U.K.* **56**, 889–907.

DAVENPORT, J. (1979a). Cold resistance in *Gammarus duebeni* Liljeborg. *Astarte* **12**, 21–26.

DAVENPORT, J. (1979b). The isolation response of mussels (*Mytilus edulis* L.) exposed to falling seawater concentrations. *J. mar. biol. Assoc. U.K.* **59**, 123–132.

DAVENPORT, J. (1979c). Is *Mytilus edulis* a short term osmoregulator? *Comp. Biochem. Physiol.* **64A**, 91–95.

DAVENPORT, J. (1981). The opening response of mussels (*Mytilus edulis* L.) exposed to rising seawater concentrations. *J. mar. biol. Assoc. U.K.* **61**, 667–678.

DAVENPORT, J. (1982). Environmental simulation experiments on marine and estuarine animals. *Adv. Mar. Biol.* **19**, 133–256.

DAVENPORT, J. (1985). *Environmental Stress and Behavioural Adaptation*. Beckenham: Croom Helm.

DAVENPORT, J., BUSSCHOTS, P. C. M. F. & CAWTHORNE, D. F. (1980). The influence of salinity upon the distribution, behaviour and oxygen uptake of the hermit crab *Pagurus bernhardus* L. *J. mar. biol. Assoc. U.K.* **60**, 127–134.

DAVENPORT, J., LØNNING, S. & KJØRSVIK, E. (1981). Osmotic and structural changes during early development of eggs and larvae of the cod *Gadus morhua* L. *J. Fish Biol.* **19**, 317–331.

DAVENPORT, J. & STENE, A. (1985). Temperature and salinity tolerance in eggs, larvae and adults of the capelin, *Mallotus villosus* Müller. *J. mar. biol. Assoc. U.K.*

DAVENPORT, J. & VAHL, O. (1979). Responses of the fish *Blennius pholis* to fluctuating salinities. *Mar. Ecol. Prog. Ser.* **1**, 101–107.

DAVENPORT, J. & VAHL, O. (1984). Desiccation resistance in the eggs of the capelin, *Mallotus villosus*. *Astarte* **12** (1979), 35–37.

DAVENPORT, J. & WANKOWSKI, J. (1973). Pre-immersion salinity choice behaviour in *Porcellana platycheles*. *Mar. Biol.* **22**, 313–316.

DIAMOND, J. M. & BOSSERT, W. H. (1967). Standing gradient flow. A mechanism for coupling of water and solute transport in epithelia. *J. gen. Physiol.* **50**, 2061–2083.

DUNSON, W. A. (1976). Salt glands in reptiles. In *Biology of the Reptilia, Physiology A*, Vol 5. (eds W. R. Dawson & C. Gans) pp. 413–445. New York: Academic Press.

DUNSON, W. A. (1979). Control mechanisms in reptiles. In *Mechanisms of Osmoregulation in Animals*. (ed. R. Gilles) pp. 273–322. Chichester: John Wiley & Sons.

DUNSON, W. A. (1984). The contrasting roles of the salt glands, the integument, and behaviour in osmoregulation of marine and estuarine reptiles. In *Osmoregulation in Estuarine and Marine Animals*. (ed. A. Pequeux) Springer-Verlag.

DUNSON, W. A. & STOKES, G. D. (1983). Asymmetrical diffusion of sodium and water through the skin of sea snakes. *Physiol. Zool.* **56**, 106–111.

EDWARDS, H. A. (1982). Free amino acids as regulators of osmotic pressure in aquatic insect larvae. *J. exp. Biol.* **101**, 153–160.

GANNING, B. (1971). Studies on chemical, physical and biological conditions in Swedish rockpool ecosystems. *Ophelia* **2**, 51–105.

GILLES, R. (ed) (1979). *Mechanisms of Osmoregulation in Animals*. Chichester: John Wiley & Sons.

GILLES-BAILLIEN, M. (1970). Urea and osmoregulation in the diamondback terrapin *Malaclemys centrata centrata* (Latreille). *J. exp. Biol.* **52**, 691–697.

GILLES-BAILLIEN, M. (1973a). Isosmotic regulation in various tissues of the diamondback terrapin *Malaclemys centrata centrata* (Latreille). *J. exp. Biol.* **52**, 691–697.

GILLES-BAILLIEN, M. (1973b). Hibernation and osmoregulation in the diamondback terrapin *Malaclemys centrata centrata* (Latreille). *J. exp. Biol.* **59**, 45–51.

GORDON, M. S., SCHMIDT-NIELSEN, K. & KELLY, H. M. (1961). Osmotic regulation in the crab-eating frog (*Rana cancrivora*). *J. exp. Biol.* **38**, 359–378.

GROSS, W. J. (1955). Aspects of osmotic regulation in crabs showing the terrestrial habit. *Amer. Nat.* **89**, 205–222.

GROSS, W. J. (1957). A behavioural mechanism for osmotic regulation in a semi terrestrial crab. *Biol. Bull. mar. biol. Lab., Woods Hole* **113**, 268–274.

HALDANE, J. B. S. (1954). *The Origin of Life: New Biology* **16**, 12. London: Penguin.

HASKIN, H. H. (1964). The distribution of oyster larvae. *Proc. Symp. Exp. Mar. Ecol. Occ. Publ. No. 2* 76–80. Graduate School of Oceanography, University of Rhode Island.

HENRY, R. P. & CAMERON, J. N. (1982). The distribution and partial characterization of carbonic anhydrase in selected aquatic and terrestrial decapod crustaceans. *J. exp. Zool.* **221**, 309–321.

HIRANO, T. & MAYER-GOSTAN, N. (1976). Eel oesophagus as an osmoregulating organ. *Proc. natn. Acad. Sci., U.S.A.* **73**, 1348–1352.

HOLLAND, H. D. (1972). The geological history of seawater – an attempt to solve the problem. *Geochim. cosmochim. Acta* **36**, 637–651.

HOLLIDAY, F. G. T. (1969). The effects of salinity on the eggs and larvae of teleosts. In *Fish Physiology*. Vol 1. (eds W. S. Hoar & D. J. Randl) pp. 293–311. New York: Academic Press.

HOLLIDAY, F. G. T. & JONES, M. P. (1967). Some effects of salinity on the developing eggs and larvae of the plaice (*Pleuronectes platessa*) *J. mar. biol. Assoc. U.K.* **47**, 39–48.

HOUSE, C. R. (1963). Osmotic regulation in the brackish water teleost *Blennius pholis. J. exp. Biol.* **40**, 87–104.

JANSSON, B. O. (1962). Salinity resistance and salinity preference of two oligochaetes *Akerdrilus monospermatecus* Knoller and *Marionina preclittochaeta* N.sp. from the intertidal fauna of marine sandy beaches. *Oikos*, **13**, 293–405.

JOWETT, P. E., RHEAD, M. M. & BAYNE, B. L. (1981). *In vivo* changes in the activity of gill A.T.P.ases and haemolymph ions of *Carcinus maenas* exposed to p,p' – DDT and reduced salinities. *Comp. Biochem. Physiol.* **69C**, 399–402.

KINNE, O. (1971). *Marine Ecology* Vol 1 Part 2. (ed. O. Kinne) pp. 821–995. New York: Wiley Interscience.

KIRSCHNER, L. B. (1979). Control mechanisms in crustaceans and fishes. In *Mechanisms of Osmoregulation in Animals.* (ed. O. Kinne) pp. 157–222. Chichester: John Wiley & Sons.

KJØRSVIK, E., DAVENPORT, J. & LØNNING, S. (1984). Osmotic changes during development of eggs and larvae of the lumpsucker, *Cyclopterus lumpus* L. *J. Fish Biol.* **24**, 311–321.

KORRINGA, P. (1952). Recent advances in oyster biology. *Q. Rev. Biol.* **27**, 266–308.

KRIJGSMAN, B. J. & KRIJGSMAN, N. (1954). Osmorezeption in *Jasus lalandii. Z. vergl. Physiol.* **37**, 78–81.

KROGH, A. (1939). *Osmotic Regulation in Aquatic Animals.* Cambridge: Cambridge University Press.

LAGERSPETZ, K. & MATTILA, M. (1961). Salinity reactions of some fresh and brackish water crustaceans. *Biol. Bull. mar. biol. Lab., Woods Hole* **120**, 44–53.

LANCE, J. (1962). Effects of water of reduced salinity on the vertical migration of zooplankton. *J. mar. biol. Assoc. U.K.* **42**, 131–154.

LILLYWHITE, H. B. & MADERSON, P. F. A. (1982). Skin structure and permeability. In *Biology of the Reptilia*. Vol. **12**. (ed. F. H. Pough) New York: Academic Press.

LOCKWOOD, A. P. M. (1961). The urine of *Gammarus duebeni* and *G. pulex. J. exp. Biol.* **58**, 149–163.

LOCKWOOD, A. P. M. (1963). *Animal Body Fluids and their Regulation*. London: Heinemann.

LØNNING, S. & DAVENPORT, J. (1980). The swelling egg of the long rough dab *Hippoglossoides platessoides limandoides* (Bloch). *J. Fish Biol.* **17**, 359–378.

LOOSANOFF, V. L. (1949). Vertical distribution of oyster larvae of different ages during the tidal cycle. Abstract, *Anat. Rec.*, **105**, 591.

MACALLUM, A. B. (1926). The palaeochemistry of the body fluids and tissues. *Physiol. Rev.* **6**, 316–355.

McLUSKY, D. A. (1970). Salinity preference in *Corophium volutator, J. mar. Biol. Assoc. U.K.* **50**, 747–752.

McDONOUGH, P. M. & STIFFLER, D. F. (1981). Sodium regulation in the tidepool copepod *Tigriopus californicus. Comp. Biochem. Physiol.* **69A**, 273–277.

McFARLAND, W. & MUNZ, F. W. (1965). Regulation of body weight and serum composition by hagfish in various media. *Comp. Biochem. Physiol.* **14**, 383–398.

MADDRELL, S. H. P. (1977). Insect Malpighian tubules. In *Transport of Ions and Water in Animals* (eds B. L. Gupta, R. B. Moreton, J. L. Oschman & B. J. Wall) pp. 541–569.

MAETZ, J. & LAHLOU, B. (1966). Les échanges de sodium et de chlor chez un élasmobranch, *Scyliorhinus*, mesurés a l'aide des isotopes ^{24}Na et ^{36}Cl. *J. Physiol. (Paris)* **58**, 249.

MAFFLY, R. H. & LEAF, A. (1959). The potential of water in mammalian tissues. *J. gen. Physiol.* **42**, 1257–1275.

MALOIY, G.M.O. (ed) (1979). *Comparative Physiology of Osmoregulation in Animals*. Vols 1 & 2. London: Academic Press.

MILNE, A. (1940) Some ecological aspects of the intertidal area of the estuary of the Aberdeenshire Dee. *Trans. Roy. Soc. Edin.*, **60**, Part 1, No. 4, 107–139.

MINNICH, J. E. (1979). Reptiles. In *Comparative Physiology of Osmoregulation in Animals*. (ed. G. M. O. Maloiy) pp. 391–641. New York: Academic Press.

MOORE, M. N., KOEHN, R. K. & BAYNE, B. L. (1980). Leucine aminopeptidase (aminopeptidase – 1), N-acetyl-ß-hexosaminidase and lysosomes in the mussel, *Mytilus edulis* L. in response to salinity changes. *J. exp. Zool.* **214**, 239–249.

NEIL, W. H. (1979). Mechanisms of fish distribution in heterothermal environments. *Am. Zool.* **19**, 305–317.

NELSON, J. (1912). Report of the Biological Department of the New Jersey Agricultural Experiment Station for the year 1911. *N.J. Agric. exp. Stat. New Brunswick, N.J.*

NEUFELD, G. J., HOLLIDAY, C. W. & PRITCHARD, J. B. (1980). Salinity adaptation of gill Na,K–ATPase in the blue crab *Callinectes sapidus*. *J. exp. Zool.* **211**, 215–224.

OPARIN, A. I. (1957). *The Origin of Life on Earth*. London: Oliver & Boyd.

PAYAN, P., GOLDSTEIN, L. & FORSTER, R. P. (1973). Gills and kidneys in ureosmotic regulation in euryhaline skates. *Am. J. Physiol.* **224**, 367–372.

PEAKER, M. (1979). Control mechanisms in birds. In R. Gilles (ed.). *Mechanisms of Osmoregulation in Animals* (ed. R. Gilles) pp. 323–348. Chichester: John Wiley & Sons.

PEAKER, M. & LINSELL, J. L. (1975). *Salt Glands in Birds and Reptiles*. Cambridge: Cambridge University Press.

PICKFORD, G. E. & GRANT, F. B. (1967). Serum osmolality in the coelocanth *Latimeria chalumnae*: urea retention and ion regulation. *Science* **155**, 568–570.

POTTS, W. T. W. & EDDY, F. B. (1973). The permeability to water of the eggs of certain marine teleosts. *J. comp. Physiol.* **82**, 305–315.

POTTS, W. T. W. & PARRY, G. (1964). *Osmotic and Ionic Regulation in Animals*. Oxford: Pergamon Press.

PRITCHARD, D. W. (1953). Distribution of oyster larvae in relation to hydrographic conditions. *Proc. Gulf. Caribb. Fish. Inst.* **1952**, 123–132.

PRUSCH, R. D. (1983). Evolution of invertebrate homeostasis: osmotic and ionic regulation. *Comp. Biochem. Physiol.* **76A**, 753–761.

RANKIN, J. C. & DAVENPORT, J. (1981). *Animal Osmoregulation*. Glasgow: Blackie.

ROBERTSON, J. D. (1957). Osmotic and ionic regulation in aquatic invertebrates. In *Recent Advances in Invertebrate Physiology* (ed. B. T. Scheer) pp. 229–246. University of Oregon, Eugene.

RORIVE, G. & GILLES, R. (1979). Intracellular inorganic effectors. In *Mechanisms of Osmoregulation in Animals* (ed. R. Gilles) pp. 83–109. Chichester: John Wiley & Sons.

SCHMIDT-NIELSEN, B. (1972). In *Nitrogen Metabolism and the Environment* (eds J. W. Campbell & L. Goldstein). New York: Academic Press.

SCHOFFENIELS, E. & GILLES, R. (1970). Osmoregulation in aquatic arthropods. In *Chemical Zoology* Vol. 5, (eds M. Florkin & B. Scheer) pp. 255–286. London: Academic Press.

SEGAL, E. & DEHNEL, P. A. (1962). Osmotic behaviour in an intertidal limpet, *Acmaea limatula*. *Biol. Bull. mar. biol. Lab., Woods Hole* **122**, 417–430.

SEYMOUR, R. (1982). Physiological and ecological adaptations of reptiles to aquatic life. In *Biology of the Reptilia* Vol. 12 (ed. F. H. Pough). New York: Academic Press.

SHUMWAY, S. E. (1977). Effect of salinity fluctuation on the osmotic pressure and Na^+, Ca^{++} and Mg^{++} ion concentrations in the haemolymph of bivalve molluscs. *Mar. Biol.* **41**, 153–177.

SHUMWAY, S. E. (1978). Activity and respiration in the anemone *Metridium senile* (L.) exposed to salinity fluctuations. *J. exp. mar. Biol. Ecol.* **33**, 85–92.

SHUMWAY, S. E. & DAVENPORT, J. (1977). Some aspects of the physiology of *Arenicola marina* (Polychaeta) exposed to fluctuating salinities. *J. mar. biol. Assoc. U.K.* **57**, 907–924.

SHUMWAY, S. E., GABBOTT, P. A. & YOUNGSON, A. (1977). The effect of fluctuating salinity on the concentrations of free amino acids and ninhydrin positive substances in the adductor muscles of eight species of bivalve molluscs. *J. exp. mar. Biol. Ecol.* **29**, 131–150.

SKADHAUGE, E. (1974). Coupling of transmural flows of NaCl and water in the intestine of the eel (*Anguilla anguilla*). *J. exp. Biol.* **60**, 535–546.

SMITH, H. W. (1931). The absorption and excretion of water and salts by the elasmobranch fishes. II. Marine elasmobranchs. *Am. J. Physiol.* **98**, 296–310.

SMITH, H. W. (1936). The retention and physiological role of urea. *Biol. Rev.* **11**, 49–82.

SOLANKI, T. G. & BENJAMIN, M. (1982). Changes in the mucous cells of the gills, buccal cavity and epidermis of the nine-spined stickleback, *Pungitius pungitius* L., induced by transferring the fish to seawater. *J. Fish Biol.* **21**, 563–575.

SPAARGAREN, D. H. (1978). A comparison of the blood osmotic composition of various marine and brackish water animals. *Comp. Biochem. Physiol.* **60A**, 327–333.

SUTCLIFFE, D. W. (1961). Studies on salt and water balance in caddis larvae (Trichoptera): I. Osmotic and ionic regulation of body fluids in *Lemnephilus affinis* Curtis. *J. exp. Biol.* **38**, 501–519.

WALL, B. J. & OSCHMAN, J. L. (1975). Structure and function of the rectum in insects. In *Excretion Fortschr. Zool.* (ed. A. R. E. Wessing) **23**, 193–222.

WATANABE, K. & YAMADA, J. (1980). Osmoregulation and the gill Na^+-K^+-ATPase activity in *Eriocheir japonicus*. *Bull. Fac. Fish. Hokkaido Univ.* **31**, 283–289.

WILSON, T. H. & MALONEY, P. C. (1976). Speculations on the evolution of ion transport mechanisms. *Fed. Proc. Fedn. Am. Socs. exp. Biol.* **35**, 2174–2179.

WOOD, L. & HARGIS, W. J. (1971). Transport of bivalve larvae in a tidal estuary. In *Fourth European Marine Biology Symposium, Bangor, Wales 1969* (ed. D. J. Crisp) pp. 29–44. Cambridge: Cambridge University Press.

Printed in Great Britain © *Society for Experimental Biology 1985*

HORMONES, IONIC REGULATION AND KIDNEY FUNCTION IN FISHES

IAN W. HENDERSON, NEIL HAZON AND KATHRYN HUGHES

Department of Zoology, University of Sheffield, Sheffield S10 2TN, U.K.

Summary

Renal osmoregulatory mechanisms in the context of hormones is considered in three types of fish: the Agnatha, the Chondrichthyes and the Osteichthyes. Particular reference is made to endocrine status and hormonal interplay in renal homeostatic mechanisms.

Among Agnatha, hagfishes display atypical osmoregulatory characteristics and their endocrine repertoire is poorly understood. Hormonal actions are unclear although the kidney appears to act as a regulator of extracellular fluid volume. Lampreys show many similarities with teleost fish with respect to osmoregulation, but again their endocrine system requires further definition.

Chondrichthyean fishes have a number of unique hormones, among them 1-α-hydroxycorticosterone from the adrenocortical homologue (interrenal gland). Their complex kidneys have not been extensively studied with respect to hormonal regulation, but a key role is certainly the maintenance of high plasma levels of urea and trimethylamine oxide. The importance of the ratio of these two compounds with respect to urea tolerance is discussed. Evidence is presented and discussed that points to 1-α-hydroxycorticosterone playing a role in osmoregulation, although its sites and mechanisms of action are not known. The presence of a non-hypophysial control of interrenal function (a renin–angiotensin system) is indicated.

The largest group of fishes, the Teleostei, are considered with respect to renal mechanisms involved in euryhalinity. Highly selective reference is made to the renin–angiotensin system and arginine vasotocin. In fresh water eels a clear negative feedback relationship exists between angiotensin II and arginine vasotocin, while in seawater-adapted animals the interplay is less clear. It is suggested that the observed increases in both arginine vasotocin and angiotensin II in eels adapted to environments hyperosmotic to their extracellular fluid in some way affects the "setting" of the feedback between the two. The possible interactions with other hormones is considered in outline.

Introduction

Fish is a popular epithet describing animals that live in water and employ gills for external gaseous exchange, or, perhaps more broadly, embraces all non-tetrapod vertebrates. In zoological terms fish (=Pisces) comprises three major groups: Agnatha (=Cyclostomata); Chondrichthyes; and Osteichthyes (Young, 1981).

It is difficult to over-emphasize the diversity of animals that exist within these classes, for among them are such contrasting types as sharks, lampreys, tunas, eels and lungfishes. Moreover the aquatic environment in which they live presents many variables in addition to the usually recognized one of salinity, that include temperature, dissolved oxygen, food supply (all often associated with the degree to which light penetrates the water) and in some cases water currents, both horizontal and vertical. Given the heterogeneity of fishes and their environments, it is hardly surprising that there is great diversity of endocrine mechanisms that regulate fluid and electrolyte homeostasis, in particular renal function – the subject of this review.

Overtly, there are many similarities in the endocrine repertoire of fishes (adrenocortical homologue, hypothalamo-hypophysial system, thyroid tissue etc.), and the osmoregulatory effector systems (gills, gut, kidney for example) seem to be uniformly present. Superimposed upon these homologies, there are, however, unique endocrine glands (e.g. Corpuscles of Stannius, urohypophysis) and special devices (e.g. rectal gland of elasmobranch fishes) with intriguing biochemical and physiological variations (Bentley, 1971).

In recent years, endocrine mechanisms that temper the homeostatic activities of the various devices regulating internal fluid volumes and compositions have come under increasingly critical scrutiny, and in no small way is this the result of the development and application of refined and sensitive technical and analytical methods. It should, however, be pointed out that current knowledge produces generalizations, as exemplified in this review, that are unlikely to be apt for the whole fish class; for example in the case of teleost fish, *Anguilla* sp., a few cyprinids and a few salmonids have been intensively studied, but how far their control processes exist in the remaining twenty or so thousand species of teleost is unknown. Similar constraints must be placed on other groups when making generalized conclusions.

The present review will consider the function of the kidney in the three major groups from the following aspects: (a) Endocrine status; (b) Hormonal interplay in the context of renal regulatory mechanisms. Only peripheral reference will be made to extrarenal processes.

There is sufficient information about vertebrates as a whole with regard to hormonal control of renal function and body fluid homeostasis to adjudge the following hormones or hormonal systems to be of especial interest and relevance: the adrenocortical (interrenal) steroids, the neurohypophysial peptides (in particular arginine vasotocin), the renin–angiotensin system and prolactin or its equivalent. In certain types, special hormones, unique to the group are also involved.

Agnatha

The Agnatha or Cyclostomata today comprise two discrete types – the Myxinoidea or hagfishes and the Petromyzonidae or lampreys. The Myxinoids are somewhat aberrant among contemporary vertebrates in that they maintain their blood plasmas at or about the same osmolality as their environmental seawater, and there are, with one or two exceptions, equal ionic activities in the two solutions (Robertson, 1960). The functional kidney consists of a small number of relatively large glomeruli sited segmentally along the archinephric ducts. The process of ultrafiltration is sensitively dependent upon arterial pressure (Riegel, 1978; Alt, Stolte, Eisenbach & Walwig, 1981). The short tubular segments are somewhat equivocally concerned with reabsorption and/or secretion of ions such as sodium, magnesium and calcium and possibly with filtered macromolecules (Munz & McFarland, 1964; Morris, 1965; Rall & Burger, 1967; Ericsson, 1967; Ericsson & Seljelid, 1968). There appears to be little or no water reabsorption along the nephron and it has been concluded that in hagfishes the kidney is primarily a volume-regulating device.

The general endocrinology of hagfishes is poorly understood, although corticosteroids appear likely, their exact site of synthesis has not been identified (see Chester Jones & Mosley, 1980) while in the neurohypophysis vasotocin may be present (Follett & Heller, 1964). There have been experiments carried out to determine hormonal actions on body composition and on renal function of hagfishes. Chester Jones, Phillips & Bellamy (1962) induced only minor changes in *Myxine* treated with a variety of materials including homologous pituitary extracts, prolactin and adrenocorticosteroids even when animals were challenged by dilution of their environmental seawater. It has been pointed out (Bentley, 1971) that myxinoid osmoregulation occurs at the cellular–extracellular boundary, rather than at the interface between the environment and the extracellular fluid, as in other vertebrates. It is therefore possible that investigations have aimed towards inappropriate indices of osmoregulation.

In summary, the basic anatomy of the myxinoid kidney suggests that perhaps renal function amounts to volume regulation, and being pressure dependent then vasoactive hormones are responsible for its functional integrity. The short tubular segments may simply act as conduits for the volume-regulating activities of the glomeruli (McFarland & Munz, 1965). Clearly the basic endocrinology and renal physiology demands extensive examination before firm statements can be made.

The second group of Cyclostomata, the lampreys, superficially at least, present many similarities with the teleost fishes in terms of their general renal function. Indeed, based on their general osmoregulatory characteristics, Youson (1982) affirms persuasively a close parallel evolution between lampreys and Osteichthyes; such parallelism is not so readily identified when the endocrine system is considered, however. In this latter context the relative dissociation of the hypothalamo–hypophysial components (Holmes & Ball, 1978), the somewhat equivocal nature of the form and secretion(s) of the adrenocortical homologue (Weisbart & Idler, 1970; Buus & Larsen, 1975; Weisbart, Youson & Wiebe, 1978; Chester Jones & Mosley, 1980; Seiler, Seiler & Claus, 1981; Seiler, Seiler, Claus & Sterba, 1983) and the possible absence of a renin–angiotensin system (Nishimura et al., 1970; Henderson, Oliver, McKeever & Hazon, 1980) are of special note.

Under particular circumstances, most notably when undergoing reproductive migrations, lampreys can adapt to both freshwater and seawater environments, and there is every reason to suppose that the underlying mechanisms permitting the adaptations are akin to those employed by euryhaline teleosts (Rankin, Henderson & Brown, 1983). Indeed Rankin and colleagues in an extensive series of studies have shown that the lamprey kidney is, like that of *Myxine* (*vide supra*), very dependent upon both blood pressure and flow for its adaptive responses to changing environmental salinity (Logan, Moriarty & Rankin, 1980; Moriarty, Logan & Rankin, 1978; Rankin et al., 1983). Arginine vasotocin is consistently diuretic, causing an increase in glomerular filtration rates, with no evidence of renal tubular actions. In this context it is of interest that heterologous, mammalian angiotensin II has no apparent effects on renal function; the latter could be viewed as supporting the evidence against a renin–angiotensin system in lampreys, although it might also reflect a failure of the lamprey angiotensin II renal receptors to respond to the heterologous peptide. The evidence for renal tubular actions of hormones in lampreys is slight. Bentley & Follett (1962, 1963) for example found sodium retention after injections of aldosterone, but not cortisol into freshwater lampreys, and an aldosterone antagonist increased sodium losses; there was some evidence that perhaps renal water excretion was also affected by aldosterone or its endogenous equivalent.

In summary, the lampreys possess kidneys that functionally resemble those of teleost fishes to a very considerable extent, and in many respects the euryhalinity of these fish depends upon appropriate and equivalent renal responses. The renal function would again appear to centre on volume regulation (Rankin & Griffiths, cited in Rankin *et al.*, 1983), although the processes involved in regulating the fractional excretion of glomerular ultrafiltrate and its contained solutes are not known. These latter processes are likely, but as yet undemonstrated, sites for hormonal action.

Chondrichthyes

Elasmobranch fishes are predominantly marine and maintain their plasma osmolalities at or slightly above that of the environmental seawater as a result of retention of urea and trimethylamine oxide. There is at the same time careful homeostasis of body fluid volume and individual solute composition. The general processes responsible for fluid and electrolyte regulation have been well described and need not be repeated (Smith, 1931; Burger, 1967; Payan & Maetz, 1970, 1971; Payan, Goldstein & Forster, 1973). Suffice to state that the conjoint actions of the gills, rectal gland and kidney are central to the process. Endocrine impingement upon these structures, more especially upon the kidney is however poorly understood and this is in part because elasmobranch fishes without digressing significantly from the general vertebrate endocrine system possess a number of unique hormones. Among the latter 1-α-hydroxycorticosterone from the interrenal gland (Idler & Truscott, 1966, 1967, 1969) and three novel neurohypophysial peptides (glumitocin, aspartocin and valitocin) in addition to small amounts of arginine vasotocin, are of particular interest. Moreover the presence of a renin–angiotensin system has not been definitively demonstrated (Nishimura *et al.*, 1970). A problem is thus immediately presented: the elasmobranch fishes employ, with respect to other vertebrates, unusual osmoregulatory habits and secrete a unique spectrum of adrenocortical and neurohypophysial hormones so that intuitive lines of investigation should not be guided too closely by findings in other vertebrate groups.

A primary function of the elasmobranch kidney would appear to be the retention of nitrogenous waste products and the elimination of divalent cations. It probably also plays a role in volume regulation, although, since the net flux of water across the gills will be minimal in the presence of almost no osmotic gradient, this function may not be so significant. Typically the elasmobranch kidney possesses extremely long nephrons which are made up of several (up to 10) distinct segments with very well-developed glomeruli (Stolte et al., 1977). Although there are brisk rates of glomerular filtration, urine production is relatively sparse and voided urine is approximately iso-osmotic with plasma. Urine is virtually urea free, and the process of urea reabsorption may be a passive (Boylan, 1972) or active sodium-linked process (Schmidt-Nielsen et al., 1972). The iso-osmotic character of the urine with respect to plasma largely results from the intense secretory activity for divalent cations (Stolte et al., 1977; Henderson, Brown, Oliver & Haywood, 1978) and some attempts in these reported studies have been made to allocate particularly secretory and/or reabsorptive functions to the many identifiable nephron segments.

There is a certain amount of admittedly circumstantial evidence that both adrenocortical steroids (or more precisely 1-α-hydroxycorticosterone) and at least one of the neurohypophysial hormones act upon the kidney. In the studies cited above regarding renal function, there are indications that the elasmobranch, unlike teleost fishes for example, adjusts its urine production more by altering renal tubular fluid reabsorption than by changing rates of glomerular filtration. Thus antidiuretic hormones may come into play in these fishes to allow both glomerular and renal tubular mechanisms to temper overall urine output (Maetz & Lahlou, 1974).

Before discussing the renal control of urea retention it is important to place the phenomenon of the 'physiological uraemia' into a proper perspective, since this substance plays such a crucial role in elasmobranch osmoregulation and yet it is for other animals a relatively toxic material, being a potent protein-denaturing agent (Hermans, 1966). Certainly the concentrations of urea that exist normally in elasmobranch plasma interfere with the structure and function of non-elasmobranch proteins and enzymes (Yancey & Somero, 1978). While some elasmobranch proteins such as haemoglobin (Martin et al., 1979) display urea tolerance, rather curiously others do not (Yancey & Somero, 1978). The problem of how they function in vivo was unsolved until the methylamine compounds, in particular trimethylamine oxide were found to act as 'biochemical antagonists' to the disruptive actions of urea. In vitro there appears to be an optimal trimethylamine oxide to urea ratio of 1:2 to achieve protection of proteins against denaturation by urea. Such a ratio has been observed in studies of the intracellular environment of some elasmobranch species.

Thus the regulation of urea production and the maintenance of appropriate amounts of trimethylamine oxide within the body fluids of elasmobranchs are of central importance to osmoregulation, particularly when the animals are exposed either experimentally or in nature to changing environmental salinities. Of course most elasmobranchs are unable to withstand abrupt transfer to significantly more dilute or concentrated environments, but a number of studies show that stepwise and gradual adaptation allows good survival of a number of purely marine species in both dilute and more concentrated seawaters (Price & Creaser, 1967; Haywood, 1973; De Vlaming & Sage, 1973; Chan & Wong, 1977; Mandrup-Poulsen, 1981). On adaptation of elasmobranchs to more dilute environments there is a reduction in total plasma osmolality with concomitant reductions in plasma sodium, chloride and urea concentrations; significantly there is usually greater reductions in urea than in the other solutes. The reduced urea concentrations may results from an increased urea excretion and/or reduced hepatic synthesis depending on species (Goldstein, Oppelt & Maren, 1968; Goldstein & Forster, 1971; Wong & Chan, 1977). Adaptation of fishes to more concentrated seawaters produces broadly opposite effects in terms of solute composition.

Virtually nothing is known of possible endocrine regulation of these vital responses to changed environmental salinity and recent studies have aimed to examine a possible role for the unusual corticosteroid, 1-α-hydroxycorticosterone, in mediating the altered metabolism of nitrogenous waste products in relation to osmoregulatory status of the dogfish, *Scyliorhinus canicula* (Hazon & Henderson, 1984). Groups of dogfish were adapted to 50 % and 140 % seawater in steps of approximately 10 % over 10-day intervals. Figure 1 illustrates the general changes in plasma composition at the various salinities and they broadly agree with other published studies cited above. The plasma constituents decline with decreasing environmental osmolality and increase with elevated salinity. It should be noted, however, that at the extremes of salinities, (120 % seawater and above and 70 % seawater and below) there are differential changes in urea and plasma sodium concentrations; thus above 120 % seawater urea appears to be preferentially retained and sodium maintained around an upper limit, while below 70 % seawater urea is preferentially reduced with sodium reaching a lower but sustained concentration. These changes were associated with

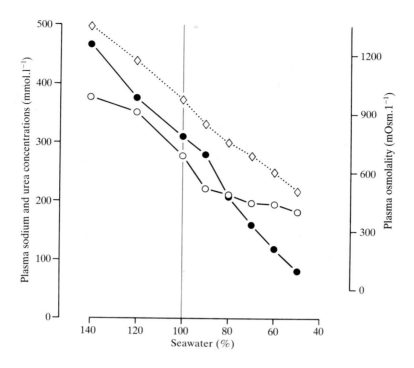

Fig. 1. Plasma sodium (○) and urea (●) concentrations and plasma osmolality (◊) in dogfish, *Scyliorhinus canicula*, adapted to varying environmental salinities. Animals were allowed at least 10 days to adapt to the environments before blood samples (caudal sinus) were collected.

some changes in 1-α-hydroxycorticosterone indicative of a possible action of this steroid in the responses. The corticosteroid concentrations in plasma were similar in fish adapted to 100, 120 and 140 % seawater, but were significantly higher in fish at lower environmental salinities. In these studies the metabolic clearance and blood production rates of 1-α-hydroxycorticosterone were determined using the constant infusion technique; results show that at lower environmental salinities the metabolic clearance and blood production rates were significantly increased while at higher salinities little change was noted. There is thus a tentative indication that the corticosteroid may moderate the production rates of urea and its renal excretion, while at the same time it participates in sodium regulation at reduced environmental salinities (Hazon & Henderson, 1984).

Clearly if corticosteroids are involved in osmoregulation in the suggested manner, then, as in other vertebrates, feedback control of their secretory patterns must be present. In this context the elasmobranch adrenocortical homologue (interrenal gland) presents some enigmatic questions. The production of the unique steroid, already discussed, the complete morphological separation of adrenocortical and adrenomedullary homologues and the relationships with hypophysial hormones are among the most pertinent aspects (Chester Jones & Mosley, 1980). Regarding the hypothalamo–hypophysial–interrenal axis, an hypothalamic capillary portal system is present (Holmes & Ball, 1974), corticotrophic activity is present in the rostral lobe of the highly specialized hypophysis (De Roos & De Roos, 1967) and an elasmobranch adrenocorticotrophic hormone has been identified (Denning-Kendall, Sumpter & Lowry, 1982). These features provide circumstantial evidence for ultimately a brain–interrenal feedback system, but there are unsolved aspects that require clarification. For example removal of the rostral lobe of the pituitary produces interrenal atrophy after 30 days (Dittus, 1941; Klesch & Sage, 1973) in some species, while other studies (Dodd, 1960; Roscoe, 1976) suggest slight control of interrenal activity by the hypothalamo–hypophysial system in other species. The interrenal in some species may thus be relatively independent of hypophysial adrenocorticotrophic hormone or perhaps other control systems exist. In many other vertebrates a second control system, the renin–angiotensin system, acts in concert with pituitary factors upon adrenocortical structure and function. Thus far, however, limited investigations have failed to identify a renal renin-like pressor material in elasmobranchs (Nishimura *et al.*, 1970) and juxtaglomerular cells have not been demonstrated with the usual criteria (Oguri, Ogawa & Sokabe, 1970; Crockett, Gerst & Blankenship, 1973). However mammalian angiotensin I produced pressor responses in *Squalus acanthias* and the effect was inhibited by an inhibitor of angiotensin I converting enzyme, SQ 20,881 (Opdyke & Holcombe, 1976). In addition dogfish renal extracts incubated *in vitro* with rat renin-substrate generated angiotensin-like pressor materials using the standard rat bioassay (Henderson *et al.*, 1980), while in the same bioassay renal extracts were also pressor. Certain of the pre-requisites suggestive of a renin–angiotensin system are thus present in some elasmobranch species.

An alternative possibility for the pressor activity of mammalian angiotensin in elasmobranchs is that actions result from stimulation of the sympathetic nervous system; catecholamine release is part of the pharmacological profile of angiotensins in other vertebrate groups (Nishimura, 1978). This possibility is supported by the observations that α-adrenergic blockade with phentolamine blocks the pressor response to exogenous mammalian angiotensins and large doses of angiotensin increase plasma catecholamine concentrations in dogfish (Opdyke & Holcombe, 1976; Opdyke, Carroll, Keller & Taylor, 1979, 1981). The exact mechanisms involved in the actions of angiotensin requires further examination, but it is of significance that mammalian angiotensin II as well as homologous renal extracts increase the production of 1-α-hydroxycorticosterone in dogfish (Hazon & Henderson, 1985).

It is clear that conclusions regarding hormonal control of renal function of elasmobranch fishes must at present be very tentative. At the same time recent observations on both the basic physiological regulatory mechanisms with special regard to the metabolism of nitrogenous waste, the 'osmotic ballast' so essential to elasmobranch osmoregulation, and the application of renal tubular micropuncture alongside sensitive assessment of endocrine status renders this area of comparative physiology an extremely fertile one.

Osteichthyes

The bony fish represent the single, largest grouping of vertebrates and may be further subdivided into holostean, chondrostean, teleostean and dipnoan types. Endocrine regulation of renal function in these groups is limited to teleosts and lungfish with few studies having been executed on animals such as the bowfin and sturgeon. The bulk of this section dealing with osteichthyeans will focus on the teleost. From the standpoint of renal osmoregulatory mechanisms three general types may be identified: stenohaline-marine; stenohaline-freshwater; and euryhaline. The euryhaline teleosts since they display such remarkable abilities to adapt to enormous environmental change have proved to be attractive and useful experimental models for furthering understanding of osmotic adjustments among fishes generally.

In freshwater, teleosts encounter a large osmotic influx of water and incipient depletion of ions, and to counter these, the kidney eliminates large volumes of osmotically free water and the gills offset ion depletion by active uptake from the environment. When in the sea, osmotically free water is at a premium for the fish, since there is osmotic loss across permeable surfaces and also there is a passive gain of sodium chloride; to gain water, marine teleosts actively imbibe the environmental water, but at the same time they obligatorily gain solute which must be eliminated. Again conjoint renal and extrarenal (predominantly gills) systems are responsible for maintaining homeostasis. Characteristically marine teleosts produce sparse volumes of urine rich in divalent ions, while the gained monovalent ions are extruded by the gills.

Conceptually and practically the glomerulus has been at the centre of the abilities of teleosts to adapt, both as a group and indeed individual species, to both freshwater and seawater environments. In addition the ability of the renal tubule to change the secretory/reabsorptive capacities is of major adaptive significance. It was noted more than fifty years ago that the glomeruli of marine teleosts were smaller than those of fresh-water species, and indeed some species living in the sea lacked these structures altogether. Moreover it was also observed that distal convoluted tubules appeared to be longer and more active in freshwater than seawater fish; indeed many marine fish lacked the structure (Smith, 1959). These features indicate the major functional characteristics of teleostean kidney in seawater and freshwater: in freshwater there are brisk rates of glomerular ultrafiltration and the distal tubule enables the generation of osmotically free water for excretion; in seawater the urine is prepared predominantly, or as in aglomerular species exclusively, by a secretory process. Moreover, even in glomerular species of marine teleost, non-filtering nephrons (*vide infra*) are capable of fluid secretion (Beyenbach, 1982).

The massive changes in glomerular filtration rates that are observed on transfer of freshwater euryhaline teleosts to seawater are in large part due to alterations in the numbers of filtering nephrons; in other words there is intermittent glomerular function (Lahlou, 1966; Hickman, 1968; Brown, Jackson, Oliver & Henderson, 1978; Brown, Oliver, Henderson & Jackson, 1980), rather than an alteration in single nephron glomerular filtration rates. Indeed in rainbow trout there appears to be an actual increase in single nephron filtration rate on entry into seawater so that the reduced total kidney glomerular filtration reflects reduced numbers of filtering tubules. The position is, however, more complex in that it is possible to identify three types of nephron within the kidney of trout: those that are actively filtering, glomeruli perfused with arterial blood but not apparently filtering and finally tubules that do not receive arterial blood to their glomeruli (Henderson & Brown, 1980; Brown *et al.*, 1980). The relative proportions of these nephron types varies with environmental salinity; for example in freshwater fish kidneys most glomeruli are arterially perfused and only 50% filter, while in equivalent seawater-adapted animals the 50% perfused are to a large extent non-filtering.

It is apparent that intrarenal blood flow with respect to glomerular perfusion, rates of filtration in single nephrons, degree of renal portal venous perfusion, filtration pressures and glomerular intermittency, is a central factor in renal adaptive responses of teleost fishes to changing environmental salinity. The control mechanisms within the kidney have only recently come under study, but it is apparent that many factors are involved including arginine vasotocin (Henderson & Wales, 1974; Babiker & Rankin, 1978), prolactin (Wendelaar-Bonga, 1976; Olivereau, 1980; Hirano & Mayer-Gostan, 1978; Hirano, 1980), adrenocortical steroids (Hirano, 1977), and the renin–angiotensin system (Brown et al., 1980). A generally accepted, if somewhat tentative view places prolactin as a key factor of freshwater adaptation, while cortisol and angiotensin are principally concerned with renal performance in seawater teleosts (Hirano & Mayer-Gostan, 1978; Rankin et al., 1983). The nature of actions of arginine vasotocin remain obscure but it is becoming increasingly clear the interplay between this peptide and the substances mentioned above is of key importance.

Recent studies in our laboratory have attempted to establish links between the release of arginine vasotocin and angiotensin in the eel, *Anguilla anguilla* L. These two hormones are intimately associated with kidney function, both producing rather dramatic actions on glomerular filtration rates in a wide variety of teleosts. Moreover in mammals the analogue of arginine vasotocin (arginine vasopressin or antidiuretic hormone) and angiotensin maintain secretory patterns that appear to regulate a balance between the input and loss of fluid from the organism. For example under most circumstances antidiuretic hormone inhibits renal renin release, while angiotensin stimulates the secretion of antidiuretic hormone. The physiological circumstances of a mammal are of course relatively constant with regard to fluxes of water with the input being entirely via the gut and losses take place through the kidney, lungs and to an extent passively across the integument. In the euryhaline teleost, however, the fluxes of water markedly contrast in freshwater and seawater environments and there are equivalent problems with respect to solute metabolism. It is therefore of considerable interest to establish a) whether there are different secretory patterns of arginine vasotocin and renin in seawater and freshwater fish; b) whether there are feedback relationships between the two hormones and whether the 'setting' changes with environmental salinity.

Specific radioimmunoassays were developed to answer these questions. Eels were adapted to a range of salinities from distilled water to normal seawater, and arginine vasotocin and angiotensin II determined. In distilled-water-adapted eels arginine vasotocin was present at a concentration of $28 \cdot 2 \pm 3 \cdot 8$ (n = 6) pg.ml^{-1}, and angiotensin II at $192 \cdot 0 \pm 63 \cdot 2$ (n = 8) pg.ml^{-1}. In normal seawater eels the concentrations were very much higher: arginine vasotocin, $778 \cdot 0 \pm 95 \cdot 8$ (n = 8) pg.ml^{-1}; angiotensin II

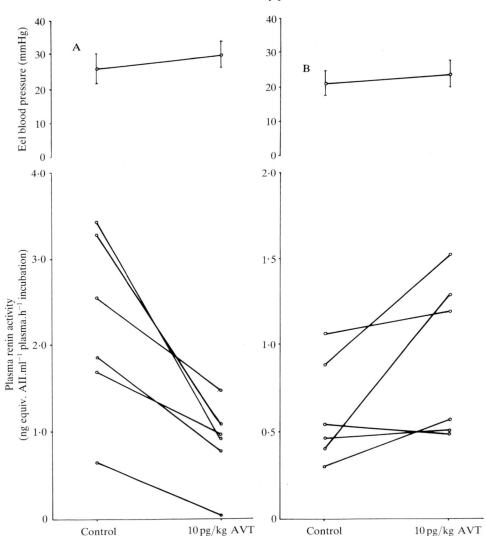

Fig. 2. Effects of a single intravenous injection of arginine vasotocin (10 pg.kg^{-1} body weight; AVT) on plasma renin activity and arterial blood pressure (pneumogastric artery). Blood samples were withdrawn 30 minutes after injection with the control sample collected immediately before. Plasma renin activity, expressed as ng equivalent angiotensin II.ml^{-1} plasma .h^{-1} incubation, was determined after incubation of plasma *in vitro* and pressor activity generated assayed on the blood pressure of the nephrectomized, pentobarbitone-anaesthetized, ganglion-blocked rat (Henderson *et al.*, 1976). (A) the responses seen in freshwater-adapted eels. (B) the responses seen in seawater-adapted eels.

$3598 \cdot 8 \pm 780 \cdot 8$ (n = 8) pg.ml^{-1}. Intermediate concentrations between these two extremes were observed in animals adapted to freshwater and 50% seawater. These differences in secretory patterns could reflect alterations in plasma volume since in freshwater the 'environmental pressure' is for hypervolaemia and in seawater hypovolaemia, or could reflect changes in plasma osmolality in the two environments.

To test the possible role of plasma volume in regulating the output of renin and vasotocin, animals were submitted to graded haemorrhage. Removal of 15% of the blood volume produced no significant effects on either arginine vasotocin or angiotensin, in freshwater-adapted eels. Thirty minutes after a haemorrhage of 30% of the blood volume, arginine vasotocin increased from $177 \cdot 3 \pm 38 \cdot 9$ to $345 \cdot 9 \pm 74 \cdot 3$ pg.ml^{-1} (n = 10; $P < 0 \cdot 01$); in the same experiments plasma angiotensin II increased from $833 \cdot 2 \pm 281 \cdot 6$ to $1205 \cdot 7 \pm 275 \cdot 7$ pg.ml^{-1} (n = 7), a change that was not statistically significant. It may be therefore that plasma volume influences the release of arginine vasotocin in a more sensitive fashion than it does renin release; it is perhaps relevant to note that in studies of the aglomerular toadfish, Nishimura, Lunde & Zucker (1979) required haemorrhage to the extent of 50% of the blood volume to produce a significant increase in plasma renin activity. This relative insensitivity of both arginine vasotocin and angiotensin to haemorrhage suggests that neither hormone is influenced physiologically by plasma volume, although some preliminary experiments suggest that the alterations in plasma volume during the initial five hours following transfer from freshwater to seawater may initiate but not sustain long-term endocrine changes. These experiments thus establish that both angiotensin and arginine vasotocin are significantly altered by environmental salinity of the teleost; the major influence would not seem to be plasma volume in terms of regulating their secretion, rather plasma sodium concentrations appear to be the best correlate so far examined. There are of course other likely regulatory influences, in particular arterial pressure itself, for Nishimura & Bailey (1982) have cogently argued at least for the renin–angiotensin system, a primary role in regulating blood pressure.

The huge differences in circulating concentrations of both arginine vasotocin and angiotensin in eels adapted to hypo- and hyperosmotic environments with respect to plasma osmolality poses the obvious question of possible feedback and its setting in the contrasting circumstances. The reciprocal relationships were therefore examined in freshwater- and seawater-adapted eels. In freshwater-adapted fish, exogenous arginine vasotocin (10 pg.kg^{-1} body weight, *i.v.*) reduced plasma renin activity from $2 \cdot 25 \pm 0 \cdot 47$ to $0 \cdot 89 \pm 0.21$ ng equivalents angiotensin II.ml^{-1}

plasma.h^{-1} incubation (n = 6, $P < 0.01$). There were no significant changes in arterial blood pressure. Conversely, mammalian angiotensin II (100 ng.kg^{-1} body weight, *i.v.*) significantly increased plasma arginine vasotocin concentrations from 164.9 ± 28.9 to 244.1 ± 39.8 pg.ml^{-1} (n = 9; $P < 0.005$). In these experiments blood pressure increased from 36.9 ± 3.8 to 47.3 ± 3.8 (n = 9; $P < 0.001$).

These apparent negative feedback relationships between arginine vasotocin and angiotensin II in the freshwater eel are less clear in seawater-adapted animals (Hughes & Henderson, 1984). Thus arginine vasotocin (10 pg.kg^{-1} body weight, *i.v.*) either increased or had no effect on plasma renin activity of seawater-adapted eels. Similarly, angiotensin II (100 ng.kg^{-1} body weight, *i.v.*) gave inconsistent change in plasma arginine vasotocin, although again the peptide increased arterial blood pressure. The somewhat equivocal reciprocal relationships between the two hormones in seawater-adapted eels may have resulted from the different status of these animals with respect to basal circulatory values of both arginine vasotocin and angiotensin II, remembering that there is at least a threefold difference in plasma concentrations between freshwater- and seawater-adapted eels. Clearly further studies of these hormonal systems are required before definitive conclusions can be reached as to their interplay, both with one another and with the endocrine system and osmoregulatory structures generally. A working hypothesis currently being tested is that in seawater, the two elements – arginine vasotocin and angiotensin II – are in positive feedback relying on plasma sodium concentrations as the driving stimulus; thus increased plasma sodium concentrations may stimulate either arginine vasotocin and/or renin release which perpetuate each other, to lower the plasma sodium concentrations to a 'set-point', below which the negative feedback seen in freshwater animals comes into play.

The actions of angiotensin II and arginine vasotocin cannot, however, be viewed in isolation, and although they demonstrably affect each other's secretory patterns, they both have primary and secondary actions on other hormonal systems and osmoregulatory structures including gills, gastrointestine and kidney. Moreover the dipsogenic actions of angiotensin II (Carrick & Balment, 1983; Hirano & Hasegawa, 1984) and the actions of the renin–angiotensin system in perhaps maintaining increased adrenocortical activity in seawater fish (Henderson, Sadi & Hargreaves, 1974; Henderson, Jotisankasa, Mosley & Oguri, 1976) must be set against synergistic and perhaps antagonistic actions of other hormones such as prolactin and possibly arginine vasotocin under varying regimes of salinity. Moreover this brief and highly selective review of teleostean renal function and hormones, has ignored many aspects that must clearly impinge. For example there have been considerable advances in recent years with regard to uncovering the physiological actions of the secretions of the Corpuscles of Stannius, the urophysis, and pars intermedia materials. In addition the possible osmoregulatory function of the pancreas (Epple & Miller, 1981) as well as establishing a role for the vitamin D_3 endocrine system (Hayes, Guilland-Cumming, Henderson & Russell, 1984) require further analysis and interpolated into a general scheme to describe the endocrine control of the kidney in both marine and freshwater teleosts.

Finally with regard to osteichthyean fishes, mention must be made of the Dipnoans or lungfishes. Sawyer, Uchiyama & Pang (1982) reviewed the subject of hormonal actions and control of renal function in these fascinating animals. They of course impose upon themselves a severe osmotic stress when aestivating effectively converting themselves from ammonotelic to ureotelic organisms. When ureotelic there is a condition of anuria (Delaney, Lahiri, Hamilton & Fishman, 1977), but on emergence into freshwaters ammonontelism develops and the animals undergo an enormous diuresis to remove retained urea. The diuretic and sometimes natiuretic phases appear to be pressure dependent and it has been persuasively argued that arginine vasotocin is a key hormone in the response (Sawyer, 1970; Sawyer, Blair-West, Simpson & Sawyer, 1976; Babiker & Rankin, 1979). Virtually nothing is known about the delicate interplay that must be necessary for the responses, with other hormones in particular the renin–angiotensin system and the adrenocortical steroids, both of which have been delineated in lungfishes.

Conclusions

In recent years it has become possible to identify and determine specific hormones or hormonal systems in the major groups of fishes. This has permitted descriptions of hormonal control of renal function in the diverse types. There are however still major gaps in our knowledge, in particular in those areas which point to synergistic and perhaps antagonistic actions and feedback relations of hormones one with another. It is anticipated that these gaps will gradually be filled and in addition it is hoped that delineation of exact regulatory mechanisms will allow, or not, the application of all embracing generalizations to the endocrine control of vertebrate osmoregulation – the often unstated, but implicit aim of comparative physiology.

References

ALT, J. M., STOLTE, H., EISENBACH, G. M. & WALWIG, F. (1981). Renal electrolyte and fluid excretion in the atlantic hagfish, *Myxine glutinosa. J. exp. Biol* **91**, 323–330.

BABIKER, M. M. & RANKIN, J. C. (1978). Neurohypophysial hormonal control of kidney function in the european eel (*Anguilla anguilla* L.) adapted to seawater or freshwater. *J. Endocrinol.* **76**, 347–358.

BABIKER, M. M. & RANKIN, J. C. (1979). Renal and vascular effects of neurohypophysial hormones in the african lungfish, *Protopterus annectens. Gen. comp. Endocrinol.* **37**, 26–34.

BENTLEY, P. J. (1971). *Endocrines and Osmoregulation.* Berlin, Heidelberg, New York: Springer-Verlag.

BENTLEY, P. J. & FOLLETT, B. K. (1962). The action of neurohypophysial and adrenocortical hormones on sodium balance in the cyclostome, *Lampetra fluviatilis. Gen. comp. Endocrinol.* **2**, 329–335,.

BENTLEY, P. J. & FOLLETT, B. K. (1963). Kidney function. in a primitive vertebrate, the cyclostome *Lampetra fluviatilis. J. Physiol.* **169**, 902–918.

BEYENBACH, K. W. (1982). Direct demonstration of fluid secretion by glomerular renal tubules in a marine teleost. *Nature* **299**, 54–56.

BROWN, J. A., JACKSON, B. A., OLIVER, J. A. & HENDERSON, I. W. (1978). Single nephron filtration rate (SNGFR) in the trout, *Salmo gairdneri.* Validation of the use of ferrocyanide and the effect of environmental salinity. *Pflug. Arch. Europ. J. Physiol.* **377**, 101–108.

BROWN, J. A., OLIVER, J. A., HENDERSON, I. W. & JACKSON, B. A. (1980). Angiotensin and single nephron glomerular filtration in the trout, *Salmo gairdneri. Amer. J. Physiol.* **239**, R509–R514.

BURGER, J. W. (1967). Problems in the electrolyte economy of the spiny dogfish, *Squalus acanthias.* In *Sharks, Skates and Rays* (ed. P. W. Gilbert, R. F. Mathewson and D. P. Rall) pp. 177–186. Baltimore: Johns Hopkins University Press.

BUUS, O. & LARSEN, L. O. (1975). Absence of known corticosteroids in blood of river lampreys (*Lampetra fluviatilis*) after treatment with mammalian corticotrophin. *Gen, comp. Endocrinol.* **26**, 96–99.

CARRICK, S. & BALMENT, R. J. (1983). The renin–angiotensin system and drinking in the euryhaline flounder, *Platichthys flesus. Gen. comp. Endocrinol.* **51**, 423–433.

CHAN, D. K. O. & WONG, T. M. (1977). Physiological adjustment to the dilution of the external medium in the lip-shark, *Hemiscyllium plagiosum* (Bennett). I Size of the compartments and osmolyte composition. *J. exp. Zool.* **200**, 71–84.

CHESTER JONES, I. & MOSLEY, W. (1980). The interrenal gland in Pisces. Part 1, Structure. In *General, Comparative and Clinical Endocrinology of the Adrenal Cortex* Vol. 3. (ed. I. Chester Jones and I. W. Henderson) pp. 395–472. London, New York: Academic Press.

CHESTER JONES, I., PHILLIPS, J. G. & BELLAMY, D. (1962). Studies on water and electrolytes in cyclostomes and teleosts with special reference to *Myxine glutinosa* L. (the hagfish) and *Anguilla anguilla* L. (the european eel). *Gen. comp. Endocrinol.* Supplement Number 1, 36–47.

CROCKETT, D. R., GERST, J. W. & BLANKENSHIP, S. (1973). Absence of juxtaglomerular cells in the kidneys of elasmobranch fishes. *Comp. Biochem. Physiol.* **44A**, 673–675.

DELANEY, R. G., LAHIRI, S., HAMILTON, R. & FISHMAN, A. P. (1977). Acid-base balance and plasma composition in the estivating lungfish (*Protopterus*). *Amer. J. Physiol.* **232**, R10–R17.

DENNING-KENDALL, P. A., SUMPTER, J. P. & LOWRY, P. J. (1982). Peptides derived from pro-opiocortin in the pituitary gland of the dogfish, *Squalus acanthias. J. Endocrinol.* **93**, 381–390.

DE ROOS, R. & DE ROOS, C. C. (1967). Presence of corticotrophin activity in the pituitary gland of chondrichthyean fish. *Gen. comp. Endocrinol.* **9**, 267–275.

DE VLAMING, V. L. & SAGE, M. (1973). Osmoregulation in the euryhaline elasmobranch, *Dasyatis sabina*. *Comp. Biochem. Physiol.* **45A**, 31–44.

DITTUS, P. (1941). Histologie und Cytologie des Interrenalorgans der Selachier unter normalen experimentellen Bedingungen. Ein beitrag zur Kenntnis der wirkungsweise des kortikotropin Harmons und des verhaltnisses von Kern zu Plasma. *Z. wiss. Zool.* **154**, 40–124.

DODD, J. M. (1960). Gonadal and gonadotrophic hormones in lower vertebrates. In *Marshall's Physiology of Reproduction* (ed. A. S. Parkes) Volume 1, Part 2, pp. 417–582. London: Longmans Green.

EPPLE, A. & MILLER, S. B. (1981). Pancreatectomy in the eel: osmoregulation effects. *Gen. comp. Endocrinol.* **45**, 453–457.

ERICSSON, J. L. E. (1967). Fine structure of ureteric duct epithelium in the north atlantic hagfish (*Myxine glutinosa* L.). *Z. Zellforsch. mikrosk. Anat.* **83**, 219–230.

ERICSSON, J. L. E. & SELJELID, R. (1968). Endocytosis in the ureteric duct epithelium of the hagfish (*Myxine glutinosa* L.). *Z. Zellforsch. mikrosk. Anat.* **90**, 263–272.

FOLLETT, B. K. & HELLER, H. (1964). The neurohypophysial hormones of bony fishes and cyclostomes. *J. Physiol.* **172**, 72–91.

GOLDSTEIN, L. & FORSTER, R. P. (1971). Osmoregulation and urea metabolism in the little skate, *Raja erinacea*. *Amer. J. Physiol.* **220**, 742–746.

GOLDSTEIN, L., OPPELT, W. W. & MAREN, T. H. (1968). Osmotic regulation and urea metabolism in the lemon shark, *Negaprion brevirostris*. *Amer. J. Physiol.* **215**, 1493–1497.

HAYES, M. E., GUILLAND-CUMMING, D., HENDERSON, I. W. & RUSSELL, R. G. G. (1984). Vitamin D₃ metabolites and their possible roles in calcium homeostasis in *Salmo gairdneri*. *Gen. comp. Endocrinol.* **53**, 495.

HAYWOOD, G. P. (1973). Hypo-osmotic regulation coupled with reduced metabolic urea in the dogfish, *Poroderma africanum*: an analysis of serum osmolarity, chloride and urea. *Marine Biol.* **23**, 121–128.

HAZON, N. & HENDERSON, I. W. (1984). Secretory dynamics of 1α-hydroxycorticosterone in the elasmobranch fish, *Scyliorhinus canicula*. *J. Endocrinol.* **103**, 205–211.

HAZON, N. & HENDERSON, I. W. (1985). Factors affecting the secretory dynamics of 1a-hydroxycorticosterone in the dogfish, *Scyliorhinus canicula*. *Gen. comp. Endocrinol.* (In Press).

HENDERSON, I. W. & BROWN, J. A. (1980). Hormonal actions on single nephron function in teleosts. In *Epithelial transport in the Lower Vertebrates* (ed. B. Lahlou) pp. 163–170. Cambridge: Cambridge University Press.

HENDERSON, I. W., BROWN, J. A., OLIVER, J. A. & HAYWOOD, G. P. (1978). Hormones and single nephron function in fishes. In *Comparative Endocrinology* (ed. P. J. Gaillard and H. H. Boer) pp. 217–222. Amsterdam: North Holland/Elsevier Biomedical Press.

HENDERSON, I. W., JOTISANKASA, V., MOSLEY, W. & OGURI, M. (1976). Endocrine and environmental influences upon plasma cortisol concentrations and plasma renin activity of the eel, *Anguilla anguilla* L. *J. Endocrinol.* **70**, 81–95.

HENDERSON, I. W., OLIVER, J. A. McKEEVER, A. & HAZON, N. (1980). Phylogenetic aspects of the renin–angiotensin system. In *Advances in Physiological Sciences*, Volume **20**: *Advances in Animal and Comparative Physiology* (ed. G. Pethes and V. L. Frenyo). XXVIII I.U.P.S., Section V, pp. 355–363. Budapest: Pergamon Press, Ademiai Kiado.

HENDERSON, I. W., SA'DI, M. N. & HARGREAVES, G. (1974). Studies on the production and metabolic clearance rates of cortisol in the european eel, *Anguilla anguilla* L. *J. Steroid Biochem.* **5**, 701–707.

HENDERSON, I. W. & WALES, N. A. M. (1974). Renal diuresis and antidiuresis after injections of arginine vasotocin in the freshwater eel *Anguilla anguilla* L. *J. Endocrinol.* **61**, 487–500.

HERMANS, J. (1966). The effect of protein denaturents on the stability of the *alpha* helix. *J. Amer. chem. Soc.* **88**, 2418–2422.

HICKMAN, C. P. (1968). Urine composition and kidney tubular function in southern flounder, *Paralichthys lethostigma* in seawater. *Can. J. Zool.* **46**, 439–455.

HIRANO, T. (1977). Prolactin and hydromineral metabolism in the vertebrates. *Gunma Symp. Endocrinol.* **14**, 45–59.

HIRANO, T. (1980). Prolactin and osmoregulation. In *Endocrinology, 1980* (ed. I. A. Cumming) pp. 186–189. Australian Academy of Sciences.

HIRANO, T. & HASEGAWA, S. (1984). Effects of angiotensins and other vasoactive substances on drinking in the eel, *Anguilla japonica. Zool. Sci.* **1**, 106–113.

HIRANO, T. & MAYER-GOSTAN, N. (1978). Endocrine control of osmoregulation in fish. In *Comparative Endocrinology* (ed. P. J. Gaillard and H. H. Boer) pp. 209–212. Amsterdam: North Holland/Elsevier Biomedical Press.

HOLMES, R. L. & BALL, J. N. (1974). *The Pituitary Gland.* Cambridge: Cambridge University Press.

HUGHES, K. & HENDERSON, I. W. (1984). Interactions between the renin–angiotensin system and arginine vasotocin in the eel, *Anguilla anguilla* L. *Gen. comp. Endocrinol.* **53**, 442–443.

IDLER, D. R. & TRUSCOTT, B. (1966). 1α-hydroxycorticosterone from cartilaginous fish: a new adrenal steroid in blood. *J. Fish. Res. Bd. Can.* **23**, 615–619.

IDLER, D. R. & TRUSCOTT, B. (1967). 1α-hydroxycorticosterone: synthesis *in vitro* and properties of an interrenal steroid in the blood of a cartilaginous fish (genus *Raja*). *Steroids* **9**, 457–477.

IDLER, D. R. & TRUSCOTT, B. (1969). Production of 1α-hydroxycorticosterone *in vivo* and *in vitro* by elasmobranchs. *Gen. comp. Endocrinol.* Supplement Number **2**, 325–330.

KLESCH, W. L. & SAGE, M. (1973). The stimulation of corticosteroidogenesis in the interrenal of the elasmobranch, *Dasyatis sabina* by mammalian ACTH. *Comp. Biochem. Physiol.* **52A**, 145–146.

LAHLOU, B. (1966). Mise en evidence d'un 'recrutement glomerulaire' dans le rein des téléostéens d'après la methode du T_m glucose. *C. r. hebd. Séanc. Acad. Sci., Paris* **262**, 1356–1358.

LOGAN, A. G., MORIARTY, R. J. & RANKIN, J. C. (1980). A micropuncture study of kidney function in the river lamprey, *Lampetra fluviatilis* adapted to freshwater. *J. exp. Biol.* **85**, 137–147.

MAETZ, J. & LAHLOU, B. (1974). Actions of neurohypophysial hormones in fishes. In *Handbook of Physiology – Endocrinology IV, Part 1* (ed. R. O. Greep and E. B. Astwood), pp. 521–543. Baltimore: Williams and Wilkins, American Physiological Society.

MANDRUP-POULSEN, J. (1981). Changes in selected blood serum constituents as a function of salinity variations in the marine elasmobranch, *Sphyrna tiburo. Comp. Biochem. Physiol.* **70A**, 127–131.

MARTIN, J. P., BONAVENTURA, J., FYHN, H. J., FYHN, U. E. H., GARLICK, R. L. & POWERS, D. A. (1979). Structural and functional studies of haemoglobins from amazon stingrays of the genus *Potamotrygon. Comp. Biochem. Physiol.* **62A**, 131–138.

McFARLAND, W. N. & MUNZ, F. W. (1965). Regulation of body weight and serum composition by hagfish in various media. *Comp. Biochem. Physiol.* **14**, 383–398.

MORRIS, R. (1965). Studies on salt and water balance in *Myxine glutinosa* L. *J. exp. Biol.* **42**, 359–371.

MORIARTY, R. J., LOGAN, A. G. & RANKIN, J. C. (1978). Measurement of single nephron filtration rate in the kidney of the river lamprey, *Lampetra fluviatilis* L. *J. exp. Biol.* **77**, 57–69.

MUNZ, F. W. & McFARLAND, W. N. (1964). Regulatory function of a primitive vertebrate kidney. *Comp. Biochem. Physiol.* **13**, 381–400.

NISHIMURA, H. (1978). Physiological evolution of the renin–angiotensin system. *Japan. Heart J.* **19**, 806–822.

NISHIMURA, H. & BAILEY, J. R. (1982). Intrarenal renin–angiotensin system in primitive vertebrates. *Kidney Intl* **22**, Supplement Number **12**, S-185–S-192.

NISHIMURA, H., LUNDE, L. G. & ZUCKER, A. (1979). Renin response to hemorrhage and hypotension in the aglomerular toadfish, *Opsanus tau. Amer. J. Physiol.* **237**, H105–H111.

NISHIMURA, H., OGURI, M., OGAWA, M., SOKABE, H. & I MAI, M. (1970). Absence of renin in kidneys of elasmobranchs and cyclostomes. *Amer. J. Physiol.* **218**, 911–915.

OGURI, M., OGAWA, M. & SOKABE, H. (1970). Absence of juxtaglomerular cells in the kidneys of chondrichthyes and cyclostomes. *Bull. Jap. Soc. Sci. Fisheries* **36**, 881–884.

OLIVEREAU, M. (1980). Kidney structure and prolactin secretion in seawater eels treated with pimozide. In *Epithelial Transport in the Lower Vertebrates* (ed. B. Lahlou) pp. 81–90. Cambridge: Cambridge University Press.

OPDYKE, D. F., CARROLL, R. G., KELLER, N. & TAYLOR, A. A. (1979). Angiotensin II releases catecholamines in dogfish. *Bull. Mt. Desert Isl. Biol. Lab.* **19**, 12–13.

OPDYKE, D. F., CARROLL, R. G., KELLER, N. & TAYLOR, A. A. (1981). Angiotensin II releases catecholamines in dogfish. *Comp. Biochem. Physiol.* **70C**, 131–134.

OPDYKE, D. F. & HOLCOMBE, R. (1976). Response to angiotensin I and II and to angiotensin I-converting enzyme inhibitor in a shark. *Amer. J. Physiol.* **231**, 1750–1753.

PAYAN, P., GOLDSTEIN, L. & FORSTER, R. P. (1973). Gills and kidneys in ureosmotic regulation in euryhaline skates. *Amer. J. Physiol.* **224**, 367–372.

PAYAN, P. & MAETZ, J. (1970). Balance hydrique et minerale chez les elasmobranches: arguments en faveur d'un contrôle endocrinien. *Bull. Inf. scient. tech. Commt. Energ. atom.* **146**, 77–96.

PAYAN, P. & MAETZ, J. (1971). Balance hydrique chez les elasmobranches: arguments en faveur d'un contrôle endocrinien. *Gen. comp. Endocrinol.* **16**, 535–554.

PRICE, K. S. & CREASER, E. P. (1967). Fluctuations in two osmoregulatory components – urea and sodium chloride – of the clearnose skate. I Upon laboratory modification of external salinities. *Comp. Biochem. Physiol.* **23**, 65–76.

RALL, D. P. & BURGER, J. W. (1967). Some aspects of hepatic and renal excretion in *Myxine. Amer. J. Physiol.* **212**, 354–356.

RANKIN, J. C., HENDERSON, I. W. & BROWN, J. A. (1983). Osmoregulation and the control of kidney function. In *Control Processes in Fish Physiology* (ed. J. C. Rankin, T. J. Pitcher and R. T. Duggan) pp. 66–88. London and Canberra: Croom Helm.

RIEGEL, J. (1978). Factors affecting glomerular functions in the pacific hagfish, *Eptatretus stouti* (Lockington). *J. exp. Biol.* **73**, 261–277.

ROBERTSON, J. D. (1960). Studies on the chemical composition of muscle tissue. I The muscles of the hagfish, *Myxine glutinosa* L. and the roman eel, *Muraena helena* L. *J. exp. Biol.* **37**, 879–888.

ROSCOE, M. J. (1976). Functional morphology and physiology of the pituitary complex and interrenal gland in elasmobranch fishes. Ph.D. Thesis, University College of North Wales, Bangor.

SAWYER, W. H. (1970). Vasopressor, diuretic and natriuretic responses by lungfish to arginine vasotocin. *Amer. J. Physiol.* **218**, 1789–1794.

SAWYER, W. H., BLAIR-WEST, J. R., SIMPSON, P. A. & SAWYER, M. K. (1976). Renal responses of australian lungfish to vasotocin, angiotensin II and NaCl infusion. *Amer. J. Physiol.* **231**, 593–602.

SAWYER, W. H., UCHIYAMA, M. & PANG, P. K. T. (1982). Control of renal function in lungfishes. *Fed. Proc.* **41**, 2361–2364.

SCHMIDT-NIELSEN, B., TRUNIGER, B. & RABINOWITZ, L. (1972). Sodium-linked urea transport by the renal tubule of the spiny dogfish, *Squalus acanthias. Comp. Biochem. Physiol.* **42A**, 13–25.

SEILER, K., SEILER, R. & CLAUS, R. (1981). Histochemical and spectrophotometric demonstration of hydroxysteroid dehydrogenase activity in the presumed steroid producing cells of the brook lamprey (*Lampetra planeri* Bloch) during metamorphosis. *Endokrinologie* **78**, 297–300.

SEILER, K., SEILER, R., CLAUS, R. & STERBA, G. (1983). Spectrophotometric analyses of hydroxysteroid dehydrogenase activity in presumed steroid-producing tissues of the brook lamprey (*Lampetra planeri* Bloch) in different developmental stages. *Gen. comp. Endocrinol.* **51**, 353–363.

SMITH, H. W. (1931). The absorption and secretion of water and salts by elasmobranch fishes. II Marine elasmobranchs. *Amer. J. Physiol.* **98**, 296–310.

SMITH, H. W. (1959). *From Fish to Philosopher*. Boston: Little Brown and Company.

STOLTE, H., GALASKE, R. G., EISENBACH, G. M., LECHENE, C., SCHMIDT-NIELSEN, B. & BOYLAN, J. W. (1977). Renal tubule ion transport and collecting duct function in the elasmobranch little skate *Raja erinacea*. *J. exp. Zool.* **199**, 403–410.

WEISBART, M. & IDLER, D. R. (1970). Re-examination of the presence of corticosteroids in two cyclostomes, the atlantic hagfish (*Myxine glutinosa* L.) and the sea lamprey (*Petromyzon marinus* L.). *J. Endocrinol.* **46**, 29–43.

WEISBART, M., YOUSON, J. H. & WIEBE, J. P. (1978). Biochemical, histochemical and ultrastructural analyses of presumed steroid-producing tissues in the sexually mature sea lamprey, *Petromyzon marinus* L. Gen. comp. Endocrinol. **34**, 26–37.

WENDELAAR-BONGA, S. E. (1976). The effect of prolactin on kidney structure of the euryhaline teleost, *Gasterosteus aculeatus* during adaptation to fresh water. *Cell Tiss. Res.* **166**, 319–338.

WONG, T. M. & CHAN, D. K. O. (1977). Physiological adjustments to dilution of the external medium in the lip shark, *Hemiscyllium plagiosum* (Bennett). II Branchial, renal and rectal gland function. *J. exp. Zool.* **200**, 85–96.

YANCEY, P. H. & SOMERO, G. N. (1978). Urea requiring lactate dehydrogenases of marine elasmobranch fishes. *J. comp. Physiol.* **125**, 135–141.

YOUNG, J. Z. (1981). *The Life of Vertebrates*. 3rd Edition. Oxford: Clarendon Press.

YOUSON, J. H. (1982). The kidney. In *The Biology of Lampreys* Volume 3 (ed. M. W. Hardisty and I. C. Potter) pp. 191–261. New York: Academic Press.

PHYSIOLOGICAL ADAPTATIONS AND THE CONCEPTS OF OPTIMAL REPRODUCTIVE STRATEGY AND PHYSIOLOGICAL CONSTRAINT IN MARINE INVERTEBRATES

P. J. W. OLIVE

Dove Marine Laboratory and Department of Zoology,
University of Newcastle upon Tyne,
Tyne and Wear NE1 7RU, U.K.

Summary

The dominant 'demographic' theory of life history evolution supposes that different lifetime patterns of reproduction are the result of selection of alternative optimal solutions for the allocation of limited resources between somatic and reproductive functions. A number of trade-off possibilities have been recognized – those between current reproductive output and residual reproductive value and between fecundity and initial offspring size being considered especially important. Many theoretical studies assume that natural selection will favour the adoption of optimal solutions, but it has been pointed out that such solutions may not be obtainable due to design constraints and the development of physiological adaptations to specific reproductive traits which limit subsequent evolutionary potential.

The validity of this idea is examined in this paper through a review of the major reproductive strategies available to marine invertebrates and the physiological adaptations associated with them. The ecologically important distinction between planktotrophic and lecithotrophic development is not necessarily associated with major physiological adaptations in the adults, but the distinction between strictly semelparous and iteroparous life histories is. This is demonstrated in a survey of the endocrinological and environmental control of reproductive processes in related organisms with contrasting modes of reproduction. Particular reference is made to the Polychaeta, in which the contrast between semelparous and iteroparous life histories is particularly marked. A similar contrast is found between cephalopoda and other mollusca, and the discussion of physiological adaptations is extended to include these groups and the Echinodermata.

I. Introduction: The 'Demographic Theory' of life history evolution and the concept of physiological constraint

A large body of theory has developed which seeks to explain the evolution of different life histories and reproductive strategies among organisms. The most widely accepted theory has been termed 'the demographic theory' of life history evolution (Tuomi, Hakala & Hankioja, 1983). The essential features of this theory are:–

  i) That natural selection acts on individual life history traits.
  ii) That natural selection optimizes adaptive strategies.
  iii) That individual life history traits are free to co-evolve.

The theory suggests that the life history is resource limited and that allocation of resources to reproduction necessarily involves a trade-off with potential allocation to somatic functions (Calow, 1979; Fisher, 1958; Gadgil & Bossert, 1970; Williams, 1966a, b). Three specific postulates of this theory can be identified; that:–

1. When the resources available to organisms are limiting, an increase in reproductive effort results in both an increase in reproductive output and a reduction in somatic investment. Increased reproductive effort will result in an increase in fecundity and/or increased survivorship of offspring due to enhanced investment in individual propagules.

2. Reduced somatic investment has a cost either in reduced adult survivorship and/or reduced future reproductive output.

3. There exists the possibility at any age of a trade-off between *current reproductive output* and *residual reproductive value,* where residual reproductive value is the lifetime product of survivorship and fecundity.

It is supposed that different patterns of reproduction are the consequence of the operation of different optimality solutions under different systems of selection, as in the r-, K- selection version (MacArthur & Wilson, 1967; Pianka, 1970; Pianka & Parker, 1975), under different schedules of mortality as in the bet-hedging version (Schaffer, 1974; Schaffer & Rosenzweig, 1977; Stearns, 1976, 1977), or under different schedules of environmental instability and unpredictability (Istock, 1981, 1984).

The underlying rationale of the theory depends on the assumption that fitness is measurable as a demographic parameter 'r' associated with populations or with the spread of genes within populations. It is also supposed that maximizing 'r' is equivalent to maximizing reproductive value at age zero. The validity of this assumption will not be discussed here, but see Caswell (1980), Charlsworth (1980), Ricklefs (1981), Schaffer (1979, 1981), Sibley & Calow (1983) and Stearns (1983) for relevant discussion.

The central trade-off in the demographic theory, namely, that between reproductive effort and residual reproductive value, can be compartmentalized, and components associated with trade-offs between pairs of individual life history traits can be identified (Calow, 1984; Sibly & Calow, 1983; Stearns, 1977). For instance, in many circumstances if reproductive effort at any age is fixed there is an inevitable trade-off between the number of offspring and initial offspring size. The optimal solution depends on schedules and causes of offspring mortality (Christiansen & Fenchel, 1979; Vance, 1973).

This idea can be expressed as an 'adaptive landscape' associated with pairs of variables within which local and global optima can occur. According to optimality theory the observed life history will be the consequence of optimization for all pairs of genetically determined traits under prevailing ecological conditions.

The validity of this general theory can be questioned on several counts.

i) It assumes a fixed pattern of resource allocation, which is only one of several which are possible (Tuomi *et al.*, 1983).

ii) It assumes that age-specific variation in reproductive effort has a significant component of genetically determined hereditability. This is not proven and observed patterns of age-specific reproductive effort will, to a large extent, be the consequence of physiological processes influenced by epigenetic variation in resource availability.

iii) It assumes an optimizing mode of selection, which seeks to optimize the adaptive strategy through the appropriate modulation of resource allocation, whereas other patterns of selection are possible (Gould & Lewontin, 1979).

iv) It ignores structural, physiological and developmental constraints which limit evolutionary potential and prevent organisms achieving a theoretically optimal solution (Stearns, 1977, 1983, 1984).

Individual reproductive traits may not be independent variables; consequently decisions taken with respect to one may carry implications for others, and syndromes such as those which it has been suggested are symptomatic of r- or K- selection (Pianka, 1970) may reflect physiological or historical couplings (Tuomi *et al.*, 1983; Olive, in press). Reproduction is the culmination of a protracted sequence of cellular differentiation and a given trait is not likely to be controlled through the operation of a single genetic locus. The adoption of a specific reproductive trait will require the evolution of an appropriate set of physiological and developmental processes controlled by a large number of genes. The refinement of appropriate patterns of cellular differentiation and their control may limit the future evolutionary potential for descendants of the particular lineage, so that all options do not remain open. *'The organism may be trapped by its evolutionary history,'* (Stearns, 1984). Stearns (1983, 1984) pointed out that some patterns of reproduction are not distributed randomly among organisms but have a strong systematic bias. He suggested three hypotheses which could account for such a bias:–

  i) The extinction (genetic inflexibility) hypothesis.
  ii) The optimality hypothesis.
  iii) The adaptation/intrinsic constraint hypothesis.

Semelparous reproduction among Polychaeta and Mollusca for instance has such a bias; most subgroups in these major taxons exhibit iteroparous reproduction but some subgroups, e.g., Nereidae and Cephalopoda, are exclusively semelparous. According to the *extinction hypothesis,* at some point during the radiation and evolution of the Nereidae and Cephalopoda all iteroparous forms became extinct and there remained insufficient genetic potential for the subsequent evolution of iteroparity. A version of this hypothesis has been proposed by Strathmann (1978a, b), to account for the distribution of feeding and non-feeding larvae among Gastropoda.

The *optimality hypothesis,* however, supposes that 'for semelparous organisms semelparity always has been, and still is, the optimal strategy favoured by natural selection' (Stearns, 1984). Iteroparity is an available option which has never been favoured.

According to the *adaptation/intrinsic constraint* hypothesis, the ancestral organism (proto-nereid or cephalopod) became semelparous while adopting a particular mode of reproduction. This in turn introduced selection for specific physiological adaptations which have subsequently become fixed and which now limit the reproductive potential of descendant organisms. Stearns (1984) concluded that the third hypothesis is the most likely explanation of the observed bias, but the implied physiological basis for this was not clear.

In this paper I shall examine in some detail the physiological adaptations associated with the adoption of different reproductive strategies by marine invertebrates and I shall pay particular attention to the adoption of semelparous and iteroparous life histories. I shall seek to determine whether specific physiological couplings of the kind proposed by Stearns (1984) and which are an integral feature of an 'Organismic theory' of life history as outlined by Tuomi *et al.* (1983) are found to exist.

In seeking to identify such couplings, particular attention will be paid to:–

  i) The co-ordinating role of the endocrine system,

  ii) the properties of the timing mechanisms and

  iii) the relative patterns of energy allocation to reproduction.

I shall seek to draw general conclusions but I will make particularly detailed reference to investigations of the physiological control of reproduction in the Polychaeta.

II. Reproductive strategies of marine invertebrates

A special feature of reproduction in marine organisms is the facility which they have to produce large numbers of small eggs which develop into pelagic often planktotrophic larvae. Marine organisms also have the opportunity to produce smaller numbers of better provisioned larvae which are either benthonic or have a short lecithotrophic pelagic life. The 'choice' between these modes has been perceived as critical and has attracted considerable discussion which seeks to explain the prevalence of the pelagic planktotrophic mode and the circumstances in which it may be non-adaptive (see Christiansen & Fenchel, 1979 for discussion).

The pelagic planktotrophic mode of development can be identified as one element in a syndrome of what are supposed to be primitive traits which include external fertilization, the production of simple round-headed spermatozoa, and the simultaneous discharge of large numbers of gametes in distinct spawning crises (Jagersten, 1972; Olive, in press). This syndrome of reproductive traits may be contrasted with an 'advanced syndrome' in which the production of well-provisioned oocytes occurs repeatedly and which requires the development of mechanisms of insemination other than the mass discharge of gametocytes. These include sperm storage by females, spermatophore production, and direct insemination or copulation. These traits are prominently developed among the smallest members of the marine invertebrate phyla and are particularly common among the marine intersitial fauna (but see Nordheim, 1984). Similar features are also found in virtually all freshwater and terrestrial invertebrates where ultimately the roles of larvae and adults as dissemules and trophic stages may be reversed.

From a physiological point of view the distinction between pelagic planktotrophic development and non-feeding modes of development is not in itself an important one for the adult although it is for the larva. The constraints which tend to prevent the redevelopment of pelagic plantotrophic larvae and so maintain the validity of the generalization that

272   P. J. W. OLIVE

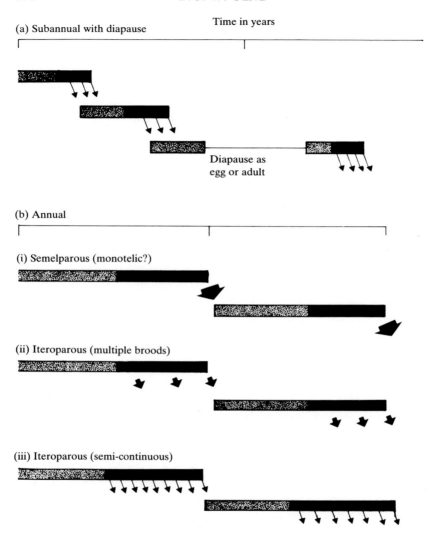

Fig. 1. A diagrammatic representation of the temporal organization of life histories among marine invertebrates. They can be subdivided as subannual, annual and perennial, or by reference to the recurrence of reproductive activity (semelparity = monotely *versus* iteroparity = polytely), or by reference to the degree of synchrony of the episodes of gametocyte discharge (discrete *versus* continuous or semicontinuous). These systems of classification are not mutually exclusive and much confusion is likely to arise from the imprecise use of technical terms.

dispersive pelagic larvae are primitive and non-feeding larvae advanced, are probably genetic ones associated with the construction of a functional pelagic larva (see above). The extent to which the reproductive strategy requires control of germ-cell production and output, and consequently of

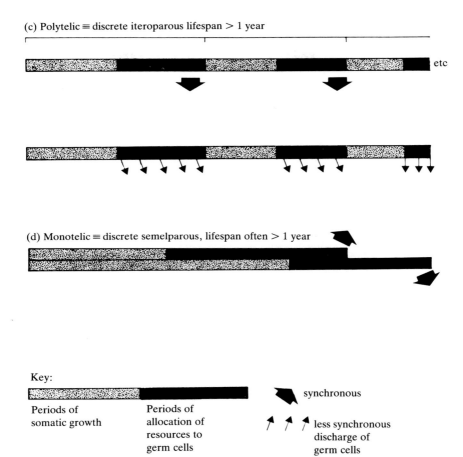

(c) Polytelic ≡ discrete iteroparous lifespan > 1 year

(d) Monotelic ≡ discrete semelparous, lifespan often > 1 year

Key:

Periods of somatic growth

Periods of allocation of resources to germ cells

synchronous

less synchronous discharge of germ cells

the partitioning of resources and of the flow of energy to germinal tissue is, however, of fundamental importance. Figure 1 illustrates in a diagrammatic way, a variety of different lifetime patterns of germ-cell output to be found in marine organisms together with the terminology used to describe them. Most require some control of energy allocation and there is a delay between the acquisition of resources and the investment of those resources in the act of gametocyte discharge. One may ask – what are the selective advantages which lead to delayed discharge? This question is necessary because there are inevitable costs due to the finite probability that mortality will occur before the investment is made, and to the maintenance of the stored energy. The following three general models can be identified which suggest reasons why delayed reproduction may yield a better return on investment than immediate reproduction:–

1. *Conditions for offspring survival are not constant*

The return per unit of energy allocated to reproduction is maximized if the investment is made at a time when larval success is likely to be maximal. Thus it is often suggested that for organisms with feeding planktotrophic larvae maximum success is likely to be associated with larvae released at the time of the spring-time phytoplankton bloom, which offers a temporarily under-exploited niche which can be utilized by a well-timed release of eggs or larvae. Moreover, reproduction early in the year will give offspring the maximum time for development before the onset of adverse conditions. Under these circumstances there is an obvious advantage in the development of physiological mechanisms which achieve this timing. This model therefore specifies both the *time* of reproduction and the *degree of synchrony*. Maximum success is associated with simultaneous discharge of eggs (or larvae) at the optimal time for larval development.

2. *Fertilization is external*

When fertilization is external, the probability that an egg will be fertilized or that a spermatozoan will encounter a suitable egg depends upon the concentration of gametes in the seawater, or, where there is some form of pairing or pseudocopulation, on the probability of a gravid animal encountering another suitably gravid individual in the population. In either case the risk that discharged gametes will be wasted through non-fertilization will be minimized if all members of the population are sexually mature and discharge gametocytes simultaneously, or if subgroups within the population spawn synchronously, or if mature individuals in the population congregate prior to gamete discharge. The advantages of synchrony decrease if sperm storage is possible.

The external fertilization model specifies the *degree of synchronization* but not the optimal time for breeding.

3. *Reproduction is risky*

When animals reproduce they may expose themselve to risks not otherwise encountered. This may be associated with finding and/or selecting a mate, or as in model 2, be associated with migration or swarming behaviour designed to increase the probability that fertilization is successful. If reproduction does carry high risks in this way, this may in turn modify the pattern of energy allocation. As energy becomes available which could be allocated to reproduction, such allocation is not made; instead the energy is invested in survivorship and growth. In terms of the demographic theory, reproductive effort at age x is minimized (in effect zero) to ensure the maximum reproductive output at some future time $(x + n)$. The demographic theory suggests that when reproduction does occur reproductive effort should be correspondingly high, but does not provide a scheme for determining when reproduction should occur. This model for delayed reproductive allocation is not mutually exclusive with models 1 and 2, but it specifies semelparous *not* iteroparous reproduction. It also predicts high-mortality schedules imposed on sexually reproducing individuals.

A notable feature of reproduction among the marine invertebrates is the scarcity of a pattern of reproduction involving more-or-less continuous production of small well-provisioned broods. Such a pattern is virtually unknown among the larger bodied members of most phyla in the marine environment but is in contrast virtually universal among the larger invertebrates in terrestrial and freshwater environments. The fact that multiple brood production is adopted by minute forms and by those in specialized habitats such as the deep sea, suggests that this mode of reproduction is not cost effective and is only adopted when morphological or environmental constraints preclude gamete accumulation and mass discharge.

Patterns of delayed allocation of resources to sexual reproduction can be achieved in a number of different ways:–

1. By progressive accumulation of gametocytes followed by synchronous discharge;
2. By accumulation and storage of specific resources followed by subsequent rapid transfer to germinal tissues;
3. By retention of fertilized eggs in a brood chamber prior to their discharge;
4. By any combination of these.

The following section will review the endocrinological control of reproductive processes and the mechanisms co-ordinating reproductive events with environmental cycles and which thus bring about the required synchronization of reproductive events. Particular reference will be made to the overall reproductive strategy that has been adopted in an attempt to determine if physiological adaptations associated with specific traits can be detected.

III. Physiological control of reproductive processes

Among marine invertebrates two contrasting patterns of reproduction are encountered which have been described as polytelic

(≡discrete iteroparous) and monotelic (≡discrete semelparous) in Fig. 1.

Both patterns of reproduction require the simultaneous discharge of large numbers of gametes and therefore require control of some or all of the following:–

a) Germ cell proliferation.
b) The flow of energy and other components to differentiating germ cells.
c) Progressive differentiation and maturation of germ cells.
d) The sudden discharge of germ cells or embryos in synchronized spawning or hatching.
e) Patterns of somatic cell and accessory gland differentiation.
f) Sexual behaviour.

The literature abounds in careful descriptions of reproductive cycles which reveal the extent to which the progress of the component processes is non-random, but an experimental programme is required to discover how the highly organized sequence of events is achieved. This is likely to involve the endocrine system in the *endogenous* regulation of reproductive processes and also some system of *exogenous* control to maintain a specific relationship between reproductive processes and real time where such a phenomenon is observed.

Figure 2 illustrates in a diagrammatic way the formal components of the regulatory system. It includes:–

1. Perception and input of environmental information.
2. Integration and summation of input.
3. Transduction of input as changes in hormonal milieu.
4. Modulation of cellular responses to the hormonal milieu through –
   a) direct effects of environmental variables (e.g. temperature):
   b) differential availability of resources which can also perhaps influence the transduction process itself.
5. The observed resultant cycle of gametogenesis and spawning.

In reviewing some aspects of this general scheme I shall in particular wish to determine whether different patterns of physiological control can be detected which could be a cause, or a consequence, of the adoption of different reproductive strategies such as discrete iteroparous and discrete semelparous reproduction.

The class Polychaeta provides an opportunity to test the idea that physiological adaptations associated with the adoption of specific reproductive strategies can act as evolutionary constraints, since strictly iteroparous and semelparous reproductive strategies are found among closely related families (Golding & Olive, 1978; Olive, 1979). The discussion will be extended, however, to include other taxonomic groups.

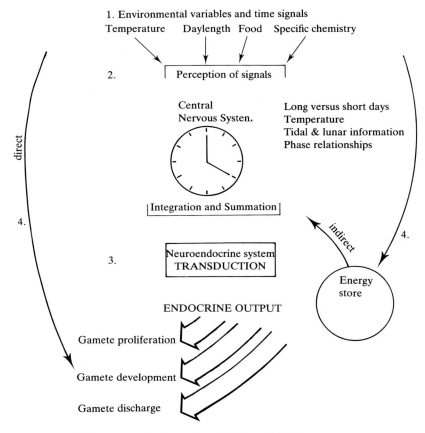

Fig. 2. A diagrammatic representation of the components of the regulatory system controlling germ cell development and discharge and hence of observed reproductive cycles.

A. *Patterns of endocrine control*

(i) *Iteroparous forms:*

Among the iteroparous polychaetes so far investigated, the endocrine system has been found to involve one or more of the following elements:–

   i) negative inhibition of germ-cell proliferation by developing gametocytes;

  ii) production of gonadotrophic hormones essential for continued gametocyte development and for the flow of energy to reproductive tissues;

iii) production and release of spawning hormones controlling maturation and/or release of the fully differentiated germ cells.

The formal evidence for the involvement of these types of endocrine
effect has been reviewed several times (see Olive, 1979; Franke &
Pfannenstiel, 1984). All three elements are not necessarily known to
occur together and knowledge of the nature of the hormones involved is
rudimentary.

The combination of gonadotrophic and spawning hormone functions
provides a flexible system which can be used to regulate a variety of
different reproductive cycles. The system also has inherent flexibility
which can be used to modulate the effective amplitude of the reproductive cycle. This system of control is found in the Nephtyidae, and the
observed reproductive cycle appears to be an expression of a temporal
sequence of hormone production and release. In *Nephtys hombergi*
gametogenesis and vitellogenesis begin in September and is associated
with the production of a gonadotrophic hormone not present in the
cerebral ganglia during the summer months (Bentley & Olive, 1982;
Olive & Bentley, 1980). In the presence of the hormone oocytes continue
to develop and accumulate. Spawning is initiated by the release of a
second cerebral hormone which can only be detected in the ganglia shortly before and during the breeding season (Olive & Bentley, 1980). The
normal reproductive cycle can therefore be interpreted as a consequence
of the endocrine regime represented diagrammatically in Fig. 3A.
Natural variations in the reproductive cycle are also thought to be an
expression of changes in the hormonal milieu. Thus in some years
premature oosorption and energy withdrawal from the developing germinal tissue are observed (Olive, Morgan, Wright & Zhang, 1984). Bentley
& Olive (in preparation) assayed gonadotrophic hormonal production in
such a year and found evidence of reduced levels of hormone production.
In yet other years they also obtained evidence that spawning hormone
was produced but not released. Those gametogenic cycles characterized

---

Fig. 3. Contrasting cycles of Gonadotrophic Hormone (GH) and Spawning Hormone (SH)
production and release observed in different years in a population of *Nephtys hombergi*.
A) A 'normal' cycle. Complete oocyte development and sexual maturity induced by sus-
tained high levels of GH production. Mass spawning induced by the synthesis and release
of SH.
B) Premature oosorption and ovary breakdown induced by low levels of GH production.
SH produced and perhaps released but poor viability of the few remaining oocytes.
C) Sustained high levels of GH production. Spawning Hormone synthesized but not
released, spawning failure followed by a prolonged period of oosorption.
All three cycles have been observed in natural populations (Bentley, unpublished observa-
tions).

by premature oosorption and/or non-spawning can therefore be interpreted as being caused by modified cycles of hormone production as
indicated in Fig. 3B,C). The combination of gonadotrophic and spawning
hormones provides a flexible system for the control of reproductive

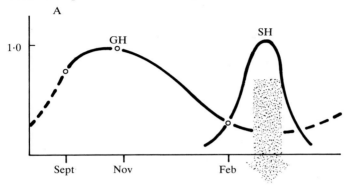

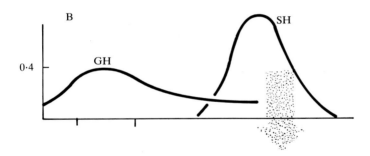

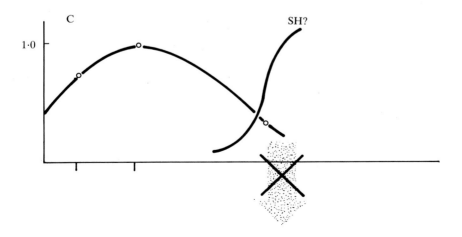

processes in iteroparous organisms, and may have evolved independently many times not only in the Polychaeta but also more widely among the different invertebrate Phyla.

We have begun the separation and characterization of several polychaete hormones including the spawning hormones of *Arenicola marina* and *Nephtys hombergi*, the existence of which were demonstrated by Howie (1963, 1966), Olive (1976) and Olive & Bentley (1980). The isolation steps carried out so far (Bentley & Olive, in preparation) indicate the activity of two structurally quite different substances.

The terms *gonadotrophic hormone* and *spawning hormone* should be regarded as generic terms rather than as the names of specific hormones, until the active substances have been at least partially characterized or their source identified, since each function may be a complex of several interacting hormones. This combination of endocrine functions does, however, seem to be widespread in the control of the discrete iteroparous reproductive cycles characteristic of so many marine invertebrates. For example the combination of Gonadotrophic Hormone and Spawning Hormone functions is involved in the regulation of the annual iteroparous reproductive cycles of the larger Asteroidea although both functions are known to be caused through the integrated action of several hormones.

The progression through the gametogenic cycle in *Asterias rubens* is associated with marked changes in steroid biosynthesis and metabolism (Voogt, Oudejans & Braertjes, 1984, for review). In particular the onset of vitellogenesis is associated with a decrease in the level of progesterone and an increase in oestrone. Injection of oestradiol-17β results in increased levels of oestrone and is associated with an increase in several indices of sexual maturity indicating stimulated vitellogenesis (Schoenmakers, Van Bohemen & Dieleman, 1981). Similarly culture of ovary fragments with oestradiol-17β is associated with enhanced vitellogenesis (Takahashi & Kanatani, 1981). It is likely that elevation of oestrone levels relative to progesterone initiates mobilization of resources stored in the pyloric caecae (De Waal, Poortman & Voogt, 1982) and that an antagonism between the two steroids is operative. Maturation and shedding of the gametes are also under complex endocrine control in Asteroidea. The chain of endocrine influences controlling gamete maturation and spawning in Asteroids was first discovered by Chaet & McConnaughty (1959) who found that a hot seawater extract of the radial nerves induced spawning when injected into the coelomic cavity of gravid male and female specimens of *Asterias forbesi*. The history of the subsequent elucidation of the chain of regulation of maturation has been reviewed by Kanatani

(1973, 1979). The substance extracted from the radial nerves is a peptide (Kanatani *et al.*, 1971) properly termed the *Gonad Stimulating Substance* (GSS). It causes the production of a *Maturation Inducing Substance* (MIS) by non-germinal cells in the ovary. MIS was identified as 1-Methyl-Adenine by Kanatani and his associates (Kanatani, 1969; Kanatani, Shirai, Nakanishi & Kurokawa, 1969), and 1-Me-Ad has been found to have maturation-inducing properties in a large number of Asteroidea (Kanatani, 1969, 1979, for review). 1-Methyl-Adenine itself does not have meiosis-inducing properties when introduced into the cytoplasm of the oocyte. 1-Methyl-adenine acts on the oocyte surface and causes the release of a substance designated the *Maturation Promotion Factor* (MPF) into the oocyte cytoplasm (Kishimoto & Kanatani, 1976, 1977). The hormonal processes involved in the control of the gametogenic development, maturation and spawning in Asteroidea are summarized in Figure 4.

Processes	Hormones	Nature of control
Gamete development		
Previtellogenesis Mobilization	Steroids Progesterone	Changing levels of steroids; ratio of progesterone to oestrone
Vitellogenesis	Oestrone	High progesterone inhibits High oestrone stimulates
Spawning Ovulation Contraction and expulsion Maturation of oocytes	Neurosecretory peptide (radial nerves) = GSS 1 methyl adenine (follicle cells) = MIS Early 2nd messenger ? Calmodulin Intracellular effector (oocyte subsurface) = MPF	radial nerves GSS ↓ + ovaries MIS ↓ + ⟨Ca^{2+}⟩ oocyte surface ↓ MPF ↓ germinal vesicle breakdown

Fig. 4. A summary of the endocrine control of gametogenesis in Asteroidea (see text for bibliographic sources).

Elements of the same dual endocrine system have been found in the marine gastropods (see Joose, 1979; Ram, 1983 for reviews), the *Egg Laying Hormone* (ELH) of *Aplysia* spp. having been investigated in particular detail.

The functional properties of the dual gonadotrophic/spawning hormone system are also appropriate to the regulation of the repeated or semicontinuous form of iteroparous reproduction characteristic of freshwater and terrestrial invertebrates. The endocrine system of the freshwater snail *Lymnea stagnalis*, for instance, is of this type and has been intensively studied (see Joose & Geraerts, 1983; Geraerts & Joose, 1984 for reviews). The gonadotrophic function is attributed to the *Dorsal Body Hormone* which stimulates vitellogenesis as well as cellular differentiation and synthetic activity in the genital tract. While the spawning hormone function is attributable to the secretions of the neuroendocrine *Cauda-Dorsal Cells* which induce ovulation, stimulate egg mass formation and initiate egg-laying behaviour (Joose, 1984).

The sequence of sexual development maturation and egg laying is orchestrated by the temporal sequence of production and release of these hormones.

Egg-laying behaviour itself is likely to be subject to a high degree of fine control and there is increasing evidence of the role of prostaglandin-like substances in this process in many different marine invertebrates (Clare, unpublished; Clare, Walker, Holland & Crisp, 1982).

(ii) *Semelparous forms*

The basic similarity in the overall pattern of endocrine control of reproduction in a variety of different groups of invertebrates where discrete annual reproductive cycles recur may be contrasted with that found in the small number of strictly semelparous groups adequately investigated. The two best known are the Nereidae among Polychaeta and Cephalopoda among the molluscs. In both groups sexual reproduction is always restricted to a single terminal phase of the entire lifespan (see Boyle, 1984 for systematic review of Cephalopod life histories).

In the Nereidae the formal properties of the endocrine system have been investigated through the analysis of cerebral ganglion ablation and replacement performed *in vivo*. Sexual maturation and the changes which accompany this process are thought to be controlled by the progressive withdrawal of a single hormone. The hormone has the capacity:–

    i) to inhibit the somatic metamorphosis (epitoky) which often accompanies sexual maturation;

ii) to inhibit male germ cell differentiation prior to the transition to meiosis I;

iii) to maintain regenerative ability following loss of caudal segments;

iv) to inhibit the later and final stages of oocyte maturation;

v) to support the successful completion of the earlier stages of oocyte development for which the presence of hormone is essential.

Two schemes for the role of the hormone in co-ordinating sexual reproduction have been proposed, both taking into account the demonstrated decline in hormonal activity of the brain during normal development. According to Durchon and his collaborators (Durchon & Porchet, 1971; Durchon, 1976) each stage of sexual development is programmed by a stage-specific titre of hormone, the concentration of which was estimated by *in vitro* assay. Golding (1983) has proposed an alternative scheme based on the results of a standardized assay for endocrine activity

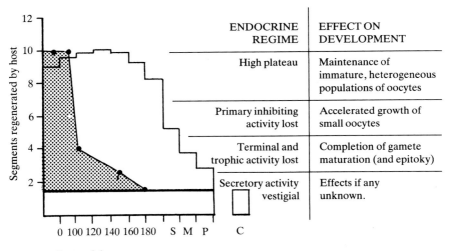

Stage of donors
0 – 180, max oocyte diameter
S, Submature
M, Mature
P, Postspawning
C, Decerebrate control

Fig. 5 Patterns of endocrine activity in relation to an index of sexual maturity in *Nereis diversicolor*. The shaded area indicates results obtained by Durchon and his collaborators (see Durchon, 1976) using an assay based on inhibition of spermiogenesis *in vitro*. The open area shows the endocrine activity as measured by the capacity to promote segment regeneration when implanted into standard immature hosts (from Golding, 1983). Interpretation (from Golding, 1983). Note the marked difference in the apparent course of hormone decline as recorded by the two systems.

in vivo in which the number of segments regenerated by a standard decerebrated host is used as an index of the secretory activity of an implanted ganglion. According to this scheme the programme of development is explained in terms of a series of different thresholds for the extinction of each of the several functions of the cerebral hormone. Figure 5 illustrates the programme of secretory activity as measured by regeneration-supporting capacity recorded for brains taken from animals at different stages of sexual maturity.

According to both schemes the progress of sexual development is orchestrated by the progressive withdrawal of the cerebral hormone – the production of which is known to be inhibited by a hormone-like substance produced by the maturing coelomic oocytes (Durchon, 1952; Porchet & Cardon, 1976; Porchet, Dhainaut & Porchet-Hennere, 1979). Since oocyte maturation is a consequence of hormone withdrawal, this acts as a positive feedback loop.

The control process is far from simple and it has proved particularly difficult to establish the role of the endocrine system in the regulation of oocyte development. The pattern of oocyte growth observed in populations in natural conditions is difficult to reconcile with the Durchon/ Porchet model (see Olive & Garwood, 1981; Fischer, 1984), and Fischer (1984) suggests that the growth rate of the oocytes is probably influenced indirectly through control of the metabolic and nutritional milieu in which they develop.

Rapid progress is being made in the biochemical analysis of the interactions between the cerebral ganglia, coelomocytes, coelomic fluid and developing germ cells which form part of a co-ordinated system (reviews by Dhainaut *et al.*, 1984; Fischer, 1984; Porchet, 1984).

The growth of the oocytes depends on the presence of macromolecular fractions (vitellogenins) in the coelomic fluid, but the oocytes also take up low relative molecular mass substances (sugars and amino acids), the incorporation and metabolism of which may be influenced by the hormonal milieu. Withdrawal of cerebral hormone also leads to the appearance in the coelomic fluid of two moderately low relative molecular mass fractions which, when injected into immature females, are found to initiate rapid sexual maturation (Porchet *et al.*, 1979). These substances, termed B_1 and B_2 by Porchet and his collaborators, are thought to enhance production of the feedback substances by the oocyte and hence are involved in the positive feedback loop (Fig. 6).

Withdrawal of the cerebral hormone with its manifold effects on sexual maturation is a relatively late event in the maturational programme. It coordinates a complex series of events and ensures that somatic maturation

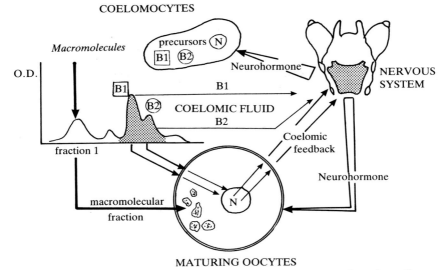

MATURING OOCYTES

Fig. 6. A summary of suggested interactions between the supraoesophageal ganglion, coelomocytes, coelomic fluid and developing oocytes of Nereidae. (Simplified from an original diagram of Porchet, 1984).
The absorbance scan based on gel filtration of the coelomic fluid suggests the presence of macromolecules produced by the coelomocytes and incorporated by the oocytes and lower relative molecular mass fractions of which B_1 and B_2 influence oocyte growth by activating production of the oocyte-produced substance which inhibits cerebral hormone production and which forms therefore part of a positive feedback loop. See text for further discussion.

(epitoky), redeployment of nutritional reserves and maturation of germ cells occur in unison, in a highly adaptive manner. It also ensures that resources are not wastefully directed to regenerative processes when the terminal reproductive event is imminent.

Withdrawal of the hormone marks an 'all or nothing' transition to a programme of sexual development and due to the operation of the positive feedback loop it is normally irreversible. Golding (unpublished) however has succeeded in reactivating the brains of maturing individuals following serial transplantation through several immature hosts.

The key event in the life history of the monotelic Nereidae is the 'decision' to initiate sexual development which in the longer-lived species occurs some 12–18 months prior to eventual reproduction. The endocrine system seems to be primarily concerned with regulating the consequences of such a 'decision', the causes of which remain unexplained.

Strictly semelparous (monotelic) reproduction occurs in some other polychaete families; the reproductive physiology of these is hardly known but it is interesting to note that a preliminary investigation of the endocrinology of the epitokous opheliid *Polyophthalmus pictus* does indicate an inhibitory system of reproductive control (Franke, 1984).

Sexual reproduction in the Cephalopoda, which is also a terminal life history event, is characterized by a massive re-allocation of resources to reproductive tissues (O'Dor & Wells, 1975). Moreover, Stearns (1984) has cited this group as one where physiological adaptation to the monotelic form of reproduction may now act as an evolutionary constraint, although it was not clear what constituted that physiological adaptation. The pattern of endocrine regulation is not the same as it is in Nereidae although functionally it is similar. It does however differ markedly from that of the iteroparous mollusca discussed above. The optic lobes of the cephalopoda are the source of a powerful gonadotrophin, the release of which is responsible for the allocation of resources to reproductive tissues. The glands are normally inhibited from functioning by their innervation. If the nerves supplying the glands are cut or the glands isolated *in vitro* the optic glands become active, continue to release hormone and co-ordinate the massive re-allocation of resources to reproduction. As in the Nereidae there is in effect an all or nothing switch from somatic growth to an outburst of reproductive activity which will terminate the life (O'Dor & Wells, 1975; Wells & Wells, 1975, 1977). The system also resembles that in the Nereidae since the endocrine system is used to put into effect the consequences of a 'decision' which is made within the central nervous system.

To conclude:

Within the two taxonomic groupings I have considered, in which iteroparous and semelparous subgroups can be found, there do seem to be major differences in the overall pattern of endocrine control which is related in a fundamental way to the reproductive strategy. Thus, in the Polychaeta iteroparous forms have been found to have components of the gonadotrophic hormone/spawning hormone system whereas semelparous forms have an inhibitory (juvenile hormone) type of control. Similar associations can be found in the Hirudinea (see Olive & Clark, 1978) but great care must be taken in interpreting these findings.

The Syllidae have complex patterns of sexual reproduction involving the detachment of free-living sexual stolons, and have a third type of endocrine system in which an inhibitory hormone is released from unknown endocrine centres in the pharyngeal region. Cyclical control of this system is imposed by a stimulatory hormone released from the prostomium (see Franke, 1983a,b; Franke & Pfannenstiel, 1984; Heacox & Schroeder, 1982 for recent developments), and this system probably represents a third independently evolved endocrine system in the phyllodocemorph polychaeta.

An inhibitory system of endocrine control has also been discovered in the Nemertea (Bierne, 1970, 1973; Bierne & Rué, 1979; Rué & Bierne, 1980), but these organisms are probably not semelparous.

A feature of the endocrine system of the semelparous species is that they are adapted to the control of a once-per-lifetime allocation of resources to reproduction and that they prevent wasteful allocation of resources to somatic functions during sexual maturation. The inhibition of caudal regeneration by maturing Nereidae at low hormone concentrations, for instance, has this functional significance (Golding & Olive, 1978). Perhaps the most important feature of all is that once sexual reproduction has been initiated it is not usually reversible and the later stages of maturation are autonomous in these organisms.

B. *Temporal control of reproductive processes*

(i) *General considerations:*

The reproductive activities of most organisms bear a fixed-phase relationship to real time. This is true for most macrofaunal invertebrates in shallow temperate seas and is also true for some organisms found in quasistable environments such as the deep sea (Lightfoot, Tyler & Gage, 1979; Tyler, Grant, Pain & Gage, 1982). Persistent phase relationships between reproductive events in a population and external cycles can be found in both iteroparous and strictly semelparous organisms but the mechanisms by which they are maintained are likely to be quite different. In the case of the iteroparous species, each individual in the population shows cyclic development of gametocytes with gamete maturation and spawning recurring at fixed, usually annual, time intervals. In the case of semelparous forms a similar cycle can be detected at the population level but individual organisms only become mature once per lifetime. Moreover the average lifespan is often greater than the spawning periodicity at a population level consequently the phase relationship cannot simply be a response by individuals to environmental conditions.

Historically environmental temperature has been regarded as the one factor likely to control the reproductive cycles of marine animals, a view deriving from the formative paper of Orton (1920).

In its simplest form the temperature regulation hypothesis maintains that environmental temperature cycles influence the reproductive cycles of organisms by defining times when conditions are suitable for reproduction to occur. This simple idea does not fit situations where specific events have a fixed recurrent relationship to real time. Moreover, there is increasing evidence that marine invertebrates like those in the terrestrial environment can respond to the predictable changes in photoperiods associated with the seasons in temperate and boreal regions. Evidence of photoperiodic regulation of reproductive events has been obtained for Echinodermata (Pearse & Eernisse, 1982); Mollusca (Dogterom, Bohlken & Joose, 1983; McCrout, Van Minuer & Duncan, 1984); Crustacea (Marcus, 1980; Steele, 1981; Steele, Steele & MacPherson, 1977); Tunicata (West & Lambert, 1976) and in several groups of Polychaeta (Franke, 1983b; Garwood, 1980; Garwood & Olive, 1982; Olive & Pillai, 1983). It is not surprising, therefore, to find that the neuroendocrine system of marine invertebrates is involved in the regulation of reproductive cycles. In the general scheme presented in Fig. 2 it was supposed that environmental factors could influence gametogenic processes either directly or indirectly via the central nervous system. The organism, or some component of it, it is supposed can act as a 'black box' which receives information from the environment and from the nutritional and physiological status of the organism. The overt reproductive cycle is the consequence of the *'transduction'* of this information. Experiments conducted in our laboratory suggest that the transduction is performed with reference to real time, implicating clock-based physiology in the control of reproductive cycles. Although the integrating, transducing function of the organism is a complex 'black box', it can be subjected to formal experimental analysis which can reveal some of its properties. Such an approach has been successful in the Insecta where the role of the central nervous system in controlling the insertion of diapause stages into successive generations with reference to photoperiod, real time and other conditions has been analysed in remarkable detail (see Beck, 1980; Saunders, 1982; Vaz Nunes & Veerman, 1982a,b; Veerman & Vaz Nunes, 1984 for recent discussion). The control of reproductive cycles in marine invertebrates can be subject to similar formal analysis and we have begun an investigation of the properties of the timing mechanisms in Polychaeta including both iteroparous and semelparous forms (see Olive, 1981a, 1984 for more detailed reviews).

(ii) *Iteroparous cycles*

There are innumerable reports in the literature of reproductive cycles of marine invertebrates in temperate regions, in which gametogenesis or vitellogenesis begins at more or less the same time each year and culminates in reproductive activity approximately six months later. There is also evidence from our own studies and reports in the literature (Bierne, 1970) that when maintained under suitable constant conditions iteroparous organisms have an innate tendency to progress towards a condition of sexual maturity. Environmental factors modulate the rate of that progression in such a way as to ensure that sexual maturity is achieved at an appropriate time. The precise way in which this is done can only be determined by laboratory experiments, although useful information can be obtained from field studies carried out under different hydrographical conditions or from the analysis of differences in cycles observed in different years.

Environmental factors which influence the rate at which gametogenic processes proceed can have powerful synchronizing (or desynchronizing) effects on populations of organisms, or cells within organisms (Olive, 1981a), especially when the relationship between the environmental variable and the process rate is not linear.

The important factors are:–

i) the time of initiation of dependent processes, and

ii) the nature of the relationship between gametogenic rate and environmental variable.

A relatively simple case, in which changes in environmental temperature play a dominant role, was found in the phyllodocid polychaete *Eulalia viridis*. In this species the rate of vitellogenesis increases strongly with environmental temperature in the range 5–20 °C (Garwood & Olive, 1978; Olive, 1981a, 1981b). The relationship is such that there will be a dramatic increase in the sexual maturity of females in late spring as the temperature passes a 10 °C threshold. However, heterochronic experiments showed that the ability to respond to elevated temperatures was influenced by some endogenous factor, which we described as being a circa-annual rhythm (Olive, 1981b), which prevented individuals from responding to elevated temperatures at an inappropriate time. The organism is known to have a gonadotrophic hormone system, and non-operation of this system perhaps with reference to endogenous factors such as nutritional state or an endogenous clock could be responsible for this restriction.

As a timing device environmental temperature is relatively noisy and there is now good evidence that many marine invertebrates are responsive to relative day length. One such organism is the polychaete *Harmothoe imbricata* which is proving to be particularly suitable for the investigation of the photoperiodic response. The response to daylength (measured as time to spawning or oocyte growth rate) is not linear, the critical daylength for the transition from slow to rapid oocyte growth being c. 11·5 h. At 5 °C a transition from short to long days in the period October to January is followed by a sharp increase in oocyte growth rate

(Fig. 7A). Oocyte growth continues, however, albeit at a relatively slow rate, in short day conditions (Fig. 7B). The behaviour of animals exposed to long days at 5 °C throughout this period is interesting; they fail to grow oocytes (Fig. 7B). Apparently some exposure to short-day lengths is required before a response to long days can be initiated and this is being investigated (Clark, S., unpublished). Several aspects of the photoperiodic response of this organism are now under investigation.

Responses such as those of *E. viridis* and *H. imbricata* to natural cycles

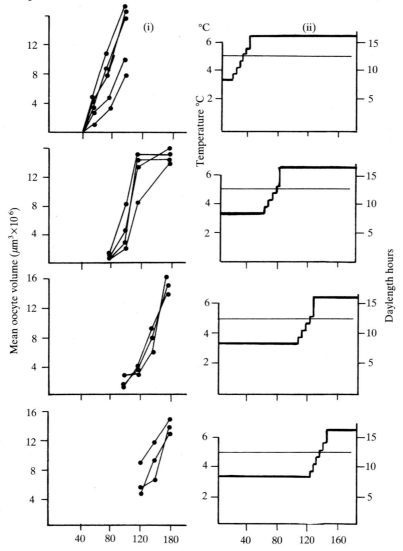

of temperature and daylength may be sufficient to bring organisms syn-chronously to a state of maturity at an appropriate time. In some cases, as in *H. imbricata*, this may lead automatically to spawning with no further specific input required to initiate this process. In many animals, especially those which are broadcast spawners, the spawning mechanism itself may require induction by environmental factors. The physiology of the initiation of this, the final stage in sexual reproduction, is not well understood; spawning may be initiated by the presence of specific sub-stances in the seawater due to the phytoplankton succession (Himmel-mann, 1979, 1981) or spawning may be related to changes in air or sea temperature or the presence of other spawning individuals. These late-

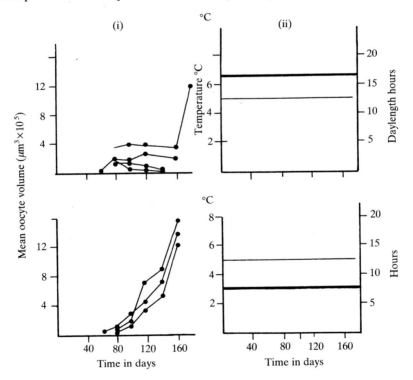

Fig. 7. (i) Patterns of oocyte growth exhibited by female *Harmothoe imbricata* exposed to a variety of daylength regimen. (ii) The corresponding temperature and daylength regimen, thicker line daylength, thinner line temperature (always 5 °C).
Animals exposed to increased daylengths from 8L : 16D to 16L : 8D show an immediate increase in the rate of oocyte growth. Animals under constant conditions show a different pattern, constant 16L : 8D inhibits gamete development. Animals under constant 8L : 16D show a spontaneous increase in oocyte growth rate. The effect of exposure to long days after short days is to accelerate and bring forward the oocyte growth (from a larger set of data of S. Clark, unpublished, with permission).

acting environmental factors are very likely to act by causing the discharge of the spawning hormones which, as described above, have been found to operate in many different groups of iteroparous organisms. There is a striking parallel between the dual system of endocrine control involving gonadotrophic and spawning hormones and the two ways in which environmental factors influence reproductive cycles –

i) by modulation of rates of gametogenesis to bring about progressive sexual maturation,

ii) by initiating or triggering spawning.

A major challenge now is to understand the relationship between the parallel environmental and endocrinological systems of control.

(iii) *Semelparous (monotelic) organisms*

As explained above, the environmental control of reproduction in semelparous organisms is not likely to be the same as that in iteroparous species. The Nereidae provide a model of such a situation in which there is a reproductive cycle with a strong rhythmic element yet individual animals spawn only once. Both annual and lunar components of rhythmicity have been described (Hauenschild, 1955, 1956, 1960; Olive, 1984; Olive & Garwood, 1983).

The observed rhythm of reproduction is a population level phenomenon and only when the phase length of the overt rhythm and the lifespan of the organism are identical is it possible to explain the cycle simply in terms of a response to specific environmental conditions. In all the cases studied the mean lifespan or generation time is greater than the phase length of the observed rhythm, and in these circumstances some other factor must determine which members of the population become sexually mature (possibly in response to some perceived signal) and which members do not.

In *Nereis diversicolor* observations so far can be 'explained' in terms of a model which supposes the existence of a persistent gated rhythm with circa-annual periodicity (Olive & Garwood, 1983). This sets a series of times when gametogenesis may be initiated. Gametogenesis and sexual maturation then proceed according to an endogenously determined programme in which the unique endocrine system plays a most important role in co-ordinating the sequence of maturational steps.

Finally the individual reaches a stage at which sexual reproduction and gamete discharge are possible. At this stage the organism is again receptive to specific environmental information. The 'déclenchement' or release of spawning behaviour may involve a complex series of behavioural and pheromonal interactions as described for *Platynereis dumerili* (Boilly-Marer, 1969, 1974) or it may require specific environmental conditions for its release. At this stage short-term rhythmicity could be imposed on a population.

A key feature of this sequence of maturational events is the 'decision' to embark on sexual reproduction. The evidence suggests that this decision in monotelic organisms is made with respect to both endogenous factors and real time.

IV. Conclusions: Physiological adaptations and the concept of optimality

I started this discussion by referring to current theories of life history evolution and addressed the problem of determining whether, as has been suggested, physiological constraints may develop which prevent species from adopting optimal patterns of life history. The following conclusions may be offered:–

1. The ecologically important distinction for marine organisms between the production of feeding and non-feeding larvae is not apparently associated with major physiological adaptation by the adults. The physiological adaptations for discrete reproduction with external fertilization are similar whether the allocation is made through the assignment of relatively small amounts of energy to a large number of offspring or larger amounts of energy to a smaller number of offspring.

2. Major differences in the reproductive physiology of predominantly semelparous and iteroparous subgroups within major taxonomic groupings can be detected. This suggests that the physiological requirements of these two types of life history are fundamentally different.

3. In iteroparous organisms a flexible system of endocrinological and environmental control of reproductive processes has developed which permits not only regulation of the timing of reproductive processes but also regulation of relative reproductive effort. Optimality theory predicts a trade-off between reproductive allocation and future fecundity, survivorship, or both. The amount of food an organism finds at any time in its lifespan is variable and animals which can breed several years in succession may tend to maintain their survivorship and fail to breed when their food input is low. Resource availability, however, is subject to epigenetic variation and the physiological properties of iteroparous organisms may be involved in homeostatic mechanisms which maintain survivorship, sometimes at the expense of current reproductive effort. For example, reproductive effort in the Polychaetes *Nephtys hombergi*

and *Harmothoe imbricata* is variable between years (Olive, Garwood, Bentley & Wright, 1984; Gremare & Olive, 1985), but there is no evidence of a reciprocal relationship between reproductive effort and survivorship, and the endocrine system of *Nephtys hombergi* is known to be involved in the onset of premature oosorption (see above).

4. The plasticity of the gonadotrophic hormone/spawning hormone system is such that it is not likely to exert a constraint over the adoption of different forms of iteroparous reproduction.

5. The physiological consequences of the adoption of a strictly semelparous (monotelic) mode of reproduction by the Nereidae and Cephalopoda seem to have been severe. In particular the endocrine control of reproductive processes differs markedly from that in related but iteroparous taxonomic groupings. The endocrine system is involved in the co-ordinated transfer of acquired energy to reproductive tissue and no trade-off between reproductive effort and residual reproductive value is possible.

Optimality theory for such organisms predicts a relatively high and uniform reproductive effort. The gating mechanism in Nereidae could be regarded as a physiological means to achieve this result since it permits reference to some endogenous criteria of condition prior to the irrevocable initiation of sexual maturation (Garwood & Olive, 1981).

A study of the allocation of energy to reproduction in *H. imbricata* and *N. diversicolor*, however, revealed similar levels of variation in the iteroparous and semelparous species (Gremare & Olive, 1985). The physiological mechanism is evidently not sufficient to eliminate epigenetic sources of variation of reproductive effort in Nereidae.

6. It may be supposed that monotelic reproduction arose in the Nereidae in conjunction with epigamy (swarming) and the evolution of the Heteronereis (Clark, 1961; Smith, 1958). The swarming heteronereis is undoubtedly subject to increased risks of predation, and delayed reproduction may have become advantageous in these circumstances following a model 3 – 'Reproduction is Risky' – hypothesis as outlined above.

The refinement of the physiological system appropriate for this pattern of reproduction seems to have been sufficient to prevent any return to iteroparity, even when the epigametic heteronereis stage has been secondarily lost. If this is so, it is not necessary to assume that semelparous reproduction is an optimal reproductive strategy for all Nereidae. These organisms may indeed be trapped by their evolutionary history.

This essay represents a synthesis of many discussions I have had with my colleagues and students. While the ideas I express and their limitations are my own, the data from which they derive are due to the work of many people. I should particularly like to express my thanks to P. R. Garwood, M. Bentley, N. Wright, A. Gremare, S. Clark and A. Grant for their sometimes hidden contributions to this work, and for making their own unpublished work available to me. I should also like to express my gratitude to the Science and Engineering Research Council and the Natural Environment Research Council, whose support has made much of this work possible.

References

BECK, S. D. (1980). *Insect Photoperiodism*. 2nd edition. New York: Academic Press.

BENTLEY, M. G. & OLIVE, P. J. W. (1982). An *in vitro* assay for gonadotrophic hormone in the Polychaete *Nephtys hombergii* Sar. (Nephtydae). *Gen. comp. Endocr.* **47**, 467–474.

BIERNE, J. (1970). Recherches sur la différenciation sexuelle au cours de l'ontogenèse et la régénération chez le nemertien *Lineus ruber* Müller. *Ann. Sci. nat. (Zool.)* **12**, 181–298.

BIERNE, J. (1973). Contrôle neuroendocrinien de la puberté chez le mâle de *Lineus ruber* (Hétéronémerté). *C. r. hebd, séanc. Acad. Sci., Paris* **276**, 363–366.

BIERNE, J. & RUÉ, G. (1979). Endocrine control of reproduction in two rhynchocoelan worms. *Int. J. Inv. Rep.* **1**, 109–120.

BOILLY-MARER, Y. I. (1969). Recherches expérimentales sur la danse nuptiale de *Platynereis dumerilii* (Aud. M. Edw.) (Annélide, Polychète). Origine et modalités d'action de la substance excitatrice. *Cah. Biol. mar.* **10**, 255–269.

BOILLY-MARER, Y. I. (1974). Étude éxpérimental du comportement nuptial de *Platynereis dumerilii* (Annélide, Polychète); Chémoréception, émission des produits genitaux. *Mar. Biol.* **24**, 167–179.

BOYLE, P. (1984). (ed.) *Cephalopod Life Histories*. Vol. 1. New York: Academic Press.

CALOW, P. (1979). The cost of reproduction – a physiological approach. *Biol. Rev.* **54**, 23–40.

CALOW, P. (1984). Exploring the adaptive landscapes of invertebrate life cycles. In *Advances in Invertebrate Reproduction*, Vol. **3** (ed. W. Engels) pp. 329–342. Amsterdam: Elsevier.

CASWELL, H. (1980). On the equivalence of maximising reproductive value and maximising fitness. *Ecology* **61**, 19–24.

CHAET, A. B. & McCONNAUGHTY, R. A. (1959). Physiologic activity of nerve extracts. *Biol. Bull. mar. biol. lab. Woods Hole, Mass.* **117**, 407.

CHARLSWORTH, B. (1980). *Evolution in Age-Structured Populations* pp. 300. Cambridge: Cambridge University Press.

CHRISTIANSEN, F. B. & FENCHEL, T. M. (1979). Evolution of marine invertebrate reproductive patterns. *Theoretical Population Biology* **16**, 267–282.

CLARE, A. S., WALKER, G., HOLLAND, D. L. & CRISP, D. J. (1982). Barnacle egg hatching: A novel role for a prostoglandin-like compound. *Mar. Biol. Lett.* **3**, 113–120.

CLARK, R. B. (1961). The origin and formation of the Heteronereis. *Biol. Rev.* **36**, 199–236.

DEWAAL, M., POORTMAN, J. & VOOGT, P. A. (1982). Steroid receptors in invertebrates: a specific 17-β-estradiol binding protein in a sea star *Asterias rubens. Mar. Biol. Lett.* **3**, 317–323.

DHAINAUT, A. (1984). Oogenesis in polychaetes. Ultra-structural differentiation and metabolism of nereid oocytes. *Fortschr. Zool.* **29**, 183–207.

DOGTEROM, G. E., BOHLKEN, S. & JOOSE, J. (1983). Effect of the photoperiod on the time schedule of egg-mass production in *Hymaates stagnalis* as induced by ovulation hormone injections. *Gen. comp. Endoc.* **49**, 255–260.

DURCHON, M. (1952). Recherches expérimentales sur deux aspects de la reproduction chez les annélides polychètes: l'épitoquie et la stolonisation. *Ann. Sci. Nat. (zool.)* 11th series **14**, 119–206.

DURCHON, M. (1976). L'endocrinologie des vers et des annélides. In *Actualités sur les Hormones des Invertébrés.* pp. 53–78. *Coll. internat. du CNRS*, no. **251**.

DURCHON, M. & PORCHET, M. (1971). Premières données quantitative sur l'activité endocrine du cerveau des Néréidiens au cours de leur cycle sexuel. *Gen. comp. Endoc.* **16**, 555–565.

FISCHER, A. (1984). Control of oocyte differentiation in nereids (Annélida, Polychaeta) – facts and ideas. *Fostschr. Zool.* **29**, 227–245.

FISHER, R. A. (1958). *The Genetical Theory of Natural Selection.* 2nd ed. 287 pp. New York: Dover Press.

FRANKE, H. D. (1983a). Endocrine control of reproductive periodicity in male *Typosyllis prolifera* (Polychaeta, Syllidae). *Int. J. Inv. Reprod.* **6**, 229–238.

FRANKE, H. D. (1983b). Endocrine mechanisms mediating light temperature effects on male reproductive activity in *Typosyllis prolifera* (Polychaeta: Syllidae).

FRANKE, H. D. (1984). Endocrine control of reproduction in the monotelic polychaete *Polyophthalmus pictus* (Opheliidae). In *Advances Invertebrate Reproduction* **3** (ed. W. Engels) p. 579. Amsterdam, New York: Elsevier Science.

FRANKE, H. D. & PFANNENSTIEL, H. D. (1984). Some aspects of endocrine control of polychaete reproduction. *Fortschr. Zool.* **29**, 53–72.

GADGIL, M. & BOSSERT, W. H. (1970). Life historical consequences of natural selection. *Am. Nat.* **104**, 1–26.

GARWOOD, P. R. (1980). The role of temperature and daylength in the control of the reproductive cycle of *Harmothoe imbricata* (L.). (Polychaeta: Polynoidae). *J. exp. mar. Biol. Ecol.* **47**, 35–53.

GARWOOD, P. R. & OLIVE, P. J. W. (1978). Environmental control of reproduction in the polychaete *Eulalia viridis* and *Harmothoe imbricata.* In *Physiology and Behaviour of Marine Organisms* (eds D. S. McLusky & A. J. Berry) pp. 331–339. Oxford: Pergamon Press.

GARWOOD, P. R. & OLIVE, P. J. W. (1981). The influence of environmental factors on the growth of oocytes in *Nereis diversicolor* (Annelida: Polychaeta). *Bull. Soc. Zool. Fr.* **106**, 399–402.

GARWOOD, P. R. & OLIVE, P. J. W. (1982). The influence of photoperiod on oocyte growth and its role in the control of the reproductive cycle of the polychaete *Harmothoe imbricata* (L.) *Int. J. Inv. Reprod.* **5**, 161–166.

GERAERTS, W. P. M. & JOOSE, J. (1984). Freshwater snails (Basommastophora). In *The Mollusca. Reproduction*, Volume 7 (ed. K. M. Wilbur) pp. 141–207. New York: Academic Press.

GOLDING, D. W. (1983). Endocrine programmed development and reproduction in *Nereis*. *Gen. comp. Endocr.* **52**, 456–466.

GOLDING, D. W & OLIVE, P. J. W. (1978). Patterns of regenerative growth, reproductive strategy and endocrine control in polychaete annelids. In *Comparative Endocrinology* (ed. P. J. Gaillard & H. H. Boer) pp. 117–120. Amsterdam: Elsevier (North Holland Biomedical Press).

GOULD, S. J. & LEWONTIN, R. C. (1979). The spandrels of San Marco and the Panglossian paradigm: a critique of the adaptationist programme. *Proc. Roy. Soc. London*, B **205**, 581–598.

GREMARE, A. & OLIVE, P. J. W. (1985). A preliminary study of fecundity and reproductive effort in two polychaetous annelids with contrasting reproductive strategies. *Int. J. Inv. Reprod.* (In press.)

HAUENSCHILD, VON C. (1955). Photoperiodizität ab Ursache des von der Mondphase abhanigen Metamorphose – Rhythmus bei dem Polychaeten *Platynereis dumerilii*. *Z. naturf.* **106**, 658–662.

HAUENSCHILD, C. (1956). Neue experimentelle Untersuchungen zum Problem der Lunaperiodizitat. *Naturwissenschaftliche* **43**, 361–363.

HAUENSCHILD, C. (1960). Lunar periodicity. *Cold Spring Harb. Symp. quant. Biol.* **75**, 491–497.

HEACOX, A. E. & SCHROEDER, P. C. (1981). A light and electron-microscopic investigation of gametogenesis in *Typosyllis pulchra* (Berkeley & Berkeley) (Polychaeta: Syllidae). I. Gonad Structure and spermatogenesis. *Cell Tissue Res.* **218**, 623–639.

HIMMELMAN, J. H. (1979). Factors regulating the reproductive cycles of two North East Pacific chitons, *Tonicella lineata* and *T. insignis*. *Mar. Biol.* **50**, 215–225.

HIMMELMAN, J. H. (1981). Synchronisation of spawning in marine invertebrates by phytoplankton. In *Adv. Inv. Reproduction* (eds W. Clark & T. Adams) Vol. **2**, 3–19. New York: Elsevier North Holland Press.

HOWIE, D. I. D. (1963). Experimental evidence for the humoral stimulation of ripening of the gametes, and spawning in the Polychaete *Arenicola marina*. *Gen. comp. Endocr.* **3**, 600–608.

HOWIE, D. I. D. (1966). Further data relating to the maturation hormone and its site of secretion in *Arenicola marina*. *Gen. comp. Endocr.* **6**, 347–360.

ISTOCK, C. (1981). Natural selection and life history variation: theory plus lessons from a Mosquito. In *Insect Life History Patterns: Habitat and Geographic Variation* (eds R. F. Denno & H. Dingle) pp. 113–127. N.Y.: Springer-Verlag.

ISTOCK, C. (1984). Variable reproductive patterns within populations: ecological and evolutionary consequences. In *Advances in Invertebrate Reproduction*, Vol. 3 (ed. W. Engels) pp. 343–355. Amsterdam: Elsevier.

JAGERSTEN, G. (1972). *Evolution of the Metazoan Life Cycle* pp. 282. New York: Academic Press.

JOOSE, J. (1979). Evolutionary aspects of the endocrine system and the hormonal control of reproduction in molluscs. In *Hormones and Evolution* (ed. E. J. W. Barrington) pp. 119–157. New York: Academic Press.

JOOSE, J. & GERAERTS, W. P. M. (1983). Hormones. In *The Mollusca* (Vol. 4) pp. 317–406. *Physiology Part 1* (eds K. M. Wilbur & A. S. M. Saleuddin). New York: Academic Press.

JOOSE, J. (1984). Photoperiodicity, rhythmicity and endocrinology of reproduction in the snail *Lymnea stagnalis*. In *Photoperiodic Regulation of Insect and Molluscan Hormones. CIBA Foundation Symposium* **104**, 204–220.

KANATANI, H. (1969). Induction of spawning and oocyte maturation by 1-methyladenine in starfishes. *Expl Cell Res.* **57**, 333–337.

KANATANI, H. (1973). Maturation-inducing substance in starfishes. *Int. Rev. Cytol.* **35**, 253–298.

KANATANI, H. (1979). Hormones in echinoderms. In *Hormones and Evolution*, Vol. 1 (ed. E. J. W. Barrington) pp. 273–307. New York: Academic Press.

KANATANI, H., IKEGAMI, H., SHIRAI, H., OIDE, H. & TAMURA, S. (1971). Purification of gonad-stimulating substance obtained from the radial nerves of the starfish, *Asterias amurensis*. *Devl. Growth, Differ.* **13**, 151–164.

KANATANI, H., SHIRAI, H., NAKANISHI, K. & KUROKAWA, T. (1969). Isolation and identification of meiosis-inducing substance in the starfish, *Asterias amurensis*. *Nature* **221**, 273–274.

KISHIMOTO, T. & KANATANI, H. (1976). Cytoplasmic factor responsible for germinal vesicle breakdown and meiotic maturation in starfish oocytes. *Nature* **266**, 321–322.

KISHIMOTO, T. & KANATANI, H. (1977). Lack of species specificity of starfish maturation promoting factor. *Gen. comp. Endocr.* **3J**, 41–44.

LIGHTFOOT, R. H., TYLER, P. A. & GAGE, J. D. (1979). Seasonal reproduction in deep sea bivalves and brittlestars. *Deep Sea Res.* **26A**, 967–973.

MACARTHUR, R. H. & WILSON, E. O. (1967). *Theory of Island Biogeography*. Princeton: Princeton University Press.

MARCUS, N. H. (1980). Photoperiodic control of diapause in the marine calanoid copepod *Lobidocera crestina*. *Biol. Bull. mar. Biol. Lab., Woods Hole* **159**, 311–318.

NORDHEIM, H. VON (1984). Life histories of subtidal interstitial Polychaeta of the families Polygordiidae, Nerillidae, Protodrilidae, Dinophilidae and Diurodrilidae from Helgoland (North Sea). *Helgoländer meeresunters* **38**, 1–20.

O'DOR, R. K & WELLS, M. J. (1975). Control of yolk protein synthesis by *Octopus* gonadotrophin *in vivo* and *in vitro*. *Gen. comp. Endocr.* **27**, 129–135.

OLIVE, P. J. W. (1976). Preliminary evidence for a previously undescribed spawning hormone in *Nephtys hombergii* (Polychaeta: Nephtyidae). *Gen. comp. Endocr.* **28**, 454–460.

OLIVE, P. J. W. (1979). Endocrine adaptations in Polychaeta. In *Hormones and Evolution* (ed. E. J. W. Barrington) pp. 73–118. London: Academic Press.

OLIVE, P. J. W. (1981a). Environmental control of reproduction in Polychaeta; experimental studies of littoral species in N. E. England. In *Advances Invertebrate Reproduction* Vol. 3 (eds. W. Clark & T. Adams) pp. 31–57. New York: Elsevier/North Holland inc.

OLIVE, P. J. W. (1981b). Control of the reproductive cycles in female *Eulalia viridis* (Polychaeta: Phyllodocidae). *J. mar. biol. Ass. U.K.* **61**, 941–958.

OLIVE, P. J. W. (1984a). Environmental control of reproduction in Polychaeta. *Fortschr. Zool.* **29**, 17–28.

OLIVE, P. J. W. (1984). Covariability of reproductive traits in marine invertebrates: implications for the phylogeny of the lower invertebrates. *Syst. Association Series* **28** (eds Conway Morris *et al.*). Oxford University Press (In press).

OLIVE, P. J. W. & BENTLEY, M. G. (1980). Hormonal control of oogenesis, ovulation and spawning in the annual reproductive cycle of the polychaete *Nephtys hombergi* (Sar.): (Nephtyidae). *Int. J. Inv. Repr.* **2**, 205–221.

OLIVE, P. J. W. & CLARK, R. B. (1978). Reproductive Physiology. In *Physiology of Annelids* (ed. P. J. Mill) pp. 271–368. London: Academic Press.

OLIVE, P. J. W. & GARWOOD, P. (1981). Gametogenic cycle and population structure of *Nereis* (Hediste) *diversicolor* and *Nereis* (Nereis) *pelagica* from N. E. England. *J. mar. Biol. Ass. U.K.* **61**, 193–213.

OLIVE, P. J. W. & GARWOOD, P. R. (1983). The importance of long term endogenous rhythms in the maintenance of reproductive cycles of marine invertebrates: a reappraisal. *Int. J. Inv. Repr.* **6**, 339–347.

OLIVE, P. J. W., GARWOOD, P. R., BENTLEY, M. G. & WRIGHT, N. (1981). Reproductive success, relative abundance and population structure of the two species of *Nephtys* in an estuarine beach. *Mar. Biol.* **63**, 189–196.

OLIVE, P. J. W., MORGAN, P. J., WRIGHT, N. H. & ZHANG, S. L. (1984). Variable reproductive output in Polychaeta: options and design constraints. In *Adv. Inv. Reprod.* **3** (ed. W. Engels *et al.*) pp. 399–408. Amsterdam, New York: Elsevier Science.

OLIVE, P. J. W. & PILLAI, G. (1983). Reproductive biology of the polychaete *Kefersteinia cirrata* Keferstein (Hesionidae). II. The gametogenic cycle and evidence for photoperiodic control of oogenesis. *Int. J. Inv. Repr.* **6**, 307–315.

ORTON, J. H. (1920). Sea temperature, breeding and distribution in marine animals. *J. mar. biol. Ass. U.K.* **12**, 339–366.

PEARSE, J. S. & EERNISSE, D. J. (1982). Photoperiodic regulation of gametogenesis and gonadal growth in the sea star *Pisaster ochraceus*. *Mar. Biol.* **67**, 121–125.

PIANKA, E. R. (1970). On 'r' and 'k' selection. *Am. Nat.* **104**, 592–597.

PIANKA, E. R. & PARKER, W. S. (1975). Age specific reproductive tactics. *Am. Nat.* **109**, 453–464.

PORCHET, M. (1984). Biochemistry of oocyte differentiation in nereids. *Fortschr. Zool.* **29**, 207–225.

PORCHET, M. & CARDON, C. (1976). The inhibitory feedback mechanism coming from oovocytes and acting on brain endocrine activity in *Nereis*. *Gen. comp. Endocr.* **30**, 378–390.

PORCHET, M., DHAINAUT, A. & PORCHET-HENNERE, E. (1979). Evidence of coelomic substances inducing genital maturation in *Perinereis cultrifera* (Annélides, Polychètes). *Wilhelm Roux. Arch. dev. Biol.* **186**, 129–138.

RAM, J. L. (1983). Gastropod egg-laying Hormones. In *Molluscan Neuro-endocrinology* (eds J. Lever & H. H. Boer) pp. 94–101. Amsterdam, New York: North Holland Publishing Co.

RICKLEFS, R. E. (1981). Fitness, reproductive value, age, structure and the optimization of life-history patterns. *Am. Nat.* **117**, 819–825.

RUÉ, G. & BIERNE, J. (1980). Contrôle endocrinien de l'oogenèse chez l'Hoplonémertien *Amphiporous lactifloreus*. *Bull. Soc. Zool. Fr.* **105**, 155–163.

SAUNDERS, D. S. (1982). *Insect clocks* 2nd edn. Oxford: Pergamon Press.

SCHAFFER, W. M. (1974). Selection for optimal life histories: the effects of age structure. *Ecology* **55**, 291–303.

SCHAFFER, W. M. (1979). Equivalence of maximizing reproductive value and fitness in the case of reproductive strategies. *Proc. natn. Acad. Sci., U.S.A.* **76**, 3567–3569.

SCHAFFER, W. M. (1981). On reproductive value and fitness. *Ecology* **62**, 1683–1685.

SCHAFFER, W. M. & ROSENZWEIG, M. L. (1977). Selection for life histories II. Multiple equilibria and the evolution of alternative reproductive strategies. *Ecology* **58**, 60–72.

SCHOENMAKERS, H. J. N., VAN BOHEMEN, CH. G. & DIELEMAN, S. J. (1981). Effects of estradiol-17β on the ovaries of the starfish *Asterias rubens*. *Devl. Growth Differ.* **23**, 125–135.

SIBLY, R. & CALOW, P. (1983). An integrated approach to the life-cycle evolution using selective landscapes. *J. theor. Biol.* **102**, 527–547.

SMITH, R. I. (1958). On reproductive pattern as a specific character among nereids. *Syst. Zool.* **7**, 60–73.

SOKOLOVE, P. G., MCCRONE, E. J., MINUTE, J. VAN & DUNCAN, W. C. (1984). In *Photoperiodic Regulation of Insect and Mollusc Hormones* (eds R. Porter & G. N. Collins). *Ciba Foundation Symp.* **104**, 189–203.

STEARNS, S. C. (1976). Life history tactics: a review of the ideas. *Q. Rev. Biol.* **51**, 3–47.

STEARNS, S. C. (1977). The evolution of life history traits. *Ann. Rev. Ecol. Syst.* **8**, 145–171.

STEARNS, S. C. (1983). On fitness. In *Fourth Bremen Symposium Biological Systematics Theory* (ed. G. Roth). New York: Gustav Fischer.

STEARNS, S. C. (1984). The tension between adaptation and constraint in the evolution of reproductive patterns. In *Advances Invertebrate Reproduction* (eds W. Engels & A. Fischer) 3, pp. 387–398. Amsterdam, New York: Elsevier Science Publishers.

STEELE, U. J. (1981). The effect of photoperiod on the reproductive cycle of *Gammarus lawrencianus* Bousfield. *J. exp. mar. Biol. Ecol.* **53**, 1–7.

STEELE, U. J., STEELE, D. H. & MACPHERSON, B. R. (1977). The effect of photoperiod on the reproductive cycle of *Gammarus setosus* Dementieva, 1931. *Crustaceana*, Suppl. **4**, 58–63.

STRATHMANN, R. R. (1978a). Progressive vacating of adaptive types during the phanerozoic. *Evolution* **32**, 907–914.

STRATHMANN, R. R. (1978b). The evolution and loss of feeding larval stages of marine invertebrates. *Evolution* **32**, 894–906.

TAKAHASHI, N. & KANATANI, H. (1981). Effect of 17β-estradiol on growth of oocytes in cultured ovarian fragments of the starfish *Asterina pectinifera*. *Devl. Growth Differ.* **23**, 565–569.

TUOMI, J., HAKALA, T. & HANKIOJA, E. (1983). Alternative concepts of reproductive effort, costs of reproduction and selection in life history evolution. *Amer. Zool.* **23**, 25–34.

Tyler, P. A., Grant, A., Pain, S. L. & Gage, J. D. (1982). Is annual reproduction in deep-sea echinoderms a response to variability in their environment? *Nature* **300**, 747–750.

Vance, R. R. (1973). On reproductive strategies in marine benthic invertebrates. *Am. Nat.* **107**, 339–352.

Veerman, A. & Vaz Nunes, M. (1984). Photoperiod reception in spider mites: photoreceptor, clock and counter. In *CIBA Foundation Symposium* **104**. Photoperiodic Regulation of Insect and Molluscan Hormones, pp. 48–64. London: Pitman.

Vaz Nunes, M. & Veerman, A. (1982a). External coincidence and photoperiodic time measurement in the spider mite *Tetranychus urticae*. *J. Insect Physiol.* **28**, 143–154.

Vaz Nunes, M. & Veerman, A. (1982b). Photoperiodic time measurements in the spider mite *Tetranychus urticae*: a novel concept. *J. Insect Physiol.* **28**, 1041–1053.

Voogt, P. A., Oudejans, R. C. H. M. & Braertjes, J. J. S, (1984). Steroids and reproduction in Starfish. In *Advances Invertebrate Reproduction* (eds W. Engels *et al.*), Vol. **3** pp. 151–161. Amsterdam, New York: Elsevier Science.

Wells, M. J. & Wells, J. (1975). Optic gland implants and their effects on the gonads of Octopus. *J. exp. Biol.* **62**, 679–588.

Wells, M. J. & Wells, J. (1977). Optic glands and the endocrinology of reproduction. *Symp. Zool. Soc. London.* **38**, 525–540.

West, A. B. & Lambert, C. C. (1976). Control of spawning in the tunicate *Styela plicata* by variations in the natural light regime. *J. exp. Zool.* **195**, 263–270.

Williams, G. C. (1966a). Natural selection, the costs of reproduction and a refinement of Lacks principle. *Am. Nat.* **100**, 687–690.

Williams, G. C. (1966b). Adaptation and natural selection. Princeton N.J.: Princeton University Press.

Printed in Great Britain © *Society of Experimental Biology 1985*

THE THEORY OF HOMEOVISCOUS ADAPTATION OF MEMBRANES APPLIED TO DEEP-SEA ANIMALS

A. G. MACDONALD

Physiology Department, Marischal College, Aberdeen University, Aberdeen
AB9 1AS, Scotland, U.K.

and

A. R. COSSINS

Zoology Department, The University of Liverpool, P.O. Box 147, Liverpool
L69 3BX, U.K.

Summary

Deep-sea organisms live at high pressure and low temperature. These two factors increase the order of the bilayer in cell membranes, and, on the basis of the homeoviscous theory of membrane adaptation, predictions are made of the fluidity and composition of deep-sea membranes. Some of the predictions have been tested using membranes from deep-sea fish and some of the results are consistent with the theory. The conclusion is that the theory receives general support from the deep sea and, conversely, adaptation of membranes to high pressure can be profitably investigated in a more detailed manner by testing further predictions based on the homeoviscous concept.

Introduction

It is now established that deep-sea organisms are adapted at the molecular level to their high ambient pressure. A certain amount is known about the properties of several enzymes from deep-sea animals, and interesting ideas about their 'fitness' to function at high pressure have been put forward (Somero, 1982; Hochachka, 1975). At the level of integrated motor activity and the behaviour of the whole animal, tolerance to high pressure has been quantified in deep-sea crustacea, clearly demonstrating the significance of the nervous system in adaptation (Macdonald, 1975; Macdonald & Gilchrist, 1982; Brauer *et al.*, 1984). This paper belongs somewhere between these two levels of organization insofar as it is concerned with membranes, but its level of analysis is clearly molecular. Our approach to the study of deep-sea membranes is based on homeoviscous theory.

The theory of homeoviscous adaptation of membranes states that organisms regulate the composition of their membranes to maintain the fluidity of the lipid bilayer within tolerable limits. Fluidity in this context means the relative motional freedom of the anisotropic and heterogeneous lipid bilayer, and in any particular case is operationally defined and quantified by the spectroscopic method used to measure it. Examples of homeoviscous adaptation to temperature changes are well known; see for instance Cossins (1983) and Thompson (1983) for examples in which fluidity adjustments are accomplished by changes in the degree of saturation of the fatty acids in membrane phospholipids. The relationship between the metabolism of fatty acids, their elongation and the insertion of double bonds is discussed in Thompson (1980) and in Hazel & Sellner (1980).

The homeoviscous concept was first applied on a bulk scale to the apparent regulation of the melting point of storage lipids in organisms which experience temperature changes. Recently a similar condition was described, but not conclusively demonstrated, in the lung surfactant lipids of the Map turtle (Lau & Keough, 1981).

The analogous phenomenon in membrane bilayers was first demonstrated by Sinensky (1974) in bacterial membrane lipids, using an electron spin resonance method to measure fluidity, but previous work showing how the membrane lipid composition of various organisms changed during exposure to different temperatures clearly prepared the foundations for the homeoviscous theory at the membrane level (Cullen, Phillips & Shipley, 1971; Haest, De Gier & Van Deenen, 1969).

The term homeoviscous adaptation was first used by Sinensky (1974) and although bilayer fluidity parameters are no longer quantified as viscosity, the term persists. Originally primarily concerned with thermal adaptation, homeoviscous theory may develop to characterize the bilayer structure which cells regulate in response to such factors as specific ions, organic xenobiotics and drugs, including anaesthetics, dietary metabolites such as fatty acids and cholesterol, and thermodynamic intensity parameters such as transmembrane voltage and ambient hydrostatic pressure. The extraordinary diversity of the lipids comprising the bilayer component of membranes requires an explanation, and it would appear that homeoviscous theory provides an appealing and testable basis for one. Thus, on the one hand membrane lipid composition is considered to be partly determined by the 'requirements' of numerous functional components (membrane-bound enzymes, ion pumps, channels, receptors, antigens etc); on the other hand it appears to be subject to homeostatic control in order to buffer the functional components from the more severe changes in the cells' environment. The central problem is to characterize the microenvironment which the lipid bilayer provides for the functional components. Such microenvironments comprise steric and structural factors, dynamic or motional factors, a dielectric constant and a solvent characterized by a solubility parameter, in which various inter-molecular forces act.

In addition to providing an appropriate bilayer for the immediate operation of its functional components, cells may provide some built-in 'anticipatory' regulation, or a safety margin. This idea comes from experiments with the sub-bacterial cell *Acholeplasma laidlawii*, and appears to demonstrate how unnecessary the complex lipid composition of its membrane is. When grown in the presence of inhibitors of fatty acid synthesis the cells' plasma membrane (its only membrane) contains a very limited number of fatty acids, yet the cell grows adequately. Silvius & McElhaney (1978) suggested the normal lipid heterogeneity provides a safety margin, preventing a drastic phase separation in the event of an abrupt temperature change, probably enabling the continued functioning of its component parts whilst regulatory adjustments follow.

Whilst homeoviscous theory is concerned with the changes in bilayer fluidity it is apparent that fluidity is inextricably related to bilayer thickness, with implications for spatial and charge separation, (Borochov & Shinitzky, 1976; Heron, Shinitzky, Hershkowitz & Samuel, 1980; Pugh, Kates & Szabo, 1980; Riordan, 1980), and to a number of specific molecular motions only now being resolved by spectroscopic techniques. In practice the theory is studied at the level of bilayer fluidity, with a particular spectroscopic parameter being measured for the bilayer as a whole. This provides an average value and in only a few cases is the fluidity of a specific lipid grouping, associated with a functional component, examined.

The theory should not be overstated. At least two reasons exist why homeoviscous adaptation should only be manifest in a partial or irregular manner. First, homeoviscous adaptation implies a kinetic role for bilayer lipids in the normal functioning of complex processes, which will be influenced by several other kinetic parameters. Compensation to a changed set of conditions may well be achieved by a means other than the lipid bilayer. Secondly, compensation for a change in rate may not be 'necessary', as, for example, during hibernation in certain mammals.

In this paper we examine homeoviscous theory applied to the fluidity of the membrane of deep-sea fish and of laboratory cells subjected to high hydrostatic pressure. We show that high hydrostatic pressure (as occurs in the deep sea) significantly reduces bilayer fluidity, and accordingly we predict the magnitude and nature of the compensations that might be expected to offset it. Some of these predictions have been tested by measuring the fluidity of the bilayers of 'high pressure' membranes, and further examined by analysing their lipid composition. We leave it to the reader to reflect on the extent to which the membranes of deep-sea animals and high pressure studies in general might ultimately contribute to an understanding of the role of fluidity in the functioning of membranes.

The deep sea

The mean depth of the world's oceans is 3800 m at which the pressure is 380 atm (38 MPa). The deep trenches extend to 10 000 m (1000 atm or 100 MPa) depth and are highly restricted environments. Animals and bacteria are distributed throughout the entire vertical range of the oceans, although their numbers and biomass are greatly attenuated at the greater depths. Below 2000 m depth the water temperature is between 4° and 0 °C (Macdonald, 1975). For the purposes of this paper the deep sea is a very simple place. If the depth of an animal is known then so too is its ambient pressure and its temperature is highly predictable from oceanographic data.

Perhaps as a consequence of the scarcity of food in the deep sea, certain animals have a low metabolic rate, including their 'energetic' tissues (Smith, 1978; Sullivan & Somero, 1980). It is conceivable that such hypometabolic creatures may not have taken up the option of adapting their membranes in homeoviscous fashion. One of the predictive points made in a later section of this paper is that organic chemistry can easily provide lipid molecules with the properties required for a viable level of membrane fluidity in the coldest and deepest reaches of the ocean. The test for the homeoviscous theory in such environments is therefore biological as well as physical. An interesting biological question is, what determines whether organisms adopt a particular physiological strategy such as homeoviscous membrane adaptation? The deep sea probably contains sufficiently diverse metabolic types to illuminate this problem, although its attraction at our present level of knowledge is primarily at the simpler, physical level of prediction.

Effects of pressure on membrane fluidity

For the present discussion membrane fluidity may be subdivided into three types. First there are the rotational and other movements of the individual phospholipid molecules within the bilayer. Secondly there are lateral and transverse ('flip-flop') movements of the bilayer lipids. These occur, respectively, in the plane of the bilayer and from one half of the bilayer to the other. And third, membrane proteins undergo rotational and other movements, which are influenced by the fluidity of the bilayer and by various other factors. Somewhat separately the phase state of the bilayer may exist in a liquid-crystalline state, which is the typical physiological condition, or in a gel state in which all kinds of fluidity parameters are markedly reduced. Certain membranes show a relatively sharp transition from one phase to the other but most do not, the transition being dampened by the heterogeneity of the fatty acids and by the presence of cholesterol or other large molecules. Different phase states and domains may coexist in a membrane (Kates & Kuksis, 1980; Karnovsky, Kleinfeld, Hoover & Klausner, 1982; Aloia, 1983; Benga & Holmes, 1984).

In the past decade the effects of pressure on membrane fluidity and phase transitions have been measured in an unprecedented flurry of interest. Phase transitions in model membranes were first studied, and it is now established that the thermodynamics of the gel-to-liquid-

Table 1. *Pressure increases the phase transition temperatures of natural membranes*

Membranes	$dT/dP \,°C\, atm^{-1}$ or $\cdot 1 MPa^{-1}$	Method	References
rabbit lung macrophage	0·027	spin labelled at C16	Gause, Mendez & Rowlands, 1974
rat liver mitochondria	0·01	estimated, freeze fracture	Wattiaux, De Coninck *et al.*, 1980
human erythrocyte membrane	0·022 0·027	pyrene excimer extracted lipids	Flamm, Okubo, Turso & Schachter, 1982
Acholeplasma laidlawii	0·016	fluorescence polarization	Macdonald & Cossins, 1983
	0·017	turbidimetry	
Halobacterium halobium	0·053	isomerization–relaxation of bacteriorhodopsin	Tsuda, Govindjee & Elvey, 1983

crystalline phase transitions are entirely orthodox, but more important, the orthodoxy is apparent in the analogous phenomena in the heterogeneous bilayers of natural membranes (Macdonald, 1984a). Table 1 summarizes the pressure coefficient of membrane transition temperatures (quasi-melting points) which are chiefly determined by the composition of the fatty acids in the bilayer and defined by the Clausius-Clapeyron equation; $dT/dP = T. \Delta V/\Delta H$. Thus high pressure 'freezes' a bilayer, raising its 'melting' or transition temperature by an amount determined by the product of the transition temperature and the molar volume expansion at the transition $(T.\Delta V)$ divided by the enthalpy of transition (ΔH). Typically dT/dP is approximately $0.02\,^{\circ}\text{C}\,\text{atm}^{-1}$ $(\cdot002\,^{\circ}\text{C}\,\text{MPa})$. *Halobacterium* is unusual (Table 1) perhaps because its lipid bilayer is dominated by the protein structure of the membrane. The data in Table 1 enable predictions to be made about the degree of adaptation or adjustment required in deep-sea membranes.

A number of bilayer fluidity measurements have been carried out at high pressure and most have used the fluorescence polarization of diphenylhexatriene (DPH). It is usual to distinguish between the rate of a specific molecular motion, and its range, or amplitude. Table 2 summarizes the available data for steady-state measurements of DPH fluorescence polarization, expressed as anisotropy. These are convenient to compare with data we have obtained from the membranes of deep-sea fish (below). Steady-state anisotropy (r_s) is a close approximation to the limiting anisotropy (r_∞) obtained from time resolved measurements, particularly when the bilayer fluidity is low. It is a measure of the structural order, or the range, of molecular motion in a bilayer and is adequate for present purposes. When bilayer fluidity is high, r_s is a less satisfactory measure, because it is an expression of two factors, the structural order r_∞ and a dynamic component. The latter dominates in very fluid bilayers whose fluorescence polarization can only be adequately studied using time-resolved methods which distinguish the two components. (Heyn, 1979; Jähnig, 1979; Van Blitterswicjk, Van Hoeven & Van Der Meer, 1981; Pottel, Van Der Meer & Herreman, 1983). Time-resolved measurements of DPH fluorescence polarization have been published by Chong & Cossins (1983) for goldfish synaptic membranes and myelin fractions and by Lakowicz & Thompson (1983) for sonicated liposomes. The interpretation of the dynamic aspects of DPH polarization at high pressure is not yet clear. It appears that pressure mimics the addition of cholesterol to a bilayer above its transition temperature insofar as it reduces the range of lipid motion (increases order parameter) with little reduction in the rate of motion (Kinosita & Ikegami, 1984). Increasing

Table 2. *An increase in pressure (A) and a decrease in temperature (B) increases r_s, the steady-state fluorescence anisotropy of DPH* in bilayers. Values shown are representative, taken from non-linear plots in some cases.*

A. Pressure	Δr_s 1000 atm^{-1} (100 MPa^{-1})	Temp °C	References
dioleoylphosphatidylcholine			
multilamellar liposomes	0·044	6	Chong & Cossins 1984
,, +0·6 mole ratio			
cholesterol	0·034	6	Chong & Cossins 1984
dioleoylphosphatidylcholine			Lakowicz & Thompson
unilamellar liposomes	0·080	30	1983
dimyristoylphosphatidylcholine			
unilamellar liposomes	0·075	45	
,, + 0·14 mol ratio			
cholesterol	0·04	30	
mineral oil	0·16	20	
Goldfish brain – synaptic vesicles	0·034	5·6	Chong & Cossins 1983
Goldfish brain – myelin vesicles	0·034	5·6	Chong & Cossins 1983
Acholeplasma laidlawii			
above transition	0·014	55	Macdonald & Cossins
mid-transition	0·054	37	1983
below transition	negligible	20	

B. Temperature	Δr_s, 20 °C^{-1}		
Goldfish			
synaptic vesicles	− 0·088	0–20	Cossins & Prosser 1982
Acholeplasma laidlawii			
above transition	− 0·009	50	Macdonald & Cossins
below transition	− 0·090	35	1983
rat liver mitochondria	− 0·066	20–40	Kinosita *et al.*, 1981
human erythrocyte	− 0·070	20–40	Kinosita *et al.*, 1981
Halobacterium halobium	− 0·033	20–40	Kinosita *et al.*, 1981

* diphenylhexatriene

the cholesterol: phospholipid ratio by 0·35–0·50 in dioeoyl phosphatidyl-choline bilayers increases the steady-state polarization of DPH by the same amount as 1000 atm, the maximum pressure in the oceans (Chong & Cossins, 1984). Order parameters obtained by other spectroscopic

Table 3. *Pressure reduces the rate of lateral diffusion of small molecules in membrane bilayers, expressed as the increase in temperature required to offset the pressure effects*

Membrane	Excimer probe	t° range of measurements	Temperature increase required to offset 100 atm	References
Sonicated liposomes of DPPC* + cholesterol 0·02 mole fraction	pyrene	48–60 °C	8 °C	Müller & Galla, 1983
Sonicated liposomes of DPPC + cholesterol 0·17 mole fraction	pyrene	50–60 °C 43–50 °C	6·6 °C 4·8 °C	
Human erythrocyte	pyrene	18–39 °C	2·6 °C	Flamm *et al.*, 1983
Multilamellar DPPC liposomes	dipyrenyl-propane	17–30 °C	1·9 °C	Viriot *et al.*, 1983

    * Dipalmitoylphosphatidylcholine.

methods applied to bilayers at high pressure are reviewed in Macdonald (1984a).

The lateral motion of membrane proteins may be influenced by cytoplasmic proteins whilst that of lipids and other small molecules is often two orders of magnitude faster and more like a diffusional movement within the plane of the membrane. Lateral diffusion of the latter type is not necessarily closely related to bilayer order parameter (Kleinfeld *et al.*, 1981). Table 3 summarizes the available data for the lateral diffusion of bilayer lipids under pressure. At the time of writing no measurements of the lateral movement of membrane proteins have been reported, but it is interesting to speculate that should pressure depolymerize membrane proteins or the restraining cytoplasmic proteins, then a net increase in lateral movement of the former might occur. Other dynamic properties of membrane proteins under pressure also await investigation, and these are likely to be most important in homeoviscous theory.

Predictions

In the normal physiological condition membranes are poised above their phase transition temperatures and accordingly the data in Table 1 may be used to predict the extent of the homeoviscous adjustment in deep-sea membranes. From $dT/dP = 0.02\,°C\,atm^{-1}$ it follows that 1000 atm (100 MPa) and 2 °C is equivalent to −18 °C at normal atmospheric pressure. Thus the membranes of organisms at Trench depths are apparently functional at the equivalent of conditions inside a domestic deep freeze. Even at abyssal depths of 4000 m (400 atm or 40 MPa) conditions are equivalent to −6 °C at normal pressure.

More useful is the prediction of the degree of compensation in the order parameters of deep-sea membranes. Using the pressure coefficient of the steady-state fluorescence anisotropy of DPH in fish membranes (Table 2), perfect compensation would require a shift of some 0.013 in 400 atm organisms. This could be achieved by an increased proportion of unsaturated fatty acids, by a reduction in membrane cholesterol and least likely of all, by a reduction in the chain length of the fatty acids. These predictions assume perfect compensation, which is rare in homeoviscous responses during temperature acclimation (Cossins, 1983). Furthermore in the deep sea they may be obscured by the prevalence of low metabolic rates in certain animals. These predictions only apply to animals confined to a limited depth range. Analogous predictions can be made for laboratory organisms subjected to a prolonged exposure to high pressure.

The maximum pressure compensation predicted for ocean depths lies well within the range of familiar membrane lipids. For instance, the decrease in the bilayer phase transition temperature brought about by the insertion of one *cis* double bond into distearoylphosphatidylcholine, converting it to 18:0, 18:1 phosphatidylcholine, is approximately 50 °C (Stubbs, Koryama, Kinosita & Ikegami, 1981; Coolbear, Berde & Keough, 1983). Any restriction to the strict application of homeoviscous adaptation in deep sea animals will probably arise from kinetic and biological factors and not, apparently, from fundamental physical-chemical limitations.

A. *Testing the predictions*

Laboratory studies have so far been restricted to the ciliated protozoan *Tetrahymena pyriformis* NT-1, which is a thermotolerant strain with a well-developed homeoviscous capacity (Thompson & Nozawa, 1977). Its microsomal desaturase enzymes alter the proportion of unsaturated to saturated fatty acids which are incorporated in membrane lipids in response to temperature changes. According to a 'cold activation' hypothesis put forward by Kasai *et al.*, (1976) the desaturases should likewise respond to changes induced by other environmental factors, such as pressure.

The practical advantages of attempting to acclimate cells rather than marine animals, are considerable. Even so, high-pressure culture experiments are complicated enough by aeration and other culture requirements (Macdonald, 1967; Taylor & Jannasch, 1976; Taylor, 1979). The experiments with *Tetrahymena* avoided these as much as possible by opting for a short incubation period at high pressure during which time-limited growth occurred. This could be matched with control cultures at normal atmospheric pressure and reduced temperature. The experiments thus compared the fatty acid composition of membranes obtained from low-temperature control cultures with that of membranes obtained from cells exposed to high pressure. The maximum pressure which the cells could tolerate at 37 °C was 260 atm which is clearly a small pressure stress when judged by the change in the fluorescence anisotropy it might produce (Table 2).

The results showed that, in the particular conditions prevailing, pressure did not change the fatty acids associated with *Tetrahymena's* phospholipids in a way consistent with homeoviscous theory (Macdonald, 1984b). Quite the reverse occurred, with the ratio of 16:0/16:1 fatty acids linearly increasing with pressure. Whilst at the cellular level *Tetrahymena* does not change its membrane fatty acids as predicted, it is still possible that the molecular ordering of the microsomal membranes could lead to the activation of the desaturases, i.e. 'cold activation'. Pressure affects many metabolic reactions which could obscure the primary effect of pressure on the microsomal desaturases. There remains considerable scope for pressure experiments with this type of cellular and membrane preparation as well as the larger scale operation of acclimating marine animals to pressure.

B. *Published data on deep-sea animals*

A number of attempts to correlate the lipid composition of marine animals with depth, and hence pressure, are worth noting. In 1962 Lewis published the fatty acid composition of whole planktonic animals from 300 m depths in arctic water and elsewhere. At best the data revealed differences which might be attributable to temperature, but not to pressure. In the same paper the point was made that protoplasmic viscosity would be reduced at depth, by pressure, and that this might be connected with the fatty acid content of the animals. The fact is that protoplasmic 'viscosity' (consistency, or 'gel-strength') is reduced by high pressure but not, as far as is known, by pressure acting on lipids. Pressure depolymerizes protein structures such as microtubules and actin filaments, and it is probably by this means that 'gel strength' is reduced. This ubiquitous phenomenon is likely to require compensatory adaptations in deep-sea eukaryote cells, but probably does not involve lipids (Swezey & Somero, 1982).

The fatty acid composition of the total phospholipid extracts from the white skeletal muscle of *Trematomus bochgrevinkii*, the antarctic ice fish, which lives at $-1.9\,°C$ and at less than 5 atm pressure has been compared with that of three species of fish living at $2-4\,°C$ and 1800 m depth (Patton, 1975). Table 4 shows the similarity between the two groups. A benevolent interpretation would be (i) the fatty acids are likely to be largely derived from membranes and (ii) the difference between the two environmental temperatures ($4-6\,°C$) might be offset by the 180 atm difference in ambient pressure, thereby accounting for the similarity between the two sets of data.

The only other attempt to relate membrane composition to depth and pressure of which we are aware, is a contemporary study of fish brain gangliosides (Avrova, 1984). Gangliosides are complex lipids of the class known as glycophospholipids. They contain sialic acid linked to a sugar residue, and a pair of hydrocarbon 'tails' which ensures they are sufficiently amphipathic to intercalate in a bilayer. One 'tail' belongs to sphingosine and the other is part of a fatty acid which is subjected to variation in the degree of saturation. Avrova (1984) showed that *Antimora rostrata* (from $2-6\,°C$ and 2000 m depth) possessed brain gangliosides which were relatively rich in mono-unsaturated fatty acids and

Table 4. *Fatty acid saturation in the phospholipids extracted from fish white muscle (From Patton, 1975).*

Species	Ambient temperature and pressure		Fatty acid type (Wt. %)		
			Saturated	Mono-unsaturated	Poly-unsaturated
Antimora rostrata (n=3)	2–4 °C	180 atm	40·5	21·0	39·0
Synaphobranchus branchiostomas (n=1)	2–4 °C	180 atm	32·1	22·9	44·8
Alepocephalus sp. (n=3)	2–4 °C	180 atm	33·0	24·9	42·6
		Mean	35·2±5·0	22·9±2·3	42·1±3·4
Trematomus borchgrevinkii (n=2)	−1·9 °C	5 atm	35·2	22·2	42·5

poor in saturated fatty acids. Table 6 includes a selection of data alongside the phospholipid fatty acid data obtained by Cossins & Macdonald (to be published) using the methods described in the following section.

C. *Recent experiments with membranes at sea*

Our attempts to test the predictions made earlier concerning the degree of saturation of membrane fatty acids and the fluidity of the intact membranes of deep-sea species have so far been limited to two cruises on RRS Challenger in the deep water southwest of Ireland. Benthic fish were trawled and three membrane fractions prepared from freshly collected animals; liver mitochondria, a brain myelin-rich fraction and a brain synaptic-membrane fraction. Centrifugation at sea limits the purity and choice of membranes. A maximum of $15\,000\,g$ was available using a bench-top refrigerated centrifuge fitted with an imbalance cut-out (I.E.C. Centra 3R-S). Steady-state fluorescence polarization measurements were carried out on all three types of membranes. Only the liver mitochondria were available in sufficient quantity to enable the lipid composition to be analysed. The initial stages of lipid extraction were begun at sea but the samples were stored and transported to our laboratories for the separation of the main phospholipids; (phosphatidylcholine, (PC); phosphatidylethanolamine, (PE); phosphatidylserine + inositol, (PS) and cardiolipin (CD). The fatty acid composition of each phospholipid was then analysed by conventional capillary gas chromatography (Carlo-Erba Fractovap 4160–00).

Our intention was to correlate (1) the normal ambient pressure and temperature of individual fish (obtained from the depth of the bottom trawl), (2) the fluidity of their membranes and (3) the fatty acid composition of the major bilayer phospholipids in these membranes.

(i) *The fatty acids*

Of the phospholipids analysed PS and CD were present in much smaller quantities than PC and PE, and the latter therefore are more relevant to bulk membrane properties. Samples generally contained less than 15 % by weight of unidentified fatty acids. A total of over 80 samples from 15 different species listed in Table 5 were analysed for over 40 different fatty acids. Fatty acid peaks on the chromatograms were identified by characteristic retention times and by the addition of known standards.

Table 6 presents the data from three species for illustrative purposes.

Table 5. *The species of deep sea fish used to prepare membranes for fluidity and fatty acid analysis*

Species	Depth of capture (m)	Species depth range in N. Atlantic (m)
Lepidorhombus whiffiagonis	200	200–540
Lophius budegassa	200	
Lophius piscatorius	200	100–1170
Helicolenus dactylopterus	200	200–950
Phycis blennoides	800	150–1030
Lepidion eques	800–900	510–2420
Mora moro	1000	500–1400
Alephocephalus bairdii	1000	650–1900
Nezumia aequalis	1000	200–2320
Coryphenoides rupestris	1300	400–2000
Hoplostethus atlanticus	1300	900–1700
Antimora rostrata	2000	700–3000
Conocara murrayi	2000	1900–2400
Histiobranchus bathybius	4000	1800–4800
Coryphenoides armatus	3800–4000	2200–4800

Note the depth-dependent increase in total mono-unsaturated fatty acids and the decrease in saturated fatty acids. Two indices are used to crudely integrate the data. The unsaturation index (UI) is the sum of the product of weight % and the number of double bonds. The saturation ratio (SR) is simply the ratio of weight % saturated: unsaturated fatty acids. Table 6 shows no particular trend in UI but shows a clear decrease in the SR values for deeper fish, which also experience lower temperatures. The full data for all species were subjected to a regression analysis of UI and SR against the depth of capture of the individual specimens, and the results are shown in Table 7. The SR for the major phospholipids, PC and PE, shows a statistically significant decrease with increase in depth of capture, and so does UI for PS. The SR is an index more likely to reflect fluidity than UI (Cossins & Lee, 1985). Clearly these results are consistent with the predictions.

Inspection of the ganglioside fatty acid data in Table 6 shows saturation is also inversely related to depth.

(ii) *Measurements of membrane fluidity at sea*

The quality of the membrane suspensions was checked retrospectively by means of electron microscopy. The myelin fraction comprised membranous vesicles and myelin whorls, and was generally satisfactory. The

Table 6. *Fatty acid composition of membrane lipids from deep-sea fish*

Species	Liver mitochondria Phosphatidylethanolamine			Brain Gangliosides		
	Phycis blennoides	*Antimora rostrata*	*Coryphenoides armatus*	*Comephorus dybowski*	*Lampanyctus australis*	*Antimora rostrata*
Depth	800 m (n=4)	2000 m (n=5)	4000 m (n=6)	15–200 m 0–7°C	500–700 m 8–9°C	2300 m 2–6°C
12:0	0·26 (0·32)		0·15 (0·24)			
14:0	0·25 (0·18)	0·19 (0·42)	0·58 (0·43)	0·8	1·8	t
15:0	0·21 (0·14)	0·28 (0·62)				
16:0	13·72 (0·60)	10·82 (1·48)	6·05 (2·31)	16·4	18·3	10·9
16:1ω9	1·30 (1·72)		0·22 (0·24)	5·1	3·0	3·1
16:1ω7	0·52 (0·45)	0·47 (0·44)	0·38 (0·18)			
17:0				t	t	t
18:0	8·97 (1·90)	4·44 (0·87)	4·35 (0·66)	28·4	43·1	18·5
18:1ω9	8·52 (1·62)	11·32 (1·29)	14·50 (1·91)	11·0	11·4	18·9
18:1ω7	4·26 (2·13)	7·9 (0·92)	10·66 (1·68)			
18:1ω5			0·68 (0·08)			
18:2ω6			0·52 (0·12)			
18:3ω6	2·14 (2·37)					
18:3ω3	0·13 (0·25)		0·64 (0·15)			
18:4ω3			0·24 (0·44)			
19:0						
20:0				t	t	t
20:1ω11			0·95 (1·51)	0·7	0·7	t
20:1ω9	1·97 (1·37)	7·72 (0·78)	7·35 (1·22)		t	6·6
20:1ω7		0·18 (0·41)	1·60 (0·40)			
20:2ω6		0·12 (0·27)	0·58 (0·10)			
20:4ω3	0·16 (0·32)			1·1		
20:4ω6	2·48 (0·44)	2·78 (0·30)	2·00 (0·41)	2·7	1·3	5·3

Table 6. *continued.*

	Liver mitochondria Phosphatidylethanolamine			Brain Gangliosides		
Species	*Phycis blennoides*	*Antimora rostrata*	*Coryphenoides armatus*	*Comephorus dybowski*	*Lampanyctus australis*	*Antimora rostrata*
Depth	800 m (n=4)	2000 m (n=5)	4000 m (n=6)	15–200 m 0–7°C	500–700 m 8–9°C	2300 m 2–6°C
20:5ω3	6·42 (1·28)	8·28 (1·89)	4·91 (0·56)	1·2		6·1
21:0					0·7	t
22:0				t	1·2	1·3
22:1ω9				1·7	1·7	9·5
22:5ω3	1·00 (0·69)	1·92 (0·69)	0·81 (0·24)			
22:6ω3	34·24 (3·67)	40·26 (5·07)	34·71 (5·61)	12·3	5·9	9·9
23:0/23:1*					1·2	
24:0				t	1·5	t
24:1ω9				17·6	5·2	9·9
Unknowns	13·43 (0·87)	3·23 (2·01)	8·07 (4·69)	—	4	—
Total	99·98	99·91	99·95	100	100	100
Total saturated	23·4 (1·4)	15·7 (2·7)	11·1 (3·5)	47·3	67·5	40·6
Total monoene	16·6 (1·4)	27·6 (2·1)	36·4 (2·6)	35·4	21·3	48·0
Total polyene	46·6 (2·4)	53·4 (5·3)	45·4 (5·3)	17·3	7·2	21·3
Unsaturation Index	276·0 (17·2)	328·4 (29·1)	287 (38·2)	130·4	61·9	159·1
Saturation ratio	0·372 (0·031)	0·196 (0·047)	0·143 (0·062)	0·897	2·37	0·585

Liver mitochondrial fractions from Cossins, A.R. and Macdonald, A.G. (to be published). Brain gangliosides from Avrova (1984) who did not specify the isomers present. The following fatty acids were not present in the liver mitochondrial studies: 14:1ω9, 16:1ω5, 16:2ω?, 16:3ω3, 16:4ω?, 20:3ω3, 20:3ω6, 22:1ω11, 22:1ω5. Values represent averages of n determinations with s.D. in the brackets. Unsaturation index was calculated by summing the ωt% multiplied by the number of double bonds for each fatty acid in the mixture. Saturation ratio was the total ωt% saturated divided by total unsaturated (i.e. monoene and polyene) fatty acids. t=trace; *=counted as 23:0 for the calculation of indices.

Table 7. *Regression analysis of saturation ratio (SR) and unsaturation index (UI) against depth of capture (Km) for phosphatide fatty acids isolated from liver mitochondria fractions of deep sea and shallow water fish (Cossins, A.R. & Macdonald, A.G. to be published).*

		n	Regression coefficient (slope)	Y-intercept	t	P
Phosphatidyl-choline	SR	43	−0·038	0·441	2·332	0·023*
	UI	43	4·55	258·5	0·765	0·545
Phosphatidyl-ethanolamine	SR	46	−0·0735	0·041	7·680	0·0001**
	UI	46	6·665	273·1	1·681	0·096
Phosphatidyl-serine	SR	9	0·777	0·167	1·967	0·088
	UI	9	−94·4	263·6	2·967	0·020*
Cardiolipin	SR	13	0·150	0·115	1·216	0·249
	UI	13	46·6	255·9	1·619	0·131

* Significant
** Highly significant

synaptic-rich fraction was more heterogeneous and included mitochondria along with synaptic vesicles but lacked myelin. Liver mitochondria were largely disrupted and also contained substantial quantities of membranous vesicles. None of the membrane suspensions examined contained oil droplets. At the tissue level the brains were uniform in appearance but the livers varied between individuals of the same species in size and in pigmentation, presumably reflecting different nutritional or physiological states.

Steady-state fluorescence polarization measurements are probably the only form of spectroscopy at present practical on an ocean-going research ship. A highly sensitive T-format spectrometer similar to that described by Jameson, Weber, Spencer & Mitchell (1980) was used. Variation in the photomultiplier tube output voltage was found to be caused by the ship's motion (not by flexing of optically aligned components) and the oscillating signal was smoothed by means of a BBC microcomputer connected to a fast 12-bit analogue-to-digital converter. The analogue signal was continuously averaged until a stable polarization ratio was achieved, and overall polarization was measured with a precision of better than ±1 % of the values of interest. All measurements were made at $4 \pm 0.1\,°C$, normal atmospheric pressure, using the three membrane fractions isolated from the species listed in Table 5. A linear regression analysis was carried out on polarization as a function of the depth of

Table 8. *The linear regression analysis of r_s, the steady-state fluorescence anisotropy of DPH* in fish membranes, with depth of capture (Cossins & Macdonald, 1984).*

Membrane fraction	n	Slope r_s 100 atm^{-1}	P	Y-intercept r_s
Brain myelin	82	$-0{\cdot}0027\pm{\cdot}00066$	$<0{\cdot}001$	$0{\cdot}271$
Brain synaptic	83	$+0{\cdot}0013\pm{\cdot}00066$	$0{\cdot}05-0{\cdot}1$	$0{\cdot}232$
Liver mitochondria	88	$+0{\cdot}0020\pm{\cdot}0013$	$>0{\cdot}1$	$0{\cdot}202$

Values represent the slope $\pm$s.e.m. of the slope. n represents the number of individual observations, P the probability and Y, the intercept, is the anisotropy value extrapolated to zero depth i.e. the surface, * diphenylhexatriene.

capture of the individual providing the material. Table 8 summarises the results. The anisotropy of brain myelin membranes shows a significant depth dependency, decreasing $0{\cdot}0027$ for each 1000 m. It is worth noting that the regression is weighted by the data from 15 specimens of *C. armatus* and 1 of *Histiobranchus bathybius* from 4000 m. However we have recently obtained more specimens of *H. bathybius* and have confirmed the data for the myelin fraction which was based on one specimen. The other two types of membrane show no change in polarization with depth.

The question is, how should the depth dependency of anistropy be interpreted? We make three assumptions. First we assume that anisotropy is measuring a state of fluidity at normal atmospheric pressure which is readily reversed by changes in pressure, as for example, during the fishes' ascent through the water column in the trawl. Secondly, we assume that the pressure coefficient for steady-state anisotropy (Table 2) obtained from shallow-water material applies to deep-sea membranes. Third, we assume a temperature coefficient may be applied likewise. All three assumptions have the support of the preliminary measurements we have made of the polarization values of deep-sea membranes using a high-pressure cuvette chamber. Fig. 1 shows that a depth-dependent decrease in r_s of $0{\cdot}0027$ 100 atm^{-1} as observed in myelin membranes (Table 2) largely offsets the effect pressure has of increasing anisotropy ($0{\cdot}0034$ 100 atm^{-1}). However, temperature changes cannot be ignored, and Fig. 1 shows the magnitude of the correction needed to estimate anisotropy *in situ*. Despite the temperature effect, it is our view that the depth-dependent increase in fluidity is consistent with the prediction made earlier, and hence with homeoviscous theory.

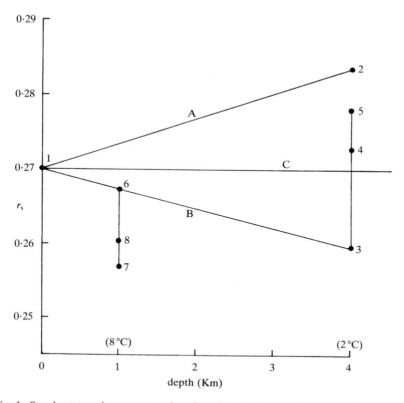

Fig. 1. Steady-state anisotropy, r_s, values for a hypothetical membrane as a function of pressure (depth) and temperature in the ocean.

The point 1, shows the r_s value of 0·270 for a membrane measured at 4 °C and normal atmospheric pressure. The line A of positive slope shows the increase in r_s caused by pressure (0·0034 100 atm^{-1}) at constant temperature, and represents the amount which homeoviscous compensation is predicted to offset. The negative slope B shows the depth dependency of r_s, as determined in myelin fractions from deep-sea fish (Table 8). The point 3 therefore corresponds to the anisotropy value for a deep sea membrane, measured at 4 °C and normal atmospheric pressure. Using the above pressure coefficient this value is corrected to 400 atm (4000 m depth), 4 °C (point 4) and to 2 °C, (point 5), a probable temperature at that depth. The difference between point 5 and the line of constant $r_s = 0·27$ (C) represents imperfect homeoviscous compensation, and the difference between point 2 and the line C shows that about half the pressure compensation has been achieved.

The non-linear temperature profile of the oceans depths makes values of r_s at intermediate depths complicated to generalize. Point 6 shows a value at 1000 m and 4 °C which, when corrected to the *in situ* temperature of 8 °C, assumes the value shown by point 7. This in turn is corrected for pressure to give the true *in situ* value at point 8.

Pressure coefficient of $r_s = 0·0034$ 100 atm^{-1} and the temperature coefficient = 0·00255 °C^{-1}.

The lack of any depth dependency in the polarization of liver mitochondria and brain synaptic membranes is probably due, at least in part, to their great variability. In the case of liver mitochondria dramatic differences were apparent in the pigmentation of both the whole liver and the derived membrane fraction. It is quite probable that the pigment had a severe quenching effect upon DPH fluorescence and thus on the anisotropy values. The saturation of the membrane fatty acids does vary with depth, as predicted by homeoviscous theory, but the lack of a statistically significant correlation of anisotropy with UI or SR suggest the DPH fluorescence polarization is indeed perturbed. The variation in the data for brain synaptic membranes does not appear to arise from artefacts. Intraspecific variation is much greater than observed in previous studies of temperature acclimated goldfish and green sunfish (Cossins, Friedlander & Prosser, 1977; Cossins, Kent & Prosser, 1980). It would be particularly interesting to know the composition of the fatty acids in the synaptic fraction, but unfortunately the small quantity of material has so far precluded this.

Conclusions

Generally, we believe that the extension of the homeoviscous theory of membrane adaptation to deep-sea fish has been successful. The limitations in centrifuging pure membrane samples at sea, the possible complications arising from postmortem changes in the animals in the trawl (Shelton, Macdonald, Pequeux & Gilchrist, 1985) and the instrumental difficulties appear insufficient to obscure at least two important findings. First, the myelin vesicle anisotropy, r_s, is related to depth, and shows that the bilayer-ordering effect of high pressure is partially offset. Second, the fatty acid composition of liver mitochondria is likewise related to depth in a manner consistent with homeoviscous theory. There are good reasons for thinking that further work, involving developments in centrifugation at sea and the collection of more individuals of the different species will resolve some of the present obscurity and enable us to proceed to more refined investigations. These could include time-resolved fluorescence spectroscopy and measurements of some physiological properties of the membranes which are closely related to their fluidity. Attempts to design experiments to test the capacity of shallow water organisms to adapt their membrane lipids to high pressure also receive some encouragement from the deep-sea work.

The work at sea was supported by a grant to AGM from the NERC.

References

ALOIA, R. C. (1983). *Membrane Fluidity in Biology*. Vol 2. (ed. R. C. Aloia) New York: Academic Press.

AVROVA, N. F. (1984). The effect of natural adaptations of fishes to environmental temperature on brain ganglioside fatty acid and long chain base composition. *Comp. Biochem. Physiol.* **78B**, 903–909.

BENGA, C. & HOLMES, R. P. (1984). Interactions between components in biological membranes and their implications for membrane function. *Prog. Biophys. Mol. Biol.* **43**, 195–257.

BOROCHOV, H. & SHINITZKY, M. (1976). Vertical displacement of membrane proteins mediated by changes in microviscosity. *Proc. natn. Acad. Sci., U.S.A.* **73**, 4526–4530.

BRAUER, R. W., SIDELYOVA, V. G., DAIL, M. B., GALAZII, G. T. & ROER, R. D. (1984). Physiological adaptation of cottoid fishes of Lake Baikal to abyssal depths. *Comp. Biochem. Physiol.* **77A**, 699–705.

CHONG, P. L.-G. & COSSINS, A. R. (1983). A differential polarised phase fluorometric study of the effects of high hydrostatic pressure upon the fluidity of cellular membranes. *Biochemistry, N.Y.* **22**, 409–415.

CHONG, P. L.-G., & COSSINS, A. R. (1984). Interacting effects of temperature, pressure and cholesterol content upon the molecular order of dioleoylphosphatidylcholine vesicles. *Biochim. biophys. Acta* **772**, 197–201.

COOLBEAR, K.P., BERDE, C. B. & KEOUGH, K. M. W. (1983). Gel to liquid crystalline phase transitions of aqueous dispersions of polyunsaturated mixed acid phosphatidyl cholines. *Biochemistry, N.Y.* **22**, 1466–1473.

COSSINS, A. R. (1983). The adaptation of membrane structure and function to changes in temperature. In *Cellular Acclimatisation to Environmental Change* (ed. A. R. Cossins & P. Sheterline) pp. 3–32. Cambridge: Cambridge University Press.

COSSINS, A. R., FRIEDLANDER, M. J. & PROSSER, C. L. (1977). Correlations between behavioural temperature adaptations of goldfish and the viscosity and fatty acid composition of their synaptic membranes. *J. comp. Physiol.* **120**, 109–121.

COSSINS, A. R. & LEE, J. A. C. (1985). The adaptation of membrane structure and lipid composition to cold. *Proc. Ist Int. Cong. Int. Union Biol. Sci. Comp. Physiol. Biochem,* (Liège). (In press).

COSSINS, A. R. & MACDONALD, A. G. (1984). Homeoviscous theory under pressure. 2. The molecular order of membranes from deep sea fish. *Biochim. biophys. Acta* **776**, 144–150.

COSSINS, A. R., KENT, J. & PROSSER, C. L. (1980). A steady state and differential polarised phase fluorometric study of the liver microsomal and mitochondrial membranes of thermally acclimated green sunfish. *Lepornis cyanellus. Biochim biophys. Acta* **599**, 341–358.

COSSINS, A. R. & PROSSER, C. L. (1982). Variable homeoviscous responses of different brain membranes of thermally-acclimated goldfish. *Biochim. biophys. Acta* **687**, 303–309.

CULLEN, J., PHILLIPS, M. C. & SHIPLEY, C. C. (1971). The effects of temperature on the composition and physical properties of the lipids of *Pseudomonas fluorescens. Biochem. J.* **125**, 733–742.

FLAMM, M., OKUBO, T., TUSSO, N. & SCHACHTER, D. (1982). Pressure dependence of pyrene excimer fluorescence in human erythrocyte membranes. *Biochim. biophys. Acta* **687**, 101–104.

GAUSE, E. M., MENDEZ, V. M. & ROWLANDS, J. R. (1974). A spin label study of the effects of hydrostatic pressure and temperature on cellular lipids. *Spectrosc. Letters* **7**, 477–490.

HAEST, C. W. M., DE GIER, J. & VAN DEENEN, L. L. M. (1969). Changes in the chemical and barrier properties of the membrane lipids of *E. coli* by variation of the temperature of growth. *Chem. Phys. Lipids* **3**, 413–417.

HAZEL, J. R. & SELLNER, R. A. (1980). The regulation of membrane lipid composition in thermally acclimated poikilotherms. In *Animals and Environmental Fitness* (ed. R. Gilles) pp. 541–560. Oxford: Pergamon Press.

HERON, D. S., SHINITZKY, M., HERSHKOWITZ, M. & SAMUEL, D. (1980). Lipid fluidity markedly modulates the binding of serotonin to mouse brain membranes. *Proc. natn. Acad. Sci., U.S.A.* **77**, 7463–7467.

HEYN, M. (1979). Determination of lipid order parameters and rotational correlation times from fluorescence depolarization experiments. *FEBS Letters*, **108**, 359–364.

HOCHACHKA, P. W. (1975). How abyssal organisms maintain enzymes of the 'right' size. *Comp. Biochem. Physiol.* **52B**, 39–41.

JÄHNIG, F. (1979). Structural order of lipids and proteins in membranes: Evaluation of fluorescence anisotropy data. *Proc. natn. Acad. Sci., U.S.A.* **76**, 6361–6365.

JAMESON, D. M., WEBER, G., SPENCER, R. D. & MITCHELL, G. (1980). Fluorescence polarization: measurements with a photon counting photometer. *Rev. Sci. Instrum.* **49**, 510–514.

KASAI, R., KITAJIMA, Y., MARTIN, C. E., NOZAWA, Y., SKRIVER, L. & THOMPSON, G. A. (1976). Molecular control of membrane properties during temperature acclimation. Membrane fluidity regulation of fatty acid observation, action. *Biochemistry, N.Y.* **15**, 5228–5233.

KARNOVSKY, M. J., KLEINFELD, A. M., HOOVER, R. L. & KLAUSNER, R. D. (1982). The concept of domains in membranes. *J. Cell Biol.* **94**, 1–6.

KATES, M. & KUKSIS, A. (1980). *Membrane Fluidity. Biophysical Techniques and Cellular Regulation*, (ed. M. Kates & A. Kuksis) New Jersey: The Humana Press.

KLEINFELD, A. M., DRAGSTEN, P., KLAUSNER, R. D., PJURA, W. J. & MATAYOSHI, E. D. (1981). The lack of relationship between fluorescence polarization and lateral diffusion in biological membranes. *Biochim. biophys. Acta* **649**, 471–480.

KINOSITA, K., KATAOKA, R., KIMURA, Y., GOTOH, O. & IKEGAMI, A. (1981). Dynamic structure of biological membranes as probed by 1,6-Diphenyl-1,3,5-hexatriene: A nanosecond fluorescence depolarization study. *Biochemistry, N.Y.* **20**, 4270–4277.

KINOSITA, K. & IKEGAMI, A. (1984). Reevaluation of the wobbling dynamics of diphenyl-hexatriene in phosphatidylcholine and cholesterol/phosphatidylcholine membranes. *Biochem. biophys. Acta* **769**, 523–527.

LAKOWICZ, J. R. & THOMPSON, R. B. (1983). Differential polarised phase fluorometric studies of phospholipid bilayers under high hydrostatic pressure. *Biochim. biophys. Acta* **732**, 359–371.

LAU, M.-J. & KEOUGH, M. W. (1981). Lipid composition of lung and lung lavage fluid from map turtles (*Malaclemys geographica*) maintained at different environmental temperatures. *Can. J. Biochem.* **59**, 208–219.

LEWIS, R. W. (1962). Temperature and pressure effects on fatty acids of some marine ectotherms. *Comp. Biochem. Physiol.* **6**, 75–89.

MACDONALD, A. G. (1967). The effect of high hydrostatic pressure on the cell division and growth of *Tetrahymena pyriformis*. *Expl Cell. Res.* **47**, 569–580.

MACDONALD, A. G. (1975). *Physiological Aspects of Deep Sea Biology*. Cambridge: Cambridge University Press.

MACDONALD, A. G. (1984a). The effects of pressure on the molecular structure and physiological functions of cell membranes. *Phil. Trans. R. Soc. Lond.* B. **304**, 47–68.

MACDONALD, A. G. (1984b). Homeoviscous theory under pressure. 1. The fatty acid composition of *Tetrahymena pyriformis* NT-1 grown at high pressure. *Biochim. biophys. Acta* **775**, 141–149.

MACDONALD, A. G. & COSSINS, A. R. (1983). Effects of pressure and pentanol on the phase transition in the membrane of *Acholeplasma laidlawii* B.

MACDONALD, A. G. & GILCHRIST, I. (1982). The pressure tolerance of deep sea amphipods collected at their ambient high pressure. *Comp. Biochem. Physiol.* **71A**, 349–352.

MÜLLER, H-J. & GALLA, H-J. (1983). Pressure variation of lateral diffusion in lipid bilayers. *Biochim. biophys. Acta* **733**, 291–294.

PATTON, J. S. (1975). The effect of pressure and temperature on phospholipid and triglyceride fatty acids of fish white muscle: A comparison of deep water and surface marine species. *Comp. Biochem. Physiol.* **52B**, 105–110.

POTTEL, H., VAN DER MEER, W. & HERREMAN, W. (1983). Correlation between order parameter and the steady state fluorescence anisotropy of 1,6-diphenyl-1,3,5 hexatriene and an evaluation of membrane fluidity. *Biochim. biophys. Acta* **730**, 181–186.

PUGH, E. L., KATES, M. & SZABO, A. G. (1980). Fluorescence polarization studies of rat liver microsomes with altered phospholipid desaturase activation. *Can. J. Biochem.* **58**, 952–958.

RIORDAN, J. R. (1980). Ordering of bulk membrane lipid or protein promotes activity of plasma membrane Mg^{2+} ATP-ase. *Can. J. Biochem.* **58**, 928–934.

SHELTON, C. J., MACDONALD, A. G., PEQUEUX, A. & GILCHRIST, I. (1985). The ionic composition of the plasma and erythrocytes of deep sea fish. *J. comp. Physiol.* (in press).

SILVIUS, J. R. & McELHANEY, R. N. (1978). Growth and membrane lipid properties of *Acholeplasma laidlawii* B. lacking fatty and heterogeneity. *Nature* **272**, 645–647.

SINENSKY, M. (1974). Homeoviscous adaptation – a homeostatic process that regulates the viscosity of membrane lipids in *E. coli. Proc. natn. Acad. Sci., U.S.A.* **71**, 522–525.

SMITH, K. L. (1978). Metabolism of abyssopelagic fishes: *in situ* measurements of the rat tail, *Coryphaenoides armatus*. *Nature* **274**, 362–364.

SOMERO, G. N. (1982). Physiological and biochemical adaptations of deep sea fishes: adaptive responses to the physical and biological characteristics of the abyss. In *The Environment of the Deep Sea* (ed. W. G. Ernst & J. G. Morin) pp. 257–278. New Jersey: Prentice Hall.

STUBBS, C. D., KORYAMA, T., KINOSITA, K. & IKEGAMI, A. (1981). Effect of double bonds on the dynamic properties of the hydrocarbon region of lecithin bilayers. *Biochemistry, N.Y.* **20**, 4257–4262.

SULLIVAN, K. M. & SOMERO, G. N. (1980). Enzyme activities of fish skeletal muscle and brain as influenced by depth of occurrence and habits of feeding and locomotion. *Marine Biology* **60**, 91–99.

SWEZEY, R. R. & SOMERO, G. N. (1982). Polymerization thermodynamics and structural stabilities of skeletal muscle actions from vertebrates adapted to different temperatures and hydrostatic pressures. *Biochemistry* **21**, 4496–4503.

TAYLOR, C. D. (1979). Growth of a bacterium under a high pressure oxy-helium atmosphere. *Appl. Environ. Microbiol.* **37**, 42–49.

TAYLOR, C. D. & JANNASCH, H. W. (1976). Subsampling technique for measuring growth of bacterial cultures under high hydrostatic pressure. *Appl. Environ. Microbiol.* **32**, 355–359.

THOMPSON, G. A. (1980). The Regulation of Membrane Lipid Metabolism. Boca Raton, CRC Inc.

THOMPSON, G. A. & NOZAWA, Y. (1977). Tetrahymena: A system for studying dynamic membrane alterations within the eukaryotic cell. *Biochim. biophys. Acta* **472**, 55–92.

THOMPSON, G. A. (1983). Mechanisms of homeoviscous adaptation in membranes. In *Cellular Acclimatisation to Environmental Change*. (ed. A. R. Cossins & P. Sheterline) pp. 33–53. Cambridge: Cambridge University Press.

TSUDA, M., GOVINDJEE, R. & ELVEY, T. G. (1983). Effects of pressure and temperature on the M412 Intermediate of the bacterorhosospin photocycle. *Biophys. J.* **44**, 249–254.

VAN BLITTERSWICJK, W. J., VAN HOEVEN, R. P. & VAN DEER MEER, B. W. (1981). Lipid structural order parameters (reciprocal of fluidity) in biomembranes derived from steady-state fluorescence polarization measurements. *Biochim. biophys. Acta* **644**, 323–332.

VIRIOT, M. L., GUILLARD, R., KAROFFMANN, I., ANDREW, J. C. & SIEST, C. (1983). Pressure effects on the apparent viscosity of artificial dipalmitoyl phosphatidylcholine and dimyristoylphosphatidylcholine membranes using intramolecular excimer probe. *Biochim. biophys. Acta* **733**, 34–38.

WALTIAUX-DE CONINCK, S., DUBOIS, F., MERTENS-STRIJTHAGEN, J., DE SCHRIJVER, C. & WALTIAUX, R. (1980). Permeability of mitochondria to sucrose induced by hydrostatic pressure. *Biochim. biophys. Acta* **600**, 173–184.

Printed in Great Britain © Society of Experimental Biology 1985

HOW TO SURVIVE IN THE DARK: BIOLUMINESCENCE IN THE DEEP SEA

PETER J. HERRING

Institute of Oceanographic Sciences, (NERC), Wormley, Godalming, Surrey
U.K.

Summary

Bioluminescent tissues in marine organisms may take the form of point source emitters, internal or external glandular organs or glands containing bacterial symbionts. In many cases additional accessory optical structures have been evolved to increase the efficiency of emission, to restrict the angular direction, to focus or collimate the light, to alter its spectral distribution or to guide it from the source to a distant point of emission. This variety of structure is matched by a variety of locations of luminous tissues and organs over the body of different animals. The time course, intensity and spectral nature of bioluminescence are equally variable.

Information can be encoded in the spatial pattern, time course and spectral characteristics of bioluminescent signals and the recognition of this information depends upon the visual abilities of the target organism. The known characteristics of the bioluminescence of certain marine organisms are compared with those that would be predicted for different functional interpretations. It is probable that each type of bioluminescent signal in deep-sea organisms is but one factor in the suite of activities which make up a particular behavioural pattern.

'*How have all the exquisite adaptations of one part of the organisation to another part, and to the conditions of life, and of one organic being to another being, been perfected? We see these beautiful co-adaptations . . . everywhere and in every part of the organic world*'. *Charles Darwin*, The Origin of Species.

Introduction

This symposium is concerned with the physiological adaptations of marine organisms. The recognition of such adaptations normally involves the experimental manipulation of the environment and either the community, individual organism or a particular system of the organism, in order to distinguish the responses of the one in relation to the other. For most deep-sea species such an approach is still largely impracticable and many of our necessarily anthropomorphic concepts of adaptation are based more on intuitive assumptions than on experimental demonstrations. Correlations between the physical characteristics of emitted bioluminescence, the visual capabilities of the community and the behavioural responses to luminescent stimuli are still in their infancy. Observation of structure alone is *not* an adequate basis for functional interpretation. This is clearly demonstrated by earlier interpretations of organs in fish and crustaceans – which we now know to be photophores – as slime glands, ears and accessory eyes. Modern zoologists are by no means blameless in this respect; unidentified glandular tissues or unusual structures in deep-sea species are still far too often interpreted as 'probably luminous'.

I shall make the assumption that where bioluminescence occurs it can be regarded as a physiological adaptation that aids survival in the dark, whether it be the permanent darkness of the deep sea or the low light levels characteristic of the mesopelagic realm during the day and the shallow surface waters during the night. I want to emphasize particularly the *variety* of luminescent expression in marine organisms, both anatomically and physiologically. Functional interpretations have been reviewed by a number of authors in recent years (e.g. Buck, 1978; Morin, 1983; Young, 1983) who have classified the possible behavioural categories (albeit still largely theoretical) in various degrees of detail. I shall therefore discuss functions only in so far as they can be directly related to the more easily observed features of the luminescent systems in different species.

1. Structural aspects

a) Single cells

The simplest structural unit for light emission is that of a single luminous cell (or photocyte) acting as an effective point source in the absence of any accessory structures. In the case of an induced luminous marine bacterium (Hastings & Nealson, 1977) the emission is a continuous glow but in most other marine examples light is produced as flashes of varying durations in response to a variety of stimuli. Luminous dinoflagellates provide the best known examples of this type though the subcellular distribution of their luminescent microsources is both complex and has a circadian variability (Sweeney, 1982). Radiolaria are the only other unicellular luminous organisms but there are numerous examples of point source emitters in other phyla. These typically include most coelenterates and echinoderms, many polychaetes (e.g. polynoids) some gastropods, crustaceans (e.g. the amphipod *Scina*) and the tunicates (*Pyrosoma, Oikopleura*). Single cells without any accessory structures are relatively uncommon in fish, cephalopods and crustaceans. In most invertebrates the photocytes are aggregated into groups in particular parts of the body but in some holothurians, the nudibranch *Phyllirrhoë* and the amphipod *Danaella*, they are scattered over much of the body surface.

b) Internal glandular organs

In a number of species the photocytes apparently produce a secretory product which is not expelled to the exterior. This occurs in the small photocytes between the fin rays and elsewhere in the epidermis of stomiatoid fishes (O'Day, 1973). There is an indication of an internal duct in the photocyte mass of the amphipod *Scina* (Herring, 1981a) and a similar situation probably applies in the copepod *Oncaea conifera* (Herring, unpublished). Bassot's (1966a) descriptions of the histology of the photophores of a number of mesopelagic fishes demonstrate a range of secretory types from the ductless *Maurolicus*, though the closed duct of *Bonapartia* to the open duct of *Gonostoma*. There is, however, no evidence yet of how the cellular secretory cycle relates to luminescence. In all such cases of internal secretory tissue it must be assumed that the product is reabsorbed and probably recycled.

c) External glandular organs

The presence of glandular tissues with an opening to the exterior through which the luminous secretory product is discharged is common to many invertebrates, particularly crustaceans. It is typified by ostracods such as *Vargula* (= *Cypridina*), in which labral glands are responsible, and *Conchoecia* in which carapace glands in a variety of positions act similarly (Angel, 1968). Similar glandular complexes occur on the body and limbs of many calanoid copepods. The luminescence need not always be discharged but can be produced within the glandular complex (e.g. *Hemirhabdus* spp.) and this seems also to occur at times in the ostracods (Angel, 1968; Morin & Bermingham, 1980). Among the most dramatic secretory luminescence is that of deep-sea decapods (Oplophoridae and Pandalidae) which produce repeated gouts of luminous secretion from the mouth. The secretory source of the luminescence is probably the hepatopancreas (Herring, 1976). The mysid *Gnathophausia* produces a similar effect from glands on the second maxilla. Luminous secretions are frequently accompanied by mucus secretion as in the annelid *Chaetop-terus* (Anctil, 1979), the bivalve *Pholas* (Bassot, 1966b), the hemichor-date *Balanoglossus* (Baxter & Pickens, 1964) and many coelenterates.

It has generally been assumed that this secretory luminescence involves the simultaneous discharge of two components of the bioluminescence reaction ('luciferin' and 'luciferase') into the water and that these two components are produced by different gland cells. There is no direct evidence for this assumption and it is not easy to reconcile observations of intraglandular luminescence with this hypothesis. It seems equally likely that the reaction system may be produced as a single intracellular package which is disrupted by ejection to the exterior. This would be commensurate with those cases (e.g. *Pholas*) where only a single secret-ory cell type can be identified. In *Chaetopterus* the single cell type obser-ved (Anctil, 1979) can be correlated with the extraction of a photoprotein (analogous to a luciferin–luciferase complex) (Shimomura, Beers & Johnson, 1968). Perhaps the most remarkable of secretory systems is that of the searsiid fishes whose postcleithral organ pours forth a mass of epithelial cells from within the gland, each cell luminescing on contact with seawater (Herring, 1972). Each ejected photocyte could in this case be regarded as a single cell emitter rather than as a secretory product.

d) Symbiont glands

The luminous organs of many fish and some cephalopods are glands containing symbiotic luminous bacteria. All such glands open to the ex-terior and it is assumed that none of the host tissue is itself also lumines-cent. (In the anglerfish *Linophryne* non-bacterial luminous organs are also present elsewhere on the body (Hansen & Herring, 1977)). The symbionts have not always been identified but in most cases are species of *Vibrio* or *Photobacterium* (Nealson & Hastings, 1979). Symbionts leak naturally into the surrounding water (Haygood, Tebo & Nealson, 1984) and in some cases can be ejected as a luminous cloud (e.g. some sepiolids and anglerfishes). In other symbiotic associations (e.g. the subocular organs of *Photoblepharon* and *Anomalops*) there is no likelihood of any active expulsion of the glandular contents.

e) Accessory optical structures

Many of the luminous tissues considered above are simple in that they consist solely of light-producing tissue, whether photocytes or secretory, and light emission from these tissues is consequently uniform in distribution (Fig. 1A). The requirement for a more clearly defined direction of emission has resulted in the development of accessory optical structures of several types.

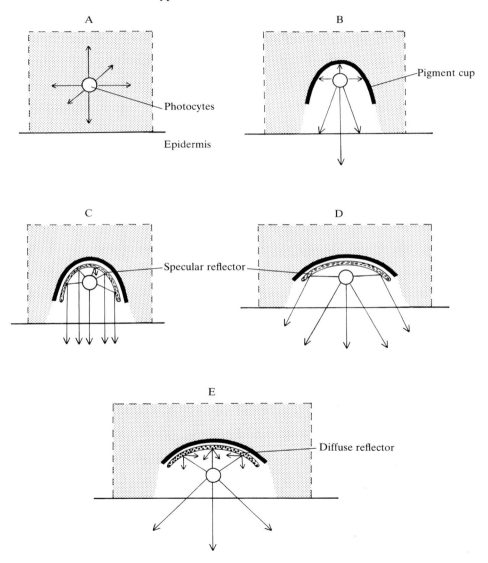

Fig. 1. The effects of pigment and reflectors on light emission: (A) point source emission of group of photocytes, (B) pigment cup restricts the solid angle of emission; reflectors of different geometries provide a more efficient emission, whether they are specular (C) and (D) or diffuse (E). Arrows indicate possible ray paths. See text for examples.

The siting of photocytes on a pigmented tissue (e.g. as in the medusa *Atolla*) inevitably limits the direction of emission. More clearly defined directionality is achieved by enclosing the photocytes in a cup of opaque pigment, restricting emission to the pigment aperture (Fig. 1B). Many of the smaller photophores on fishes and some cephalopods are of this type (e.g. Brauer, 1908). It is necessarily wasteful in the sense that much of the light that is produced is absorbed by the pigment and never emerges from the photophore. The efficiency of emission is therefore greatly enhanced by the incorporation of a reflector system within the pigment layer (Fig. 1C–E). This general arrangement of reflector and pigment cup is that found in the great majority of photophores in fish, cephalopods and crustaceans. Reflectors differ in their appearance and composition and their effects range from uniformly diffuse reflectance to highly specular. Many tissues have some reflective capability and in the ommastrephid squids, for example, the photocyte aggregates rest on a sheet of relatively opaque white connective tissue, providing a diffuse reflectance. Where collagen fibrils are employed there is the potential for some degree of specular reflectance if the fibrils are appropriately aligned (Land, 1972). Collagen fibrils form the reflectors of several squid photophores (Herring, Clarke, Boletzky & Ryan, 1981; Butcher, Dilly & Herring, 1982) but the most highly organized is that in *Abralia* (Young & Arnold, 1982) in which the regularity of the fibril arrangement would suggest an effective degree of specular reflectance. Diffuse reflectors are infrequent in fishes but do occur in the photophores of juveniles of the searsiid *Holtbyrnia*. Granular diffuse reflectors of this type are present in several decapod crustaceans (Dennell, 1940; Herring, 1981b).

Far more usual is the presence of a constructive interference reflector composed of multiple layers of alternating high and low refractive index. These produce the high specular reflectance that characterizes the photophores of many fish, cephalopods and crustaceans. Land (1972), following Huxley (1968), has provided a theoretical treatment of such systems from which it is clear that their efficiency is very high. For an 'ideal' system giving maximum reflectance of a given wavelength (λ) the optical thickness of each layer should be $\lambda/4$. The low refractive index material is assumed to be cytoplasm and the high refractive index material is usually chitin or protein in invertebrates and guanine in fishes (Denton & Land, 1971; Herring & Locket, 1978; Brocco & Cloney, 1980). Most systems are assumed to be 'ideal' $\lambda/4$ reflectors but the layer arrangement has rarely been examined in sufficient detail to rule out the subtleties of non-ideal systems. Not all fish reflectors are guanine based; in the alepocephalids *Photostylus* and *Xenodermichthys* the lamellate reflectors lack guanine (Best & Bone, 1976).

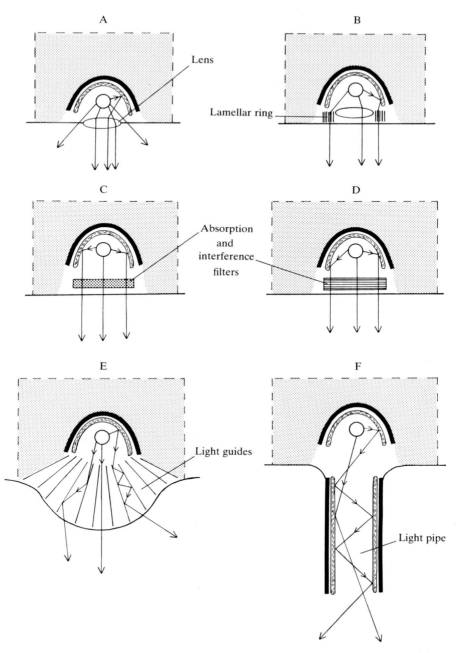

Fig. 2. Effects of accessory structures: (A) lens alone, (B) lens and lamellar ring, (C) pigmented absorption filter, (D) interference filter, (E) light guide diffuser and (F) light pipe. See text for examples.

Many photophores with reflector and pigment layers also have a structure in their aperture which appears to be a lens (Fig. 2). In myctophid fishes the lens is a thickened portion of the overlying scale (Lawry, 1973). In many decapods and euphausiids the lens is chitinous and, in the latter, denser towards its centre. The position and refractive properties of these lenses leave little doubt about their functional identity. Many fish and cephalopod photophores have lenticular structures, which probably function as collimating lenses, in their apertures (Brauer, 1908; Chun, 1910) but nothing is known of their composition, refractive index or effect on light emission.

Associated with the lens in many photophores is a lamellar ring, filling the gap between the reflector aperture and the lens (Bassot, 1966a; Herring & Locket, 1978; Young & Arnold, 1982). The role of these structures is not clear but they probably collimate the emitted light by intercepting light that would otherwise emerge off-axis (Fig. 2B).

A number of photophores lack any collimating tissues and the directionality of the light beam derives from the geometry and structure of the reflector. This is the case in the large suborbital photophores of many stomiatoid fishes and of *Anomalops* and *Photoblepharon*, the snout photophores of *Diaphus* and the occlusible arm-tip photophores of many cephalopods.

A defined direction of emission can also be achieved by the use of light-guide systems (Fig. 2E) with or without the provision of a lens. In the photophores of many enoploteuthid and lycoteuthid cephalopods bundles of collagen fibres form a near-hemispherical cushion of light guides over the photocytes (Butcher *et al.*, 1981). In the large subocular organs of cranchiid squids connective tissue fibres perform the same function and the illuminated area may be many times greater than that of the photocyte surface. The emission cone from each light guide, and hence the whole organ, will depend on the critical angle which is in turn related to the refractive index of the materials employed. There has been no analysis of the physics of these systems and it is not even possible to rule out wave guide effects.

Even more dramatic and extensive are the light-channelling structures in many fishes, particularly those which utilize bacterial symbionts in one or a very few light organs (Herring & Morin, 1978). Many species use internal reflective systems, including the swim bladder (McFall-Ngai, 1983), linked to the light-conducting properties of muscle and/or connective tissues to distribute the luminescence over a large surface area. Similar effects are achieved by the midwater fishes *Opisthoproctus* and *Winteria* (Bertelsen & Munk, 1964; Herring, 1975). In the former genus the entire ventral sole forms a highly reflective light pipe; similar light pipes are present in many ceratioid anglerfish in which the light is transmitted down the pipe from the bacterial source. In *Chaenophryne* the light pipe increases in length as the animal develops (Munk & Bertelsen, 1980) and in *Himantolophus* several such light pipes may present the appearance of multiple light sources (Haneda, 1968).

A further refinement of photophore structure is the possession of a pigmented tissue plug in the aperture. This is particularly common in stomiatoid and gonostomatid fishes in which a reddish or lilac pigment is present. Similarly coloured tissues occur in *Xenodermichthys* (Best & Bone, 1976), the squid *Histioteuthis* (Dilly & Herring, 1981) and some decapod photophores, both cuticular and hepatic. The pigments have been investigated in few cases but range from carotenoproteins to porphyrins. Pigment plugs also occur in the bacterial photophores of *Opisthoproctus* and *Monocentris*. The effects of such pigments must be to modify the spectral nature of the emitted light (Denton, Gilpin-Brown & Wright, 1970; Denton & Herring, 1978; Denton *et al.*, 1985). Multiple reflective platelets in the photophore aperture of enoploteuthid and other squids (Arnold, Young & King, 1974; Butcher *et al.*, 1981) are believed to act as interference filters similarly affecting the photophore emission.

Switching the luminescence on and off usually occurs at the photocyte level, but in a number of animals, particularly those with bacterial photophores, additional methods may be employed. These may involve

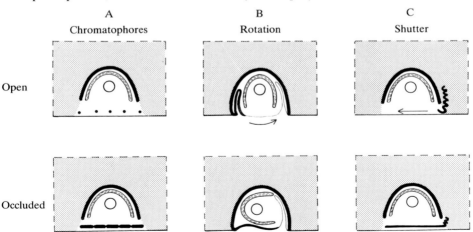

Fig. 3. Three different means whereby a photophore may be occluded: (A) with chromatophores, (B) by rotating the organ into a pigmented pocket and (C) by drawing a pigmented shutter across the aperture.

the expansion of occluding chromatophores, the rotation of the organ inwards or the raising of a pigmented curtain (Fig. 3).

The sheer morphological complexity of even very small photophores (e.g. Young & Arnold, 1982) makes it difficult to assign a function to many of the observed structures without a similar detailed knowledge of the output of the organ. Many photophore structures, therefore, cannot yet be interpreted. The complexities of the escal structure of many angler-fish and the bewildering variety of reflector (iridosome) organization in many cephalopod photophores are notable examples. Our interpretations of the operation and optical subtleties of many photophores are probably still extremely naïve.

2. Position of luminous structures

The location of luminous tissues and organs on an animals body demonstrates almost as much variety as does their structure. There are relatively few animals in which photocytes are dispersed randomly over the whole body but there are considerably more in which the luminescence *appears* to be uniformly distributed, by virtue of either the diffusive effects of the tissues or the small size of the animal. The medusa *Pelagia* and nudibranch *Phyllirrhoë* have a wide distribution of photocytes, as do fishes such as *Echiostoma*, and a similar impression is given by the epithelial photocytes of the siphonophore *Hippopodius* (Bassot *et al.*, 1978) and amphipods *Danaella* and *Scina marginata* (Herring, 1981a). A colony of *Pyrosoma* appears uniformly illuminated, though the light is produced by two small clusters of photocytes in each zooid.

When an animal has a clearly segmented organization the photocytes are often also segmentally repeated whether they are of the internal or glandular type (e.g. *Chaetopterus*, *Tomopteris*, some copepods, decapods, euphausiids, ophiuroids and crinoids). The segmental arrangement of photophores is particularly prominent in many fishes, notably the stomiatoids and myctophids.

A dorsal distribution of photocytes (e.g. some holothurians, copepods and amphipods) is relatively rare. Far more frequent is a ventral one. Most luminous pelagic species of decapod and euphausiid crustaceans, fish and cephalopods have predominantly ventrally placed photophores. This is regardless of whether the photophores are superficial (e.g. the cephalopods *Abralia* and *Ommastrephes*, many stomiatoid fishes and the decapods *Oplophorus* and *Sergia*) or internal (e.g. the cephalopods *Megalocranchia* and *Pyroteuthis*, some apogonid and leiognathid fishes, *Coccorella* and *Opisthoproctus*, the decapods *Sergestes* and

Parapandalus). This ventral predominance has been the subject of considerable discussion (McAllister, 1967; Marshall, 1979) and some examples, at least, are explicable in terms of ventral camouflage (Clarke, 1963; Herring, 1982; Young, 1983). Ventrally positioned luminescence also characterizes the marine gastropod *Planaxis* and the pycnogonid *Colossendeis*.

The luminous tissues or organs are often sited at the periphery of the animal. The luminous bodies in stomiatoid fishes are located not only along the dorsal and ventral margins of the body but also down the length of each fin ray (O'Day, 1973). In other fishes luminous organs are sited on the tails of the unusually elongate genera *Idiacanthus* and *Saccopharynx*, on the escas and barbel tips of anglerfish and melanostomiatids and the tip of the elongate dorsal fin ray of *Chauliodus*. Peripheral sites are common in invertebrates. Arm and/or tentacle tip photophores occur in many cephalopods (Herring, 1977a) while tail photophores are present in lycoteuthids (Voss, 1962). The amphipods *Megalanceola* and *Scina* luminesce from the tips of certain appendages and in the medusae *Aequorea* and *Atolla* the brightest luminescence is distributed round the edge of the umbrella.

Photophores are frequently associated with the eye. Subocular photophores are common in cephalopods and indeed are the only photophores in *Gonatus pyros*, *Brachioteuthis* and most cranchiids. Many stomiatoids have a particularly large sub- and/or postorbital photophore in addition to smaller photophores round the orbit (e.g. Tchernavin, 1953). Pre- and supraorbital photophores in some gonostomatid and myctophid fishes actually shine into the eye and the large bacterial photophores in the anomalopids are situated beneath the eye. Photophores on the eyestalk are a feature of euphausiid and many decapod crustaceans.

Photophores are associated with the mouth in several fishes. *Neoscopelus*, *Chauliodus* and *Sternoptyx* have photophores within it (Nafpaktitis, 1977; Tchernavin, 1953; Herring, 1977b) and the pinecone fish *Cleidopus* has a bacterial organ on the floor of the mouth (Paxton, 1973). The luminous oral ring in adult females of the octopods *Vitreledonella* and *Japetella* is a rare example among the invertebrates (Robison & Young, 1981).

Luminous organs associated with the gut are common in fishes, particularly those harbouring luminous symbionts. They are most frequently rectal or anal diverticula, or portions of rectal epithelia (*Coccorella*, *Howella*). Pyloric and/or intestinal caeca form luminous organs in *Lumiconger* (Castle & Paxton, 1984), *Coccorella*, pempherids and some apogonids, and oesphageal diverticula in leiognathids and other

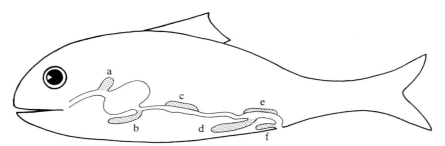

Fig. 4. Regions of the gut modified in different fishes to form luminous organs or tissues: (a) oesophageal diverticula, (b) pyloric caeca, (c) intestinal wall, (d) rectal diverticula (e) rectal wall and (f) anal diverticula.

apogonids (Fig. 4). Bacterial light organs of cephalopods do not open into the gut lumen.

'Hepatic' photophores are present in several decapods (e.g. *Sergestes*) and the luminous secretion of others (e.g. *Oplophorus*) is produced by the hepatopancreas. The digestive gland of the squid *Megalocranchia* has photophores situated on it, but not formed from it (Voss, 1980) while there is some evidence for luciferin accumulation in the digestive gland of certain other squids (Young *et al.*, 1979).

Many other sites for luminous tissue are known, particularly among the invertebrates (e.g. *Pholas*, *Pyrosoma*, *Oikopleura*, *Gnathophausia*, ctenophores) and in a few cases the ovaries, too, are luminous (some echinoderms and medusae). It is clear that there is virtually no tissue that is not modified either to form a luminous region or to be the bearer of photophores.

3. Physical characteristics

The structure of the luminous tissues of many marine organisms can be investigated comparatively readily but determination of the physical characteristics of the emitted light is much more difficult. It requires the simultaneous functioning of the luminescing animal, investigator and measuring system, a triumvirate only achieved with considerable difficulty, if at all, for most deep-sea species. Despite these problems sufficient is known for it to be apparent that the physiological variety matches that of the morphology and distribution.

a) Time course

Induced bacteria luminesce steadily and continuously and individual dinoflagellates have a dim steady luminescence in addition to their other emissions. Most live animals, however, emit light only briefly, the intensity decaying over periods varying from a few milliseconds to several minutes (Morin, 1983). The long periods (several minutes) of relatively steady luminescence have been observed in euphausiid and decapod crustaceans, some cephalopods and fishes such as the ceratioids, squaloids, leiognathids, monocentrids, myctophids and hatchetfishes. Durations of several seconds to minutes have been seen in *Planaxis*, *Pyrosoma*, *Pholas*, *Megalanceola*, *Colossendeis*, hemichordates, *Porichthys* and many coelenterates. In colonial species, and in whole animals with numerous photocytes, asynchronous scintillation of individual photocytes may give an overall impression of steady luminescence. Different responses can be obtained by different methods. The hatchetfish *Argyropelecus* glows steadily when alive but electrical stimulation of isolated photophores can produce very short flashes (Baguet, Christophe & Marechal, 1980). Postorbital organs of stomiatoid fishes produce brief (< 1 s) flashes in live animals but glow steadily on adrenaline treatment or just after death. 'Terminal glows' are features of several groups of animals and must not be mistaken for normal responses. Some secretory luminescence may persist for many minutes albeit at much reduced intensity. Most invertebrates with non-secretory luminescence have flash or pulse durations of 50–2000 ms (Morin, 1983). Flashes of the photophores of many fishes are equally brief (myctophid caudal organs, astronesthids, stomiatoid postorbital organs). Luminous pulses produced by fish with bacterial photophores tend to be longer (>1 s) as in the anomalopids (Herring & Morin, 1978). Leiognathids have a repertoire of different responses and durations in different circumstances (McFall-Ngai & Dunlap, 1983). It is very probable that this applies equally to many fish and cephalopods in which different photophores with different time constants may be used for different purposes.

Many species will produce a series of flashes and/or a conducted wave of light in response to a single stimulus. This is particularly common in coelenterates (Chang, 1954; Morin, 1974; Bassot *et al.*, 1978) but also occurs in Radiolaria, ophiuroids, polychaetes, hemichordates and some fishes. Multiple pulses are occasionally produced by secretory species such as ostracods and copepods but most species give a 1 : 1 stimulus : response ratio (Morin, 1983). Electrical stimuli are those most often employed in experimental work and the responses frequently differ depending on whether whole animals or isolated tissues are examined. Isolated preparations frequently fail to give repetitive responses obtainable from the whole animal. The effects of high voltages delivered to small tissue preparations are particularly difficult to interpret (e.g.

Baguet, 1975) and data from such *in vitro* experiments give much more information about the physiology of the photophore than about the normal *in vivo* bioluminescence.

b) Intensity

Intensity measurements, other than *in vivo*, are equally likely to be misleading and necessarily only provide a minimum value. In general the larger the organism the less is the experimentally determined intensity likely to approach that *in vivo*, and the intensity measurements available (e.g. Nicol, 1978; Morin, 1983) should therefore only be regarded as an indication of the order of magnitude of relative potential output. Where careful investigations have been made on live organisms some of the most interesting results have been the potential variability in the emission intensity of single organisms, whether they be light/dark-adapted dinoflagellates or countershading cephalopods. It is generally assumed that the intensity is under the organisms control, either through facilitation or recruitment, but this has rarely been clearly demonstrated (Bassot, 1979). Indeed many of the suggested functions of bioluminescence would be equally well served by an all-or-none response.

c) Spectral distribution

The spectral nature of bioluminescent light varies considerably between species (Herring, 1983; Widder, Latz & Case, 1983). Nevertheless, most pelagic species have emission maxima in the blue-green (450–490 nm) which correlates closely with the waveband of maximum transmission in oceanic water and the maximal visual sensitivity of most oceanic animals. Half bandwidths are typically broad (>80 nm) and the spectra unimodal. There is an indication that many benthic species have longer wavelength emission maxima (500–520 nm) commensurate with the transmission effects and visual sensitivities in this more turbid and productive environment. Indeed it has been suggested that the scotopic pigments of California nearshore fishes are adapted to match the spectral characteristics of twilight and bioluminescence (Hobson, McFarland & Chess, 1981). Exceptions to the general rule of unimodal emission are known in several phyla but the physicochemical basis for these spectra is not understood, though energy transfer effects are undoubtedly responsible for some of them (Ward, 1979). Additional complexities are provided by the few cases of temporal changes in emission spectra (e.g.

searsiid fishes and *Parapronöe*). The correlations between the emission maxima, visual pigments and water transmission are less clear for those species with emission maxima outside the expected range. The most remarkable exceptions are those few fishes (e.g. *Malacosteus*) which have a far-red-emitting photophore (λ_{max} 705 nm) as well as a blue one. The red emission is probably a combination of energy transfer and absorption filtering (Widder, Latz, Herring & Case, 1984). Other unusual cases are the coelenterate *Umbellula*, which emits green and blue light from different regions of the colony, the pennatulid *Stachyptilum* in which different colonies have different emission maxima and *Parazoanthus* in which individuals in the same colony have different emission maxima (Widder *et al.*, 1983). The spectral characteristics can result solely from the biophysical nature of the reaction system, as in most secretory luminescence, but can also be modified by the effects of spectrally selective filters or reflectors. Such external structures can only narrow the emitted bandwidth. Absorption filtering occurs in the hatchetfish *Argyropelecus*, selective reflection in the lanternfish *Diaphus*, and both effects operate in *Opisthoproctus* (Denton & Herring, 1978; Denton *et al.*, 1985). In each case the final spectral emission is a very close match to that of downwelling light in the sea.

Superimposed on the physical features of the emissions (outlined above) are longer term variations induced by rhythmic behaviour patterns. The best documented examples are the dinoflagellates, some of which have a very marked circadian rhythm of stimulable luminescence, allied in *Pyrocystis* to intracellular movements of the luminescent microsources (Sweeney, 1982). Luminescence is repressed during the day and reaches a maximum at night. The rhythm persists in continuous darkness and can be phase shifted by a variety of procedures. Many other luminous organisms are inhibited by light. In ctenophores the evidence suggests that light inhibition involves direct inactivation of the photoprotein (Ward & Seliger, 1976). In the pennatulid *Renilla*, however, light inhibition appears to operate at the neurophotocyte junction i.e. the conduction process rather than the luminescent potential (Morin, 1974). A rhythmic light inhibition is suggested by work on the hemichordate *Ptychodera* (Baxter & Pickens, 1964) and euphausiids are subject to a short-lived light inhibition after a photoflash or continuous weak light source (Kay, 1965). The situation in these animals is complicated by a light stimulation effect as well. The latter is a feature of many other organisms, including those not known to show any light inhibition or rhythms (e.g. *Pyrosoma*, ostracods, *Porichthys*). These responses are probably indicative of a more general neural sensitivity.

4. Functional interpretations

What should we make of this remarkable diversity of structure, expression, and control in the bioluminescent systems of marine organisms? The ecology of bioluminescence cannot be separated from that of vision. The reception of bioluminescent signals is dependent upon the visual capabilities of the target organism. This may be the emitter itself in those cases in which a photophore points directly into the eye and those in which objects or organisms are detected by their reflection of bioluminescent light. For intraspecific communication other individuals of the same species are the targets. In all these circumstances a close relationship between the visual and bioluminescent systems is to be expected. The most 'secure' communication channel in these conditions will be a narrow bandwidth emission to which the emitting species' eye is uniquely sensitive. This is the case in the red-emitting fishes (*Malacosteus, Aristostomias, Pachystomias*) with a narrow bandwidth far red emission (Widder *et al.*, 1984). The eyes of these fishes are certainly unusually sensitive to red light, for they contain red-sensitive visual pigments enhanced, in *Malacosteus*, by a red tapetum.

Where reflection from nearby objects is concerned the spectral quality of light received by the observer will be a product of the emission and reflectance characteristics. Monochromatic light may be poorly reflected by some targets and a broader bandwidth emission may increase the prospects of a detectable signal from a variety of targets. Similar arguments can be proposed for other situations in which luminescence is employed. It is therefore appropriate to consider how the diversity noted earlier can be interpreted as adaptations to these various circumstances.

Information in bioluminescent signals can be encoded in the flash frequency, and in the spectral and spatial distribution of the luminous sources. The degree to which each of these factors can be recognized by the observer is critical. Information encoded in the signal frequency ($\equiv$ flash rate) will not be distinguished unless it is below the flicker fusion frequency ($<10\,\mathrm{s}^{-1}$ at low intensities and deep-sea temperatures for crustaceans and for fishes). Spectrally coded information will be unintelligible to an observer without adequate spectral discrimination and spatial (pattern) information depends upon the observer's visual acuity.

In the simplest bioluminescent interactions, such as a response to a potential predator, the information content of the signal may be low. The flash of the dinoflagellate or secretion of a decapod are typical of this type. These responses are probably employed in contact with a variety of species rather than one particular predator. Anticipated characteristics will be a short duration (to prevent the prey being localized) a broad spectral emission (to encompass a range of predator spectral sensitivities) and a high intensity (quantum rate) for maximum shock effect. An omni-directional response is also likely. Just such characteristics (adaptations) are recognizable in many examples. Thus the dinoflagellates have a brief ($\sim$100 ms) flash of high intensity (10^8–10^{10} q. s^{-1} flash^{-1}) resulting from a reaction system modelled by Hastings (1983a) as 'a laser-like burst of activity'. It is non-directional but of relatively narrow half bandwidth ($\sim$40 nm). The latter feature is unexpected but, since the emission maximum (475 nm) falls at the peak sensitivity of most oceanic animals, probably has little consequence. It is presumably largely employed against grazing crustaceans, particularly copepods, and its effectiveness has been elegantly demonstrated (Esaias & Curl, 1972; Buskey, Mills & Swift, 1983).

Decapod (and other) secretory responses have a relatively broad half bandwidth ($\sim$70 nm) and omnidirectional effect but are relatively long lasting. This is an appropriate characteristic in a situation in which the emitter itself remains dark and the secretion has a decoy effect. In these contact situations an all-or-none response is most appropriate, though repeated responses of diminishing intensity (and therefore effect?) are possible. Repeated flashes may reinforce the initial response and a burst of rapid bright flashes is indeed produced by many coelenterates and fishes. Most deep-sea species have eyes clearly adapted to achieve sensitivity at the expense of acuity and a bright flash at short range is likely to be intimidatory. It is possible that the effects of a bright flash may be longer lived than expected, for recent work has demonstrated that for some coastal crustaceans, at least, exposure to high light intensities results in a permanent impairment of vision (Loew, 1976; Nilsson & Lindstrom, 1983). The intensities necessary for damage in these animals are, however, much greater than those of marine bioluminescence.

The size of a secretory response may be intimidatory (e.g. *Thalassocaris* (Herring & Barnes, 1976)) and the presence of photocytes at the periphery of an animal, as noted earlier, may give a similarly false impression of size, particularly if the appendages are elongate. O'Day (1973) considered this was the role of the silhouetting luminescence of many stomiatoids.

Many responses usually ascribed to a startle, distract or confuse role only poorly match the expected characteristics of such a function. For example, *Pyrosoma* responds with a long-lived glow, *Scina* and *Oncaea* with intracellular flashes of shorter wavelength than those of most other species. Responses of this type are probably associated with some behavioural event, such as escape swimming. In *Photoblepharon* it has been described as a 'blink and run' tactic and it is certainly a feature of decapod and copepod crustaceans. It is important to realize that bioluminescence in these situations is only one component of a behavioural response.

Temporary blinding is one method of hiding from a predator but there are other bioluminescence tactics which involve camouflage, of which counterillumination is the best documented (Clarke, 1963; Herring, 1982; Young, 1983). What luminescent adaptations could be expected in a counterilluminating animal? The prime requirement must be to match the ambient light so that there is zero contrast between the animal and its background. Thus one would expect that the luminescence will be steady, the intensity, spectral and angular distribution and polarization of the light will match that of the environment and that the animal can change these characteristics appropriately as the environmental light conditions change. Photophores should be present along the ventral surface of the animal, beneath opaque tissues, be absent from transparent species and present only in the mesopelagic realm at depths where ambient light is significant.

Luminous systems conforming to these criteria are present in many fish, cephalopods and crustaceans. The observed luminescence is steady and in some cases has been seen from submersibles (Beebe, 1935). In the most carefully conducted experiments intensity fluctuations of captive animals are proportional to the ambient light (Case, Warner, Barnes & Lowenstine, 1977; Warner, Latz & Case, 1979; Young *et al.*, 1980). The spectral distribution of light from these photophores is an excellent match of ambient light in the sea, with a narrow half bandwidth and a peak between 470 and 480 nm (Herring, 1983). Colour filters are present in many of these photophores and modify the emitted spectrum so that a better spectral match with down-welling light is achieved (Denton & Herring, 1978; Denton *et al.*, 1985). In *Diaphus* the reflector is spectrally selective. There is no detailed information on the construction of the reflector but in theory (Land, 1972) the required narrow bandwidth is achieved most effectively by non-ideal stacking of platelets, albeit with more layers than that of an 'ideal' $\lambda/4$ system of similar efficiency. Denton, Gilpin-Brown and Wright (1972) have shown that the angular distribution of the ventral luminescence of some fishes closely matches that of the background light and similar results have been obtained for euphausiids and decapods (Herring, 1976; Herring & Locket, 1978; Latz & Case, 1982). The elaboration of accessory optical structures in these photophores   is   probably   responsible   for   the   resulting angular distribution. There are no published comparisons between the polarization of the luminescence and that of ambient light but preliminary observations on *Argyropelecus* (Denton, unpublished) indicate that the anticipated close match is not achieved.

Variations in intensity match the background over a wide range but there is little information on other parameters. Animals moving from deep water during the day to near surface at night will be subject to variations in the spectral and angular distributions of light during their migrations. No example is known of an animal altering the angular distribution of light from its photophores, though both euphausiids and some decapods rotate their photophores to maintain constant the angular distribution of ventral luminescence despite changes in the orientation of the body (Hardy, 1962; Latz & Case, 1982).

Evidence for changes in the spectral emission of counterillumination bioluminescence to match those of ambient light is very limited. Young & Mencher (1980) have shown that the squid *Abralia trigonura* can alter its spectral emission from a sunlight match at depth during the day to a moonlight match near surface at night, both by the involvement of different types of photophore and spectral modifications of one particular type. The spectral change appears to be triggered by changes in water temperature (Young & Arnold, 1982).

The distribution of ventral photophores generally accords with the hypothesis that if they are for counterillumination they should be present only in those mesopelagic species subject to an ambient light background. In general ventral photophores are absent from transparent species or, as in many squids, present only beneath opaque structures such as the eyes and liver. The transparent larvae of fish such as the scopelarchid *Benthalbella* lack ventral photophores – but develop them as they metamorphose into opaque adults. The largely transparent euphausiid *Stylocheiron* has only a single ventral abdominal photophore, in contrast to the four present in other, more opaque, genera. Even photophores located on the flanks of many animals are in fact ventrally directed. The only photophore in the hatchetfish *Argyropelecus* that is not ventrally directed is the preorbital, pointing into the eye. This is presumed to act as a reference standard for comparison with background light and has the expected filter pigment but lacks the external reflector systems that provide the appropriate angular distribution for the ventral photophores. The preorbital ($\equiv$ oral) organs of *Sternoptyx* are not directed into the eye – and lack the filter pigment with which the counterilluminating ventral photophores are equipped (Herring, 1977b).

Compelling though the evidence is for ventral counterillumination it is unlikely that *all* ventrally placed photophores are employed for this purpose. McAllister (1967) voiced some doubts about the generality of the hypothesis and there are indeed anomalies in the observed characteristics and distribution of ventral photophores in a number of species that conflict with the requirements of the hypothesis. The spectral emission of several species departs substantially from a match with ambient light in the sea (Herring, 1983). If the spectral distribution is not critical it is surprising that so many other species have adaptations designed to produce such a match even at the expense of reduced intensity (Denton *et al.*, 1985). *Argyropelecus* and many other animals have photophores almost completely obliterating their ventral surface but many species have only a very few ventral photophores (e.g. *Benthalbella*, macrourids, *Onychoteuthis*, *Parapronoë*). These can hardly provide an even camouflage and may perhaps be more disruptive than counterilluminating. Morin (1983) has suggested a similar rôle may apply to leiognathids and other fish living in the optically complex turbid coastal environment. He also notes that ventral camouflage may increase the success of predators foraging on the bottom. The gonostomatids *Yarella* and *Polymetme* are also primarily near-bottom species but retain a full array of ventral photophores equipped with pigmented filters.

Light organs used to lure prey should have rather different characteristics and one might expect fairly uniform distribution of light, broad spectral emission and a steady intensity. More complex characteristics will be necessary if the lure is to mimic a particular prey organism. Luminous bacteria on faecal pellets provide a uniform intensity and it has been suggested that one ecological benefit of bacterial luminescence is to attract a predator to the faecal pellets and re-establish the population in the nutrient-rich environment of the gut. Young (1983) further suggests that the luminous lures of oceanic species are mimicking luminous faecal pellets. The location of small photophores at the tip of appendages such as the dorsal fin ray of *Chauliodus*, tail of *Saccopharynx* and the barbels and escas of stomiatoids and angler fish suggests such a purpose. The elaboration of some of these 'lures', whose multiple luminous filaments or light guides provide a mass of luminous sources, does not seem intended to provide a particular pattern as the filaments are highly mobile and the pattern must be constantly changing. Only a siphonophore might provide a similar appearance (cf. Robins, 1966). The minute variations in the escal structures of different ceratioids are almost certainly beyond the resolution of the limited acuity of most deep-sea eyes, including those of the corresponding males. These 'lures' are therefore unlikely to provide a species-specific sexual signal, despite their presence only in the females. They (and the barbels of stomiatoids) undergo very extensive changes in structure (and hence luminous pattern?) during development, further complicating the problems of specific recognition (Bertelsen, 1951; Morrow & Gibbs, 1964).

Specific identification of luminescent signals, whether by friend or foe, necessitates the sensory ability to discriminate the information encoded in the emitted signal. Species of lanternfish have characteristic photophore patterns on their flanks and it has been suggested that they are used in species recognition. However, the light from these flank photophores, as noted above, is directed downwards and is barely visible from the side. In addition recognition of the pattern will require considerable visual acuity. A 2 mm difference in the position of a photophore seen at a range of 1 m will subtend an angle of only about 10 minutes of arc at the eyes and in actively swimming animals will be very difficult to resolve.

For intraspecific recognition of bioluminescence a close correlation between the luminescence and visual abilities is to be expected. Long-range communication probably requires a broad cone of emission but once the correspondent is located a narrow beam of light would be most effective to avoid interception by potential predators. A close correlation is found in *Odontosyllis* whose luminescence is largely confined to sexual aggregations closely tuned to a lunar cycle and which has λ_{max} at ~510 nm (Shimomura, Johnson & Saiga, 1963). Its electroretinogram has a maximum amplitude at 510–520 nm significantly different from the shorter wavelength visual maxima of the non-luminous worms *Nereis* and *Vanadis* (Wilkens & Wolken, 1981). The midshipman fish *Porichthys* has luminescence maxima at 485 and 507 nm (Tsuji *et al.*, 1975) and corresponding visual sensitivity maxima (Fernandez & Tsuji, 1976). This is a coastal fish whose photophores are ventrally distributed, yet the close correlation suggests a more intraspecific function than counterillumination, supporting earlier reports of its role in courtship (Crane, 1965). Dartnall (1975) has noted that the correlation between sensitivity maxima and spectral maxima need not be exact as there is only a small reduction in sensitivity with quite marked differences in visual pigments, particularly where the retinal density is as high as in deep sea fishes. Nevertheless, it is surprising to find in the squid *Ctenopteryx* a sexually dimorphic photophore emitting at ~420 nm (Herring, 1983) when oegopsid visual pigments have absorption maxima at about 480 nm (Muntz, 1983).

A clear instance of correlation between sensitivity and spectral emission is found in those fishes emitting red light. All three genera have both red and blue luminescence and all three have twin visual pigments in marked contrast to most deep-sea fishes (O'Day & Fernandez, 1974;

Denton *et al.*, 1970). The additional red-sensitive visual pigment is potent evidence that the luminescence is used either in an intraspecific rôle or for illuminating prey. Photophores used in this way, as illumination systems, must emit light to which the eye is sensitive and must be bright enough to offset the losses involved in transmission and reflection from a distant object. Efficient reflector systems are particularly likely in these photophores, typical of which are the large postorbital photophores of stomiatoids, the nasal organs of *Diaphus* and the suborbital organs of the anomalopids. Observations on the latter have demonstrated their role in prey capture (Morin *et al.*, 1975). When stomiatoids are handled these same postorbital photophores flash repeatedly and can equally be employed as a defensive system.

Flashing photophores or photocytes can encode a great deal of information, as is particularly the case in fireflies (Lloyd, 1983) but observations in the sea are very limited. Sexual signalling between pairs of anomalopids has been observed (Morin & Harrington, unpublished) and synchronous flashing of the ostracod *Vargula* in mating displays (Morin & Bermingham, 1980). There are many reports of synchronously flashing patches observed at sea, some of which probably represent similar types of lekking displays by so far unidentified organisms. The luminescent responses to light stimuli demonstrate the behavioural potential for a luminescent dialogue between individuals. Any such dialogue will entrain much of its information in the flash frequency and time course. By extrapolation from observations on fireflies one might also expect that stereotyped patterns of movement in the water by a luminous animal might provide specific information to an observer. If such dialogues do occur it would be most interesting to know how defined they are and whether local 'dialects' could be distinguished in wide-ranging species. Unfortunately there are no *in situ* measurements on repetitively flashing animals.

Conclusions

It is clearly possible in some cases to relate the features of photophore distribution, structure, and operation to their function. The diversity observed in the luminous structures of marine organisms suggests (1) that they are functionally highly diverse and (2) that they represent many instances of independent evolution with a considerable degree of convergence (Hastings, 1983b). In recognizing the identifiable adaptations of many bioluminescent systems it is immediately apparent that they represent only one of a suite of physiological adaptations. To consider, for example, photophore structure without photophore control, luminous responses without associated locomotory responses, bioluminescent emission without visual capabilities, is to erect artificial barriers to any attempts to understand the relationship between the animal and its environment.

We can note, with appropriate humility, how many of our own efforts in illumination technology merely duplicate those already constantly employed in the unremitting struggle for survival in the sea. Emission geometry controlled by pigment absorption, reflectors both diffuse and specular, lenses, collimating systems, iris diaphragms and shutters, interference and absorption filters, intracellular fluors, fibre optic systems, information transfer by pulsed signals, even the equivalent of a 'sniperscope': all are present in marine organisms. No doubt many other subtleties still await recognition.

Animals with bacterial symbionts are restricted (for reasons that are not understood) to only one to three photophores. In these cases different luminous functions (and hence signals) are achieved by control of the photophores and associated behavioural activities (Morin *et al.*, 1975; McFall-Ngai & Dunlap, 1983). However, most luminous animals achieve a multiplicity of functions by means of an equivalent variety of luminous organs (each presumed to have their own signal characteristics) and their differential distribution over the body. In contrast to this means of *emitting* a variety of signals their *detection* is achieved by signal differentiation within a very few sensory structures (the eyes) rather than by increasing the number of eyes and dedicating each type to recognition of a particular signal. It is therefore probable that the elaboration and diversification of the retinal regions in fish and cephalopods, and of the ommatidia in the compound eyes of deep-sea crustaceans, are adaptations to the different types of bioluminescent information ($\equiv$signals) necessary for the species.

The problem of surviving in the dark of the oceans has many different bioluminescent solutions. Probably only a minority have yet been recognized.

References

ANCTIL, M. (1979). The epithelial luminescent system of *Chaetopterus variopedatus*. *Can. J. Zool.* **57**, 1290–1310.

ANGEL, M. V. (1968). Bioluminescence in planktonic halocyprid ostracods. *J. mar. biol. Ass. U.K.* **48**, 255–257.

ARNOLD, J. M., YOUNG, R. E. & KING, M. V. (1974). Ultrastructure of a cephalopod photophore. II. Iridophores as reflectors and transmitters. *Biol. Bull. mar. biol. Lab., Woods Hole* **147**, 507–521.

BAGUET, F. (1975). Excitation and control of isolated photophores of luminous fishes. *Progr. Neurobiol.* **5**, 97–125.

Baguet, F., Christophe, B. & Marechal, G. (1980). Luminescence of *Argyropelecus* photophores electrically stimulated. *Comp. Biochem. Physiol.* **67A**, 375–381.

Bassot, J.-M. (1966a). On the comparative morphology of some luminous organs. In *Bioluminescence in Progress* (ed. F. H. Johnson & Y. Haneda) pp. 557–610. Princeton: University Press.

Bassot, J.-M. (1966b). Données histologiques et ultrastructurales sur les organes lumineux du siphon de la Pholade. *Z. Zellforsch. mikrosk. Anat.* **74**, 474–504.

Bassot, J.-M. (1979). Sites actifs et facilitation dans trois systèmes bioluminescents. *Archs Zool. exp. gén.* **120**, 5–24.

Bassot, J.-M., Bilbaut, A., Mackie, G. O., Passano, L. M. & Pavans de Ceccatty, M. (1978). Bioluminescence and other responses spread by epithelial conduction in the siphonophore *Hippopodius*. *Biol. Bull. mar. biol. Lab., Woods Hole* **155**, 473–498.

Baxter, C. H. & Pickens, C. E. (1964). Control of luminescence in hemichordates and some properties of a nerve net system. *J. exp. Biol.* **41**, 1–14.

Beebe, W. M. (1935). *Half Mile Down*. London: The Bodley Head.

Bertelsen, E. (1951). The ceratioid fishes. Ontogeny, taxonomy and distribution. *Dana Rep.* No. **39**, 272 pp.

Bertelsen, E. & Munk, O. (1964). Rectal light organs in the argentinoid fishes *Opisthoproctus* and *Winteria*. *Dana Rep.* No. **62**, 17 pp.

Best, A. C. G. & Bone, Q. (1976). On the integument and photophores of the alepocephalid fishes *Xenodermichthys* and *Photostylus*. *J. mar. biol. Ass. U.K.* **56**, 227–236.

Brauer, A. (1908). Die Tiefsee-Fische. II. Anatomischer Teil. *Wiss. Ergebn. dt. Tiefsee-Exped. 'Valdivia'* **15**, 1–266.

Brocco, S. L. & Cloney, R. A. (1980). Reflector cells in the skin of *Octopus dofleini*. *Cell Tissue Res.* **205**, 167–186.

Buck, J. (1978). Functions and evolutions of bioluminescence. In *Bioluminescence in Action* (ed. P. J. Herring) pp. 419–460. London: Academic Press.

Buskey, E., Mills, L. & Swift, E. (1983). The effects of dinoflagellate bioluminescence on the swimming behavior of a marine copepod. *Limnol. Oceanogr.* **28**, 575–579.

Butcher, S., Dilly, P. N. & Herring, P. J. (1982). The comparative morphology of the photophores of the squid *Pyroteuthis margaritifera* (Cephalopoda: Enoploteuthidae). *J. Zool., Lond.* **196**, 133–150.

Case, J. F., Warner, J., Barnes, A. T. & Lowenstine, M. (1977). Bioluminescence of lantern fish (Myctophidae) in response to changes in light intensity. *Nature, Lond.* **265**, 179–181.

Castle, P. H. J. & Paxton, J. R. (1984). A new genus and species of luminescent eel (Pisces: Congridae) from the Arafura Sea, Northern Australia. *Copeia* **1984**, 72–81.

Chang, J. J. (1954). Analysis of the luminescent response of the ctenophore *Mnemiopsis leidyi* to stimulation. *J. cell. comp. Physiol.* **47**, 489–492.

Chun, C. (1910). Die Cephalopoden. I. Oegopsida. *Wiss. Ergebn. dt. Tiefsee-Exped. 'Valdivia'* **18**, 1–401.

Clarke, W. D. (1963). Function of bioluminescence in mesopelagic organisms. *Nature* **198**, 1244–1246.

Crane, J. M. (1965). Bioluminescent courtship display in the teleost *Porichthys notatus*. *Copeia* **1965**, 239–241.

Dartnall, H. J. A. (1975). Assessing the fitness of visual pigments for their photic environment. In *Vision of Fishes* (ed. M. A. Ali) pp. 543–563. New York: Plenum Press.

Dennell, R. (1940). On the structure of the photophores of some decapod Crustacea. *Discovery Rep.* **20**, 307–382.

Denton, E. J., Gilpin-Brown, J. P. & Wright, P. G. (1970). On the 'filters' in the photophores of mesopelagic fish and on a fish emitting red light and especially sensitive to red light. *J. Physiol., Lond.* **208**, 72–73P.

DENTON, E. J., GILPIN-BROWN, J. P. & WRIGHT, P. G. (1972). The angular distribution of the light produced by some mesopelagic fish in relation to their camouflage. *Proc. R. Soc. B*, **182**, 145–158.

DENTON, E. J. & HERRING, P. J. (1978). On the filters in the ventral photophores of mesopelagic animals. *J. Physiol., Lond.* **284**, 42P.

DENTON, E. J., HERRING, P. J., WIDDER, E. A., LATZ, M. I. & CASE, J. F. (1985). The roles of filters in the photophores of oceanic animals and their relation to vision in the oceanic environment. *Proc. R. Soc. B* (in press).

DENTON, E. J. & LAND, M. F. (1971). Mechanism of reflexion in silvery layers of fish and cephalopods. *Proc. R. Soc. A*, **178**, 43–61.

DILLY, P. N. & HERRING, P. J. (1981). Ultrastructural features of the light organs of *Histioteuthis macrohista* (Mollusca: Cephalopoda). *J. Zool., Lond.* **195**, 255–266.

ESAIAS, W. E. & CURL, H. C. (1972). Effect of dinoflagellate bioluminescence on copepod ingestion rates. *Limnol. Oceanogr.* **17**, 901–906.

FERNANDEZ, H. R. & TSUJI, F. I. (1976). Photopigment and spectral sensitivity in the bioluminescent fish *Porichthys notatus*. *Mar. Biol.* **34**, 101–107.

HANEDA, Y. (1968). Observations on the luminescence of the deep sea luminous angler fish, *Himantolophius groenlandicus*. *Sci. Rep. Yokosuka Cy Mus.* **14**, 1–6.

HANSEN, K. & HERRING, P. J. (1977). Dual bioluminescent systems in the anglerfish genus *Linophryne* (Pisces: Ceratioidea). *J. Zool., Lond.* **182**, 103–124.

HARDY, M. G. (1962). Photophore and eye movement in the euphausiid *Meganyctiphanes norvegica* (G. O. Sars). *Nature* **196**, 790–791.

HASTINGS, J. W. (1983a). Chemistry and control of luminescence in marine organisms. *Bull. mar. Sci.* **33**, 818–828.

HASTINGS, J. W. (1983b). Biological diversity, chemical mechanisms and the evolutionary origins of bioluminescence. *J. molec. Ecol.* **19**, 309–321.

HASTINGS, J. W. & NEALSON, K. H. (1977). Bacterial bioluminescence. *A. Rev. Microbiol.* **31**, 549–595.

HAYGOOD, M., TEBO, B. M. & NEALSON, K. H. (1984). Luminous bacteria of a monocentrid fish (*Monocentris japonicus*) and two anomalopid fishes (*Photoblepharon palpebratus* and *Kryptophanaron alfredi*): population sizes and growth within the light organs, and rates of release into the seawater. *Mar. Biol.* **78**, 249–254.

HERRING, P. J. (1972). Bioluminescence of searsiid fishes. *J. mar. biol. Ass. U.K.* **52**, 879–887.

HERRING, P. J. (1975). Bacterial bioluminescence in some argentinoid fishes. *Proc. 9th europ. mar. Biol. Symp.* (ed. H. Barnes) pp. 563–572. Aberdeen: Aberdeen University Press.

HERRING, P. J. (1976). Bioluminescence in decapod Crustacea. *J. mar. biol. Ass. U.K.* **56**, 1029–1047.

HERRING, P. J. (1977a). Luminescence in cephalopods and fish. *Symp. zool. Soc. Lond.* **38**, 127–159.

HERRING, P. J. (1977b). Oral light organs in *Sternoptyx*, with some observations on the bioluminescence of hatchet-fishes. In *A Voyage of Discovery* (ed. M. V. Angel) pp. 553–567. Oxford: Pergamon Press.

HERRING, P. J. (1981a). Studies on bioluminescent marine amphipods. *J. mar. biol. Ass. U.K.* **61**, 161–176.

HERRING, P. J. (1981b). The comparative morphology of hepatic photophores in decapod Crustacea. *J. mar. biol. Ass. U.K.* **61**, 723–737.

HERRING, P. J. (1982). Aspects of the bioluminescence of fishes. *A. Rev. Oceanogr. mar. Biol.* **20**, 415–470.

HERRING, P. J. (1983). The spectral characteristics of luminous marine organisms. *Proc. R. Soc. B*, **220**, 183–217.

HERRING, P. J. & BARNES, A. T. (1976). Light stimulated bioluminescence of *Thalassocaris crinita* Dana (Decapoda, Caridea). *Crustaceana* **31**, 107–110.

HERRING, P. J., CLARKE, M. R., BOLETZKY, S. V. & RYAN, K. P. (1981). The light organs of *Sepiola atlantica* and *Spirula spirula* (Mollusca: Cephalopoda); bacterial and intrinsic systems in the order Sepioidea. *J. mar. biol. Ass. U.K.* **61**, 901–916.

HERRING, P. J. & LOCKET, N. A. (1978). The luminescence and photophores of euphausiid crustaceans. *J. Zool., Lond.* **186**, 431–462.

HERRING, P. J. & MORIN, J. G. (1978). Bioluminescence in fishes. In *Bioluminescence in action* (ed. P. J. Herring) pp. 287–329. London: Academic Press.

HOBSON, E. S., McFARLAND, W. N. & CHESS, J. R. (1980). Crepuscular and nocturnal activities of Californian nearshore fishes, with consideration of their scotopic visual pigments and the photic environment. *Fish. Bull. U.S.* **79**, 1–30.

HUXLEY, A. F. (1968). A theoretical treatment of the reflexion of light by multi-layer structures. *J. exp. Biol.* **48**, 227–245.

KAY, R. H. (1965). Light-stimulated and light-inhibited bioluminescence of the euphausiid *Meganyctiphanes norvegica* (G. O. Sars). *Proc. R. Soc. B*, **162**, 365–386.

LAND, M. F. (1972). The physics and biology of animal reflectors. *Prog. Biophys. molec. Biol.* **24**, 75–106.

LATZ, M. I. & CASE, J. F. (1982). Light organ and eyestalk compensation to body tilt in the luminescent midwater shrimp, *Sergestes similis. J. exp. Biol.* **98**, 83–104.

LAWRY, J. V. (1973). Dioptric modifications of the scales overlying the photophores of the lantern fish *Tarletonbeania crenularis* (Myctophidae). *J. Anat.* **114**, 55–63.

LLOYD, J. E. (1983). Bioluminescence and communication in insects. *A. Rev. Entomol.* **28**, 131–160.

LOEW, E. R. (1976). Light, and photoreceptor degeneration in the Norway Lobster *Nephrops norvegicus* (L.). *Proc. R. Soc. B*, **193**, 31–44.

McALLISTER, D. E. (1967). The significance of ventral bioluminescence in fishes. *J. Fish. Res. Bd Can.* **24**, 537–554.

McFALL-NGAI, M. (1983). Adaptations for reflection of bioluminescent light in the gas bladder of *Leiognathus equulus* (Perciformes: Leiognathidae). *J. exp. Zool.* **227**, 23–33.

McFALL-NGAI, M. J. & DUNLAP, P. V. (1983). Three new modes of luminescence in the leiognathid fish *Gazza minuta*: discrete projected luminescence, ventral body flash and buccal luminescence. *Mar. Biol.* **73**, 227–237.

MARSHALL, N. B. (1979). *Developments in Deep-sea Biology*. Poole: Blandford Press.

MORIN, J. G. (1974). Coelenterate bioluminescence. In *Coelenterate Biology. Reviews and New Perspectives* (ed. L. Muscatine & H. M. Lenhoff) pp. 397–438. New York: Academic Press.

MORIN, J. G. (1983). Coastal bioluminescence: patterns and functions. *Bull. mar. Sci.* **33**, 787–817.

MORIN, J. G. & BERMINGHAM, E. L. (1980) Bioluminescent patterns in a tropical ostracod. *Am. Zool.* **20**, 851.

MORIN, J. G., HARRINGTON, A., NEALSON, K., KRIEGER, N., BALDWIN, T. O. & HASTINGS, J. W. (1975). Light for all reasons: versatility in the behavioral repertoire of the flashlight fish. *Science, N.Y.* **190**, 74–76.

MORROW, J. E. & GIBBS, R. H. (1964). Family Melanostomiatidae. In *Fishes of the Western North Atlantic* (ed. Y. H. Olsen). *Mem. Sears Fdn mar. Res.* No. 1, Pt. 4, 351–511.

MUNK, O. & BERTELSEN, E. (1980). On the esca light organ and its associated light-guiding structures in the deep-sea anglerfish *Chaenophryne draco* (Pisces, Ceratioidei). *Vidensk. Meddr dansk. naturh. Foren.* **142**, 103–129.

MUNTZ, W. R. (1983). Bioluminescence and vision. In *Experimental Biology at Sea* (ed. A. G. Macdonald & I. G. Priede) pp. 217–238. London: Academic Press.

NAFPAKTITIS, B. G. (1977). Family Neoscopelidae. In *Fishes of the Western North Atlantic* (ed. R. H. Gibbs) *Mem. Sears Fdn mar. Res.* No. 1, Pt. 7, 1–12.

NEALSON, K. H. & HASTINGS, J. W. (1979). Bacterial bioluminescence: its control and ecological significance. *Microbiol. Rev.* **43**, 496–518.

NICOL, J. A. C. (1978). Bioluminescence and vision. In *Bioluminescence in Action* (ed. P. J. Herring) pp. 367–398. London: Academic Press.

NILSSON, H. L. & LINDSTRÖM, M. (1983). Retinal damage and sensitivity loss of a light-sensitive crustacean compound eye (*Cirolana borealis*): electron microscopy and electrophysiology. *J. exp. Biol.* **107**, 277–292.

O'DAY, W. T. (1973). Luminescent silhouetting in stomiatoid fishes. *Contr. Sci.* No. 246, 8 pp.

O'DAY, W. T. & FERNANDEZ, H. C. (1974). *Aristostomias scintillans* (Malacosteidae): a deep-sea fish with visual pigments apparently adapted to its own bioluminescence. *Vision Res.* **14**, 545–550.

PAXTON, J. R. (1973). Bioluminescence in the Australian monocentrid fish, *Cleidopus gloria-maris*. In *Oceanography of the South Pacific* (ed. R. Fraser) p. 521. Wellington: N.Z. Nat. Com. UNESCO.

ROBINS, C. R. (1966). Additional comments on the structure and relationships of the mirapinniform fish family Kasidoroidae. *Bull. mar. Sci.* **16**, 696–701.

ROBISON, B. H. & YOUNG, R. E. (1981). Bioluminescence in pelagic octopods. *Pacif. Sci.* **35**, 39–44.

SHIMOMURA, O., BEERS, J. R. & JOHNSON, F. H. (1968). *Chaetopterus* photoprotein: crystallization and cofactor requirements for bioluminescence. *Science, N.Y.* **159**, 1239–1240.

SHIMOMURA, O., JOHNSON, F. H. & SAIGA, Y. (1963). Partial purification of the *Odontosyllis* luminescence system. *J. cell. comp. Physiol.* **61**, 275–292.

SWEENEY, B. M. (1982). Microsources of bioluminescence in *Pyrocystis fusiformis* (Pyrrophyta). *J. Phycol.* **18**, 412–416.

TCHERNAVIN, V. V. (1953). The feeding mechanisms of a deep-sea fish *Chauliodus sloani* Schneider. *British Museum (N.H.) Special Publication,* 101 pp.

TSUJI, F. I., NAFPAKTITIS, B. G., GOTO, T., CORMIER, M. J., WAMPLER, J. E. & ANDERSON, J. M. (1975). Spectral characteristics of the bioluminescence induced in the marine fish *Porichthys notatus,* by *Cypridina* (Ostracod) luciferin. *Molec. cell. Biochem.* **9**, 3–8.

VOSS, G. L. (1962). A monograph of the Cephalopoda of the North Atlantic. 1. The family Lycoteuthidae. *Bull. mar. Sci.* **11**, 264–305.

VOSS, N. A. (1980). A generic revision of the Cranchiidae (Cephalopoda; Oegopsida). *Bull. mar. Sci.* **30**, 365–412.

WARD, W. W. (1979). Energy transfer processes in bioluminescence. *Photochem. Photobiol. Rev.* **4**, 1–58.

WARD, W. W. & SELIGER, H. H. (1976). Action spectrum and quantum yield for the photoinactivation of mnemiopsin, a bioluminescent protein from the ctenophore *Mnemiopsis* sp. *Photochem. Photobiol.* **23**, 351–363.

WARNER, J. A., LATZ, M. I. & CASE, J. F. (1978). Cryptic bioluminescence in a midwater shrimp. *Science, N.Y.* **203**, 1109–1110.

WIDDER, E. A., LATZ, M. I. & CASE, J. F. (1983). Marine bioluminescence spectra measured with an optical multichannel detection system. *Biol. Bull. mar. biol. Lab., Woods Hole* **165**, 791–810.

WIDDER, E. A., LATZ, M. I., HERRING, P. J. & CASE, J. F. (1984). Far red bioluminescence from two deep-sea fishes. *Science, N.Y.* **225**, 512–514.

WILKENS, L. A. & WOLKEN, J. J. (1981). Electroretinograms from *Odontosyllis enopla* (Polychaeta; Syllidae): initial observations on the visual system of the bioluminescent fireworm of Bermuda. *Mar. Behav. Physiol.* **8**, 55–66.

YOUNG, R. E. (1983). Oceanic bioluminescence: an overview of general functions. *Bull. mar. Sci.* **33**, 829–845.

YOUNG, R. E. & ARNOLD, J. M. (1982). The functional morphology of a ventral photophore from the mesopelagic squid, *Abralia trigonura*. *Malacologia* **23**, 135–163.

YOUNG, R. E., KAMPA, E. M., MAYNARD, S. D., MENCHER, R. M. & ROPER, C. F. E. (1980). Counterillumination and the upper depth limits of midwater animals. *Deep-Sea Res.* **27A**, 671–691.

YOUNG, R. E. & MENCHER, F. M. (1980). Bioluminescence in a mesopelagic squid: diel color change during counterillumination. *Science, N.Y.* **208**, 1286–1288.

YOUNG, R. E., ROPER, C. F. E., MANGOLD, K., LEISMAN, G. & HOCHBERG, F. G. (1979). Luminescence from non-bioluminescent tissues in oceanic cephalopods. *Mar. Biol.* **53**, 69–77.

Printed in Great Britain © *Society for Experimental Biology 1985*

BIOLUMINESCENCE IN THE SEA:
PHOTOPROTEIN SYSTEMS

OSAMU SHIMOMURA

Marine Biological Laboratory, Woods Hole, MA 02543, USA, and
Department of Physiology, Boston University School of Medicine, Boston,
MA 02118, USA

Summary

Photoproteins are the primary reactants of the light-emitting reactions of various bioluminescent organisms. A photoprotein emits light in proportion to its amount, like a luciferin, but its light-emitting reaction does not require a luciferase. There are about two dozen types of bioluminescent organisms for which substantial biochemical knowledge is presently available, and about one third of them involve photoproteins. Most photoproteins are found in marine organisms.

There are various types of photoproteins: the photoproteins of coelenterates, ctenophores and radiolarians require Ca^{2+} to trigger their luminescence; the photoproteins of the bivalve *Pholas* and of the scale worm appear to involve superoxide radicals and O_2 in their light-emitting reactions; the photoprotein of euphausiid shrimps emits light only in the presence of a special fluorescent compound; the photoprotein of the millipede *Luminodesmus*, the only known example of terrestrial origin, requires ATP and Mg^{2+} to emit light.

The Ca^{2+}-sensitive photoproteins of coelenterates have been most frequently studied and most widely used. Therefore, they are overwhelmingly popular compared with other types. All coelenterate photoproteins, including aequorin, halistaurin, obelin and phialidin, have relative molecular masses close to 20000, contain an identical functional group, and emit blue light in aqueous solution when a trace of Ca^{2+} is added, in the presence or absence of molecular oxygen.

Aequorin contains an oxygenated form of coelenterazine in its functional group. When Ca^{2+} is added, aequorin decomposes into three parts, i.e., apo-aequorin, coelenteramide and CO_2, accompanied by the emission of light. Apo-aequorin can be reconstituted into active aequorin indistinguishable from the original sample, by incubation with an excess of coelenterazine in a buffer containing 5mM-EDTA and a trace of

2-mercaptoethanol, even at 0 °C. Thus, aequorin and other coelenterate photoproteins can be luminesced and recharged repeatedly. The regeneration of coelenterate photoproteins in this manner probably takes place *in vivo*, utilizing stored coelenterazine.

The photoproteins of coelenterates, and their chemically modified forms, are useful in measuring and monitoring calcium ions in biological systems, especially in single cells.

Introduction

An unusual protein was isolated from the jellyfish *Aequorea* in 1961 and named 'aequorin' after its genus name (Shimomura, Johnson & Saiga, 1962). It had a capability of emitting light in aqueous solutions merely by the addition of a trace of Ca^{2+}, even in the absence of oxygen. In 1966, another unusual bioluminescent protein was found in the polychaete annelid *Chaetopterus* (Shimomura & Johnson, 1966). This protein emitted light without participation of an enzyme when a trace of Fe^{2+} and an organic peroxide were added in the presence of O_2. These two examples were clearly out of place in the classical concept of the 'luciferin–luciferase' bioluminescence, in which 'luciferin' is customarily a relatively heat-stable, diffusible organic substrate and 'luciferase' is an enzyme that catalyses a luminescent oxidation of the luciferin.

Accordingly, we have introduced a new term 'photoprotein' as a convenient, general designation for the bioluminescent proteins of the *Aequorea* and *Chaetopterus* types (Shimomura & Johnson, 1966). Thus, a photoprotein is a protein that directly participates in the light-emitting chemical reaction of a living organism, that does not turn over in the reaction, and that is capable of emitting light in proportion to the amount of the protein. The proportionality of emitted light sets a clear distinction between the photoprotein and the enzyme luciferase.

When examined from the functional aspects, photoproteins are the molecules that contain both the functions of luciferin (substrate) and luciferase (enzyme) in each molecule, thus resembling various enzyme–substrate complexes. The photoproteins occur in nature, however, as the major molecular species of bioluminescence systems and not as the transient, unstable intermediates commonly formed in enzyme–substrate reactions. Bacterial luciferase, by reacting with $FMNH_2$ and O_2, forms an unstable, photoprotein-like intermediate which emits light when a fatty aldehyde is added (Hastings & Gibson, 1963; Hastings & Nealson, 1977). To avoid possible confusion, such an intermediate should not be termed a photoprotein unless it exists in luminous bacteria as a major component of the luminescence system.

One may sometimes be confused concerning definitions of photoprotein and luciferin, owing to the lack of universally accepted definitions for these terms. Thus, differing from the definition of photoprotein given above and used in this chapter, Cormier (1978) had defined photoprotein as 'a stabilized, oxygenated intermediate of a protein–luciferin complex that reacts with Ca^{2+} to produce light', therefore excluding bioluminescent proteins of all other types, even the bioluminescent protein of *Chaetopterus* for which the term 'photoprotein' was originally designated.

Various photoproteins

There are about two dozen types of bioluminescent systems for which substantial biochemical knowledge is presently available (Shimomura, 1982; Hastings, 1983), and about one third of them involve photoproteins. The photoproteins that have been isolated and confirmed are listed in Table 1, and briefly explained below.

Coelenterate photoproteins

Photoproteins obtained from hydrozoan jellyfishes, and also from hydroids, emit blue light when Ca^{2+} is added, in the presence or absence of O_2. The photoproteins of this type are suitable for use in detecting and measuring trace amounts of Ca^{2+} and have been widely used in the studies of Ca^{2+} in various biological systems including single cells (cf. Blinks, Prendergast & Allen, 1976; Ashley & Campbell, 1979). Overwhelming popularity of this type of photoprotein compared with other types sometimes leads to a misconception that photoproteins are aequorin-type Ca^{2+}-sensitive bioluminescent proteins.

All photoproteins of this type have relative molecular masses close to 20 000. Concentrated solutions of the purified proteins are slightly yellowish and non-fluorescent except for ordinary protein fluorescence. After Ca^{2+}-triggered luminescence, the solutions turn colourless and become brightly blue fluorescent; the intensities of the blue fluorescence are dependent on the concentrations of the spent protein and Ca^{2+}. In the case of aequorin, the emission spectrum of blue fluorescence is superimposable on the spectrum of Ca^{2+}-triggered luminescence, indicating that the blue-fluorescent chromophore formed in the luminescence reaction is the light emitter (Shimomura & Johnson, 1970).

The chemistry of the bioluminescent reaction of aequorin has been clarified in considerable detail (see pages 362–3). The reaction mechanisms of

Table 1. *List of photoproteins which have been isolated*

Source	Name	M_r	Cofactors required	Luminescence maximum (nm)
PROTOZOA				
Thalassicola sp.[1]	Thalassicolin		Ca^{2+}	440
COELENTERATA				
Aequorea aequorea[2]	Aequorin	20 000	Ca^{2+}	470
Halistaura sp.[3]	Halistaurin		Ca^{2+}	470
Obelia geniculata[4]	Obelin	20 000	Ca^{2+}	475
Phialidium gregarium[5]	Phialidin	23 000	Ca^{2+}	474
CTENOPHORA				
Mnemiopsis sp.[6]	Mnemiopsin-1	24 000	Ca^{2+}	485
	Mnemiopsin-2	27 500	Ca^{2+}	485
Beroë ovata[6]	Berovin	25 000	Ca^{2+}	485
ANNELIDA				
Chaetopterus variopedatus[7]		120 000 184 000	Fe^{2+}, hydroperoxide and O_2	460
Harmothoë lunulata[8]	Polynoidin	500 000	Fe^{2+}, H_2O_2 and O_2	510
MOLLUSCA				
Pholas dactylus[9]	Pholas luciferin	34 600	Luciferase, or peroxidase, or Fe^{2+} and O_2	490
CRUSTACEA: EUPHAUSIDAE				
Meganyctiphanes norvegica[10]		360 000 900 000	"F" and O_2	476
Euphausia pacifica			"F" and O_2	476
DIPLOPODA				
Luminodesmus sequoiae[11]		104 000	ATP, Mg^{2+} and O_2	496

References: [1] Campbell *et al.*, 1981; [2] Shimomura & Johnson, 1979; [3] Shimomura, Johnson & Saiga, 1963; [4] Campbell, 1974; [5] Levine & Ward, 1982; [6] Ward & Seliger, 1974*a,b*; [7] Shimomura & Johnson, 1969*a*; [8] Nicolas *et al.*, 1982; [9] Michelson, 1978; [10] Shimomura & Johnson, 1969*b*; [11] Shimomura, 1981.

all other photoproteins in this group are believed to be essentially the same as that of aequorin. In addition to the four species listed in Table 1, a number of other species, probably all luminous medusae and hydroids including scyphozoan *Pelagia noctiluca*, appear to contain aequorin-type photoproteins. In contrast, luminous anthozoans contain a luciferin (coelenterazine) and a species-specific luciferase, as well as small amounts of a Ca^{2+}-activated photoprotein in some instances; the

Table 2. *Sensitivities to Ca^{2+} and luminescence emission maxima of aequorin, halistaurin, phialidin and some modified forms of aequorin*†

Photoprotein	Median sensitivity*		Emission maximum (nm)
	1 mM-citrate	0·1 M-KCl	
Aequorin	7·15	5·9	465
Halistaurin	6·84	5·6	470
Phialidin	6·2	5·1	474
Acetylated aequorin	7·6	6·2	460
Ethoxycarbonylated aequorin	7·6	6·25	450
Fluorescamine-aequorin	7·5	6·1	463
Fluorescein-aequorin	7·4	6·1	518

* Median sensitivity is the pCa value at which the intensity of luminescence is equal to $\sqrt{I_0 I_{max}}$, where I_0 is the intensity when no calcium is added and I_{max} is the intensity when $0·01$ M-Ca^{2+} is added. The maximum sensitivities are roughly 1·5–2·0 units greater than the median sensitivities shown. The citrate buffer, pH 7·0, contained 1 mM-sodium citrate plus a calculated amount of calcium citrate to set pCa value, based on the stability constant of calcium citrate at $10^{4·5}$ (cf. Shimomura & Shimomura, 1984). The KCl buffer, pH 7·0, contained 1 mM-MOPS plus an amount of calcium chloride to set pCa value, in addition to $0·1$ M-KCl. All at 22–25 °C. † Unpublished data.

sea pen *Ptilosarcus gurneyi* and the sea cactus *Cavernularia obesa* contain photoproteins which have not been fully characterized in addition to their luciferins and luciferases, but the sea pansy *Renilla mulleri* contains only its luciferin and luciferase (Shimomura & Johnson, 1979a).

Spent aequorin that has been luminesced with Ca^{2+} can be converted into an active form, that is indistinguishable from the original aequorin in every aspect of properties, by incubating the coelenterazine in the presence of O_2 and a trace of 2-mercaptoethanol (Shimomura & Johnson, 1975; see also page 363). The yield of the regeneration is practically 100 %. Thus, a sample of aequorin can be luminesced and recharged repeatedly. The regeneration of spent photoprotein takes place also with obelin (Campbell, Hallet, Daw, Ryall, Hart & Herring, 1981) and with halistaurin and phialidin (unpublished results).

The sensitivities to Ca^{2+} of aequorin, halistaurin and phialidin, together with their luminescence emission maxima, are shown in Table 2.

Ctenophore photoproteins

Mnemiopsins and berovin are Ca^{2+}-activated photoproteins similar to aequorin in major aspects, but with some marked differences in certain properties (Ward & Seliger, 1974a, b). The absorption maximum of mnemiopsin-2 is at 435 nm which is about 20 nm shorter than that of aequorin. A more striking difference is that mnemiopsin and berovin are extremely sensitive to light (Hastings & Morin, 1968), being easily inactivated by a broad spectrum of light from 230 nm to 570 nm (Ward & Seliger, 1976). In contrast, aequorin is not photosensitive.

Photoinactivated mnemiopsin, as well as spent mnemiopsin after Ca^{2+}-triggered luminescence, can be reconstituted into its active form by incubation with coelenterazine in the presence of O_2, similarly to aequorin; however, the reconstruction takes place only at pH 9·0 (Anctil & Shimomura, 1984).

Radiolarian photoproteins

Campbell et al., (1981) reported that thalassicolin obtained from the luminous radiolarian *Thalassicola* sp. was a Ca^{2+}-activated photoprotein similar to those found in coelenterates. It is of interest as the only example of radiolarian photoprotein presently known.

Pholas luciferin

The boring clam *Pholas dactylus* was one of the first examples in the modern biochemical study of bioluminescence, and it was for this system that Dubois (1887) first coined the terms 'luciferase' and 'luciferin'.

According to Michelson (1978), *Pholas* luciferin (M_r 34 600) is a glycoprotein, and *Pholas* luciferase is a glycoprotein containing two atoms of copper per molecule (M_r 310 000). The luciferin emits light (λ max 490 nm) when the luciferase is added in the presence of O_2. The luminescence of luciferin can be elicited equally well by the addition of horseradish peroxidase or Fe^{2+} plus a ligand such as phosphate or pyrophosphate, in the presence of O_2.

The emission of light from *Pholas* luciferin caused by *Pholas* luciferase and that caused by Fe^{2+} in the presence of a suitable ligand are similar, resulting in the same quantum yield and the same spectral distribution (Henry & Michelson, 1973). Accordingly, it appears that there is no direct interaction or binding between the luciferin and luciferase during the light-emitting chemical reaction. Thus, the molecules of *Pholas* luciferase would not be directly involved in the light-emitting reaction itself despite its designation. In the absence of an essential luciferase function, it would be proper to classify *Pholas* luciferin into the category of photoprotein.

The absorption spectrum of *Pholas* luciferin shows an absorption band at 307 mn (ε 11 800) in additon to a protein absorption band at 280 nm. After luminescent oxidation, the former band disappears and concurrently a new band appears at 355–360 nm. The chromophore is still not chemically identified.

Chaetopterus photoprotein

The photoprotein of the parchment worm *Chaetopterus* purified by chromatography is an amorphous protein with a relative molecular mass of 120 000. The material, however, can be converted into a crystalline form having an increased relative molecular mass of 184 000 by slowly precipitating with ammonium sulphate (Shimomura & Johnson, 1968a). The essential factors required in the light-emitting reaction of this photoprotein are Fe^{2+}, O_2 and a hydroperoxide such as those that form spontaneously during storage of dioxane or tetrahydrofuran. Two kinds of additional activators were found, but they have not been identified chemically.

The absorption spectrum of this photoprotein shows no significant deviation from those of common, simple proteins, despite the fact that this protein shows a fluorescence excitation peak at 377 nm. When excited at 377 nm, the resulting fluorescence (λ max 455 nm) is similar, in its maximum and spectral distribution, to the bioluminescence of this photoprotein elicited by trace amounts of Fe^{2+} and aged dioxane containing peroxide (λ max 460 nm).

Polynoidin

A membrane photoprotein isolated from the scales of the scale worm *Harmothoë lunulata* was named 'polynoidin' (Nicolas, Bassot & Shimomura, 1982). This photoprotein (M_r 500 000) emits light (λ max 510 nm) when H_2O_2 and Fe^{2+}, or other reagents that produce superoxide radical or hydroxyl radical, are added in the presence of oxygen. This photoprotein is not fluorescent (except usual protein fluorescence) after the bioluminescence reaction or before the reaction. Similarity between the bioluminescence systems of *Pholas*, *Chaetopterus* and scale worms in cofactor requirements and certain other properties may suggest involvement of similar reaction mechanisms in these systems.

A green-fluorescent substance (fluorescence emission maximum 520 nm) isolated from the scales has been suggested to be the reaction product of bioluminescent reaction (Fresneau, Arrio, Lecuyer, Dupaix, Lescure & Volfin, 1984). This fluorescence substance, however, cannot be the reaction product of the primary light-emitting reaction of polynoidin, because the bioluminescence reaction product of polynoidin does not show any green fluorescence (Nicolas *et al.*, 1982). The green-fluorescent substance is possibly a product of a reaction which is coupled to the primary light-emitting reaction involving polynoidin. Nevertheless, a possibility that the green-fluorecent substance is an *in vivo* light emitter, excitable by energy transfer from the excited state of polynoidin, cannot be excluded at present.

Euphausiid photoproteins

Most of the euphausiids are bioluminescent (Harvey, 1952), and the bioluminescent systems involved are perhaps identical or, at least, nearly the same. The bioluminescence of euphausiids is unusual in two aspects. Firstly, euphausiids are the only group that is known to contain photoproteins among numerous bioluminescent crustaceans; all other groups of luminous crustaceans, including decapods and ostracods, contain coelenterazine (a luciferin) or *Cypridina* luciferin plus a specific luciferase in their bioluminescence systems.

the second unusual point of euphausiid bioluminescence is the biochemical uniqueness of its luminescence system. The system requires two components, i.e., an organic compound of relatively small molecular size and a protein, in addition to molecular oxygen, thus resembling, at least superficially, the luciferin-luciferase system. In euphasiid bioluminescence, however, the organic compound acts as a catalyst in the luminescent oxidation of the protein component, as if the roles were reversed in a luciferin-luciferase system.

The purified photoprotein obtained from *Meganyctyphanes norvegica* contained two sizes of molecules (M_r 340 000 and 900 000). A compound having strong blue fluorescence extracted and purified from *M. norvegica* was designated 'F' (Shimomura & Johnson, 1967, 1968b). The same compound was also obtained from *Euphausia pacifica* recently (unpublished results). The solutions of the photoprotein and 'F' separately dissolved, are both very unstable and are spontaneously inactivated without light emission, even at 0 °C. Mixing of the photoprotein and 'F' in the presence of oxygen results in the emission of blue light (λ max 476 nm). the emission peak of the luminescence is identical to that of the fluorescence of 'F,' suggesting that 'F' is the light emitter of the bioluminescence. The quantum yield in reference to 'F' is over ten, and the values in reference to the photoprotein are 0·55 and 0·22 for the molecular species of M_r 900 000 and M_r 360 000, respectively.

The compound 'F' was found to be a novel type of bile pigment having a structure that is derived from chlorophyll rather than heme, although the complete structure is still unknown (Shimomura, 1980). No information is available at present concerning the chemical nature of the functional group of euphausiid photoprotein.

Luminodesmus photoprotein

This is the only example of photoprotein of terrestrial origin at present. The specimens of the millipede *Luminodesmus sequoiae* (Loomis & Davenport, 1951) emit light from their whole body continuously day and night, seemingly until they are dead. The photoprotein extracted and purified from this organism emits light (λ max 496 nm) when ATP and Mg^{2+} are added in the presence of O_2 (Hastings & Davenport, 1957; Shimomura, 1981). Thus, the luminescence system of *Luminodesmus* resembles that of the fireflies in requiring ATP and Mg^{2+} but differs in requiring only the photoprotein instead of the luciferin and luciferase that are required in the firefly system. The relative molecular mass of the photoprotein was found to be 104 000, which is close to the relative molecular mass of firefly luciferase (100 000). Although one may suspect, based on this information, that the photoprotein might be a complex of a firefly-type luciferase and firefly-type luciferin, firefly luciferin itself was not detected in this photoprotein. Recently, the presence of a porphyrin chromophore was reported in the photoprotein, but the role of this chromophore in the light-emitting reaction is not clear at present (Shimomura, 1984).

Extraction and purification of photoproteins

Photoproteins are usually highly reactive, unstable substances, like luciferins. They are easily lost by spontaneous light emission and various other causes. In isolating active photoproteins, it is important to pay special attention to prevent the loss of their activity. Compared to the isolation of luciferins, however, techniques available for isolating photoproteins are somewhat limited owing to their protein nature.

The basic principle is to extract a photoprotein with an aqueous solution and purify it by various means of protein purification, all under conditions that prevent luminescence and keep the photoprotein molecules intact. Namely, the luminescence system must be reversibly inhibited during the extraction and purification of a photoprotein. The method of reversible inhibition differs depending on the nature and cofactor requirement of the system. For example, the calcium chelator EDTA is used to inhibit the luminescence of the Ca^{2+}-activated photoproteins of coelenterates and ctenophores, such as aequorin, obelin and mnemiopsin (Shimomura *et al.*, 1962; Campbell, 1974; Hastings & Morin, 1968; Ward & Seliger, 1974a). To inhibit the luminescence systems of *Chaetopterus* and *Pholas*, the metal ion inhibitors 8-hydroxyquinoline and diethyldithiocarbamate, respectively, were used (Shimomura & Johnson, 1966; Henry & Monny, 1977).

The ionic strength and pH of buffers are also important, and these conditions should be chosen to optimize the yield of active photoprotein. The use of acidic buffers, pH 5·6–5·8, was very effective in suppressing spontaneous luminescence during the extraction of the photoproteins of euphasiids and *Luminodesmus* (Shimomura & Johnson, 1967,; Shimomura, 1981). In the extraction of the membrane photoprotein polynoidin, all easily soluble impurities were removed before the solubilization of the photoprotein with Triton X-100, thus making the use of an inhibitor unessential (Nicolas *et al.*, 1982)

Extraction of aequorin

Aequorin is the photoprotein that has been extracted most frequently and used most widely in various applications. In extracting aequorin from the jellyfish *Aequorea*, the first step is to cut off the circumferential margin of umbrella, making thin strips of 1–3 mm wide which are commonly called 'rings.' The rings can be cut efficiently using cutting devices (Johnson & Schimomura, 1978; Blinks, Mattingly, Jewell, van Leeuwen, Harrer & Allen, 1978) or, less efficiently, by scissors. The rings (about 0·5 g each) that contain photogenic organs are kept in cold sea water, and the rest of the bodies (average 50 g each) that contain no photogenic tissues are discarded, thus eliminating a large amount of impurities therein.

The rings are hand shaken vigorously with cold saturated $(NH_4)_2SO_4$ containing 50 mM-EDTA (Johnson & Shimomura, 1972) or with seawater (Blinks *et al.*, 1978) to dislodge photogenic particles from the rings. Then, the rings are removed by filtering through a net of Dacron or Nylon (50–100 mesh), and the photogenic particles suspending in the filtrate are collected in a cake of Celite on a Büchner funnel. The photogenic particles in the cake are cytolysed and aequorin therein is extracted by shaking with cold 50 mM-EDTA (pH 6·5). After filtration, crude aequorin is precipitated by saturation with $(NH_4)_2SO_4$.

It seems important here to compare the two methods of shaking rings mentioned above. Shaking rings in seawater will doubtlessly result in much cleaner crude extracts than is obtainable by shaking in saturated

$(NH_4)_2SO_4$ containing EDTA. On the other hand, saturated $(NH_4)_2SO_4$ considerably inhibits the luminescence response of the photogenic particles to mechanical stimulation such as shaking and stirring, and it also salts out and stabilizes aequorin that have leaked out from the particles, thus resulting in somewhat better yield of aequorin than that obtainable by shaking in seawater. Vigorously shaking over one litre of liquid by hand is not easy. This author has been using an electric cake mixer successfully for the past ten years to dislodge photogenic particles from the rings that are soaked in saturated $(NH_4)_2SO_4$ containing EDTA, instead of shaking by hand.

In regard to the purification of aequorin, Blinks *et al.* (1978) described a well-designed method for purifying an aequorin extract that has been obtained by the 'seawater shaking' method. The method included gel filtration on Sephadex G-50 and ion-exchange chromatography on DEAE-Sephadex A-50 and QAE-Sephadex A-50. The ion exchangers were effectively used to separate the green-fluorescent protein from aequorin. For the purification of the crude extract obtained by shaking rings in saturated $(NH_4)_2SO_4$, gel filtration on Sephadex G-75 or G-100 using buffers containing $1 \text{ M-}(NH_4)_2SO_4$ and not containing $(NH_4)_2SO_4$, and ion-exchange chromatography on DEAE-cellulose have been used (Johnson & Shimomura, 1972; Shimomura & Johnson, 1969, 1976). The green-fluorescent protein was separated from aequorin mainly on Sephadex G-75 or G-100 based on the property of aequorin to aggregate in the presence of $1 \text{ M-}(NH_4)_2SO_4$. Using Sephadex G-50 is not recommended, at least for the initial step, owing to the presence of a large amount of high relative molecular mass impurities in the extract obtained by shaking with saturated $(NH_4)_2SO_4$.

The luminescence of aequorin

Properties of aequorin

Aequorin is a conjugated protein having a relative molecular mass of approximately 20000 (Blinks *et al.*, 1976), and it contains a functional chromophore corresponding to roughly 2 % of the mass. A concentrated solution of aequorin is yellowish owing to its absorption peak (λ max about 460 nm) in addition to a protein absorption peak at 280 nm ($E^{1\%}_{cm}$ 27·0; Shimomura & Johnson, 1969). It is a mixture of isoproteins, containing several isomers (Blinks *et al.*, 1976). The isoelectric points of those isoproteins lie between 4·2 and 4·9 (Blinks & Harrer, 1975). The solubility of aequorin in aqueous buffers is generally greater than

30 mg/ml (Shimomura & Johnson, 1979b). Aequorin can be salted out from aqueous buffers with $(NH_4)_2SO_4$, although the salting out can be incomplete even after the complete saturation of $(NH_4)_2SO_4$ if the solutions contain 0·1 mg/ml or less of aequorin. One milligram of aequorin emits $4·3–4·5 \times 10^{15}$ photons at 25 °C when Ca^{2+} is added, at a quantum yield of 0·15 (Shimomura & Johnson, 1969, 1970, 1979b).

The stability of aequorin in the absence of Ca^{2+} varies widely depending upon such conditions as temperature, pH, concentrations of salts, and impurities. The effect of temperature is especially strong; aequorin in solutions, freeze-dried aequorin, and aequorin precipitated from saturated $(NH_4)_2SO_4$ are all satisfactorily stable at −75 °C or below, whereas all those forms of aequorin are rapidly inactivated at temperatures above 30 °C. The half-life of a sample of pure aequorin in 10 mM-EDTA (pH 6·5) at 25 °C was 7 days (Shimomura & Johnson, 1979b). According to the experience of this author, aequorin is most stable when precipitated with saturated $(NH_4)_2SO_4$.

Aequorin is non-fluorescent, except for a weak ultraviolet fluorescence due to its protein moiety. By Ca^{2+}-triggered luminescence reaction, one molecule of aequorin is turned into three different molecules, i.e., coelenteramide, CO_2 and apo-aequorin (Shimomura, Johnson & Morise, 1974; Shimomura & Johnson, 1975) as shown in Fig. 1. The apo-aequorin molecule can reversibly bind with the molecule of coelenteramide in the

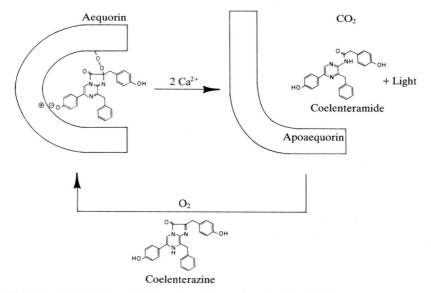

Fig. 1. A simplified schematic illustration of aequorin molecule and of its luminescence and regeneration reactions.

presence of Ca^{2+}, forming a complex that fluoresces in blue. The dissociation constant of the complex was found to be $3\cdot6 \times 10^{-6}$ at pH $7\cdot4$ at $25\,°C$ based on the relative molecular mass of the protein at $20\,000$ (Morise *et al.*, 1974). Thus, the bioluminescence reaction product of aequorin is usually blue-fluorescent, except when the concentrations of aequorin used are too low (much lower than $1\,\mu M$) to form the fluorescent complex. The blue fluorescence of the complex (λ max $470\,nm$) is spectrally indistinguishable from the bioluminescence emission of aequorin, giving a basis to the postulation that the fluorescent complex is the light emitter of aequorin bioluminescence (Shimomura & Johnson, 1970).

The log–plot of the luminescence intensity *versus* Ca^{2+}-concentration gives a sigmoid curve having a maximum slope of about 2 in low ionic-strength buffers not containing any inhibitor (Shimomura & Johnson, 1976; Shimomura & Shimomura, 1982), suggesting that two Ca^{2+} are required to trigger the luminescence of aequorin.

Regeneration of aequorin

Apo-aequorin can be reconstituted into aequorin by incubating with coelenterazine in the presence of O_2 and 2-mercaptoethanol, wherein the last chemical appears to protect the functional sulphydryl group of apo-aequorin during the course of the regeneration (Shimomura & Johnson, 1975). For the regeneration, there is no need to separate coelenteramide from apo-aequorin. In practice, the product of the luminescence reaction is incubated at $0–5\,°C$ in a buffer, pH $7\cdot5$, containing $5\,mM$-EDTA, $3\,mM$-2-mercaptoethanol and an excess of coelenterazine (at least $5\,\mu g/ml$ more than the calculated amount). The regeneration is usually $50\,\%$ complete within $30\,min$ and practically $100\,\%$ complete after $3\,h$.

A simplified model of the molecule of aequorin is shown in Fig. 1. Note that the protein conformation of aequorin is considerably more rigid and compact than that of apo-aequorin, reflecting the results obtained by the fluorescence polarization studies and the papain digestion of those proteins (La & Shimomura, 1982). The binding of oxygen to the carbon atom adjacent to the carbonyl group of coelenterazine moiety in aequorin has been recently confirmed by the C-13 nuclear magnetic resonance spectrometry (Kishi & Shimomura, unpublished results). Thus, a model previously presented (Hori *et al.* 1975; Cormier, 1978, 1981) in which aequorin contains one molecule of unsubstituted coelenterazine plus one molecule of O_2, both tightly bound to the protein part, needs to be revised.

When the regeneration reaction of apo-aequorin is carried out in the presence of an excess of free Ca^{2+}, instead of in $5\,mM$-EDTA, the result is a continuous, weak light emission from the reaction mixture. This weak luminescence lasts many hours. In contrast, the short, bright flash of aequorin in the presence of an excess of Ca^{2+} has the rate constants of $100-500 \sec^{-1}$ for the rise and $0\cdot6-1\cdot25 \sec^{-1}$ for the decay (Loschen & Chance, 1971; Hastings, Mitchell, Mattingly, Blinks & van Leeuwen, 1969). The weak luminescence in the presence of Ca^{2+} can be intensified several times by the addition of $0\cdot5\%$ diethylmalonate (Shimomura & Shimomura, 1981).

In the emission of the weak luminescence described above, apo-aequorin appears to be acting like an enzyme that catalyses the luminescent oxidation of coelenterazine. The mechanism involved might be a simple, straightforward one: aequorin is first formed, then it instantly reacts with Ca^{2+} to emit light. This simple mechanism, however, has no experimental support at present; the regeneration reaction of aequorin in the presence of EDTA was not activated by diethylmalonate, suggesting either that Ca^{2+} is needed in the activation by diethylmalonate or that aequorin is not an intermediate in the reaction mechanism of the weak luminescence in the presence of Ca^{2+} (Shimomura & Shimomura, 1981). Whatever the mechanism, apo-aequorin must be a highly unusual enzyme if it is an enzyme. Apo-aequorin has a turnover number of 1–2 per hour. (Shimomura & Johnson, 1976) and does not exist in nature independently.

Luminescence of aequorin

The luminescence of aequorin can be divided into three categories. The first category, by far the most important, is the luminescence triggered in aqueous solutions by certain metallic ions, especially by Ca^{2+} (Shimomura & Johnson, 1973; Blinks et al., 1976). Some lanthanides ions can efficiently trigger the luminescence, almost as strongly as Ca^{2+}. The only other metallic ions with significant activities are Sr^{2+}, Pb^{2+} and Cd^{2+}, all of which are, however, much weaker than Ca^{2+} in triggering the luminescence of aequorin. Thus, in the study of Ca^{2+} in biological systems, aequorin can be considered to be highly specific to Ca^{2+}.

The second category of aequorin luminescence is caused by various kinds of thiol-modification reagents, such as p-benzoquinone, Br_2, I_2, N-bromosuccinimide, N-ethylmaleimide, iodoacetic acid and p-hydroxy-mercuribenzoate (Shimomura et al., 1974). The luminescence is weak, but lasts for more than one hour. The quantum yields in this type of luminescence never exceed 15% of that of the Ca^{2+}-triggered luminescence. The luminescence is probably caused by spontaneous decomposition of the functional group of aequorin, i.e., coelenterazine peroxide, when an SH group that has been stabilizing the functional group is blocked with a thiol reagent (Shimomura *et al.*, 1974). To prevent this type of luminescence occurring in experiments using aequorin, any reagents that might react with an SH group should be avoided.

The third category of the luminescence is intrinsic to the molecules of aequorin. Luminescence of low levels can be detected from solutions of aequorin that have been made 'Ca^{2+} free' by using high concentrations of a Ca^{2+} chelator, such as EDTA or EGTA, and from aequorin precipitated by saturating with $(NH_4)_2SO_4$ and even from samples of freeze-dried aequorin. The light emission increases with rises in temperature, generally reaching the maximum intensity at around 60 °C. Suspending freeze-dried aequorin in various organic solvents also causes the intensity of the intrinsic luminescence to increase (Shimomura & Johnson, 1979b).

Inhibition of aequorin luminescence

All thiol-modification reagents, which cause weak, spontaneous luminescence of aequorin in the absence of Ca^{2+}, are in effect inhibitors in the Ca^{2+}-triggered luminescence of aequorin, owing to much lower quantum yields with the thiol reagents than with Ca^{2+} (see above).

Bisulphite, dithionite and p-dimethyaminobenzaldehyde are all strongly inhibitory even at micromolar concentrations (Shimomura *et al.*, 1962). It has been found that the functional group of aequorin, i.e., an oxygenated form of coelenterazine, decomposes without light emission when the photoprotein is treated with bisulphite or dithionite, being transformed into a hydroxy-coelenterazine or coelenterazine, respectively (Shimomura & Johnson, 1978).

EDTA and EGTA can inhibit the Ca^{2+}-triggered luminescence of aequorin in two ways. Firstly, the removal of free Ca^{2+} by chelation causes inhibition. Secondly, direct interaction between the molecules of aequorin and the free (unchelated) forms of these chelators causes inhibition (Shimomura & Shimomura, 1982; Ridgway & Snow, 1983). The second type of inhibition, previously unnoticed, is strong in solutions of low ionic strength, but is relatively weak in the presence of 0·1 M-KCl (Shimomura & Shimomura, 1984), presumably because aequorin is already inhibited with KCl. Therefore, attention must be paid if EDTA or EGTA is used in low-ionic-strength calcium buffers for measuring aequorin luminescence, especially when the total concentration of chelator is kept constant to make solutions of various pCa values, i.e., when a solution of lower Ca^{2+}-concentration contains a higher concentration of the free, inhibitory form of chelator.

At high concentrations (>50 mM) a number of inorganic and organic substances can inhibit the Ca^{2+}-triggered luminescence reaction of aequorin. Thus, KCl (100–150 mM) used in physiological buffers is inhibitory. Magnesium ions are inhibitory at millimolar concentrations, probably by competing with Ca^{2+} (cf. Blinks *et al.*, 1976).

Chemical modification of aequorin

Various protein-modification reagents for modifying primary amino groups tend to cause spontaneous light emission from aequorin, eventually resulting in a large, if not complete, loss of the luminescence activity. The effect observed resembles that of thiol-modification reagents, suggesting that the amino-modification agents probably react with the functional SH-groups instead of, or in addition to, the amino groups intended. Despite this difficulty, four kinds of modified aequorin that may be of use as calcium indicators have been prepared (Shimomura & Shimomura, unpublished results). The data on sensitivity to Ca^{2+} and on luminescence spectra of those modified proteins are included in Table 2.

All modified forms of aequorin are more sensitive to Ca^{2+} than is native aequorin. In the case of acetylated aequorin, the Ca^{2+}-sensitivity in reference to luminescence intensity can be as high as eight times that of native aequorin when measured in 1 mM-citrate buffer (low ionic strength), and about four times in a buffer containing 0·1 M-KCl. The emission spectrum is also affected by modification. Fluoroescein-aequorin, which emits yellow light apparently by an energy transfer, is of special interest for possible use in the quantitative assay of Ca^{2+} concentration.

Bioluminescence of living organisms
Green luminescence of coelenterates

The majority of live bioluminescent coelenterates emit green light, whereas the photoproteins isolated from them emit blue light. This is due to the presence of green-fluorescent proteins in the photophores of those organims (Morin & Hastings, 1971a, b). The green-fluorescent proteins of most coelenterates, including those of *Aequorea* and *Obelia*, fluoresce with an identical emission maximum at 508–509 nm (Morin & Hastings, 1971a; Cormier, Hori & Anderson, 1974; Herring, 1983). The only exception previously reported is the green-fluorescent protein of *Phialidium* which fluoresces with an emission maximum at 497 nm

(Levine & Ward, 1982). According to this author's recent, unpublished data, however, the green-fluorescent protein of *Halistaura* also fluoresces with an emission maximum at 496 nm, close to that of *Phialidium*.

In living organisms, it has been postulated that an efficient energy transfer takes place from the excited state of photoprotein light emitter to the molecule of a green-fluorescent protein (Morin & Hastings, 1971b) probably mostly by the Förster-type mechanism.

In the case of the bioluminescence of *Aequorea*, Morise, Shimomura, Johnson & Winant (1974) found that the photoprotein aequorin (M_r 20 000; bioluminescence quantum yield 0·15) and the green-fluorescent protein (fluorescence quantum yield 0·72) do not bind each other in solutions to cause an efficient, radiationless energy transfer between them. However, the same authors have demonstrated that, when the two proteins have been co-adsorbed on DEAE-cellulose or DEAE-Sephadex, an efficient energy transfer takes place upon addition of Ca^{2+} resulting in the emission of green light (quantum yield 0·15), and they suggested the involvement of a Förster-type mechanism in the *in vivo* luminescence of *Aequorea*. The radiationless energy transfer in *Aequorea* was not fully supported by Cormier (1978) and Ward (1979). Cormier found it unlikely because no increase in photon yield had been observed. This argument is not convincing, however, because a radiationless energy transfer need not always increase a quantum yield. Ward stated that, regardless of the mechanism, *in vivo* energy transfer is likely to be very efficient in the presence of a high concentration of green-fluorescent protein (5–10 %), but failed to mention that a considerable distortion of the emission spectrum is also likely to occur if the transfer occurs mostly by radiative mechanism.

Control mechanisms of in vivo *luminescence*

The mechanism of triggering light by stimulation in living animals is complicated. The discussion below is limited to only the immediate step of triggering light-emitting reactions.

The light flashes of coelenterates and ctenophores are almost certainly caused by the free Ca^{2+} that is released in the photophores by various causes of stimulation. The spontaneous luminescence of the millipede *Luminodesmus* is probably controlled by the supply of ATP.

Regarding the luminescence systems of *Pholas* and scale worms, it has been postulated that the immediate reactants to trigger the light emission of the photoproteins are O_2^- (superoxide radical) or another activated oxygen species, in addition to O_2 (Michelson, 1978; Nicolas *et al.*, 1982).

It seems reasonable to adopt this postulation for the luminescence system of *Chaetopterus* which is similar to those of *Pholas* and scale worms in cofactor requirements. It must be noted here, however, that the requirement of two oxygen species, i.e., O_2^- and O_2, probably means two steps of reaction in each system. If so, one of the oxygen species must not be the immediate reactant of the light-emitting reaction. Further details of the reaction mechanisms are needed to clarify this point.

The bioluminescence system of euphausiid shrimps, i.e., a photoprotein system, resembles that of dinoflagellates, i.e., luciferin–luciferase system, in at least two aspects. Compound 'F' of the former system and the luciferin of the latter are structurally similar bile pigments derived from chlorophylls (Shimomura, 1980; Dunlap, Hastings & Shimomura, 1981), and these two systems can be cross reacted (Dunlap, Hastings & Shimomura, 1980). Both systems are extremely pH sensitive. The luminescence of a mixture of euphausiid photoprotein and 'F' is caused by a slight increase of alkalinity (Shimomura & Johnson, 1967), and a dark mixture of the luciferin and luciferase of dinoflagellate can be made luminous by a slight increase of acidity (Hastings, 1978). Thus, pH is probably the factor that controls the *in vivo* luminescence of those systems. Possibly, pH is also the controlling factor in the reactivation of photoinactivated mnemiopsin in the ctenophore *Mnemiopsis* (Anctil & Shimomura, 1984).

Functions of photoproteins

The most special and obvious characteristic of photoproteins is the capability of emitting light. The light emission from the bodies of organisms, or sometimes from their secretions, possibly has important biological roles, and this subject has been discussed in detail by Buck (1978). Photoprotein systems may also have biochemical functions in addition to the emission of light, but our present knowledge concerning this subject is limited.

It has been postulated, as already noted, that the bioluminescence systems of *Pholas*, *Chaetopterus* and scale worms require O_2^- in addition to O_2 in their light-emitting reactions. If the involvement of O_2^- is firmly proved, then the luminescence reaction in those systems can be considered a process of detoxication.

The photoproteins of coelenterates and ctenophores contain an oxygenated form of coelenterazine as their functional groups. Coelenterazine was found in a wide variety of bioluminescent marine organisms, including shrimps, squids, fishes and coelenterates, as the luciferin of their bioluminescence systems, and a food-chain relationship involving this compound has been suggested (Cormier, 1978; Shimomura, Inoue, Johnson & Haneda, 1980). Coelenterazine was also found in some types of non-bioluminescent shrimps and fishes very recently (unpublished data). Based on these findings, it seems probably that the coelenterazine in various marine organisms has a more general, fundamental role than the emission of light.

The author is grateful for research support by the National Science Foundation and the National Institutes of Health.

References

ANCTIL, M. & SHIMOMURA, O. (1984). Mechanism of photoinactivation and re-activation in the bioluminescence system of the ctenophore *Mnemiopsis*. *Biochem. J.* **221**, 269–272.

ASHLEY, C. C. & CAMPBELL, A. K., Eds. (1979). *Detection and Measurement of Free Ca^{2+} in Cells*, 461 pages, Amsterdam: Elsevier/North-Holland Biomedical Press.

BLINKS, J. R. & HARRER, G. C. (1975). Multiple forms of the calcium-sensitive bioluminescent protein aequorin. *Fedn. Proc. Fedn Am. Socs. exp. Biol.* **34**, 474.

BLINKS, J. R., PRENDERGAST, F. G. & ALLEN, D. G. (1976). Photoproteins as biological calcium indicators. *Pharmac. Rev.* **28**, 1–93.

BLINKS, J. R., MATTINGLY, P. H., JEWELL, B. R., VAN LEEUWEN, M., HARRER, G. C. & ALLEN, D. G. (1978). Practical aspects of the use of aequorin as a calcium indicator: assay, preparation, microinjection, and interpretation of signals. *Methods in Enzymology* **57**, 292–328.

BUCK, J. B. (1978). Functions and evolutions of bioluminescence. In *Bioluminescence in Action* (ed. Herring, P. J.), pp. 419–460, London: Academic Press.

CAMPBELL, A. K. (1974). Extraction, partial purification and properties of obelin, the calcium-activated luminescent protein from the hydroid *Obelia geniculata. Biochem. J.* **143**, 411–418.

CAMPBELL, A. K., HALLETT, M. B., DAW, R. A., RYALL, M. E. T., HART, R. C. & HERRING, P. J. (1981). Application of the photoprotein obelin to the measurement of free Ca^{2+} in cells. In *Bioluminescence and Chemiluminescence (eds)* Deluca, M. A. & McElroy, W. D.), pp. 601–607. New York: Academic Press.

CORMIER, M. J. (1978). Comparative biochemistry of animal systems. In *Bioluminescence in Action* (ed. Herring, P. J.), pp. 75–108, London: Academic Press.

CORMIER, M. J. (1981). *Renilla* and *Aequorea* bioluminescence. In *Bioluminescence and Chemiluminescence* (eds. DeLuca, M. A. & McElroy, W. D.), pp. 225–233, New York: Academic Press.

CORMIER, M. J., HORI, K. & ANDERSON, J. M. (1974). Bioluminescence in coelenterates. *Biochem. biophys. Acta* **346**, 137–164.

DUBOIS, R. (1887). Note sur la fonction photogenique chez le *Pholas dactylus. C. r.Séanc. Soc. Biol.* **39**, 564–566.

DUNLAP, J. C., HASTINGS, J. W. & SHIMOMURA, O. (1980). Crossreactivity between the light-emitting systems of distantly related organisms: novel type of light-emitting compound. *Proc. Natn. Acad. Sci., USA* **77**, 1394–1397.

DUNLAP, J. C., HASTINGS, J. W. & SHIMOMURA, O. (1981). Dinoflagellate luciferin is structurally related to chlorophyll. *FEBS Lett.* **135**, 273–276.

FRESNEAU, C., ARRIO, B., LECUYER, B., DUPAIX, A., LESCURE, N. & VOLFIN, P. (1984). The fluorescent product of scale worm bioluminescence reaction: an *in vitro* study. *Photochem. Photobiol.* **39**, 255–261.

HARVEY, E. N. (1952). *Bioluminescence*, 649 pages, New York, Academic Press.

HASTINGS, J. W. (1978). Bacterial and dinoflagellate luminescent systems. In *Bioluminescence in Action* (ed. Herring, P. J.), pp. 129–170, London: Academic Press.

HASTINGS, J. W. (1983). Biological diversity, chemical mechanisms, and the evolutionary origins of bioluminescent systems. *J. molec. Evolution* **19**, 309–321.

HASTINGS, J. W. & DAVENPORT, D. (1957). The luminescence of the millipede, *Luminodesmus sequoiae. Biol. Bull. mar. biol. Lab., Woods Hole* **113**, 120–128.

HASTINGS, J. W. & GIBSON, Q. H. (1963). Intermediates in the bioluminescent oxidation of reduced flavin mononucleotide. *J. biol. Chem.* **238**, 2537–2554.

HASTINGS, J. W. & MORIN, G. M. (1968). Calcium activated bioluminescent proteins from ctenophores (*Mnemiopsis*) and colonial hydroids (*Obelia*). *Biol. Bull. mar. bid. Lab., Woods Hole* **135**, 422.

HASTINGS, J. W. & NEALSON, K. H. (1977). Bacterial luminescence. *A. Rev. Microbiol.* **31**, 549–595.

HASTINGS, J. W., MITCHELL, G., MATTINGLY, P. H., BLINKS, J. R. & VAN LEEUWEN, M. (1969). Response of aequorin bioluminescence to rapid changes in calcium concentration. *Nature* **222**, 1047–1050.

HENRY, J. P. & MICHELSON, A. M. (1973). Studies in bioluminescence. VIII. Chemically induced luminescence of *Pholas dactylus* luciferin. *Biochimie* **55**, 75–81.

HENRY, J. P. & MONNY, C. (1977). Protein-protein interaction in the *Pholas dactylus* system of bioluminescence. *Biochemistry* **16**, 2517–2525.

HERRING, P. J. (1983). The spectral characteristics of luminous marine organisms. *Proc. R. Soc. Lond.* B**220**, 183–217.

HORI, K., ANDERSON, J. M., WARD, W. W. & CORMIER, M. J. (1975). *Renilla* luciferin as the substrate for calcium induced photoprotein bioluminescence. *Biochemistry* **14**, 2371–2376.

JOHNSON, F. H. & SHIMOMURA, O. (1972). Preparation and use of aequorin for rapid microdetermination of Ca^{2+} in biological systems. *Nature New Biol* **237**, 287–288.

JOHNSON, F. H. & SHIMOMURA, O. (1978). Introduction to the bioluminescence of medusae, with special reference to the photoprotein aequorin. *Methods in Enzymology* **57**, 271–291.

LA, S. Y. & SHIMOMURA, O. (1982). Fluorescence polarization study of the Ca^{2+}-sensitive photoprotein aequorin. *FEBS Lett.* **143**, 49–51.

LEVINE, L. D. & WARD, W. W. (1982). Isolation and characterization of a photoprotein, "phialidin," and a spectrally unique green-fluorescent protein from the bioluminescent jellyfish *Phialidium gregarium. Comp. Biochem. Physiol.* **72B**, 77–85.

LOOMIS, H. F. & DAVENPORT, D. (1951). A luminescent new xystodesmid milliped from California. *J. Wash. Acad. Sci.* **41**, 270–272.

LOSCHEN, G. & CHANCE, B. (1971). Rapid kinetic studies of the light-emitting protein aequorin. *Nature New Biol.* **233**, 273–274.

MICHELSON, A. M. (1978). Purification and properties of *Pholas dactylus* Luciferin and luciferase. *Methods in Enzymology* **57**, 385–406.

MORIN, J. G. & HASTINGS, J. W. (1971a). Biochemistry of the bioluminescence of colonial hydroids and other coelenterates. *J. cell. Physiol.* **77**, 305–311.

MORIN, J. G. & HASTINGS, J. W. (1971b). Energy transfer in a bioluminescent system. *J. cell. Physiol.* **77**, 313–318.

MORISE, H., SHIMOMURA, O., JOHNSON, F. H. & WINANT, J. (1974). Intermolecular energy transfer in the bioluminescent system of *Aequorea. Biochemistry* **13**, 2656–2662.

NICOLAS, M.-T., BASSOT, J.-M. & SHIMOMURA, O. (1982). Polynoidin: a membrane photoprotein isolated from the bioluminescent system of scale-worms. *Photochem. Photobiol.* **35**, 201–207.

RIDGWAY, E. B. & SNOW, A. E. (1983). Effects of EGTA on aequorin luminescence. *Biophys. J.* **41**, 244a.

SHIMOMURA, O. (1980). Chlorophyll-derived bile pigment in bioluminescent euphausiids. *FEBS Lett.* **116**, 203–206.

SHIMOMURA, O. (1981). A new type of ATP-activated bioluminescent system in the millipede *Luminodesmus sequoiae*. *FEBS Lett.* **128**, 242–244.

SHIMOMURA, O. (1982). Mechanism of bioluminescence. In *Chemical and Biological Generation of Excited States* (eds Adam, W. & Cilento, G.), pp. 249–276, New York: Academic Press.

SHIMOMURA, O. (1984). Porphyrin chromophore in *Luminodesmus* photoprotein. *Comp. Biochem. Physiol.* **79B**, 565–567.

SHIMOMURA, O. & JOHNSON, F. H. (1966). Partial purification and properties of the *Chaetopterus* luminescence system. In *Bioluminescence in Progress* (eds Johnson, F. H. & Haneda, Y.), pp. 495–521, Princeton, New Jersey: Princeton University Press.

SHIMOMURA, O. & JOHNSON, F. H. (1967). Extraction, purification and properties of the bioluminescence system of the euphausiid shrimp *Meganyctiphanes norvegica*. *Biochemistry* **6**, 2293–2306.

SHIMOMURA, O. & JOHNSON, F. H. (1968a). Chaetopterus photoprotein: crystallization and cofactor requirements for bioluminescence. *Science* **159**, 1239–1240.

SHIMOMURA, O. & JOHNSON, F. H. (1968b). Light-emitting molecule in a new photoprotein type of luminescence system from the euphausiid shrimp *Meganyctiphanes norvegica*. *Proc. Natn. Acad. Sci., U.S.A.* **59**, 475–477.

SHIMOMURA, O. & JOHNSON, F. H. (1969). Properties of the bioluminescent protein aequorin. *Biochemistry* **8**, 3991–3997.

SHIMOMURA, O. & JOHNSON, F. H. (1970). Calcium binding, quantum yield, and emitting molecule in aequorin bioluminescence. *Nature* **227**, 1356–1357.

SHIMOMURA, O. & JOHNSON, F. H. (1973). Further data on the specificity of aequorin luminescence. *Biochem. biophys. Res. Commun.* **53**, 490–494.

SHIMOMURA, O. & JOHNSON, F. H. (1975). Regeneration of the photoprotein aequorin. *Nature* **256**, 236–238.

SHIMOMURA, O. & JOHNSON, F. H. (1976). Calcium-triggered luminescence of the photoprotein aequorin. *Soc. exp. Biol. Symp.* **30**, 41–54.

SHIMOMURA, O. & JOHNSON, F. H. (1978). Peroxidized coelenterazine, the active group in the photoprotein aequorin. *Proc. Natn. Acad. Sci., U.S.A.* **75**, 2611–2615.

SHIMOMURA, O. & JOHNSON, F. H. (1979a). Comparison of the amounts of key components in the bioluminescence systems of various coelenterates. *Comp. Biochem. Physiol.* **64B** 105–107.

SHIMOMURA, O. & JOHNSON, F. H. (1979b). Chemistry of the calcium-sensitive photoprotein aequorin. In *Detection and Measurement of Free Ca^{2+} in Cells* (eds Ahsley, C. C. & Campbell, A. K.), pp. 73–83, Amsterdam: Elsevier/North-Holland Biomedical Press.

SHIMOMURA, O., INOUE, S., JOHNSON, F. H. & HANEDA, Y. (1980). Widespread occurrence of coelenterazine in marine bioluminescence. *Comp. Biochem. Physiol.* **65B**, 435–437.

SHIMOMURA, O., JOHNSON, F. H. & MORISE, H. (1974). Mechanism of the luminescent intramolecular reaction of aequorin. *Biochemistry* **13**, 3278–3286.

SHIMOMURA, O., JOHNSON, F. H. & SAIGA, Y. (1962). Extraction, purification and properties of aequorin, a bioluminescent protein from the luminous hydromedusan, *Aequorea. J. cell. comp. Physiol.* **59**, 223–240.

SHIMOMURA, O., JOHNSON, F. H. & SAIGA, Y. (1963). Extraction and properties of halistaurin, a bioluminescent protein from the hydromedusan *Halistaura. J. cell. comp. Physiol.* **62**, 9–16.

SHIMOMURA, O. & SHIMOMURA, A. (1981). Resistivity to denaturation of the apoprotein of aequorin and reconstitution of the luminescent photoprotein from the partially denatured apoaequorin. *Biochem. J.* **199**, 825–828.

SHIMOMURA, O. & SHIMOMURA, A. (1982). EDTA-binding and acylation of the Ca^{2+}-sensitive photoprotein aequorin. *FEBS Lett.* **138**, 201–204.

SHIMOMURA, O. & SHIMOMURA, A. (1984). Effect of calcium chelators on the Ca^{2+}-dependent luminescence of aequorin. *Biochem. J.* **221**, 907–910.

WARD, W. W. (1979). Energy transfer in bioluminescence. *Photochem. Photobiol. Rev.* **4**, 1–57.

WARD, W. W. & SELIGER, H. H. (1974a). Extraction and purification of calcium-activated photoproteins from the ctenophores *Mnemiopsis* sp. and *Beroe ovata. Biochemistry*, **13**, 1491–1499.

WARD, W. W. & SELIGER, H. H. (1974b). Properties of Mnemiopsin and Berovin, calcium-activated photoproteins from the ctenophores *Mnemiopsis* sp. and *Beroe ovata. Biochemistry* **13**, 1500–1510.

WARD, W. W. & SELIGER, H. H. (1976). Action spectrum and quantum yield for the photoinactivation of mnemiopsin, a bioluminescent photoprotein from the ctenophore *Mnemiopsis. Photochem. Photobiol.* **23**, 351–363.

Printed in Great Britain © Society of Experimental Biology 1985

ASPECTS OF PHOTORECEPTION IN AQUATIC ENVIRONMENTS

J. N. LYTHGOE

Department of Zoology, Bristol University, Woodland Road, Bristol BS8 1UG

Summary

Photoreceptors are found in several different parts of the body in addition to the eyes, and as in the eyes, rhodopsin may be one of the photopigments responsible. Visual photoreceptors are photon counters, but at low light levels it is uncertain exactly when and where a photon will arrive. Thus a basic problem of vision is statistical and the maximum number of photons must be sampled to get statistically reliable information about visual contrasts, detail and movement. Sample size can be increased by extending the retinal integration time or the integration area, but this carries the cost of reduced ability to see detail and to resolve moving images. For scotopic vision the spectral absorption of visual pigment may be arranged to maximize sensitivity without greatly increasing physiological noise which reduces the perception of contrast. Photopic vision is usually mediated by from two to four cone types containing different visual pigments which allow the possibility of colour vision. Natural waters differ greatly in colour, and influence both the photopic visual pigments possessed by fishes and their coloration.

The functions of light-sensitive systems

In their simplest form photoreceptors merely record the presence of light, yet even this can be very useful to an animal. Because the succession of night and day is the archetype of regular timekeeping, animals can use light to regulate the processes that bring their bodily functions into a state that anticipates the requirements of the time of day and of the season. Even a crude sensitivity to light enables animals that have no visual sense themselves to know if they are vulnerable to sighted predators. By being aware of the changes of light intensity with time, simple photoreceptors that have no form vision, are able to detect a shadow moving across them that might betray the presence of a predator.

Vision itself is one of the most important of the senses, although being so dependent on it ourselves, we probably overestimate its importance to animals in general. Like any sense, its potential is set by the properties of the physical system that mediates it, but the part of the electromagnetic spectrum that we see as light has some important characteristics that make it an unusually good carrier of information. Light travels so fast that the time delay between an event and its representation as a retinal image is minimal and it travels in straight lines so that the retinal image is an accurate representation of the outside scene. The wavelength of light is short which means that the image carries fine spatial detail, and the range of wavelengths within the visible waveband coupled to the fact that different surfaces do not absorb all wavelengths equally make colour vision a useful sense.

The distribution of visual pigments in light-sensitive systems

The main pigments mediating vision in both vertebrate and invertebrate eyes are based on opsin proteins conjugated to a chromophore group of either retinol (rhodopsins), or dehydroretinol (porphyropsins). Another pigment, retinochrome also appears to play a part in vision in cephalopods (for a review see Knowles & Dartnall 1977). On the basis of immunohistochemical studies it is also known that the pineal of fishes, amphibia, reptiles and birds contain opsin-based light-sensitive pigments (Vigh, Vigh-Teichmann, Rohlich & Aros 1982). They are also present in the light-sensitive iridophores in the skin of at least one fish, the Neon tetra (Lythgoe, Shand & Foster 1984). Action spectra obtained by measuring morphological, electrical or hormonal changes, suggest that visual pigments are also present in the melanophores of larval Lamprey (Young 1935), Hag (Steven 1955) and *Xenopus* skin (Lythgoe & Thompson 1984), but it should be borne in mind that action spectra are a notoriously insecure basis for characterizing the underlying photoreceptor. Extraretinal photoreceptors are also known in many other animals (for reviews see Menecker 1977, Wolken & Mogus 1979, Weber 1983, Lythgoe 1980). Perhaps the best characterized extraretinal sense is the dermal light sense of echinoderms (Millott 1968, Gras & Weber 1983). For example, the sea urchin *Centrostephanus longispinus* has melanophores that can be isolated and change shape from ovoid to stellate when illuminated. They have a maximum sensitivity between 430 and 450 nm, and it is interesting that this blue-sensitivity is typical of the non-visual light senses of many different animals from widely different phyla (Shropshire 1980) although this is difficult to explain in relation to the spectral distribution of the environmental light.

The mode of action of visual pigments

Visual pigment molecules form an integral part of the plasma membranes of invertebrate retinular cells and vertebrate rod and cone outer segments. In the living eye most of the visual pigment molecules are in the 11-cis configuration, but when a photon is absorbed by a molecule it isomerizes to the all-trans form. In a process that is not fully understood this leads to the mobilization of a cascade of Ca^{2+}ions that block Na^+ channels in the outer segments and hence alter the polarity of the cell, and initiate a nerve impulse (for a review see Knowles & Dartnall 1977). In the vertebrate rod it only requires about 10 photons to be absorbed by a group of perhaps 300 rods within about 0·1 seconds for a visual sensation to be produced (Pirenne 1967, Ripps & Weale 1976). Visual pigments therefore act as photon counters, and at this level the basic information for vision is digital.

Light underwater

The number of reviews on light underwater possibly outnumber the investigations they describe. It therefore seems more sensible to refer the reader to some of the reviews that are already published (Jerlov 1976, Tyler & Smith 1970, Lythgoe 1979) rather than to add to their number here. One problem is that the measurements required to make reliable predictions on underwater vision are difficult and expensive and at the time of writing there seems to be no set of data that provides quantities for all the variables required to complete a set of calculations on through-water vision, even though we are reasonably sure what those variables are (Duntley 1962, 1963).

When daylight reaches the water surface, some is reflected back and the rest penetrates underwater. The more oblique the angle of incidence of the light, the more is reflected back and the less passes through the interface. Within the top 10 m or so in clear water, the lens-like action of the waves directs sunlight into a series of bright shafts, which form a ripple pattern of bright light on horizontal surfaces underwater (McFarland & Loew 1983), although on an overcast day these ripples are not visible. To depths of at least 50 m in clear water a diver looking upwards can see the circular 'Snells window' which subtends an angle of about 98° and into which the entire above-water hemisphere is compressed. Snells window subtends the same angle at all depths, but beneath about 50 m it becomes indistinct and then lost due to the forward scattering action of the water. This is only true of clear water as may be found in the Mediterranean and clear tropical oceans.

In most inshore and inland waters scattering by suspended particles in the water is much greater and the structure of the underwater light distribution is much less affected by the optics of the air–water interface.

Beneath the optically complex layer near the surface, the diffuse downwelling light becomes attenuated in an exponential fashion. This downwelling light is composed of both direct unscattered light and light that has been scattered by suspended particles and the water molecules themselves. It is only the unscattered light that is capable of forming an image, so that any mathematical model of underwater vision has to include both the attenuation coefficient for a broad beam of light which includes both scattered and unscattered light, and the narrow beam attenuation coefficient which includes only unscattered, image–forming light. As the distance between eye and object increases, so diffuse, non-image forming light is scattered from the intervening water mass into the eye forming a veil of brightness that effectively reduces visual contrasts. When the radiance presented by the object is sufficiently close to that presented by the water background that the eye can no longer distinguish it, the object becomes invisible, (Duntley 1962, 1963; Lythgoe 1979). The background radiance itself depends upon the angular direction of view. The background light looking in the upward direction can be at least 100 times brighter than when looking directly downwards, and about 20 brighter than when looking horizontally through the water (Jerlov, 1976).

Pure water is most transparent to blue light of wavelength between about 470 and 490 nm. At the longwave end of the spectrum, almost all red light above about 600 nm is absorbed within about 25 m of the surface. At the shortwave end u.v. light is also rapidly attenuated, and the near u.v. of wavelength near 350 nm is mostly absorbed within the top 60 m. The result is that below the surface 60–100 m or so the visually useful daylight spectrum is limited to the blue and green parts of the spectrum. However much water is not pure and blue, for it contains green phytoplankton, the yellow products of vegetable decay both of marine and terrestrial origin, and different coloured silts and sands carried in suspension. According to the concentration and composition of these various impurities, natural water can vary from the blue of the open oceans, through the green of much inshore and productive waters, to the yellow green, brown and even red of very peaty fresh water.

Photons and vision

The fact that photons are delivered in discrete packages of energy called photons points to the direct relationship between brightness, acuity, contrast and the perception of moving objects. The reason is that photoreceptors are photon counters, and the problems of vision can be approached by considering how large a sample of photons needs to be collected to make reliable judgements about the nature of the outside world (Snyder, Laughlin & Stavenga 1977, Barlow 1981, Land 1981). As in any statistical problem large differences between populations can be detected by relatively few samples, whereas small differences require much larger samples. Put into visual terms this means that it requires good light to see fine detail, moving objects, subtle gradations of grey and brightness, and an efficient optical system for forming a bright image on the retina.

Contrast

In a situation where two areas of the retinal image differ only in brightness, the brighter of the two areas receives more photons per unit area and unit time than the darker area. However it is not possible to predict exactly where and when each photon will be delivered, or indeed if any particular photon will be absorbed by the photoreceptor, or pass through unaltered. Using the Poisson distribution Land (1981) has calculated the sample size required to discriminate two areas of different brightness at various probability levels between 80 and 90 %, and it is clear that for an eye such as the human, contrast perception begins to fall away quite markedly even around sunset, and on a starlit night, the eye has difficulty in discriminating 20 % differences in brightness, compared to a less than 1 % difference in good light.

Sensitivity

Within the present context, sensitivity is taken as the proportion of photons that arrive in the vicinity of the animal that are absorbed and contribute to a visual signal. The photon catch can be increased in several ways. First the optics of the eye can be designed so that the image is as bright as possible. For point sources of light against a dark background (a situation that might describe the experience of a deep-sea fish), sensitivity is proportional to the pupil aperture, A. When there are more extended light areas, as there are in almost every other visual situation, the brightness of the image is A/f, where f is the focal length. A/f is the well-known f number of photographers, but applies as well to eye design. Fish are particularly interesting because most have round lenses of refractive index of about 1·65. Thus the ratio of lens diameter to focal length tends to be about the same for all species (this is Mathessons ratio and is 2·55), and gives them a minimum f number of about ·78, compared to an f number for man of about 2·1 with pupil dilated, and ·89 for the cat (see Land 1981; Lythgoe 1980 for reviews). Just as it is uncertain exactly where a photon will arrive, it is also uncertain exactly when. However, the longer the time period over which photons are collected, the larger will be the sample size, and the finer the contrast discriminations that can be made. Of course the snag is that if the collecting period (the Integration Time) is very long, the retinal image will have changed because either the object of interest, or the observer, or both have moved, so that elements of the retinal image that are in motion will not be discriminated. There is always a compromise between very short integration times giving good vision for moving objects (insects for example tend towards this solution), and a long integration time that tends to give good spatial and contrast vision in dim light, provided the retinal image is not changing too rapidly. This is the solution that one would expect of ambush predators which would tend to be most successful in dim light. The integration time has been directly measured in few animals besides man, but it is related to the flicker fusion frequency, which is the frequency that a flashing light can just be distinguished from a continuous one.

Flicker fusion frequencies are considerably higher in bright light than they are in dim. Man is a typical vertebrate in this respect having a flicker fusion frequency that varies from about 50 Hz in bright light to as little as 20 Hz in dim light near the periphery of the field of view (Tansley 1965). McFarland & Loew (1983) and Protasov (1970) have listed the critical fusion frequencies for a number of fishes. They range from 87 Hz for some active diurnal teleosts, to only 7 Hz for sharks in dim light. Apart from fishes few other marine animals have been investigated. *Octopus* and *Limulus* have critical fusion frequencies of 70 and 15 respectively in bright light, but there seem to be no data for dim light. Perhaps slow-moving nocturnal animals that feed by browsing or grazing, or that ambush slow-moving prey, have slower than average retinal integration times, because the retinal image will be relatively stationary, and they can sacrifice the perception of moving objects for increased sensitivity.

For non-visual photoreceptor systems a fast integration time allows transient changes in brightness to be detected. This should be useful for marine animals that need to detect a sudden decrease in illumination that may indicate a predatory animal swimming overhead. The dermal photoreceptors in sea urchins, or the photoreceptors of feather-duster worms may come into this category. However non-visual photoreceptors do not always need to detect transient changes in illumination, especially if their function is to serve the mechanisms that control circadian activity or breeding cycle with the seasons, or indeed merely to signal that an animal has successfully hidden itself in the substrate. For mechanisms like these it may make sense to increase sensitivity by increasing the integration time rather than by increasing receptor pigment concentrations or by increasing the receptor area. There are not yet many examples to quote. Integration times of 120 mins in the hypothalmus receptor in the quail that controls the hormone levels that lead to gonad development have been measured by Follett & Milette (1982). In the Hagfish, which appears to use its dermal photoreceptors to sense whether it is buried in the substrate, there are integration times of 1–4 mins. (Newth & Ross 1955, Steven, 1955).

Acuity

The finest detail that any eye can resolve depends ultimately on the number of photons that go to form the retinal image, and upon the wavelength of light. In almost all visual situations under water, except possibly near the surface in daylight, it is probably the number of photons that limits the quality of the retinal image. As has been described above, a large photon sample size is required to make fine contrast discriminations, and this requires a long integration time (with the consequential loss of moving images). It also requires larger image elements to be sampled in order to increase the photon sample size, and this has to mean that fine detail is lost. Enlarging the area of the image elements can either be achieved anatomically or neurally. The cones of many ambush predator fishes appear to be larger than for other fish, and it may also be that the double or triple cones in many teleost retinas are designed to maximize the photon-catching area. More obvious examples are to be found in the grouped rods of some deep-sea fish where a bundle of rods that can scarcely be optically insulated from each other are enclosed in a mirror-like tapetal cup (Lockett 1977).

Other devices for maximizing photon catch also tend to reduce acuity. For example, ordinary tapeta that are designed to reflect back light that has already made one pass of the photoreceptors, so that there is a second chance to absorb photons, will reduce acuity because of the optical imperfections of the system. The same may well be true of the layered retina of several deep-sea fishes and more shallow-living nocturnal species such as the conger and squirrel and soldier fishes. In these retinas there are several layers of rods giving a much better chance that photons will be absorbed, but almost certainly at the expense of acuity. An increased integration area may also be achieved neurally, by arranging that the signal from many rods may synapse on a single ganglion cell (Walls 1942; Tansley 1965; Rodieck 1973).

Wavelength and vision

Sensitivity

The familiar bell-shaped spectral absorbance curve of the visual pigments has the obvious consequence that photons delivered at some wavelengths are more likely to be absorbed than at others (Knowles & Dartnall 1977). It follows that a visual pigment that absorbs maximally at wavelengths where photons are most plentiful will give the greatest sensitivity. For some photoreceptor systems it is sufficient to detect solely the presence of light, but in visual systems the animal needs to wrest the maximum amount of information from the retinal image. An efficient photon-capturing system is useful because it helps to increase the number of photons that go to make up an image, and hence to increase the amount of spatial, temporal and contrast information that the neural retina and brain can glean from it.

There is now a considerable body of information about the way that the visual pigments of both vertebrate and invertebrates adapt to the spectral quality of the underwater light climate (Goldsmith 1972, Menzel 1975, Suzuki 1984, for invertebrates; Lythgoe 1980 for a review of vertebrates). In summary the rod visual pigments do show a tendency to match their spectral sensitivity curve to the colour of the ambient light. The match is near perfect in the homochromatic blue waters of the oceanic mesopelagic zone and deeper, but as the water becomes more stained with chlorophyll and the yellow products of vegetable decay, the match becomes progressively less good. It is also interesting to note that the scotopic visual pigments in the rods of our own eyes with a maximum absorbance at 498 nm are considerably too blue-sensitive to match the spectral quality of the night sky. Indeed in this respect the most red sensitive of our three cone types, with an absorbance maximum of 564 nm, would be the more suitable for nocturnal vision (Dartnall 1975).

The apparent paradox that animals often possess visual pigments that do not confer the greatest possible sensitivity in the prevailing light climate may be partly explained by considering the quality of information provided by the retinal image. Contrast is defined as $T-B/B$ where T is the number of photons absorbed from one element of the image, and B is the number absorbed from surrounding elements. The greater the difference between (T–B) and B, the smaller B needs to be for a statistic-ally significant difference between B and (T–B) to be registered. Contrasts are often reduced when both T and B are increased by the addition of non-image-forming light, N. In this case contrasts are reduced to (T–B)/(B+N). Non-image-forming light is familiar to us the light scattered from suspended water droplets on a foggy day, or by light reflected back into our eyes by net curtains hanging at a window. Under-water scattered veiling light is a major reason why visibility is almost always less than 40 m underwater, and frequently less than 1 m.

There may be an equivalent situation at the visual pigment level if the occasional visual pigment molecule undergoes a chemically induced rather than a light-induced isomerization from the 11-cis to the all-trans form. Some substances known to be present in the rod outer segment membranes are known to induce this isomerization which would lead to a spurious visual signal. The chromophore group is normally protected from isomerizing substances by being embedded within the opsin molecule. But in the vertebrate eye (although not in invertebrates) a chromophore that has undergone the light-induced 11-cis to all-trans isomerization has to move from its bed within the opsin molecule to pigment epithelium that surrounds the outer segment, there to be enzymically re-isomerized back to the 11-cis form, and then re-embedded within the opsin molecule. The speculation is that cones, which need to replenish the 11-cis retinal faster than the rods require an easier passage of the chromophore group in its journey in and out of the opsin molecule. Perhaps this easy pathway also allows the entry of isomerizing substance such as naturally occurring phosphatidylethanolamine (Groenendijk, Jacobs, Bonting & Daemen 1980). Other substances such as borohydride and hydroxylamine are known to attack the chromophore group in cones but not in most rods. The missing link in the argument is that it has yet to be shown that visual pigment molecules that offer maximum protection from the chromophore group are also likely to absorb maximally in the 480–520 spectral range, which is the spectral region where most scotopic rhodop-sins are located, and corresponds to the analogue porphyropsin range of 490–557 nm (Dartnall & Lythgoe 1965) in freshwater fishes and larval amphibia.

Contrasts are degraded by the imposition of non-image-forming light across the whole area of the image. This non-image-forming light may come from scatter in the environment outside the eye or from scatter and multiple reflections within it. In either case the visual pigment will be isomerized just as effectively as by useful image-forming light. However, if the image-forming light has a wavelength component that is not present in the non-image-forming veiling light, then it is helpful if the eye is only sensitive to light that is unique to the image-forming component. This solution will sacrifice sensitivity, but will improve image quality. There are indications that in several visual systems, including some bioluminescence visual systems, animals do indeed sacrifice sensitivity to increase contrast discrimination (Muntz 1976, Lall, Biggeley & Lloyd 1980, Seliger, Lall, Lloyd & Biggeley 1982).

In shallow water suspended objects are chiefly illuminated by the bright daylight that has travelled the direct path from the surface, but they are viewed against the water background spacelight which is derived from light scattered from suspended particles and water molecules. This light travels a greater distance through the water and hence undergoes greater wavelength-selective absorption. When an object is viewed horizontally or from above, it will be relatively richer in wavelengths that are most strongly absorbed by the water. Photoreceptors located in regions of the spectrum that are offset from the wavelength of maximum transmission of light will be relatively more sensitive to a bright object than to the water background spacelight and the visual contrast of the object will be enhanced (Lythgoe 1968, 1979). The offset visual pigments in the rods of fishes that will certainly reduce sensitivity may be counteracted by the improved visual contrasts. It should be emphasized however that in deep water, or for dark objects, or objects seen in silhouette, visual contrasts will be best using visual pigments that absorb most strongly at wavelengths where the water is most transparent.

A similar situation may well occur in the eyes of surface-feeding gulls. Like most birds, gulls have cones that contain yellow, orange and red oil droplets, although in these gulls the proportion of red droplets is unusually high (Muntz 1972). It is likely that the red oil droplets filter light travelling through the red-sensitive cones containing a rhodopsin of maximum absorption of around 565 nm. The red oil droplets effectively block all wavelengths shorter than about 600 nm, so that the cone is likely to be sensitive to a more narrow spectral band (Bowmaker 1977) and sensitivity is reduced by at least half. Using these red-sensitive cones, the gull would see floating objects on the water surface with enhanced contrast (Lythgoe 1979). On the other hand underwater skilled hunters – the penguin is a good example – lack red oil droplets, and have a visual system best suited to discriminate between the blue-green colours that are likely to predominate in Antarctic waters (Bowmaker & Martin 1984).

Colour vision

When there is only one type of photoreceptor in operation there is no way of telling whether a surface appears bright because it is reflecting strongly at wavelengths where the photoreceptor is very sensitive, or whether the surface is radiating more strongly than its background. However the eye can resolve the question by introducing a second receptor type, surveying the same element of the image, but most sensitive to a different region of the spectrum. With two or more photoreceptor types it becomes possible to recognize surfaces that have characteristic spectral reflectance properties. This information is coded as colour and it is independent of the brightness of the surface. One reason why colour vision is such an important sense is that it is possible to recognize the characteristic colour of an object no matter whether it lies in shade or full daylight. Under water the problem of light and shade is likely to be even more difficult because the waves act as cylindrical lenses throwing an ever-moving reticulated ripple pattern on the bottom, and colour vision is likely to be very helpful in giving the greatest possible information about the components of the visual scene.

The range of wavelengths that can be seen by a visual system depends ultimately on the spectral absorption properties of the visual pigments. The most short-wave-sensitive visual pigment known is the 345 nm pigment of the fly *Ascalaphus* (Schwemer *et al.*, 1971), and the most long-wave-sensitive pigment appears to be the 625 nm porphyropsin of several freshwater fishes (Loew & Lythgoe 1978, Levine & MacNicholl 1979). The actual range of wavelengths that can be detected is greater. At short wavelengths it is set by the absorption of the amino acid components of proteins, and is probably around 300 nm (Lythgoe 1979). The long-wave limits of vision are more difficult to define, since the long-wave limb of the visual pigment spectrum is still capable of capturing enough light for a visual response even though the absorbance of the pigment at these long wavelengths is too small to measure. Much fresh water is heavily stained with the tea-coloured products of vegetable decay, sometimes to such an extent that the water is most transparent to far-red, or indeed infrared light (Muntz 1978, Muntz & Mouat 1984). The most red-sensitive human cone pigment has an absorption maximum at around 654 nm, in contrast to the 625 nm porphyropsins of several species of freshwater fishes (Loew & Lythgoe 1978, Levine & MacNicholl 1979). If it were possible for fishes to make such a pigment it would probably benefit them to have cone pigments sensitive to even longer wavelengths, and it seems likely that the 625 nm porphyropsin is the most long-wave-sensitive visual pigment that can be achieved.

Therefore it is safe to say that the colour of the water has a strong influence on the visual pigments they possess, the lifestyle of the individual species is clearly very important as well. Relatively deep-living teleosts where the available light is narrowed by the selective spectral absorption of the water, have a correspondingly narrow spread of cone visual pigment wavelengths. The roach, which is a shallow-living species, possesses u.v.-sensitive cones (Avery, Bowmaker, Djamgoz & Downing 1982) and it appears to be a general rule that shallow-living teleosts have a class of cones absorbing most strongly in the deep violet part of the spectrum. In the top few centimetres of even the most yellow-stained water, and in the top metre or so of clearer water there is a measurable quantity of unabsorbed u.v. light (Jerlov 1976), but we do not as yet have any very clear idea about why it should be helpful to see it. Even at wavelengths that we can see, we do not know enough about either the physics and physiology of underwater colour vision, or about the lifestyle of the individual species to come to many conclusions, but it is clear that the ecology of colour vision is a fascinating study for the future.

References

AVERY, J. A., BOWMAKER, J. K., DJAMGOZ, M. B. A. & DOWNING, H. E. G. (1982). Ultraviolet receptors in a freshwater fish. *J. Physiol.* **334**, 23–24P.

BARLOW, W. B. (1981). Critical limiting factors in the design of the eye and visual cortex. *Proc. roy. Soc. Lond.* B. **212**, 1–34.

BOWMAKER, J. K. (1977). The visual pigments, oil droplets, and spectral sensitivity of the pigeon. *Vision Res.* **17**, 1129–38.

BOWMAKER, J. K. & MARTIN, G. R. (1984). Colour vision in the penguin *Spheniscus humboldti*: A microspectrophotometric study, Vision Research (in press).

DARTNALL, H. J. A. (1975). Assessing the fitness of visual pigments for their photic environment. In *Vision in Fishes.* (ed. M. A. Ali), pp. 543–563, New York: Plenum Press.

DARTNALL, H. J. A., & LYTHGOE, J. N. (1965). The spectral clustering of visual pigments. *Vision Res.* **5**, 81–100.

DUNTLEY, S. Q. (1962). Underwater visibility. In *The Sea*, (ed. M. N. Hill), pp. 452–455, London: Interscience.

DUNTLEY, S. Q. (1963). Light in the sea. *J.Opt. Soc. Amer.* **53**, 214–233.

FOLLETT, B. K. & MILETTE, J. J. (1982). Photoperiodism in quail testicular growth and maintenance under skeleton photoperiods. *J. Endocrinology* **93**, 83–90.

GOLDSMITH, T. H. (1972). The natural history of invertebrate visual pigments. In *Handbook of Sensory Physiology VII/2.* (ed. H. J. A. Dartnall), pp. 685–719, Berlin: Springer–Verlag.

GRAS, H. & WEBER, W. (1983). Spectral light sensitivity of isolated chromatophores of the sea urchin *Centrostephanus longispinus*. *Comp. Biochem. Physiol.* **76A**, 279–281.

GROENENDIJK, G. W. T., JACOBS, C. M. M., BONTING, S. L. & DAEMEN, F. J. M. (1980). Dark isomerization of retinals in the presence of phosphatidylethanolamine. *Eur. J. Biochem.* **106**, 119–128.

JERLOV, N. G. (1976). *Marine Optics*, London: Elsevier.

KNOWLES, A. & DARTNALL, H. J. A. (1977). Spectroscopy of visual pigments. In *The Eye*, (ed. H. Davson), p. 73, New York, London: Academic Press.

LALL, A. B., BIGGELEY, H. H. & LLOYD, J. E. (1980). Ecology of colors of bioluminescence in fireflies. *Science* **210**, 560–562.

LAND, M. F. (1981). Optics and vision in invertebrates. In *Handbook of Sensory Physiology Vol. VII/6B*. (ed. H. Autrum), pp. 471–592, New York: Springer.

LEVINE, J. S. & MACNICHOLL JR. (1979). Visual pigments in teleost fishes: effects of habitat microhabitat and behavior on visual system evolution. *Sensory Processes* **3**, 95–130.

LOCKETT, N. A. (1977). Adaptations to the deep-sea environment. In *Handbook of Sensory Physiology Vol. VII/5* (ed. F. Crescitelli), pp. 67–192, Berlin: Springer–Verlag.

LOEW, E. R. & LYTHGOE, J. N. (1978). The ecology of cone pigments in teleost fishes. *Vision Res.* **18**, 715–722.

LYTHGOE, J. N. (1968). Visual pigments and visual range underwater. *Vision Res.* **8**, 997–1012.

LYTHGOE, J. N. (1979). *The Ecology of Vision*. Oxford: Clarendon Press.

LYTHGOE, J. N. (1980). Vision in fishes: ecological adaptations. In *Environmental Physiology of Fishes*, (ed. M. A. Ali), New York: Plenum.

LYTHGOE, J. N. & THOMPSON, M. (1984). A porphyropsin-like action spectrum from Xenopus melanophores. *Photochem. Photobiol.* **40**, 411–412.

LYTHGOE, J. N., SHAND, J. & FOSTER, R. W. (1984). Visual pigment in fish iridocytes. *Nature* **308**, 83–84.

McFARLAND, W. N. & LOEW, E. R. (1983). Wave produced changes in underwater light and their relation to vision. In *Predators and Prey in Fishes*. pp. 11–22, (eds D. I. G. Noakes, D. G. Lindquist, G. S. Helfman & J. A. Ward), The Hague, Boston, London: Junk.

MENECKER, M. (1977). Extraretinal photoreceptors. In *The Science of Photobiology*. (ed. K. C. Smith), pp. 227–240, New York: Plenum.

MENZEL, R. (1975). Colour receptors in insects. In *The Compound Eye and Vision in Insects*. (ed. G. A. Horridge), pp. 121–153, Oxford: Clarendon Press.

MILLOTT, N. (1968). The dermal light sense. In *Invertebrate Photoreceptors*. (eds J. D. Carth & G. E. Newells), pp. 1–36, New York: Academic Press.

MUNTZ, W. R. A. (1972). Inert absorbing and reflecting pigments. In *Handbook of Sensory Physiology VII/1*. (ed. H. J. A. Dartnall), Berlin: Springer–Verlag.

MUNTZ, W. R. A. (1976). On yellow lenses in mesopelagic animals. *J. mar. biol. Assoc.* **56**, 963–976.

MUNTZ, W. R. A. (1978). A penetacao de luz nas aguas de Rio Amazonicos. *Acta Amazonica,* **8**, 613–619.

MUNTZ, W. R. A., & MOUAT, G. S. V. (1984). Annual variation in the visual pigments of brown trout inhabiting lochs providing different light environments. *Vision Research* (in press).

NEWTH, D. R. & ROSS, D. M. (1955). On the reaction of light of *Myxine glutinosa* L. *J. exp. Biol.* **32**, 4–21.

PIRENNE, M. H. (1967). *Vision and the eye*. London: Chapman & Hall.

PROTASOV, V. R. (1970). *Vision and near orientation of fish* (translated from the Russian). *Israel Prog. Sci. Transl.*, Jerusalem.

RIPPS, H. & WEALE, R. A. (1976). The visual stimulus. In *The Eye*. (ed. H. Davson), pp. 89–90, London, New York: Academic Press.

RODIECK, R. W. (1973). *The Vertebrate Retina*. San Francisco: Freeman.

SCHWEMER, J., HAMDORF, F. & GOGOLA, M. (1971). Der UV – Sehrfarbstoff der Insekten: Photochemie *in vitro* und *in vivo*. *Z. vergl. Physiol.* **75**, 174–188.

SELIGER, H. A., LALL, A. B. LLOYD, J. E. & BIGGELEY, W. H. (1982a). The colors of firefly luminescence–1. Optimization model. *Photochem. Photobiol.* **36**, 673–680.

SHROPSHIRE, W. (1980). Carotevoids as primary receptors. In *The Blue Light Syndrome*. (ed. J. Senger), pp. 172–186, Berlin: Springer–Verlag.

Snyder, A. W., Laughlin, S. B. & Stavenga, D. G. (1977). Information capacity of eyes. *Vis. Res.* **17**, 1163–1175.

Steven, D. M. (1955). Experiments in the light sense of the Hag, *Myxine glutinosa L., J exp. Biol.* **32**, 22–38.

Suzuki, T. (1984). Rhodopsin-porphyropsin system of crayfish. *Vision Res.* (in press).

Tansley, K. (1965). *Vision in Vertebrates*, New York: Chapman & Hall.

Tyler, J. E. & Smith, R. C. (1970). *Measurements of Spectral Irradiance Underwater*. New York: Gordon & Breach.

Vigh, B., Vigh–Teichmann, I., Rohlich, P. & Aros, B. (1982). Immunoreactive opsin in the pineal organ of reptiles and birds. *Z. mikrosk.-anat. Forsch., Leipzig.* **96**, 113–129.

Walls, G. L. (1942). *The Vertebrate Eye and its Adaptive Radiation*. Hafner.

Weber, W. (1983). Photosensitivity of chromatophores. *Amer. Zool.* **23**, 495–506.

Wolken, J. J. & Mogus, A. (1979). Extraocular photosensitivity. *Photochem. Photobiol.* **29**, 189–196.

Young, J. Z. (1935). The photoreceptors of lampreys: 1. light-sensitive fibres in the lateral line nerves. *J. exp. Biol.* **12**, 229–238.

Printed in Great Britain © Society of Experimental Biology 1985

CHEMORECEPTION IN THE SEA: ADAPTATIONS OF CHEMORECEPTORS AND BEHAVIOUR TO AQUATIC STIMULUS CONDITIONS

JELLE ATEMA

Boston University Marine Program, Marine Biological Laboratory, Woods Hole, Massachusetts 02543, U.S.A.

In this paper I make an attempt to understand the environmental constraints that may have led to the great variety in structure and physiology of different chemoreceptor cells and organs that we find even in a single aquatic species, let alone in different species. The focus is on the aquatic stimulus environment. I will argue that the different receptor organs, cells and membranes live in different microenvironments, each presenting the receptor with different signals, background chemistry, and signal-to noise ratios. Receptor cell physiology and receptor organ structure serve to interface efficiently with the environment. Even some specific behaviours – stimulus acquisition behaviour – are designed to improve stimulus 'interception'. In addition to these environmental constraints receptor organs are under behavioural constraints. Ultimately, all receptors serve behavioural needs. Thus, receptor organs, whose structure and behaviour are designed at one (peripheral) end to facilitate stimulus access to the receptor cell, serve at the other (central) end to organize the neural information in specialized areas of the nervous system.

To avoid generalities, I will frequently use the lobster, particularly *Homarus americanus*, as a specific example, because it provides a good case in aquatic chemoreception where both chemoreceptor physiology and chemoreceptive behaviour have been studied in one species in some detail.

I. The chemical stimulus environment

A. *Signal-to-noise ratio and signal detection*

The sea, and in the broadest sense every body of water from oceanic to cellular proportions, is an aqueous solution of chemical compounds. In addition to soluble compounds the sea also contains less-soluble material in a suspension of lipid droplets and solid particles; these droplets can act as solvents for lipophylic compounds, and the particles can act as adsorption surfaces for a variety of different materials. Any compound that can interact with a receptor membrane can be a chemical stimulus for an organism: the sea is indeed a rich broth of potential chemical stimuli. Which compounds actually do serve as signals is dependent on their local signal-to-noise ratios.

A signal can stand out against the noise background if it is sufficiently different in quality and/or quantity. Qualitative differences, which I will call 'spectral contrast', are provided by chemical compounds that are either rare or unique for the particular environment in which the signal is to be detected; more commonly, spectral contrast is provided by unique *mixtures* of compounds, even common compounds. Another way to stand out is by 'dynamic contrast, by which I mean that even a common chemical compound can be a signal if it appears in unusual quantity. To be quantitatively unusual it must appear suddenly as a pulse, or a series of pulses, above its local background level. The rise time of the pulse must exceed the adaptation rate of the receptor cells (Schmidt & Ache 1978). Some insects practise pulsed release of sex pheromones (Connor *et al.* 1980; Carde & Baker 1984), but even without such elaboration – often characteristic of communication systems – natural odour distributions generally appear as pulses to a measuring device with temporal resolution below 1 s and/or spatial resolution below a few cm (Murlis & Jones 1981; Fig. 1), such as chemoreceptors. That is, at this spatiotemporal scale, odours are rarely distributed homogeneously.

Any organism needs to identify certain targets, such as objects and areas for feeding, sheltering, and social interaction. Most targets give off (or are coated with) peculiar odours by which they can be identified. I will use the term 'odour' from here on to mean the chemical mixture emanating from (or attached to) a source regardless of the sense organ that perceives it. These odours are blends of compounds; occasionally one single compound may dominate. Since the world consists entirely of odour sources, the resulting chemical noise is great and selective filtering for specific targets becomes essential for one or another species. To identify, for instance, a food source in the sea one must select those chemical compounds that are uniquely associated with food and that are capable of surviving sufficiently long to be detected under ambient conditions; i.e. the signal must be above threshold and above noise. For completeness I should add that parts of organisms, such as organs and cells, particularly during development, search for chemical targets as well, and that gradient search and signal-to-noise ratios may be equally important at

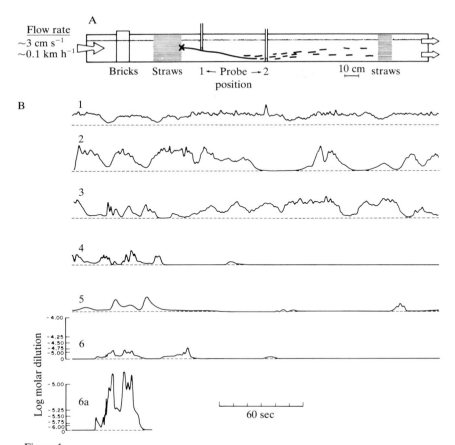

Figure 1
(A) Diagrammatic side view of seawater flume for the measurement of dye distribution at
the time and size scale of (lobster) chemoreceptor organs. Dye was released at X in near-
laminar flow over three different substrate textures (smooth, gravel, rock). Dye density was
measured at two positions with a spectrophotometer probe with spatial resolution of 1 cm³,
the approximate sampling volume of one flick of a lobster antennule.
(B) Dye concentration measurements at two probe positions and over three substrates: At
position 1 over smooth (1), gravel (2) and rock (3) substrates and at position 2 over smooth
(4), gravel (5) and rock (6) substrates. The initial segment of (6) is shown in vertically
expanded scale in (6a) and a log molar dilution scale is given for both based on calibration
curves; the scale of (6) applies to all other traces. Non-homogeneous mixing results in
'pulsed' appearance of dye concentration. Commonly observed concentration peaks are
1–3 s duration and 0.1–1.0 log steps above background. (From Atema *et al.*, in prep.).

that level of organization. In addition, signal-to-noise ratios, but not
actual search, are important in signal detection by sedentary receivers
such as sessile animals and plants, postsynaptic membranes and target
organs for hormones. Many principles of chemoreception apply at these
different levels of biological organization.

B. *The quality of the signal: spectral properties – a chemical picture of the source*

Mixtures more than any one single compound can uniquely identify a source, although rare compounds (i.e. those for which there is low ambient background noise) and common compounds in otherwise restricted situations can also serve as specific signals. The few presently identified marine sex or alarm pheromones are often uniquely structured hydrocarbons (Table 1). They are often labile under natural conditions. While this property has not facilitated chemical structure identification, it is a requisite for signals in general: they must not persist. It was common not long ago to think of all pheromones as single unique compounds (e.g. bombykol, Schneider 1969) that serve to identify the target in search for a mating partner. However, upon closer inspection it has become clear that (perhaps all) insect and vertebrate pheromones are mixtures of several, often chemically related compounds, and that specific mixture ratios are important (Silverstein & Young 1976; Epple, Golob & Smith 1979; Roelofs 1979; Carde & Baker 1984; O'Connell 1985). Unfortunately, thus far too few marine pheromones are known to generalize but there is no reason to believe that aquatic constraints on target identification are different from the terrestrial in this respect. Similarly, experiments on bait attractiveness generally show that mixtures are also more stimulatory than single compounds in feeding behaviour. This has been found for fish (Atema 1980a,b; Carr 1982) and crustacea (McLeese 1970; Mackie 1973; Carr, Netherton & Milstead 1984). Identification of unique mixtures is thus an important task for chemoreceptor organs. Lobsters, for instance, are not only capable of discriminating between the natural body odours of two mussel species (*Mytilus edulis* and *Modiolus demissus*) but even to change their perceptual sensitivity to either species' odour with experience (Derby & Atema 1981).

Occasionally, however, single common compounds such as the amino acid glycine (Pawson 1977), the tripeptide glutathione (Loomis 1955) and the amine betaine (Carr 1977) can cause full or nearly full feeding excitement. Such is the case also for settling and metamorphosis in abalone larvae, where the amino acid GABA is the critical signal (Table 1). Needless to say such common compounds do not provide much specificity and represent a very large class of possible targets. It is the equivalent of visually responding to any moving object of about the right size and speed (Ewert 1980). In some cases generality may be advantageous (fish feeding), in other cases context may provide sufficient specificity (substrate settling).

Table 1. *Aquatic chemical signal compounds**

Structure	Name	Threshold	Function	Reference
1	Ectocarpene	10^{-6} M	gamete attractant	Mueller 1977
2	Fucoserratine	10^{-7} M	gamete attractant	Mueller 1977
3	Multifidene	10^{-6} M	gamete attractant	Mueller 1977
4	Anthopleurine	$3 \cdot 5 \times 10^{-10}$ M	alarm substance	Howe & Sheikh 1975
5	Navenone A	(mixture	alarm substance	Sleeper *et al.* 1980
6	Navenone B	ratio	alarm substance	Sleeper *et al.* 1980
7	Navenone C	4:2:1)	alarm substance	Sleeper *et al.* 1980
8	GABA	10^{-6} M	settling & metamorphosis	Baloun & Morse 1984
9	Betaine	—	feeding	Carr 1982
10	Glutathione	—	feeding	Loomis 1955
11	Glycine	—	feeding	Pawson 1977

*Structure diagrams of compounds shown to serve as significant single compound stimuli

Indeed, the latter case may demonstrate that single common compounds can serve as unique signals in situations where confusion with
other signals is unlikely. Dramatic examples of this are found in the

'micromarine' environment of the chemical synapse. Here, single ordinary compounds such as acetylcholine, GABA, glutamate, glycine or proline (among many other transmitter substances, Bloom 1984) are suddenly released in high concentrations (for example 10^{-4} M-acetylcholine) against a moderately low ambient background (10^{-8} M, maintained by rapid enzymatic degradation of the transmitter; Giraudat & Changeux 1981). Three important constraints allow the use of common compounds as unequivocal signals; all three are well-known features of synaptic signal transmission but may well apply to other situations. First and perhaps most importantly, unique and specific detection of such a signal requires narrowly tuned receptors. Second, no other chemically similar compounds that might still trigger the receptor are present in (equally) large quantities. And third, the signal is released as a sudden pulse with steep (milliseconds) rise time. This leads us to discuss dynamic signal properties, the other major feature besides spectral contrast that determines signal detection.

C. *The pulsed distribution of chemical signals in time and space: dynamic properties*

The chemical synapse illustrates well another aspect of marine signal detection: signal degradation. In the chemical synapse, transmitter concentration must be lowered quickly to allow the following signal to be received. This is accomplished by enzymatic transformation of the signal compound, resulting in rapid return to background concentrations. Similar processes operate in the sea but at a different scale of space and time. Here, various microorganisms, particularly bacteria, use amino acids, amines and peptides as a metabolic substrate. (What is a chemical stimulus for one species is food for another.) The constant production of these compounds by all living and dying organisms and their constant uptake by bacteria leads to an equilibrium background concentration which lies at about 10^{-8} M for most major amino acids in coastal marine waters (Mopper & Lindroth 1982), surprisingly and perhaps fortuitously similar to synaptic acetylcholine transmitter background levels. It is against this background that signal detection must take place in the sea.

Very different from the micron distances in chemical synapses are the distances over which signals often must travel in the marine environment to be useful to target identification. Molecular diffusion over these distances becomes an irrelevant process compared with turbulent mixing and odour transport on carrier currents. A source of stimulus release, whether it remains still or moves away, produces its unique mixture of compounds. Currents on the scale of the source, let us say centimetres to metres, carry the odour away. In the oceans or in large rivers, these currents are part of macroscale water movements with dimensions of 1–1000 kilometres, which cause an odour plume to develop from an

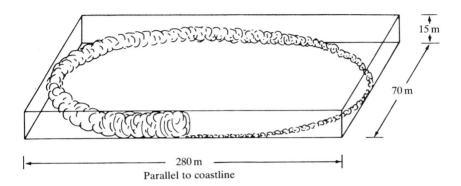

280 m
Parallel to coastline

15 m

70 m

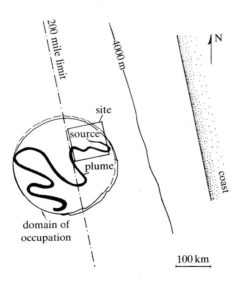

200 mile limit

4000 m

N

site

source

plume

coast

domain of
occupation

100 km

Figure 2
(A) Distribution of a tracer one tidal period (12.4 h) after starting continuous release from a point source at a deep (4000 m) Pacific site; on a one day time scale tidal currents ($2\,cms^{-1}$ parallel to the coast, $0\cdot5\,cms^{-1}$ perpendicular to the coast) dominate the horizontal current field near the bottom.
(B) 'Active space' (or 'domain of occupation') of a hypothetical tracer plume after 100 days of continuous release.
(Both from Kupferman & Moore, 1981).

emitting source (Fig. 2). In addition, these currents contain various dimensions of turbulence; the larger ones cause the plume to meander, while the smaller ones cause the plume to break up at the edges into small eddies. The result is the appearance of filaments and eddies of higher signal strength in a plume of lower or even zero signal strength. Ultimately the odour distribution will approach homogeneity and its signal value will fade into the background noise; the plume has dissolved. Events at these large size and time dimensions may be important to fish or turtle migrations but not to receptor organs.

Measurements of dye distributions at the size and time scale of chemoreceptor organs show clearly the pulsed nature of the dye signal as it travels on a carrier current away from the source past the 'receptor' (Fig. 1). Signal distribution becomes more homogeneous at increasing distance from the source of release; substrate texture greatly influences turbulent mixing. Near the source, the concentration of chemical signal pulses can be several orders of magnitude above background. Further away only a slightly variable signal is present; its steady state ('DC') value can still be measured above 'zero' background with absolute detectors, such as spectrophotometers, but most sense organs are relative (adapting) detectors and as such almost certainly measure only the small superimposed 'AC' values. Sensitive chemical detectors such as the taste organs of catfish can still respond in behavioural experiments to a signal that is 10–25 % above its artificially greatly elevated background (Stewart, Bryant & Arema 1979), such as one would find within a rather well-mixed odour plume. Chemically less-sensitive animals may have to leave a near-homogeneous plume to detect its presence. In fully mixed odour plumes all animals presumably must leave the plume to detect its presence. This is suggested for river migration of salmon (Hasler & Scholtz 1983; Johnsen & Hasler 1980). Døving, however, has suggested that salmonids can measure absolute levels of constant odour by using a large number of randomly adapting and disadapting receptor cells (Døving pers. comm.). The critical experiments to resolve this issue have not been done.

In sum, it should be clear that each odour distribution has a characteristic size and time scale. At the scales of relevance for biological species, distribution of odour is rarely homogeneous and chemical signals appear to receiving organisms as series of pulses of different concentration. Measurements were made in aerial and aquatic tracer plumes (Murliss & Jones 1982, and Atema et al. unpubl. Fig. 1.) The size and frequency of such pulses may well contain important information about the direction of and distance to the odour source.

D. *Viscosity*

Odour receivers face another constraint. Within a centimetre or so of a solid surface the viscous properties of water begin to dominate (Vogel 1981) and turbulence begins to cease, leaving molecular diffusion as the major mechanism for odour molecule transport. At first glance such viscous boundary layers seem to present a barrier for efficient access to odour stimuli. However, at the size and time scale of chemoreceptors molecular diffusion may not be severely limiting (Futrelle 1984; Mankin & Mayer 1984; Boeckh, Kaissling & Schneider 1965). In fact, in some species, receptor structures appear designed to *maximize* viscosity of their immediate surroundings. The densely packed tufts of aesthetasc sensilla in crustacea (Fig. 3) inhibit water flow and odour access; similarly, fish olfactory epithelia are folded up over lamellae (Fig. 4) enclosed in two small pockets in the rostral head, preventing water flow and odour access. Similar organization is seen in gastropod olfactory organs (Fig. 4). These adaptations will be discussed later: they probably serve to enhance contrast by allowing the animal to *control* flow over the nose and hence stimulus access.

II. Stimulus acquisition behaviour

Species of different size and mobility are confronted with different dimensions of odour distributions; this defines the extent to which chemical signals are useful to them. Fish can actively swim and intercept an odour plume in which eddies and filaments of odour present a dynamic stimulus pattern that may contain information about distance and direction of the source. They can sample a large area quickly. However, copepods are wrapped up in the viscous boundary layer, settled barnacles do not swim, and even bacteria and algal gametes locate odour sources. Organisms employ different behavioural techniques to have efficient access to (chemical) stimuli: I will use the term 'Stimulus acquisition behaviour' to identify its function among many the other functions of behaviour observed in organisms.

A. *Information currents*

Many aquatic species generate water currents; these serve at once to facilitate gas exchange, the uptake and excretion of metabolic products, and the transport (delivery and reception) of chemical stimuli. Filter

Figure 3.   Lateral antennules of (A) the lobster *Homarus americanus* and (B) the blue crab *Callinectes sapidus* with aesthetasc sensilla and, in the lobster, larger guard hairs: note dense packing of aesthetasc sensilla. In (B) the medial antennule is shown also; it bears no aesthetasc sensilla and does not flick. (B, courtesy of Dr. Richard Gleeson.)

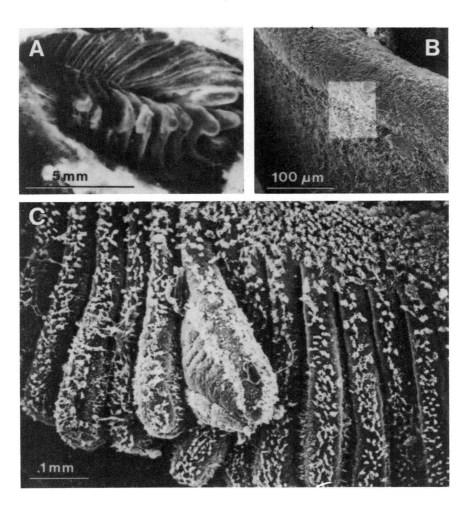

Figure 4. Catfish (*Ictalurus nebulosus*) and mud snail (*Illyanassa obsoleta*) noses:
(A) Catfish olfactory 'rosette' of lamellae in natural position under water, exposed by removing the entire roof of the olfactory chamber.
(B) Detail of individual lamella with motile cilia on top of the ridge and olfactory cilia down the flanks (SEM).
(C) Part of the osphradium of the mud snail (SEM) with tufts of motile cilia; one lamella pulled out to show the line of cilia along the flank: these may contain the chemosensory cilia.

feeding copepods provide a clear example (Strickler 1982 and this Symposium). These small animals (mm size) generate powerful currents which, due to viscosity, are laminar and undisturbed by unpredictable turbulence; hence they are constant and under the animal's control. Some copepods feed on algal cells; body odours emanate constantly from such cells. The copepod's laminar current draws this algal body odour toward the copepod in such a predictable pattern that the arrival of the odour source (the algal cell) is at a specified time and place within the striking distance of the copepod's feeding appendages. Hence, this current is known as a feeding current; however, it clearly serves also as a chemical information current.

Several chemical information currents are found in the lobster and other large decapod crustacea which do not exist within the boundary layer (although their receptor organs do). With the scaphognatite – functioning as a peristaltic pump – lobsters generate a continuous, high-velocity current which draws water into the gill chamber from ventral pores between the walking legs; this gill current exits anteriorly through a small pore, one for each of the bilateral gill chambers. A short distance away the two currents join into one and together project to five to seven animal lengths anterior in mature animals (Fig. 5). In juveniles this current projects only one to three animal lengths before dissolving in turbulence (McPhie & Atema 1984). Since this current is continuous it gives the animal no control over the delivery of body odour. Chemical communication (as practised in social behaviour) requires such control. To this purpose lobsters employ a fan organ composed of the three maxilliped exopodites: fanning abruptly redirects the forward gill current and blows it back along the flanks of the lobster to about the middle of its abdomen. In addition, the fan current draws water from an area of about 0·3 animal lengths around the lobster's head (McPhie & Atema 1984), a space regularly sampled by the antennules (to be discussed below). Fanning is controlled by the animal; it is a commonly observed behaviour in response to a variety of stimuli, particularly chemical stimuli, and it is seen extensively in feeding and social behaviour. It is probably significant that urine is released from the small pores that project directly into the gill current. Body odour and urine contain sex-specific cues (Cowan & Atema 1984). Although not experimentally tested, the implications seem clear: when not fanning lobsters project their body odour forward,

---

Figure 5. Information currents of *Homarus americanus* (From Atema & McPhie, in prep.): (A) Gill currents with mean and standard deviations; top view of three different-sized animals (15, 55, and 80 mm CL) and (4) side view of (3) or mature animal (broken line indicates that vertical expansion of plume is limited by horizontal stratification of water). Arrows indicate water uptake into gill chamber. AL, Animal length from rostrum to tail; CL, carapace length from eye socket to posterior carapace margin, the standard measurement for lobsters.
(B) Exopodite 'fan' current. Direction 1 is commonly observed; directions 2 and 3 occur occasionally. Small arrows show water flow drawn toward the lobster.

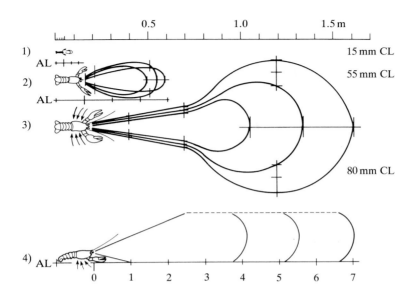

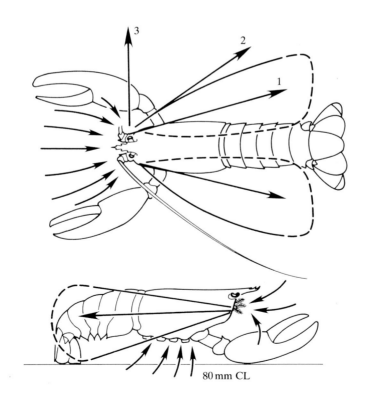

80 mm CL

particularly in mature-sized animals, and urine can be injected into this current allowing the animal to send chemical signals. This may occur for instance when females court males, during which time they repeatedly approach the entrance of dominant male shelters (Atema *et al.* 1979). Males often respond with yet another current: they beat their pleopods near the second shelter entrance, thus drawing a very large current through their shelter entering from the first entrance, where the female stands.

B. *'Sniffing'*

In addition to odour distribution over currents of animal-size dimensions, the lobster's chemoreceptor organs which operate at the scale of millimeters must have efficient access to the (pulsed) chemical stimulus distributions within these larger currents. To overcome the severe viscosity problems that dominate the (sub)millimetre scale, they employ 'flicking', a vigorous, high velocity beat of the antennular lateral branch. Behavioural experiments have shown that this appendage is essential in efficient orientation in odour plumes (Reeder & Ache 1980; Devine & Atema 1982). It allows spatial and temporal sampling ('digitizing') of the chemical environment. Physiological experiments have shown (Schmidt & Ache 1979) that between flicks the receptors are adapted to the chemical composition of the viscous layer surrounding the receptors, while odour pulses may drift by which hardly influence the layer. A flick causes a rapid water exchange around the receptor sensilla which are now suddenly exposed to the new water chemistry. Thus, even if the odour plume itself were not clearly pulsed, flicking superimposes a pulsed reception which differentiates between the odour that was and the odour that is. It is likely that it is the flicking behaviour that allow the spatial and temporal resolution necessary to detect the presence of odour plumes and their internal structure. Thus, increasing viscosity by dense packing of sensilla (see also Gleeson 1982) and rapid physiological adaptation of aesthetasc receptor cells may serve as mechanisms to *prevent* odour reception between flicks; this would serve to enhance stimulus contrast during flicks, and – most importantly for behaviour – from one flick to the next.

Functionally, flicking resembles sniffing (Macrides & Chorover 1972) and tongue flicking in tetrapods. Flicking is seen commonly in lobsters responding to external, particularly chemical, stimuli. This is often accompanied by exopodite fanning which draws in water from anterior regions toward the antennules. During courtship, both animals exchange currents while vigorously flicking their antennules; i.e. they 'sniff' each others body odour while still at a distance of one to a few animal lengths.

Fish do not flick but they do generate nasal currents. This allows the animal control of a laminar flow over its olfactory epithelium, not too different from copepod currents. There are a variety of nasal irrigation mechanisms (Døving & Thommesen 1977; Døving, Dubois-Dauphin, Holley & Jourdan 1977), the most efficient of which is found in the macrosmatic eels and catfishes. Here a ciliary driven current draws water into the anterior naris over the extensively folded nasal epithelium and blows it out from the posterior naris (Fig. 4). In catfish, the nasal current appears to be under the animal's control: the chemically stimulated side increases its velocity (Chen, unpubl. in Bardach & Villars 1974). Such a mechanism could serve to enhance left–right control. Other mechanisms involve accessory olfactory sacs: hydrostatic pumps operated by jaw movements (Melinkat & Zeiske 1979); during food odour introductions tuna often show jaw snapping movements (Atema, Holland & Ikehara 1980) which may well serve as 'sniffs'.

Much like fish noses marine gastropods draw ciliary currents from a siphon into their gill cavity which contains a very large 'nose', the osphradium, resembling the catfish nose in gross morphology. In the mud snail, *Ilyanassa obsoleta* (formerly *Nassarius obsoletus*) this current keeps the often buried animal informed of its environmental chemistry; food odour induces down-stream animals to emerge from the mud and to approach the source in a nearly straight line while swinging their siphons left to right, presumably sampling the odour plume (Atema & Burd 1975).

C. *Locomotor adaptations to odour distributions ('chemotaxis')*

One might expect that mobile organisms exhibit source localization behaviour patterns that are adapted to the odour distribution patterns found in nature at the size scale relevant to the particular species. Recent work with moths flying in pheromone plumes (Cardé 1984) shows this to be the case. Earlier concepts of 'active space', i.e. that volume of air or water in which the chemical stimulus is above behavioural threshold, are based on time averaged Gaussian models in which odour is assumed to be evenly diluting away from the source (Bossert & Wilson 1963). Apart from theoretical objections, observed animal behaviour is difficult to explain under the assumptions of this theoretical model; the advantage of this model is that it can be expressed in a mathematical equation and hence it serves the useful purpose of comparing between types of odour

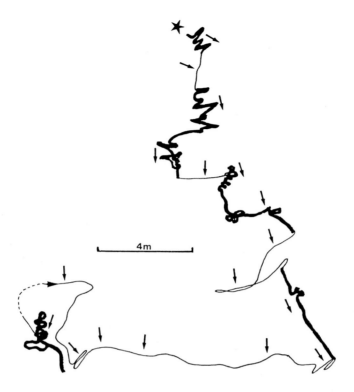

Figure 6. Upwind orientation toward and localization of a continuously releasing pheromone source by a male gypsy moth. Flight path shown by thin line when outside odour plume filaments, by thick line when inside odour. Odour plume visualized with soap bubbles. (Courtesy Dr. Charles David.)

plumes. Current 'instantaneous' plume models, such as described earlier in this paper, match well with observed behaviour (but are impossible to describe mathematically). Observed moth behaviour (Fig. 6) can be described by two simple decision rules: "when you smell the odour fly upwind, when you do not smell it cast across-wind" (David *et al.* 1982). This requires that the animal can determine wind direction, which in moths is probably largely visual (Kuenen & Baker 1982). Fast-flying tsetse flies employ a different method of odour source localization: they sit and monitor wind direction, aim for the source, frequently overshoot, loop back downwind, may again overshoot and loop back upwind, and then use vision in final approach (Bursell 1984). There is no comparable body of knowledge for aquatic animals, but it seems reasonable to assume that similar decision rules may be employed by fish, crustacea, and molluscs as long as the environmental conditions are comparable, in particular the condition that current direction can be determined. The latter should be the case in benthic animals which are in visual and/or mechanical contact with the (stationary) substrate, but not so easily in pelagic species where stationary visual and mechanical cues are often absent as the organism drifts with the current. Only Kalmijn (1984) has proposed a reasonable but yet untested model of current detection based on electric fields induced by the earth's magnetic field; and this model would operate only in electrically sensitive fish such as sharks. Thus, even large-scale oceanic hunters such as tuna may be forced to behave like bacteria when it comes to odour source localization.

Bacteria, which live in the viscous world of molecular diffusion, have a different set of simple decision rules that govern their food localization behaviour: they 'cast' (i.e. swim straight) in a random direction, stop, tumble around, cast in the next random direction, stop, etc. The rule is that when odour concentration is higher at the next stop, the frequency of tumbling decreases thus increasing the length of the following random cast; conversely, when odour concentration at the next stop is lower the tumbling frequency increases (Macnab & Koshland 1972). This simple rule results in bringing the organism – eventually – to the area of highest odour concentration. Tuna in large tanks get excited about food odour, increase their swimming speed and change swimming patterns; at higher odour concentrations they make short runs and quick turns. They do not localize the odour source but occasionally mill about in the general area of highest odour concentration (Atema *et al.* 1980; pers. obs.). In that area they strike visual targets, a fact known by many fishermen.

When current direction can be determined, the decision rule in some animals – comparable to the moths discussed above – is to swim up-current when odour is present ('chemically stimulated rheotaxis'). This is the case in the mostly pelagic lemon sharks (Hodgson & Mathewson 1971), whereas the mostly benthic nurse sharks appear to engage in direc-ted chemical gradient search ('chemotaxis'), as do catfish (Bardach Todd & Crickmer 1967), lobsters (Devine & Atema 1982; Reeder & Ache 1980), and mudsnails (Atema & Burd 1975) to name a few – benthic – representatives of different phyla. An extensive review of fish olfactory orientation behaviour can be found in Kleerekoper (1969).

D. *Summary of stimulus acquisition behaviour*

Aquatic chemoreception is intimately connected with currents, includ-ing self-generated 'information' currents, micro- and macro-scale tur-bulence and long-distance bulk transport. To understand the mechanisms of aquatic chemoreception one must understand these different currents, which determine the relevant odour distribution patterns and the odour sampling techniques of various species. Depending on their life style (sessile mussels and tunicates, mobile lobsters and tuna, small scale gametes and bacteria) different species and developmental stages will employ different mechanisms to stay informed of their environmental chemistry, which is often the dominant sensory cue regulating their behaviour.

As soon as odours are released they begin to travel on the various current systems, and their mixture components are affected differentially by physical, chemical and biological factors. Thus, not only does the entire odour mixture disperse and eventually dissipate into background noise, its mixture composition changes over time as well. For long-distance odour localization one can therefore expect chemoreceptors to focus on chemically and biologically stable compounds that are sufficiently unique or abundant to stand out against the background water chemistry. In close encounters the odour signal need not be so stable as long as it is sufficiently unique to identify the source, be it a social partner, a food item, or a habitat. When other sensory cues set an unmistakable context the odour signal may not need to be specific either; it could serve only to coordinate behaviour in time as may occur in certain phases of courtship behaviour, in feeding attack, and in settling and metamorphosis. An appreciation of these different requirements is necessary to understand the performance constraints on chemoreceptor cells and the organization of chemoreceptor organs, an area of research that has seen significant developments in the last decade.

III. Receptor cell adaptations

It is the business of chemoreceptor cells to identify behaviourally important chemical compounds against ambient backgrounds of chemical noise. They are the selective amplifiers that provide the first level of the transduction of chemical energy in the form of environmental odour molecules into ion fluxes across the receptor membrane. For bacteria, protists, and gametes, these electrochemical events may rather directly control behaviour; for plants and lower invertebrates such as coelenterates the electrochemical events may spread across tissues and regulate behaviour amongst different cells; and for animals with a more complex nervous system these events may be only the first of a long series of subsequent neural filtering processes.

Chemoreceptor cells selectively filter different chemical compounds, depending on the micro environment in which they operate and the behavioural function they serve. To exaggerate the point: a human taste cell rarely encounters and has no need to respond to the silk moth sex pheromone, bombykol, while the moth antennal receptor cells do not come across and are not interested in detecting sugars. Less obvious may be that lobster olfactory cells and taste cells 'look at' different parts of the chemical spectrum that surrounds them even though the two operate in much the same marine environment. Similarly, catfish senses of smell and taste show somewhat different focus on the amino acids in their common freshwater environment (Caprio 1982). Spectral response differences may point to differences in the actual microenvironment of the receptor cells, but they could also reflect different behavioural functions. This is well demonstrated in catfish, where two different taste organs regulate food intake (Atema 1971) while the nose is preferred for learning novel situations (Atema 1977) and is involved in conspecific body odour recognition used in social behaviour (Herbert & Atema 1977). In general, different spectral filters can be expected in different chemoreceptor organs, and when investigated, some have been found.

Receptor cells must not only perform spectral filtering but also deal with great dynamic fluctuations in stimulus and noise intensities. In the marine environment, amino acid receptors must be able to operate over a dynamic range of 10^{-8} M (the natural amino acid background in coastal water) to 10^{-2} M (the maximum amino acid concentrations in animal tissue). Since most, but not all (Hatt & Bauer 1982), cells have an instant working range of only about two orders of magnitude (Bauer, Dudel & Hatt, 1981; Derby & Atema 1982b; Johnson, Borroni & Atema 1984, 1985; Fig. 7) there must be various adaptation mechanisms to deal with the much larger range of concentrations found in the environment. In sum, chemoreceptor cells must deliver reliable dynamic and spectral information under greatly fluctuating conditions of stimulus and background composition.

A. *Spectral filters*

At the level of molecular events the best-known chemoreceptors are the acetylcholine receptors of the postsynaptic membrane of the vertebrate neuromuscular junction. I will use this as a model for the narrowly tuned amino acid receptors of some crustacea, whose narrow response spectrum in turn makes them easier to understand than the complex and unpredictable response spectra seen in smell and taste receptor cells of most animals studied thus far. The acteylcholine receptor

CELL NUMBER

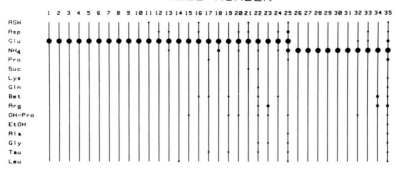

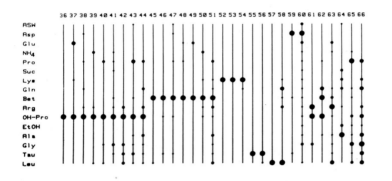

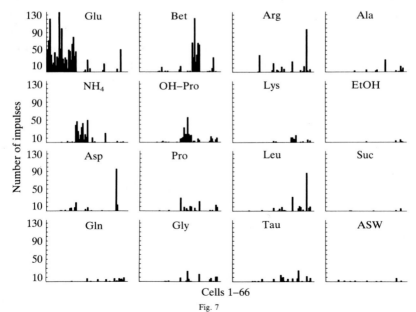

Cells 1–66

Fig. 7

lives in a highly specialized environment, a micron-sized space, carefully controlled by enzymes and ionic pumps, which maintain a reasonable chemical homeostasis under normal conditions. Acetylcholine secreted from the presynaptic membrane is the relevant signal for the receptor, which is narrowly tuned for its task. The receptor is a 5-subunit protein with 2 binding sites for acetylcholine. The subunits are arranged around and form a central channel that crosses the cell membrane. When the receptor sites are occupied by acetylcholine – a fast, transient random state, the frequency of which depends on the concentration of acetylcholine – the channel briefly opens, resulting in massive ionic flux (Na^+ and K^+) driven by the large electrochemical gradient across the membrane (Conti-Tronconi & Raftery 1982; Changeux, Devillers-Thiery & Chemouilli 1984).

The crustacean neuromuscular junction operates similarly but with a different transmitter; its chemical signal is glutamate (Nistri & Constanti 1979). When, a few years ago, it was discovered that lobsters have narrowly tuned glutamate receptors not only in the specialized microenvironment of the neuromuscular synapse but also in their walking leg taste receptors (Derby & Atema 1982b,c) a comparison between the two was inevitable. So far, we know that the two receptors are highly specialized for glutamate binding: they have much lower affinity for compounds with structural similarity such as aspartate and glutamine. However, they differ in other respects: for instance, kainate stimulates the neuromuscular receptor (Shank & Freeman 1976) but is not very effective at the taste receptor. This leads one to believe that the two receptor proteins are synthesized under, at least partially, different genetic control. (A detailed discussion of this subject will distract us too far from

---

Figure 7. Spectral filtering of 66 individual primary chemoreceptor cells of *Homarus americanus* legs each stimulated with 15 different compounds in 1 s pulses (see Figure 9) of each compound in artificial sea water (ASW).
(A) Response magnitude categorized in four different dot sizes scaled to the cell's largest response (largest dot): many cells respond exclusively to one compound; few cells respond significantly to more than one compound. Largest dot: 100 %, decreasing dot size: 70–100 %, 30–70 % and less than 30 %. 'No dot' indicates no response to that compound. The largest receptor cell population is narrowly tuned to glutamate; there are also tuned populations for ammonium, hydroxyproline and betaine, as well as smaller populations for lysine, taurine, leucine and aspartate.
(B) Responses of all 66 cells (arranged along horizontal axis of each diagram in the order of Figure 7A) to the 15 compounds and control (ASW, artificial seawater). Each bar represents the total number of impulses elicited in one cell by the compound listed in the diagram. The across-fibre patterns clearly show the dominant responses to glutamate, ammonium, betaine and hydroproline.
(From Johnson *et al.* 1984.)

the main topic of this paper.) However, the great surprise is not that the two glutamate receptors are different, but that the taste receptor is so narrowly tuned.

Narrowly tuned receptor cells form a good basis in principle for a 'labelled line' coding system, in which stimulus quality is given by the fact that the particular cell fires, and stimulus intensity by the firing rate of the cell. Such a cell responds only if its 'labelled' stimulus is present supraliminally; the neuromuscular junction is a clear case of a labelled line. In contrast, coding based on patterns generated across fibres depends on simultaneous comparison of many fibres, whose activity rates form patterns that vary with both stimulus quality and intensity. In order to generate different patterns of activity, the receptor cells of such a system must be broadly tuned and have different stimulus specificities (Erickson 1982). The cells of most chemoreceptor organs are broadly tuned; there are compelling theoretical reasons – such as conservation of neuronal space – why across-fibre comparisons are most efficient for coding a great variety of stimuli. This makes the discovery of narrow tuning the more intriguing: different populations of narrowly tuned cells could serve as multiple labelled lines for important chemical signal compounds; or they could participate in across-fibre patterns; or they could do both.

Prior to the discovery of narrow tuning in crustacean chemoreceptors, the classic example of narrowly tuned chemoreceptors was found in pheromone receptors of some insects; here, as in neuromuscular junctions, a specialized communication function is obvious. In both situations, a chemical message is sent that must be understood without mistake by the receiver; mistakes in either case are costly: neurophysiological and reproductive malfunctioning, respectively. This enforces severe constraints on the fine tuning of sender and receiver. In lobster chemoreceptors, where it is not likely that the constraints of communication apply, we can only speculate as to the function of narrow tuning. We can, however, be certain that narrow tuning is the predominant characteristic of lobster chemoreceptors, both those associated with smell and with taste

---

Figure 8. Dose response functions for three different chemoreceptor cell populations of *Homarus americanus* when stimulated with 1 s pulses (see Figure 9) of their best compound alone (solid lines) or as part of a 15-compound equimolar mixture (broken lines). Mean values and standard errors. Asterisk: significant ($P < 0.05$) differences between single and mixture stimuli.
(A) Hydroxyproline cells of antennules.
(B) Taurine cells of antennules.
(C) Glutamate cells of walking legs.
(From Johnson *et al.* 1985.)

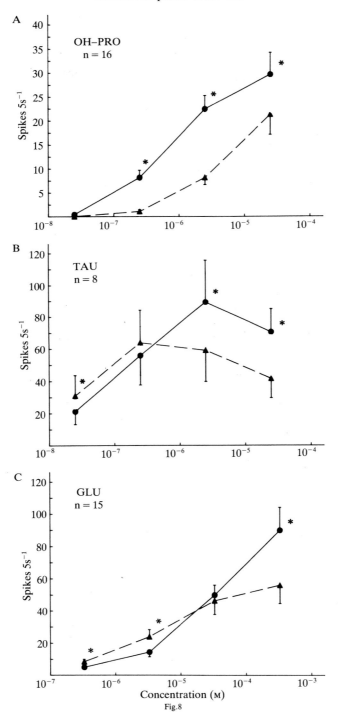

Fig.8

functions (Derby & Atema 1982c; Johnson, Voigt, Borroni & Atema 1984; Johnson & Atema 1983).

While we may not yet be able to propose a clear hypothesis concerning the behavioural function of narrow tuning in the lobster's receptors, we can begin to sketch out how these receptors function in their natural environment of sea water. At present, the lobster chemoreceptors provide us with the best example of 'interfacing with the marine chemical environment'. When presented with single amino acids and amines in a low organic background of artificial seawater, both legs and antennules of lobsters demonstrate the presence of several receptor cell populations that are narrowly tuned each to one particular compound, such as glutamate, betaine, ammonium, taurine, hydroxyproline, aspartate, lysine, and glycine (Johnson *et al.* 1984; Johnson & Atema 1983). This narrow tuning is maintained even at the relatively high stimulus concentrations (3×10^{-4}M) found in the lobster's natural prey such as mussel flesh (Fig. 7). The same cells, when presented with mixtures of these compounds, show reduced responses (Johnson & Atema 1983; Gleeson & Ache 1983). A more detailed investigation of the effects of mixtures showed that one cell population (narrowly tuned for OH-proline) gave systematically suppressed responses to its best compound when presented in an equimolar mixture of 14 other compounds that themselves do not or hardly stimulate these cells; two other cell populations (narrowly tuned for glutamate and taurine, respectively) showed enhanced responses at low concentrations and suppressed responses at high concentrations of the mixture stimulus (Fig. 8) (Johnson *et al.* 1984). The net effect is that a particular mixture stimulates the different cell populations differently depending on its concentration; curiously, this could result – at least in theory – in different odour quality reception depending on odour concentration. Concentration-dependent quality perception is known in human taste (Bartoshuk 1978). However, since response suppression appears far stronger and more prevalent then enhancement, the overall effect is that the narrowly tuned receptor cells are less excited by mixture

---

Figure 9. Stimulus delivery to lobster leg.
(A) The stimulus delivery (C) and the response recording chamber (F); water flow ('in' at A, 'out' at D), stimulus injection (B); rubber septum (E).
(B) The 1 s 'odour' pulse measured as conductivity change of distilled water after injection of 50 μl of 1 M-salt solution. Mean and standard errors of ten repeated injections. Inset: recording electrodes in lobster leg to create same turbulence for conductivity measurements as for chemical stimuli.
(From Johnson *et al.* 1984)

TOP VIEW

A

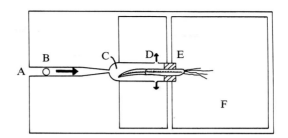

SIDE VIEW

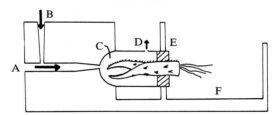

B

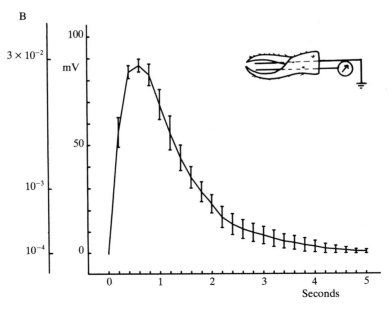

Fig. 9

stimuli than by single compounds, but yet maintain their ability to re-spond to specific compounds in the mixture. The weak responses seen in narrowly tuned cells to compounds other than the best stimulus may well be completely suppressed in mixtures; thus, mixture stimuli would actu-ally sharpen the tuning focus of each population. In addition, response suppression would allow the cell to expand its dynamic response range beyond the two orders of magnitude commonly found in controlled low-background conditions. Natural stimulus intensities range over at least six orders of magnitude. To generate a better understanding of the impor-tance of stimulus intensity fluctuations we need to investigate the dynamic response properties of receptor cells.

B. *Dynamic Filters*

When spectral analysis showed that of all the cell populations studied in lobsters the glutamate cells of the legs were simultaneously the most commonly encountered and the most narrowly tuned, we chose this population for an initial investigation of their adaptation and disadapta-tion properties (Voigt & Atema 1984). We stimulated single cells repeatedly with standard $50 \mu l$, $1 s$, 3×10^{-4} M-glutamate pulses (Fig. 9) resembling the pulse shapes (time and peak height) seen in simulated odour plumes (Fig. 1). Pulse intervals of $80 s$ and longer caused no inter-pulse adaptation; $40 s$ intervals caused a 25% drop in response intensity and duration after the first one or two stimuli (Fig. 10). Pulse intervals of $20 s$ caused systematically decreasing responses, both in response dura-tion, maximum spike frequency, and total numbers of spikes (Fig. 11). Not all cells have the same dynamic response properties. Most cells gave phasic–tonic responses and showed adaptation; other cells giving only short phasic responses showed no interpulse adaptation even at $10 s$ pulse intervals. A third type of glutamate cell responded with double bursts and showed significant adaptation with $20 s$ interpulse intervals. Thus, while the glutamate cells form a consistent spectral group, their dynamic re-sponse properties vary considerably, and subgroups appear which are defined by their dynamic properties. Differences in dynamic properties of receptor cells would allow the receptor organ as a whole greater resolution in measuring different rates of change in stimulus concentra-tion. While we do not know what molecular properties allow the receptor cells to have different stimulus adaptation and disadaptation time courses, the pulsatile character of natural odour plumes may well have enforced this feature of chemoreceptors.

Interpulse interval: 80 s

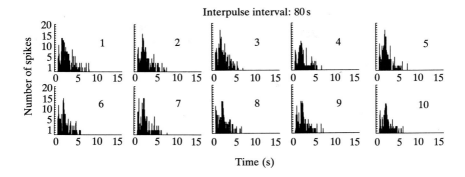

Time (s)

Interpulse interval: 40 s

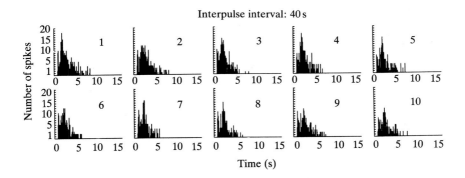

Time (s)

Interpulse interval: 20 s

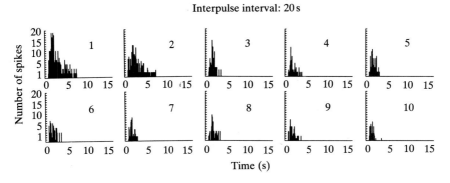

Time (s)

Figure 10. Response (post-stimulus histogram of number of spikes in 100 ms time bins) of single lobster leg glutamate receptor cells to a series of ten repeated 1 s glutamate pulses at three different interpulse intervals: 80 s, 40 s, 20 s. The phasic–tonic responses adapt somewhat with 40 s and adapt significantly with 20 s interval stimulation. Stimulus pulse profile as in Figure 9. (From Voigt and Atema, unpublished.)

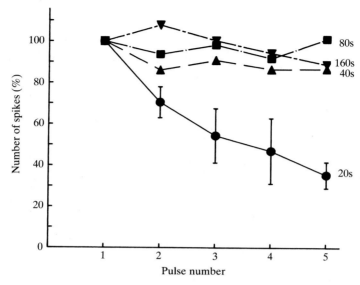

Figure 11. Adaptation of lobster glutamate cells to five repeated 1 s glutamate pulses delivered with pulse intervals of 20, 40, 80 or 160 s. Means of five different cells in each case; for clarity standard error bars shown only for cell responses to 20 s intervals. Stimulus pulse profile as in Figure 9. (From Voigt and Atema, unpublished.)

IV. Organization of chemoreceptor organs

In higher metazoans, receptor cells are organized into receptor organs with distinct behavioural functions, served by particular neural organizations within the nervous system. Once again, the lobster will serve as an example. It is richly endowed with many distinct chemoreceptor organs (Fig. 12, Table 2), each with its own task in serving the behavioural needs of the animal. If Eskimos have a dozen different names for various forms of what Europeans simply call snow, then lobsters probably have as many names for their chemoreceptor organs, where we humans generally speak of only smell and taste. Meanwhile, the human terms can be used for some of the lobsters' chemoreceptor organs provided one applies proper biological criteria (Atema 1977, 1980a).

To summarize a great deal of information on the behavioural function of different chemoreceptor organs, it may be easiest to follow a lobster on its way to its food, a distant mussel. The lobster orients to the mussel's body odour plume emanating from the mussel's feeding current by using predominantly its lateral antennular branches (Fig. 3) (Devine & Atema 1982), with its prominent aesthetasc sensilla (Ghiradella, Case & Cronshaw 1968; Snow 1973; Laverack & Ardill 1965). Removal of these

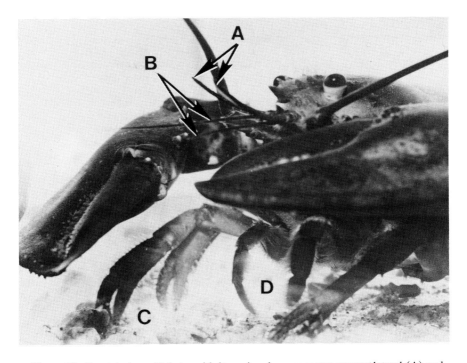

Figure 12. Frontal view of lobster with its major chemoreceptor organs: lateral (A) and medial (B) branch of antennules, chelate walking legs (C), and third maxillipeds (D).

sensilla impairs but does not completely eliminate efficient orientation (Devine & Atema 1982), leading us to believe 1) that there are non-aesthetasc chemoreceptors on this branch and 2) that it is the flicking behaviour of this organ – and not specifically the presence of aesthetasc sensilla – that makes it uniquely adapted to orientation, because the equally chemoreceptive (spiny lobster *Panulirus argus*: Fuzessery, Carr & Ache 1978; clawed lobster *Homarus americanus*: Johnson unpubl.), but non-flicking, medial branch does not play a role there. As argued earlier, flicking allows spatial and temporal sampling of the chemical environment. The function of the medial branch remains unknown. The walking legs, which move about but do not flick, aid in orientation. This was seen in animals missing one lateral branch: functional leg chemoreceptors prevented 'circus movements', i.e. turning in circles toward the side of the remaining lateral branch (Devine & Atema 1982). Thus, despite excellent chemical sensitivity, the legs and their receptor cells appear not or less specifically designed for spatial or temporal sampling.

In the vicinity of the mussel the lobster starts probing about using the

Table 2. *Chemoreceptor organs of* Homarus americanus

Appendage	Chemoreceptive function
1. aesthetasc sensilla of lateral branch of antennule (Figs. 3, 12)	orientation in odour plumes odour identification, social cues
2. non-aesthetasc sensilla of lateral branch of antennule	orientation in odour plumes odour identification
3. medial branch of antennule (Fig. 12)	odour identification?
4. chelate walking legs (Figs. 12, 13)	feeding and food recognition, grooming?, mating?
5. non-chelate walking legs	grooming?
6. third maxillipeds (Fig. 12)	feeding and food recognition (distinct from walking legs), grooming?, mating?
7. first and second maxillipeds, maxillae	feeding?
8. oesophagus	food palatability?
9. general carapace, tail and claws	food recognition?
10. antennae	food recognition?

chemoreceptors on its first two pairs of legs (Fig. 13) to recognize the mussel as a piece of food. Eliminating the leg chemoreceptors, but not the mechanoreceptors, results in non-recognition and blocks the feeding behaviour sequence at that stage (Derby & Atema 1982b). The first two pairs of legs appear to be critical in this respect (Borroni, Handrich & Atema 1985) and could be called 'hands' functionally. These legs take the mussel and 'hand' it over to the maxillipeds, where chemoreceptors examine it once again: lack of maxilliped chemoreceptor function results in breaking off the feeding behaviour sequence at this stage (Derby & Atema 1982b). If accepted by the maxillipeds, the legs take the mussel to the claws: the crusher claw cracks the shell while the seizer claw, as in a nutcracker, prevents the mussel from jumping out during the cracking. The 'hands' then begin to pick out the meat from the mussel; their 'hedgehog' sensilla (Fig. 13) dig with their 'spines' into the flesh, liberating tissue fluid; this would allow sampling of the organic content of the food for final palatability. The legs hand over pieces of flesh to the maxillipeds and then onwards into the mouth which consists of two other pairs of maxillipeds, two pairs of maxillae, and a pair of mandibles, all

Figure 13. Taste organ of *Homarus americanus*.
(A) Chelate walking legs with tufts of large sensilla and row of small 'hedgehog' sensilla along biting edges of claw (arrows).
(B) Row of 'hedgehog' sensilla.
(C) Enlargement of one sensillum showing 'spines'. (B and C from Derby, 1982.)

Fig. 13

supplied with still unknown chemoreceptors. Finally, there are chemoreceptors in the oesophagus (Robertson & Laverack 1978) of unknown behavioural function.

In addition to a role in feeding behaviour where the amino acids and amines are important stimuli, the antennules, legs, and maxillipeds play a role in courtship and mating behaviour (Atema & Engstrom 1971; Atema et al. 1979) where urine and body odour cues convey sex identification (Cowan & Atema 1984). Prominent use and activity of these three major chemoreceptor organs in the process of turning over the female just prior to copulation suggests the use of (yet unidentified) chemical cues.

The presence of abundant hedgehog sensilla on the fourth pair of walking legs (Derby 1982) which are not used in feeding behaviour, suggests a distinct behavioural role perhaps in grooming: the chemical recognition and removal of parasites, or – in females – diseased eggs from the abdomen. The fourth pair of legs is used extensively for these grooming functions.

The lobster example serves to illustrate that different chemoreceptor organs even in one animal at once serve different behavioural functions (e.g. grooming *versus* spatial orientation) and operate in different microenvironments where they encounter chemical stimuli that differ in mixture composition, absolute stimulus strength, and pulse pattern. The gross morphology of the organs (e.g. hedgehog *versus* aesthetasc) as well as their behaviour (e.g. grabbing *versus* flicking) are adapted to special behavioural needs. One might expect that the spectral and dynamic response properties of the receptor cells will show similar specializations with respect to the peculiar conditions of their microenvironment: for instance, aesthetasc receptors are expected to have faster adaptation and disadaptation rates than hedgehog receptors, since flicking antennules serve a function in spatial orientation within filamentous odour plumes. Considering their function in detecting distant and thus dilute odours, antennular receptors are also expected to have lower thresholds than leg receptors. This could depend on the natural state of adaptation due to stimulus background noise or on intrinsic physiological properties of receptor cells: Derby & Atema (1982a) reported (unusual?) leg receptor responses to 10^{-14} m-NH_4, whereas Thompson & Ache (1980) measured antennular responses in spiny lobsters to 10^{-12} m-taurine which they extrapolated to far lower thresholds. The lobster also serves to draw attention to the importance of generating information currents to obtain (and deliver) chemical signals. While details are naturally peculiar to each species, the general principles that are beginning to emerge from research on lobsters may well be useful in our concepts of aquatic chemoreception in general. There principles are that chemoreceptor organs show specific adaptations to their microenvironment in terms of gross morphology, behaviour, receptor cell physiology, and central connections. It is illuminating to consider each organ in its various functional relationships with its own microenvironments.

Summary

1. The chemical stimulus environment is pulsed in nature.

2. Mixtures can identify an odour source with great specificity, and (hence) most chemical signals are mixtures, even when initial research may seem to indicate that single compounds are sufficient to release complete behaviour.

3. Information currents are often necessary to receive chemical stimuli.

4. Receptor cell physiology reflects the microenvironment in which the receptor organ operates. Receptor cells interface with the stimulus environment in such a way as to enhance signal-to-noise ratios and to cover the naturally occurring dynamic stimulus range.

5. Different chemoreceptor organs are designed to perform a number of different behavioural tasks. This is equally true for aquatic species that sample one (aqueous) medium as for terrestrial species that sample air and aqueous media. Hence, most of these principles are not unique to aquatic chemoreception.

This paper was written during a period of research supported by the Whitehall Foundation and the U.S. National Science Foundation (BNS 8411969). I thank my students past and present for their enthusiasm and critical support; in addition, their work figures prominently in the data upon which this paper is based.

References

ATEMA, J. Structures and functions of the sense of taste in the catfish (*Ictalurus natalis*). *Brain, Behav. Ecol.* **4**, 273–294.

ATEMA, J. (1977). Functional separation of smell and taste. In *Olfaction and Taste VI.* (ed. J. Le Magnen & P. MacLeod.) pp. 165–174. London. Information Retrieval Ltd.

ATEMA, J. (1980a). Smelling and tasting underwater. *Oceanus* **23**, 4–18.

ATEMA, J. (1980b). Chemical senses, chemical signals and feeding behavior in fishes. In *Fish Behavior and Its Use in the Capture and Culture of Fishes*, (ed. J. E. Bardach, J. J. Magnuson, R. C. May & J. M. Reinhart.) pp. 57–94. Manila; ICLARM.

ATEMA, J. & BURD, G. D. (1975). A field study of chemotactic responses of the mud snail, *Nassarius obsoletus. J. chem. Ecol.* **1**, 243–251.

ATEMA, J. & ENGSTROM, D. G. (1971). Sex pheromone in the lobster *Homarus americanus. Nature* **232**, 261–263.

ATEMA, J., HOLLAND, K. & IKEHARA, W. (1980). Olfactory responses of yellowfin tuna (*Thunnus albacares*) to prey odors: chemical search image. *J. chem. Ecol.* **6**, 457–465.

ATEMA, J., JACOBSON, S., KARNOFSKY, E., OLESZKO-SZUTS, S. & STEIN, L. (1979). Pair formation in the lobster *Homarus americanus*: behavioral development, pheromones and mating. *Mar. Behav. Physiol.* **6**, 277–296.

BALOUN, A. J. & MORSE, D. E. (1984). Ionic control of settlement and metamorphosis in larval *Haliotis rufescens* (Gastropoda). *Biol. Bull. mar. biol. Lab., Woods Hole* **167**. 124–138.

BARDACH, J. E., TODD, J. H. & CRICKMER, R. (1967). Orientation by taste in fish of the genus *Ictalurus*. *Science* **155**, 1276–1278.

BARDACH, J. E. & VILLARS, T. (1974). The chemical senses of fishes. In *Chemoreception in Marine Organisms*. (ed. P. T. Grant & A. M. Mackie) pp. 49–104. (New York: Academic Press).

BARTOSHUK, L. M. (1978). Gustatory system. In *Handbook of Behavioral Neurobiology*, Vol. I., *Sensory Integration* (ed. Masterton) pp. 503–567.

BAUER, U., DUDEL. J. & HATT, H. (1981). Characteristics of single chemoreceptive units sensitive to amino acids and related substances in the crayfish leg. *J. comp. Physiol.* **144**, 67–74.

BLOOM, F. E. (1984). The functional significance of neurotransmitter diversity. *Am. J. Physiol.* **246**, C184–C194.

BOECKH, J., KAISSLING, K. E., & SCHNEIDER, D. (1965). Insect olfactory receptors. *Cold Spring Harbor Symp. Quant. Biol.* **30**, 263–280.

BORRONI, P. F., HANDRICH, L. S. & ATEMA, J. (1985). The role of narrowly tuned taste cell populations in lobster (*Homarus americanus*) feeding behavior. *Behav. Neurosci.* (in press).

BOSSERT, W. H. & WILSON, E. O. (1963). The analysis of olfactory communication among animals. *J. theoret. Biol.* **5**, 443–469.

BURSELL, E. (1984). Observations on the orientation of tsetse flies (*Glossina pallidipes*) to wind-borne odours. *Physiol. Entomol.* **9**, 133–137.

CAPRIO, J. (1982). High sensitivity and specificity of olfactory and gustatory receptors of catfish to amino acids. In *Chemoreception in Fishes, Developments in Aquaculture and Fisheries Science*, Vol. **8**. (ed. T. J. Hara) pp. 109–134. Amsterdam: (Elsevier).

CARDÉ, R. T. (1984). Chemo-orientation in flying insects. In *Chemical Ecology of Insects*. (ed. W. J. Bell & R. J. Cardé) pp. 111–124. London: Chapman and Hall Ltd.

CARDÉ, R. T. & BAKER, T. C. (1984). Sexual communication with pheromones. In *Chemical Ecology of Insects*. (ed. W. J. Bell & R. J. Cardé) pp. 355–383. London: (Chapman and Hall Ltd.).

CARR, W. E. S. (1977). Chemoreception in the shrimp, *Palaemonetes pugio*: the role of amino acids and betaine in elicitation of a feeding response by extracts. *Comp. Biochem. Physiol.* **61**, 127–131.

CARR, W. E. S. (1982). Chemical stimulation of feeding behavior. In *Chemoreception in Fishes, Developments in Aquaculture and Fisheries Science. Vol.* **8**. (ed. T. J. Hara) pp. 259–274. Amsterdam: (Elsevier).

CARR, W. E. S., NETHERTON III J. C., & MILSTEAD, M. L. (1984). Chemoattractants of the shrimp, *Palaemonetes pugio*: variability in responsiveness and stimulatory capacity of mixtures containing amino acids, quaternary ammonium compounds, purines and other substances. *Comp. Biochem. Physiol.* **77A**, 469–474.

CHANGEUX, J. -P., DEVILLERS-THIERY, A. & CHEMOUILLI, P. (1984). Acetylcholine receptor: an allosteric protein. *Science* **225**, 1335–1345.

CONNOR, W. E., EISNER, T., VANDER MEER, R. K., GUERRERO, A., GHIRINGELLI, D., & MEINWALD, J. (1980). Sex attractant of an Arctiid Moth (*Utetheisa ornatrix*): A pulsed chemical signal. *Behav. Ecol. Sociobiol.* **7**, 55–63.

CONTI-TRONCONI, B. M. & RAFTERY, M. A. (1982). The nicotinic cholinergic receptor: correlation of molecular structure with functional properties. *Ann. Rev. Biochem.* **51**, 491–530.

COWAN, D. & ATEMA, J. (1984). Sex discrimination in lobsters: urine cues. *Biol. Bull. mar. biol. Lab. Woods Hole* **167**, 525.

DAVID, C. T., KENNEDY, J. S., LUDLOW. A. R., PERRY, J. N., & WALL, C. (1982). A reappraisal of insect flight towards a distant point source of wind-borne odor. *J. Chem. Ecol.* **8**. 1207–1215.

DERBY, C. D. (1982). Structure and function of cuticular sensilla of the lobster *Homarus americanus. J. Crust. Biol.* **2**, 1–21.

DERBY, C. D. & ATEMA, J. (1981). Selective improvement in responses to prey odors by the lobster, *Homarus americanus*, following feeding experience. *J. Chem. Ecol.* **7**, 1073–1080.

DERBY, C. D. & ATEMA, J. (1982a). Chemosensitivity of walking legs of the lobster *Homarus americanus*: Neurophysiological response spectrum and thresholds. *J. exp. biol.* **98**, 303–315.

DERBY, C. D. & ATEMA, J. (1982b). The function of chemo- and mechanoreceptors in lobster (*Homarus americanus*) feeding behavior. *J. exp. Biol.* **98**, 317–327.

DERBY, C. D. & ATEMA, J. (1982c). Narrow-spectrum chemoreceptor cells in the walking legs of the lobster *Homarus americanus*: taste specialists. *J. comp. Physiol.* A **146**, 181–189.

DEVINE, D. & ATEMA, J. (1982). Function of chemoreceptor organs in spatial orientation of lobster, *Homarus americanus*: differences and overlap. *Biol. Bull mar. biol. Lab., Woods Hole* **163**, 144–153.

DØVING, K. B. & THOMMESEN, G. (1977). Some properties of the fish olfactory system. In *Olfaction and Taste VI.* (ed. J. Le Magnen & P. MacLeod) pp. 75–183. London: Information Retrieval.

DØVING, K. B., DUBOIS-DAUPHIN, M., HOLLEY, A. & JOURDAN, F. (1977). Functional anatomy of the olfactory organ of fish and the ciliary mechanism of water transport. *Acta Zool. Stockholm* **58**, 245–255.

EPPLE, G., GOLOB, N. F. & SMITH III, A. B. (1979). Odor communication in the tamarin *Saguinus fuscicollis* (Callitrichidae); behavior and chemical studies. In *Chemical Ecology: Odour Communication in Animals,* (ed. F. J. Ritter). pp. 117–130. Amsterdam: (Elsevier/North-Holland Biomedical Press).

ERICKSON, R. P. (1982). The across-fiber pattern theory: an organizing principle for molar neural function. In *Contributions to Sensory Physiology,* Vol. **6**, (ed. W. D. Neff). pp. 79–110. New York: Academic Press.

EWERT, J. P. (1980). *Neuroethology.* New York: (Springer-Verlag).

FUTRELLE, R. P. (1984). How molecules get to their detectors. The physics of diffusion of insect pheromones. *TINS April*, 116–120.

FUZESSERY, Z. M., CARR, W. E. S., & ACHE, B. W. (1978). Antennular chemosensitivity in the spiny lobster, *Panulirus argus*: studies of taurine sensitive receptors. *Biol. Bull. mar. biol. Lab., Woods Hole* **154**, 226–240.

GHIRADELLA, H. T., CASE, J. F. & CRONSHAW, J. (1968). Structure of aesthetascs in selected marine and terrestrial decapods: chemoreceptor morphology and environment. *Am. Zool.* **8**, 603–621.

GIRAUDAT, J. & CHANGEUX, J. P. (1981). The acetylcholine receptor. In *Towards Understanding Receptors I.* (ed. J. W. Lamble) pp. 34–43. Amsterdam: (Elsevier).

GLEESON, R. A. (1982). Morphological and behavioral identification of the sensory structures mediating pheromone reception in the blue crab, *Callinectes sapidus. Biol. Bull. mar. biol. Lab., Woods Hole* **163**, 167–171.

GLEESON, R. A. & ACHE, B. W. (1983). Mixture suppression of primary chemoreceptor responses: neurophysiological evidence in taurine sensitive cells. *Neurosci. Abst.* **13**, 1024.

HASLER, A. D. & SCHOLTZ, A. T. (1983). *Olfactory Imprinting and Homing in Salmon*. New York: (Springer Verlag). 134 pp.

HATT, H. & BAUER, U. (1982). Electrophysiological properties of pyridine receptors in the crayfish walking leg. *J. comp. Physiol. A* **148**, 221–224.

HERBERT, P. & ATEMA, J. (1977). Olfactory discrimination of male and female conspecifics in the bullhead catfish, *Ictalurus nebulosus*. *Biol. Bull. mar. biol. Lab., Woods Hole* **153**, 429–430.

HODGSON, E. S. & MATHEWSON, R. F. (1975). Chemosensory orientation in sharks. *Ann. N. Y. Acad. Sci.* **188**, 175–182.

HOWE, N. R. & SHEIKH, Y. M. (1975). Anthopleurine: a sea anemone alarm pheromone. *Science* **189**, 386–388.

JOHNSEN, P. B. & HASLER, A. D. (1980). The use of chemical cues in the upstream migration of coho salmon, *Oncorhynchus kisutch* Wolbaum. *J. Fish Biol.* **17**, 67–73.

JOHNSON, B. R. & ATEMA, J. (1983). Narrow-spectrum chemoreceptor cells in antennules of the American lobster, *Homarus americanus*. *Neuroscience Letters* **41**, 145–150.

JOHNSON, B. R., BORRONI, P. F. & ATEMA, J. (1985). Mixture effects at primary olfactory and gustatory receptor cells from the lobster. *Chem. Senses* (in press).

JOHNSON, B. R., VOIGT, R., BORRONI, P. F. & ATEMA, J. (1984). Response properties of lobster chemoreceptors: tuning of primary taste neurons in walking legs. *J. comp. Physiol. A* **155**, 593–604.

KALMIJN, A. J. (1984). Theory of electromagnetic orientation: a further analysis. In *Comparative Physiology of Sensory Systems*. (ed. L. Bolis, R. E. Keynes, & S. H. P. Maddrell) pp. 525–560. Cambridge: Cambridge Univ. Press.

KLEEREKOPER, H. (1969). *Olfaction in Fishes*. Bloomington, IN: (Indiana University Press).

KUENEN, L. P. S. & BAKER, T. C. (1982). Optomotor regulation of ground velocity during flight to sex pheromone at different heights. *Physiol. Entomol.* **7**, 193–202.

KUPFERMAN, S. L. & MOORE, D. E. (1981). Physical oceanographic characteristics influencing the dispersion of dissolved tracers released at the sea floor in selected deep ocean study areas. *SAND* 80–2573 Sandia National Laboratory, 30 pp.

LAVERACK, M. S. & ARDILL, D. J. (1965). The innervation of the aesthetasc hairs of *Panulirus argus*. *Q. Jl. microsc. Sci.* **106**, 45–60.

LOOMIS, W. F. (1955). Glutathione control of the specific feeding reactions of hydra. *Ann. N. Y. Acad. Sci.* **62**, 209–228.

MACKIE, A. M. (1973). The chemical basis of food detection in the lobster *Homarus gammarus*. *Mar. Biol.* **21**, 103–108.

MACNAB, R. M. & KOSHLAND JR, D. E. (1972). The gradient-sensing mechanisms in bacterial chemotaxis. *Proc. natn. Acad. Sci. U.S.A.* **69**, 2509–2512.

MACRIDES, H. R. & CHOROVER, E. H. (1972). Olfactory bulb units: activity correlated with inhalation cycles and odor quality. *Science* **175**, 84–87.

MANKIN, R. W. & MAYER, M. S. (1984). The insect antenna is not a molecular sieve. *Experientia* **40**, 1251–1252.

McLEESE, D. M. (1970). Detection of dissolved substances by the American lobster (*Homarus americanus*) and olfactory attraction between lobsters. *J. Fish. Res. Bd. Can.* **27**, 1371–1378.

McPHIE, D. & ATEMA, J. (1984). Chemical communication in lobsters: information currents. *Biol. Bull. mar. biol. Lab., Woods Hole* **167**, 510–511.

MELINKAT, R. & ZEISKE, E. (1979). Functional morphology of ventilation of the olfactory organ in *Bedotia geayi* Pellegrin 1909 (Teleostei, Atherinidae). *Zool. Anz. Jena* **203**, 354–368.

MOPPER, K. & LINDROTH, P. (1982). Diel and depth variations in dissolved free amino acids and ammonium in the Baltic Sea determined by shipboard HPLC analysis. *Limnol. Oceanogr.* **27**, 336–347.

MÜLLER, D. G. (1977). Chemical basis of sexual approach in marine brown algae. In *Marine Natural Products Chemistry* (ed. D. J. Faulkner, W. H. Fenical). *NATO Conference Series IV: Marine Sciences.* pp. 351–366. New York: (Plenum Press).

MURLIS, J. & JONES, C. D. (1981). Fine-scale structure of odour plumes in relation to insect orientation to distant pheromone and other attractant sources. *Physiol. Entomol.* **6**, 71–86.

NISTRI, A. & CONSTANTI, A. (1979). Pharmacological characterization of different types of GABA and glutamate receptors in vertebrates and invertebrates. *Prog. Neurobiol.* **13**, 117–235.

O'CONNELL, R. J. (1985). Responses to pheromone blends in insect olfactory receptor neurons. *J. comp. Physiol.* (in press).

PAWSON, M. G. (1977). Analysis of a natural chemical attractant for whiting, *Merlangus merlangus* L. and cod, *Gadus morhua* L. using a behavioral bioassay. *Comp. Biochem. Physiol.* **56A**, 129–135.

REEDER, P. B. & ACHE, B. W. (1980). Chemotaxis in the Florida spiny lobster, *Panulirus argus. Anim. Behav.* **28**, 831–839.

ROBERTSON, R. M. & LAVERACK, M. S. (1978). Inhibition of oesophageal peristalsis in the lobster after chemical stimulation. *Nature* **271**, 239–240.

ROELOFS, W. (1979). Production and perception of lepidopterous pheromone blends. In *Chemical Ecology: Odour Communication in Animals* (ed. F. J. Ritter) pp. 159–168. Amsterdam: (Elsevier/North-Holland Biomedical Press).

SCHMITT, B. C. & ACHE, B. W. (1979). Olfaction: response enhancement by flicking in a decapod crustacean. *Science* **205**, 204–206.

SCHNEIDER, D. (1969). Insect olfaction: deciphering system for chemical messages. *Science* **163**, 1031–1037.

SHANK, R. P. & FREEMAN, A. R. (1976). Agonistic and antagonistic activity of glutamate analogs on neuromuscular excitation in the walking limbs of lobsters. *J. Neurobiol.* **7**, 23–36.

SILVERSTEIN, R. M. & YOUNG, J. C. (1976). Insects generally use multicomponent pheromones. In *Pest Management With Insect Sex Attractants and Other Behavior-Controlling Chemicals.* (ed. M. Beroza) pp. 1–29. Washington, D. C: Amer. Chem. Society.

SLEEPER, H. L., PAUL, V. J., & FENICAL, W. (1980). Alarm pheromones from the marine opisthobranch *Navanax inermis. J. Chem. Ecol.* **6**, 57–70.

SNOW, P. (1973). Ultrastructure of the aesthetasc hairs of the littoral decapod, *Paragrapsus gaimardii. Z. Zellforsch. mikrosk. Anat.* **138**, 489–502.

STEWART, A., BRYANT, B. & ATEMA, J. (1979). Behavioral evidence for two populations of amino acid receptors in catfish taste. *Biol. Bull. mar. biol. Lab., Woods Hole* **157**, 396.

STRICKLER, R. (1982). Calanoid copepods, feeding currents and the role of gravity. *Science* **218**, 158–160.

THOMPSON, H. & ACHE, B. W. (1980). Threshold determination for olfactory receptors of the spiny lobster. *Mar. Behav, Physiol.* **7**, 249–260.

VOGEL, S. (1981). *Life in Moving Fluids: The Physical Biology of Flow.* Boston, MA: (W. Grant Press).

VOIGT, R. & ATEMA, J.(1984). Chemoreceptor adaptation: responses of glutamate cells to repeated stimulation. *Biol. Bull. mar.. biol. Lab., Woods Hole* **167**, 534.

Printed in Great Britain. © *Society of Experimental Biology 1985*

THE MECHANICAL SENSES OF AQUATIC ORGANISMS

A. D. HAWKINS

Marine Laboratory, Aberdeen, Scotland

Introduction

In looking at sensory systems in a particular environment, the sea, it is useful to concentrate on the various kinds of stimulation – the potential information – available to the organism. This paper looks at the mechanical properties of seawater, and identifies those mechanical stimuli which are there to be detected and utilized by marine organisms.

The science of mechanics deals with the laws governing the movement of objects, and mechanoreceptors are sense organs responding to those forces which can induce motion of a medium and the objects within it. The forces themselves may be gravitational, frictional, or viscous, or arise from contact with moving bodies or fluids. Their effect within the medium may be to exert pressure or stress, induce a fluid flow, or to propagate travelling waves of motion and pressure through the medium. All these potential stimuli may act upon the animal, touching, stretching, compressing, moving or deforming the body, and providing a basis for detection.

Water differs from air in being much more dense, less compressible and elastic, and more viscous. In water, the main mechanical stimuli or disturbances which an organism encounters are those due to gravity itself, changes in the local pressure, water currents, local water movements and turbulence, wave motion at the air/water interface, particle oscillations and sound.

Gravity

Most marine organisms respond to gravity. In many of the simple metazoans these responses do not appear to be mediated by any particular sense organs, the stresses set up in the body of the organism providing an indication of orientation with respect to the earths gravitational field. Rapid gravitational responses are more usually mediated by simple statocysts, however, which appear to have evolved independently, many times, in different groups (Laverack, 1981). The essential feature of a statocyst is a heavy mass, often a calcareous accretion, mounted on sensory cells which commonly bear a series of non-motile sensory cilia. Examples are found in the carnivorous ctenophores of the marine plankton, the many marine medusae, the annelids, the decapod crustaceans, the cephalopod molluscs, and in all the vertebrates. The statocyst organs enable these animals to maintain their posture and balance, and often provide a basis for complex compensatory reactions, enabling the animal to regain its balance after movement. In the more active animals, including many decapods, cephalopods, and fish the statocysts play a role not only as gravity sensors but as detectors of linear accelerations by the animal, often in the three main axes of yaw, tilt and pitch (Laverack, 1981). Horridge (1971) has suggested that in all these groups statocysts evolved as gravity detectors from stiff cilia which were originally underwater vibration receptors.

Hydrostatic pressure

The absolute pressure, or hydrostatic pressure is a function of gravitational forces. It is proportional to depth in water, and increases at a rate of about 1 atmosphere every 10 m, a much greater range that that encountered on land. In the deep ocean pressures may be as high as 1000 atmospheres. Large changes in hydrostatic pressure are more characteristic of shallow seas subjected to wave action and tides. A behavioural sensitivity to sudden changes in pressure is well established for many marine organisms, some of them being able to perceive changes of the order of 1 % (Blaxter 1978). Those having a gas phase, like fish with swimbladders, appear to be more sensitive than others (Blaxter 1980). Sensitivity to relatively slow changes in pressure, like those caused by tidal variations in water depth, is less firmly established, and it is still not clear whether any animal has an absolute sense of pressure. Moreover, where a pressure sense has been established the sense organs responsible have yet to be identified. In larvae of the herring, *Clupea harengus*, the development of gas within the otic bulla is associated with an improvement in pressure sensitivity (Blaxter & Denton, 1976), suggesting that the gas phase is important to the operation of the receptor. Qutob (1962) concluded that changes in the volume of the gas-filled swimbladder resulted in changes in the tension of the walls of this organ which were detected by proprioceptors. In decapod crustaceans, which do not have a gas phase, Digby (1972) has propounded the theory that pressure influences potentials across the cuticle, but the evidence for this serving as a pressure receptor is scanty. Shear forces between tissues of differing compressibility have also been suggested as a possible basis for pressure reception in crustaceans (Enright, 1963). In general, however, we are remarkably ignorant of the mechanisms of pressure reception in marine organisms.

Water currents

It is widely believed that water currents play a considerable part in directing the course of movement or marine organisms, and especially fish, though the mechanisms by which this direction might be brought about are not always described. Certainly, water currents are a dominant and pervasive feature of the marine environment, and have a far-reaching effect upon even the larger more active marine organisms.

There is some confusion in defining and classifying the responses made by organisms to water flow. The terms rheotaxis and rheotropism have been used to describe, respectively, the orientation of an animal with respect to water flow, and a general response to water currents (see Arnold 1974, for more precise definitions). However, in many cases

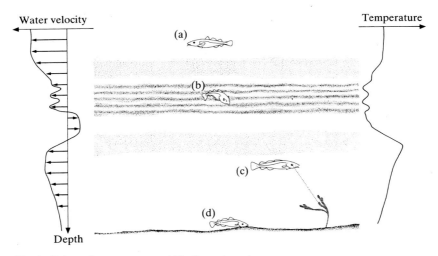

Fig. 1. Orientation to currents within the water column.
(A) An organism out of sight of the bottom, or in darkness, in a current of uniform velocity is often unable to orientate, and is carried passively with the current. (B) An organism in a turbulent layer, or where the current velocity profile changes within dimensions comparable with the size of the body, may be able to orientate with respect to the water currents. (C) an organism within sight of the bottom, or (D) in contact with it can orientate itself relative to the current.
Note that by vertical migration an animal can influence its transport direction by reference to cues such as temperature gradients, without detecting water movements. (Modified from Westerberg, 1984).

where these terms are applied it is not certain that the organism is responding to the water flow *per se*. For a neutrally buoyant animal immersed in a body of water moving at a constant velocity the detection of the movement itself presents a major problem (Fig. 1). A blind fish in mid-water, in a non-turbulent flowing stream clear of the bottom, does not head up-stream as is commonly supposed but is carried passively with the flow (Lyon, 1904; Dijkgraaf, 1933). It can only detect its own motion if it can see or is in contact with some fixed reference point in the environment, like the sea bed. It is well established that in the latter circumstances many animals do hold their position and stem the current by observing their own displacement relative to the seabed. Such animals can often be induced to move as if they were in a moving current simply by moving a visible background. In shallow water the tactile sense is particularly important in enabling fish to align themselves with respect to the direction of water flow. Lyon (1904) described how blinded killifishes, *Fundulus*, released into a tideway were carried steadily down-stream, but even slight and momentary contact with aquatic vegetation allowed the fish instantly to orientate themselves against the current.

There is an indirect mechanism available to marine fish which might enable them to determine that they are being carried passively over the ground in a moving body of water. Large scale electrical fields are generated by ocean currents flowing through the earth's magnetic field and may inform electroreceptive animals of their passive drift in tidal or ocean currents. Likewise, when swimming through the earth's magnetic field, the fish may induce electrical fields of their own (Kalmijn, 1971). Comparison of the sensitivity of electroreceptive fish, and especially the sharks and rays, with the strength of natural electric fields does show a small overlap and in principle this may provide these fish with a real compass sense (Kalmijn, 1981). Pals & Schoenage (1979) have also measured strong local variations in the electric field close to the seabed, and have suggested that these geoelectric fields may present orientation cues or information about local properties of the environment to benthic fish.

For most animals, however, remote from the seabed, or under conditions where vision is impaired, passive drift appears to be difficult for the animal to detect as well as difficult to compensate for. Thus, passive drift with water currents is a fact of life for many marine organisms especially for the smaller species of zooplankton. Many oceanic species may spend their whole lives within an oceanic eddy or gyral, with their life cycles synchronized with their drift from place to place. Individual neritic organisms may also find themselves caught up in offshore currents and may often be carried passively to unfavourable areas, from which they cannot hope to return. Nevertheless, there is increasing evidence that some organisms which one might expect to be at the whim of wind-driven and tidal currents are able to stay in particular areas, or make use of currents for transport (Leggett, 1984). This independent movement does not have to be the result of directed active swimming against the current, but may be mediated in other ways. For example, by quite small vertical movements the animals may take advantage of opposing currents at different depths (Fig. 1). There can be large mesoscale variations in the vertical structure of water masses, with great variations not only in current speed but other parameters with depth (Westerberg, 1984). The temperature, salinity, density and concentration of dissolved materials may vary with depth on a scale of 1–10 m. Vertical migration, perhaps mediated by gravitational, hydrostatic pressure or phototactic responses, and modulated by the tidal or diel cycle, may translate the animal from one moving water mass to another resulting in it moving in a given direction, or in it maintaining its station relative to the seabed. The particular bodies of water may be detected on the basis of their thermal or chemical characteristics. Behaviour of this kind seems to be especially prevalent in estuaries and coastal waters, and several examples are given by Leggett (1984). Selective tidal stream transport by the plaice *Pleuronectes platessa* in the North Sea is perhaps the best example (Greer Walker, Harden Jones & Arnold 1978), both juvenile and adult fish, with relatively poor swimming abilities, are able to move in a particular direction by selection of the appropriate tidal stream, the fish resting on the sea bed when the current opposes that direction.

It is not entirely clear how behaviour of this kind is mediated, or whether a directed response to the current itself plays any part. In some cases, the organism may simply show rhythmic vertical movements synchronized with tidal changes in the hydrostatic pressure. Where there is a response to the currents themselves it is possible that cues to the animal being in a moving body of water are provided by very small scale discontinuities in the water mass. That is, by local differences in the velocity of water movement on a scale comparable in dimensions with the body of the animal (Fig. 1). The organism may in principle detect the direction of motion by means of local water motion detectors on the body especially where there are strong gradients in current velocity across the direction of motion. Many organisms do possess mechanoreceptors projecting from the integument (described later). These are sensitive to shearing forces though it should be stressed that in a non-turbulent mass of water, moving at constant velocity, they are unlikely to be stimulated. Dijkgraaf

(1933), in a series of very careful experiments, demonstrated that blinded
fish could orientate with respect to water jets, and that the lateral line
system of mechanoreceptors was implicated in the response. Orientation
of this kind is familiar to us all from swimming past the water inlet in a
swimming pool.

Under some circumstances inertial receptors, like the statocyst organs
mentioned earlier, might serve for the detection of movement in a water
current. It is clear that many organisms including decapod crustaceans,
cephalopods and fish are sensitive to both angular and linear accelerations, and are well able to detect the direction of these accelerations
relative to the body axis (Laverack, 1981). Though a neutrally buoyant
inactive organism in a laminar flow of water moving at constant velocity
will not experience acceleration, it will experience it at any boundary with
a current moving at a different velocity, and this may lead to compensatory movements of the body.

Given that some organisms can detect linear and angular accelerations,
can they make use of inertial navigation to maintain a course or compensate for drift due to water currents? Modern techniques of inertial navigation certainly allow ships to determine their geographic position, or to
compensate for the effects of deflecting currents. Such systems rely on
accelerometers mounted on a system of gyroscopes, the latter providing
spatial reference. The aquatic vertebrates possess accelerometers in the
form of semicircular canals and otolith organs, able to detect angular and
linear accelerations respectively, but there is no evidence that these
organs allow marine fish to navigate with precision over long time
periods. However, Jones (1984) has recently argued that inertial
guidance may take place in some fishes which maintain a fixed heading in
the absence of any obvious external cues. He suggests that these animals
update their headings at regular intervals by reference to features like
sand waves on the seabed, using inertial guidance in the intervening
period.

Local water movements

A range of organisms from taxonomically quite distinct groups possess
water motion detectors projecting from the integument, which are
strikingly similar (Laverack, 1981). Most of these organs consist of
relatively short projections from the body (usually less than 0.1 mm −
100 μm), often arrayed in tracts or groups. Some comprise single or
groups of stiff cilia, which are presumed to be non-motile, but which are
free to move at the base. They may or may not be associated with a

secreted cap, or cupula. Others are hard but articulated cuticular structures, like bristles or fans. The receptors may be naked and fully exposed
to the water or even mounted on hillocks, or they may be enclosed in pits,
canals or tubes. Some have a definite axis of sensitivity or are constrained
to move in a direction by the possession of hinge-like joints, or through
placement within a groove or duct.

Examples of these water movement detectors can be found in a wide
range of aquatic organisms, including the arrow worms, or chaetognaths;
the comb-jellies, or ctenophores; the crustaceans, especially the larger
decapods; pelagic and sessile tunicates, cephalochordates and
vertebrates. Horridge (1966) has suggested that similar sense organs
based on non-motile cilia may serve a similar function in a variety of
coelenterates, annelids, molluscs and other smaller phyla, while a range
of cuticular hairs, bristles and fans might play a similar role in many
aquatic insects. Where these receptors have been found and examined it
has usually been possible to show that they are sensitive to water currents
and in some cases also to oscillatory motions of the medium generated by
sources close to the animal.

In the chaetognath *Spadella cephaloptera*, and indeed most other
chaetognaths, there are regular arrays of sense organs over the surface of
the body (Fig. 2), visible sometimes as bristles in the living animal but
essentially consisting of regular flat planar projections, extending up to
about 100 μm from the body (Bone & Pulsford, 1978). Each projection
consists of a fence of 75–100 closely packed stiff cilia, with the typical
$9 + 2$ structure of microtubules, arising from a group of spindle-shaped
sensory cells. Each sensory cell has an axon which passes to the ventral
ganglion of the central nervous system. The central doublets of the cilia
are aligned parallel to the axis of the fence, and it is inferred that the
organs are sensitive to deformation of the ciliary fence by water motion
in a plane transverse to the axis of the fence. This axis of sensitivity
remains to be verified, however. Other types of projection which are
presumed to be sensory are found elsewhere on the body and also have
a ciliary structure.

Horridge & Boulton (1967) suggested that these sensory structures of
the arrow worm are sensitive to the oscillatory motions set up by vibrating
sources in the near vicinity of the animal. By vibrating a nearby glass
probe (within 1–3 mm) animals could be induced to turn and seize the end
of the probe within their jaws. They attacked the probe only if it was
vibrated at frequencies between 9 and 20 Hz, at source amplitudes of
100–500 μm. The eyes of chaetognaths are relatively simple, but these
animals are active predators able to capture prey even in darkness.

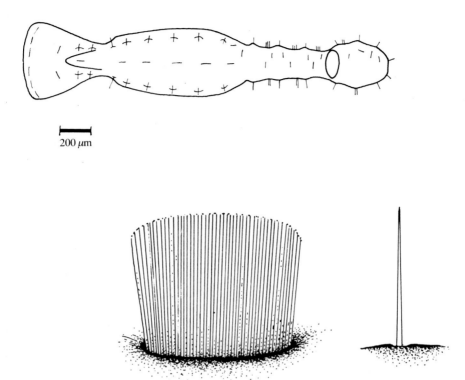

200 μm

10 μm

Fig. 2. The arrangement of ciliary fences on the chaetognath *Spadella* (re-drawn from Bone & Pulsford, 1978). In the living animal the fences, which are made up of cilia, stand out rigidly from the surface of the body. *Spadella* is able to detect the low-frequency water oscillations set up by its prey organisms (copepods).

Horridge and Boulton concluded that prey capture was achieved by detection of the water movements set up by the prey. This suggestion was confirmed by Newbury (1972), who established that the animal responded best to probes vibrating at frequencies corresponding to the beating rates of the feeding appendages of copepods, their natural prey. Indeed, Newbury speculated that chaetognaths recognize the vibration rates produced by specific copepods. More recent experiments by Feigenbaum & Reeve (1977) have confirmed these results and have shown that there can be significant differences in the frequency sensitivity of different species. *Sagitta hispida* gave a peak response at 105Hz, and also responded to non-vibrating sweeps of the probe. Attack distances were invariably extremely short (< 3 mm).

Organisms which rival chaetognaths as predators amongst the marine plankton are the ctenophores. Hyman (1940) pointed out that the epidermis of ctenophores is liberally provided with projecting bristles from sensory cells. It is possible that these serve to detect water movements generated by prey. Feeding strategems vary within the group. Some, like *Pleurobrachia*, catch their prey with long tentacles, others, like *Beröe*, swallow their prey whole. Horridge (1964) has described the capture of prey by *Leucothea*, a species which has muscular 'fingers' which are suddenly extended to capture prey. Simple non-motile cilia up to 100 μm long, issuing from axon-bearing cells, are found at the tips of the fingers. The fingers themselves are sensitive to water displacements (Horridge, 1964). A vibrating glass probe evokes extension of the whole finger as it is brought very close to the tip. Similarly, a vibrating needle brought close to a tentacle of *Pleurobrachia* will stimulate contraction of the tentacle and movement of the whole body. In this species Horridge (1966) has suggested that non-motile cilia on the tentacles are the responsible receptors.

Aquatic arthropods, and especially the decapod crustaceans (perhaps the most amenable to study) show a great variety of articulated pegs, bristles, hairs and fans distributed across the outer surface of the exoskeleton, which are associated with sensory cells inserted at their base (Bush & Laverack, 1982). These organs may be present on the body or appendages. They consist sometimes of short pegs, projecting barely above the exoskeleton, to long hair-like projections or setae. The latter may be long and slender, or short and fat. Some are smooth, while others are branching or serrated. Some are stiff, and others flexible. A great many of them appear to be tactile in function and are insensitive to water motion, but others are acutely sensitive to small water currents. Laverack (1962a, b), has investigated the properties of hair fan organs found on the chelae and carapace of the lobster *Homarus gammarus* L. (formerly *vulgaris*). These organs resemble flower buds, or small artichokes, about 75 μm long, buried within cuticular pits (Fig. 3). Though they appear to be mounted on a base allowing movement in all directions it is possible that their motion is constrained along an axis. There is evidence that they are innervated by two directionally sensitive units, each responding to a different direction of movement. The organs are extremely sensitive to oscillatory patterns of water flow, with a response synchronized with the stimulating waveform at frequencies up to 100 Hz. Rather different

A   B

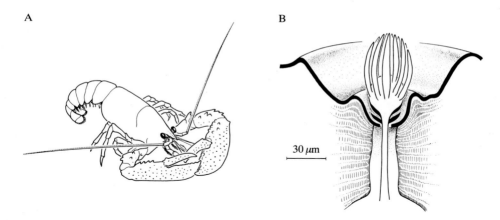

Fig. 3. Hair fan organs of the lobster *Homarus*. These cuticular receptors are contained
within shallow depressions on the surface of the cuticle, and are distributed on the chelae
and carapace of the lobster (A). The hair fan (B) is articulated at the base, and responds
to water currents by movement. The receptor cells pass through a narrow aperture in the
cuticle. Experimental evidence indicates that two directionally sensitive units are present,
each responding to a different direction of movement. (Redrawn from Laverack, 1962b).

water-movement-sensitive sensory hairs are found on the chelae of the
crayfish *Cherax destructor*, and have been examined by Tautz &
Sandeman (1980). Here, the sensory hairs are again contained within pits
and are usually grouped together. Some of the hairs are feathered, while
others are smooth, their lengths ranging from 20–400 μm. When
stimulated by oscillatory water movements the thresholds of the response
indicated greatest sensitivity within the frequency range 150–300 Hz,
with a water particle displacement threshold of about 0·2 μm. Weise
(1976) has calculated thresholds of about 0·1 μm at 100 Hz for sensory
hairs on the telson of the crayfish *Procambarus clarkii*, described earlier
by Mellon (1963).

    These various mechanoreceptors in crustaceans are sensitive to a wide
variety of forms of mechanical stimulation including tactile stimuli (Solon
& Kass-Simon, 1981) water currents (Laverack 1962a; Mellon, 1963;
Vedel & Clarac, 1976), pressure gradients (Laverack, 1962b), and vibration (Tazaki, 1977). Some are sensitive to displacement of the surrounding water and others to the velocity of motion of the water, (Tautz, 1979:
Solon & Kass-Simon, 1981).

    Organs which appear to have a mechanoreceptive function have also
been described for several species of tunicate, including both pelagic and
sessile forms. In the pelagic larvacean *Fritillaria*, ciliated cells are found
on the lower lip, and may well respond to local water movements. These

sensory organs are unusual for invertebrates in that the sensory cells are in contact at their base with the axons of central nervous cells (Bone, Gorski & Pulsford, 1979). In the sessile tunicate *Ciona*, and also in the filter feeding salps, cupular organs resembling those of the vertebrate lateral line system of sense organs are found (Bone & Ryan, 1978). In *Ciona* these organs are located in the zone of the atrial (exhalent) siphon, about 75–100 individual organs being present. Each one consists of a hillock, bearing an elongate cupula up to 250 μm long (Fig.4A,D). The cupulae are free to bend at their junction with the sensory organ. Several kinds of cells bearing cilia contribute to the organ, all of them being

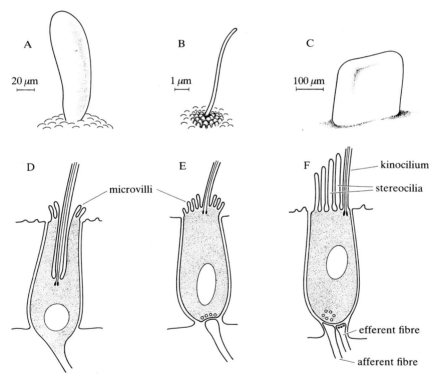

Fig. 4. Integumentary mechanoreceptors and their associated sensory hair cells. (A) The cupular organ of the tunicate *Ciona* found on the exhalent siphon. Several cilia-bearing cells contribute to the organ. Note that each is a primary sensory cell, (D), bearing its own axon. (After Bone & Ryan, 1978). (B, E) Cilia-bearing cells with a sensory function from the cephalochordate *Amphioxus*. These cells are found on the body surface, buccal cirri and velar tentacles. They synapse with central axons. (After Bone & Best, 1978). (C, F) A neuromast from the lateral line system of the aquatic toad *Xenopus*, with its sensory hair cells. Note the eccentrically placed kinocilium which gives the hair cell its pronounced morphological and physiological polarization.

primary sensory cells, bearing their own axons. Bone & Ryan (1978) showed that *Ciona* was sensitive to a vibrating probe placed near the atrial siphon over a wide frequency range. The similarity of these cupular organs to those of the lateral line system or aquatic vertebrates led Bone and Ryan to suggest that the organs offered a suitable morphological starting point for the evolution of the acoustico–lateralis system in vertebrates. They suggested that the presence of the cupula, lacking in the simpler ciliated mechanoreceptors of other tunicates, reflected the need to stiffen a rather longer receptor. In the same way, the vibration receptors of chaetognaths might derive their stiffness from the cilia being packed together to form fences.

Sensory cells bearing single cilia without a cupula are also found on the body surfaces, buccal cirri and velar tentacles of the cephalochordate *Amphioxus* (Fig. 4B,E). There are two different types (Bone & Best, 1978), each synapsing with central axons. Bone and Best have suggested that these cells normally respond to deformation of the cilium by water currents. Those on the velar tentacles show a remarkable multiplication of microtubules in the rather stiff cilia. In both types the cilium is surrounded by elongate microvilli, which might stabilize the structure and give it greater rigidity. As in the vertebrate lateral line system, the sensory cells synapse with central axons, and are not primary sensory cells of the typical invertebrate type. In this they differ from similar cells in the cupular organs of *Ciona*.

The lateral line system of vertebrates is perhaps the best-studied system of integumentary mechanoreceptors. It consists of a series of individual sense organs, or neuromasts, distributed on the head and trunk, sometimes as free receptors, but often in grooves or canals. Each individual neuromast consists of a group of receptors cells, the hair cells, surrounded by supporting cells. At their distal ends, the sensory processes of the hair cells are surmounted by a gelatinous cupula, projecting into the surrounding medium. The hair cells are morphologically polarized (Fig. 4F). The sensory processes are made up of a group of similar cilia, the stereocilia, and a single eccentrically placed kinocilium, with the familiar $9 + 2$ fibrillar structure. The physiological response of the hair cell is similarly polarized. A bending or deflection of the cupula, and cilia, in the direction of the kinocilium results in a depolarization across the hair-cell membrane and firing of the afferent nerve fibre. Deflection in the opposite direction results in a hyperpolarization, and inhibition of the afferent fibre. Each neuromast contains a mixed population of hair cells polarized in each of two opposing directions. The opposing sensory cells synapse with different afferent nerve fibres. By this means the receptor is bilaterally sensitive, and able to discriminate between deflection in the two opposing directions. The functioning of the lateral line system has been reviewed by Dijkgraaf (1963), Kuiper (1967) and Sand (1981).

There seems little doubt that these various projections from the integument serve a common function. In addition to being sensitive to mechanical stimulation, they often have a distinct axis of sensitivity and can even distinguish in some cases between motion in two opposing directions. In many organisms they are based on cilia. It is well established that motile cilia may respond to bending forces with a power stroke, for example, the cilia of the feeding apparatus of the echinoderm pluteus larva reverse their beat when encountering a solid particle (Strathmann, Jahn & Fonseca, 1972). Cilia appear to be readily modified to serve a mechano-sensory function.

The constraints which determine the form of these various integumentary sense organs have yet to be analysed in detail. It is clear that viscous shearing forces are especially important in determining the action of water movement upon the smallest organs. For a sensory hair to detect motion of the adjacent medium it must project well beyond the thin boundary layer which lies close to the body. Boundary layers depend on the water velocity but are generally thinner in water than in air. Any projecting setae for the detection of water currents can therefore be shorter in water than in air (Tautz, 1979). Increased sensitivity to the water flow outside the boundary layer can be achieved by harnessing

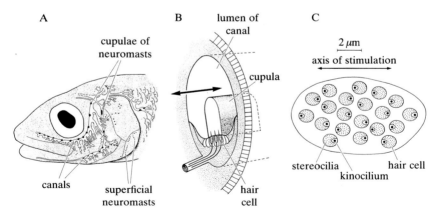

Fig. 5. The lateral line system of the herring *Clupea harengus* (A) Head of juvenile herring showing the positions of the head canals, and the cupulae within them. Superficial neuromasts are also shown. (B) Schematic cross section of a canal neuromast. Note that the long axis of the cupula is aligned with the direction of water motion. (C) Diagram of the neuromast viewed in cross section to show the hair cells predominantly orientated in two opposing directions. (Based on Blaxter, Gray & Best, 1983).

viscous forces through an increase in the surface area of the projecting process by the addition of branching, tree-like extensions. Where a cupula is present it may be a planar structure with its long axis orientated parallel to the direction of flow as in some of the lateral line neuromasts of fish (Fig. 5). Presumably this conformation provides the organ with a degree of stiffness to resist the shear forces applied through friction drag. On a larger scale, where the friction drag is proportionately small, some immunity is gained to the effects of viscosity. Sensitivity to the pressure drag set up by acceleration of the adjacent water may be obtained by an increase in frontal area exposed to the moving water. However, it seems that for most organisms a very large planar sensory structure, placed across the direction of the flow is disadvantageous (perhaps through the resistance it would offer to movement), indicating that the structure of these organs is essentially a compromise between sensory and other functions.

In many cases the integumentary mechanoreceptors clearly have the detection of local water movements or turbulence as their primary function. In most cases the water movements are set up by particular local sources, including other fish, but in other cases, as in the blind cave fish *Anoptichthys*, there is experimental evidence that stationary objects are detected by analysis of the pattern of water movement generated between those objects and the fish (Campenhausen, von Reiss & Weissert 1981).

Surface waves

We can gain particular insight into the way the integumentary mechanoreceptors function by considering their use for a specialized function – the detection of surface waves. The perception of surface waves by aquatic organisms has proved more amenable to experimental study than the response to turbulence, perhaps because the stimulus is easier to reproduce. A variety of surface-feeding fish (Schwartz, 1971), amphibians (Gorner, 1976), and aquatic insects (Wiese, 1972) make use of surface waves to locate prey trapped or moving on the water surface with great precision. In fish, the receptive structures are lateral line organs on the dorsal side of the head and trunk. The main neuromasts are contained within bilaterally symmetrical sacs and canals, open to the exterior, each group of neuromasts differing in their orientation with respect to the body axis (Fig. 6).

These surface-feeding fish determine both the distance of the source and its direction (Bleckmann, 1980). Source distance is determined most precisely with the fish close to a natural source. The amplitudes of the

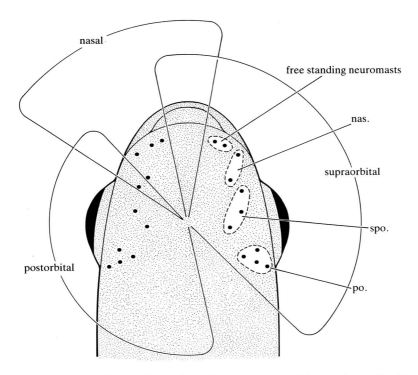

Fig. 6. Surface wave detection by the lateral line sense organs of the topminnow *Fundulus notatus*. The various canals are raised slightly above the surrounding skin, close to the water surface. Each canal is particularly sensitive to waves approaching within a particular sector. The receptive fields of the three systems are shown, as determined from extirpation experiments. The receptive field of the group of two free standing neuromasts is not shown, nor are the symmetrically located fields. (After Schwartz & Hasler, 1966).

different frequency components of the wide band signals from insect prey vary with distance (Fig. 7). Experiments have confirmed the importance of the frequency spectrum of the wave as a basis both for discriminating prey from non-prey signals, and for determining source distance (Hoin-Radkovsky, Bleckmann & Schwartz, 1984).

Determination of direction in these fish appears to depend on comparison of the activity of the distributed neuromasts. Though the fish can determine the presence of a source with the numbers of neuromasts reduced, its ability to locate the source is abolished when only one neuromast remains intact (Muller & Schwartz 1982). Moreover, ablation of the neuromasts on one side of the body results in a misinterpretation of target angles. There are two possible mechanisms for the directionality. One is that because the neuromasts are orientated in different directions and are scattered about the body, they are stimulated to a

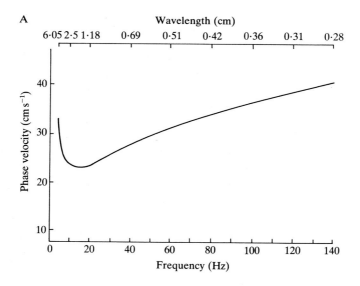

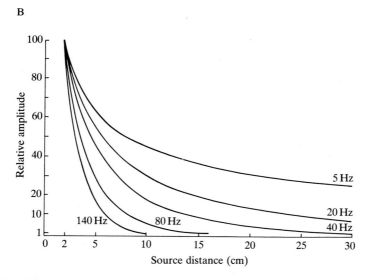

Fig. 7. (A) Propagation velocities of surface waves of different frequency and wavelength. Note that the velocities are much lower than the velocities of sound (1500 ms^{-1}). (B) The attention of water surface waves is dependent upon frequency, and distance from the source of vibration. Thus the frequency spectrum of the wave from a particular source will change with distance. Surface-wave-sensitive fish have been shown to use the frequency structure of the wave to determine source distance (see text for details). (Redrawn from Hoin-Radkovsky *et al.* 1984).

differing degree by a stimulus from a given source. Location might then be based on amplitude differences at the different neuromasts. The other is that because surface waves travel relatively slowly (particularly in comparison with sound waves) there are differences in the time of arrival of the wave at the different neuromasts. It has been suggested that it is timing, rather than amplitude cues that form the basis of directionality, at least in the aquatic toad *Xenopus laevis* (Elepfandt, 1982). Elepfandt points out that this animal does not locate wave direction by evaluating the intensity gradient along the body, and does not always orientate towards the direction of maximum sensitivity of its activated receptors. It is possible, however, that the method of processing wave direction in *Xenopus* may differ from that in surface-feeding fish.

That fish and other organisms orientate not only to surface waves but to local turbulence within the water column is well established. It is rather surprising that more is not known about the way these organisms evaluate and analyse the received signals. In particular a better understanding of the means by which the arrays of mechanoreceptors locate the sources of hydrodynamic stimuli is needed.

Particle oscillations

A key feature of the response pattern of the various mechanoreceptors, including the lateral line, is that they are often particularly sensitive to oscillatory motion. Indeed in some cases the organs are tuned to quite high frequencies of motion, and at the same time shielded from direct exposure to the large slow water movements by being placed inside ducts or canals, as shown in Fig. 5 for the herring.

Particle oscillations are set up by the movement of any object within an elastic medium. As the source moves, it imparts kinetic energy to adjacent particles of the medium which in turn are moved, generating a wave which propagates away from the source. The propagation velocity is very much faster than that for hydrodynamic phenomena like surface waves, or turbulent eddies and depends upon the elastic constants of the medium. The velocity is higher in a stiff, less compressible medium like water (about $1500\,\mathrm{ms^{-1}}$ for seawater, compared with $340\,\mathrm{ms^{-1}}$ for air).

Within the propagated wave the component particles of the medium are alternately forced together and then apart. The motion can be described by the mean velocity of the oscillating particles, or by the amplitude of motion, or displacement. The displacements may be very small – of the order of nanometers – much smaller than the movements associated with hydrodynamic stimuli. Always accompanying the particle

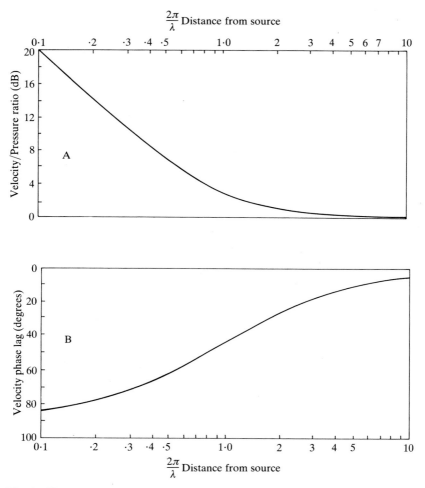

$\frac{2\pi}{\lambda}$ Distance from source

Fig. 8. Changes in the relationship between particle velocity and sound pressure with distance from a monopole sound source. The velocity/pressure ratio is highest close to the source, (A), where velocity shows a phase lag with respect to pressure. Distant from the source, in the far field, the velocity always bears the same proportion to the pressure and is in phase with it. (Modified from Siler, 1969).

oscillation, however, is a pressure change above and below the hydrostatic pressure of the medium. Distant from a source, and in the absence of reflecting boundaries the magnitudes of the two parameters, the velocity and pressure, are proportional to one another, the proportionality depending on the density and elasticity. In water, which is both more dense and less elastic than air, the particle oscillations are less than those in air by a factor of 3500.

In considering these acoustic waves, or sounds, propagating away from a source it is useful to distinguish between the so-called near field and far field. In the far field, in the absence of reflecting boundaries, the propagated sound is described by the well-known plane wave equation. The velocity of particle motion is simply proportional to the oscillatory change in pressure (the sound pressure) and is in phase with it (Fig. 8). Both velocity and pressure diminish with $\frac{1}{r}$, where r is the distance from the source (following an inverse square law of intensity). Close to the source, however, within the near field, very much larger particle velocities accompany a given sound pressure. Here, the component particles of the medium are moving around the moving source, rather than alternately towards and away from it, and quite large particle oscillations can take place without significant accompanying pressures. These effects vary with the type of source. They are quite small for a monopole source like an air bubble in water, expanding and contracting in size. Here the velocity decreases with $\frac{1}{r^2}$ in the near field. The motion is much larger for a dipole source like a simple oscillating object showing no volume changes. Here the velocity diminishes with $\frac{1}{r^3}$. Within the near field there is also a difference in the phase of velocity relative to pressure, the former lagging behind the latter (by 90° close to the source).

The extent of the near field depends on the dimensions of the source and the frequency of the propagated wave. The latter is of course dependent upon the pattern of motion of the source. Approximately, the near field extends a distance $r = \lambda/2\pi$ from the source, where λ is the wavelength ($\lambda = c/f$, where c is the velocity of propagation for the medium, and f is the frequency in Hz). Wavelengths and therefore the dimensions of the near field are particularly large in water, for example a 100 Hz signal has a wavelength of 15 m, and the nearfield extends almost 2 m from the source.

Any process projecting from the surface of an animal's body may be stimulated by particle oscillation. Effectively, the base of the process is anchored to the body of the animal, while the tip projects into the oscillating surrounding medium. The magnitude of shearing force set up at the base of the hair by the oscillation of the medium will depend on a number of factors, however. It will first of all depend on the nature of the body to which it is anchored. If it is attached to a large, dense body with a high inertia, or if the body is effectively rigid, and differing in composition from the surrounding medium, then the shearing force will be large. With a much smaller body, similar in density and elasticity to the surrounding medium, then the shearing forces will be small. The shearing force will also depend on the dimensions of the process and its rigidity. Some sensory hairs will be driven by viscous forces, especially if they are small, light and highly feathered. Others will be driven mainly by inertial forces. An example of the latter is the otolith organ of teleost fish, which we will be considering later in the context of sound reception.

There has been some controversy whether integumentary sense organs which are sensitive to particle oscillation, like the lateral line, are organs of hearing or not. On the one hand, some authors have stressed their role as 'low-frequency vibration receptors' or as a 'short-range auditory system', implying that they detect sounds and are acoustic receptors (van Bergeijk, 1967; Tavolga & Wodinsky, 1963). On the other hand, authors have stressed their sensitivity to water displacements and local water currents like the hydrodynamic waves and eddies produced by moving objects in water, and have referred to them as 'distance-touch' receptors (Dijkgraaf, 1963).

In practice it has not been established that these simple integumentary organs are sufficiently sensitive to respond to the particle displacement amplitudes found distant from sound sources, in the far field. Hair-like receptors on the telson of the crustacean *Procambarus clarkii* exhibit a threshold to particle displacements of $0 \cdot 1 \, \mu$m at 100 Hz, while sensory hairs on the chelae of the crayfish *Cherax destructor* have yielded a threshold of $0 \cdot 6 \, \mu$m at 100 Hz. The lateral line of the aquatic toad *Xenopus laevis* conveys a threshold to water displacements of $0 \cdot 3 \, \mu$m at 20 Hz (Görner, 1976), while the surface-feeding fish *Aplocheilus* responds to surface wave amplitudes of $0.013 \, \mu$m at 100 Hz (Bleckmann, 1980). These sensitivities are characteristic of the near field of sound waves, rather than the far field. Auditory receivers, like the otolith organs of fish, showing a significant elaboration of structure compared with these simple mechanoreceptors, respond to sounds with particle displacement amplitudes of about $1 \times 10 \, \mu$m at 75 Hz (Hawkins & Johnstone, 1978). Lateral line organs also show a rather restricted frequency response compared with auditory organs. A detailed study of individual lateral line organs of the aquatic toad *Xenopus laevis* has shown a decline in sensitivity at about 40 Hz, the frequency response curve (Fig. 9) clearly demonstrating that the organ functions as a detector of particle velocity (Kroese, van Zalm & van Bercken, 1978). This is consistent with the proposal that deflection of the cupula is due to viscous forces (Harris & Milne, 1966). Other authors have sometimes reported a rather wider frequency response from the lateral line. For example Kuiper (1967) has reported peak sensitivities ranging from 50 to 150 Hz for different specimens of the same species and Bleckmann (1980) reports a response tuned to about 100 Hz in *Aplocheilus*, though these frequencies are still rather lower

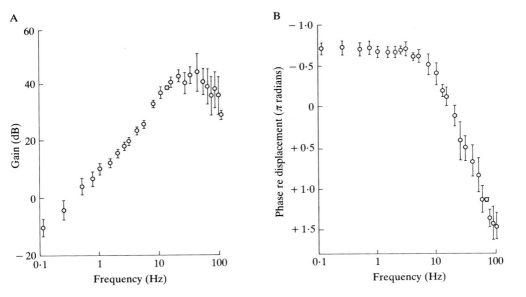

Fig. 9. The frequency response of the lateral line organ of *Xenopus laevis*. (A) Gain and (B) phase with respect to displacement for different stimulus frequencies. (Redrawn from Kroese *et al.* 1978).

than those reported for the fish auditory system (see later).

Though the various integumentary mechanoreceptors are not sufficiently sensitive to be regarded as auditory organs there is little doubt that they can respond to high-amplitude sound waves in the near field. Indeed, evidence is accumulating that fish may detect and orientate to low-frequency sound sources in their close vicinity by means of the lateral line. Denton & Gray (1982) have recently compared the oscillations of the fish and seawater at various positions around low-frequency vibrating sources. They have shown that fish are effectively rigid longitudinally, and that there may be large local differences in the amplitude of motion of the fish, and the adjacent medium (Fig. 10). When the fish is close to a source of vibration the amplitudes, signs, and patterns of stimulation along the lateral line system change strikingly with the position of the fish relative to the source. Under these circumstances the lateral line system can therefore play a major sensory role. As Denton & Grey (1982) and Schuijf (1981) have pointed out, however, when the distance from the source is great relative to the length of the animal (and this can happen well within the near field), the pattern of motion of the water at the head will be very similar to that at the tail. Any difference in motion between

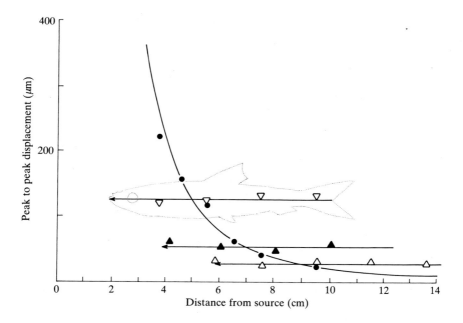

Fig. 10. The longitudinal rigidity of a fish (the sprat *Sprattus sprattus*) in the presence of a vibrating source. The observed displacements of the surrounding water are shown at different distances from the source (●). The triangles indicate the position of the fish on three different occasions. The displacements shown by the fish are almost the same at all points along the body, confirming that the body is longitudinally rigid. Thus, there are local differential movements between the fish and surrounding seawater, especially close to the source. Further away from the source, in the far field, there is little difference in motion between the animal and the water. (Redrawn from Denton & Gray, 1982).

the animal and the water will be very small, and stimulation of the lateral line (or of any similar receptors in other organisms) will be minimal. Moreover, since the oscillations are propagated at the speed of sound, there will only be very small differences in the timing or phase of the wave at different points along the body, ruling out the use of such cues for detection.

Sounds

Hearing, or the detection of sound waves in the far field, where particle oscillations vary very little over the body of the animal, has been clearly established for the marine vertebrates (Hawkins & Myrberg, 1983). The organs employed to detect sounds in the fish are based on sensory membranes, or maculae, within the ears, composed of hair cells loaded with a heavy calcareous mass, or otolith, but otherwise rather similar to the

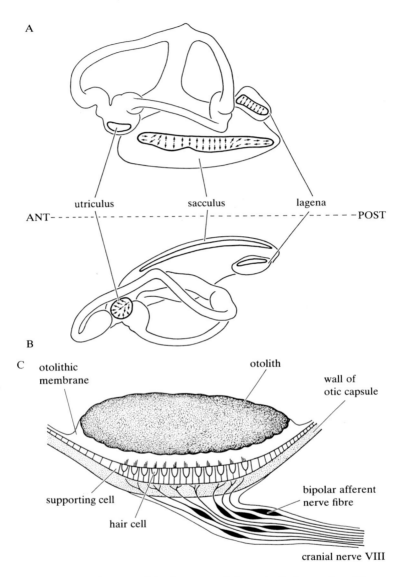

Fig. 11. The principle parts of the inner ear of the cod, *Gadus morhua*. The sensory membranes or maculae of the three otolith organs are shown, with the polarity of hair cell fields indicated by arrows. (A) Lateral view of left ear, (B) Dorsal view of left ear. (C) Schematic cross section through the utriculus, showing the otolith mounted above the hair cells and separated from them by an otolithic membrane.

neuromast organs of the lateral line system. There are three otolith organs to each ear, the sacculus, lagena, and utriculus (Fig. 11). The relative sizes of the otolith organs can vary substantially from one fish to another. In each organ, the calcareous otolith is separated by a thin membrane from the sensory cilia of a large number of hair cells, and as in the neuromasts of the lateral line system the individual hair cells are morphologically and physiologically polarized. Commonly, they are arrayed in fields or zones of differing orientation within the macula. The relative sizes of the otoliths, their orientation and suspension with respect to the sensory maculae, and the patterns of orientation of the hair cells themselves within the macula can vary greatly from one otolith organ to another and from one species to another (Popper & Coombs, 1982). The utricular macula and its otolith generally lie in the horizontal plane, while the saccular or lagenar maculae and their respective otoliths lie mainly in vertical planes.

The otoliths of the inner ear move under the action of gravitational forces and linear accelerations, as mentioned earlier. These movements have been studied in detail by de Vries (1950). However, in addition, the otolith organs are also sensitive to propagated sound waves. Early extirpation experiments showed that removal of the otolith organs abolished the sensitivity of fish to sounds. Since then there has been experimental confirmation that the otolith organ is a detector of particle oscillation (Hawkins & MacLennan, 1976; Chapman & Sand, 1974), rather than sound pressure. A mechanism for this, proposed both by Pumphrey (1950) and Dijkgraaf (1960), is that the tissues of the fish head are essentially similar in their acoustic properties to the surrounding seawater. The head will therefore oscillate back and forth in phase with the particle oscillations of the medium. The dense otolith, however, will lag behind by virtue of its inertia, giving rise to shearing forces at the macula which will excite the hair cells. De Vries (1950) considered an equation of motion for an otolith organ and concluded that the organ would be driven in phase with the particle acceleration at low frequencies, reaching an upper cut-off frequency in the region of several hundred Hertz (depending on the mass of the otolith, its resistance to motion, and any elastic restoring forces) above which its motion would decline steeply. Schuijf (1981) has recently reconsidered the mechanics of the otolith, and has confirmed de Vries' analysis. In particular he has stressed that it is the particle acceleration in the incident sound wave which provides the stimulus. Schuijf, like others before him, has stressed that the acceleration is a vector quantity, the oscillations taking place along a particular axis from the source.

Frequency response curves prepared for some fish have confirmed de Vries (1950) suggestion that the upper frequency limit of the otolith organ is rather sharply curtailed. However, many fish show a more

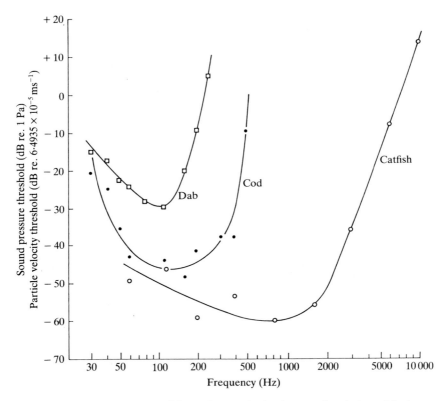

Fig. 12. Auditory thresholds at different frequencies for three species of teleost fish, determined from behavioural experiments. The thresholds for the cod, *Gadus morhua* (Chapman & Hawkins, 1973) and freshwater catfish *Ictalurus nebulosus* (Poggendorf, 1952) are given in terms of sound pressure. Both these species have a gas-filled swimbladder, the catfish having the swimbladder linked to the ear by the bones of Weber. The thresholds for the dab *Limanda limanda* (Chapman & Sand 1974) are expressed in terms of particle velocity. This species lacks a swimbladder.

In the far field the thresholds for all three species are directly comparable (the reference velocity of 6.4935×10^{-5} ms^{-1} corresponds to a sound pressure of 1 Pa).

extended frequency range, and a higher sensitivity than others (Fig. 12). There is now clear evidence that in the so-called hearing specialists sound reception is enhanced by the presence of a particular organ, the gas-filled swimbladder. Removal of gas from the swimbladder of the cod, *Gadus morhua*, significantly reduces sensitivity to sounds at higher frequencies (Sand & Enger, 1973), while conversely, placing an artificial swimbladder (a flaccid air-filled balloon) close to the head of a fish lacking a swimbladder, the dab *Limanda limanda*, increases its sensitivity and extends its upper frequency response (Chapman & Sand, 1974). Conduction mechanisms are found in some species, coupling the swimbladder to the inner ear, as in the Ostariophysi and Clupeidae (Blaxter, 1981), while within a particular family, the Holocentridae, the frequency range and auditory sensitivity depends on the degree of association between the swimbladder and the inner ear (Coombs & Popper, 1979).

An explanation for the increased sensitivity of fish with the inner ear associated with the swimbladder has been provided by von Frisch (1936), Pumphrey (1950) and van Bergeijk (1967). They have suggested that because the gas-filled cavity of the swimbladder is more compressible than the surrounding water it acts as a pressure-release material. The incident sound pressures associated with any sound result in the walls of the swimbladder pulsating, generating large particle oscillations in the immediate vicinity of the swimbladder wall. These may stimulate the nearby otolith organs directly, as in the cod, or may be coupled directly to the otolith organs by an anatomical linkage. The swimbladder is effectively acting as an acoustic transformer, converting the relatively large pressure changes associated with sounds in water into large local particle oscillations, which stimulate the particle-acceleration-sensitive end organs. The acoustics of the cod swimbladder have been studied in some detail by Sand & Hawkins (1973) who showed that enhancement of the particle oscillation amplitudes at the level of the ear is provided over a wide frequency range (Fig. 13). The swimbladder of the cod is heavily damped and tuned to a resonant frequency rather higher than the frequency range of the fish, producing little phase distortion, and preserving the ability of the auditory system to respond rapidly to changes in amplitude of the applied stimulus. Pressure is of course, a scalar rather than a vector quantity, and acts in all directions. The otolith organs stimulated by way of the swimbladder will always receive their stimulation from the same direction, the received signal always having the same phase; regardless of the initial direction of the sound stimulus. This observation led van Bergijk (1964) to assert that though such a system served to enhance the sensitivity of the ear, it effectively destroyed its ability to determine the direction of a sound source. Sounds would always appear to the fish as if they emanated from the swimbladder.

Field experiments to establish directional hearing in fish have concentrated on a particular species, the cod (Schuijf & Buwalda, 1980). They have shown that cod are able to discriminate between spatially separated sound sources in both the horizontal and vertical planes and also that they can orientate directly towards particular sources, often at substantial distances. The abilities of fish to locate a source may even exceed those of terrestrial vertebrates, since cod can discriminate between sound sources at different distances (Schuijf & Hawkins, 1983),

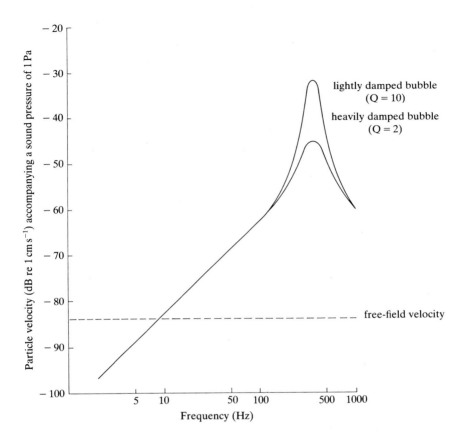

Fig. 13. Curves illustrating the radial pulsation of a damped air bubble in an underwater sound field. The particle velocities are given at the periphery of a spherical bubble for a constant sound pressure of 1 Pa. The values shown are for a 1·5 cm radius bubble at a depth of 20 m, resonating at about 380 Hz. The particle velocities accompanying the same sound pressure for a propagated plane wave in a free field are given for comparison. Note that there is an amplication of particle velocity over a wide range of frequencies and not only at the resonant frequency. In practice, the amplification is likely to be less with the swim-bladder spaced apart from the ear. Moreover, measurements from intact cod *Gadus morhua* have shown that the frequency is much higher than predicted, well above the hearing range of the fish, and the damping is quite high. Curves calculated by the method described in Sand & Hawkins (1973).

and discriminate between diametrically opposed loudspeakers in both the horizontal and vertical planes (Buwalda, Schuijf & Hawkins, 1983), abilities which are especially poor in man.

Any particle oscillation detector is inherently directional. Depending on the suspension of the otolith, the shape of the maculae and the pattern of orientation of the sensory hair cells, the otolith organs will respond

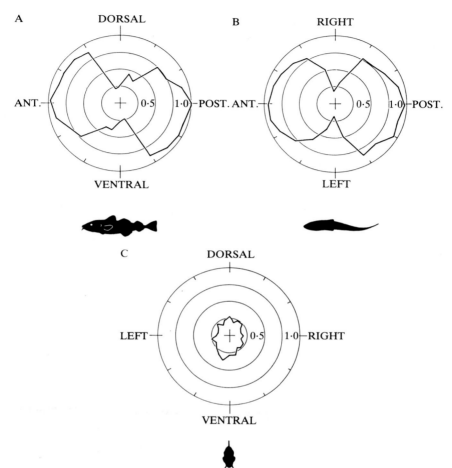

Fig. 14. Directionally of a single unit recorded from the left, anterior sacculus of the cod *Gadus morhua,* by oscillating the fish on a three-dimensional vibrating table. The polar diagrams show the relative response (in terms of spikes per Hz) from a single primary afferent nerve fibre, at different angles, in three mutually perpendicular planes. The response is bidirectional in both the median vertical and horizontal planes (Hawkins & King, unpublished).

differently to sound waves incident from different directions. The primary afferent nerve fibres from the otolith organs of cod are strongly directional in their response to oscillatory motion, as shown in Fig. 14. Moreover, units from different parts of the otolith organs, or from different otolith organs, show quite different axes of sensitivity (Hawkins & Horner, 1981). The response is always bidirectional, essentially reflecting the oscillatory nature of the stimulus, the particular individual unit firing only on one half cycle of the stimulus, indicating that each nerve fibre synapses only with hair cells having a particular polarity. The fact that the maculae are often divided into areas of opposing polarity, and that this polarity is preserved at the level of the afferent nerve fibres, points to the importance to fish of information about the phase of the incident sound wave.

It is attractive to conclude that the direction of a sound source can be determined, at least in the absence of a swimbladder, by comparison of the outputs of differently aligned directional receivers, these being provided by the different otolith organs. There is a serious flaw to this argument, however. Such a system has an inherent bidirectionality or ambiguity, so that the fish would be unable, for example, to discriminate between a source in front of the head and one behind it. Though the organization described enables the fish to discriminate positive and negative phases of a received signal, in a free sound field the instantaneous phase of particle oscillation bears no relation to propagation direction. The particle accelerations occur alternately towards and away from the source. Not even the starting phase of the sound can be used to resolve the ambiguity, since sounds can start with either a compression or a rarefaction. In addition, a satisfactory explanation must also take account of the presence of the swimbladder, since particle oscillations reradiating from this organ and carrying no directional information must dominate the direct vectorial input, at least in parts of the auditory system.

A model has been developed by Schuijf (1975, 1976, 1981) which reconciles these difficulties. This proposes that directional detection consists of two processes; determination of the axis of propagation, and removal of the remaining ambiguity. The first of these is achieved by vector weighing of the direct input at the different otolith organs (perhaps performed bilaterally). The ambiguity is then resolved by a direct comparison of the phase of particle acceleration with the phase of sound pressure. Figure 15 shows that there is a phase reversal of particle oscillation as a sound source is moved to a diametrically opposed position, on the other side of the fish. On the other hand the sound pressure signal, received by the swimbladder and transformed into particle oscillation which then stimulates the ear, retains the same phase regardless of the position of the source relative to the fish. Differences in shape or cross-sectional area of the swimbladder viewed from different angles do not affect the amplitude or phase since the organ is very small in relation to the wavelengths of sound. Thus, far from interfering with the directional hearing abilities of the fish, the swimbladder may be essential for resolving ambiguities.

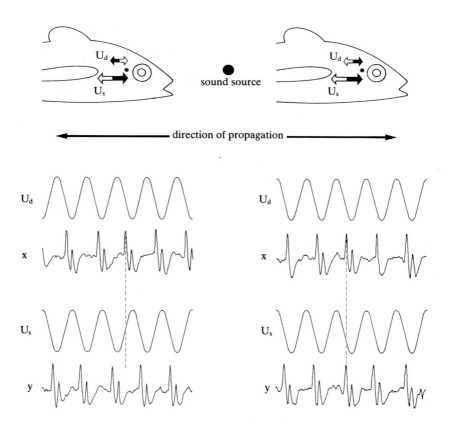

Fig. 15. The principle of 'phase' analysis in a teleost fish with a swimbladder. The particle velocity in the unperturbed sound field, with the fish absent, is denoted by U_d. The scattering of sound from the swimbladder results in a particle velocity U_s at the location of the ear. Note that as the fish moves from one side of the source to the other there is a reversal in the phase of U_d, but the phase of U_s remains the same. Provided the fish is able to separate the incident wave from the near field of the swimbladder, it can in principle discriminate between the two source positions. x and y represent the hypothetical responses of the ear to the two waves. It is well established that the primary afferent fibres show a response which is strongly phase locked to the stimulus. (Modified from Schuijf, 1976).

There is evidence to support Schuijf's model; recent experiments in free-field conditions under a raft in a Scottish sea loch (Buwalda *et al.* 1983) have confirmed not only that cod can discriminate sounds from opposing directions but that the discrimination is based on the phase relationship between particle motion and sound pressure. A phase reversal of sound pressure with respect to particle motion is experienced by the cod as a 180° change in direction.

Schuijf's model of directional detection does seem to be valid. However, there is still a long way to go before the actual principles of phase analysis can be understood, and the actual mechanisms operating within the ear elucidated. In particular, the segregation of the direct oscillatory signal and the indirect signal emanating from the swimbladder is not understood. Nevertheless a particular prediction of the model has already been tested. It is known that the phase relationship between particle acceleration and sound pressure varies with distance from a source. If the cod is able to detect phase differences between these two quantities might it not be able to determine its distance from a source? Experiments by Schuijf & Hawkins (1983) have confirmed that cod can discriminate between pure tones emitted alternately from two aligned sound projectors at different distances. These results fit the model and confirm that the cod is well able to locate sound sources in three-dimensional space.

References

ARNOLD, G. P. (1974). Rheotropism in fishes. *Biol. Rev.* 49, 515–576.

BLAXTER, J. H. S. (1978). Baroreception. In *Sensory Ecology* (ed. M. A. Ali). New York: Plenum Publishing Corporation.

BLAXTER, J. H. S. (1980). The effect of hydrostatic pressure on fishes. In *Environmental Physiology of Fishes* (ed. M. A. Ali). New York: Plenum Publishing Corporation.

BLAXTER, J. H. S. (1981). The swimbladder and hearing. In Hearing and Sound Communications in Fishes. (ed. W. N. Tavolga, A. N. Popper & R. R. Fay) pp. 61–72. New York: Springer-Verlag.

BLAXTER, J. H. S. & DENTON, E. J. (1976). Function of the swimbladder – inner ear-lateral line system of herring in the young stages. *J. mar. biol. Ass. UK* 86, 487–502.

BLAXTER, J. H. S., GRAY, J. A. B. & BEST, A. C. G. (1983). Structure and development of the free neuromasts and lateral line system of the herring. *J. mar. biol. Ass. UK* 63, 247–260.

BLECKMANN, H. (1980). Reaction time and stimulus frequency in prey localisation in the surface-feeding fish *Aplocheilus lineatus*.

BONE, Q. & BEST, A. C. G. (1978). Ciliated sensory cells in amphioxus (Branchiostoma). *J. mar. biol. Ass. UK* 58, 479–486.

BONE, Q., GORSKI, G. & PULSFORD, A. L. (1979). On the structure and behaviour of *Fritillaria* (Tunicata: Larvacea). *J. mar. biol. Ass. UK* 59, 399–411.

BONE, Q. & PULSFORD, A. (1978). The arrangement of ciliated sensory cells in *Spadella* (Chaetognatha). *J. mar. biol. Ass. UK* 58, 565–570.

BONE, Q. & RYAN, K. P. (1978). Cupular sense organs in *Ciona* (Tunicata: Ascidiacea). *J. Zool.* 186, 417–429.

BUSH, B. M. H. & LAVERACK, M. S. (1982). Mechanoreception. In *The Biology of Crustacea*, Vol. 3, pp. 399–468. New York: Academic Press.

BUWALDA, R. J. A., SCHUIJF, A. & HAWKINS, A. D. (1983). Discrimination by the cod of sounds from opposing directions. *J. comp. Physiol.* 150, 175–184.

CAMPENHAUSEN, C. VON, REISS, I. & WEISSERT, R. (1981). Detection of stationary objects by the blind cave fish *Anoptichthys jordani* (Characidae). *J. comp. Physiol.* 143, 369–374.

CHAPMAN, C. J. & HAWKINS, A. D. (1973). A field study of hearing in the cod, *Gadus morhua*. *J. comp. Physiol.* 85, 147–167.

CHAPMAN, C. J. & SAND, O. (1974). Field studies of hearing in two species of flatfish *Pleuronectes platessa* (L.) and *Limanda limanda* (L.) (fam. Pleuronectidae). *Comp. Biochem. Physiol.* **47**, 371–386.

COOMBS, S. & POPPER, A. N. (1979). Hearing differences among Hawaiian squirrelfish (family Holocentridae) related to differences in the peripheral auditory system. *J. comp. Physiol.* **132A**, 203–207.

DENTON, E. J. & GRAY, A. B. (1982). The rigidity of fish and patterns of lateral line stimulation. *Nature* **297**, 679–681.

DE VRIES, H. (1950). The mechanics of the Labyrinth. *Acta Otolaryngologica*, **38**, 262–273.

DIGBY, P. S. B. (1972). Detection of small changes in hydrostatic pressure by crustacea and its relation to electrode action in the cuticle. *Symp. Soc. exp. Biol.* **26**, 445–471.

DIJKGRAAF, S. (1933). Untersuchungen uber die funktion der seitenorgane an fischen. *Z. vergl. Physiol.* **20**, 162–214.

DIJKGRAAF, S. (1960). Hearing in bony fishes. *Proc. R. Soc. Lond. Ser. B.* **152**, 51–54.

DIJKGRAAF, S. (1963). The functioning and significance of the lateral line organs. *Biol. Rev.* **38**, 51–106.

ELEPFANDT, A. (1982). Accuracy of taxis response to water waves in the clawed toad (*Xenopus laevis* Daudin) with intact or with lesioned lateral line system. *J. comp. Physiol.* **148**, 535–545.

ENRIGHT, J. T. (1963). Estimates of the compressibility of some marine crustaceans. *Limnol. Oceanogr.* **8**, 382–387.

FEIGENBAUM, D. & REEVE, M. R. (1977). Prey detection in the chaetognatha: response to a vibrating probe and experimental determination of attack distance in large aquaria. *Limnol. Oceanogr.* **22**, 1052–1058.

GORNER, P. (1976). Source localisation with labyrinth and lateral line in the clawed toad (*Xenopus laevis*). In *Sound Reception in Fish*. (ed. A. Schuijf, A. D. Hawkins) pp. 171–184. Amsterdam: Elsevier.

GREER WALKER, M., HARDEN JONES, F. R. & ARNOLD, G. P. (1978). The movements of plaice (*Pleuronectes platessa*) tracked in the open sea. *Journal du Conseil International pour l'exploration de la Mer* **38**, 58–86.

HARRIS, G. G. & MILNE, D. C. (1966). Input-output characteristics of the lateral-line sense organs of *Xenopus laevis*. *J. Acoust. Soc. Am.* **40**, 32–42.

HAWKINS, A. D. & HORNER, K. (1981). Directional characteristics of primary auditory neurons from the cod ear. In *Hearing and Sound Communication in Fishes*. (ed. W. N. Tavolga, A. N. Popper & R. R. Fay) pp. 311–327. New York: Springer-Verlag.

HAWKINS, A. D. & JOHNSTONE, A. D. F. (1978). Hearing of Atlantic salmon, *Salmo salar*. *J. Fish Biol.* **13**, 655–673.

HAWKINS, A. D. & MACLENNAN, D. N. (1976). An acoustic tank for hearing studies in fish. In *Sound Reception in Fish*. (ed. A. Schuijf & A. D. Hawkins) pp. 149–169. Amsterdam: Elsevier.

HAWKINS, A. D. & MYRBERG, A. A. (1983). Hearing and sound communication under water. In *Bioacoustics, A Comparative Approach*. (ed. B. Lewis) pp. 347–405. London: Academic Press.

HOIN-RADKOVSKY, I., BLECKMANN, H. & SCHWARTZ, E. (1984). Determination of source distance in the surface-feeding fish *Pantodon Buchholzi* Pantodontidae. *Anim. Behav.* **32**, 840–851.

HORRIDGE, G. A. (1964). Non-motile sensory cilia and neuromuscular junctions in a ctenophore independent effector organ. *Proc. Roy. Soc. B.* **162**, 333–350.

HORRIDGE, G. A. (1966). Some recently discovered underwater vibration receptors in invertebrates. In *Some Contemporary Studies in Marine Science*. (ed. H. Barnes) pp. 395–405. London: Allen and Unwin Ltd.

HORRIDGE, G. A. (1971). Primitive examples of gravity receptors and their evolution. In *Gravity and the Organism*. (ed. Gordon and Cohen) Chicago: Univ. of Chicago.

HORRIDGE, G. A. & BOULTON, P. S. (1967). Prey detection by chaetognatha via a vibration sense. *Proc. Roy. Soc. B.* **168**, 413–419.

HYMAN, L. H. (1940). *The Invertebrates. I. Protozoa through Ctenophora.* New York: McGraw Hill.

JONES, F. R. H. (1984). Could fish use inertial clues when on migration. In *Mechanisms of Migrations in Fishes.* (ed. J. D. McCleave, *et al.*) pp. 67–78. NATO Conf. Series.

KALMIJN, A. J. (1971). The electric sense of sharks and rays. *J. exp. Biol.* **55**, 371–383.

KALMIJN, A. J. (1981). Biophysics of geomagnetic field detection. *IEEE Transactions on Magnetics* Vol. Mag. **17**, No. 1.

KROESE, A. B. A., ZALM, J. M. VAN DEN & BERCKEN, J. VAN DEN. (1978). Frequency response of the lateral-line organ of *Xenopus laevis. Pflugers Arch.* **375**, 167–175.

KUIPER, J. W. (1967). Frequency characteristics and functional significance of the lateral line. In *Lateral Line Detectors* (ed. P. Cahn) pp. 105–121. Indiana University Press.

LAVERACK, M. S. (1962a). Responses of cuticular sense organs of the lobster *Homarus vulgaris* (crustacea) I. Hair-peg organs as water current receptors. *Comp. Biochem. Physiol.* **5**, 319–325.

LAVERACK, M. S. (1962b). Responses of cuticular sense organs of the lobster, *Homarus vulgaris* (crustacea) II. Hair fan organs as pressure receptors. *Comp. Biochem. Physiol.* **6**, 137–145.

LAVERACK, M. S. (1981). The adaptive radiation of sense organs. In *Sense Organs.* (ed. M. S. Laverack & D. Cosens) Edinburgh: Blackie.

LEGGETT, W. C. (1984). Fish migrations in coastal and estuarine environments: A call for new approaches to the study of an old problem. In *Mechanisms of Migrations in Fishes.* (ed. J. D. Cleave *et al.*) 159–178. NATO Conf. Series.

LYON, E. P. (1904). On rheotropism. I. Rheotropism in fishes. *Am. J. Physiol.* **12**, 12.

MELLON, DE F. (1963). Electrical responses from dually innervated tactile receptors on the thorax of the crayfish. *J. exp. Biol.* **40**, 137–148.

MULLER, U. & SCHWARTZ, E. (1982). Influence of single neuromasts on prey localising behaviour of the surface-feeding fish, *Aplocheilus lineatus. J. comp. Physiol.* **149**, 399–408.

NEWBURY, T. K. (1972). Vibration perception by chaetognaths. *Nature* **236**, 459–460.

PALS, N. & SCHOENHAGE, A. A. C. (1979). Marine electric fields and fish orientation. *J. Physiol.* **75**, 349–353.

POGGENDORF, A. (1952). Die absoluten Horschwellen des Zwergwelses (*Ameiurus nebulosus*) und Beitrage zur Physik des Weberschen Apparate der Ostariophysen. *Z. vergl. Physiol.* **34**, 222–257.

POPPER, A. N. & COOMBS, S. (1982). The morphology and evolution of the ear in actinopterygean fishes. *Am Zool.* **22**, 311–328.

PUMPHREY, R. J. (1950). Hearing. In *Physiological Mechanisms in Animal Behaviour. Symp. Soc. Exp. Biol.* **4**, 1–18.

QUTOB, Z. (1962). The swimbladder of fishes as a pressure receptor. *Arch. Neerl. Zool.* **15**, 1–67.

SAND, O. (1981). The lateral line and sound reception. In *Hearing and Sound Communication in Fishes.* (ed. W. N. Tavolga, A. N. Popper & R. R. Fay) pp. 459–480. Springer-Verlag.

SAND, O. & ENGER, P. S. (1973). Evidence for an auditory function of the swimbladder in the cod. *J. exp. Biol.* **49**, 405–414.

SAND, O. & HAWKINS, A. D. (1973). Acoustic properties of the cod swimbladder. *J. exp. Biol.* **58**, 797–820.

SCHUIJF, A. (1975). Directional hearing of cod (*Gadus morhua*) under approximate free field conditions. *J. comp. Physiol.* **98**, 307–332.

SCHUIJF, A. (1976). The phase model of directional hearing in fish. In *Sound Reception in Fish.* (ed. A. Schuijf & A. D. Hawkins) pp. 63–86. Amsterdam: Elsevier.

SCHUIJF, A. (1981). Models of acoustic localisation. In *Hearing and Sound Communication in Fishes* (ed. W. N. Tavolga, A. N. Popper & R. R. Fay) pp. 267–310. New York: Springer-Verlag.

SCHUIJF, A. & BUWALDA, R. J. A. (1980). Underwater localisation – a major problem in fish acoustics. In *Comparative Studies of Hearing in Vertebrates*. (ed. A. N. Popper & R. R. Fay) pp. 43–77. New York: Springer-Verlag.

SCHUIJF, A. & HAWKINS, A. D. (1983). Acoustic distance discrimination by the cod. *Nature* **302**, 143–144.

SCHWARTZ, E. (1971). Die ortung von Wasserwellen durch oberflacherfische. *Z. Vergl. Physiol.* **74**, 64–80.

SCHWARZ, E. & HASLER, A. D. (1966). Reception of surface waves by the blackstripe topminnow, *Fundulus notatus*. *J. Fish. Res. Bd. Canada* **23**, 1331–1352.

SILER (1969). Near- and far-fields in a marine environment. *J. Acoust. Soc. Am.* **46**, 483–484.

SOLON, M. H. & KASS-SIMON, G. (1981). Mechanosensory activity of hair organs on the chelae of *Homarus americanus*. *Comp. Biochem. Physiol.* **68A**, 217–223.

STRATHMANN, R. R., JAHN, T. L. & FONSECA, J. R. C. (1972). Suspension feeding by marine invertebrate larvae: clearance of particles by ciliated bands of rotifer, pluteus and trochophore. *Biol. Bull. mar. biol. Lab. Woods Hole* **142**, 505–519.

TAUTZ, J. (1979). Reception of particle oscillation in a medium – an unorthodox sensory capacity. *Naturwiss.* **66**, 452–61.

TAUTZ, J. & SANDEMAN, D. C. (1980). The detection of waterborne vibration by sensory hairs on the chelae of the crayfish. *J. exp. Biol.* **88**, 351–356.

TAVOLGA, W. N. & WODINSKY, J. (1963). Auditory capacities in fishes: Pure tone thresholds in nine species of marine teleosts. *Bull. Am. Museum Nat. Hist.* **126**, 179–239.

TAZAKI, K. (1977). Nervous responses from mechanosensory hairs on the antennal flagellum in the lobster *Homarus gammarus* (L.). *Mar. Behav. Physiol.* **5**, 1–18.

VAN BERGEIJK, W. (1964). Directional and non-directional hearing in fish. In *Marine Bio-acoustics* (ed. W. N, Tavolga) pp. 281–299. Oxford: Pergamon Press.

VAN BERGEIJK, W. (1967). The evolution of vertebrates hearing. In *Contributions to Sensory Physiology*. (ed. W. D. Neff) pp. 1–46. New York: Academic Press.

VEDEL, J. P. & CLARAC, F. (1976). Hydrodynamic sensitivity of cuticular sense organs in the rock lobster *Palinurus vulgaris*. Morphological and physiological aspects. *Mar. Behav.* **3**, 235–251.

VON FRISCH, K. (1938). Uber die Bedeutung des Sacculus und der Lagena fur den Gehor-sinn der Fische. *Z. vergl. Physiol.* **25**, 703–747.

WESTERBERG, H. (1984). The orientation of fish and the vertical stratification of fine – and micro-structure scales. In *Mechanisms of Migration in Fishes*. (ed. J. D. Cleave *et al.*) pp. 179–204. NATO Conf. Series.

WIESE, K. (1972). Das mechanorezeptorische Beuteortungssytem von *Notonecta*. I. Die Funktion des tarsalen Scolopidialorgans. *J. comp. Physiol.* **78**, 83–102.

WEISE, K. (1976). Mechanoreceptors for near-field water displacements in crayfish. *J. Neurophysiol.* **39**, 816–33.

Printed in Great Britain © *Society for Experimental Biology 1985*

FEEDING CURRENTS IN CALANOID COPEPODS: TWO NEW HYPOTHESES

J. RUDI STRICKLER

Department of Biological Sciences, University of Southern California, Los Angeles, CA 90089–0371, USA

Summary

The interaction between planktonic herbivorous calanoid copepods and their food, planktonic algae, is investigated to increase our understanding of the physiological adaptations these small marine animals have acquired in the course of evolution. Emphasis is given to the centimetre – second scale where calanoids encounter algae, select and capture them, or reject them either passively or actively. Most calanoid copepods create feeding currents which can be subdivided into three cores: motion, viscous, and sensory cores. Algae contained in the sensory core are perceived and then re-routed towards the capture area. The perimeter encompassing all the points of these re-routings can be defined as the reactive field of awareness surrounding the calanoid.

An analysis of typical biological oceanographic feeding experiments reveals that direct observations are necessary to understand the feeding behaviours and strategies of calanoid copepods. To facilitate further studies, a new experimental set-up has been described and two hypotheses have been formulated. The method allows direct observations, in all three dimensions, of free-swimming herbivorous calanoids and their food in a 6-litre vessel.

The two hypotheses are based on the fact that calanoids create feeding currents and orient their bodies within the water column. The first hypothesis states that calanoid copepods create species-specific, and maybe even age-specific, feeding currents. The second one proposes that ambient water motions may act as a mechanism for niche separation in herbivorous calanoid copepods. This latter hypothesis is based on the inference that ambient water motions may interfere with the flow field of the feeding current thereby making it more difficult for calanoids to successfully re-route algae contained in the sensory core of the feeding current.

Introduction

'Seeing is believing' is an expression which holds true in all sciences. For example, nuclear physicists use large and expensive machines to verify their theories and hypotheses on the composition of matter in a visual way, and neuroscientists use sophisticated scanning devices to formulate hypotheses on how brains work. It is logical then that biological oceanographers have adopted the same guiding theme, 'seeing is believing', to verify one of their paradigms, namely that herbivorous calanoid copepods are filter-feeders.

For years, 'filter-feeding' was the accepted mechanism used by calanoids to capture algae from the surrounding water (Cannon, 1928). It was also thought that the size and shape of the algae were the only criteria for successful capture (Marshall, 1973; Jørgensen, 1966). However, this notion was based on very little direct evidence and a great deal of inference. In the last few years, by using laboratory techniques which were appropriate to the problems of observing small animals, it has been possible to look closer at individual calanoids feeding. The results have introduced a paradigm shift away from the filter-feeding model. To date, there has been no new paradigm established; alternative hypotheses are still at the stage of being formulated.

The calanoid copepod – algae interaction

Since the first scientific investigations into open-water marine, estuarine, and fresh-water ecosystems 150 years ago, the interaction between planktonic calanoid copepods and their food has been the focus of much attention and controversy (Claus, 1891; vom Rath, 1892; Pütter, 1909, 1924; Esterly, 1916; Storch & Pfisterer, 1926; Cannon, 1928; Storch, 1929; Boyd, 1976; Frost, 1977; Longhurst & Herman, 1981; Ortner, Wiebe & Cox, 1981; Paffenhöfer, 1984). This emphasis is understandable because the interaction is an important trophic link in the aquatic food web. For example, it is estimated that 50 % of the marine phytoplankton production in the western Atlantic is consumed every day by herbivorous calanoid copepods (Dagg & Turner, 1982). Calanoids are, in turn, eaten by fish and carnivorous invertebrates. Thus, the flow of matter and energy to these higher trophic levels is largely governed by calanoid grazing.

Due to the size of copepods (0·3 to 5 mm in length), the fineness of their body structures (2 to 100 μm in diameter), and the speed of their movements (appendages oscillating at 4 to 70 Hz; swimming speeds of 1 to 500 bodylengths per second), it is not surprising that their feeding and swimming behaviours are still not adequately understood. Earlier researchers lacked techniques to observe live animals at appropriate time and length scales (Alcaraz, Paffenhöfer & Strickler, 1980; Koehl, 1984). Additionally, live copepods must swim in large vessels while being observed because of the possible interference between the boundary layer around the animal and the nearest wall of the vessel (Zaret, 1980; Vogel, 1981). This fact makes it even more difficult to observe the fine details and high-speed performances of feeding and swimming animals directly. For example, to observe an alga of 10 μm diameter in the feeding current near the mouthparts (speed of flow is around 1 cm sec^{-1}), one has to employ an exposure/observation time of less than 100 μsec to have a blur of less than one tenth of a diameter. Additionally, to track the path of the alga, single observations have to be made at least every 4 msec. At the same time, long working distance, large depth of field, and high optical resolution set other constraints on the experimental researcher.

Recent investigations have resolved many of the technical difficulties and allowed direct observations of the feeding behaviour of living animals. Some of these studies have used high-speed, high-magnification microcinematography to observe food capture and handling by tethered animals (Alcaraz *et al.* 1980, Cowles & Strickler, 1983; Koehl, 1984; Koehl & Strickler, 1981; Paffenhöfer, Strickler & Alcaraz, 1982; Price & Paffenhöfer, 1985*a,b*; Price, Paffenhöfer & Strickler, 1983; Rosenberg, 1980; Strickler, 1984). The methods employed allow resolutions of 1·3 μm and 2 msec with a field of observation smaller than 1 mm. Other studies have analysed swimming patterns by using low-magnification optics to observe free-swimming copepods (e.g. Strickler, 1970; Buskey, 1984), but these methods have not resolved the copepods' food simultaneously.

To date, only one study has employed a technique which is capable of resolving both the free-swimming calanoid copepods and their food (Strickler, 1982). The present contribution is a follow-up report with additional results obtained using the same technique. It also attempts to formulate hypotheses for further research on calanoid copepod – algae interaction. At the same time it demonstrates the kind of physiological adaptations small marine animals have acquired over evolutionary times.

Our most detailed information on the feeding biology of herbivorous calanoid copepods comes from cinematographic observations of *Eucalanus pileatus* and *E. crassus*. We now know that these calanoids are capable of complex feeding behaviours. Observations on other species suggest that this plasticity is universal to copepods (Strickler, 1984). Therefore, I assume that most calanoid copepods will behave similarly to these two *Eucalanus species*.

In this contribution I will address four topics: one, the methods employed to observe swimming calanoid copepods and their food; two, the trophic interactions within the centimetre – second range; three, the benefits for biological oceanography of further research into this interaction; and four, a possible mechanism for niche separation among calanoid copepods.

Observations on free-swimming animals

To directly observe a calanoid copepod swimming freely in a large volume of water, a special optical set-up is necessary (Strickler, 1982). This set-up must be capable of resolving not only the copepod, but also nearby suspended algae. Fig. 1 shows one frame from a 16 mm cinematographic recording of a feeding calanoid. In this figure, the animal was swimming in five litres of natural seawater and was 4 cm away from the nearest wall. The algae were about 15 μm in diameter. One can see that the technique allows a large range of depth of focus. Out-of-focus particles (or the distal ends of the first antennae and their setae) are registered as double images instead of becoming blurred and fading away. The farther apart the two images are, the farther the particle is out of focus.

A 10-sec sequence of 25 frames per second (i.e. 250 frames) gives a detailed picture of the movements of the animal and its effects on nearby

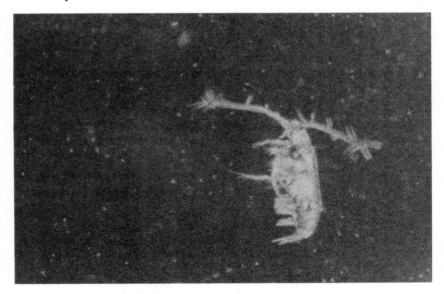

Fig. 1. One frame of a 16 mm film showing *Eucalanus crassus* during a feeding bout. The light source was a Krypton Ion Laser (530·9 nm).

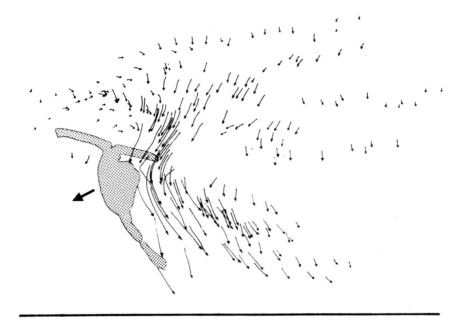

Fig. 2. Flow field of *Eucalanus crassus* during feeding. Each arrow shows the pathline of an alga during a 0·4 sec time interval (from Strickler, 1982; with permission of AAAS, Washington). Bar equals 1 cm.

algae and on the surrounding water. The evaluation of this sequence reveals the flow field generated by the copepod while creating a feeding current (Fig. 2, from Strickler, 1982).

The optical technique used works best at very low concentrations of algae; concentrations as low as one alga/ml can be observed. Indirect methods (e.g. Coulter counter, ^{14}C- labelling) do not allow quantitative observations at such low concentrations. The sizes of the algae can also be deduced from the pictures thereby enabling identification to the species level. Thus, it is possible to observe grazing on mixed algal assemblages which may reveal selection for or against a particular type of algae.

Optical pathway

The basic system is a modification of a Schlieren optical pathway as designed by Toepler (1866). A collimated light beam is focused by the condensing lens (Fig. 3). At the focal point, a small black spot stops the light from reaching the image plane. Hence, there is only a dark exposure.

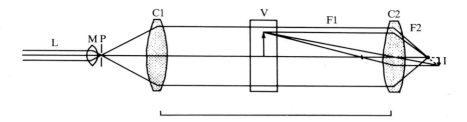

Fig. 3. Optical pathway used to obtain Fig. 1. The collimated light beam (4 cm diameter) is an enlarged laser beam (L) which passed a spatial filter (M = microscope lens, P = pinhole, C1 = collimator lens). All collimated light is focused by the condenser lens (C2) onto the black dot in the back focus (F2). The image (I) of the object in the vessel (arrow in V) is formed by diffracted light (F1 = front focal point). Bar equals ~ 100 cm.

However, any light scattered by an object which is situated in the collimated light beam will miss the black spot and reach the image plane, forming a light image on the dark background (see Fig. 1). In this way, any change in optical density within the collimated beam is registered. Solid particles also form an image because their boundaries diffract some of the light.

Out-of-focus particles do not form a sharp picture on the image plane. If the particle is only a few centimetres out of focus its image will still be useful, especially in cinematographic studies. Fig. 1 shows that the distal ends of the first antennae form a double picture giving some idea of the distance to the object plane; however, to calculate three-dimensional resolution from these double pictures is neither efficient nor accurate. It can only serve as a first approximation.

Three-dimensional resolution

Fig. 2 shows an oblique view of a feeding calanoid and its feeding current. For a better understanding of the flow field, the energy involved to create it, and the encounter rate with algae it provides, one must observe the flow field from very special viewpoints. For example, in Fig. 4 a cross section through the flow field shows the speeds of the flow in a plane parallel to the body axis and the stretched-out first antennae. The plane was also 0·5 mm away from the surface of the body. The figure shows that the animal took more water from the left than from the right and coordinated this flow with a motion of the abdomen. This asymmetry in the flow field may enable early perception of incoming algae of desired food value (Strickler, 1982; Andrews, 1983). Observing flow in other planes (e.g. symmetry plane of the body, planes perpendicular to the flow) could help the researchers in estimating flow parameters important for fluid dynamical calculations.

Observations of flow fields generated by calanoids can be labour intensive. For Fig. 4, we had to wait for hours until an animal swam parallel to the optical axis and within the collimated light beam. This figure could have been obtained more efficiently if the original observations were made with three-dimensional resolution. That is, two pictures (as in Fig. 2) taken at the same time and at different discrete angles could then be combined to produce the three-dimensional image. This image could be rotated using computer analyses until the desired plane or viewpoint has been achieved.

In order to obtain these two pictures, two collimated light beams (Fig. 3) could be intersected at a small angle allowing stereo viewing as in humans. This arrangement would, however, result in a larger error in the direction of the viewing than in the plane perpendicular to this direction.

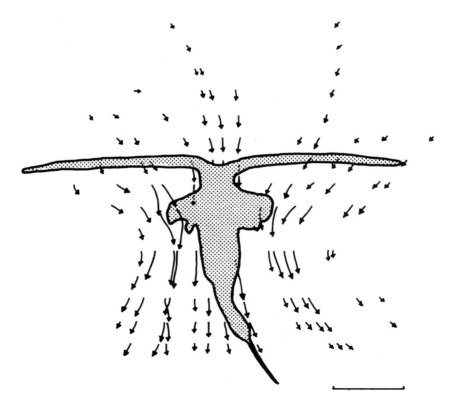

Fig. 4. Slice through the flow field of *Eucalanus crassus*. The slice was taken parallel to the body axis, 0·5 mm away from the body surface. Arrows show pathlines of algae during 0·2 sec time intervals. Bar equals 0·1 cm.

With two beams intersecting at 90° one can read the X and Z (vertical) coordinates from one beam and the Y and Z coordinates from the other one. Time synchronization assures true X–Y–Z values, while reading the Z coordinate twice serves as a control.

In a preliminary study, I mounted a 1-litre vessel on translation slides which were air cushioned and allowed translations in the three coordinate axes only. One person could easily adjust the vessel to any location and then follow a swimming copepod. However, secondary currents in the water would always develop, interfering with exact measurements. To avoid this problem, I am now building a new set-up where the optical system is movable in the X and Y direction while the vessel moves in the Z direction only. Since calanoid copepods swim mostly in the horizontal plane with only small changes in the Z direction (hop and sink swimming behaviour) the vessel will not be moved as often and so the generation of secondary currents will be minimized.

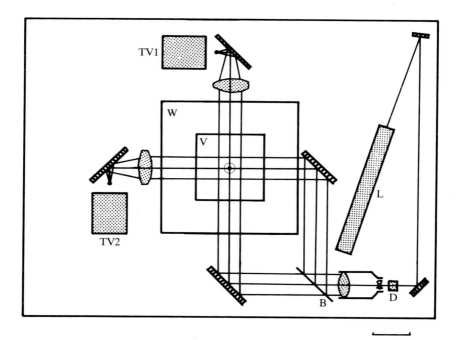

Fig. 5. Schematic of experimental set-up. The HeNe laser (L; 632 nm) serves for adjustments of the optics; the infrared laser diode (D; 820 nm) is used during observations. Beam splitter (B; 50/50) allows two light paths according to Fig. 3 with two television cameras (TV1, TV2) as recording devices. The vessel (V) within the water jacket (W) is movable only in the vertical direction (circle = axis) while the whole set-up is movable in the horizontal plane by 20 cm in both axes. Bar equals 10 cm.

Keeping a swimming animal within the focus of both optical systems and, at the same time, within the frames of the two image planes is a difficult task. Due to the different refractive indices of air and water, the wall of the vessel acts as an additional, non-moving lens. Therefore, as the animal changes its position, the distance between the object plane and the condenser lens changes. To overcome this distancing problem a water jacket around the observational vessel will move with the optical system ensuring constant distances between the object, the condenser lens and the image plane. Additionally, a circulating water bath regulates the temperature in the water jacket and, therefore, in the vessel. Fig. 5 shows a schematic view of this new arrangement.

The inside dimensions of the vessel are $18 \times 18 \times 18$ cm giving a total volume of 5832 ml of water. The volume of water in focus (i.e. the window) is about 0·5 ml ($8 \times 8 \times 8$ mm). In this window, any particle larger than 10 μm is resolved and its position in all three dimensions determined with an absolute accuracy of 12 μm. Particles in the shadow of other particles (or animals) will be resolved in only two dimensions. Particles very close to the animal cannot be resolved because in both beams they are in the shadow of the animal. However, the resolution capabilities of this experimental set-up enables the observer to track the fate of every alga entering the window, even when the alga is lost for a short time in the animal's shadow (Fig. 4). Algae that are ingested will initially appear anteriorly of the animal but will not reappear after passing the mouthparts. Rejected algae will be seen again, usually within one second (pers. obs.). Therefore, one can determine the proportions of algae ingested, algae rejected, and those not captured at all. One can also determine the points of entry of algae into the flow field.

Trophic interactions within the centimetre – second range

The interaction between a herbivorous, planktonic calanoid copepod and the suspended algae encompasses many spatial and temporal scales. These can be conveniently divided into three groupings:
1) Searching for patches of food to maximize encounters occurs within the decimetre – tens of seconds range;
2) Encounter and food recognition prior to capture occur within the centimetre – second range; and
3) Food capture, handling movements, and ingestion occur within the millimetre – millisecond range.

Even on larger scales (e.g. hundred of metres – days) much of the distribution and abundance of calanoid species may also be linked to feeding behaviour (Longhurst, 1976; Bohrer, 1980; Ortner, Wiebe & Cox, 1980; Longhurst & Herman, 1981; Ortner *et al.*, 1981). However, before any observed population pattern within the larger ranges can be interpreted, detailed knowledge of the interactions within the three smaller scales is required. Information at these levels will advance our understanding of calanoid feeding behaviour and complement studies using standard biological oceanographic methods and experimental designs (e.g. Edmondson & Winberg, 1971).

Each of the three smaller scales has received varying degrees of attention from the scientific community. The smallest scale, food capture and handling, has attracted the most attention (see above). The largest scale, searching for food patches, has also received considerable attention because of its similarity with predator – prey interactions (e.g. Kerfoot, 1978). However, the middle scale has not yet been adequately studied. In this range, calanoids encounter algae, guide them to the capture area, reject them at distance before exerting energy to capture them, and lose them due to non-perception or multiple encounters.

The following scenario of the interactions within this middle range is based on many observations. However, it should be considered as a scenario only, since too many pieces are still missing and too much inference holds it together.

Capture of algae

One of our first direct observations on feeding *E. crassus* showed that the animal uses its maxillipeds individually to capture single algae and bring them forward to the area between the mandibles and the endites of the first maxillae (Strickler, 1984). We described this motion pattern as 'chopstick' feeding, pointing out that the animal has to perceive the position of the algae precisely (Alcaraz *et al.*, 1980). We observed the same mechanism executed with other mouthparts and in other species. This observation did not agree with the paradigm which describes the mechanism of food gathering by copepods as simple filter-feeding/sieving (Barrington, 1967; Marshall & Orr, 1972; Meglitsch, 1972; Barnes, 1974; Margalef, 1974).

Analyses of many more films confirmed the suggestion that the 'second maxillae ... should open like the wings of a butterfly and suck the alga into the space between the setae' (Alcaraz *et al.* 1980). Koehl & Strickler (1981) argued and Strickler (1984) showed evidence for a 'fling and clap' mechanism; a motion that produces lift at low Reynolds numbers (Weis–Fogh, 1973). This motion pattern has two effects: one, it produces a feeding current which brings the alga close to the mouthparts (see below), and two, it provides the animal with a mechanism to suck the alga in between the mouthparts. Once the alga is between the second maxillae it is then transported by endites to the mandibles (Paffenhöfer *et al.*, 1982).

For both of these capture mechanisms (i.e. chopstick, and fling and clap) to work, the alga must be near the mouthparts. The calanoids perform only two to three motions to catch an alga, and algae beyond the reach of these few motions are not captured. There is a clearly defined space around the mouthparts in which algae can be caught. This space is called the capture area (Strickler, 1982).

Generation of the feeding current and enhancement of capture rate

Most calanoid copepods create a feeding current which carries algae into the capture area. *E. crassus*, for example, establishes a current about 8 mm long (fig. 2, Strickler, 1982). Generation of the feeding current is based on the 'fling and clap' mechanism (see figs. 2,3,4 in Strickler, 1984). The feeding current moves at speeds of up to 1 cm sec^{-1} through the capture area. For an adult female *E. crassus*, this area is 0·5 mm^2. This means that the flow through the capture area was 345 ml day^{-1} (see fig. 2 in Strickler, 1982).

Other calculations showed that the Reynolds number of this current is 0·75 (Andrews, 1983). Therefore, viscosity governs the flow field and the behaviour of the feeding current. Viscous forces transport layers of water adjacent to the part of the current which passes through the capture area. Therefore, not all algae entrained in the moving water can be captured. It would seem then that a copepod wastes energy moving these algae.

The energy, however, is not wasted. Numerous observations show that when an alga is entrained in the flow field anterior of the capture area, but destined to pass outside the capture area, a copepod can alter its flow field to direct the alga into the capture area (for motion pattern, see Fig. 4). This alteration of the flow field is produced by modulating the stroke angle of the beating maxillipeds and endopodites of the second antennae (see fig. 5 versus fig. 4 in Strickler, 1984). This behaviour pattern is best described as re-routing.

Re-routing entails perception of the location and direction of algae in the flow field anterior of the capture area and beyond the perimeter of flow directed through the capture area. In one observation, an alga was perceived 1·25 mm in front of the capture area (approx. 0·8 bodylengths), or 430 msec before capture (Strickler, 1982). It appears that a sensory perimeter anterior to the capture area exists. Algae passing through this perimeter can be detected and re-routed. This perimeter is termed the reactive field because it is similar in concept to Holling's reactive field of awareness (Holling, 1966; Curio, 1976).

The signal used by copepods to locate algae is unknown. A chemical(s) released by algae has been suggested (Friedman & Strickler, 1975; Hamner & Hamner, 1977; Alcaraz *et al.*, 1980; Poulet & Marsot, 1978, 1980; Koehl, 1984). Several researchers are currently trying to identify the signal. Assuming a chemical is the signal, we hypothesized (Alcaraz *et al.*, 1980; Strickler, 1980; Andrews & Strickler, 1981; Andrews, 1983) that the chemical(s) forms an active space (Wilson, 1970) around individual algae. Once an alga enters the flow field, the active space is extended along an axis in the direction of the flow. This hypothesis was pursued by Andrews (1983) who determined that deformation of the active space could provide early warning of the presence and direction of an incoming alga.

The above description of the feeding current and its role in enhancing the capture rate is still only a scenario which must now be tested. Afterall, only a few years ago, the food-gathering apparatus of calanoids was described as a 'leaky' sieve (Boyd, 1976) so it may seem that this scenario is a little 'far-fetched'.

The techniques proposed here allow us to observe the animals while they feed. For example, when algae are captured, their pathlines will stop at the capture area (Fig. 6). Analysis of many pathlines will result in the determination of the capture area, the flow through the capture area (clearance rate), and the points of entry of algae into the flow field.

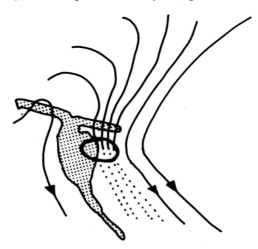

Fig. 6. Hypothetical diagram showing pathlines of algae and determination of capture area.

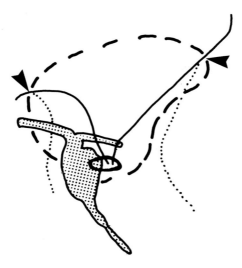

Fig. 7. Hypothetical diagram showing points of re-routings of algae (arrows) and the perimeter of the reactive field (dashed line).

Re-routings can be observed by backtracking algae to the points of entry (Fig. 7). Two algae may have the same point of entry but enter at different times. Let us assume that one alga is selected for while the other does not motivate the animal for capture. The latter one will pass the animal outside the capture area whereas the first one is re-routed (Fig. 7). The perimeter formed by the many points where the pathlines of such pairs of algae separate, circumscribes the reactive field (Fig. 7). When such sequences are re-examined with special emphasis on the motions of animals, one can see the movements executed by animals to achieve these re-routings. With such detailed evaluation, it will be possible to test the scenario and, even if proven incorrect, the full complexity of the calanoid copepods' foraging behaviour can be assessed.

Biological oceanography and microcinematography

It seems paradoxical that biological oceanographers should try to gain an understanding of the trophodynamics of the oceans by observing zooplankters glued to dog hairs and submerged in optical vessels, but there are three reasons for using this approach. Firstly, the 'sphere of influence' of a zooplankter is only a few millilitres even in the largest of all water bodies (Alcaraz *et al.*, 1980). Secondly, high-speed microcinematography is essential to observe zooplankters since their movements, influenced by viscosity (Strickler, 1984), are executed so quickly. Thirdly, tethering herbivorous calanoids does not restrict their movements greatly due to their relatively slow swimming speeds. Therefore, knowing the processes and their underlying principles within these small volumes should increase our understanding of aquatic ecosystems. The following example gives us an appreciation of today's state of the art.

Grazing experiments are classically conducted by placing copepods in bottles containing the same volumes of water with known concentrations of algae. Usually, bottles without animals serve as controls for changes in algal concentrations. After a time interval of a few hours (up to 24 h), the difference between the algal concentrations in the bottles allows calculations of copepod grazing rates. Differences are often expressed as the 'volume swept clear per unit time' (clearance rate). However, these approaches have resulted in estimates that vary over one order of magnitude for animals of similar size. I have chosen three examples to illustrate this point (Table 1).

For the interpretations of these results, I have assumed that flow rates through the capture area in the above species are similar to that of *E. crassus*, i.e. 345 ml day^{-1}, or at least within 20 %, about 280 to 410 ml day^{-1}. This assumption is based on the similarities in size and morphology of the species involved. I also assume that an animal cannot vary the flow of its feeding current more than 20 % because of physical and fluid-mechanical constraints. Rosenberg (1980) has shown that food concentrations do not regulate the beat frequency of the mouthparts to a significant degree. The animals can, however, stop feeding completely (Cowles & Strickler, 1983), which means that their intake can be less than 410 ml day^{-1} but not more. By the way, using a time period of one day to calculate the clearance rates is for convenience only. The amount of time that calanoid copepods feed in one day is not yet known. For this argument, it matters only that there is a upper limit for the volume of water passing through the capture area.

In Frost's (1972) experiment, the clearance rate of 151 ml day^{-1} is lower than the lower limit for flow through the capture area (280 ml day^{-1}). This may have been because:

1a) the animals made many breaks in feeding due to the concentration of desired food items being too low for continuous feeding (see Cowles & Strickler, 1983). Also, changing this concentration did not stimulate the animals to change the frequencies of breaks and feeding bouts; and/or

1b) the experimentally introduced water motion to keep the algae suspended may have reduced the capture rate. This motion may have

Table 1. Results of feeding experiments

Copepod	Algae Species	Volume of cell (μm^3)	Conc. (cells ml^{-1})	Volume swept clear ($ml \cdot day^{-1}$)[d]	Number of cells eaten $hour^{-1}$
Calanus pacificus[a] (adult females)	Coscinodiscus augstii	26000	100 20	151 151	629 126
Calanus helgolandicus[b] (pacificus, CV, females)	Prorocentrum micans	7000	16 43	1600 619	1067 1109
Eucalanus pileatus[c] (CV)	Leptocylindrus danicus	12100	47	319	625

[a] Frost (1972)
[b] Paffenhöfer (1976)
[c] Paffenhöfer & Knowles (1978)
[d] time base of one day for convenience only (see text)

interfered with the perception of nearby algae or may have stimulated the animal to swim rather than feed.

In Paffenhöfer's (1976) experiment, the clearance rates are greater than the higher limit for flow through the capture area (410 ml day^{-1}). This may have been because:

2a) the animals re-routed many algae through the capture area. Re-routing occurred more at the lower density of food than the higher one. The animals seem to optimize for a constant ingestion rate (around 1100 cells hour^{-1}); and/or

2b) the experimentally introduced water motion did not interfere with the perception of nearby algae. It also did not distribute the algae homogeneously. Therefore, the animals may have found patches of food, allowing ingestion at maximum rates (i.e. 1100 cells hour^{-1}).

In Paffenhöfer & Knowles' (1978) experiment, the clearance rate (319 ml day^{-1}) is similar to the flow through the capture area (345 ml day^{-1}) for *E. crassus* (Strickler, 1982). It appears that no re-routings were necessary to obtain food at the experimental food density. However, there are possibly two reasons to explain this result:

3a) the animals were incapable of re-routings and there were no adverse factors introduced (see 1b above); and/or

3b) the concentration of 47 cells ml^{-1} is high enough for the type of food offered and so the animals did not need to introduce costly re-routings (see 2a above).

The three investigations cited were made at a time when the calanoid's complex repertoire of feeding behaviours was unknown. Today, it is mandatory first of all to observe feeding animals. Afterwards, the 'bottle' (black box) approach may be used again, with either a slightly or a radically improved design. This is the only way to deduce reasonable data about the energy transfer between the algae and herbivorous calanoid copepods.

Feeding currents and water motion

Feeding currents: a new model of feeding in herbivorous calanoids

Let us firstly summarize the above scenario. Calanoid copepods generate flow fields where the flow has a low Reynolds number and, consequently, is laminar. Shear deforms the active spaces around incoming algae, giving the copepods advanced warning of algae entering the reactive field. The copepods then alter their flow fields, re-route the algae into the capture areas where individual algae are seized. Thus, by creating

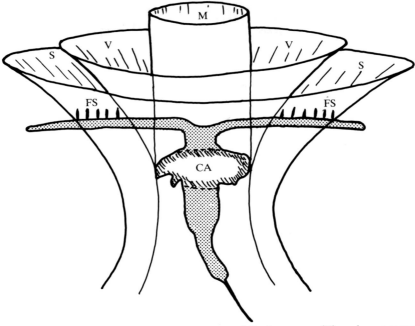

Fig. 8. Diagram explaining the terms motion core (M), viscous core (V), and sensory core (S). See text for details. CA, capture area; FS, sensory fields on first antennae.

feeding currents herbivorous calanoid copepods maximize encounter and capture rates.

This scenario is only valid for algae above a certain size (e.g. 10 μm). Algae below this limit are captured using a different motion pattern (Price *et al.*, 1983; Price & Paffenhöfer, in press) where the second maxillae act as motile-particle deposition filters (Rubenstein & Koehl, 1977) rather than as grabbing instruments (Price & Paffenhöfer, 1985*b*). However, to date this whole motion pattern is not fully understood. Observing very small algae in the feeding current is still an overwhelming technical challenge.

The scenario is visually explained in Fig. 8. The inner core of the feeding current (motion core, Fig. 8) is the volume of water which always passes through the capture area. It does not matter whether the animal moves through the water or whether the water moves through the area while the animal remains at the same position. A human analogy would be either a lawn mower or a rotary planer. However, calanoid copepods create feeding currents. The speed of flow is highest in the vicinity of the capture area. Therefore, water is drawn in from a larger area than the forward projected capture area (viscous core, Fig. 8). The human analogy would be a vacuum cleaner. Very small algae which do not elicit capture motions come from within this core. However, large algae approaching the calanoid can be perceived from within the layers surrounding the viscous core (sensory core, Fig. 8). Re-routing these algae from their projected pathlines will bring them into the capture area. In this case the human analogy would be a person using a vacuum cleaner and seeing single particles on the floor.

This scenario/model favours animals that generate large flow fields with good temporal stabilities. Larger flow fields permit larger volumes of water to be scanned, increasing the encounter rate. More stable flow fields permit better prediction of the presence and direction of incoming algae allowing capture at low energetic costs.

The model would also cover animals which do not have sophisticated sensory systems. The proportions of the sizes of the three cores (motion, viscous, and sensory) will be different for different species. The proportions depend on the sizes of the sensory receptor fields, sizes of the capture areas, and the propulsion systems. However, they not only depend on morphological differences but also, as we will see later, on behavioural ones.

Because of the inter-relationships between aspects of calanoid morphology and the sizes, shapes, and temporal stabilities of their feeding currents, one would expect very few differences between individuals of a particular developmental stage of any species. Therefore, one could formulate a hypothesis: calanoid copepods create species-specific, and maybe even age-specific, feeding currents. The differences between species should be greater than between age stages because the ontogenetic differences in morphology are not of the same order of magnitude as between species. However, one could also expect that the differences between species are smaller at the earlier stages than at adult ones. For the moment, let us assume that this hypothesis is true and continue to test the consequences of such a strong inter-relationship between the animal and the motions of its surrounding water.

The calanoid copepod – feeding current unit

If herbivorous calanoid copepods create flow fields which match their morphologies, one could consider an individual animal and its feeding current as a unit. This would be a similar concept to entomologists pairing spiders with their webs (Levy, 1978) or, to Strickler & Twombly (1975) associating swimming copepods with their fluid-dynamical disturbances. Hence, many such units exist in nature and the question arises as to whether these units are of ecological importance. What dimension of the N–dimensional niche concept would separate the units? Do differences between the units prevent competition?.

While the above questions will be answered using the methods described earlier, we can already infer that many animal – feeding currents units will be significantly different from each other. One has only to examine the animal's body orientation in the water and determine the physical forces involved in enabling this orientation.

It has been observed that while grazing many herbivorous calanoids glide slowly in a horizontal plane (e.g. Hutchinson, 1967). Since these animals are generally negatively buoyant, an equilibrium exists between the buoyant forces (e.g. lift) and gravity. Another observation is that swimming behaviour during feeding bouts is very controlled, either by constant speeds (Strickler, 1984) or by periodically repeated patterns (e.g. hop and sink). Additionally, while creating feeding currents, animals experience a force preventing them from swimming into the current. Emlet & Strathman (pers. comm.) compare this to the action of a sea anchor.

I hypothesized (Strickler, 1982) that five forces act upon calanoids that generate feeding currents: gravity, drag, pressure gradient, buoyancy, and torque. Gravity and buoyancy oppose each other; usually with gravity as the larger force. However, if these two forces are combined into a single one, excess gravity, the rotational force that animals experience would be ignored. This force is created by gravity and buoyancy acting upon different centres. The torque force generated by movements of the abdomen counteracts this rotation and keeps the animals at distinct angles to the horizontal plane. Torque also counteracts any rotation created by drag and the pressure gradient (originating from the ventrally located feeding current). All of these five forces act together in determining the animals' body orientations, their swimming velocities, and the flow fields of their feeding currents (Strickler, 1982). Therefore, if two calanoid copepods differ in their body orientations and/or swimming patterns while feeding, their animal – feeding current units must also be different.

Strickler (1982) showed that calanoids orient differently during feeding bouts. In the lab one frequently identifies free swimming copepods by their body orientations. For example, *Eucalanus crassus* points anterior-side up when feeding; its feeding current is long (8 mm) and narrow (fig. 2, Strickler, 1982). This contrasts with *E. monachus* which feeds ventral-side up (Strickler, 1982); its feeding current is short (1 mm) and has a large cross-sectional area (pers. obs.). The vast difference in the shapes of the animal – feeding current units of these two closely related calanoid species suggests that the proportions of the cores of their feeding currents (Fig. 8) will not be the same. Therefore, their reactive fields and the perception of the algae in the surrounding water will also differ.

Changes in body orientation are not the only ways to vary the reactive fields of calanoid copepods. Reactive fields are the results of several factors. One of these factors is the shear field created by the copepods. A large shear field enhances early perception of incoming algae (Andrews, 1983). To create large shear fields the animal must be 'well anchored' within its environment (to follow the suggestion of Emlet & Strathman about sea anchors). The two forces involved are excess gravity and drag. Emlet & Strathman (1985) estimated that animals below 0·6 mm in length will be anchored by drag rather than by excess gravity, whereas the reverse is seen for animals above this size limit.

Calanoid copepods exhibit a variety of swimming behaviours. While some glide slowly when feeding, others such as *Centropages typicus*, alternate feeding bouts with breaks, swimming upwards during feeding and sinking during the breaks. The timing of these two activities depends on the quality and quantity of the algae (Cowles & Strickler, 1983). This swimming pattern is commonly described as 'hop and sink' (for energetic reasoning, see Haury & Weihs, 1976). The important point is that during feeding bouts, these animals are not as anchored as the gliding ones. Hence, their feeding currents have different structures (see fig. 2B in Strickler, 1982). With periodically fluctuating swimming speeds, the reactive fields will also change over time. This means that swimming behaviour is just as much a component of the animals' 'gestalt' as body orientation.

Differences between animal – feeding current units may indicate separate ecological niches. For example, *E. crassus* may find its food at very low densities in still waters, surviving where calanoids with short feeding currents and small sensory cores (Fig. 8) cannot. On the other hand, *E. monachus* may find scarce food in mixing, turbulent environments where the water motion interferes with the feeding current. This introduction of the ambient water motion of the animal's environment into our thinking may prove useful in explaining the abundances and distributions of the different calanoid copepod species. Let us first examine fluid motions which have the same time and length scales as the animal – feeding current units, and then consider the question of niche separation.

Fluid motion at the centimetre spatial scale

The water surrounding calanoid copepods may be in motion due to wind forcing, water currents, tides, mixing layers, and similar physical phenomena. Motions on large scales (e.g. eddies with diameters of decametres to kilometres) do not directly affect the feeding behaviour of calanoids because the copepods' sensory systems do not allow perception at these spatial scales. However, these motions are important in terms of gene flow and distribution of the species (e.g. Wroblewski, 1980). When the kinetic energy of the fluid motions is transferred to internal energy, most of the large-scale motion dissipates into smaller scale motion. If this scale is within two orders of magnitude of the scale of the feeding currents, interference between the two fluid motions occurs. Ambient fluid motions, especially those at random (e.g. turbulence), will interact with the flows generated by the feeding animals (Fig. 9). The results are less predictable flow fields around calanoid copepods.

Temporal (and random) changes of the flow fields will affect calanoids. If animals capture their food from within the motion and viscous cores of

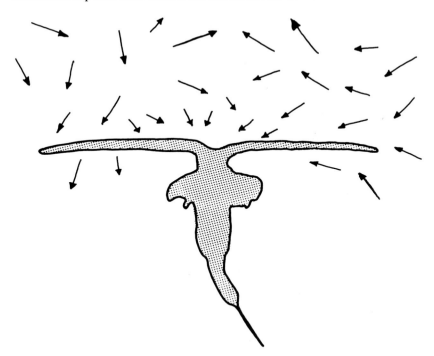

Fig. 9. Hypothetical diagram showing interference between ambient water motion and flow field around a calanoid copepod. Compare with Fig. 4.

the feeding currents only, they will still encounter the same amount of food. The ambient motion may even increase the encounter rates. However, animals which capture algae from the sensory cores will find it harder to re-route these particles successfully (Fig. 9). The incoming signals will be received in a scrambled fashion and particles will be lost. Observations show that herbivorous calanoid copepods which glide horizontally while feeding execute many jumps and do not feed when contained in constantly mixing environments. However, carnivorous calanoids (e.g. *Epischura* spp.) which neither produce nor depend on feeding currents continue swimming in their usual fashion (pers. obs.).

A study by Oviatt (1981) shows circumstantial evidence for the validity of the above scenario. Nutrients, algae, and zooplankters were kept in large containers (13 000 l). Some containers were continuously mixed, others periodically mixed, and others not mixed at all. In the mixed microcosms the density of algae increased but calanoid copepod levels dramatically decreased. Oviatt pointed out that this result cannot be explained as a possible increase of resuspended particles of low nutritional value. She also remarked that the observed decrease may not be a 'straightforward effect of turbulence'. In Narragansett Bay where these zooplankters were even more abundant than in any of the microcosms, turbulence measurements suggested higher mixing energies than in the containers. However, the fluid motions in the mixed microcosms may have contained components at the appropriate spatial and temporal scales to interfere significantly with the feeding mechanisms of the zooplankters. On the other hand, the zooplankters in the Bay may have found refuge in water masses where no such components existed.

Fluid motion as a possible mechanism for niche separation

When herbivorous calanoid copepods share the same food resources, the question of the relationships between species arises. Hutchinson (1951, 1967, 1978) reviewed this topic and found that most sympatric species differ in size. Based on the assumption that these animals were filter feeders, hypotheses on whether size differences were correlated with mesh-size differences and, therefore, with size-selective feeding were tested (reviewed in Koehl, 1984). However, recent results which are based on more detailed analyses support a change of perspective. One may now assume that the mechanisms of capture, handling, and ingestion of algae by these animals are similar for all species (Strickler, 1984). Selection may then be based on olfaction and taste rather than on size and shape. The sole exception is feeding on very small particles. Price *et al.*

(1983) demonstrated that calanoids feed differently on small particles than on larger ones. Price & Paffenhöfer (in press) showed that there is a switch in motion pattern which occurs in small calanoids at smaller particle sizes than in larger species.

Hutchinson (1967) also reviewed cases where the calanoid species were about the same size. From feeding data obtained by Fryer (1954) and Lowndes (1935) he concludes: '(this observation) suggests that some sort of truly behavioural selection of food is possible. This should be considered in all cases in which two species of the same size are living together' (p.686).

From direct and indirect observations (e.g. Donaghay, 1980; Poulet & Marsot, 1978, 1980; and lit. given above) one can conclude that calanoids display true feeding behaviour (capturing, handling, and ingesting on the basis of sensory input and past experience). Hence, one can assume that selection is based on behaviour patterns. Selection for certain food items is always combined with rejection of other items present at the same time.

Rejection of particles occurs at two levels (Strickler, 1984). At the first level, the animals reject particles passively by not capturing them at all. These rejections may occur for two reasons: either the particles are not perceived or particles are perceived but no capture responses are elicited (Strickler, 1984). In both cases particles are not re-routed and, thus, the animals do not expend any energy to 'taste' these items. At the second level, particles are captured and then actively rejected (Paffenhöfer *et al.*, 1982). Rejection at this level costs the animals energy. Because of the reversibility of viscous flows it costs as much energy to reject particles as to capture them in the first place (Strickler, 1984). Therefore, it is advantageous to reject (select) at the first level.

Niche separation may occur at both levels of rejection (and selection). Separation may be on the basis of food recognition using, for example, chemical cues for information. It may also happen at the first level of rejection (and selection) when ambient water motion interferes with the feeding currents thereby reducing the numbers of successful re-routings and captures. The example of the two related *Eucalanus* species is a case in point.

E. crassus generate large feeding currents and select food items at the first level. They reject undesired items mostly passively (pers. obs., see also Fig. 4). Selected particles must be re-routed in order to pass through the capture area. *E. monachus*, however, create small feeding currents. Most of the particles contained in these currents pass through the capture area anyway. Therefore, this species is not as dependent on re-routing as *E. crassus*. In calm waters this difference between the two species may not play a large role. However, in environments where ambient water motions are at the same scale as the feeding currents, *E. crassus* cannot select food as efficiently as in calm waters. If the ambient water motions interfere with the foraging mechanisms during most of the animals lifespan (e.g. copepodite IV through to adulthood) the abundance and distribution of this species will be adversely affected.

The example of the two *Eucalanus* species may not survive closer scrutiny. However, it prompts the formulation of a second hypothesis: ambient water motions may act as a mechanism for niche separation in herbivorous calanoid copepods. This poses a number of questions. What nature and intensities of water motions will interfere with the life of the calanoids? Are there certain calanoid copepod – feeding current units which fit the ambient water motion environment better than others? In lakes and ponds where there is less water motion, could niche separation be based on differences in size rather than in copepod – feeding current units?

It will be interesting to test the two hypotheses proposed in this contribution and be able to consider the flow fields created by these animals as part of their whole appearance. Even if these ideas prove to be false, the results from these investigations will enhance our understanding of the fluid environments of calanoid copepods.

I thank Prof. M. S. Laverack and the Society for Experimental Biology for inviting me to this symposium. I conceived the ideas for this contribution while I was at the Australian Institute of Marine Science. Many thanks to the Institute's Director, Dr J. S. Bunt, for his support. Many thanks also to the University of Southern California for providing a challenging opportunity, and to Dr G.-A. Paffenhöfer for providing Table 1. I acknowledge the support of a NSF-grant (OCE 8416261).

References

Alcaraz, M., Paffenhöfer, G.-A., & Strickler, J. R. (1980). Catching the algae: a first account of visual observations on filter-feeding calanoids. In: *Evolution and Ecology of Zooplankton Communities*, (ed. W. C. Kerfoot), pp. 241–248. Univ. Press of New England.

Andrews, J. C. (1983). Deformation of the active space in the low Reynolds number feeding current of calanoid copepods. *Can. J. Fish. Aquatic Sci.* **40**(8), 1293–1302.

Andrews, J. C. & Strickler, J. R. (1981). Deformation of the active space in the feeding currents of calanoid copepods. *Absr. 1981 AMSA Conference, Brisbane, Australia*, 9–10 May 1981.

Barnes, R. D. (1974). *Invertebrate Zoology*, p. 536. Philadelphia: Saunders.

Barrington, E. J. W. (1967). *Invertebrate Structure and Function*, pp. 204–205. Boston: Houghton Mifflin.

Bohrer, R. N. (1980). Experimental studies on diel vertical migration. In *Evolution and Ecology of Zooplankton Communities*, (ed. W. C. Kerfoot), pp. 111–121. Univ. Press of New England.

BOYD, C. M. (1976). Selection of particle sizes by filter-feeding copepods: A plea for reason. *Limnol. Oceanogr.* **21**, 175–180.

BUSKEY, E. J. (1984). Swimming pattern as an indicator of the roles of copepod sensory systems in the recognition of food. *Mar. Biol.* **78**, 53–57.

CANNON, H. G. (1928). On the feeding mechanisms of the copepods *Calanus finmarchicus* and *Diaptomus gracilis*. *J. exp. Biol.* **6**, 131–144.

CLAUS, C. (1891). Ueber das Verhalten des nervoesen Endapparates an den Sinneshaaren der Crustaceen. *Zool. Anz.* **14**, 363–368.

COWLES, T. J. & STRICKLER, J. R. (1983). Characterization of feeding activity patterns in the planktonic copepod *Centropages typicus* Kroyer, under various food conditions. *Limnol. Oceanogr.* **28**, 106–115.

CURIO, E. (1976). *The Ethology of Predation*. Berlin: Springer–Verlag.

DAGG, M. J. & TURNER, J. T. (1982). The impact of copepod grazing on the phytoplankton of Georges Bank and the New York Bight. *Can. J. Fish. Aquatic Sci.* **39**, 979–990.

DONAGHAY, P. L. (1980). Grazing interactions in the marine environment. In *Evolution and Ecology of Zooplankton Communities*, (ed. W. C. Kerfoot), pp. 234–240. Univ. Press of New England.

EDMONDSON, W. T. & WINBERG, G. G. (1971). *A Manual on Methods for the Assessment of Secondary Productivity in Fresh Waters*. Oxford: Publ., (IBP Handbook No. 17). Blackwell Sci.

EMLET, R. R. & STRATHMANN, R. R. (1985). Gravity, drag, and feeding currents of small zooplankton. *Science* **228**, 1016–1017.

ESTERLY, C. O. (1916). The feeding habits and food of pelagic Copepoda and the question of nutrition by organic substances in solution in the water. *Univ. California Public. Zool.* **16**.

FRIEDMAN, M. M. & STRICKLER, J. R. (1975). Chemoreception and feeding in calanoid copepods (Arthropoda: Crustacea). *Proc. natn. Acad. Sci., U.S.A.* **72**, 4185–4188.

FROST, B. W. (1972). Effects of size and concentration of food particles on the feeding behavior of the marine planktonic copepod *Calanus pacificus*. *Limnol. Oceanogr.* **17**, 805–815.

FROST, B. W. (1977). Feeding behavior of *Calanus pacificus* in mixtures of food particles. *Limnol. Oceanogr.* **22**, 472–491.

FRYER, G. (1954). Contributions to our knowledge of the biology and systematics of the freshwater Copepoda. *Schweiz. Z. Hydrol.* **16**, 64–77.

HAMNER, P. & HAMNER, W. M. (1977). Chemosensory tracking of scent trails by the planktonic shrimp *Acetes sibogae australis*. *Science* **195**, 886–888.

HAURY, L. & WEIHS, D. (1976). Energetically efficient swimming behavior of negatively buoyant zooplankton. *Limnol. Oceanogr.* **21**, 797–803.

HOLLING, C. S. (1966). The functional response of invertebrate predators to prey density. *Mem. Entomol. Soc. Canada* **48**, 1–86.

HUTCHINSON, G. E. (1951). Copepodology for the ornithologist. *Ecology* **32**, 571–577.

HUTCHINSON, G. E. (1967). *A Treatise on Limnology*. Vol. **II**, *Introduction to Lake Biology and the Limnoplankton*. New York: John Wiley & Sons.

HUTCHINSON, G. E. (1978). *An Introduction to Population Ecology*. New Haven: Yale University Press.

JØRGENSEN, C. B. (1966). *Biology of Suspension Feeding*. Oxford: Pergamon Press.

KERFOOT, W. C. (1978). Combat between predatory copepods and their prey: *Cyclops*, *Epischura*, and *Bosmina*. *Limnol. Oceanogr.* **23**, 1089–1102.

KOEHL, M. A. R. (1984). Mechanisms of particle capture by copepods at low Reynolds numbers: possible models of selective feeding. In *Trophic Interactions within Aquatic Ecosystems*, (eds D. G. Meyers & J. R. Strickler), pp. 135–166. Boulder: Westview Press.

KOEHL, M. A. R. & STRICKLER, J. R. (1981). Copepod feeding currents: Food capture at low Reynolds number. *Limnol. Oceanogr.* **26**, 1062–1073.

LEVY, H. W. (1978). Orbweaving spiders and their webs. *Amer. Sci.* **66**, 734–742.

LONGHURST, A. R. (1976). Interactions between zooplankton and phytoplankton profiles in the eastern Tropical Pacific Ocean. *Deep-Sea Res.* **23**, 729–754.

LONGHURST, A. R. & HERMAN, A. W. (1981). Do oceanic zooplankton aggregate at, or near, the deep chlorophyll maximum? *J. mar. Res.* **39**, 353–356.

LOWNDES, A. G. (1935). The swimming and feeding of certain calanoid copepods. *Proc. Zool. Soc. Lond. 1935, 687–715.*

MARGALEF, R. (1974). *Ecologia*, p. 491. Barcelona: Ediciones Omega.

MARSHALL, S. M. (1973). Respiration and feeding in copepods. *Adv. Mar. Biol.* **11**, 47–120.

MARSHALL, S. M. & ORR, A. P. (1972). *The Biology of a Marine Copepod*, pp. 98–100. New York: Springer–Verlag.

MEGLITSCH, P. A. (1972). *Invertebrate Zoology*, p. 535. New York: Oxford Univ. Press.

ORTNER, P. B., WIEBE, P. H., & COX, J. L. (1980). Relationships between oceanic epizooplankton distributions of the seasonal deep chlorophyll maximum in the north-western Atlantic Ocean. *J. mar. Res.* **38**, 507–531.

ORTNER, P. B., WIEBE, P. H., & COX, J. L. (1981). Reply to 'Do oceanic zooplankton aggregate at, or near, the deep chlorophyll maximum?' *J. mar. Res.* **39**, 357–359.

OVIATT, C. A. (1981). Effects of different mixing schedules on phytoplankton, zooplankton and nutrients in marine microcosms. *Mar. Ecol. Prog. Ser.* **4**, 57–67.

PAFFENHÖFER, G.-A. (1976). Continuous and nocturnal feeding of the marine planktonic copepod *Calanus helgolandicus*. *Bull. mar. Sci.* **26**, 49–58.

PAFFENHÖFER, G.-A. (1984). Does *Paracalanus* feed with a leaky sieve? *Limnol. Oceanogr.* **29**, 155–160.

PAFFENHÖFER, G.-A. & KNOWLES, S. C. (1978). Feeding of marine planktonic copepods on mixed phytoplankton. *Mar. Biol.* **48**, 143–152.

PAFFENHÖFER, G.-A., STRICKLER, J. R., & ALCARAZ, M. (1982). Suspension-feeding by herbivorous calanoid copepods: a cinematographic study. *Mar. Biol.* **67**, 193–199.

POULET, S. A. & MARSOT, P. (1978). Chemosensory grazing by marine calanoid copepods (Arthropoda: Crustacea). *Science* **200**, 1403–1405.

POULET, S. A. & MARSOT, P. (1980). Chemosensory feeding and food gathering by omnivorous marine copepods. In *Evolution and Ecology of Zooplankton Communities*, (ed. W. C. Kerfoot), pp. 198–218. Univ. Press of New England.

PRICE, H. J. & PAFFENHÖFER, G.-A. (1985a). Perception of food availability in calanoid copepods. In *The Role of Food Limitation in Structuring Zooplankton Communities*, (ed. W. Lampert). Plön: *Arch, Hydrobiol. Ergeb. Limnol.*

PRICE, H. J. & PAFFENHÖFER, G.-A. (1985b). Capture of small cells by the copepod *Eucalanus elongatus*. *Limnol. Oceanogr.* (in press)

PRICE, H. J., PAFFENHÖFER, G.-A., & STRICKLER, J. R. (1983). Mechanisms of cell capture in calanoid copepods. *Limnol. Oceanogr.* **28**, 116–123.

PÜTTER, A. (1909). *Die Ernaehrung der Wassertiere und der Stoffhaushalt der Gewaesser.* Jena.

PÜTTER, A. (1924). Die Ernaehrung der Copepoden. *Arch. Hydrobiol.* **15**.

ROSENBERG, G. G. (1980). Filmed observations of filter feeding in the marine planktonic copepod *Acartia clausii*. *Limnol. Oceanogr.* **25**, 738–742.

RUBENSTEIN, D. I. & KOEHL, M. A. R. (1977). The mechanisms of filter feeding: Some theoretical considerations. *Am. Nat.* **111**, 981–994.

STORCH, O. (1929). Analyse der Fangapparate niederer Krebse auf Grund von Mikro-Zeitlupenaufnahmen. *Biol. Gen.* **5**, 39–59.

STORCH, O. & PFISTERER, O. (1926). Der Fangapparat von *Diaptomus*. *Z. vergl. Physiol.* **3**, 330–376.

STRICKLER, J. R. (1970). Ueber das Schwimmverhalten von Cyclopoiden bei Verminderungen der Bestrahlungsstaerke. *Schweiz. Z. Hydrol.* **32**, 150–180.

STRICKLER, J. R. (1980). Active space, chemoreception, and calanoid copepods: a mathematical model. Abstr. 21 Congress Intern. Assoc. Limnol., Kyoto, 24–31 Aug. 1980.

STRICKLER, J. R. (1982). Calanoid copepods, feeding currents, and the role of gravity. *Science* **218**, 158–160.

STRICKLER, J. R. (1984). Sticky water: a selective force in copepod evolution. In *Trophic Interactions within Aquatic Ecosystems*, (eds D. G. Meyers & J. R. Strickler), pp. 187–239. Boulder: Westview Press.

STRICKLER, J. R. & TWOMBLY, S. (1975). Reynolds number, diapause and predatory copepods. *Int. Ver. Theor. Angew. Limnol. Verh.* **19**, 2943–2950.

TOEPLER, A. (1866). Ueber die Methode der Schlierenbeobachtung als mikroskopisches Hilfsmittel, nebst Bemerkungen zur Theorie der schiefen Beleuchtung. *Poggendorf's Ann. Phys. Chem.* **127**, 556–580.

VOGEL, S. (1981). *Life in Moving Fluids*. Boston: Willard Grant Press.

VOM RATH, O. (1982). Ueber die von C. Claus beschriebene Nervenendigung in den Sinneshaaren der Crustaceen. *Zool. Anz.* **15**, 96–101.

WEIS-FOGH, T. (1973). Quick estimates of flight fitness in hovering animals, including novel mechanisms for lift production. *J. exp. Biol.* **59**, 169–230.

WILSON, E. O. (1970). Chemical communication within animal species. In *Chemical Ecology*, (eds E. Sondheimer & J. B. Simeone), pp. 133–155. London: Academic Press.

WROBLEWSKI, J. S. (1980). A simulation of the distribution of *Acartia clausii* during Oregon upwelling, August 1973. *J. Plank. Res.* **2**, 43–68.

ZARET, R. E. (1980). The animal and its viscous environment. In *Evolution and Ecology of Zooplankton Communities*, (ed. W. C. Kerfoot), pp. 3–9. Univ. Press of New England.

Printed in Great Britain © *Society for Experimental Biology 1985*

LOCOMOTOR ADAPTATIONS OF SOME GELATINOUS ZOOPLANKTON

Q. BONE

Marine Biological Association Laboratory, Citadel Hill, Plymouth, PL1 2PB, U.K.

Summary

Swimming behaviour and locomotor adaptations are described in chaetognaths, larvacean tunicates, some cnidaria, and thaliacean tunicates. The first two groups swim by oscillating a flattened tail, the others by jet propulsion. In chaetognaths, the locomotor muscle fibres are extensively coupled and relatively sparsely innervated, they exhibit compound spike-like potentials. The motoneurons controlling the rhythmic activity of the locomotor muscle lie in a ventral ganglion whose organization is briefly described. Rhythmic swimming bursts in larvaceans are similarly driven by a caudal ganglion near the base of the tail, but each caudal muscle cell is separately innervated by two sets of motor nerves, as well as being coupled to its neighbours. The external epithelium is excitable, and linked to the caudal ganglion by the axons of central cells. Mechanical stimulation of the epithelium evokes receptor potentials followed by action potentials and by bursts of rapid swimming. The trachyline medusa *Aglantha* and the small siphonophore *Chelophyes* also show rapid escape responses; in *Aglantha* these are driven by a specialized giant axon system lacking in other hydromedusae, and in *Chelophyes*.

Slow swimming in *Aglantha* apparently involves a second nerve supply to the same muscle sheets used in rapid swimming, whereas in *Chelophyes* slow swimming results from the activity of the smaller posterior nectophore.

Slow swimming in siphonophores is more economical than the rapid responses. In the hydrozoan medusa *Polyorchis* (as in *Chelophyes*) action potentials in the locomotor muscle sheet change in shape during swimming bursts, and their duration is related to the size of the medusa; they are not simply triggers of muscular contraction.

The two groups of thaliacean tunicates are specialized differently. *Doliolum* is adapted for single rapid jet pulses (during which it achieves instantaneous velocities of 50 body lengths s-1), whilst salps are adapted for slow continuous swimming. The cost of locomotion is greater in *Doliolum*.

Few gelatinous zooplankton show special adaptations both for rapid escape movements, and for slow sustained swimming, those that do deserve further study.

Introduction

Many animal groups have gelatinous representatives in the zooplankton, as larvae, or as larvae and adults, and these range in size from protozoa and small larval forms to quite large animals, for example the big heteropod molluscs like *Carinaria* and *Pterotrachea* and large scyphomedusae. The great majority however, are only a few mm or cm long and operate at Reynolds numbers well below 5×10^{-3}. Even so,

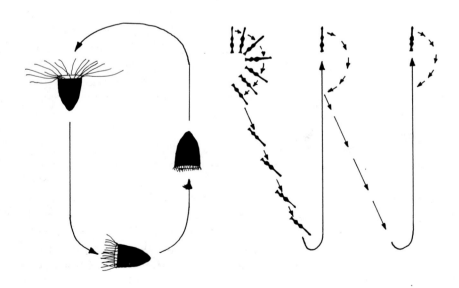

Fig. 1. Swimming patterns of alternate upwards swimming and passive sinking in the trachyline medusa *Aglantha* (after Mackie, 1980), and on the right, in *Sagitta hispida* (after Feigenbaum & Reeve, 1977).

some of these smaller animals achieve instantaneous velocities of 30 cm s^{-1} or so, which may correspond to 50 body lengths s^{-1}. Rapid swimming of this order is obviously only of brief duration, during attack or escape responses; most gelatinous zooplankton spend the greater part of their lives passively floating (excluding SO_4^{2-} to attain neutral or near neutral buoyancy, Denton & Shaw, 1962; Bidigare & Biggs, 1980), or slowly swimming intermittently or continuously as part of their feeding pattern. Thus, as Mills (1981) elegantly demonstrated, some hydrozoan medusae are neutrally buoyant and hang in the water with extended tentacles, waiting for their prey to blunder into them, whilst other negatively buoyant species search for their food by a regular cycle of swimming upwards and sinking down as swimming ceases. The trachyline medusa *Aglantha* shows this latter pattern (Fig. 1A) swimming upwards in the water column with its tentacles retracted and then sinking down inverted fishing with extended tentacles (Mackie, 1980). Similarly, chaetognaths show patterns of passive sinking alternating with bursts of activity driving them upwards (Fig. 1B); Feigenbaum & Reeve (1977) have shown how *S. hispida* thereby extends the area of water searched for prey. The energetic advantage of this kind of behaviour has been considered by Haury & Weihs (1976).

Such patterns of activity (and inactivity) are shown by animals that are on the whole, whatever group they belong to, characterized by simplicity of design, and economy in the number of elements they use in locomotion. Perhaps the most striking demonstration of economy of construction is shown by fritillariid larvaceans, where there may be only four chromosomes (Colombera & Lazzaretto-Colombera, 1977), and cell numbers are greatly reduced, but most gelatinous zooplankton animals have a rather simple locomotor apparatus and simple control system, with relatively small numbers of neurons, often using epithelia not only as permeability barriers or to secrete test and mesogloeal material, but also as conduction pathways. It is remarkable that even though the locomotor systems are 'simplified' they may double in different groups not only for cruising locomotion, but also for rapid escape responses.

The locomotion of rather few planktonic animals has been studied in any detail, and this short review will deal only with some cnidaria, with chaetognaths, and with pelagic tunicates. Many interesting forms are unfortunately omitted, such as the planktonic molluscs and veliger larvae, or the planktonic polychaetes like *Tomopteris* and the larger *Alciopa* (which would make interesting comparisons with the nereids examined by Clarke & Tritton, 1970).

The examples chosen generate forward thrust by two quite different methods: by oscillating a flattened body and tail (like fishes) and by expelling propulsive jets (like squid). Since both methods are employed by quite unrelated groups of animals, independent solutions to similar problems are available for comparison.

Oscillatory propulsion of chaetognaths

Thrust generation by oscillating a flattened tail is used by chaetognaths and larvacean tunicates. In both groups, swimming is intermittent, and there is a characteristic pattern of regular short swimming bursts. During these bursts, *Sagitta setosa*, the only species as yet studied in any detail (Bone & Pulsford, 1984), oscillates the tail at 40–50 Hz, it is an active predator and if disturbed, makes very rapid darting escape movements. Since it is denser than seawater, *Sagitta* sinks slowly between the regular swimming bursts for 15–20 s and then a swimming burst drives it upwards to maintain its position in the water column. The regular swimming bursts persist if the animal is seized by the tail with a suction electrode (Fig. 2), and persist after decapitation, so that they are not controlled by the ganglia of the brain, but rather, by the large ventral ganglion lying about one third of the way down the body.

Rhythmic activity can be recorded from the isolated ganglion (Fig. 2) and ceases if the ganglion is removed; the motoneurons responsible for innervation of the locomotor musculature lie within the ganglion.

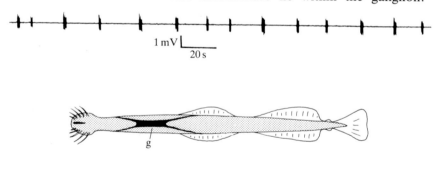

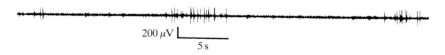

Fig. 2 *Sagitta setosa* showing position of ventral ganglion (g). Upper record: suction electrode on tail of decapitated specimen showing rhythmic swimming bursts; lower record: rhythmic activity recorded by suction electrode on isolated ventral ganglion. (From Bone & Pulsford, 1984).

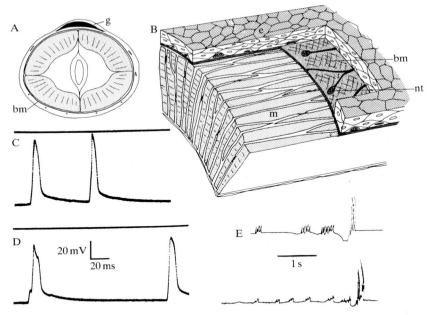

Fig. 3. Locomotor system of *Sagitta*. (A) Transverse section of body at level of ventral ganglion showing quadrants of locomotor muscle and position of ventral ganglion (g) external to basement membrane (bm); (B) simplified stereogram of muscle innervation. The muscle cells (m) are extensively coupled and covered with a basement membrane (bm) containing collagen fibres. Nerves and nerve terminals (nt) lie external to the basement membrane, the terminals do not contact the muscle cells. A multi-layered external epithelium (e) is not excitable. (C,D) Spike-like potentials recorded from locomotor muscle cells during spontaneous activity. Note compound nature of first potential in D, and difference in form of successive potentials. (E) Large and small spontaneous tail movements recorded by suction electrode placed on tail (C-E from Bone & Pulsford, 1984).

Curiously enough, the rather similar swimming bursts of larvaceans are also driven by a ganglion near the base of the tail, and are not interrupted if the brain is removed. However, the similarity between the two ends there for each group has a very different pattern of organization of the locomotor system.

In chaetognaths, the flattened tail lies in the horizontal plane, and the body flexes dorsoventrally during swimming. The locomotor muscles are arranged in four quadrants, two dorsal and two ventral, so that directional swimming such as the attack response to vibrating probes (Horridge & Boulton, 1967; Feigenbaum & Reeve, 1977) must depend upon unequal activation of these muscle quadrants. Each is composed of small spindle-shaped cross-striated muscle fibres which are extensively coupled to each other with numerous gap junctions. No nerve terminals are seen on the muscle fibres; a curious situation which led Grassi (1883) to doubt whether *Sagitta* had any motor nerves! The paradox was recently resolved by Duvert & Barets (1983) who showed that vesicle-filled nerve terminals lay *outside* the tough basement membrane containing helical collagen fibres which surrounds the musculature. Apart from the brain ganglia and 16 axons in the two nerve bundles of the gut, the entire nervous system of *Sagitta* is external to this thick basement membrane. It seems likely that the basement membrane functions during swimming in the same way as the helical connective tissue fibres in the skin of sharks (Wainwright, Vosburgh & Hebrank, 1978; Wainwright, 1983), but this speculation has not been tested. Prof. E. R. Trueman (personal communication) has made preliminary measurements on the internal pressure in large specimens of *Sagitta* which indicate that during bending of the body, internal pressure peaks of around 1 KPa are observed, and work in this direction would be worth pursuing. The relative numbers of nerve terminals and muscle fibres in each quadrant are not known, but the rarity of terminals in sections of the body makes it clear that not all fibres are innervated, probably relatively few, and the majority are excited via the gap junctions connecting them to innervated fibres.

Fig. 3 illustrates the arrangement. Intracellular records from the locomotor muscle fibres obtained from animals cut open and pinned out on Sylgard show that during the locomotor bursts (which continue under these conditions) the electrical activity of the fibres consists of rapid spike-like events which are evidently compound (Fig. 3C,D) and do not overshoot. *Sagitta* is able to grade the activity of the locomotor muscles to make small and large movements (Fig. 3E) and it seems that gradation is brought about by recruiting different numbers of innervated fibres which excite varying numbers of fibres coupled to them by decremental

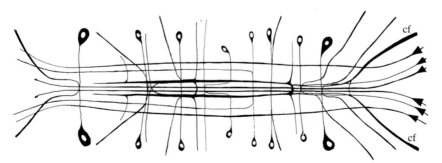

Fig. 4. Arrangement of larger fibres in ventral ganglion, anterior to right. The three pairs of fibres arrowed enter from the anterior ganglia. The largest fibres (cf) supply ciliary fence organs at the base of the head. (modified from Bone & Pulsford, 1984).

conduction, an economical solution to the problem of grading muscular activity that is not known so far in other planktonic animals. Two types of muscle fibres have been described in *Sagitta* (see Duvert & Salat, 1979) but the less common type is coupled by gap junctions to the more abundant, and its role is not known.

The ventral ganglion, which controls the locomotor muscles, is built upon a rather regular scalariform plan (Fig. 4) which shows a number of large fibres up to 6μm in diameter that are constant in number and position between individuals, and very similar between species (Bone & Pulsford, 1984). Some of these are known to connect with the anterior brain ganglia, and others pass to the ciliary fence vibration receptors arrayed around the body, but details of the 'wiring diagram' of the ventral ganglion remain to be investigated. Since isolated ventral ganglia show the same rhythmic activity as seen in the muscle responses of intact animals it seems clear that this activity is not initiated or regulated by proprioceptive input, and no proprioceptors have been observed histologically. Acetylcholine and L-glutamate have no effect on this rhythmic activity, but it seems from some recent preliminary experiments that acetylcholine may be the neuromuscular transmitter.

I am not aware of any kinematographic analyses of *Sagitta* swimming, although these would make a rewarding comparison with other animals swimming in the oscillatory mode, and behavioural observations are limited to the escape responses evoked by touch and attack responses evoked by near field vibrations. Other sense organs are known in *Sagitta*, apart from the eyes, and these are chiefly found on the head, where there are what appear on histological grounds to be chemoreceptors at the margins of the mouth, and mechanoreceptors on the ventral surface of the head. The role that these may play in locomotor behaviour is unknown.

Oscillatory propulsion of larvaceans

The organization and behaviour of the other group swimming by oscillatory propulsion, the larvaceans, is better known, although here again, kinematographic analyses are lacking. Larvaceans oscillate a flattened tail, as do chaetognaths, but in this case, instead of a fluid-filled body cavity providing a hydrostatic skeleton, the tail is chordate like, with a central notochord flanked by ten pairs of rectangular thin muscle cells, and with a dorsal nerve cord containing motoneuron somata (Fig. 5). Oikopleurid larvaceans have quite a wide repertoire of tail movements (Bone & Mackie, 1975) which they use to enter their houses and to pump them up, and to pump water through the house filtering system (Flood,

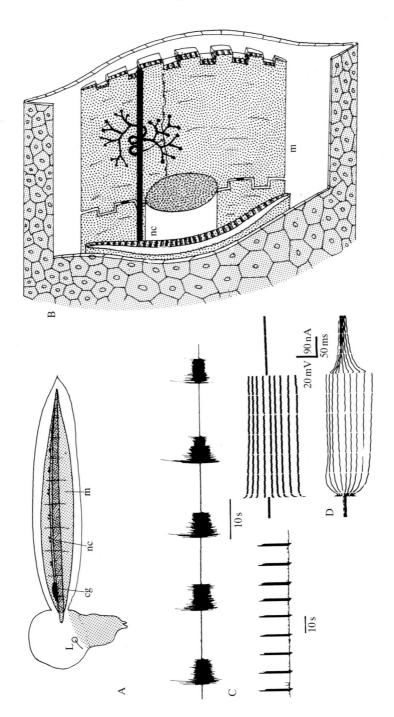

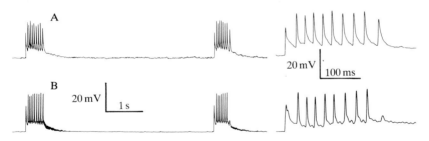

Fig. 6. Electrical activity of caudal muscle cells in *O. dioica*. Simultaneous intracellular records from two caudal muscle cells along trunk. Note similarity of records, but difference in amplitude of last potential of burst in lower trace. (From Bone, 1985).

1978) as well as for swimming. Normally, they sit quietly in the house, oscillating the tail at around 2 Hz (in *O. dioica*) to draw water through the house filters. If disturbed, they leave the house rapidly, and swim around in intermittent bursts, during which tail oscillation in *O. dioica* is around 20 Hz (Fig. 5C), and the animal swims at some $3 \, \text{cm s}^{-1}$, equivalent to $15.6 \, \text{l.s}^{-1}$. These swimming bursts are driven by a caudal ganglion at the base of the tail, which contains some 40–50 cell bodies (Martini, 1909). As in chaetognaths, the muscle cells are electrically coupled (Fig. 5D), although gap junctions have not yet been demonstrated histologically. The caudal muscle cells are cross striated, and receive two separate types of motor innervation (Flood, 1973, 1975; Bone & Mackie, 1975). One of these consists of large corymbiform motor terminals, below which acetylcholinesterase is found (Flood, 1973), the other simple elongate endings which do not show acetylcholinesterase staining. The motoneuron somata providing these terminals lie along the dorsal nerve cord.

This combination of electrical coupling between muscle cells with a dual motor innervation provides a situation that is not easy to analyse in functional terms, but obviously will permit several ways in which a single muscle cell may be activated. During the regular swimming bursts, electrical activity from the caudal muscle cells (Bone, 1985) consists of a

Fig. 5. Locomotor system of *Oikopleura*. (A) *Oikopleura dioica* (tail rotated for clarity) showing notochord (nc), muscle cells (m) and dorsal nerve cord containing caudal ganglion (cg) near tail base. Apart from the house-secreting epithelium (dotted) on the anterior part of the trunk, the entire outer epithelium is excitable. A pair of mechanoreceptors (L) lie on either side of the trunk near the junction of the two types of epithelia. (B) Stereogram of portion of tail showing interdigitated muscle cells (m), notochord (nc) and dorsal nerve cord containing cell bodies which supply corymbiform and elongate motor end plates to the muscle cells. (C) Rhythmic swimming bursts. Regular bursts of swimming in *O. labradoriensis* (upper) and *O. dioica* (lower) recorded with suction electrodes on tail tip. (D) Current pulses injected into one muscle cell (upper) are seen in a second muscle cell further along tail (lower). (Upper record in C from Bone & Mackie, 1975).

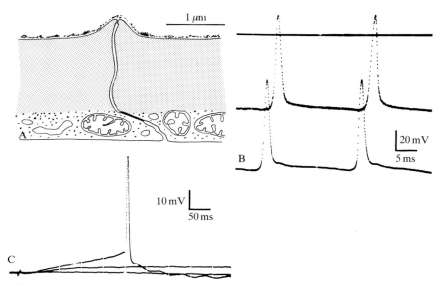

Fig. 7. Properties of external epithelium in *Oikopleura*. (A) Scheme of structure of epithelium in *O. dioica*. Note outer fine-fibril layer (dotted) covering inner mitochondrial zone. The two cells are coupled by gap junctions in the inner zone, and a tight junction is found at the external surface. (B) Propagated action potentials recorded from epithelial cells along tail of *O. longicauda*. (C) Epithelial action potential preceded by receptor potential recorded from epithelial cell where the outer membrane was mechanically stimulated by the recording electrode tip. (B and C from Bone, 1985).

series of rapid potentials around 50 mV, which therefore do not overshoot the 70 mV resting potential (Fig. 6A). Simultaneous records from different muscle cells show very similar activity in each, but often, the posterior cell along the tail shows an 'extra' potential at the end of the burst, which is only seen at much lower amplitude in the anterior cell (Fig. 6B). Perhaps the larger potentials in each cell represent the activity of nerve terminals, and the smaller potential in the anterior cell at the end of the burst corresponds to a potential arising from nerve activity in the posterior cell which is decrementally transmitted along the muscle cell chain via gap junctions. A striking feature of the potentials recorded from the muscle cells is that mechanical stimulation of the outer epithelium of the animal evokes potentials that are significantly larger and may overshoot resting potential (Fig. 6C). During the swimming bursts evoked by mechanical stimulation, in addition to increase in amplitude of the muscle potentials, they also increase in frequency. In the large species, *O. labradoriensis*, for example, the frequency increases from 5 Hz during a normal swimming burst, to 20 Hz in a burst evoked by mechanical stimulation.

The external epithelium in *Oikopleura* is mechanosensitive, and when stimulated mechanically, propagates overshooting action potentials which arise from depolarizing generator potentials provided these reach the threshold value of some 7 mV from resting potentials around 80 mV (Fig. 7B,C). This excitable epithelium covers the whole of the body, apart fom the anterior trunk region which secretes the filtering house, and is linked to the caudal ganglion via two axons arising from cell bodies in the caudal ganglion. These pass to two bristle-bearing mechanoreceptors on either side of the posterior part of the trunk, which were first described

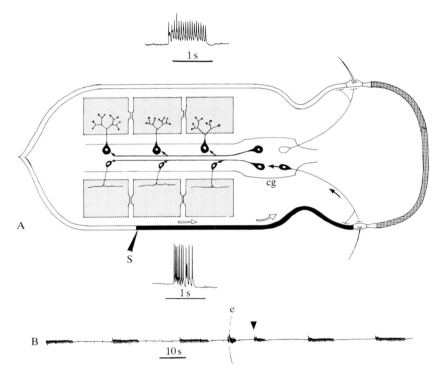

Fig. 8. Epithelial action potentials and locomotion in *Oikopleura*. (A) Schematic diagram illustrating operation of the system. Upper half of diagram, normal rhythmic swimming (intracellular record from caudal muscle cell at top). Lower half of diagram, epithelial action potentials travel along tail from stimulus site (S) and pass to the caudal ganglion (cg) via the axon linking the trunk mechanoreceptor to the ganglion. They then evoke rapid swimming bursts during which amplitude of potentials in caudal muscle cells (below) is larger than during the normal swimming bursts. (B) Suction electrode records caudal muscle activity of normal swimming bursts in *O. labradoriensis* followed by an out of sequence burst evoked by mechanical stimulation which begins with a larger epithelial action potential (e). This is followed by a second out of sequence burst (arrowed) evoked by direct stimulation of the mechanoreceptor bristle. (Intracellular records from Bone, 1985, suction electrode record from Bone & Ryan, 1979).

by Langerhans (1877). Here, the axon branches to form gap junctions with the base of the receptor cell, and with an adjacent epithelial cell, so that input to the caudal ganglion, and thence to the caudal muscle cells is identical whether the receptor itself is stimulated, or any point on the skin is stimulated (Fig. 8). In other words, the outer epithelium extends the field of the receptor cells, and the response evoked is a non-specific escape burst of high-speed swimming.

Apart from the two vibration receptors, *Oikopleura* has a statocyst, and chemoreceptors near the mouth, but nothing is known of the role of either; the statocyst does not seem to be involved in any kind of righting reflex since larvaceans do not appear to adopt any preferred attitude in the water.

Oikopleura operate at Reynolds numbers up to about 150, a region intermediate between that of very small oscillatory swimmers such as sperm, and larger animals like small fish, so that hydrodynamic analysis of their swimming should prove rewarding. It seems likely from preliminary kinematic records, which show large lateral movements of the trunk as the tail oscillates, that efficiency is low, and that swimming is energetically expensive. Since *Oikopleura* normally does not swim but slowly pumps water through its house, high-cost escape swimming can be accepted.

Rapid jet propulsion in hydrozoan medusae and siphonophores

In contrast to the oscillatory swimmers, jet-propelled animals in the plankton have received more attetion, both from the hydrodynamic aspect, and from the design and control of the muscles involved. For medusoid forms, Gladfelter (1973) has provided an interesting comparative analysis of shape and mesogleal properties in a variety of medusae and a diphyid siphonophore, whilst Daniel (1983) has modelled the mechanics and energetics of medusan jet propulsion, and Bone & Trueman (1982) have examined swimming in two siphonophore species from a combination of chamber pressure and kinematic records.

The properties of the neuromuscular systems in such forms have been studied by several workers, chiefly in hydrozoa (see Spencer & Schwab, 1982), which are well adapted for electrical recording, but there is also recent work on scyphozoa and cubozoa (see Passano, 1982). For the pelagic tunicates which swim by jet propulsion, the salps and doliolids, preliminary accounts have been given by Bone & Trueman (1983, 1984).

In both cnidaria and tunicata, some species are adapted for slow continuous cruising, where economy of operation must be paramount; whilst others show adaptations for short-term rapid-escape responses where maximum speed is more important than economy. We shall examine the independent solutions achieved by the two groups to these two very different requirements, and how each have sometimes reconciled the two.

A fundamental difference between the two phyla is that the jet chamber of the medusoid forms has but a single posterior jet aperture, so that refilling has to be via the same aperture as the propulsive jet, and negative thrust must therefore be generated during refilling. In the tunicates, the jet chamber is provided with an anterior aperture as well as a posterior one, and refilling when the animal is swimming forwards is mainly via the anterior aperture, largely avoiding this negative thrust component of the cycle, as well as allowing the possibility of swimming in either direction by appropriate closure of the valves at each aperture.

Although most medusoid forms swim relatively slowly, rapid short bursts of escape swimming are found in diphyid siphonphores and in some Trachymedusae like *Pantachogon* and *Aglantha*. *Aglantha* is capable of instantaneous velocities of 50 cm s^{-1}, *Chelophyes* up to 30 cm s^{-1} (Fig. 9). A single contraction of *Aglantha* can drive it 8 cm, and Donaldson,

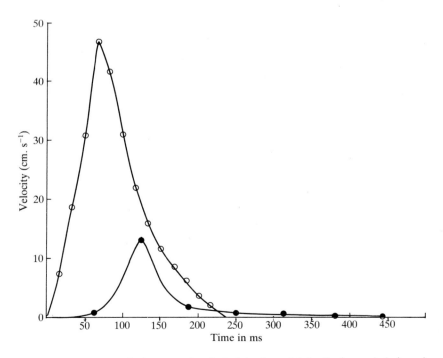

Fig. 9. Instantaneous velocity curves for single jet pulses of *Aglantha* (open circles), and *Chelophyes* (solid circles). *Aglantha* plotted from data in Donaldson et al. (1980).

Mackie & Roberts (1980) have shown that such single jet pulses suffice to break the medusa free from the embrace of the larger *Aequorea* and are indeed effective escape responses. Maximum accelerations during the movements of *Aglantha* are up to $7 \cdot 8 \, \text{m s}^{-2}$; in *Chelophyes* up to $5 \cdot 3 \, \text{m s}^{-2}$.

Aglantha makes up to three jet pulses in succession, of which the first is the most effective, since subsequent pulses begin before the bell has completely refilled and so drive the animal only 40–60 % of the distance it is driven by the first pulse.

The thrust produced during the jet pulse (mu_e) is the product of the mass of water ejected (m) and the velocity of ejection (u_e): evidently if the jet chamber is completely refilled, negative thrust during inhalation will be the product of the same mass and the velocity of inhalation (u_i). Unless u_i is less than u_e, the animal will simply oscillate backwards and forwards and there will be no net forward motion. During several jet pulses, *Aglantha* does reduce m, since the jet chamber is not completely refilled, but u_i is also reduced by increasing the duration of the refilling phase (three to four times the length of the expulsion phase), and by increasing the size of the aperture. During the jet pulse, the velar aperture is reduced by contraction of the velar muscles, which relax during inhalation.

In *Chelophyes*, the escape response is a burst of jet pulses (up to ten or more at frequencies up to 8 Hz) and here, the ratio of the refilling phase of the cycle to the expulsion phase is only $1:1 \cdot 4$, since refilling has to be rapid to permit such a rapid series of jet pulses. Positive thrust exceeds negative thrust in this case almost entirely because the jet aperture is reduced by about 50% during the expulsion phase, during which maximum jet velocity is up to $121 \, \text{cm s}^{-1}$.

In both *Aglantha* and *Chelophyes*, the muscle contracting the jet chamber is a thin sheet of coupled cross-striated myoepithelial cells which propagate action potentials at around $30 \, \text{cm s}^{-1}$. In *Aglantha* these myoepithelial cells do not have internal sarcoplasmic reticular tubules, nor invaginations of the cell membrane equivalent to a T-system, and thus it seems probable that the action potential is a mixed Na^+/Ca^{2+} event or carried by Ca^{2+} alone. In *Chelophyes* however, although an SR is absent, an analogue of the T-system is provided by regular invaginations of the basal membrane (Mackie & Carré, 1983; Chain, Bone & Anderson, 1981). Here, the action potential appears to be carried only by sodium ions, and the T-system analogue has been suggested to be responsible for calcium release during contraction (Bone, 1981). Not unexpectedly, in view of these different arrangements, the action potentials of *Aglantha* are relatively longer lasting events, compared to those of *Chelophyes* (Figs. 10 & 11).

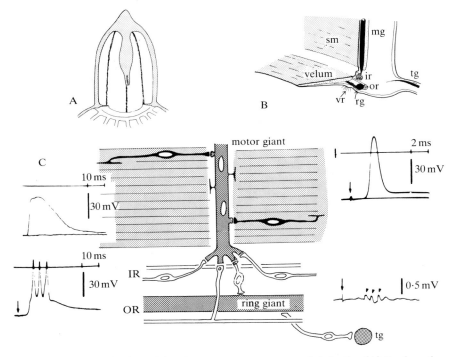

Fig. 10. The organization of the giant axon escape system of *Aglantha*. (A) Section of medusa showing subumbrellar muscle sheet divided by radial canals and radial nerves. (B) Stereogram of bell margin, showing third order motor giant (mg) running up subumbrellar muscle (sm) from inner nerve ring (ir) A ring giant axon (rg) lies in the outer nerve ring (or) and is coupled to tentacle giant axons (tg). Vibration receptors (vr) lie around the base of the velum. (C) schematic diagram of connexions involved in rapid escape response. mg: motor giant, synapsing directly with subumbrellar muscle (sm) and indirectly with the muscle via lateral neurons (ln) coupled to it. The motor giant is coupled to many small neurons in the inner ring (ir), and via chemical synapses to the ring giant (rg) in the outer nerve ring (or). The ring giant is coupled to the tentacle giant (tg). On left: action potential from subumbrellar muscle in high Mg^{2+} seawater (upper) and three spikes in ring giant (lower). On right: action potential from motor giant (upper) and suction electrode record of three spikes in tentacle giant (lower) recorded simultaneously to those in ring giant shown on left. A and B and electrical records in C from Donaldson *et al.* (1980) and Roberts and Mackie (1980); remainder of C based on Weber *et al.*, 1982.

In *Chelophyes* however, remarkably enough, the action potentials change form during the burst, from that shown above, to a much longer potential resembling that of *Aglantha* (and other medusae such as *Polyorchis*, Spencer & Satterlie, 1981). The functional explanation for this change in form is not clear, but as the action potentials lengthen (and increase in amplitude with magnificent overshoots up to 70 mV!) the tension exerted increases and pressures in the jet chamber during successive pulses rise (Fig. 11), so that the first few jet pulses of a burst are less powerful than the succeeding pulses. Perhaps this allows the animal to withdraw its long fishing stem before maximum escape velocity is reached. In *Aglantha*, the fishing tentacles are much shorter, and there is no danger that they might be damaged by the first powerful contraction of the bell.

The nervous mechanisms controlling these two rapid swimming forms have been examined by Mackie and his colleagues (Roberts & Mackie, 1980; Mackie & Carré, 1983), and are interesting variations on the same basic plan. In *Aglantha*, (Fig. 10) eight large diameter ($40 \mu m$) third-order motor giant axons (accompanied by 15–20 smaller ($0.3 - 1 \mu m$) axons) run up the subumbrellar sheets from the inner nerve ring at the base of the velum, and make motor synapses with the muscle. Tracer injections of these multinucleate giants show that they give off short lateral branches to the muscle, and are coupled to small motor neurons running laterally across the subumbrellar muscle and innervating it. Since Lucifer yellow injections into the giant axon spread into the lateral motoneurons, but HRP does not, it seems likely that the lateral motoneurons are coupled to the motor giants by gap junctions (Weber, Singla & Kerfoot, 1982). Lucifer yellow injected into the motor giants similarly spreads into the small neurons of the inner nerve ring at the base of the velum indicating gap junction connexions. Axons from the outer nerve ring form chemical synpases with the motor giants; this outer nerve ring contains a single first-order ring giant (up to $24 \mu m$ in diameter). There are also smaller (up to $7.8 \mu m$) 'giant' axons along each tentacle coupled to the ring giant (or perhaps branches of it). Fig. 10 shows the arrangement. Roberts & Mackie (1980) found that stimulation which evokes a short burst of spikes in the ring giant is followed by a single spike in each of the motor giants, and by a short identical burst in the tentacle axons (Fig. 10). Stimuli evoking ring giant activity, and escape swimming are water vibrations or mechanical stimuli to the tentacles, velum and bell margin. Numerous ciliated receptors around the bell margin probably mediate these responses.

In slow swimming medusae, the response to strong stimulation is involution of the bell (the crumpling response) which involves an epithelial pathway, but the crumpling response is absent in *Aglantha* and epithelial conduction systems play no part in the escape response.

In *Chelophyes*, although the basic plan of the system is similar, epithelial conduction systems here play an important role. The myoepithelial sheet is innervated only around the bell margin, there are no nerves upon the subumbrellar myoepithelial sheet itself. The inner nerve ring, which innervates the subumbrellar sheet at the bell margin, consists of a chain of a few bipolar neurons whose axons are only some 2–3 μm in diameter; there are no giant fibres. Some sensory cells with long processes occur in the inner ring, these are presumably mechanoreceptors; the margin of the bell is very sensitive to light touch. The outer nerve ring also contains mechanoreceptors, and numerous epithelial cells of a special type which are richly innervated. Again, giant fibres are absent.

The ectodermal epithelium of the nectophore is excitable, and propa-

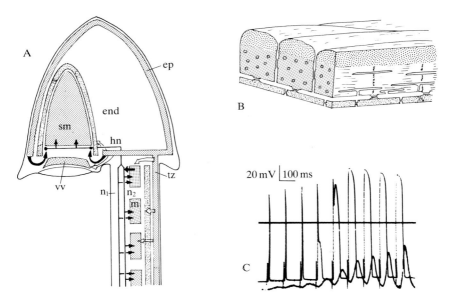

Fig. 11. The locomotor system in *Chelophyes*. (A) Organization of anterior nectophore and stem. Epithelial action potentials (open arrows) in the exumbrellar epithelium (ep) pass to the nectophore endoderm (end) which is coupled to the ectoderm at the bell margin, and to the radial muscles of the velum (rv). The nerve ring at the base of the nectophore is connected with the ectodermal epithelium by epithelio-neural synapses (solid arrows) as the two nerves (n1 and n2) of the stem. The latter connect with the nerve ring by a hydroecial nerve (hn). The subumbrellar swimming muscle (sm) is innervated by the nerve ring only at the nectophore base. In the stem, epithelial action potentials pass to the endoderm coupled to the ectoderm, and in a transitional zone near the base (tz) drive n1 and n2 which innervate the ectodermal stem muscles (m). Activity in these nerves if sufficiently large, evokes action potentials in the stem ectoderm at the transitional zone and thence drives swimming. (B) diagram showing arrangement of swimming subumbrellar muscle. The muscle cells have an outer mitochondrial zone (coarse stipple) and an inner myofilament zone containing regularly arranged tubular invaginations of the basal membrane. The cells are coupled to each other and to the underlying endoderm. c: burst of stimulated action potentials from subumbrellar muscle showing increase in tension (bottom trace) during successive potentials associated with increasing duration of action potential as a plateau phase develops. (A) redrawn from Mackie & Carré, 1982; (B) redrawn from Chain *et al.*, 1981; (C) from Bone, 1981).

gates impulses at 50 cm s^{-1}, when stimulated mechanically anywhere on its surface, these action potentials pass around the nectophore to reach the outer nerve ring, and evoke nervous activity which passes to the inner ring and activates the subumbrellar muscle sheet.

Rapid escape swimming bursts are also triggered by touching the velum and nectophore margin; presumably here the inner nerve ring may be directly stimulated via its sensory cells, as well as indirectly via the sensory cells of the outer nerve ring.

Fig. 11 summarizes the rapid escape system of the anterior nectophore, in comparison with that of *Aglantha* (Fig. 10). The situation in the siphonophore is however, more complex than has so far been described, because there is in addition a smaller posterior nectophore, and a long muscular trailing stem. Both epithelial and nervous pathways link the excitable epithelia of the anterior nectophore with two large axons (10 μm) running down the stem, which innervate the smooth myocytes in the stem; there is also a superficial plexus of small neurons. The nerve

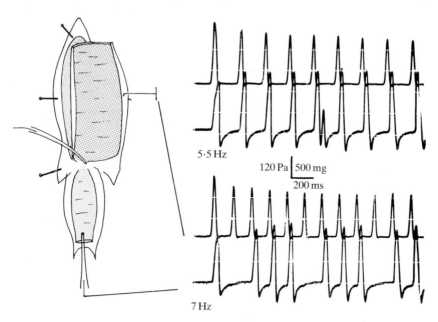

Fig. 12. Co-ordination between the anterior and posterior nectophores in *Chelophyes*. The anterior bell is pinned out and attached to a strain gauge, a suction electrode stimulates the nerve ring at its base. Pressure pulses from the intact posterior nectophore are recorded by a catheter placed in the velar aperture. At a stimulation frequency of 5·5 Hz (upper records) pressure pulses from the posterior nectophore (lower trace) follow contractions of the subumbrellar muscle of the anterior nectophore. At 7 Hz, the posterior nectophore is unable to follow 1 for 1 for more than a few contractions.

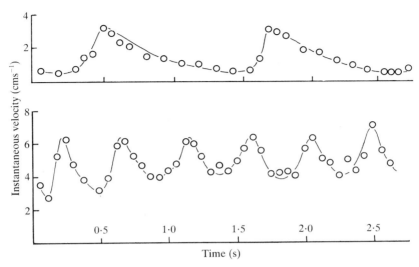

Fig. 13. Slow swimming in *Chelophyes* with the smaller posterior nectophore alone active, and in *Abylopsis* (lower) using the larger posterior nectophore. (From Bone & Trueman, 1982).

rings of the posterior nectophore are not directly connected to the nerve fibres within the stem, but the small nerve plexus synapses with the ectodermal epithelium at the apical peduncle of the posterior nectophore, and it is probable that these neuroepithelial synapses drive epithelial action potentials (such synapses are also known in salps) and the posterior nectophore, like the anterior, is stimulated via conducting epithelia.

During escape responses, when both anterior and posterior nectophores contract, maximum instantaneous swimming velocity is 25% higher than when the anterior nectophore alone contracts. In pinned-out preparations, contraction of the two is closely coupled at frequencies below 4·5 Hz when the preparation is stimulated on the velum of the anterior nectophore, but the posterior nectophore fails to follow at higher frequencies (Fig. 12). The close coupling at lower frequencies suggests a physiological mechanism, but as Mackie & Carré point out, it is possible that the posterior nectophore is simply stimulated mechanically by the contraction of the anterior.

Chelophyes and *Aglantha* are evidently designs specialized for rapid short-term escape swimming, and are both elongate (*Chelophyes* has a fineness ratio of 3–4, *Aglantha* somewhat less). Both however are also able to swim slowly. *Chelophyes* does so by using the smaller posterior nectophore alone, contracting at a frequency below 1 Hz. During such slow swimming, maximum instantaneous velocities are $3·5\,\mathrm{cm\,s^{-1}}$

(Fig. 13A). Here, the same muscle sheet is used as in escape swimming, but at this low contraction frequency, the action potentials do not develop the maximum plateaus seen at higher frequency, and hence contract less forcefully, producing less powerful jets. *Aglantha* also uses the same muscle sheet for slow swimming as for rapid swimming, but in contrast to *Chelophyes*, electrical events in the muscle sheet during slow swimming are not the same as they are in escape swimming. During slow swimming, extracellular records show that propagated spikes (as are found during escape swimming) do not occur; it seems that the subumbrellar muscle sheet receives a dual innervation, and that the slow nerve system is incapable of generating propagated muscle spikes.

This is an interesting situation, paralleling the gradation mechanism in crustacean muscle, and it certainly appears that the rapid escape control system of *Aglantha* with its giant motoneurons is a specialization added on top of the usual single medusan slow system, as Mackie (1980) suggests. However, in *Polyorchis* a slow swimming hydrozoan medusa, the subumbrellar muscle sheet propagates muscle action potentials, although there is only a single motor innervation.

It would be interesting to examine slow muscle responses in *Aglantha* with intracellular electrodes, as Mackie (1968) has done for

Table 1.

Organism	Jet cycles	Mean forward velocity (cm s^{-1})	Work (J.kg^{-1}) (underlined values for organisms designed for maximum escape velocity)
Siphonophora			
Chelophyes	30	16·0	28·2
Abylopsis	60	3·0	2·86
Tunicata			
Doliolum			
small	50	0·5	6·16
large	25	8·0	5·58
Salpa fusiformis			
* small blastozooid	52	3·8	2·5
† medium blastozooid	70	1·6	1·07
* large oozooid	30	6·6	0·55
blastozooid chain			
(16 zooids, 12 active)	400	6·2	1·15

* Animals operating at maximum performance.
† Estimated cruising operation.
Modified from Bone & Trueman (1984).

the dual innervated muscle of the stem of *Nanomia*.

Slow swimming by jet propulsion in hydrozoan medusae and siphonophores

Most medusoid forms swim much more slowly than do *Aglantha* and *Chelophyes* during their escape responses. The slow swimming siphonophore *Abylopsis* for example swims at $3 \, \text{cm s}^{-1}$ during which it achieves maximum instantaneous velocities of $8 \, \text{cm s}^{-1}$ (Fig. 13B). Similar values were found by Gladfelter (1973) for a range of hydrozoan medusae, mean velocities being from $1 \cdot 2 - 7 \cdot 5 \, \text{cm s}^{-1}$; maximum instan-

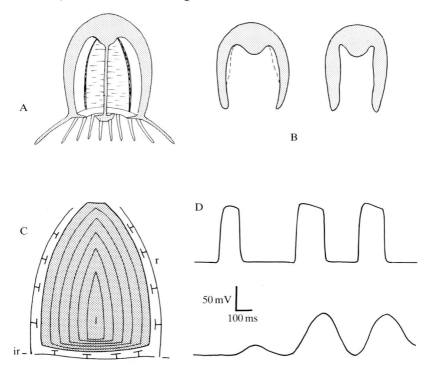

Fig. 14. The locomotor system in *Polyorchis*. (A) The sub-umbrellar sheet is divided into quadrants by radial canals and radial nerves (r). (B) Sections of *Polyorchis* during contraction cycle. On left, fully expanded (stippled) dotted lines showing beginning of contraction at apex of jet chamber. On right, fully contracted at end of jet pulse. (C) Invasion of one quadrant of subumbrellar muscle sheet by action potentials in sheet propagating at different velocities in radial and circumferential directions from neuromuscular junctions with inner ring nerve (ir) and radial nerves (r). Successive positions of wavefront outlined at 10 ms intervals. (D) Change in shape of action potentials and increase in tension with successive potentials (cf. Fig. 11,C). (A and B redrawn from Gladfelter, 1972; C, redrawn from Spencer, 1982; D, from Spencer & Satterlie, 1981).

taneous velocities being up to $11·8\,\mathrm{cm\,s^{-1}}$. We should expect that this sustained slow swimming behaviour should be less costly than the escape responses of the rapid forms, and analysis of the pressure pulses of *Abylopsis* (Bone & Trueman, 1982) compared with those of *Chelophyes* (in the way outlined later (section 6)) indicates that *Abylopsis* performs about half the work during each jet cycle than does *Chelophyes*, although it expels about five times as much water (Table 1).

Similar figures are not available for hydrozoan medusae, although the valuable theoretical analysis of the mechanics and energetics of medusan jet propulsion by Daniel (1983) provides the basis for future comparisons.

Although some slow-swimming hydrozoan medusae (e.g. *Stomatoca*, Mackie & Singla, 1975; Mackie, 1975) show less complex swimming behaviour than others, such as *Polyorchis* (Gladfelter, 1972), the organization of their swimming muscles and neural control systems is probably similar in all. The subumbrellar muscle sheet is divided into segments by the radial canals, and innervated both by axons running up in radial nerves, and from the inner nerve ring around the bell margin (Singla, 1978; Spencer, 1979) (Fig. 14). In *Polyorchis*, Gladfelter's (1972) kinematic analysis of swimming showed that the bell contracted in such a way as to expel water progressively from the apex to the orifice, and Spencer (1982) pointed out that this could be simply achieved as a result of the difference in conduction velocity across the subumbrellar muscle segments in different directions. He found (Spencer, 1979) that conduction was approximately three times as fast in the circular direction (along the muscle cell axes) as in the radial direction, so that contraction in each segment of the subumbrellar muscle efficiently pushed water out of the velar aperture (Fig. 14). In *Abylopsis*, conduction velocity across the unsegmented subumbrellar myoepithelium is probably uniform in all directions, as it is in *Chelophyes*, and since the sheet is innervated only around the velar margin (see Fig. 11), the jet chamber does not contract 'peristaltically'.

Perhaps the most interesting locomotor adaptation of *Polyorchis* is that the action potential does not simply trigger contraction of the swimming muscle, but, as Spencer & Satterlie (1981) point out, it also carries information about the required duration of contraction! These authors found that the plateaued square-wave-form action potentials changed in length (by prolongation of the plateau) not only during successive action potentials of a swimming burst (Fig. 14), but also according to the size of the medusa, so that small medusae had short action potentials and larger medusae, larger potentials (Fig. 15). Change in action potential duration (and concomitant increase in tension in the subumbrellar muscle) during

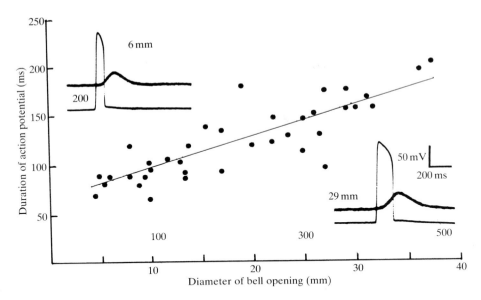

Fig. 15. Change in action potential duration with size in *Polyorchis*. Inset: stimulated action potentials and contractions in a medusa of bell opening 6 mm (left) and 29 mm (right). Scale bars: 50 mV, 200 ms. (From Spencer & Satterlie, 1981).

swimming bursts) is shown in a similar but much more striking manner in the siphonophore *Chelophyes*, but changes related to change in scale are unique. It seems reasonable to suppose as Spencer and Satterlie suggest, that larger jellyfish need longer contraction durations to eject water than do smaller, and that this is achieved by increasing action potential duration. Both Na^+ and Ca^{2++} are involved in the action potential, so that if the contractile process depends in part upon extracellular Ca^{2+} and Ca^{2+} enters during the plateau phase, then increasing action potential duration will increase contraction duration. Further investigations of this interesting situation are obviously desirable, and it seems probable that it may prove to be general in medusoid forms.

It is rather disappointing that neither slow-swimming medusae nor salps seem to increase their swimming efficiency by pulsing appropriately to induce vortex ring interaction in their wakes, in the way suggested by Weihs (1977). At least this seems true for hydromedusae (Daniel, 1983) and salps; perhaps scyphomedusae or cubomedusae are more ingenious.

Rapid jet propulsion in *Doliolum*

The two groups of pelagic tunicates that swim by jet propulsion are quite differently adapted, for whilst salps swim slowly and continuously filtering food particles from the inhaled water, doliolids filter feed with an elaborate ciliated gill apparatus and give one or two rapid contractions at long irregular intervals or when they are stimulated. The apparently spontaneous contractions at irregular intervals shoot the animal upwards in the water column (they sink very slowly in an oblique attitude), a single contraction in an animal 1·5 mm long can drive it forwards 45 mm or more (Fedele, 1923). Similar contractions evoked by water vibrations or mechanical stimuli are evidently escape responses; depending upon the stimulus site the animal moves rapidly forwards or backwards.

In contrast, salps when stimulated mechanically merely accelerate or reverse the normal swimming rhythm; these reactions are much less effective escape responses.

Although doliolids are small animals, it has proven possible to obtain kinematic records of their swimming responses, as well as records of chamber pressures and intracellular records from the muscle bands. The animals are barrel shaped (Fig. 16) encircled by eight or nine thin muscle hoops; as in medusoid forms, restoration of body shape after contraction is brought about by elastic energy stored in the thin tunic. Both anterior

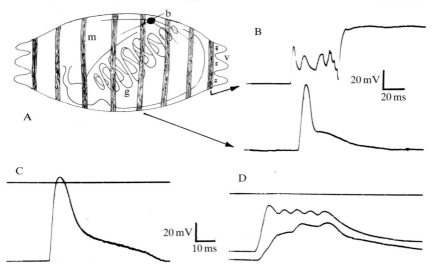

Fig. 16. The locomotor system in *Doliolum*. (A) diagram of animal showing muscle bands encircling animal (m), dorsal brain (b), anterior (right) and posterior flap valves (v), and gill apparatus (g). (B) Simultaneous records from anterior lip muscle band (upper) and locomotor muscle band (lower) showing sustained activity in lip band and single spike-like potential in locomotor band. (C and D) Electrical events in locomotor muscle bands associated with single contraction (C) and sustained contraction (D). In D simultaneous records from two regions of muscle band. (Modified from Bone & Trueman, 1984).

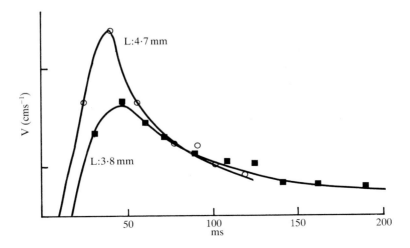

Fig. 17. Instantaneous velocity curves for single jet pulses in *Doliolum* of different sizes. (From Bone & Trueman, 1984).

and posterior apertures are provided with flap valves (Fig. 16) and forward or reverse locomotion is brought about by a sustained contraction of the anterior or posterior band, accompanied by a rapid contraction of the other muscle bands (around $8.5 \, L/s^{-1}$ at $17 \, °C$). Single contractions produce instantaneous velocities up to $30 \, \text{cm s}^{-1}$. (Fig. 17) with maximum accelerations up to $550 \, \text{cm s}^{-2}$. The jet pulses are rapid ($50 \, \text{ms}$ or so), chamber pressures are related to the size of the animal and can exceed 500 Pa, producing efflux velocities up to $80 \, \text{cm s}^{-1}$ negative pressure during inhalation after the single jet pulse are only -20 Pa or less, reflecting the fact that water is inhaled both through the anterior as well as the posterior aperture, as well as a reduced exhalant aperture size during the jet pulse.

Preliminary investigation of the muscle bands encircling the jet chamber has shown that they are multiply innervated, and that contraction involves decremental spike-like potentials of characteristic form (Fig. 16). Since the obliquely striated muscle fibres in the bands are very small ($3 \, \mu\text{m}$ wide by $40 \, \mu\text{m}$ deep), and apparently have no internal tubular systems, it is probable that the potentials seen in Fig. 16 are mixed Na^+–Ca^{2+} events, but their ionic basis remains to be studied.

The continued contraction of the anterior or posterior muscle bands during the jet pulse involves a train of similar events (Fig. 16), such tetani are also sometimes seen in the locomotor muscle bands if the animal remains contracted for a short time as Fedele (1923) occasionally observed.

It might be expected in view of the synchrony required for the contrac-

tion of the locomotor muscle bands during the jet pulse that their
motoneurons might be electrically coupled, but no gap junctions have
been observed in the brain.

Doliolid jet propulsion is obviously adapted for rapid escape movements (as in *Aglantha* a stimulus usually evokes only a single jet pulse),
and it would be expected therefore that the system is specialized for
maximum power output rather than economy. That this is so can be
inferred from estimates of the work done during the jet pulse, obtained
in the following way from records of the pressure pulses. Since volume
changes follow pressure changes, provided the aperture remains constant
during the pulse, the work done is given by the product of the pressure
pulse and its integral (the volume change). A similar estimate of the work
done during refilling can be obtained from records of the negative
pressure pulse during inhalation, and if it is assumed that the resilience
of the test material (whose expansion in all cases is solely responsible
for the refilling of the jet chamber) remains at 100 %, then the total
work done during the jet cycle by the locomotor muscles overcoming
test elasticity and expelling the jet is simply the sum of the work cal-

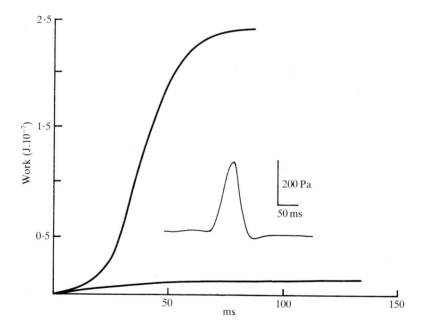

Fig. 18. Work performed by 2·1 mm *Doliolum* to expel jet (upper trace) and to overcome
test elasticity (lower) during jet pulse, obtained as outlined in text. Inset: pressure pulse
analysed. (From Bone & Trueman, 1984).

culated from the two phases of the jet cycle (Fig. 18).

In order to compare the cost of locomotion in different animals which use jet propulsion for slow cruising and for short rapid bursts of escape swimming (Table 1) we may imagine that the latter could be stimulated to cover 1m at the same rate as during their much shorter escape swimming bursts. Table 1 shows that both *Chelophyes* and *Doliolum*, which are designed for rapid escape responses operate very much less economically than the cruising salps and *Abylopsis*.

Cruising jet propulsion in salps

Only one species, *Salpa fusiformis*, has been studied in detail by the same methods used for *Doliolum* (Bone & Trueman, 1983), but so far as known, all species have the same continuous rhythmical slow swimming pattern. In *S. fusiformis*, this slow forwards swimming results from rhythmic jet pulses at frequencies between 0·5 and 2 Hz, which give oscillatory instantaneous velocities up to $12·5\,\mathrm{cm\,s^{-1}}$, and mean forward velocities of $1·3 - 6·6\,\mathrm{cm\,s^{-1}}$ (Fig. 19).

Slow continuous swimming of this sort is obviously very different to the

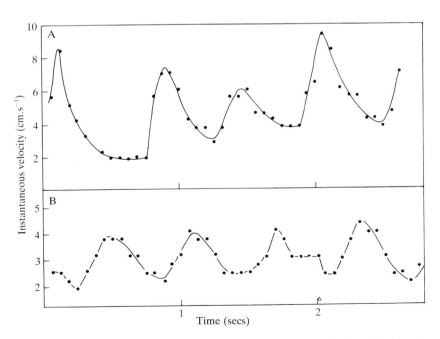

Fig. 19. Instantaneous velocity curves for slow sustained swimming by *S. fusiformis*. Oozooid (A) and blastozooid (B). (From Bone & Trueman, 1983).

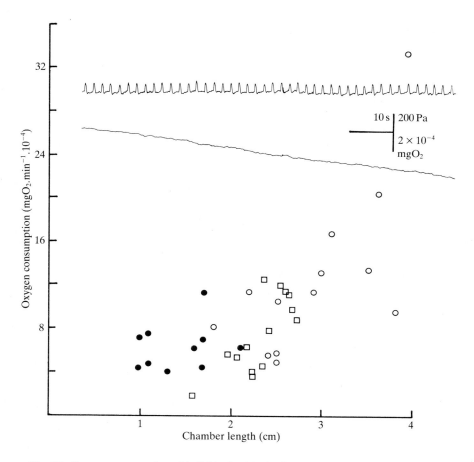

Fig. 20. Oxygen consumption of individuals of *S. fusiformis* swimming in a respirometer chamber. Oozooids: open symbols; blastozooids; solid circles. (From Trueman *et al.*, 1984).

rapid escape responses of doliolids, and the salp locomotor system is designed on a different basis. The thrust produced is the product of the mass ejected per second and its exhalant velocity (mu), but since the power needed to accelerate the fluid ejected is the rate at which kinetic energy is given to it (0·5 mu^2/s), it is more economical to eject a large mass of fluid at low velocity via a large aperture. Moreover, the efficiency of momentum transfer between the exhaled jet and the ambient water rises as the jet velocity approaches the forward velocity of the animal. Maximum economy therefore requires that the salp should emit large-diameter low-velocity jets during the jet pulse, and this is (not unexpectedly) what they do. Chamber pressures are relatively low (maximum values being only 45–100 Pa), the jet pulse is long (250–300 ms), and calculated mean jet velocities are between 18·5 and 33·5 cm s^{-1}. These values were obtained from salps tethered in small dishes, where they were probably stimulated to pulse in a way corresponding to rapid continuous cruising, rather than the slower more economical normal cruising whilst they are filter feeding. Unfortunately, the animals are so delicate that it is not possible to measure chamber pressures in free-swimming animals using indwelling pressure catheters. Nevertheless, even the values obtained under experimental conditions indicate that salps operate economically; a similar analysis of the pressure pulse records to that in *Doliolum* showed that the work performed during each jet cycle ranged from 4·5 F 10·65 × 10^{-5} J, and to cover a metre, salps perform 0·55 – 2·5 J/kg body weight (Table 1), about half the doliolid value.

Results from oxygen consumption studies (Trueman, Bone & Brac-

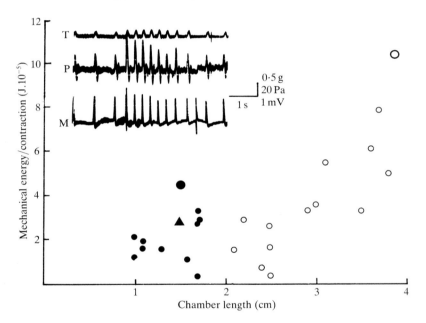

Fig. 21. Work performed during single jet cycles of oozooids (open circles) and blastozooids (solid circles) of *S. fusiformis* based on oxygen consumption data. The larger circles show work performed during single cycles at maximum performance (calculated from analysis of the pressure pulses). The triangle shows work performed similarly calculated for cruising performance.

Inset: acceleration escape response of tethered oozooid of *S. fusiformis* showing abrupt change in frequency and amplitude of pressure pulses (P) and tension (T). Compound muscle potentials (m) recorded from a muscle band of the rear lips show less obvious amplitude changes, and this suction electrode also records an epithelial action potential at the beginning of stimulation (arrow) as well as at the end of the burst of accelerated swimming. (Modified from Trueman *et al.*, 1984).

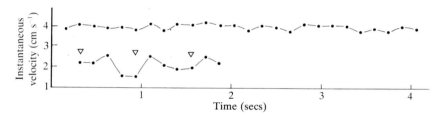

Fig. 22. Instantaneous velocity curves for the same 13-member chain of blastozooids when all zooids were active (upper), and when only a single zooid was active, showing flattening of curve due to lack of co-ordination between contractions of different zooids. (From Bone & Trueman, 1983).

conot, 1984) of salps swimming quietly in a respirometer chamber (Fig. 20) accord with the view that the salps tethered in small Petri dishes were operating above their normal slow rate, for the work they performed in the respirometer chamber (calculated assuming 20% efficiency of conversion of chemical to mechanical energy in the muscles) was half or less than that calculated from analysis of the pressure pulses in rapid cruising (Fig. 21).

As in doliolids, salp muscles contract synchronously, and are multiply innervated by nerves radiating from the brain, they do not propagate action potentials. Bursts of potentials in motoneuron axons evoke summating compound muscle potentials, whose size depends upon stimulation frequency and upon the distance of the recording electrode from an innervated site; salps grade their swimming not only by changing jet pulse frequency, but also by varying the contraction of the locomotor muscle fibres which are relatively slow, contracting at $1.5\,\mathrm{l\,s^{-1}}$, less than 1/5th the speed of doliolid fibres. Escape reactions involve the same system, but salps are unable to swim very rapidly, and can only increase chamber pressures and cycle frequency by relatively small amounts, perhaps doubling their normal slow cruising velocity for a few seconds before returning to the normal rate (Fig. 21, inset).

Like medusae, solitary salps show oscillations of forward velocity as a result of the intermittent jet propulsion system. Acceleration and decelerations of this kind are less efficient than operation at constant forward velocity as they result in drag increases. The blastozooid generation in *S. fusiformis* normally consists of a long chain of linked individuals aligned with their long axes along the chain. Since, when cruising along undisturbed, the jet pulses of the individual zooids along the chain are not co-ordinated, although they cycle at approximately the same rate, the forward velocity of the chain shows only minor oscillations (Fig. 22). Partly for this reason perhaps, the blastozooids are linked in chains, where they swim more efficiently than if separated. It is interesting that Gladfelter (1973) found that in the siphonophore *Diphyes* contraction of the two linked nectophores was staggered, so smoothing the forward velocity curve, no doubt for the same reason. Curiously, no evidence for this was found for the related *Chelophyes*, where both nectophores seem normally to contract together (see Fig. 12).

Conclusions

Although the animals discussed are on the whole rather delicate and quite small, and above all are only available for study at certain favoured marine laboratories where plankton can be collected in good condition close to the shore, the past decade has produced a lot of information about their locomotor systems. The discovery and exploitation of suitable nerve muscle preparations in medusoid forms and the beginnings of intracellular recording from chaetognaths and tunicates have advanced our knowledge of the control systems in locomotion, whilst kinematic studies and theoretical analyses have in the same period allowed some estimates of locomotor efficiency and economics, at least for jet-propelled forms. It is unfortunate that no kinematic analyses for oscillatory swimmers have been made, so that comparisons between the two methods of generating thrust (see Alexander, 1978) are not yet possible.

Perhaps the least surprising feature to emerge from this survey is that different medusoid forms, whatever their taxonomic position, are specialized either for rapid swimming, or for slow cruising; in a few forms only are the locomotor systems capable of both kinds of activity. In most hydromedusae for instance, the response to a strong stimulus is 'crumpling', mediated by the excitable epithelium covering the bell, which causes the medusa to curl inwards, only in *Aglantha* is this response absent, and strong stimuli evoke rapid escape swimming, although the same muscle sheet is normally employed as it is in other hydromedusae for slow swimming. To evoke slow and fast responses from the same muscle sheet *Aglantha* apparently has evolved a dual motor innervation, and this situation seems to have arisen also in larvaceans for the same purpose. But in most forms, there is only a single type of response from the muscle, and a single motor innervation; gradation being brought about centrally by changing the discharge frequency of motoneurons (salps) or the number of motoneurons involved (chaetognaths, doliolids). In some medusoid forms, appropriate changes in muscle contraction as the animal increases in size (*Polyorchis*) or during a swimming burst (*Chelophyes*) result from changes in action potential form, a peripheral mechanism not yet known in other animals. Finally, only a few locomotor adaptations in a few animals have been touched upon here; there is no question but that other groups of gelatinous animals in the plankton offer fascinating material for neurophysiologists interested in locomotor behaviour; although in medusae progress has been made in the analysis of the central pattern generators driving locomotor activity, it is perhaps here that we can expect most progress in other forms.

To zoologists familiar with rhythmic activity in other animals, it may seem strange that the role of proprioceptive input has not been mentioned, but no evidence exists for proprioceptors in any of the forms discussed; perhaps some neurons themselves may be stretch sensitive in some forms.

References

ALEXANDER, R. McN. (1978). In *Mechanics and Energetics of Animal Locomotion*, (ed. R. McN. Alexander and G. Goldspink), pp. 222–248. London: Chapman and Hall.

BIDIGARE, R. R. & BIGGS, D. C. (1980). The role of sulphate exclusion in buoyancy maintainance by siphonophores and other oceanic gelatinous zooplankton. *Comp. biochem. physiol.* **66A**, 467–471.

BONE, Q. (1981). The relation between the form of the action potential and contractions in the subumbrellar myoepithelium of *Chelophyes* (Coelenterata: Siphonophora). *J. comp. physiol.* **14A**, 555–558.

BONE, Q. (1985). Epithelial action potentials in *Oikopleura* (Tunicata: Larvacea). *J. comp. physiol.* (In press).

BONE, Q. & MACKIE, G. O. (1975). Skin impulses and locomotion in *Oikopleura* (Tunicata: Larvacea). *Biol. bull. mar. lab. Woods Hole* **149**, 267–268.

BONE, Q. & PULSFORD, A. (1984). The sense organs and ventral ganglion of *Sagitta* (Chaetognatha). *Acta. Zool. Stockh.* (In press).

BONE, Q. & Ryan, K. P. (1979). The Langerhans receptor of *Oikopleura* (Tunicata: Larvacea). *J. mar. biol. Ass. U.K.* **59**, 69–75.

BONE, Q. & TRUEMAN, E. R. (1982). Jet propulsion of the calycophoran siphonophores *Chelophyes* and *Abylopsis*. *J. mar. biol. Ass. U.K.* **62**, 263–276.

BONE, Q. & TRUEMAN, E. R. (1983). Jet propulsion in salps (Tunicata: Thaliacea). *J. Zool. Lond.* **201**, 481–506.

BONE, Q. & TRUEMAN, E. R. (1984). Jet propulsion in *Doliolum* (Tunicata: Thaliacea). *J. exp. mar. biol. ecol.* **76**, 105–118.

CHAIN, B. M., BONE Q. & ANDERSON, P. A. V. (1981). Electrophysiology of a myoid epithelium in *Chelophyes* (Coelenterata: Siphonophora). *J. comp. physiol.* **143**, 329–338.

CLARKE, R. B. & TRITTON, D. J. (1970). Swimming mechanisms in nereidiform polychaetes. *J. Zool. Lond.* **161**, 257–271.

COLOMBERA, D. & LAZZARETTO-COLOMBERA, I. (1978). Chromosome evolution in some marine invertebrates. In *Marine Organisms, Genetics, Ecology and Evolution*, (ed. B. Battaglia & J. A. Beardmore). pp. 487–525. New York: Plenum Press.

DANIEL, T. L. (1983). Mechanics and energetics of medusan jet propulsion. *Can. J. zool.* **61**, 1406–1420.

DENTON, E. J. & SHAW, T. I. (1962). The buoyancy of gelatinous marine animals. *J. physiol. Lond.* **161**, 14–15.

DUVERT, M. & SALAT, C. (1979). Fine structure of muscles and other components of the trunk of *Sagitta setosa* (Chaetognatha). *Tissue and Cell* **11**, 217–230.

DUVERT, M. & BARETS, A. L. (1983). Ultrastructural studies of neuromuscular junctions in visceral and skeletal muscles of the chaetognath *Sagitta setosa*. *Cell Tiss. Res.* **233**, 657–669.

DONALDSON, S., MACKIE, G. O. & ROBERTS, A. (1980). Preliminary observations on escape swimming and giant neurons in *Aglantha digitale* (Hydromedusae: Trachylina). *Can. J. Zool.* **58**, 549–552.

FEDELE, M. (1923). Attivita dinamiche e sistemo nervoso nella vita dei *Dolioli. Pubbl. Staz. Zool. Napoli* **4**, 129–240.

FEIGENBAUM, D. L. & REEVE, M. R. (1977). Prey detection in the Chaetognatha: response to a vibrating probe and experimental determination of attack distance in large aquaria. *Limnol. oceanogr.* **22**, 1052–1058.

FLOOD, P. R. (1973). Ultrastructural and cytochemical studies on the muscle innervation in Appendicularia, Tunicata. *J. microscopie*, **18**, 317–326.

FLOOD, P. R. (1975). Scanning electron microscope observations on the muscle innervation of *Oikopleura dioica* Fol (Appendicularia, Tunicata) with notes on the arrangement of connective tissue fibres. *Cell Tiss. Res.* **164**, 357–369.

FLOOD, P. R. (1978). Filter characteristics of appendicularian food catching nets. *Experientia* **34**, 173–175.

GLADFELTER, W. B. (1972). Structure and function of the locomotory system of *Polyorchis montereyensis* (Cnidaria: Hydrozoa). *Helgoland. wiss. Meeres.* **23**, 38–79.

GLADFELTER, W. B. (1973). A comparative analysis of the locomotory systems of medusoid Cnidaria. *Helgoland. wiss. Meeres.* **25**, 228–272.

GRASSI, G. B. (1883). I Chetognathi. *Fauna u. Flora des Golfes V. Neapel* **5**, pp 126.

HAURY, L. & WEIHS, D. (1976). Energetically efficient swimming behaviour of negatively buoyant zooplankton. *Limnol. oceanogr.* **21**, 797–803.

HORRIDGE, G. A. & BOULTON, P. S. (1967). Prey detection by Chaetognatha via a vibration sense. *Proc. Roy. Soc. Lond., B* **168**, 413–419.

LANGERHANS (1877). Zur Anatomie der Appendicularien. *Monat. Kon. Preuss. Akad. Wiss. Berlin,* **1877**, 561–556.

MACKIE, G. O. (1968). The control of fast and slow muscle contractions in the siphonophore stem. In 'Coelenterate ecology and behaviour', ed. G. O. Mackie, pp. 647–659. Plenum Press: New York.

MACKIE, G. O. (1975). Neurobiology of *Stomatoca*. II. Pacemakers and conduction pathways. *J. neurobiol.* **6**, 357–378.

MACKIE, G. O. (1980). Slow swimming and cyclical 'fishing' behaviour in *Aglantha digitale* (Hydromedusae: Trachylina). *Can. J. Fish. aquat. Sci.* **37**, 1550–1556.

MACKIE, G. O. & CARRÉ, D. (1983). Coordination in a diphyid siphonophore. *Mar. Behav. Physiol.* **9**, 139–170.

MACKIE, G. O. & SINGLA, C. L. (1975). Neurobiology of *Stomatoca*. I. Action systems. *J. neurobiol.* **6**, 339–356.

MARTINI, E. (1909). Studien über die Konstanz histologischer Elemente. I. *Oikopleura longicauda. Z. wiss. Zool.* **92**, 563–626.

MILLS, C. E. (1981). Diversity of swimming behaviours in hydromedusae related to feeding and utilization of space. *Mar. biol.* **64**, 185–189.

PASSANO, L. M. (1982) Scyphozoa and cubozoa. In *Electrical Conduction and Behaviour in 'Simple' invertebrates.* (ed. G. A. B. Shelton). pp 149–202. Oxford: Clarendon Press.

ROBERTS, A. & MACKIE, G. O. (1980). The giant axon escape system of a hydrozoan medusa, *Aglantha digitale. J. exp. biol.* **84**, 303–318.

SINGLA, C. L. (1978). Fine structure of the neuromuscular system of *Polyorchis penicillatus* (Hydromedusae, Cnidaria). *Cell. Tiss. Res.* **193**, 163–174.

SPENCER, A. N. (1979). Neurobiology of *Polyorchis*. II. Structure of effector systems. *J. neurobiol.* **10**, 95–117.

SPENCER, A. N. (1982). The physiology of a coelenterate neuromuscular synapse. *J. comp. physiol.* **148**, 353–363.

SPENCER, A. N. & SATTERLIE, R. A. (1981). The action potential and contraction in subumbrellar swimming muscle of *Polyorchis penicillatus* (Hydromedusae). *J. comp. physiol.* **144**, 401–407.

SPENCER, A. N. & SCHWAB, W. E. (1982). The Hydrozoa. In *Electrical Conduction and Behaviour in 'Simple' Invertebrates*, (ed. G. A. B. Shelton), Oxford: Clarendon Press.

TRUEMAN, E. R., BONE, Q. & BRACONNOT, J. C. (1984). Oxygen consumption in swimming salps (Tunicata: Thaliacea). *J. exp. biol.* **110**, 323–327.

WAINWRIGHT, S. A. (1983). To bend a fish. In *Fish Biomechanics*,, (ed. P. W. Webb & D. Weihs), pp 68–91. New York: Praeger.

WAINWRIGHT, S. A., VOSBURGH, F. & HEBRANK, J. H. (1978) Shark skin: function in locomotion. *Science* **202**, 747–749.

WEBER, C., SINGLA, C. L. & KERFOOT, P. A. H. (1982). Microanatomy of the subumbrellar motor innervation in *Aglantha digitale* (Hydromedusae: Trachylina). *Cell Tiss. Res.* **223**, 305–312.

WEIHS, D. (1977). Periodic jet propulsion of aquatic creatures. *Fortschr. Zool.* **24**, 171–175.

Printed in Great Britain © *Society of Experimental Biology 1985*

SWIMMING ACTIVITY IN MARINE FISH

C. S. WARDLE

DAFS, Marine Laboratory, PO Box 101, Aberdeen, U.K.

Summary

Marine fish are capable of swimming long distances in annual migrations; they are also capable of high-speed dashes of short duration, and they can occupy small home territories for long periods with little activity. There is a large effect of fish size on the distance fish migrate at slow swimming speeds. When chased by a fishing trawl the effect of fish size on swimming performance can decide their fate. The identity and thickness of muscle used at each speed and evidence for the timing of myotomes used during the body movement cycle can be detected using electromyogram (EMG) electrodes. The cross-sectional area of muscle needed to maintain different swimming speeds can be predicted by relating the swimming drag force to the muscle force. At maximum swimming speed one completed cycle of swimming force is derived in sequence from the whole cross-sectional area of the muscles along the two sides of the fish. This and other aspects of the swimming cycle suggest that each myotome might be responsible for generating forces involved in particular stages of the tail sweep. The thick myotomes at the head end shorten during the peak thrust of the tail blade whereas the thinner myotomes nearer the tail generate stiffness appropriate for transmission of these forces and reposition the tail for the next cycle.

Introduction

This paper discusses the swimming of those fish like cod, *Gadus morhua L.*, salmon, *Salmo salar L.*, saithe, *Pollachius virens (L.)*, and mackerel, *Scomber scombrus L.* These species have a rounded cross-section to their body, a streamlined shape and a well-developed tail fin for propulsion. My aim is to bring together a number of observations, not all of which are well established, but when put side by side indicate fresh views of how these fish swim. Much of what is known of the swimming of fish is tentative and not well established partly because of the difficulties of observing and recording the swimming of fish, but even more important is the difficulty of investigating the physiological and hydrodynamical properties of the fish while it is swimming. Recent papers by Hess & Videler (1984) and Videler (1985), analysing new high-speed cine films made of saithe swimming in the tanks at the Marine Laboratory, Aberdeen, challenge current ideas of how fish pass their muscular energy to the water. They have concluded that the left and the right lateral muscles must produce alternate contractions simultaneously over the whole length of the body. In contrast the present paper evolves those more conventional ideas where the myotomes are thought to contract in sequence, forming a wave of bending that moves tailwards along the body of the fish, sweeping the tail and driving the fish forwards. The fact that there are these different ways of considering the swimming of fish indicate that there are weaknesses in the existing knowledge and that more observations and alternative approaches are needed to consolidate the facts.

Fish move slowly over long distances

Observing fish and the results from tagging fish indicate that fish swim slowly but sometimes over very long distances. If fish are watched in an aquarium, in films made on coral reefs, or directly as a SCUBA diver the impression given is that fish swim gently with slow erratic movements and only occasionally make quick dashes away from danger, collision or to take food. The observation that fish volunteer slow movements for most of their lives is also found when tags that transmit their position by ultra sound, are attached to fish that are caught and returned to the wild. Trout and cod have been followed in this way in Scottish lochs and their hour-to-hour movements are surprisingly slow compared with their potential abilities (Holliday, Tyler & Young 1974, Hawkins, Maclennan, Urquhart & Robb 1974). Direct observations of saithe which school on reefs in the sea lochs of Scotland also show these active fish to swim slowly back and forth as it were patrolling the reef. Saithe have been found clustered close together in a ball-like group with each neutrally buoyant fish quite still and pointing in a different direction. As each fish in the ball detects the diver approaching, it first reacts in its own direction and time, and starts to move out of the ball structure. Analysis of cine film made while approaching such a group shows that, very shortly after the first reactions of individual fish, all the fish turn from their original course to move in the direction taken by the fish that moved first. The whole group of fish take up a polarized motion all moving on parallel courses. These fish can be made to dash away at high speed, for example by the diver startling them by breathing out suddenly, but if approached carefully they can be followed and they maintain a distance of only 1 or 2 metres ahead of the diver. They choose to swim slowly and economically maintain a safe distance by keeping one eye on the following diver (Wardle 1983). Many species of active swimming fish typically move around slowly and they rarely dash at high speed and then only for short distances. Within this framework different species of fish have adapted to live at different levels of activity; some are continuously active, others are generally inactive and even sluggish and examples of this range of fish types are described by Lindsey (1978). Some species of tuna and the mackerel *Scomber scombrus* have no swim bladder and they are heavier than water and sink if they do not continuously gain lift by swimming. Tuna species like *Euthynnus affinis* (with no swim bladder) have been shown to have a minimum swimming speed of 2 Ls^{-1}, at 30 cm fork length when swimming around a 7·3 m diameter tank (Magnuson 1970, 1978). A 30 cm mackerel when cruising in a school of mackerel around a 6 m by 10 m tank was found to have a voluntary swimming speed never below 1 Ls^{-1} (0·3 ms^{-1}) unless the school was confined to only 5 cubic metres of water when the body took a steep angle as large as 27° to the horizontal and a minimum speed of 0·2 ms^{-1}. (He & Wardle unpublished). Although a speed of 1 Ls^{-1} (0·3 ms^{-1}) seems slow, if it is kept up continuously the mackerel moves 1080 m per hour or 25·9 km per day or 9467 km per year. Mackerel migrate annually back and forth along the length of the British Isles some 3000 km (Rankine & Walsh 1982) and similar distances along the eastern coast of the U.S.A. and Canada. Size has a large effect on the distance a fish can swim at these low sustained swimming speeds (see Table 1). Two large blue-fin tuna, *Thunnus thynnus*, lengths 2·5 and 2·8 m, were tagged and caught again after crossing 7778 km of the north Atlantic in less than 118 and 119 days, a minimum average speed of 65·9 km day^{-1}, 0·76 ms^{-1} or 0·3 fish lengths second^{-1} (Mather 1962). The Southern blue-fin tuna, *Thunnus maccayi*, are thought to have a single

Table 1. *The distance fish of different length will swim if they continuously maintain speeds of 1·0 length per second*

fish length (m)	0·05	0·1	0·2	0·4	0·8	1·6	3·2
km per hour	0·18	0·36	0·72	1·4	2·9	5·8	11·5
km per day	4·3	8·6	17	35	69	138	277
km per year	1555	3110	6221	12442	24883	49766	99533

For reference the circumference of the earth is 40074 km., 3000 to 7000 km crosses the Atlantic Ocean, 3000 km circles the British Isles, 1200 km from Shetland to the deep water south of Ireland. Ships cruise at speeds between 18 to 36 km h^{-1}. Tidal currents often reach 1 to 4 km h^{-1} and in some coastal areas can reach 15 km h^{-1}.

spawning ground, between N. Australia and Java, yet the adults are caught around the three southern oceans between 25° and 50° South (Harden Jones 1982).

Salmon (*Salmo salar*) are known to leave the rivers of the U.K. as smolts (20 cm long) and tagged smolts have been recaught a year or more later at the feeding areas on the west coast of Greenland. Of some 758 tagged in Scotland and recaught in Greenland none have been caught in less than a year after tagging. During their first year in the sea smolts grow to 60 to 70 cm long. A salmon (*Salmo salar*) smolt 20 cm long was tagged on the river Usk, Wales in April 1960 and was caught off Greenland in October 1961 as a 73 cm male (Swain, Hartley & Davies 1962). During their first year of sea growth the distance that could be swum by such a salmon at 1 Ls^{-1} will increase from 6221 km per year at 20 cm to 24 883 km per year at 80 cm (see Table 1). The tag returns were from the commercial gill net fishery on the Greenland coast which was developed between 1960 and 1971. It is unlikely that the gill net would have taken salmon smaller than 70 cm if they had arrived in less than one year. Between 1974 and 1982 there were eight records of salmon smolts tagged in Scotland being caught about 2 years later in Newfoundland and Labrador rivers (Reddin, Shearer & Burfitt 1984). An adult salmon used for hatchery spawning in Scotland was tagged and released on 23rd October 1955 and was caught 15th October 1956 on the coast of Greenland 3203 km away (Menzies & Shearer 1957).

Given plenty of time these long distances are covered by many different species of fish. The ability of fish to move so easily so far might indicate that the observed migrations are wanderings from one food-rich area to another. However the remarkable thing about so many of the recorded fish migrations is that they do follow predictable seasonal routes where fishermen find and catch them.

Currents in the coastal areas can have significant effects on the ability of fish to move effectively at slow swimming speeds and the behavioural tactics whereby the fish makes use of the tidal streams have been discovered and described by Arnold & Cook (1982). Many other species show long-distance migrations and those of salmon, eels, herring, cod and plaice, carefully studied over long periods by fisheries scientists, are reviewed by Harden Jones (1968) and McCleave, Arnold, Dodson & Neill (1982).

Swimming of fish in otter trawls

It was mentioned earlier that fish move away keeping just ahead of an approaching diver and only dash away when startled. Fishing gears towed across the sea bed stimulate fish in a similar way generating a valuable source of observations of fish behaviour and swimming performance at the gear towing speeds. The development of towed underwater observation vehicles and underwater TV cameras has made it possible to observe and record the behaviour of fish in towed otter trawls (Wardle 1983, Main & Sangster 1983). Otter trawls are towed at speeds between 1·5 and 2 ms^{-1}. Fish are herded into the mouth of the trawl and then turn and swim forwards holding station with the moving patterns of the netting. This action gathers together groups of different species and different sizes of fish all swimming at the same speed. When small and large fish are swimming side by side in the mouth of an otter trawl at 2 ms^{-1}, the smaller fish are observed to have a very short endurance becoming rapidly exhausted and give up swimming long before the larger fish. At the same towing speed the largest fish have been seen to swim for the whole of an observation period of half an hour and these fish were not in the catch when the net was hauled an hour or so later. Mackerel have been seen, at slower towing speeds, to explore the net, feed on exhausted sandeels and then swim faster than the net out through the mouth. These sorts of observations confirm tank and flume experiments where it has repeatedly been shown that large fish can swim continuously at speeds below sustained swimming speeds without showing fatigue (Brett 1972). Respirometer experiments have demonstrated that the activity level of sustained swimming is supported by the uptake and transport to the tissues of a continuous supply of oxygen and the consumption of oxygen is related to the swimming speed (Brett & Glass 1973, Tytler 1969). If those fish, swimming in the mouth of a trawl, are startled by the observer they are able to dash forwards at their much higher burst speed and clear the net and they then swim using anaerobic respiration and have limited endurance (see Johnston, this volume).

The smaller fish swimming in the mouth of the net show fatigue due to their much higher tail beat frequency. When swimming at a steady speed a fish moves forwards about 0·7 of its length (L) for each complete tail cycle (Hunter & Zweifel 1971). In practice a fish 1 m long moves forwards 0·7 m per tail beat whereas a 10 cm (L = 0·1 m) long fish only moves 7 cm (·07 m). If both these fish swim 2 metres in one second, as forced to in the mouth of the trawl, the larger fish must complete 3 tail beats and the smaller fish 29 tail beats each second. Although the speed of swimming is the same for both fish the physiological rates of work are different in terms of frequency of muscle contraction and its metabolic support. The small fish moves at its maximum burst speed supported by anaerobic breakdown of glycogen to lactic acid whereas the larger fish is possibly still at a sustained swimming speed cruising aerobically. The Reynolds number of the smaller fish is 1×10^5, the larger fish 1×10^6 and both may swim with laminar flow over their bodies. The larger fish has a greater drag mainly due to its bigger surface area which is proportional to L^2 (Wardle 1975). The mass of cod growing from $0 \cdot 20$ m to $1 \cdot 00$ m is proportional to L^3. Muscle mass of cod was found to reduce from $47 \cdot 4$ % of total fresh mass at $0 \cdot 20$ m to $37 \cdot 8$ % for fish $1 \cdot 0$ m long, the muscle mass being equal to $3 \cdot 75\ L^{2 \cdot 86}$ (Wardle 1977). One might guess that the small fish is using its whole lateral muscle to swim at $2\,\mathrm{ms}^{-1}$ whereas the large fish swimming at the same speed, with only a little more drag, is probably using a similar cross-sectional area of muscle to the small fish, but this is only a tiny proportion (at most 5 %) of its much larger muscle cross-sectional area. What do we know about the forces used during swimming and which muscles and what proportion of them are used?

Fish swimming hydrodynamics and drag force

The amount of force F, required to overcome the drag on a fish-like body, of surface area A, moving through water of density ϱ, with a fineness ratio $1 \cdot 2$ and a drag coefficient Cf, at a speed U is summarized in the formula:

$$F = \varrho\,AU^2 1 \cdot 2Cf.$$

The coefficient of friction Cf is affected by the state of flow around the body of the fish. This flow can be laminar or turbulent or part laminar and part turbulent, the transition from laminar to turbulent occurring as the Reynolds number rises from 1×10^6 to 3×10^6. The appropriate Reynolds number is the product of length of the fish, multiplied by the speed through the water divided by a constant kinematic viscocity. Both of the fish discussed in the previous section were estimated to be swimming with Reynolds number below this critical level. There is as yet no direct way of knowing which Reynolds number is relevant to fish except by consulting hydrodynamic examples such as those for flat plates or cylinders in books like that by Hoerner (1965). It is perhaps surprising that there is no successful technique for systematically demonstrating this change in flow over the surface of the fish as size or speed is increased. So many aspects of the swimming of fish would be clarified if a practical method of flow visualization that did not disturb the fish could be devised. For further discussion of the hydrodynamic principles involved in fish swimming – see Blake (1983). The force used at different swimming speeds can be estimated from the drag formula and will, in a later section, be compared with muscle force, but first where does the force for swimming come from?

The segmental motor of fish

The lateral swimming muscles of fish are divided into segmental units known as myotomes. There have been many views on why the myotomes are arranged in their particularly complex overlapping structure. Some of these were reviewed and new ideas added by Wardle & Videler (1980). The unit of motor control is the myotome which is the shortest length of the lateral muscle that can contract in isolation. Each myotome may act alone, all myotomes may act together in synchrony (the Mauthner reflex of Eaton, Bombardieri & Meyer (1977) and Zottoli (1977)) or they may act in controlled sequences. The number of muscle fibres contracting, at any one time, within each myotome will determine the force. In these various ways the great variety of fish movements are generated. The control systems for the contraction of the motor units are discussed by Roberts (1981). The muscle fibres were shown to be arranged in the myotomes in such a fashion that wherever the fibre is positioned in the thickness of the body all contracting fibres shorten a similar amount during bending movements (Alexander 1965). Other points relevant to the structure and function of the segmental motor are (a) a new finding that the contraction time of the muscle changes over the length of the fish and (b) more obviously that the cross-sectional area of the muscle tissue is thick at the head end reducing to the caudal tail peduncle. These points will be expanded in the later sections.

Relating the electromyogram to movement and force

A block of lateral swimming muscle from a freshly killed fish can be made to shorten by electrical stimulation. If the stimulus pulse is made short (20 V, 10 μs) two distinct events can be detected one after the other following the stimulus. Firstly, the muscle action potential (MAP), lasting 2 to 5 ms, can be detected by the bared tips of insulated stainless steel wires joined to a suitable amplifier and oscilloscope. Secondly, the contraction of the muscle lasting between 20 and 100 ms can be shown and timed by either a movement sensor or a tension transducer linked to the same oscilloscope. An example of the response is shown in Fig. 1 where it can be seen that the action potential is completed long before the muscle develops tension or shortens. The contraction time of muscle is the period between the stimulus pulse and the completion of shortening

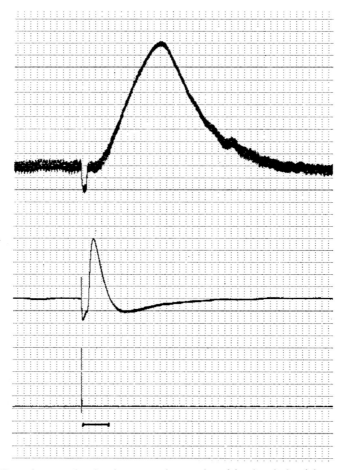

Fig. 1. Recorder trace showing the temporal separation of the electrical and the mechanical activity in a block of lateral swimming muscle of a cod (length 30 cm at 14 °C). A) Muscle tension rising to a peak at 30 ms. B) Muscle action potential (MAP). C) Stimulus pulse 10 μs. Time scale (horizontal bar) 10 ms.

or of maximum force development. The contraction time of the muscle sample depends on the anatomical position of the muscle, it also decreases with an increase in temperature and increases with an increase of the size of the fish (Wardle 1980, Wardle 1975). It should be noted (Fig. 1) that between the end of the muscle action potential (MAP) and the end of the muscle shortening no electrical activity is picked up in the electromyogram (EMG) electrodes. In the isolated preparation discussed above the excited muscle cells are synchronized by the initial stimulating pulse. When EMG electrodes are placed in muscle of intact vertebrates the voluntary movements produce a much less clear-cut record. Studies of the relationship between the MAP recorded as EMG are possible in human volunteers. Sudden voluntary movements of a limb or a knee jerk reflex in humans have been used to demonstrate time delays, similar to those measured in fish, between the EMG activity and the subsequent shortening forces developed by the muscle (Ralston, Todd & Inman 1976, Corser 1974). For this reason, as pointed out by Corser (1974), great care is needed in interpreting the detected EMG activity as evidence for the timing of the forces that generate the movement. The timings are best understood by first measuring the associated delays in force production of the particular muscle tissue as in the example shown in Fig. 1.

When fish are swimming at their fastest speed they bend their body back and forth in a period close to twice the twitch contraction time (Wardle 1975). In the example of a muscle twitch shown in Fig. 1, the lateral muscle of a 30 cm cod at 14 °C has a muscle cell action potential (MAP) peaking at 5 ms (trace b) and a twitch contraction time of 30 ms (trace a) which would allow a maximum tail beat frequency of 16·7 Hz. During a maximum speed swim one should expect to pick up EMG spikes from a location in the muscle of the fish lasting no more than 5 ms and the muscle should not complete its shortening for a further 25 ms (see Fig. 1). In fish, as in other vertebrates, more prolonged shortening of isolated muscle tissue can be stimulated by an appropriate rapid sequence of electric pulses causing a tetanic contraction (Johnston 1981). During slow voluntary movement of the human arm or leg muscles, a sequence of MAPs detected as EMG are coincident with the development of force indicating a tetanic contraction. After the EMG spikes have finished the muscle contraction continues for a brief period which is similar to the muscle twitch contraction time (Ralston *et al.*, 1976).

EMG activity can be interpreted to indicate which muscle cells shorten within which myotomes and for what period during the swimming of the fish. The detection of the EMG is dependent on the proximity of the electrode/s to the depolarizing muscle cells and the intensity and number of the action potentials in the neighbouring tissue. It is important to know how close those muscle cells that are generating action potentials must be to the tip of the electrode before EMG spikes are detectable with the amplification system used. Electrodes carefully positioned at known positions in the myotome can then indicate which muscle fibres are used at which speed. Electrodes placed in different myotomes along the length of the body can indicate which myotomes are triggered during which frame of a filmed sequence of swimming. A major handicap in EMG studies of the swimming fish are the wires running from the swimming muscle back to the recording apparatus. The fish must either be trained to swim in a flume of moving water or a tight circular track or it swims for only a very short distance before encumbered by the wires. Self-contained transmitting tags using modulated ultrasound to carry the physiological signals to the side of large aquarium tanks and from open water were successfully used to transmit the changes of heart activity as ECG during swimming (Wardle & Kanwisher 1974; Priede & Tytler 1977). There were problems monitoring the heart rate during the faster swimming bursts due to the oscillatory movements generating doppler interference on the ultra-sonic carrier wave. Further development of this type of approach, perhaps using one of the electromagnetic carrier waves may allow the monitoring of the EMG in the faster bursts of freely swimming fish.

Despite the difficulties, EMG monitoring with wires has been successfully used to demonstrate the use of the red muscle alone at slow sustained swimming speeds and the increased use of the thicker white, anaerobic muscle in short bursts of fast swimming or as the tail beat frequency reached $3\cdot05$ to $3\cdot6$ Hz (Hudson 1973). Others have used EMG electrodes to confirm that as speed increases deeper pink and white muscle fibres are recruited (Davison, Johnston & Goldspink 1976, Bone, Kiceniuk & Jones 1978, Johnston, Davison & Goldspink 1977). Grillner & Kashin (1976) showed that as swimming speed increases the periods of EMG activity at each monitored location in the lateral muscle become shorter and the wave of onset of the EMG activity passes more rapidly from rostral to caudal myotomes. Blight (1976) demonstrated a wave of EMG activity moving towards the tail at $1\ \mathrm{ms}^{-1}$ through three positions on each side of a $0\cdot165$ m long tench as the tench swam forwards at $0\cdot7\ \mathrm{ms}^{-1}$.

At the relatively slow swimming speeds, in the few examples reported, the EMG wave has been observed to move towards the tail at about the speed of the body bending wave (Blight 1976, Grillner & Kashin 1976). Studies of films of swimming fish have shown this wave of bending to move 30 % faster tailwards than the fish moves headwards through the water (Wardle & Videler 1980). When there is exactly one wavelength of bending movement on the length of the fish body this relationship causes the fish to move forwards $0\cdot7$ body length for each completed tail-beat cycle. The wave of bending and the wave of EMG activity may not be expected to coincide at all speeds due to the relative differences between the period of EMG activity and the contraction time of the muscle. There is evidence of a change in this timing in both the findings of Blight (1976) and Grillner & Kashin (1976). In both these studies the periods of EMG activity get shorter as they progress towards the tail of the fish. We shall see later how the contraction time gets longer towards the tail of those fish species that have been measured.

Swimming force and cross-sectional area of muscle used

In my lecture I showed a photograph of an Olympic weight-lifting champion holding above his head 200 kg and in the next slide he was holding his unloaded arms above his head in triumph. The first picture demonstrated that, although skilful technique and other things may be equal, the thicker the cross-sectional area of the muscles available the greater is the force developed. In comparison with the every day scientist, even if he or she be trained as a weight lifter, the muscles of the champion are thicker and more weight can be lifted. The second picture indicated that the same muscles can raise the weight lifter's unloaded arms above his head but we can guess that a very small proportion of the cross-section of each of his muscles was actually being used. A third point is that the muscles of the arms are mainly involved in organizing the transmission of the force via the skeleton, the lifting of 200 kg involves forces being transmitted to the weights from every part of the body and particularly the largest forces from the extremely thick leg and trunk muscles.

Using an ultrasonic technique for measuring muscle cross-section in humans, Ikai & Fukanaga (1968) showed force was closely linked to cross-sectional area in the muscle bending the arm and that training increased this force mainly by increasing the cross-sectional area. For a range of subjects including boys, girls, men, women and athletes trained in Judo the muscle force varied between 40 and 90 Newtons cm^{-2} and no group was notably weak or strong. Training has been found to increase muscle force from 60 to 100 Ncm^{-2} suggesting an untrained muscle might achieve about twice its strength by training (Ikai & Fukanaga 1970, Komi 1979). These relative figures serve as a useful basis, in the absence of similar fish measurements, for the discussion of the cross-sectional area of the muscle used by a fish at different speeds.

The forces involved in the maximum speed of fish swimming were estimated by Bainbridge (1961) from the drag involved in moving the fish's body through the water. He then estimated the strength of the fish's lateral muscle based on that of a rowing crew. If we know that the maximum force generated by a muscle is proportional to its whole cross-sectional area and that the muscle has a limited variation in its maximum potential force per square metre of cross-section, we can determine what proportion of the fish's lateral muscle is being used to generate a particular force. Using the drag formula, which can predict the force needed for a fish body to maintain a particular speed through the water, it should be possible to predict what proportion of the cross-sectional area of the fish's swimming muscle is used at each speed.

A fish moving at its maximum swimming speed is by definition using maximum force from 100 % of the appropriate cross-sectional area of its muscle. It is likely that some small proportion of the muscle, such as the red muscle, may not have a short enough contraction time to contribute force at the fastest swimming speed. It is reasonable to guess that most of the white lateral muscle is used to swim at the maximum speed. The cross-section of muscle needed at half this speed can be calculated from the drag force. Drag force was shown to be proportional to speed, $U^{1\cdot8}$ (Wardle & Videler 1980, Wardle & Reid 1977). This tells us that 30 % of the muscle cross-section will be used at half maximum speed, 10 % of the whole cross-section is needed when the speed is halved again and 3 % when halved again. Applying this calculation to a 0·37 m mackerel, the swimming speed and muscle cross-sectional areas used are as shown in Table 2. The values for area of muscle cross-section shown in the table are those for the thickest part of the swimming muscle. The cross-sectional area of muscle and how it varies along the length of the body of a mackerel is shown in Fig. 2. The force transmitted to the water by the tail blade of a fish like cod, saithe or mackerel has been estimated by analysis of films recording steady-speed swimming (Wardle & Reid 1977, Videler & Wardle 1978). These estimates as one might expect from casual observation of the cyclic movement of the tail blade, show the pulsed nature of

Table 2. *Prediction for the cross sectional area of muscle used and the time for the EMG wave to pass from myotome 2 to myotome 26 in a 30 cm mackerel (column 5) at the swimming speeds shown*

Tail beat frequency (Hz)	swimming speed (ms^{-1})	(Ls^{-1})	Area muscle used (mm^2)	EMG wave myotome 2 to 26 (ms)	Tail cycle period (ms)	EMG activity period (ms)
16·6	3·5	11·7	1500	24	60	<5
8·3	1·7	5·7	450	48	120	>30
4·2	0·9	3·0	147	96	240	>90
2·1	0·44	1·5	45	192	480	>210
1·0	0·2	0·7	15	384	960	480?

Assuming a muscle contraction time of 30 ms in the anterior myotomes the last column shows the predicted period of EMG activity in the anterior myotomes to maintain each speed (see text).

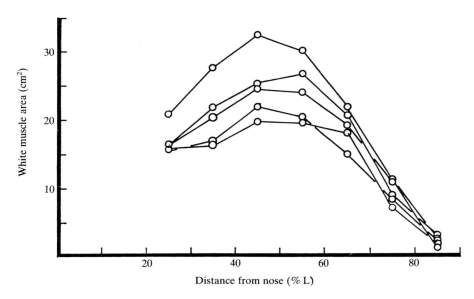

Fig. 2. White lateral swimming muscle cross sectional area (cm²) measured in sections cut at various distances from the nose (% Length) of five mackerel lengths 35 to 41 cm (from He & Wardle unpublished).

the force. The maximum force occurs when the tail blade sweeps across the centre line and zero force is measured as the tail tip reaches the extreme amplitudes (see Fig. 3). Figure 2, which shows the muscle cross-section plotted against distance along the fish, might be seen as representing a graph of force available during the passage of the wave of bending along the body during half of a tail-beat cycle at maximum swimming speed.

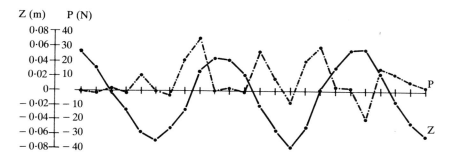

Fig. 3. Instantaneous power output (dotted line P) from a cod (Length 73·4 cm) swimming at 1·9 to 2·0 ms⁻¹ and related to the tail tip track (firm line Z). The horizontal scale shows time, 0·02 s per division (from Wardle & Reid, 1977).

Contraction time increases towards the tail

The time taken for isolated white lateral muscle blocks to complete their contraction following an electric stimulus was used to predict the maximum tail beat frequency and the maximum swimming speed of fish (Wardle 1975). The muscle samples were taken from a middle region of the lateral muscle and a large effect of size (Wardle 1975) and temperature (Wardle 1980) on the contraction time was noted. In order to make the measurement of contraction time more practical when at sea or in the field, Wardle devised a simple portable transducer (Fig. 4). Measurements using this device, have shown that the twitch contraction times of myotomes near the head end of the fish are nearly half those near the tail. The increase in the contraction time plotted against distance along the body of a mackerel is shown in Fig. 5. A similar increase of the contraction time along the length of the body has been measured in cod, haddock and saithe (Wardle & Smith unpublished). The fastest muscle is

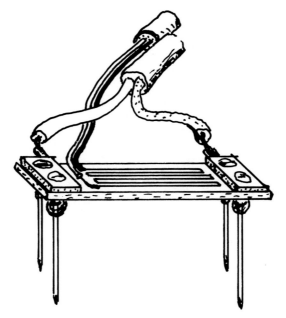

Fig. 4. The tension transducer used to record the contraction times shown in Fig. 5 and to make the record shown in Fig. 1. Four stainless (Record) hypodermic needles 23 gauge by 25 mm were tapped and screwed through brass terminal strips to the two ends of a pvc rectangle (25×10×1 mm). Foil strain gauges (13×4 mm) were glued to the top and bottom faces forming one half of a resistance bridge. The needles were inserted into the lateral muscle of decerebrate fish and stimulation pulse applied via the needles caused the shortening muscle to distort the gauge.

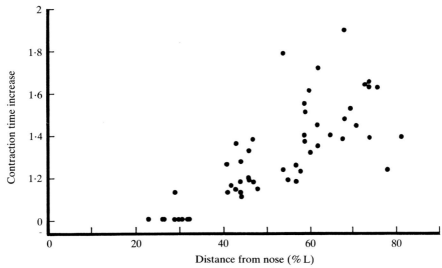

Fig. 5. The increase in muscle contraction time along the body of eight mackerel (length 28–33 cm). In each case the shortest contraction times (just behind the head) were divided into the longer contraction times of the same fish and the result plotted against position along body (from Wardle & Smith unpublished).

just behind the head and Fig. 5 should be compared with Fig. 2 where the area of cross-section of the same regions of the body indicate that the fastest muscle is in the thickest region and there is much less of the slower muscle towards the tail.

A model of stiff bending in fish

During electric fishing investigations into why fish swim to the anode when exposed to pulsed electric fields it was found that electrically stimulated isolated muscle blocks (prepared as in Wardle 1975) contracted with slightly less force (measured with an isometric force transducer) if the tissue was shielded from the anode by other tissue or the skin left on the preparation. In these tests the muscle block was mounted in an isometric transducer frame positioned in isosmotic saline symmetrically between the stimulating plates forming the anode and cathode. Also it was observed that when a large piece of muscle was stimulated, the side nearer the anode could be seen to contract more vigorously than the side nearer the cathode. To show this effect more clearly, the body of a newly killed cod (0·3 m), with head and viscera removed and neural cord destroyed, was suspended horizontally, 0·10 m deep by threads from two ping-pong balls in a 3 m-diameter fibre-glass tank of sea water 1·0 m deep.

Stainless steel electrodes were arranged in the tank 1·5 m apart so that exponential-shaped DC pulses ($\tau = 40$ ms and mean field strength of 20 volts per m) were passed at 1 second intervals through the tank. When the fish body was positioned with its right side towards the anode the first pulse caused the body to bend with the head and tail curving towards the anode. In this way the tail was flipped to the right and this action, repeated each second, drove and steered the preparation towards the anode. After several seconds the fish was pointing towards the anode with a straight body and both lateral muscles contracting with equal force at each pulse. If it swung past this point the opposite side bent towards the anode and so on. In this preparation both lateral muscles are stimulated at the same instant, the side nearer the anode contracts slightly more strongly than the side towards the cathode, the vertebral column does not compress, and the stiffened fish bends towards the stronger contraction (Wardle & P. A. M. Stewart unpublished observation).

Why one wave of bending on the body of a fish?

Analysis of films of fish swimming at a steady speed have shown that there is about one wavelength of bending present on the length of the body at any time during the swimming cycle (Videler & Wardle 1978). Wardle & Videler (1980) filmed cod and showed that the bending of the backbone very closely followed the shape of a sine wave having the formula where the lateral displacement of $Y = D \sin 2\pi X/\lambda$ where X is the longitudinal coordinate, D the amplitude and λ the wave length on the body close to 1. A model drawn using this formula is shown in Fig. 6 where λ is 1 and D is 0·2. Each line shows subsequent images where the body has moved forwards 0·07 body length per image (i.e. to the left Fig. 6) and the wave of bending is moving backwards at 0·1 body length per image (i.e. to the right Fig. 6). Now imagine the shaped muscle on either side of the backbone in accordance with Fig. 2 and imagine the right-hand

Fig. 6. A set of waves drawn according to the formula $Y = D \sin 2\pi X/\lambda$ with $\lambda = 1$. The wave of bending moves 0·1 length to the right in each image and the images are moved 0·07 length to the left. See text for discussion.

end (Fig. 6) of each line to be a tail blade. Notice how the initial formation and development of the small amplitude bends at the left-hand end (Fig. 6), involving thick muscle, coincide with the sweep of the tail blade. Notice, during this sweep, how the tip of the tail blade makes a track outside the blade of the tail indicating that here it is pressing on the water. Neither of these points are true if more or less than one wave length are included on the body. Notice as the bend, which developed in the thick muscle, at the left-hand end (Fig. 6), moves into the region of thinner muscle, towards the tail end, it is involved with the turning or tacking (as used in sailing) of the tail blade at the end and the start of each tail blade sweep.

Putting together the swimming fish

These separate descriptions of the various limits to the physiology and performance of a fish can be put together in order to consider the whole swimming action of fish. Consider first which are the relevant observations when a fish is swimming at maximum speed. The maximum swimming speed is limited by the contraction time. The swimming force of the tail on the water is cycling from zero through the maximum and back to zero. The sequence of forces shed by the tail blade as it sweeps from left to right (Fig. 3) coincides with the progression of the wave of shortening of the myotomes of the right side. Muscles with thicker cross-sectional area develop more force than thinner muscles. The shortening of the head end half of the lateral muscle which is the thickest and the fastest, coincides with the major force output as the tail sweeps through the centre line. The force of the thicker head end myotomes somehow pulls the tail blade through that part of the tail stroke that pushes with most force on the water. It follows that there is one wavelength of bending on the body in order that the thicker myotomes are always associated with the same tail blade position and related force output at the tail tip. The assumption that maximum tail beat frequency, and so speed of swimming, is limited by the muscle contraction time is based on reasoning that the maximum force needed to move at maximum speed would be reduced if the contractions of opposing myotomes at the head end overlapped. It is possible to achieve higher frequencies with overlapped contractions of opposing muscles, but when opposing muscles are contracting simultaneously less of the muscle force is available as swimming force. The caudal myotomes have up to twice the contraction time of the head end myotomes, but must contract at the same frequency as the head end myotomes and must therefore be continuously made to shorten one side against the other in a cyclical manner generating stiff bending.

In fastest swimming the muscle in the caudal half of the body is continuously contracting stiffening this region while the thick muscle at the head end is pulling the tail blade through its power stroke by, as it were, hauling on the stiffened rear half of the body. It is tempting to think of the caudal half of the fish's body as equivalent to the arm of the weight lifter being organized to transmit the forces from the deeper thicker rostral muscle and so push the fish forwards. The athlete's action in 'putting the shot' seems an even more appropriate example where the relatively frail structure of the arm transmits, by its stiffness, the forces from the legs and the trunk via the finger tips to the shot (see Dyson 1977). The finger tips are the equivalent of the fish tail fin rays and the mechanisms for the appropriate adjustment of stiffness of the caudal fin rays by muscular attachments to their bases is described by Videler (1977).

Notice how the thickness of the muscle involved at each level along the body (Fig. 2) reflects the force needed to support the different phases of the tail-beat cycle. As the wave of contraction passes through the thick rostral part it reaches the thickest muscle with the strongest force in the zone at 40 to 50 % along the body (Fig. 2). The muscle available gets thinner towards the tail and the bending forces become less during the tack and the repositioning of the tail in readiness for the next power stroke derived from the opposite side. A natural extension of this model would be to suggest that each myotome is responsible for, and specialized to deal with, a particular part of the tail sweep during steady-speed swimming.

The evidence needed to test this model of swimming will come from comprehensive studies of the EMG picked up from appropriate muscle locations, transmitted from the free swimming fish and recorded simultaneously and in synchrony with accurate high frame rate images of the same fish swimming at different speeds.

References

ALEXANDER, R. McN. (1965). The orientation of muscle fibres in the myomeres of fish. *J. mar. biol. Assoc., U.K.* **49**, 263–290.

ARNOLD, G. P. & COOK, P. H. (1982). Fish migration by selective tidal transport: First results with a computer simulation model for the European continental shelf. In *Mechanisms of Migration in Fishes*. (ed. J. D. McCleave, G. P. Arnold, J. J. Dodson & W. H. Neill), NATO Conference series IV: Marine Sciences. pp. 22–261. New York & London: Plenum Press.

BAINBRIDGE, R. (1961). Problems of fish locomotion. *Symp. zool. Soc. Lond.* **5**, 13–32.

BLAKE, R. W. (1983). *Fish Locomotion*. Cambridge University Press. p. 208.

BLIGHT, A. R. (1976). Undulatory swimming with and without waves of contraction. *Nature* **264**, 352–354.

BONE, Q., KICENIUK, J. & JONES, D. R. (1978). On the role of the different fibre types in fish myotomes at intermediate swimming speeds. *Fish Bull U.S.A.* **76**, 691–699.

BRETT, J. R. (1972). The metabolic demand for oxygen in fish, particularly salmonids, and a comparison with other vertebrates. *Respiration Physiology* **14**, 151–170.

BRETT, J. R. & GLASS, N. R. (1973). Metabolic rates and critical swimming speeds of Sockeye salmon (*Oncorhynchus nerka*) in relation to size and temperature. *J. Fish Res. Board Can.* **30**, 379–387.

CORSER, T. (1974). Temporal discrepancies in the electromyographic study of rapid movement. *Ergonomics* **17**, 389–400.

DAVISON, W., JOHNSTON, I. A. & GOLDSPINK, G. (1976). The division of labour between fish myotomal muscles during swimming. *J. Physiol., Lond.* **263**, 185–186.

DYSON, G. H. G. (1977). *The Mechanics of Athletes*. Hodder & Stoughton Ltd. 7th edition.

EATON, R. C., BOMBARDIERI, R. A. & MEYER, D. L. (1977). Mauthner–initiated startle response in teleost fish. *J. exp. Biol.* **66**, 65–81.

GRILLNER, S. & KASHIN, S. (1976). On the generation and performance of swimming in fish. In *Neural Control of Locomotion (1976)*. (ed. R. M. Herman, S. Grillner, P. S. G. Stein & D. G. Stuart). pp. 181–201. New York & London: Plenum Publishing Corp.

HARDEN JONES, F. R. (1968). *Fish Migration*. pp. 325. London: Edward Arnold (publishers) Ltd.

HARDEN JONES, F. R. (1982). A view from the ocean. In *Mechanisms of Migration in Fishes*. (ed. J. D. McCleave, G. P. Arnold, J. J. Dodson & W. H. Neill), NATO Conference series IV: Marine Sciences. pp. 1–26. New York & London: Plenum Press.

HAWKINS, A. D., MACLENNAN, D. N., URQUHART, G. G. & ROBB, C. (1974). Tracking cod in a Scottish sea loch. *J. Fish Biol.* **6**, 225–236.

HESS, F. & VIDELER, J. J. (1984). Fast continuous swimming of Saithe (*Pollachius virens*): A dynamic analysis of bending moments and muscle power. *J. exp. Biol.* **109**, 229–251.

HOERNER, S. F. (1965). *Fluid Dynamic Drag*. 2nd ed. Published by the author, Brick Town, N.J., U.S.A.

HOLLIDAY, F. G. T., TYTLER, P. & YOUNG, A. H. (1974). Activity levels of trout in Airthrey Loch, Stirling and Loch Leven, Kinross. *Proc. Roy. Soc. Edinburgh* **75B**, 315–331.

HUDSON, R. C. L. (1973). On the function of the white muscles in teleosts at intermediate swimming speeds. *J. exp. Biol.* **58**, 509–522.

HUNTER, J. R. & ZWEIFEL, J. R. (1971). Swimming speed, tail beat frequency, tail beat amplitude and size in jack mackerel, *Trachurus symmetricus*, and other fish. *Fish Wild. Serv. Fish Bull.* **69**, 253–266.

IKAI, M. & FUKUNAGA, T. (1970). A study on training effect on strength per unit cross-sectional area of muscle by means of ultrasonic measurement. *Int. Z. angew. Physiol.* **28**, 173–180.

JOHNSTON, I. A. (1981). Structure and function of fish muscle. *Symp. zool. Soc. Lond.* **48**, 71–113.

JOHNSTON, I. A., DAVISON, W. & GOLDSPINK, G. (1977). Energy metabolism of carp swimming muscle. *J. comp. Physiol.* **114**, 203–216.

KOMI, P. V. (1979). Neuromuscular performance: Factors influencing force and speed production. *Scand. J. sports sci.* **1**(1) 2–15.

LINDSEY, C. C. (1978). Form, function and locomotory habits in fish. In *Fish Physiology, Vol. VII, Locomotion*. (ed. W. S. Hoar & D. J. Randall). pp. 1–100. New York: Academic Press Inc.

MAGNUSON, J. J. (1970). Hydrostatic equilibrium of *Euthynnus affinis* a pelagic teleost without a gas bladder. *Copea* (1970) 56–85.

MAGNUSON, J. J. (1978). Locomotion by scombrid fishes: Hydromechanics, morphology and behavior. In *Fish Physiology, Vol. VII, Locomotion*. (ed. W. S. Hoar & D. J. Randall). pp. 239–313. New York: Academic Press Inc.

MAIN, J. & SANGSTER, G. I. (1983). TUVII – A towed wet submersible for use in fishing gear research. *Scottish Fisheries Research Report*. **29**, 1–19.

MATHER, F. F. (1962). Transatlantic migration of two large blue-fin tuna. *J. Cons. perm. int. Explor. mer.* **27**, 325–327.

McCleave, J. D., Arnold, G. P., Dodson, J. J. & Neill, W. H. (1982). *Mechanisms of Migration in Fishes.* NATO Conference series IV: Marine Sciences. p. 574. London: Plenum Press.

Menzies, W. J. M. & Shearer, W. M. (1957). Long distance migration of salmon. *Nature* **179**, 790.

Priede, I. G. & Tytler, P. (1977). Heart rate as a measure of metabolic rate in teleost fishes; *Salmo gairdneri, Salmo trutta* and *Gadus morhua. J. Fish Biol.* **10**, 231–242.

Ralston, H. J., Todd, F. N. & Inman, V. T. (1976). Comparison of electrical activity and duration of tension in the human rectus femoris muscle. *Electromyogr. clin. Neurophysiol.* **16**, 277–286.

Rankine, P. A. & Walsh, M. (1982). Tracing the migrations of Minch mackerel. *Scottish Fisheries Bulletin* **47**, 8–13.

Reddin, D. G., Shearer, W. M. & Burfitt, R. F. (1984). Inter-continental migrations of Atlantic salmon (*Salmo salar* L.). *ICES Anadromous and catadromous fish committee.* CM 1984/m:11. pp. 1–9.

Roberts, B. L. (1981). The organization of the nervous system of fishes in relation to locomotion. *Symp. zool. Soc. Lond.* **48**, 115–136.

Swain, A., Hartley, W. G. & Davies, R. B. (1962). Long-distance migration of salmon. *Nature* **195**, 1122.

Tytler, P. (1969). Oxygen consumption and swimming speed in the haddock. *Nature* **221**, 274–275.

Videler, J. J. (1977). Mechanical properties of fish tail joints. *Fortschr. Zool.* **24**, 183–194.

Videler, J. J. (1985). Fish swimming movements: A study of one element of behaviour. *Netherlands J. Zool.* **35**, 169–185.

Videler, J. J. & Wardle, C. S. (1978). New kinematic data from high speed cine film recordings of swimming cod (*Gadus morhua*). *Neth. J. Zool.* **28**, 465–484.

Wardle, C. S. (1975). Limit of fish swimming speed. *Nature* **225**, 725–727.

Wardle, C. S. (1977). Effects of size on swimming speeds of fish. In *Scale Effects in Animal Locomotion.* (ed. T. J. Pedley). pp. 299–313. London, New York & San Francisco: Academic Press.

Wardle, C. S. (1980). Effects of temperature on the maximum swimming speed of fishes. In *Environmental Physiology of Fishes.* (ed. M. A. Ali). pp. 519–532. New York & London: Plenum Publishing Corp.

Wardle, C. S. (1983). Fish reactions to towed fishing gears. In *Experimental Biology at Sea.* (ed. A. Macdonald & I. G. Priede). pp. 167–195. London & New York etc: Academic Press.

Wardle, C. S. & Kanwisher, J. W. (1974). The significance of heart rate in free swimming cod, *Gadus morhua*: Some observations with ultra-sonic tags. *Mar. Behav. Physiol.* **2**, 311–324.

Wardle, C. S. & Reid, A. (1977). The application of large amplitude elongated body theory to measure swimming power in fish. In *Fisheries Mathematics.* (ed. J. H. Steele). pp. 171–191. London, New York & San Francisco: Academic Press.

Wardle, C. S. & Videler, J. J. (1980). Fish swimming. In *Aspects of Animal Movement.* (ed. H. Y. Elder & E. R. Trueman). pp. 125–150. Cambridge University Press.

Zottoli, S. J. (1977). Correlation of the startle reflex and Mauthner cell auditory responses in unrestrained goldfish. *J. exp. Biol.* **66**, 243–254.

INDEX OF AUTHORS

INDEX OF SUBJECTS